To J

w and

Colin P. Mitchell is Assistant Professor of History at Dalhousie University in Halifax, Canada. After completing his Ph.D. at the University of Toronto, he has held both a Social Sciences and Humanities Research Council Fellowship and a Mellon Postdoctoral Fellowship at Cornell University.

I.B.Tauris & BIPS Persian Studies Series

Series ISBN 978 1 84885 203 7

The I.B.Tauris / BIPS Persian Studies Series publishes scholarly works in the social sciences and humanities on Iran. Such works include: original research monographs, including biographies and suitably revised theses, specially planned books deriving from conferences, specially commissioned multi-authored research books, academic readers and translations.

1. *The Practice of Politics in Safavid Iran: Power, Religion, Rhetoric*
   Colin P. Mitchell
   978 1 84511 890 7

2. *The Ilkhanid Book of Ascension: A Persian-Sunni Prayer Manual*
   Christiane Gruber
   978 1 84511 499 2

3. *Hafiz and his Contemporaries: A Study of Fourteenth-Century Persian Love Poetry*
   Dominic Brookshaw
   978 1 84885 144 3

THE PRACTICE OF POLITICS IN SAFAVID IRAN

Power, Religion and Rhetoric

COLIN P. MITCHELL

TAURIS ACADEMIC STUDIES
an imprint of
I.B.Tauris Publishers
LONDON • NEW YORK
BIPS Persian Studies Series
A Joint Publication with the British Institute of Persian Studies

Published in 2009 by Tauris Academic Studies
An imprint of I.B.Tauris & Co Ltd
6 Salem Road, London W2 4BU
www.ibtauris.com

Distributed in the United States and Canada exclusively by Palgrave Macmillan
175 Fifth Avenue, New York NY 10010

BIPS Persian Studies Series
A Joint Publication with the British Institute of Persian Studies
Volume 1

ISBN 978 1 84511 890 7

A full CIP record for this book is available from the British Library
A full CIP record for this book is available from the Library of Congress

Library of Congress catalog card: available

Printed and bound in India by Thomson Press (India)
Camera-ready copy edited and supplied by the author

For Jill

CONTENTS

Note on Transliteration ix
Acknowledgments xi

INTRODUCTION 1
Cycles of Persian Mytho-history and Abrahamic Prophecy: Locating "Formational" Safavid Iran 1
Working with Rhetoric and Letter-writing in Perso-Islamic History 6
Inshā and *Munshīs*: A Discursive Forum 11
The Practice of Politics in Safavid Iran: Structure and Scope 16

1. IMPERIALIZING THE APOCALYPSE, 1501–32 19
The Parousia (*ẓuhūr*) of Ismā`īl, 1494–1514 20
Heralding Noah's Flood: Messianic and Mystical Innovations in the Safavid Chancellery 30
Recovery of Persian Bureaucratic Culture and the Imperializing of Epistolary Rhetoric, 1514–24 46
Early Years of Ṭahmāsp and the Persian-Turk Paradigm, 1524–32 58

2. COMPETING COSMOLOGIES, 1532–55 68
Invective Rhetoric: al-Karakī and Models of Shi`ite Apologetic Discourse 71
Qāḍī-yi Jahān Qazvīnī and the "Men of the Pen" 88
Mystical Impulses and the Safavid *Inshā* Tradition 95

3. THE SECOND REPENTANCE, 1555–76 104
Reorientation to Qazvīn and the East 104
Solomonic Tropes 120
Polychromatic Impulses: `Abdī Beg Shīrāzī and the Chancellery 137

4. REX REDUX, 1576–98 145
Shāh Ismā`īl II's Challenge to the Hierocrats 145
The Emergence of a New Esprit de Corps under Khudābandah 158
Narrating and Mapping a New Safavid Dominion, 1588–98 176

CONCLUSION 198

Notes 203
Bibliography 264
Index 287

NOTE ON TRANSLITERATION

Common Arabic and Persian terms and names which have entered the English language, such as sultan, hadith, Shari`ah, have been anglicized. Place and personal names, however, have been fully transliterated.

Persian and Arabic characters have been transliterated according to the table given below.

ا	a, i, u
آ	ā
ب	b
پ	p
ت	t
ث	s̲
ج	j
چ	ch
ح	ḥ
خ	kh
د	d
ذ	dh
ر	r
ز	z
ژ	zh
س	s
ش	sh
ص	ṣ

ض	ḍ
ط	ṭ
ظ	ẓ
ع	`
غ	gh
ف	f
ق	q
ک	k
گ	g
ل	l
م	m
ن	n
و	ū
ه	h
ی	ī
ء	’
و	dipthong: au
ی	dipthong: ai

ACKNOWLEDGEMENTS

The writing and completion of this book would have been impossible without the assistance and advice from a number of individuals and institutions. First and foremost, I would like to express my gratitude to my former supervisor, Maria Subtelny, for her never-ending support and inspiration. It was she who introduced me to the intricate world of medieval Perso-Islamic epistolography, and I imagine I would still be mired in an array of didactic epistolary manuals if not for her patient and insightful guidance. Other sources of scholarly tutelage during my doctoral degree include Virginia Aksan and Roger Savory, who both provided a wealth of suggestions and tips while writing a dissertation on the medieval Safavid dynasty. I would also like to thank Robert McChesney whose remarks as external examiner were invaluable.

The transformation of this project from a doctoral dissertation to a formal academic text has taken me on a lengthy journey, during which I visited places and met individuals who each played a unique and often invaluable role. I would formally like to thank the Social Sciences and Humanities Research Council of Canada and the Andrew W. Mellon Foundation for providing me with post-doctoral scholarships that allowed me to teach and research at the Department of Near Eastern Studies, Cornell University. While sharing co-appointments to Near Eastern Studies and the Society for the Humanities at Cornell, I was able to significantly broaden the scope and depth of this research project. These fellowships also allowed research trips to Iran and Europe, and I would like to thank the Institut Français de Recherche en Iran for providing lodging and institutional support while staying in Tehran. A number of individuals were especially helpful during these sojourns, including Nasrullah Pourjavady, Ehsan Eshraqi, Reza Pourjavady, Ziva Vesel, Justine Lundau, and John Davidson. I would also like to thank the staff and administration of the Central University Library of Tehran University as well as the Library of the Majlis-i Shura-yi Islami. In addition, I would like to express my gratitude to the British Library, particularly Dr. Isa Waley, as well as the staff of the Bodleian Library at Oxford University and the Bibliothèque Nationale in Paris.

Various individuals have been involved to some degree in helping this project along, either in the form of practical advice or taking time to read sections or chapters. These include: Maria Subtelny, Sholeh Quinn, Bill Hanaway, Paul Losensky, Rudi Matthee, C.E. Bosworth, Sajjad Rizvi, Bert Fragner, Christoph Werner, Maria Szuppe, and Reza Pourjavady. I would also like to indicate my gratitude to Nasrin `Askari for her help with particularly problematic Persian texts. Likewise, I would like to thank my colleague, Amal Ghazal, for her assistance with Arabic translations. I would like to acknowledge the financial and intellectual support of my department and the Faculty of Arts and Social Sciences of Dalhousie University. The logistical and financial assistance from the BIPS' Persian Studies series, headed by Vanessa Martin, was very much appreciated, and I'd also like to thank the anonymous, external reviewers for their detailed, insightful comments on my manuscript. On the editorial front, I'm indebted to Paula Sarsen and Brenda Conroy for their tireless efforts.

I would like to thank my parents and extended family, and I am grateful to my sons, Maxwell and Thomas, for providing distractions when they were most needed. Above all else, I cannot understate the sense of indebtedness I feel to my wife Jill for her unwavering support and love.

INTRODUCTION

Knowledge is the shaper of words, pouring ideas into the moulds of letters.
— Ḥusain Vā`iẓ Kāshifī, *Makhzan al-inshā*
("Treasury of Epistolary Composition"), *MS*, Paris,
Bibliothèque Nationale, Supplément persan, no. 73, fol. 3a.

Cycles of Persian Mytho-history and Abrahamic Prophecy: Locating "Formational" Safavid Iran

The popular interpretation of the emergence of a robust empire under the Safavid dynasty in 906/1500–01 as a watershed in Iranian history is no surprise, given that one of the more dynamic historiographical undercurrents in this field has been the question of Iran's ability to survive as a distinct cultural entity after successive periods of domination by Arabs, Turks, and Mongols.[1] While the ethnic origins of the Safavid family remain unclear, this "Persian" dynasty promulgated Twelver Shi`ism as state doctrine and arguably laid the foundation in Iran for a well-entrenched and aggressive class of Shi`ite jurists and theologians, who were governed principally by a religious and legal framework first formed in the Arab world. More satisfying explanations for understanding the endurance of an "Iranian" identity probably lie with the impressive variegation of Persian culture that had developed leading up to the Safavid period. Dating back to the Indo-Aryan large-scale migrations of the second millennium BCE, the Iranian Plateau has been an arena of acculturation on a dramatic scale: Mesopotamian jurisprudence, Zoroastrian dualism, Buddhist mystical philosophy, Indian mathematics, Semitic universalism, and Hellenistic political philosophy and ethics. The seventh-century spread of Islam and the subsequent supremacy of Arabo-Islamic culture between the eighth and eleventh centuries only added another dimension to the well-established traditions of syncretism in the region. With the strong Hellenistic and Byzantine influences at work, some have hypothesized an "Irano-Mediterranean" cultural frontier in which Islam "consummated" the monarchical and monotheistic trends of late antiquity.[2] With the ongoing Turkic migrations from the Steppe Region after the tenth century and the dramatic arrival of the Mongols in the thirteenth century, "Greater Iran"—Āzarbāijān, `Irāq, the Iranian Plateau, Khurāsān, and Transoxania—had indeed emerged as a part of the Islamic world that was unsurpassed in religious and cultural plurality.

This plurality—or at least the perception of it—was seriously challenged with the advent of the modern era. Beginning in the nineteenth century, strands of nationalist historiography emerged that openly praised the glories of pre-Islamic Iran while vilifying the stultification and backwardness of Muslim Arab civilization. This invigorated program of Persian cultural authority was bolstered by rereading and popularizing a number of "Iran-glorifying" texts, and as Tavakoli-Targhi has noted, mytho-historical texts like the *Shāh nāmah* gained authority and were recited popularly towards a "process of cultural transference that intensified the desire for a recovery of the 'forgotten history' of ancient Iran."[3] Intellectuals and literary figures of the Qajar period developed a narrative of a timeless "homeland" (*vaṭan*) and "patriotism" (*ḥubb-i vaṭan*), but it should be noted that some of this was in response to the imperial ambitions of the Ottoman, Russian, and British empires.[4] If such Iranian nationalists worked stolidly to inflate the grandeur of pre-Islamic Persian history, they were frenetic in their efforts to distance themselves from Arabic culture and the Islamic faith; as the acerbic Arabophobe, Mīrzā Fatḥ `Alī Akhundzādah (1812–78), stated: "the Arabs were the cause of the Iranian people's misfortune.... It has been 1,280 years now that the naked and starving Arabs have descended upon [Iran] and made [its] life miserable."[5] This concept of "Iranian-ness" was reinforced and promoted even more so during the Pahlavī era, and Mohammed Reza Shah did his utmost to link the regime with his ancient "Aryan" predecessors.[6] For those elements of modern Iranian society that were deemed inconsistent with this greater cultural agenda, such as Arabic and Qur'ānic scholars working in theological seminaries in Qum or popular Azeri cultural movements based in Tabrīz, there was little accommodation.

In 1979, Iran was set on a theocratic course, and the argument of a pre-Islamic age of glory became anathema, at least to the new clerical custodians. For the Ayatollah Khomeini, those mythical and historical kingships of ancient Iran were products of the "age of ignorance" (*zamān-i jahāliyya*). Moreover, those caliphates and kingships that ruled after the seventh-century revelation of the message of Islam to the Prophet Muḥammad were a clear abrogation of Twelver Shi`ite doctrine: only a descendant of Muḥammad through `Alī, an Imam, could lead the Muslim community. Predictably, the Persian cultural predilections developed during the Qajar and Pahlavi periods were refashioned. Those pre-Islamic kings and heroes who dominated ancient Iranian mytho-history, like Darius and Rustam, were superceded by an Arab and Judaic "prophetography," whereby Adam, Moses, Solomon, Jesus, and Muḥammad now stood in their place. The ancient Iranian religion of Zoroastrianism had enjoyed a certain degree of official sentimentality from the Pahlavi regime, as had the Baha'i community, but Zoroastrians and Baha'is alike found themselves marginalized after 1979.

On account of Twelver Shi`ite doctrine and orthopraxy, Arab personalities like `Alī, Ḥasan, and Ḥusain were especially vaunted, and religious rituals such as the `Ashūra commemoration of Ḥusain's martyrdom at Karbalā became popular after decades of religious antipathy on the part of the Pahlavi regime. Officials of the Islamic Republic of Iran threatened to abolish the celebration of certain pre-Islamic Iranian festivals dating back to the Achaemenian period, most notably the marking of the New Year during the spring equinox. Concurrently, senior hierocrats directed state resources and manpower towards exclusive commemoration of events associated with early Arabo-Islamic history, such as the birth and death of the Prophet and the various martyrdoms of the Prophet's descendants.

These political turns and shifts have had no small impact on the historical study of Safavid Iran. Particularly, debate has persisted regarding the extent to which medieval Iranian dynasties like the Safavids balanced the respective appeals of pre-Islamic Iranian mytho-history and the golden Prophetic Age of seventh-century Medina and Mecca as sources of "collective self-view," to use Dürkheimian language. As noted by Colin Heywood in his celebrated essay on mytho-history and Ottoman studies, this notion of Islamic societies being moulded and characterized by appeals to different elements of their past has been a tenacious historiographical feature.[7] The varying ramifications for such "classicism" was first articulated with any coherency by the notable Islamic historian, G. E. Von Grunebaum, who suggested that classicism in the Islamic context was in reality "a tool to assist in the realization of the aspirations of the age that elects to seek fulfillment on the conjured-shadow of an authoritative model past."[8] In terms of how such classicism dictated medieval Perso-Islamic dynasties like the Safavids, there remains much to be done.[9]

This study contends that the Safavid state developed a dynastic legitimacy that operated on a multiplicity of levels which, in turn, reflected the complex and multifaceted nature of the medieval eastern Islamic world. In building their dynastic ideology, the Safavid shahs successfully incorporated an extremely variegated collection of political, cultural, and religious identities in a way that later regimes of Iran were unable, or unwilling, to do. The Safavid appreciation for "mythistory"[10] was not confined to Achaemenian and Sasanian periods, nor was their religious program defined strictly by orthodox Islamic interpretations of prophecy and eschatology. They were not exclusive in their patronage of different ethnic elements, and they would at times show religious tolerance toward indigenous and foreign non-Muslims. In Safavid official rhetoric, distributed both within and without Iran, imperial and pre-Islamic Persian icons stood side -by side with the greatest figures of Islamic prophecy and Shi`ite hagiography: King Darius and the Prophet Muḥammad, King Jamshīd and Imām `Alī, Emperor Anūshīrvān and the sixth Imām Ja`far Ṣādiq. This in itself is not entirely surprising, given that the medieval Islamic period was known for its amalgamation of Islamic orthodoxy with pre-Islamic Iranian concepts of justice, kingship, and social hierarchy.[11] Rulers representing the dynasties of the Timurids, the Qarā

Qoyūnlūs, the Āq Qoyūnlūs, the Uzbeks, the Mughals, and the Ottomans all accessed and rhetorically compared themselves to the mythical heroes and historical kings of Iran found in the *Shāh nāmah*, while at the same time standing as pious Muslim rulers who were implementing the Qur'ānic Shari`ah.

In the Safavid case, however, the dynasty was expected to rule on behalf of the Imamate (the twelve direct descendants of the Prophet Muḥammad) and cast themselves as both the custodians of the Shi`ite traditions and the legal plenipotentiaries of the *ahl al-bait* (Family of the Prophet). This issue of religious and cultural hybridity in premodern Iran has been recently examined by Kathryn Babayan in her study, *Mystics, Monarchs, and Messiahs.* Herein she identifies and examines a medieval Iranian "semiosphere," in which symbols and coded language reflect two distinct pre-Islamic Persianate and Islamic-Alid *ethoi* and "cultural systems," but Babayan notes that they are often merged and overlapped by religious scholars and bureaucrats during the Safavid period.[12]

In addition to these trilateral appeals—to pre-Islamic Iranian glory, the Abrahamic Prophetic traditions, and Imami hagiography and history—the Safavids also patronized and incorporated the Turkic and Mongolian elements of the Central Asian Steppe. The most visible manifestation of this dynamic was the Safavid promotion of Turkic amirs to prominent court positions and the use of their tribal clans and kinsmen for military purposes. This was not simply a policy of convenience for the Safavid shahs. They spoke Turkish, occasionally wrote poetry in Turkish, and remained true to the Central and Inner Asian tradition of an elaborate tent culture and a peripatetic royal court, despite popular categorizations of this dynasty as a "Persian" political renaissance. The Safavids had no problem rationalizing the inclusion of Turco-Mongolian titles of honour (*khān*, *bahādur*) to their ever-growing corpus of titulature, not to mention traditional Turco-Mongol notions of corporate familial sovereignty. The initial ethnic dichotomy in the Safavid court between Persian and Turk would soon become multitudinous as Shāh Ismā`īl and his successors patronized, supported, and incorporated Kurds, Arabs, Georgians, Circassians, and Armenians into the Safavid imperial project.

The Safavid ideological framework showed remarkable creativity and malleability with respect to different religious doctrines and their interpretation in the Safavid court. The decision by Shāh Ismā`īl to propagate Twelver Shi`ism was an endorsement of both the Qur'ānic-biblical cycle of prophecy, beginning with Adam and ending with Muḥammad, as well as the sanctity of the Imamate, or `Alī (son-in-law of the Prophet) and his descendants. This young ruler, however, emerged in a milieu defined by millenarian anxieties, which he manipulated by claiming divine sanction and support for a string of victories in his first ten years of power. The central Islamic world of the early sixteenth century was an unprecedented era with respect to contested space and competitive legitimacies, and the resulting ideological programs of investing political sovereignty with spiritual authority were undoubtedly "best illustrated in the triumph of the Safavi movement."[13]

Much to the distaste of orthodox Sunni and Shi`ite elements alike, Shāh Ismā`īl would continue to present himself in a messianic light to his Turkic tribal adherents as long as he continued to enjoy military and political success. The presentation of the Safavid shah as "the Perfect Man" (*al-insān al-kāmil*), in turn, reflected a strong Neoplatonic/Gnostic influence at work, which had been articulated systematically by the school of mystical philosophy rooted in the writings of Ibn `Arabī. While these proclivities would be tempered, vestiges of such apocalyptic and Gnostic imagery would continue to be represented in Safavid ideology throughout the sixteenth century. In addition to mollifying Turkic Qizilbāsh[14] supporters, any mystical dimension to Safavid dynastic rhetoric was instrumental in securing the support of the large number of different Sufi orders, or *ṭarīqahs*. Such *ṭarīqahs* dominated the religio-political landscape of sixteenth-century Iran and Central Asia, and their support and ultimate assimilation were considered imperative for a nascent dynasty like the Safavids.

Thus, it is difficult to see the "formational" reigns of Ismā`īl (1501–24), Ṭahmāsp (1524–76), and `Abbās (1589–1629) through an exclusive lens of Persian Twelver Shi`ism, which in turn allowed for the formation of a national identity.[15] This is not to deny the centrality of Twelver Shi`ism to the Safavid imperial project but simply to point out that there was a panoply of important religious, ethnic, and political constituencies in play during the sixteenth century. Indeed, the underlying premise of this present work is that Safavid ideological pretensions in the sixteenth century were reflections of this unparalleled heterogeneity, and that this malleability allowed them to survive the transition from parochial mystical movement to political empire and emerge as a viable, premodern Islamic state. During this period, the Safavid shahs relied on an impressively variegated range of legitimization, which included `Alid messianic rhetoric (to mobilize their zealot nomadic adherents); Turco-Mongol symbols and apocryphal legends (to accentuate martial traditions and a sense of loyalty to Steppe); legalistic and orthopraxic aspects of Twelver Shi`ite doctrine; ancient, pre-Islamic Iranian notions of divine kingship and statecraft; and, lastly, a vigorous commitment to citing Abrahamic Prophetic history.

This issue of shifting legitimacies in Safavid Iran has been studied from a variety of perspectives, including Kathryn Babayan and Sholeh Quinn.[16] Whether it was court chronicles like Khvāndamīr's *Ḥabīb al-siyar* and Iskander Beg Munshī's *Tārīkh-i `ālam ārā-yi `Abbāsī* or Shāh Ṭahmāsp's memoirs (*Tazkirah-yi Ṭahmāsp*), various episodes in the history of the Safavids as both a religious movement and an imperial dynasty were interpreted and profiled to best suit the legitimacy that was in vogue at the time. This present study operates from similar premises but instead focuses on the Safavid state chancellery (*dīvān-i inshā* or *dār al-inshā*) to best understand these issues of collective and elite self-view in sixteenth-century Iran. The Safavids inherited and developed a healthy respect for diplomatic correspondence (*tarassul*), which will be discussed in more detail further on, and we thankfully have access to a sizeable corpus of epistolary evidence for the sixteenth and seventeenth centuries. While the majority of these letters, missives, and epistles have been collected and edited,[17] little has been done by way of approaching them with a greater historiographical agenda.[18] The overarching approach of this project is that diplomatic epistolary evidence from the Safavid court is a valuable index to this aforementioned issue of shifting legitimacies in the sixteenth century, whereby a number of paradigmatic discourses (mystical, millenarian, hierocratic, kingly, imperial) were adopted and exchanged in a relatively short period of time. The different constituent sections of such letters—*salutatio*s, *intitulatio*s, *inscriptio*s, *narratio*s, poetry, rhymed prose—comprise a wealth of prose and poetic material, which rhetorically manipulate and provide commentary on this wide-ranging collection of mythical, historical, and religious personalities. With each modification in dynastic legitimacy, Safavid epistolary stylists (*munshīs*) and secretaries (*kātib*s) incorporated a new body of tropes, metaphors, similes, and allusions to best present their current shah to the court and the outside world. At the same time, Safavid chancellery officials were subject to stylistic influences from both pre-existing dynasties (Timurids, Āq Qoyūnlū) as well as contemporaries (Ottomans, Mughals). The rhetorical epistolary tools available to the average Safavid stylist or chancellor were indeed wide in scope and deep in complexity.

Working with Rhetoric and Letter-writing in Perso-Islamic History

In addition to the corpus of historical chronicles, memoirs, prosopographies, biographies, traveller accounts, and other materials, this study places particular emphasis on epistolary texts produced by the Safavid chancellery. Focusing on such literature against the backdrop of rhetoric and legitimacy can be fraught with misunderstandings and misconceptions; therefore, it is critical to appreciate the unique understanding of epistolography (*inshā*) in the Perso-Islamic context and why it occupies such a compelling epistemological space for medieval Iranian culture. The general ethos of *inshā* as a formal genre of prose literature undoubtedly has its roots in the administrative impulses of the Umayyad and early `Abbasid state, in which official state correspondence, letters, communiqués, and other documents were formally subsumed under offices such as the *dīvān al-inshā wa al-rasā'il*.[19] It should be noted that much of what defined this administrative ethos and practice was inherited from older Sasanian Iranian traditions that had been preserved partially after the Arab invasions and reinvigorated enthusiastically thanks to the translation movement of the ninth and tenth centuries under the stewardship of `Abbasid intellectuals like Ibn al-Muqaffa'.[20]

With the advent of the `Abbasids and their program of synthesizing a broad brand of pre-Islamic traditions from the Sasanian, Roman, Greek, and Sanskrit contexts, the production of epistolary material was framed to some extent by Pahlavi and Hellenistic definitions of both epistolography and rhetoric. As well-established Iranian families of administrators and bureaucrats like the Barmakids were sponsored and encouraged by `Abbasid authorities, humanistic and scholastic appreciation for the rhetorical (*balāghat*) and oratory (*khaṭābat*) arts grew exponentially. The medieval Islamic world, like its European counterpart, soon understood rhetoric to be one of the principal and acceptable forms of discourse inherited from the Classical world.[21] The medieval preoccupations of the Christian and Islamic worlds alike with the principals of rhetoric were undoubtedly a result of their wholesale adoption of Aristotle's *Organon*, to which the Stagirite's *Rhetorica* was appended.[22] While no evidence exists that medieval Arab and Persian scholars worked with influential Roman texts on rhetoric such as Quintillian's *Institutatio oratoria* and Cicero's *De inventione*, they did continue to be influenced by Aristotelian definitions of rhetoric and poetics into the twelfth and thirteenth centuries.[23] Indeed, the most prominent Islamic philosophers provided a number of commentaries and discussions (extant and non-extant)[24] of Aristotle's *Rhetoric*, including the *Kitāb al-khaṭaba* by Abū al-Naṣr al-Fārābī,[25] *Didascalia in Rethoricam Aristotelis ex glosa alpharabii* (a Latin translation of a now lost text by al-Fārābī), *al-Ḥikma al-`arūḍiyya* by Ibn Sīnā,[26] as well as a short commentary by Ibn Rushd.[27]

Concurrently with these humanistic and philosophical explorations of rhetoric, Classical Arab philologists and exegetes began in the ninth and tenth centuries to analyze and debate Arabic poetry and Qur'ānic revelation in terms of sophisticated grammatical constructions.[28] The strict logical frameworks that dictated the study of the Qur'ān and Arabic grammar were extended to the art of *balāghat*, and we see this field imbued with a distinct taxonomical imperative.[29] The ensuing categorization of rhetoric as a "transmitted" science (*`ilm al-naql*) along with, for example, Qur'ānic exegesis (*tafsīr*) and jurisprudence (*fiqh*), ensured that *balāghat* stood side by side with Arabic grammar (*naḥw*) and syntax (*ṣarf*) as a formal field of inquiry. One of the earliest works in this regard was Ibn al-Mu`tazz's (d. 295/908) *Kitāb al-badī`* ("The Book of Rhetorical Embellishment"). This work constituted an extensive discussion on the use of rhetorical devices—metaphors, paronomasias, antitheses—in contemporary and pre-Islamic poetry and prose, including the Qur'ān.[30] It is conventionally understood that the art of literary rhetoric in both prose and poetry was being studied, discussed, and codified by Arabic grammarians and literary critics, but Natalia Chalisova has most recently pointed out that the new "embellished" style (*badī`*) had been closely linked with earlier poets of Persian origin, such as Bashshār ibn Burd (d. 166/783) and Abū Nuwās (d. 198/814), who were consciously emulating "the poetic and musical court traditions of Sasanid Iran."[31]

When tenth-century Mu`tazilites began to use rhetorical inquiry as a means of disputing the *`ijāz al-Qur'ān* (inimitability of the Qur'ān), one of the most celebrated texts on *balāghat* and systemization of Arabic literary devices was produced as an orthodox response by `Abd al-Qāhir al-Jurjānī (d. 408/1018): the "Secrets of Eloquence" (*Asrār al-balāghat*).[32] Literary rhetoric would be further expanded in the thirteenth century thanks to abridgements by individuals such as Fakhr al-Dīn al-Rāzī (d. 605/1209) and Abū Ya`qūb Yūsuf al-Sakkākī (d. 626/1229). Al-Sakkākī's work, *Miftāḥ al-`ulūm* ("Key to the Sciences"), contained a chapter on stylistics and imagery that organized al-Jurjānī's previous work into three broad components: *`ilm al-ma`ānī* (study of syntax), *`ilm al-bayān* (study of figurative language, i.e., similes, metaphors, tropes), and *`ilm al-badī`* (study of rhetorical embellishment).[33] It was on account of the *Miftāḥ al`ulūm* and later commentaries like Qazvīnī's *Takhlīṣ al-miftāḥ* that madrasahs began to include *`ilm al-balāghat* as a formal recognizable component of their curricula, a trend which would continue into the modern era.[34] By the thirteenth century, the genre of Arabic *inshā* had undergone a fairly intense process of hybridization, whereby scribes and secretaries were expected to produce chancellery materials and formal correspondence with prose tools and devices (borrowed extensively from the poetic traditions) that had been systemized by medieval grammarians like al-Jurjānī and al-Sakkāki. In this sense, we find a strong penchant for parallelism and assonance and the dominance of rhymed (*musajj`a*) epistolary style, which initially bloomed during the Buyid period and continued well into the twelfth and thirteenth centuries.[35]

With the advent of New Persian as the dominant administrative language in central and eastern Islamic lands during the Ghaznavid and Saljuq periods, this hybridity only further intensified as both scribe and litterateur attempted to reconcile the Arabic and Persian traditions in their respective settings. Indeed, the profusion of didactic texts in the twelfth and thirteenth centuries on the tradition of *inshā* appears to be a response to the frustrations of new generations of Persian administrators as they sought to navigate this increasingly difficult discursive practice in the chancellery setting. Some formative texts in Persian on rhetoric and prose writing took the form of technical prosodic manuals and, as such, demonstrate how poetic structures, metres, rhyming patterns, and other devices were borrowed and adapted to prose writing, specifically epistolary prose. The interdependence of prose and poetic traditions in medieval Islamic courts can make it difficult to consign poets (*shā`ir*s) and prose stylists (*munshī*s) to different realms; it would probably be better to think of these individuals first and foremost as litterateurs, or *adīb*s, who operated comfortably in a number of genres.

One of the most well-known Persian works on prosody and prose was Muḥammad ibn `Umar Rādūyānī's *Tarjuman al-balāghat* ("The Interpreter of Rhetoric," ca. 493/1100). He noted the dearth of material to date on Persian and expressed frustration at the degree to which Arabic monopolized analyses of rhetoric and poetic technique.[36] Rādūyānī laid the foundation for Persian *inshā* with his exposition of the literary devices that are borrowed from Arabic and applied to New Persian, including various types of *tajnīs* (paronomasia), *tashbiyyah* (simile), *isti`ārah* (metaphor), and specific devices such as *irdāf* (synonym), *iltifāt* (transition), and *iltizām* (amalgamation of new and old verses).[37] Much of Rādūyānī's schemata were paralleled by Rashīd al-Dīn Vaṭvāṭ in his own influential work on prosody, the *Ḥadā'iq al-siḥr fī daqā'iq al-shi`r* (ca. 544/1150), but Vaṭvāṭ appears to have been more accommodating with respect to Arabic poetry.[38] Shams al-Dīn Muḥammad ibn Qais al-Rāzī (Shams-i Qais) later assembled his unequalled manual on Perso-Arabic poetic rules and devices in the *Al-Mu`jam fī ma`āyir ash`ār al-`ajam* ("A Compendium of the Standards of Persian Poetry") in 629/1232.[39] These last two works would, in many ways, mould subsequent centuries of Persian literary analysis as Marta Simidchieva demonstrated recently in her treatment of Ḥusain Vā'iẓ Kāshifī's own prosodic contribution, the *Badāyi` al-afkār fī ṣanāyi` al-ash`ār*, during the late Timurid period.[40] This medieval penchant for establishing taxonomies of literary devices and their implications for the organization and perception of specific societal groups (including secretaries and poets) is also discernible in other works like Kay Kāvūs's *Qābūs nāmah*, Muḥammad Maihānī's *Dastūr-i dibīrī* and Niẓāmī `Arūḍī Samarqandī's *Chahār maqālah*.[41]

Buttressed significantly by individuals like Vaṭvāṭ and Shams-i Qais, the medieval epistolary sciences (*`ulūm al-inshā*) blossomed as an intricate literary genre in the Persianate world after the thirteenth century. On a more practical level, the adoption of Persian by a number of different Turkic and Mongol dynasties and the emergence of Persian as the principal diplomatic medium only reinforced the importance of the epistolary sciences, however ornate and artificial they may have been. While some Arabic manuals on epistolography and features of chancellery culture had been produced during this period, the overwhelming bulk of medieval Muslim works on *`ilm-i inshā* were produced in Persian. Medieval scholars like Muntajab al-Dīn Badī` Atabeg al-Juvainī (author of *`Ataba al-kataba*) and Bahā' al-Dīn al-Baghdādī (author *of al-Tavassul īlā al-tarassul*), however, would reiterate the centrality of Arabic grammar, rhetoric, and syntax.[42] In the celebrated fourteenth-century *Dastūr al-kātib fī ta`yyīn al-marātib* ("Manual of the Scribe on Affixing Ranks"), Muḥammad ibn Hindūshāh Nakhjūvānī hoped to "inform the disciple of *inshā* with the medicines of language and the compounds of acknowledgment by drinking from the vessels of the science of inflection and syntax [*`ilm-i naḥw va ṣarf*] which were [ultimately] drawn from the watering-holes of the Arabic [literary] customs [*muvārad-i aqsām-i `arabiyyat*]."[43]

Following the debilitating Mongol invasions and Ilkhanate era of the thirteenth and fourteenth centuries, the Timurid period of the late fifteenth century saw a resurgence of interest in *inshā* by Persian scholar-bureaucrats—to borrow Cemal Kafadar's term[44]—with the *Risālah-yi qavānīn* by Mu`īn al-Dīn Muḥammad Zamchī Isfizārī, the *Manshā al-inshā* by Niẓām al-Dīn `Abd al-Vāsi`, the *Munsha'āt* of `Abd al-Raḥmān Jāmī, the *Nāmah-yi nāmī* by Khvāndamīr, and the well-known *Sharaf nāmah* by `Abd Allah Marvārīd.[45] Elsewhere, I have argued that the Timurid period represented a high period for *inshā* writing, during which scholar-bureaucrats like Marvārīd and `Abd al-Vāsi` were intent on approaching epistolary composition as a mode of high literary style and not simply as a means to instruct scribes on the mundane protocol of drafting imperial decrees and letters.[46] While there were a number of didactic *inshā* works, it also became increasingly in vogue to present works on *inshā* in the form of compendiums of letters, imperial orders, administrative decrees, and other sundry bureaucratic documents. The sixteenth-century Safavids were very much beneficiaries of this multifaceted and multidimensional practice of *inshā*. The profusion of didactic and formulaic *inshā* manuals after the sixteenth century suggests that epistolography continued to be a popular genre among litterateurs in not only the Safavid court[47] but also in the Mughal[48] and Ottoman[49] empires. The best review of this genre of material dealing with chancellery writing is Dāneshpazhūh's seminal 1973 bibliographical article, "Nivīsandagī va dabīrī," which itemizes the hundreds of *inshā* manuals and collections of *munsha'āt* material produced between 1200 and 1900, and in doing so, underscores the centrality of the *`ulūm-i inshā* to both medieval literary standards as well as administrative procedures and customs.[50]

Returning to the methodology of this current study, we find then our principal body of evidence operating within defined, yet certainly complex, frameworks of ontology and epistemology. To label such epistolary texts as simply "belles-lettres" is a gross oversimplification, and they cannot be dismissed simply as flowering rhetorical exercises.[51] In light of the ultimate objective of *The Practice of Politics in Safavid Iran*—namely using epistolary material to locate and identify dominant ideological trends within the sixteenth-century Safavid court—there are some relatively important implications to consider with respect to the provenance of *inshā* and its use by litterateur administrators in the medieval context. The concept of stylized epistolography, although crystallized in the `Abbasid period and increasingly polished in the Perso-Islamic context, was rooted in much older fifth- and sixth-century Sasanian literary traditions and administrative practice.[52] This is not altogether surprising, given the degree to which later `Abbasid secretaries and litterateurs like Ibn al-Muqaffa', Qudāma ibn Ja`far, and Ibn Qutaibah revived such older Iranian administrative traditions.[53] We know that a number of middle Persian technical administrative terms were adopted and continued by `Abbasid-era secretaries, while various manuals on courtly ethics and etiquette, such as the *Advēnak-nāmak i Nipēshishnīh* ("Models of Epistolary Style"), found themselves rearticulated (either in full or in part) in later Arabic translations and commentaries like the *Kitāb al-tāj* of pseudo-al-Jāḥiẓ and the *Tajārib al-umam* of Ibn Miskawaih or referred to by Ibn al-Nadīm in his *Fihrist*.[54]

More profound, perhaps, was the interdependence of epistolography and political ethics that developed in Sasanian court and society. The Middle Persian genre of "wisdom literature" (*andarz*), which saw collections of political, religious, and ethical maxims and aphorisms presented in both epistolary and testamentary frameworks, was of great interest to later Arab and Iranian Muslim scholars. It can be safe to assume that the profusion of political advice manuals (*akhlāq*) in the eleventh and twelfth centuries was inspired by these recirculated traditions from the ancient Sasanian period.[55] The most popular example of this epistolary gnomic literature was the *Tansar nāmah*, a letter allegedly sent by the ruler Ardashīr to King Goshnāsp of Ṭabaristān that used the rhetorical flourishes and discursive tools of the day to persuade Goshnāsp to accept Sasanian suzerainty and convert to Zoroastrianism.[56] This text, first translated from Pahlavī into

Arabic by Ibn al-Muqaffa', was later translated into Persian and popularized by the thirteenth-century scholar, Muḥammad ibn Ḥasan ibn Isfandiyār. In addition to discussing proper kingly behaviour and the application of justice, such texts would profile traditional Iranian societal orders and stratifications. In the case of the *Tansar nāmah* and the other popular testament known as the *`Ahd Ardashīr*, secretaries (*dabīrān*) and administrators not surprisingly accorded themselves a relatively high rank among the priests and warriors of Sasanian elite society.[57] Among the earliest Arabo-Islamic literary forms were such political epistles (*risālat*s) and testaments (*waṣiyyat*s) from religious scholars that advised and admonished caliphs and rulers on proper kingly behaviour during the Umayyad and `Abbasid ages.[58] From the orthodox Shi`ite perspective, this dynamic was clearly reified in `Alī's collections of sermons (*khuṭṭāb*) and letters (*rasā'il*) to supporters and enemies alike.[59]

These conceptions of epistolography, rhetoric, and the role of the rhetorician in a model society would become further nuanced and refined as ninth- and tenth-century Arabo-Islamic civilization incorporated various aspects of Hellenic culture. Luminaries such as Abū Naṣr al-Fārābī (referred to as "the Second Teacher" after Aristotle) sought specifically to rationalize these "ancient sciences" (*al-`ulūm al-awā'il*) with Islamic monotheistic orthodoxy.[60] Al-Fārābī and subsequent philosophers like Ibn Sīnā and Ibn Rushd would emulate the Classical world's respect for the rhetoricians (*khuṭabā, fuḍalā*) in society. In his Arabo-Islamic version of *The Republic*, the *al-Madīna al-fāḍila* ("The Perfect City"), al-Fārābī wrote of how "the 'orators' who have complete mastery of an efficient and artistic prose style can convince non-philosophical minds of ultimate truth."[61] As John Watt has noted, al-Fārābī discounted the logical status of rhetorical discourse in philosophy but accepted it as a "means to instruct the multitude and for use in public business."[62]

In this sense, medieval Muslim philosophers embraced Aristotelian divisions of rhetoric, e.g., "deliberative" and "epideictic," which addressed respectively the maintenance of a *polis* and the acknowledgement of virtue and vice in a society.[63] If not entirely accepted as a forum of philosophical dialectic, rhetoric nonetheless underwent intense systemization and commentary as a multifaceted literary tool. Medieval Muslim scholarship clearly embraced the Aristotelian notion of rhetoric and how it provided "the faculty of observing the means of persuasion on almost any subject presented to us," while understanding that Aristotle's advocacy of the use of figurative language within rhetorical discourse had far-reaching implications.[64] In this sense, the oratorical and argumentative rhetoric (*khaṭābat*) associated with the ancients was supplanted by an understanding of rhetoric as a vehicle of tropes and other figurative language, or what came to be known as the science of *balāghat* (*`ilm al-balāghat*).[65]

Inshā and *Munshīs*: A Discursive Forum

In the context of a medieval Perso-Islamic court like that of the Safavids, the custodians of this hybridized discourse of epistolography and rhetoric were undoubtedly the Persian *ahl al-qalam* ("men of the pen"). These very same individuals defined the administrative class, which was responsible for the smooth maintenance of a state's bureaucracy and overall polity.[66] It was these urbanite bureaucrats who found patronage through serving the central, provincial, and municipal authorities in a variety of capacities: assessing and collecting taxes, drafting and promulgating royal decrees, overseeing religious endowments (*auqāf*), and clerical administrating. Furthermore, it was these men of the pen, or "scholar-bureaucrats," who created, preserved, copied, and transmitted the most popular and compelling literary, scientific, philosophic, and religious discourses of the medieval period. Such men were products of the *adab* tradition, which could be understood as the Hellenistic notion that happiness and social stability are rooted in education and scholarly study of all pertinent aspects of Arabo- and Perso-Islamic civilization.[67]

Despite the categorization of rhetoric as a "transmitted" science and its prescription as a formal field of inquiry in the study of Arabic grammar and syntax, there is good reason to believe that literary rhetoric was understood by Persian *ahl al-qalam* within the context of political philosophy and ethics as defined in the Pahlavi and Hellenistic worlds. Early formulations of *adab* education were framed significantly by the Pahlavi and Graeco-Arabic translation enterprise in the `Abbasid court, wherein Iranian and Hellenistic treatises and pseudo-texts were used to centralize the role of rhetoric and ethics in the education of young men.[68] An early biography of Aristotle, appearing in Abū Sulaimān al-Sijistānī's *Siwān al-ḥikmat*, reflected in particular the importance of refined speech and rhetoric as a socio-political tool:

> [Philosophy] must be expressed by means of the most valid reasoning; most eloquent speech; purist language; and noblest expression, furthest from defect, vulgarity, and solecism.... Aristotle said that man's superiority over beasts is in speech, and the most worthy of humanity is the most accomplished in his speech and the most skilled in apposite and concise self-expression.[69]

For those `Abbasid and post-`Abbasid scribal custodians of *adab* culture, rhetoric was inextricably linked with coherent philosophical and ethical discourse. This particular appreciation for rhetoric was never lost in the medieval Perso-Islamic world; the ethical and poetical works by the intellectual leviathan Naṣīr al-Dīn al-Ṭūsī (d. 672/1274) echo these trends quite distinctly.[70] Al-Ṭūsī's politico-ethical treatise, the *Akhlāq-i Nāṣirī,* reiterated the need for and the high rank of rhetoricians in society. Like al-Fārābī, he positioned the exclusive "Perfect Philosophers" (*ḥukamā*)—ideally rulers and prophets—in the highest societal rank, while insisting that the second class, "the Masters of the Tongue" (*zū al-lisān*), were needed "to bring the common people and the lower elements to degrees of relative perfection."[71] "Masters of the Tongue" here was not meant to be understood in a literal fashion, i.e., as orators, since their craft is wide-ranging and "comprises the sciences of Scholastics, Jurisprudence, Elocution, Rhetoric, Poetry, and Calligraphy."[72] Later political ethics manuals from the fifteenth century, like al-Davvānī's *Akhlāq-i Jalālī* and Kāshifī's *Akhlāq-i Muḥsinī*, would replicate the models set forth by al-Ṭūsī and underscore the centrality of this stream of political ethics.[73] For instance, when the English humanist traveller, John Fryer, visited Iran in the late 1670s, he observed how the books of Khvājah Naṣīr al-Dīn al-Ṭūsī were still in the "greatest vogue" despite being written five hundred years earlier.[74]

In terms of political philosophy, the Nasirean framework set forth by al-Ṭūsī extolled those practitioners of rhetoric who had grown to be associated with a highly ranked class of society that was mandated to uphold political and societal order. It was in the fifteenth century and continuing throughout the period from 1501 to 1598 that we see increasingly acknowledgment of this role for scribes, calligraphers, and chancellery stylists in a typical Perso-Islamic court.[75] The Safavid bureaucracy, certainly along with its Ottoman and Mughal counterparts in Istanbul and Agra, grew in size, sophistication, and relative importance during the sixteenth and seventeenth centuries. In this context, rhetoric and its manifestation in official chancellery materials assume a distinction as a means of persuasive discourse—as Stephen D. O'Leary calls it, a "socially constituted utterance discipline located at the intersection of aesthetics, politics, and ethics"—which was especially significant in an era of increasing confessional apologetics. In this vein, epistolography and chancellery culture in sixteenth-century Safavid Iran were understood as arenas for Persian men of the pen to amalgamate the technical, literary tools of rhetoric—or the "interplay of style, form, content, and context," as O'Leary describes it—with an appreciation of their value towards political and religious legitimization.

Faced with texts that were arguably tautological and periphrastic, historians have impinged upon the value of such diplomatic correspondence on the basis that it offers little in the way of "real" historical information.[76] Such scholarly stances are obviously rooted in modern definitions of rhetoric as "empty discourse," which has no other purpose than flattery and mollification. Undoubtedly, this aversion is linked at least partially to the highly literary nature of the *inshā* genre and its methodological proximity to poetic devices and metrical constructs.[77] However, the *munshī* desired above all to use written language to convey meaning to his intended addressee, and in this sense, epistolary rhetoric reflects very much the root meaning of *balāghat*: "to reach out" and thus convey meaning. This conveyance was primarily through the use of figurative language that often denoted complex ideas and traditions, and it is these nuanced tropes and metaphors that abound in introductory protocols and narratives of medieval diplomatic correspondence. Metaphoric language was not designed to liken simply one thing to another, i.e., a ruler to a lion or a king to a star, but was meant to evoke instantly a set of ideas and emotions in a fashion that required little or no explication to the audience.[78] The strategic importance between concepts and images in rhetoric was noted by Kenneth Burke with respect to the Aristotelian impulse to "place an idea before our very eyes" through metaphors:

> There is a difference between an abstract term naming the "idea" of, say, security and a concrete image designed to stand for this idea, and to "place it before our very eyes." For one thing, if the image employed the full resources of imagination, it will not represent merely one idea, but will contain a whole bundle of principles.[79]

Exciting and manipulating the imagination (*khiyāl*) of an audience was considered a fundamental feature of metrics and poetry by medieval Persian scholars; in fact, the concept of *takhyīl*, the evoking of images of subjects in the minds of listeners by means of figurative language, shared ontological primacy in both poetry and rhetoric. In her masterful study *Structure and Meaning in Medieval Arabic and Persian Poetry*, Julie Scott Meisami reiterates this interpretation of metaphor and figurative language as largely designed to persuade or influence: "metaphors, comparisons, images, are not merely decorative, fanciful, descriptive, nor even (primarily) affective, but argumentative."[80] Metaphors, above all, function as persuasive devices, and the art of persuasion is a collective enterprise whereby assemblies of rhetoricians manipulate contemporary symbols and icons for a particular constituency. Thus, it is only rhetoricians and poets who can use their literary skills to access a reservoir of fables, anecdotes, parables, aphorisms, dictums, and narratives about various historical and legendary figures towards sophisticated metaphorical constructs. A set of specialized skills such as these were the purview of the Perso-Islamic *adībs* (both poets and *munshīs*), and they sought and found support and patronage in milieus where their skills could be most effectively employed: dynastic courts and chancelleries.

This all assumes the premise that the respective partners in an epistolary exchange are working with the same cognitive tools. In those climes where Persian literature, Islamic prophetography, and Sufi-Shi`ite hagiography dominated both elite and popular culture (Ottoman Turkey, Caucasus, Iran, Central Asia, Indian subcontinent), *munshīs* could maximize an extensive system of intricate allusions, tropes, similes, metaphors, and other literary devices. The Safavids' "classicist" appeals to pre-Islamic Persia and the Prophetic Near East and Arabia were also part of a common corpus of images and memories for those same products of *adab* culture in the Ottoman, Uzbek, and Mughal chancelleries. The reader who encounters the metaphorical use of a heroic, monarchic, or Prophetic exemplar, such as Rustam, Solomon, or Muḥammad, consciously or subconsciously associates with it a rich assortment of tales, legends, aphorisms, and maxims. Kathryn Babayan has made similar observations in her recent study of Safavid religious culture whereby she identifies a web of symbols and imagery, or in her words: "Persianate and Alid idioms [which] mediated Safavi actions and narratives through cultural constructs of authority, loyalty, honor and piety."[81] Historical memory was pivotal in this context, and it was to the Safavids' credit that they were able to employ and amalgamate a wide array of "clusters of symbols" from Iran's pre-Islamic and Islamic heritage. The employment of such idioms and historical exemplars in diplomatic titulature was designed to graft or superimpose their religious and political significance to a contemporary individual.

In the *adab* world of the Persian "men of the pen," the rhetorical use of exemplars when lionizing an addressee or sender was designed to signal particular virtues or ethics. For instance, the mythic king Jamshīd was associated with justice and *hubris*; the Arab king Zahhak was the embodiment of tyranny and paranoia; Solomon was the paragon of wisdom and innovation; Alexander was the military strategist par excellence; while Shi`ite Imamate personalities like `Alī, Ḥusain, and Ja`far al-Ṣādiq were associated with bravery, martyrdom, and erudition respectively. This is not to say that such mytho-historical figures could not embody a multiplicity of virtues, but in terms of exemplary rhetoric, such signalling was often meant to evoke particular characteristics.[82] We also cannot forget that much of the Safavid program in its earlier manifestation was predicated upon revolutionary, millenarian sensibilities, and the communicative power of manipulating sets of certain icons and figures towards a program of dynastic and familial support was crucial. In the Safavid context, it was a question of when and how to substitute one set of icons for another as they morphed and changed from one religio-political entity into another during the sixteenth century.

This concept of exemplarity in rhetoric has been discussed by Timothy Hampton, who analyzed how humanists like Erasmus, Montaigne, and Cervantes rhetorically manipulated exemplars from Classical and Biblical antiquity.[83] Particularly, he argues that the "praise of the ancient as model of selfhood appears throughout humanist advice literature" and points out how "one of the normalizing functions of exemplarity is to offer images of coherent, ideologically marked subjects whose bodies and histories function in harmony."[84] Julie Scott Meisami has likewise argued for the fundamental importance of this idea of exemplarity in the context of medieval Iranian culture: "The exemplary function of literature does not reflect a reductionary process by which the individual is deprived of value, but precisely the opposite: a conviction that the individual validates the general principle."[85] These observations resonate strongly here as we try to understand how epistolary rhetoric was used to project political and religious legitimization both within Iran and to the outside Islamic world. Exemplary behaviour, or `*ibra*, was already a central component in the structure of political advice manuals and works of history in the medieval period.[86]

In the case of epistolary rhetoric, narratives were known to have been included, but more often than not the formulaic reference to a particular mytho-historical personality was meant to convey a larger corpus of ideas and concepts to the reader as was practiced in panegyric court poetry.[87] As early modern humanist scholars used the image and actions of Aeneas, Cyrus, and Marcus Aurelius to model themselves and hopefully "inflate" and "excite" their readers toward deed and action, likewise the Safavid scholar-bureaucrats accessed a cast of mythical and historical kings, heroes, and prophets to defend, promote, and extend Safavid sovereignty. Seen from a broader perspective, epistolary rhetoric was part of a strong tradition in Arabo- and Perso-Islamic civilization, which approached theories of kingship and statecraft largely on the basis of narratives of exemplary political and religious behaviour.[88] Moreover, when we acknowledge that political elites were invested in the inherent control of language, speech, and discourse as a necessary tool for articulating and defending authority, we can begin to see the merit in understanding more about the relationship between state epistolography and rhetoric.

A study linking diplomatic and courtly rhetoric with the formulation and articulation of dynastic legitimacy is invaluable for examining this syncretist period of Iranian history, when Prophetic history intermingled easily with apocryphal and heroic legends from the pre-Islamic Iranian Plateau as well as the Central Asian Steppe. Why Safavid rulers like Ismā`īl, Ṭahmāsp, Muḥammad Khudābandah, and a young `Abbās looked to domestic and foreign imperial correspondence as a means of projecting their ever-dynamic ideologies is rooted in the understanding that such rhetorical texts were understood primarily in a "Nasirean," or ethico-political, light. In other words, the Safavid bureaucratic elite worked within the tradition of Naṣīr al-Dīn al-Ṭūsī's teachings and specifically upheld the rhetorical sciences as a means of achieving and ensuring political stability in a model state or kingdom. In this fashion, we must understand that the writing of diplomatic correspondence within the *dīvān-i a`lā* was as important as its despatching to the outside Muslim world.

The creation of these documents by administrative agents of the Safavid state and their vetting by higher bureaucratic officials such as the *munshī al-mamālik* (chief chancellor) and the vizier along with the likelihood that such texts were recited publicly all combine to suggest that diplomatic materials enjoyed a considerable circulation and range of audience at home and abroad. More importantly, royal letters were often copied, preserved, and exchanged amongst both literati and the provincial chancelleries, and as such these texts functioned as important internal disseminators of legitimizing principles.[89] We have a broad spectrum of ideologies at work in the Safavid dynasty during the sixteenth century, and the *bricolage* of mythical icons and historical figures developed by the Safavid *ahl al-qalam* reflected in turn a creativity that was unsurpassed in Perso-Islamic history. Sixteenth-century Safavid ideology, however unwieldy and Chimera-like, was fundamental to their transition from parochial millenarian movement to political empire during the sixteenth century. This study contends that epistolary rhetoric is one of the best contemporaneous tools available to navigate and chart these ideological currents.

The Practice of Politics in Safavid Iran: Structure and Scope

The temporal scope of this present study is the sixteenth century, beginning with the millenarian ambitions of a young Shāh Ismā`īl surrounded by Türkmen zealots and concluding with the beginning years of the most successful ruler of the dynasty, Shāh `Abbās. This period is arguably the most varied and kinetic with respect to dynastic legitimization and most in need of clarification despite the recent contributions of Sholeh Quinn, Kathryn Babayan, and Maria Szuppe.[90] This book seeks to explore the multitudinous and dynamic nature of sixteenth-century Safavid dynastic legitimacy, and its dialectical relationship with the rhetoric produced by chancellery officials in administrative documents and imperial correspondence abroad.

By focusing on chancellery culture and the role its custodians played in the building of this imperial project during the pivotal reigns of Shāh Ismā`īl, Shāh Ṭahmāsp, Muḥammad Khudābandah, and a young Shāh `Abbās, this study will address a lacuna of some proportion in contemporary Safavid studies. The various types of imperial correspondence and decrees (*munsha'āt, maktūbāt, farāmīn*) available in *inshā* compilations from the Safavid chancellery, as well as those Safavid letters preserved in Ottoman, Mughal, Uzbek, and Deccani *inshā* works, are relatively unexplored yet valuable tools. Scholarly interest in chancellery culture and epistolography has been seen in Mughal and Ottoman studies,[91] but relatively little has been produced in Safavid scholarship.[92] Hopefully, a study of Safavid *munsha'āt*, framed by larger questions of legitimacy, identity, and rhetorical expression, will find a receptive audience among specialists and non-specialists alike. For those interested in the perennial debate over Iranian identity and where the Safavids fit in the "continuous narrative" of the Persian people, this study offers a perspective that is hitherto unexplored.

While the structure of this book is broadly based on chronology, particular emphasis is placed on not only analyzing Safavid chancellery materials but also exploring the composition of the Safavid chancellery in relation to larger, ongoing political and religious trends. This study's ambitions go beyond philological and hermeneutical readings of such epistolary texts. Rather, these *inshā* documents will be juxtaposed with the narrative of political and administrative events and developments. As such, they will provide more nuanced dimensions to the Safavid narrative in the sixteenth century, while also shedding light on the administration and how it evolved during this period. Two of the main Safavid manuscript collections (*majmū`ah*)—`Abd al-Ḥusain al-Ṭūsī's *Munsha'āt al-Ṭūsī* and Abū al-Qāsim Ḥaidar Beg Īvūghlī's *Nuskhah-yi jāmi`a-i al-murāsalāt-i ulul albab*—have been used extensively in conjunction with `Abd al-Ḥusain Navā'ī's edited collections of Persian documents. In addition to anonymous collections and lesser-known works on *inshā*, valuable and underused epistolary texts can be found in mainstream Safavid court chronicles like Qāḍī Aḥmad's *Khulāṣat al-tavārīkh*. It should be noted that this study focuses primarily on Persian diplomatic letters sent abroad by the Safavid chancellery. There is a relatively large body of internal decrees, imperial orders, and proclamations (e.g., *farmāns*, *manshūrs*, *ruq`as*, *misāls*), which are not necessarily analyzed here. In part, this is rationalized by the emphasis of this study that Safavid dynastic articulations were at their strongest in formal, imperial *tarassul*. Lesser decrees, while arguably important for domestic consumption, were not conceived of by *munshīs* in the same ethico-political light and were not considered ideal forums necessarily for fully fledged discursive enterprises. Substantial discussions of issues of legitimacy and the employment of mythico-historical topoi are relatively rare in such quotidian literature. It should be stated, however, that this study does examine some occasional and unique decrees that fall outside the norm for such administrative literature. In terms of laying out the political and administrative narrative, this study also makes use of a wide breadth of recently published Safavid sources, such as Khūrshāh ibn Qubād's *Tārīkh-i īlchī-yi Niẓāmshāh* and Būdāq Munshī's *Javāhir al-akhbār*.

Chapter 1, "Imperializing the Apocalypse, 1501–1532," examines the "emergence" and reign of Shāh Ismā`īl and how chancellery documents help us understand the transition of the Safavid movement from Sufi *ṭarīqah* to imperial polity as well as determine the degree of influence exerted by the militant, millenarian ethos of the Safavid empire in its earliest years under Shāh Ismā`īl. Chapter 1 also explores how ideological pretensions were shifted considerably with the wholesale incorporation of Timurid bureaucratic culture in the 1510s and 1520s. These ex-Timurid scholar-bureaucrats in many ways had been the principal custodians of Perso-Islamic literary civilization in the post-Mongol world, and their patronage by the Safavid court was no insignificant development. Chapter 2, "Competing Cosmologies, 1532–1555" examines the arrival of the famous juridical Shi`ite scholar al-Karakī to the court of Shāh Ṭahmāsp, and how a growing presence of *fiqh*-minded, orthopraxic Twelver Shi`ites played an increasingly substantial role in the Safavid chancellery and its production of epistolary texts. By the 1530s, the millenarian rhetoric of Shāh Ismā`īl's earlier rule had been perceptibly lessened in tone, and chancellery officials were encouraged to incorporate not only tropes and metaphors but also sayings and deliberations associated with the Imami traditions. At the same time, however, we see the rise in administrative power of scions of long-standing bureaucratic families, namely men like Qāḍī-yi Jahān Qazvīnī, who challenged the brass-bounded orthodoxy of al-Karakī, and an increasing sense of cultural and religious competition appeared within the Safavid chancellery.

Chapter 3, "Second Repentance, 1555–1576," details how the chancellery was changed by the shah's decision to move the royal capital from Tabrīz to Qazvīn and the new theocratic dynamic that emerged with the establishment of various networks of Persian sayyid classes. Lastly, Chapter 4, "Rex Redux 1576–1598," details chancellery composition and comportment during the reigns of Ismā`īl II and Muḥammad Khudābandah and seeks to at least partially rehabilitate these rulers on the grounds that many of the greatest litterateurs, administrators, and historians during the later reign of Shāh `Abbās received their education, training, and early experience in the late 1570s and 1580s. This chapter also examines the new directions in style and technique of the Safavid administration during the first decade of Shāh `Abbās's rule before he initiated the plethora of political, military, administrative, and social reforms that characterized the last three decades of his reign.

1

IMPERIALIZING THE APOCALYPSE, 1501–32

This chapter is concerned with the emergence of the Safavid empire beginning in 1501 under Ismā`īl ibn Ḥaidar ibn Junaid Ṣafavī and its subsequent development in the next three decades under both Ismā`īl and his successor, Shāh Ṭahmāsp. Numerous profound and sweeping changes in Safavid political and religious culture occurred in the temporal scope studied here (1501–32). Ismā`īl was a charismatic religious authority who took a loose yet militant mystical organization of several thousand Sufis based parochially in Gīlān and Āzarbāijān and managed to carve out and consolidte a significant empire from the Caucasus to the region of Khurāsān in the east. Ismā`īl set the Safavid religious order on an imperial course, and the new shah worked to bridge the gap between millenarian mysticism and centralized, bureaucratized imperial polity. The intensity of this mélange of extreme *ghuluww* mysticism, `Alid Shi`ism, and ancient pre-Islamic Iranian concepts of both authority and religion is logically best represented in the poetry of Shāh Ismā`īl.[1] Chancellery discourse produced between 1501 and 1512 underlines these tendencies and illustrates them further and as such broadens our appreciation for how ideologies and legitimacies could be creatively articulated. By 1512, however, new constituencies of bureaucrats and litterateurs from the former Timurid empire negotiated their entry and participation in this seedling imperial project, and chancellery discourse was substantially reoriented away from the earlier millenarian imperiative first introduced by Shāh Ismā`īl. Following the accession of Shāh Ṭahmāsp in 1524, this Timurid influence, with respect to a distinctly monarchical ideology and articulation of legitimacy, continued to grow.

The composition and culture of the Safavid chancellery—a fluid network of scholar-bureaucrats, literati, and religious personalities appended to courts at the central and local levels—between 1501 and 1532 defy structural categorization. To be sure, formal bureaucratic culture was anathema in the halcyon days of Qizilbāsh militancy and territorial expansion, and Shāh Ismā`īl was quick to nominate Turkic tribal amirs to the central court positions as well as gubernatorial appointments in these newly conquered Iranian cities. Until the initial momentum of violence and retribution began to lose pace after the Battle of Chāldirān (1514), we find relatively little evidence of a politically assertive administrative and chancellery culture. This can also be explained by a relative paucity of contemporary documentary or chronological material that talks about chancellery features in any kind of structural capacity during these early decades. While we might not be able to confidently map out the chancellery in terms of its structural manifestation, we can certainly flush out this corporate entity by assembling a prosopography of who was involved in staffing the chancellery and how this might influence the articulation of legitimacy and authority.

The Parousia *(ẓuhūr)* of Ismā`īl, 1494–1514

While there is indeed evidence to suggest that both the Persian nobility and the clerical elite prospered to some degree under early Safavid rule, Jean Aubin stripped Ismā`īl clean of any overtly religious or sentimental nationalist trappings in 1988 with his seminal article, "L'avènement des Safavides reconsidéré."[2] Contrary to previous historical models, Aubin's image of Ismā`īl is uncompromisingly raw: a ruthless young man under the control of a band of Turco-Mongol nomads intent on destruction and mayhem. To suggest that Ismā`īl made a sudden transition from mystical outcast to urbane Persian *pādshāh* would ignore a significant body of historical material that points to a continuation and, in some cases, an intensification of long-standing traditions of violent millenarianism and popular Türkmen tribal customs.[3] Jean Calmard has cautioned, however, we should be alive to the idea that archaic Turco-Mongol practices (ritualistic cannabalism, exhumation of bodies) were distinct from those traditions we associate with extremist *ghuluww* movements in Islamic heresiography (decapitation, cremation).[4] In this sense, Isma`il catered to long-standing messianic and Turkic traditions, which had defined a new "paradigm of leadership" within medieval central Islamic world in the fifteenth and sixteenth centuries.[5]

Āzarbāijān and eastern Anatolia were a pastiche of various orthodox and heterodox Islamic practices as well as numerous popular non-Islamic traditions. The Safavid Order in the fourteenth and fifteenth centuries was undoubtedly influenced by this malleable landscape. Evidence suggests that Ismā`īl's father and grandfather had begun a process whereby apocalyptic violence and millenarian rhetoric were introduced and practiced regularly. The Safavid *ṭarīqah* began to embrace a distinctive martial quality as Qizilbāsh Türkmen tribal groups responded favourably to Safavid preachers—broadcasting a message of social justice and impending millenarian revolution against the Ottoman and Qarā Qoyūnlū empires—in the hinterland of northern Syria and eastern Anatolia, and they rushed forward to declare allegiance to Isma`il's grandfather, Shaikh Junaid.[6]

Between 1456 and 1459, Junaid interwove political agendas with this mystical order by arranging a diplomatic marriage alliance with the ascending Āq Qoyūnlū chief Ūzūn Ḥasan. Under the protectorship of Ūzūn Ḥasan, Junaid led several campaigns into northern Anatolia (Trebizond) and Circassia, but he was killed in 11 Jumāda I 864/March 1460 during a battle against Sulṭān Khalīl Allāh ibn Shaikh Ibrāhīm, the shah of Shīrvān, near Ṭabarsarān.[7] Thus far, the Sunni world remained unconvinced, and Rūzbihān Khunjī Iṣfahānī wrote that "the fools of Rūm, who are a crowd of error and a host of devlish imagination ... openly called Shaykh Junaid 'God' [*ilāh*] and his son 'son of God' [*ibn Allāh*]."[8] Sulṭān Ḥaidar (1460–88) adopted wholesale the Safavid agenda of ushering in a millenarian revolution. Khunjī Iṣfahānī likewise railed against the worldy demeanour: "The shaikh in a regal way arrived with the numerous army of Sufis; instead of multicoloured tatters [*muraqqa`*], they had donned armour, instead of Safavi caps [*tāj*] they had helmets, and on swift steeds and with drawn swords they came to the battlefield."[9]

Born on 25 Rajab 892/17 July 1487, Ismā`īl was, very early on, both a victim and beneficiary of the surrounding political climate.[10] Āq Qoyūnlū authorities had imprisoned the remaining members of Ḥaidar's family, including the very young Ismā`īl.[11] His mother, one remaining brother Ibrāhīm, and Ismā`īl himself were taken and installed in the citadel-prison of Istakhr in the distant province of Fārs. They were released eventually and made their way to the Safavid lodestar of Ardabīl in Shawwāl 898/August 1493.[12] Echoing long-established Near Eastern traditions of providential boy-kings escaping the agents of a local government (Moses, Zal, Cyrus, Jesus, Muḥammad al-Mahdī[13]), Safavid sources revel in depicting how the Āq Qoyūnlū sent five thousand "hypocrites and cursed ones" (*munāfiqān va mallā`īn*) to seek out the young Isma`il and eliminate him.[14] Ismā`īl was secreted away, and he was conveyed by devotees to the neighbouring region of Gīlān.[15] Ismā`īl left behind his older brother, Ibrāhīm, who was installed by the Āq Qoyūnlū as the new and co-opted supervisor of the Safavid Order in Ardabīl.[16] Ismā`īl spent the next six years in Lāhījān under the protection and tutelage of the Kār Kiyā dynasty that ruled intermittently over Gīlān, Daylam, and Māzandarān.[17] The regions of Daylam and Ṭabaristān were host to a number of such heterodox groups, an unsurprising development given the strong presence of the esoteric Zaidī Shi`ite movement in the region since the ninth century.[18] Devotees began arriving in Lāhījān to pay homage to the young Safavid shaikh, and these included powerful Persian notables like Amīr Najm Rashtī, as well as two Kār Kiyā princes, Sulṭān Ḥusain and Amīr Hāshim.[19]

More importantly, powerful Türkmen amirs began coalescing in the Lāhījān area, ostensibly to be close to their new spiritual mentor but more likely manipulating the violent millenarian milieu to launch local campaigns and raids. Ismā`īl's wardens worked in concert with various tribal elements to accelerate the imminent collapse of the Āq Qoyūnlū dynasty in the late 1490s and captured a number of key areas in the process, including Ṭārum and Qazvīn.[20] Meanwhile, young Ismā`īl continued to receive instruction from a local scholar, Shams al-Dīn Lāhījī, in Persian and Turkish poetry and literature as well as the religious sciences.[21] It would appear that Shams al-Dīn Lāhījī adhered to a number of the heterodox doctrines that had flourished in the Iranian and Anatolian hinterlands in the post-Mongol period of the fourteenth and fifteenth centuries, namely the Shi`ite-rooted doctrines of human infallibility (*`iṣmat*), resurrection (*ma`ād*), and the belief in an imminent apocalyptic event (*sā`at al-sa`a*). In this politically fractured environment, charismatic leaders of different stripes surfaced to manipulate and channel the pervasive millenarian expectations among the populace. In doing so, they drew heavily on existing Shi`ite traditions of occultation and apocalypticism. Likewise, the doctrine of metempsychosis (*tanāsukh*) had become fashionable in various mystical movements, whereby `Alī and the Imāms, along with a number of other famous religious personalities, were now in a constant state of reincarnation. The belief in reincarnation and the veneration of `Alī as a divine manifestation of God in human form became the doctrinal *goût du jour* for the fifteenth-century Turco-Iranian religious landscape. Irène Mélikoff noted: "If one examines popular religious tendencies, one finds consistently the same ideology: under a thin veneer of Sufism and Shi`ism, the belief in reincarnation, the manifestation of the divine in human form, and the possibility of a multiplicity of forms."[22] Undoubtedly, the religiously ambiguous environment of Lāhījān only intensified as numbers of nomadic Turks responded to Safavid millenarian preachers and arrived from the hinterland to join the young Ismā`īl in his quest to usher in the Apocalypse.

The signs of the emergence of the Mahdī (*al-`alāmāt al-ẓuhūr*) were indicators of the catastrophic events (*al-`alāmāt al-sa`a)* that would precede the Apocalypse and had been referred to in the Qur'ān and commented on by the Prophet himself.[23] For Shi`ites, the appearance of the Mahdī is synonymous with the meting out of justice to culprits who had wronged the family of the Prophet. Shi`ites of the day are promised an emotional release (*faraj*) for centuries of pent-up grief and anger, as in the popular Shi`ite prayer: "May God hasten release from suffering through his [Mahdī's] rise."[24] For this reason, a distinct militancy characterizes the emergence of the Mahdī, whereby the Qā'im al-Mahdī will rise with a sword (*al-qā'im bi'l-saif*) and annihilate the apostates (*kāfirs*) and irreligionists (*ahl al-ilḥād*), namely those Sunni apostates who had suppressed the "true religion" (*dīn al-ḥaqq*) of Shi`ite Islam. Indeed, the political and revolutionary function of the Qā'im al-Mahdī grew so prominent that Imami theologians writing in the eleventh and twelfth centuries more or less equated the emergence of the Mahdī with widespread revolution and anarchy for the Sunni authorities.

Returning to Isma`il's "emergence" (*ẓuhūr*) from his occultation in the forests of Lāhījān, Aubin is clear regarding the young shaikh's lack of agency in this environment and instead looks to an advisory group (*ahl-i ikhtiṣāṣ*) consisting of seven key personages: Ḥusain Beg Shāmlū (Lala Beg), `Abdāl `Alī Beg (Dada Beg), Khādim Beg Ṭālish (Khulafā Beg), Qarā Pīrī Beg Qajar, Ilyās Beg Aighūr-ūghlī, Rustam Beg Qarāmānlū, and Bairam Beg Qarāmānlū. These men were staunch supporters of the Safavid Order and contributed directly to the movement's raison d'être—paving the way for the Mahdī through frontier raiding and social disorder. After 906/1500, the Safavid army was sufficiently large to begin an explicit campaign, but indecision and lack of concensus appear to have been an issue. The plan to "liberate" the Safavid centre of Ardabil was abandoned, and suggestions from Türkmen chiefs to wage war in the Christian Caucasus and Diyār Bakr were dismissed.[25] Ismā`īl was adamant that the Shīrvānshāh, Farrukh Yasār, be punished for killing his father Ḥaidar, and he sanctified this decision by claiming that he had been visited in a dream by one of the Twelve Imāms and told to proceed against Farrukh Yasār.[26] The orgy of violence that ensued was conspicuous, and we should not be overly impressed with comments from later Safavid historians, like Iskander Beg Munshī: "Even at this early age, the ornament of imperial rule was visible on [Ismā`īl's] auspicious brow."[27] While en route to the region of Shīrvān, two large raiding expeditions were sent out with the millenarian mandate of "punishing the wicked." Khūrshāh ibn Qubād narrates how, after defeating a Georgian Christian settlement, Khulafā Beg assembled the remaining citizens in the town square and had them massacred; an abundance of riches were then taken, and any prizes of great significance were brought to the shah.[28] Meanwhile, Ilyās Beg successfully laid siege to Mantash and ravaged citizenry and town alike.[29] The Safavid *ghāzīyān* destroyed the Shīrvānshāh's forces near Gulistān in Jumāda I 906/December 1500 and continued northwards to capture the Āzarbāijānī city of Bākū.

The Shīrvān campaign of 1500 in many ways inaugurated Ismā`īl's militant *ẓuhūr,* and the Safavid success on the plains near Gulistān was vaunted as divine punishment for the killing of Ismā`īl's grandfather (Junaid) and father (Ḥaidar) by Farrukh Yasār's ancestors. Ḥusain Beg Shāmlū ordered his attendant, Shāh Kaldī Āqā, to decapitate the captured Shīrvānshāh and deliver the head to the teenaged Ismā`īl, while the corpse was burnt and pyramids were made with all the heads of the Shīrvānī victims, a typical Turco-Mongol custom.[30] To the north, Khulafā Beg levelled most of the old city of Bākū and distributed gold, jewels, and other valuables among his soldiers, while at the same time ordering the exhumation, burning, and public scattering of Khalīl Allāh Shīrvānshāh's body.[31] For the Safavid Qizilbāsh, the scope and intensity of this violence inflicted on Farrukh Yasār and his people were very probably also a reflection of the release of emotion and anger (*faraj*) that prefaced the advent of the Mahdī. On one level, the Qizilbāsh revelled in punishing those responsible for the death of two exalted shaikhs of the Safavid Order; on another level, a victory of this magnitude functioned as an allegory for the promised millenarian retribution for those villainous Sunnis who had martyred the third Imām Ḥusain on the plains of Karbalā so many centuries before. Moreover, storytellers (*qiṣṣah-khvānān*) recited epic poems such as the *Abū Muslim nāmah* with the deliberate intention of paralleling Abū Muslim's exaction of revenge on the impious Umayyads with Shāh Ismā`īl's defeat and humiliation of the Shīrvānshāhs. The chronicler `Abdī Beg Shīrāzī describes the battle of Gulistān with metaphors that leave no ambiguity: the army of Farrukh Yasār equalled the number (twenty thousand) of those vile ones who had massacred Ḥusain at Karbalā (*`adad-i Yazīdān-i Karbalā*); the sword of `Alī (*Zū al-Faqār*) had swung down on Farrukh Yasār, a descendant of Yazīd (*Yazīdān-i Sāsānī tabār-i Shīrvānshāh*), that Umayyad caliph who had ordered the slaughter at Karbalā. They made the blood of the Shīrvānīs flow in rivers, and heads and body parts rose in waves and foam.[32]

By this time, Ismā`īl's popularity among the Türkmen populations was unrivalled, and conscripts continued to flock to the Safavid millenarian cause. Būdāq Munshī recounts hearing how in the summer of 907/1501, Ismā`īl had agreed to receive an official Ottoman ambassador in the Āzarbāijānī city of Marāgha. Purportedly, thousands tried to climb the minaret of the public mosque in the hope of catching a glimpse of Ismā`īl, and "in the twinkling of an eye," over a hundred people fell to their death.[33] When Ismā`īl and his army marched uncontested into Tabrīz in the summer of 907/1501, all were stunned by the reversal of Āq Qoyūnlū and Safavid fortunes. During the crowning, Ismā`īl decreed that the "garden of Islamic law was irrigated by the work of the *mujāhidīn*'s swords, and that Islam was cultivated by the red-coloured sword of [his] blood-drinking *ghāzīs*."[34] The Qizilbāsh recited publicly one of the shah's most favourite verses from the Qu'ran, *āyāh fatḥ* ("The Victory Ayah"), as well as a popular verse from the chapter of "The Pilgrimage": "Fight in the way of God with a fight worthy of Him" (22: 78).[35] The shah also commanded that everyone would subscribe to the Twelver Shi`ite creed, and he appointed a number of *tabarrā'iyān* agents—those who anathematize the first three caliphs—to go out into the streets and coerce the urban population to renounce any vestiges of Sunni faith. Safavid chroniclers and poets saw this effacing of Sunnism as analogous to Abraham's momentous destruction of the pagan idols. `Abdī Beg Shīrāzī replicates a poem describing the *tabarrā'iyān* in Tabrīz: "With the coming of the *tabarrā'iyān*, the idols of Sunnism were shattered in the exact same way [that happened] with the blow of Ibrāhīm, son of Āzar."[36] The bulk of the population acceded to these conditions, but some prominent religious personalities like Shaikh Ibrāhīm Gulshanī, the head of the Khalvatiyyah mystical movement, fled Safavid dominion.[37]

Ismā`īl spent the spring extirpating the last remnants of Āq Qoyūnlū resistance in Āzarbāijān, and in Zū al-Ḥijja 907/June 1502 their military encampments were destroyed, large-scale massacres were perpetrated against Āq Qoyūnlū prisoners, and prodigious property and possessions were looted.[38] By this time, rumours had been circulating, and foreign observers (notably Venetian merchants) had noted that "after Ismā`īl's first victory, the members of his sect flocked to join him because in their books they found it foretold that a prophet of their religion would come and they must support and exalt him."[39] In this way, these accounts describe how "everyone and particularly his soldiers consider [Ismā`īl] immortal," and that he is seen as "the holy of holies, full of divinatory power, for he takes counsel from no one ...his every act is divine-inspired."[40] Clearly the millenarian propaganda of Ismā`īl's preaching deputies (*khalīfahs*) was having the desired effect, and sections of the population openly acknowledged the charismatic Ismā`īl as the Mahdī and his role during the imminent Hour of Judgement.

This propensity for violence translated into a discernible policy of intimidation and spectacular violent displays, and in the spring of 1503, Ismā`īl shifted orientation and launched a broad campaign against the central Iranian highlands.[41] Ismā`īl first approached Iṣfahān from the west. The citizens there had obviously heard the rumours of this agent of apocalypse and the public massacre of ten thousand prisoners at Qizil Ūzūn (near Hamadān) only a month before, and the city gates were enthusiastically opened. Meanwhile, rival Sufi elements were targeted, and we hear that close to four thousand members of the Kāzirūnī mystical movement based in Fārs were executed, while all the tombs and mausoleums of various Sufi shaikhs of the region were desecrated.[42] A later Shi`ite source, *Rauḍāt al-jinān va jannāt al-jinān* by Ḥāfiẓ Ḥusain Karbalā'ī Tabrīzī, describes how "Ismā`īl crushed all the *silsilah*s [Sufi orders]; the graves of their ancestors were destroyed, not to mention what befell their successors ... he made despondent and eradicated most of the *silsilah*s of sayyids and shaikhs."[43] When the shah's forces arrived from the south in the environs of Kāshān in the late summer of 909/1504, notables rushed from the city to welcome Ismā`īl. Obsequious capitulation has its place, and the governors of Kāshān, Qāḍī Muḥammad Kāshānī and Maulānā Jalāl al-Dīn Mas`ūd, organized massive three-day-long festivals to celebrate their new ruler's arrival. The city grandees quite astutely decreed that the markets (*asvāq*) and shops (*dakākīn*) close for the festival but ordered that the shop owners paint and adorn their businesses with treasures from Istanbul, Syria, and Europe.[44] Obviously, they realized that the Qizilbāsh would plunder their city regardless, and decided they could avoid damage, terror, and misery by simply hanging up their valuables as decorative bribes.

By 909/winter of 1504, dissent began to appear in peripheral areas in the northern half of the Iranian Plateau. The main perpetrator was Ḥusain Kār Kiyā, a Zaidī Shi`ite who had carved out a small fiefdom in Simnān and Fīrūz Kūh. When Ismā`īl's forces neared the region, Ḥusain Kār Kiyā fled, and a number of villages and settlements like Gul-i Khandān ("Smiling Flower") and Damāvand were ransacked in Ramaḍān 909/March and April 1504. Two months later, the ten thousand refugees and soldiers holed up in Astā were put to the sword, and the fort was razed to the ground.[45] Safavid sources discuss how two notables, Murād Beg Jahān Shāhī and Sāyaltamash Beg, were skewered, roasted alive, and eaten by each of the Safavid amirs until "there was not a trace of meat or bone."[46] Ismā`īl pressed on after this victory and ordered the execution of most of the population of the nearby city of Abarqūh for their alleged support of Muḥammad Karrah, another rebellious governor based out of Yazd.[47] Ismā`īl organized the public execution of Muḥammad Karrah along with the burning of Ḥusain Kār Kiyā's corpse for the courtly entertainment of a visiting Ottoman delegation while camped in the city of Iṣfahān. Khvāndamīr reports that "the burning of [both] Ḥusain Kiyā and Muḥammad Karrah, and his followers took place in that emissary's presence, and as a result he fled to his homeland in complete fear and anxiety."[48] After the conquest of Yazd in 1505, the Safavids promised safe conduct to Shāh Ni`mat Allāh, the *pīr* of the Ni`matullāhī Order and a local urban-notable, but when he emerged from hiding the *ghāzī*s entered the house and massacred his entire family.[49] `Abdī Beg Shīrāzī adds that the general populace of Yazd was slaughtered.[50] In Shawwāl 910/March 1505, every citizen of the Khurāsānī city of Ṭabas—some seven thousand people—was killed.[51]

By the spring of 911/1506, the nucleus of the Order was in Sulṭāniyyah and concentrating on resolving the thorny issue of Diyār Bakr and its ruler, `Alā' al-Daula Zū al-Qadar. After a failed diplomatic venture,[52] the Safavids marched westwards into Anatolia and northern Syria in 913/summer of 1507 to deal with `Alā' al-Daula once and for all. No one was spared from the wrath of the shah: two grandchildren of `Alā' al-Daula were not only burned alive and eaten, but also their heads were sent to Ismā`īl as trophies.[53] Ismā`īl's main advisor, Ḥusain Lala Shāmlū, was on an overextended campaign in the southwestern mountains of Anatolia but was suprised and badly routed; Ismā`īl faced his first significant defeat since his parousia seven years earlier.[54] Safavid troops continued onwards to the borders of the Mamluk sultanate. In the following year, Ismā`īl placed the campaign against the Zū al-Qadar in the hands of one of his seven "advisors," Muḥammad Khān Ustājlū, who invaded Kurdistān with several thousand men and forced a final battle with `Alā' al-Daula at the city of Qarā Ḥamīd.

The Zū al-Qadar were defeated soundly, and the heads of some hundred prisoners were sent as gifts to the shah, who was camped in Hamadān. With Kurdistān now subdued, as well as various Iranian centres, the shah's attention turned towards the ancient `Abbasid capital of Baghdad to the southwest. Despite the public submission of the city's governor, Bārīk Purnāk, the Safavids insisted on a public display of violence: the Qizilbāsh Türkmen amir `Abdāl `Alī Beg massacred every Āq Qoyūnlū notable found in Baghdad, and Ismā`īl enjoyed the spectacle while floating on the Tigris River and drinking wine.[55] In the same summer campaign of 914/1508, Ismā`īl marched southwards to subjugate the irksome Musha`sha` of Ḥuvaizah and, with the city in flames and its citizens brutalized, emissaries from the neighbouring independent territories of Dizfūl, Shūshtar, and Khurramābād arrived to proffer timidly the allegiance of their rulers to the Safavid Order.[56] Millenarian rhetoric continued unabated, and while the Qizilbāsh tribes remained committed to plundering and punishing the wicked, urban populations wearied of this apocalyptic fervour and coercive rule.

A partial solution to these problems came with Ismā`īl's invasion of Khurāsān in 1510 and the capture of numerous former Timurid cities from their recent overlord, Muḥammad Shībānī Khān. The Timurid empire under Sulṭān-Ḥusain Bāiqarā (r. 873–911/1469–1506) had been undone by fratricide, civil war, and Uzbek invasion, but there is little doubt that the Timurids had been integral to the preservation and dissemination of Perso-Islamic civilization in the post-Mongol age.[57] Eastern centres of the Persianate world—Herāt, Samarqand, Bukhārā—enjoyed relative prosperity under Timurid rule in the fifteenth century. The prolific production of poetry, literary texts, dictionaries, miniature paintings, epistolographic manuals, hagiographies, exegetical works, astrology texts, and agronomic treatises suggest that these cities had become the principal repositories of Persian literary, scientific, and administrative culture. Also impressive is the intensity and commitment with which the Timurids expressed themselves in terms of Persian monarchical and courtly rhetoric.[58] This Timurid empire had been overrun by the nomadic Uzbeks, and by 914/1508 it was clear that the Safavid and Uzbek states were on a direct course of collision.

In Jumāda I/II 916/July or August 1510, the shah's armies approached Dāmaghān, the most westerly Khurāsānī Uzbek possession. The notables promptly handed over control of the city, as did the chief officials of the city of Astarābād, some 50 kilometers to the north.[59] Ismā`īl's forces then went on to Mashhad and the tomb of Imām `Alī al-Riḍā and were able to enter the city unopposed—not a surprising development given the Shi`ite orientation of the city.[60] In Sha`bān 916/November 1510, the shah reached the walled city of Marv, and his *ghāzīs* were able to surprise and rout the Uzbek army nearby on 20 Sha`bān 916/2 December 1510 at the Maḥmūdī River.[61]

The Safavids had succeeded in capturing a number of Khurāsānī cities, but there is no doubt that possession of the Timurid capital of Herāt was key to the eastern campaign. A Safavid courtier, Qulī Jān Beg, was sent to Herāt "to blow the breeze of wonderful news into the city's meadow of desire for stability."[62] While the Safavid emissary was enjoying the pomp and ceremony of the reception organized by Herāt's notables,[63] the bailiffs (*shiḥnahān*) of the city, Muḥammad Lakūra and Muḥammad `Alī `Isā, were seized and assassinated (along with one hundred Uzbeks) by the Herātīs. Qulī Jān Beg brought the *fatḥ nāmah* to the congregational mosque and had it read from the pulpit to the nobles and notables of Marv by the *ḥāfiẓ* Zain al-Dīn Ziyāratgāhī.[64] Safavid proclivities towards millenarianism and violence could not be contained, and when the preacher failed to sufficiently exalt `Alī in his *khuṭbah*, Qulī Jān drew his sword and struck the preacher down right in the mosque. Panic and fear of a massacre spread quickly throughout the city.[65]

Such violence, again, was consistent with the violence expected of Shi`ites against Sunnis on the eve of the Apocalypse, and we can be sure that the *ghuluww*-minded would have remembered the *Abū Muslim nāmah* and its relation of a story in which Abū Muslim kills an Umayyad preacher during his sermon in a mosque.[66] Another attempt was made to assuage the population, and Khvājah Saif al-Dīn Muẓaffar Bitikchī, recently joined to the Safavid cause and former vizier of the nearby city of Astarābād, was despatched "to conciliate and comfort the people of Herāt."[67] Khvājah Kamāl al-Dīn Maḥmūd Sāgharchī, another former Timurid administrator who had joined the Safavid ranks, was sent ahead of Ismā`īl's arriving retinue, reading a royal decree (*farmān*) that addressed the new taxation policy, the shah's guarantees of security, and the imposition of Shi`ism.[68] It was also Sāgharchī who convinced Khvājah Khurd, the *kutvāl* (commandant) of the Herātī citadel of Ikhtiyār al-Dīn, to surrender peacefully.[69] As Khūrshāh ibn Qubād commented, "All those sayyids and `*ulamā* [in Herāt] who were knowledgable in Shi`ism were distinguished with royal favour."[70]

The ensuing period of negotiation and diplomatic activity—a peace treaty with the Uzbeks in early 917/spring of 1511, a mutual alliance between Ismā`īl and the fugitive Mughal Bābur—was undoubtedly a product of these incorporated Timurid bureaucratic elements.[71] Nonetheless, there appears to have been little attenuation in the Safavid use of mass violence. When a Safavid force arrived in eastern Khurāsān to help Bābur's forces against the Uzbeks, it embarked on a zealous campaign of intimidation against Sunni people and institutions. The popular and well-known poet Mullā Banā'ī was executed. The tomb of the famous Naqshbandiyyah mystic and poet, Jāmī, was desecrated. Such atrocities were overshadowed by the wholesale massacre of the entire city population of Qarshī—some fifteen thousand people.[72] Meanwhile, geopolitics in the west shifted considerably with the enthronement of the new Ottoman sultan, Salīm "the Grim," in 1512, but the Safavids were little prepared for the threat of invasion and the imminent disaster that would play out at Chāldirān in 1514.[73]

By 1514, the Safavid Order had more than succeeded in filling "le remplissage d'un vide" left by the Āq Qoyūnlū and Qarā Qoyūnlū dynasties.[74] The Safavids were in at least nominal control of those cities that had constituted the heart of the Türkmen confederacies—Tabrīz, Ardabīl, Yazd, Kāshān, Hamadān, Iṣfahān, Shīrāz, Diyār Bakr, Baghdad—and lucrative postings had been appointed to those who were most committed to the Safavid Order. It was Qizilbāsh style to receive nominal governorship of a city and then pass the actual duties on to either a responsible vizier or a relative from their *uymāq*. Ismā`īl himself was far removed from administering his domains and "was content to allow the governors the right to name their own deputy governors."[75] Many of the existing Āq Qoyūnlū administrative approaches to formal imperial decrees, promulgations, investitures, and other mundane bureaucratic transactions were adopted wholesale by the Safavids. Administration was largely left to whoever had the most experience: those urban notables of Persian centres who had served for generations as viziers, bailiffs (*dārūghah-hā*), tax collectors (*`ummāl*), financial officers (*mustaufīyān*), and notables of the state (*a`yān-i daulat*) for the Qarā and Āq Qoyūnlū dynasties.

The first significant Āq Qoyūnlū administrative family to join Safavid ranks was that of Khvājah Muḥammad Kukajī (or Kujajī) Tabrīzī, who was later given the title of Amīr Zakariyā. His title of *khvājah* itself was a reference to a high title of respect (*khvājagān*) used by the Saljūq amirs for the Iranian administrators.[76] He had served for many years as vizier and *mushrif-i dīvān* (chief audior) to both Sulṭān Ya`qūb Beg and his son, Alvand. Amīr Zakariyā came from a long line of sayyids and bureaucrats who had served previous Turco-Mongolian dynasties like the Jalāyirids, the Timurids, the Qarā Qoyūnlū, and the Āq Qoyūnlū.[77] Zakariyā astutely decided to proffer his allegiance to the Safavid Order at Muḥammadābād in Shawwāl 906/May 1501.[78] He was immediately made *vazīr-i dīvān-i a`lā,* and it is no accident that he was styled "the key to Āzarbāijān" (*kalīd-i Āzarbāijān*).[79]

The Āq Qoyūnlū administrator, Sharaf al-Dīn Maḥmūd Daylamī Qazvīnī, followed Amīr Zakariyā Kukajī one year later, and while Būdāq Munshī describes his new title as *vazīr-i shāh-i `ālam*, Yaḥyā Qazvīnī tells us that he was acting as co-*vazīr* with Amīr Zakariyā.[80] Daylamī had occupied one of the highest rungs in Alvand's bureaucracy, and his family had a long history of serving Türkmen administration from the city of Qazvīn.[81] Maḥmūd Daylamī had originally been entrusted with the collection of taxes and arrears *(ẓabt-i amvāl va jihāt-i bāqiya)* for the province of Fārs under Sulṭān Khalīl; he was later named as vizier and *mushrif* under Ya`qūb.[82]

Another important family of administrators who sought out Safavid patronage was the Sāvajīs. Qāḍī Ḍiyā al-Dīn Nūr Allāh, who would serve as Ismā`īl's ambassador to Muḥammad Shībānī Khān in 916/1510, was the son of Qāḍī Darvīsh Muḥammad ibn Sukhr Allāh, a prominent member of Rustam Beg Bāyandur's chancellery. Qāḍī Ḍiyā al-Dīn's brother, Qāḍī Nūr al-Dīn `Abd al-Raḥmān, was the chief *qāḍī* of Tabrīz for twenty years, until his death in 929/1523.[83] The incorporation of settled Persian *dīvānī* families continued with Ismā`īl's "liberation" of the predominantly Shi`ite city of Qumm in 909/1503 and the defection of a number of prominent bureaucrats and literati. Particularly noteworthy was the city's *kalāntar*, Āqā Kamāl al-Dīn Ḥusain Musībī, who came from an old family of *dīvānī*s that had administered Qumm on behalf of the Timurid ruler, Shāh Rukh. Along with Musībī, the city's "`*ulamā*, pious ones, eloquent ones, and *faqīr*s who had earlier served Ḥasan Pādshāh and Ya`qūb Pādshāh, eagerly entered the shah's service."[84] Qāḍī Muḥammad Kāshānī, the former governor of Kāshān, was appointed "second *ṣadr*" to Shams al-Dīn Lāhījī and eventually given control of Yazd.[85] Ismā`īl's honorific title, Abū al-Muẓaffar, was directly inherited from the titles used in decrees by Ya`qūb (884/1479),[86] Alvand (904/1490),[87]and Rustam (902/1497),[88] and reads as follows: *al-mulk li-llāhi Abū Muẓaffar Ismā`īl Bahādur sözūmïz*. On the face of it, Ismā`īl's bureaucratic structure was largely a continuation of its Āq Qoyūnlū counterpart and its Turco-Mongolian traditions.[89]

The overall structure and form of Safavid decrees granting *suyūrghāl*s (revenue grants) and *tiyūl*s (grants of district control in exchange for an annual supply of military forces) deviated little from Āq Qoyūnlū practice. There was an effort to change those conspicuous symbols and markings that were associated with a particular previous dynasty. This fine line of preserving overall form while altering certain visible features was "on the one hand documenting the changeover and continuation of power, while on the other hand demarcating and characterizing those qualities a new power would see as typical."[90] Herrmann demonstrates convincingly that there were, in fact, four seals in use during Ismā`īl's reign,[91] contrary to Renate Schimkoreit's assertion that there were only two.[92] Other seals point to even further connections between Āq Qoyūnlū and Safavid chancellery practices. One document, dated 909/1503, is typically Türkmen in its design with a round seal and a Qur'ānic verse in the top portion, while the bottom lists Ismā`īl's genealogy: Ismā`īl ibn Ḥaidar ibn Junaid Ṣafavī.[93] We find, however, the appearance of a seal directly invoking the sovereignty of the Twelve Imāms and geneaologically connecting Ismā`īl with this most holy of families on documents dated 914/1508 and 918/1512. These read: "May the prayers of God be on Muḥammad Muṣṭafā `Alī Murtaẓā Ḥasan ibn Murtaẓā Ḥusain Shahīd-i Karbalā Muḥammad Bāqir Ja`far Mūsā al-Kāẓim `Alī ibn Mūsā Riḍā Muḥammad Taqī `Alī Naqī Ḥasan `Askarī Muḥammad Mahdī, the slave Ismā`īl ibn Ḥaidar Ṣafavī."[94] In terms of formal diplomatic correspondence and the rhetorical genre of *inshā*, we find remarkable changes from what the Āq Qoyūnlū had presented in terms of themes, topics, allusions, and other literary devices. In the case of the early Safavids, this malleability allowed the chancellery to profile a *Weltanschauung* that was unprecedented in medieval Islamic history.

Heralding Noah's Flood: Messianic and Mystical Innovations in the Safavid Chancellery

In a postscript to the year 906/1501, Qāḍī Aḥmad wrote that "Khvājah `Abd al-Ḥayy Munshī, who had been employed in the service of Sulṭān Abu Sa`īd writing imperial correspondence, died in the capital of Tabrīz."[95] The death of such a venerable Timurid *munshī* in the new Safavid capital within months of Shāh Ismā`īl's royal ascension symbolized to some extent the attrition of a past order and the beginning of a new one. Shāh Ismā`īl and his coterie of Qizilbāsh tribal amirs, despite their nomadic history and initial contempt for all things urban, made increasing use of pre-existing chancellery structures in various cities after 1501. While previously relying on preachers and demagogues for proselytization and recruitment, the Safavid Order adopted new strategies with their new imperial setting and increasingly looked to chancellery centres as a means of "arguing the Apocalypse" or, in other words, using evocative imagery and inspiring metaphors towards a chiliastic revolution and the violent reversal of a corrupt social order. While the underlying theories explaining the appeal of apocalyptic rhetoric in different societies, like those offered by Norman Cohn[96] or Michael Barkun,[97] are beyond the scope of this present study, we are nonetheless attracted to the idea that the success of an apocalyptic movement is dependent on the ability of said movement to persuade an audience "of their situation within the particular historical pattern of temporal fulfillment represented in its mythic imagery."[98] As we have seen, the regions of northwestern Iran and eastern Anatolia had long embraced a wide range of heterodox doctrines, which employed a number of religious icons and historical personalities. The belief in an imminent apocalyptic event, which would be ushered in violently by a divinely sanctioned descendant of the Prophet (the Mahdī), was ubiquitous.

Texts were produced in the early Safavid court (*dargāh*) and administration (*dīvān*) to support the young Ismā`īl as a harbinger of the Apocalypse. While some of these texts were designed for internal consumption, a number of diplomatic letters were sent abroad to surrounding Muslim powers. The concepts of violence, intimidation, and imminent retribution that characterized the Safavid narrative between 1501 and 1514 were incorporated to no small degree into chancellery correspondence. New Safavid chancellery officials, who had only recently been serving either the Türkmen Āq Qoyūnlūs or the Timurids, presented their ruler Ismā`īl as a divine agent whose mandate was to avenge the calamities inflicted on the Shi`ite community. Moreover, we note the assertive use of both candid and veiled mystical tropes and imagery in Ismā`īl's correspondence. We find that the administration between 1501 and 1514 was also periodically influenced by educated urban Sufis who stood well apart from their antinomian brethren. Of course, the bulk of bureaucratic officials who would come to serve the Safavid chancellery were trained in well-acknowledged and established methods of bureaucracy and state governance. As Ismā`īl endeavoured to stabilize his realm, we find this group of Persian elite enjoying a healthier and increased role in producing such epistolary texts. As we shall see, the different chancellery texts available for this period reflect different levels of syncretism and tension between the populist, millenarian agenda of the young shah, the mystical traditions pervading Āzarbāijān and Anatolia, and the bureaucratic imperative to provide stability and order for taxation purposes.

The first propagandist texts worth noting are the emotive verses penned by Khaṭā'ī, or Shāh Ismā`īl himself, and how these Turkish verses were used by the Safavid authorities to attract people to the Safavid cause in its millenarian heyday. This poetry and its evocative message had a greater audience than a few languishing courtiers due to the collaborative efforts of state calligraphers (*khūsh-nivīsān*) and popular storytellers (*qiṣṣah-khvānān*).[99] Jean Calmard tells us that "itinerant Sufi-minstrels," or *`āshiqs*, sung Khaṭā'ī's poetry at popular gatherings,[100] while we know that copies of Khaṭā'ī's *Dīvān* were distributed until the eighteenth century.[101] The recitation of popular texts, such as the *Abū Muslim nāmah*, the *Mukhtār nāmah*, the *Shāh nāmah*, and the *Junaid nāmah,* was a growing phenomenon in fifteenth-century Anatolia and Āzarbāijān, and we know that Khaṭā'ī's *Dīvān* was no exception to a trend that was practiced in tribal camp and city centre alike.[102] Both Sulṭān Ḥaidar and Shāh Ismā`īl are known to have employed such *qiṣṣah-khvānān* in Ardabīl to read the *Abū Muslim nāmah* and draw clear parallels between the Safavid *ṭarīqah* and the "historical memory" of the hero and demagogue par excellence, Abū Muslim.[103] Safavid *qiṣṣah-khvāns* were particularly keen to point out how Ismā`īl's grandfather, Junaid, shared the same name of Abū Muslim's grandfather—a hero and protagonist in his own epic poem, the *Junaid nāmah*, which prefaces the *Abū Muslim nāmah.* Sām Mīrzā mentions in his biographical dictionary a number of prominent and very popular *qiṣṣah khvāns*—Āshiftah Qiṣṣah Khvān, Ḥasan Mushtāqī Shīrāzī, Maulānā Zain al-`Ābidīn—who served the court of Shāh Ismā`īl directly.[104] As Babayan points out, the public performance of the *Abū Muslim nāmah* and other apocalyptic texts was pervasive and disruptive enough that it warranted its public ban by the powerful Shi`ite religious scholar, `Alī al-`Alī al-Karakī in 940/1534.[105] In short, Ismā`īl's *Dīvān* and other texts played a significant role in using metaphorical imagery and mytho-historical exemplars to excite and inflate the imagination of adherents and would-be supporters.

Minorsky and others have commented on the strong mystical dimension of Ismā`īl's poetry and its emphasis on death, judgement, retribution, and sin.[106] In the context of this present discussion, it seems prudent to examine how Shāh Ismā`īl himself chose to express his temporal and divine mandate, and in doing so, determine the extent to which this powerful imagery was extrapolated to official correspondence.

It is clear that Ismā`īl saw poetry as a powerful vehicle for presenting an eschatological message that drew on a panopoly of spiritual, mythical, and historical metaphors and imagery. Ismā`īl's emergence is perhaps the most consistent theme in the *Dīvān*; audiences interpreted these verses in an eschatological light and understood that the Safavid shah/*pīr* was cloaking himself in the robe of the Mahdī and saw the Safavid campaign as the preamble to the Day of Judgement.[107] Along with announcing his own arrival as a pre-eternal *Agens Absolutus* and *Oculus Dei* (to borrow Minorsky's terms), Ismā`īl promises revenge, punishment, and bloodshed for those who have violated the family of Ḥaidar. Of course, this is a literary dalliance alluding to the fact that Ismā`īl's father, Ḥaidar, shared the same name as one of the *laqab* for the much-venerated `Alī.[108] The promised violence of the Mahdī's arrival and the punishment of those "irreligious ones" who transgressed the path of `Alī was clearly popular with Ismā`īl: "May my head be a sacrifice on the path of the Guide of Truth: there are hundreds like me [ready to] destroy their lives.... The blood of Shah Ḥaidar is still [unavenged]; Yazīd still awaits a crushing defeat."[109]

We also see Sufi mystical ideas—most notably the notion of pre-eternal Gnostic illuminationism and the doctrine of metempsychosis—combined with this powerful apocalyptic imagery. At least until his humble defeat at Chāldirān in 1514, Ismā`īl subscribed publicly to the belief that he was a manifestation of not just the spirit of `Alī but also a wide array of mythical and historical icons. In addition to being a reincarnation of the first Imām, as well as Ḥusain, the Mahdī, and any one of the numerous other `Alid personalities, he also a claimed to be a manifestation of the divine light of investiture (*farr*) that had emanated in kingly figures—Darius, Anūshīrvān, Shāpūr—since the halcyon days of the Achaemenids and Sasanians. Here we detect some of the clearest examples of those rich and resonating Safavid "image clusters," which combined Qur'ānic prophetography, `Alid martyrology, and pre-Islamic Persian grandeur.[110]

Chancellery material from the first fifteen years of Ismā`īl's reign provides fascinating insights into these aforementioned issues of apocalyptic thought and heterodox, mystical religious doctrines. Three *fatḥ nāmah*s, or victory letters, that Ismā`īl sent after a number of pivotal battles are of particular interest here: his conquest of Fīrūz Kūh and Astā in 909/1504, the defeat of the Syrian notable `Alā' al-Daula in 915/1509, and the rout of the Uzbeks and killing of Muḥammad Shībānī Khān at Marv in 916/1510. *Fatḥ nāmah*s, of course, have a long history in the Islamic world of diplomatics, dating back to the days of the Prophet. This study contends here that this particular genre of epistolary composition—rhetoricizing a battle to epic proportions—allowed *munshī*s and stylists to broadcast the early Safavid millenarian agenda to the outside Islamic world with Qur'ānic quotations, Prophetic hadiths, eschatological allusions, and mystical prose and poetry. At the same time, the writing of such correspondence, and its distribution within the court and empire, was a powerful tool in the shahs' quest to reinforce or anchor their multifaceted and malleable legitimacies in the Iranian and Central Asian landscape.

The first letter was written to Sulṭān-Ḥusain Bāiqarā by the Safavid chancellery shortly after the conquests of the Iranian Plateau cities of Fīrūz Kūh, Gul-i Khandān, and Astā from Ḥusain Kiyā Chulāvī in Ramaḍān 909/March 1504.[111] The numerous rhetorical devices and oblique paronomasia suggest a *munshī* of considerable skill and acumen, while mystical language and allusions combined with the motifs of human vanity and divine retribution point to a chancellery official who was adequately versed with the early messianic agenda of the Safavids. After the standard praise for God and the Prophet and felicitations for Sulṭān-Ḥusain Bāiqarā, the scribe announces the recent decision of Ismā`īl to promulgate Shi`ism. This is framed by the device of *muṭābaqah* (antithesis), wherein we read how Ismā`īl had placed the hand of both abstinence and desire (*arādat va i`tiṣām*) on the handle of true religion (*`urwatu al-wusqā*), with the latter being a Qur'ānic *iqtibās* from 2: 256: "He who disbelieves in idols and believes in God has grasped hold of the firmest handle".[112] Prefacing with an Arabic expression (*maqāl*)—"He moistened the tongue and sweetened the meaning"—the scribe inserts a line of poetry that was consistent with the Safavid tendency to manipulate Shi`ite rhetoric: "Everyone has sought refuge from to somewhere from what is within/For us, the place of refuge is the family of Ḥaidar."[113] The Safavid *munshī* was paralleling the family of the Imāms (*āl-i Ḥaidar*) with that of Ismā`īl (son of Ḥaidar), and we are reminded again how the Safavids "placed themselves within the drama surrounding the story of the `Alid victims of Umāyyad and `Abbāsid oppression."[114] After a short admonition to Sulṭān-Ḥusain Bāiqarā to observe more closely his rebellious son, Muḥammad Muḥsin Mīrzā, the scribe expands on this apocalyptic motif and begins his epistolary narrative of the subjugation of Ḥusain Kiyā Chulāvī and the towns of Fīrūz Kūh, Gul-i Khandān, and Astā.

The terms used to describe these transgressors are those normally reserved for the most villainous of the Sunni world, whereby Ḥusain Kiyā is named "wicked Yazīd" (*Yazīd-i palīd*) and his troops "comported themselves with different types of hideous acts and scourge-like conduct" (*a`māl-i shanī`ah va af`āl-i qabīḥah*). Listening to the "seductive call of that Damned group of suspicious Turks [Āq Qoyūnlū?]" (*jamā`at-i makhzūl al-`āqibat-i Turkmān-i badgumān*), the cities saw their fortune turn ruinous when they decided it was necessary to build defensive fortification for their cities and citadels.[115] The scribe then uses the rhetorical devices of *i`tirāz* and *iqtibās* by quoting the partial Qur'ānic phrase of "he who does evil acts" (*min yu`amalu su'an*), which was an admonitory *āyah* (4: 110) to Muslims to realize that no one can plead on behalf of impious transgressors on the Day of Resurrection (*yaum al-qiyāmat*). "In order that they receive their just punishment," the scribe writes, "Ismā`īl set out from his winter camp in Qumm towards these rebellious areas." The themes of human arrogance, heresy, and divine punishment continue in the *munshī*'s narrative of the conquest of the citadel of Astā, where Ḥusain Kiyā and his notables had retreated after Ismā`īl had conquered the first two cities of Fīrūz Kūh and Gul-i Khandān. This citadel was extremely well built, durable, and "situated high on a mountain" (*bālā-yi kūh-i buland vāqi` shudah*). The tower was fortified and strengthened at five levels (*panj martabah*), with each level of the tower built for warfare (*muḥārabat*) and fighting (*mujāladat*). The army encircled the *qil`ah*, and the citadel was like "the centre of a circle" (*chūn markaz-i dā'irah*), a description which is then reinforced with a poem: "Like a circle, one should surround the enemy so that not one dot will find an exit from the centre." Realizing that the citadel of Astā was unassailable, Ismā`īl ordered the river supplying the citadel's water resevoir be dammed and redirected.[116] Ḥusain Kiyā, discovering the untenability of his situation, rallied his forces and sallied forth from Astā to face the Safavid besiegers. After the battle and slaughter of most of the citadel's defenders, the people of Astā capitulated and drank (*dar kashīdand*) from the verse of 2: 239, "we have no strength."[117] Readers understood the capitulation of Astā as an allusion to the Qur'ānic tale of Saul and his epic battle with Goliath. Here, Saul rejoins a certain body of his followers who, in deciding to drink from a nearby river, demonstrate their lack of faith in God's ability to guide and provide perseverance: "God will test you by a stream. Whoever drinks its water will not be of me; but those who do not drink shall be on my side."

The Qizilbāsh *ghāzīs* then read *āyah* 4: 95: "God has exalted those in rank who fight for the faith," to the supplicants, and "close to 10,000 people, including Murād Jahānshāhlū, Aslamas, and all of Ḥusain Kiyā's kinsmen and dependants were brought to reckoning."[118] There is little mistaking the *munshī*'s decision to describe Ḥusain Kiyā and his followers with Qur'ānic language associated with those transgressors of God's law during the pre-Islamic era as well as those who had violated the sanctity of the Twelve Imāms. Astā's ten thousand denizens, according to the letter, had been led astray and suffered divine judgement for their sins, not unlike the tribes of `Ād and Thamūd. In fact, the terms normally associated with mass slaughter (*kashtan, ba-qatl rasānīdan*) are eschewed by the scribe in favour of *ba-siyāsat rasānīdan* ("to bring one to account"). Astā continued to suffer several days of "fire of punishment" (*ātash-i qahr*), and we are reminded how one of the most popular means of conveying the impending chastisement for Hell's damned in both written and oral traditions was through the imagery of fire and immolation.[119] In light of the Qur'ānic remarks and the eschatological tenor here, one is also tempted to interpret the description of the citadel, or tower, of Astā as a deliberate reference to the Tower of Babel. The legend of the Tower of Babel was part of the post-Biblical religious lore circulating the Levant and was certainly known in the medieval Islamic world. Many geographers and historians understood the construction of Babel by Nimrod to be one of the landmarks of impiety from the post-Deluvian era. When the Safavid letter describes its height at five levels (*panj martaba*), we are reminded of the Arab geographer al-Bakrī's remarks that the Tower of Babel had been 5,000 cubits high.[120] Moreover, the occupants of Astā showed their conceit and vanity over the indestructibility of their citadel (*maghrūr va masrūr bi dān gashtah*).

The destruction of the citadel at Astā and the burning of its citizenry described in this letter were construed as allegories for Ḥusain Kiyā's unwillingness to accept the sanctity of Shāh Ismā`īl's presence.[121] The motif of the four earthly elements (earth, air, fire, water) used earlier is replicated in the description of the fate of Ḥusain Kiyā, and we read how "the impure dust of that water-seeking Ḥusain Kiyā was scattered to the wind."[122] Acknowledging the earlier characterization of Ḥusain Kiyā as that "wicked Yazīd" and the reference here to the inability of the rebels to secure a water source, we discover a second set of metaphorical images specific to the martyrological dynamic of `Alid Shi`ism. Shāh Ismā`īl's isolation of the cornered rebels and the initiatives he took to deprive them of water on the eve of battle are, on a certain cognitive level, designed to profile the Safavids as vindicators of the suffering, sun-blistered family of Ḥusain at Karbalā. A second Qur'ānic allusion of 7: 43: "We are grateful to God for guiding us here," plays on the motif of water but with paradisical overtones. Readers understood this allusion in light of its larger eschatological context: "Behold the garden before you! Ye have been made its inheritors, for your deeds, reference to the companions of the Garden." We have here a wonderful dual rhetorical device designed to exalt Ismā`īl's kingdom as an earthly replica of the Paradisical garden, as well as continue the earlier theme of riverine engineering and irrigation.[123] The scribe waxes how, on account of Shāh Ismā`īl, "the rosegarden of that region has been cleansed of the thorn of opposition [planted] by that lowly group."[124]

The second of these millenarian-minded *fatḥ nāmah*s was written to the Uzbek ruler, Muḥammad Shībānī Khān. This letter describes the defeat of `Alā' al-Daula Zū al-Qadar at Mardīn and was despatched in the summer of 1510 as Ismā`īl approached Khurāsān with a full contingent of Qizilbāsh troops. Following the benedictions to God, the Prophet, and `Alī, the letter begins with a less than eloquent but nonetheless significant poem about Ismā`īl's status as both a shaikh and a divine recipient of esoteric knowledge.[125] The *fatḥ nāmah* turns to the matter at hand: narrating the shah's victory over `Alā' al-Daula Zū al-Qadar at Mardīn. Similar to the earlier *fatḥ nāmah*, the Safavid *munshī* in question chose to depict this battle and its aftermath with metaphors and similes specific to both Sufi *ghuluww* and Shi`ite historical consciousnesses. After learning that `Alā' al-Daula Zū al-Qadar had attacked a Safavid force under Ḥusain Beg Shāmlū and `Abdāl `Alī Beg, Ismā`īl decided that the fortune of the Zū al-Qadar leader had turned ruinous, warning that "whomever falls on the family of `Alī will die."[126] A Safavid force of fourteen thousand brave warriors—a symbolic number referring to the Fourteen Innocent Ones (the Twelve Imāms, Muḥammad, and Fāṭima)—was sent to do battle against fifteen thousand Türkmen who are referred to as as *ẓulmānī*, a favourite term among Shi`ites to denote the Sunni oppressors of the family of `Alī. The scribe's narration reaches a crescendo: "We dissolved twelve thousand men with the love of the twelve Imāms, and we entered from twelve different directions," all the while saying: "'From the east to the west, if there is an imam/`Alī and his family are everything to us!'"[127] This, in fact, is a relatively well-known poetic acclamation from the mystical poet, Farīd al-Dīn `Aṭṭār.[128] The results were disastrous for `Alā' al-Qadar Zū al-Qadar and, after enumerating the casualties (almost certainly exaggerated), the scribe adds a *bait* of poetry: "The smashing of peace and disturbing of the penumbra/Is contrary to the hand of friendship and the head of prudence."[129]

The *fatḥ nāmah* shifts from narration to rebuke when the scribe details how Ismā`īl had received a royal letter from "that refuge of sovereignty, he who symbolizes Saturn, Muḥammad Shībānī Khān," and learned that the capital of Herāt had been conquered and Sulṭān-Ḥusain Bāiqarā and his children had been killed.[130] Attached to this narrative is the poetic admonition: "Friend! When you pass by the funeral bier of [your] enemy/Do not rejoice because the same will happen to you."[131] The letter adds that Ismā`īl was en route to Mashhad to adorn Imām `Alī Riḍā's tomb (*rauḍat al-muqaddasa*) with 70 *vazn* (a unit of weight) of jewels—an allusion to the Shi`ite hadith (reported by the sixth Imām Ja`far Ṣādiq), which alledges that God said to `Alī: "Oh Abū al-Ḥasan, Allāh has certainly made your descendents and your tomb areas and yards of Paradise. He who visits the tombs of your descendents will have the renewal of 70 times of recommended Ḥajj."[132] The letter ends with a final *bait* that casts Ismā`īl as Noah shortly before the flood: "Grasp the hem of the skirt of Ḥaidar and worry not/Whoever rides with Noah, why should he worry about the Flood?"[133] This was certainly a deliberate reference to one of the more popular Prophetic traditions—among both Shi`ites and Sunnis—known as the *ḥadīth-i Safīna*, whereby the Prophet stated: "Behold! My Family are like the Ark of Noah, whoever embarked in it was saved, and whoever turned away from it was drowned."[134] At some point during the medieval period, this particular tradition was "Shi`itized" to the extent it was understood that the pre-eternal Family of the Prophet, namely Muḥammad, `Alī, Ḥusain, and Ḥasan, had been on a ship during a great deluge. Ships representing seventy different religions and heresies capsized and drowned, while the *ahl al-bait* was able to navigate its way safely to land.[135] The iconographic import of this tradition is clear as a number of medieval Perso-Islamic chroniclers chose to depict this event in their universal histories.[136] Moreover, the predestined relationship between Noah and `Alī subsequently emerged as one of the favourite themes in the Imami Shi`ite traditions.[137] According to one tradition describing Ḥusain's and Ḥasan's funeral preparations for `Alī in Najaf, while digging the grave they discovered a shield with the depiction: "This is one of the things which Noah has stored for `Alī ibn Abī Ṭālib."[138]

Our third and last "victory letter" was written after the defeat of the aforementioned Muḥammad Shībānī Khān and was sent to the Mamluk ruler Sulṭān al-Ghaurī in Shawwāl 916/January 1511.[139] Predictably, the intention was to boast of the recent news of this defeat and how it was a "divine victory for the warriors of Islam."[140] Besides an ornamented copy of the Qur'ān, a prayer carpet, and a crossbow, emissaries also presented a ritual covering (*kiswah*) for the Ka`bah in Mamluk-controlled Mecca. They also allegedly presented the Mamluk Sulṭān with an elaborate Safavid genealogical document that "authenticated Isma'il's membership in the ahl-i bayt as heir through Ali to Muḥammad himself," which, in turn, proved Ismā`īl as the "rightful lord of Mecca, Egypt, and the whole of Syria."[141]

The letter narrates the invasion of Muḥammad Shībānī Khān and Ismā`īl's divinely sanctioned defeat of the Uzbeks outside the city of Marv. While we see Muḥammad Shībānī Khān described as "a branch from that Chingizid tree of impiety," the letter at this point eschews, at least temporarily, the standard Safavid theme of divine retribution to date and adopts a clearly imperial justification for Ismā`īl's decision to do battle with the Uzbeks: "Due to the need to protect God's laws and uphold the rules of the caliphate and imperial rule demanded that [Ismā`īl's army] be sent to Khurāsān to extirpate that rotten branch."[142] The scribe then writes that "on that day the two armies clashed in the *dār al-mulk*, Marv," but the portion "the two armies clashed" is in fact a Qur'ānic *iqtibās* from 8: 41, which describes the miraculous Battle of Badr between the Medinans and the pagan Meccans. In this sense, we see the victory at Marv over the Chingizid infidel Muḥammad Shībānī Khān through the metaphorical lens as the historical conflict at Badr, a "day of redemption/deliverance" (*yaum al-furqān*), characterizing the golden age of Islam.[143] Here, the letter takes on a graphic dimension in descriptions of total war and conflict (*muḥārabat va mujādalat-i tammām vāqi` shud*), with the conflagration of bloodshed, killing, and burning, and it was determined that fear and anxiety would be banished by the "sword that drinks blood" (*bahrām-i khūn-āshām*). This latter term, of couse, has *ghuluww* resonances and was understood by all as a reference to `Alī's sword, the Zū al-Faqār.[144]

The Safavid chancellery pattern of combining prose rhetoric with poignant lines of poetry continues here as the *munshī* appends these verses to his narrative of the battle at Marv:

From every direction, shots of arrows flowed
You said that the angel of death had fled
(But) the blood flowed like water
And the heads of the vain ones (floated) like bubbles.

This menacing, graphic tone was clearly provocative, and the references to arrows (*tīr-i nāvak, paik*) very likely alluded to the crossbow that was presented to the Mamluk ruler as an informal summons to war. Any ambiguity about the Safavid letter's metaphorical agenda is dispelled with the following poem:

The sword and the dagger are our flowers
For shame on the narcissus and the myrtle
Our wine is the blood of our enemies
And our cup is the skull of a head.[145]

This, of course, alluded to *la pièce de résistance* of the gift presentation: the hollowed out, silver-lined skull of Muḥammad Shībānī Khān, which Ismā`īl had been using as a goblet. The line, "Our wine is the blood of our enemies/ And our cup is the skull of a head," appeared in a letter from Sulṭān Ya`qūb Āq Qoyūnlū to Sulṭān Bayāzīd after describing how he had exacted a major victory over "the land of the greatest of the *kafīr*s and infidels, the Qarābāghdān."[146] Interestingly, this verse was based on a quatrain ascribed to `Alī ibn Abī Ṭālib himself, and the self-fashioning here as a macabre punisher of the wicked would have certainly resonated.[147] The decapitation of a rival and use of the head for ornamental purposes were certainly consistent with medieval Turco-Mongol customs, but this poetic emphasis on the image of the skull was also reflective of deeper religio-literary Islamic soteriological traditions. In the thirteenth century, Farīd al-Dīn `Aṭṭār had penned the *Jumjumah nāmah*, a poetic recounting of a much older, post-Biblical legend—the *Dastān-i jumjumah-yi sulṭān*—about Jesus discovering a skull in the wilderness and bringing it back to life. Telling its tale, the skull described how it had come from a ruler who had refused to heed the prophetic warnings of Elijah, and the ruler, *sans tête*, was cast into Hell. This was apparently a popular parable among the Turco-Mongol converts to Islam and was later translated into Khvārazmian and Turkish.[148]

*Fatḥ nāmah*s originating from the Safavid chancellery between 1501 and 1514 were more than promulgations of victory to the outside Islamic world. The texts examined here suggest that Ismā`īl and his chancellery coterie used the epistolary medium, specifically the genre of *fatḥ nāmah*s, to allude to a corpus of pre-Islamic and Islamic stories and legends about divine wrath and the millenarian agents who usher it in. Realizing that *fatḥ nāmah*s such as these were despatched not only abroad to the outside Islamic world but also were written and distributed internally among the cities and provincial courts, we find such correspondence serving an important aspect of the early Safavid agenda of motivating support for Shāh Ismā`īl as a divinely mandated agent of the Apocalypse. For instance, after the conquest of Marv, *fatḥ nāmah*s were despatched with envoys to the provinces of `Irāq-i `Ajam and `Irāq-i `Arab, Fārs, Kirmān, Ārrān, Āzarbāijān, Shīrvān, Māzandarān, and Khurāsān.[149]

While we have examined the extent to which chancellery material from the early Safavids was framed by millenarian tropes and language, we have yet to investigate the degree to which theosophy played a role. With the conquest of Tabrīz in 1501, the Safavid Qizilbāsh-dominated *ṭarīqah* encountered a nexus of different mystical movements and a centre of religious syncretism. We know that unorthodox mystical orders, such as the Ḥurūfiyyah and the Nūrbakhshiyyah, had significant representation in eastern Anatolia and Āzarbāijān, as did other, less controversial movements, such as the Niʿmatullāhiyyah and the Naqshbandiyyah.[150] Moreover, Sufi artisans and confraternities were notably active in Tabrīz since the Mongol era.[151] The relationships among the Safavids and these orders and mystical confraternities have been studied from a variety of perspectives, but often these have focused on the political, cultural, and administrative dynamics.[152] Historiographically, the implementation of doctrinal Shiʿism has been anchored with the arrival of Arab Shiʿite scholars from the Jabal ʿĀmil region.[153] Relatively little has been done regarding whether prevalent networks of Shiʿite-minded Sufis stepped forward as important sources of information with respect to Shiʿite Qur'ānic exegesis, hadiths, hagiography, and the doctrines of *waṣiyyat* (designation) and *walāyat* (Imami authority).[154] Some scholars, however, like Shahzad Bashir, have noted profound institutional and doctrinal changes in fifteenth-century Shiʿism and *taṣawwuf*, whereby Persianate Sufism was defined by notions such as the Seal of Sainthood (*khātam-i vilāyat*) and the Perfect Man (*insān-i kāmil*). In turn, we see an "increasing theoretical significance of the shaikh in Sufi cosmologies, and the reformulation of Shiʿism under the influence of Sufi ideas in the post-ʿAbbasid world."[155] In terms of the Safavid *ṭarīqah* itself, it would appear that this was definitely the case, but there is little doubt that this Sufi-Shiʿite ideological discourse, until 914/1508 at least, was framed by an imperative of violence and retribution. With the Safavid incorporation of the religiously heterodox centres of Tabrīz, Kāshān, Iṣfahān, and Yazd, the Safavid shah and court initiated a series of relationships with various mystical orders that shared the Safavid prediliction for both Shiʿite definitions of Mahdism and the Imamate as well as Sufi cosmologies but who drew well short of armed violence and social upheaval as a means of ushering in their different versions of the Day of Judgement.

We can shed light on at least some of the aspects of this early religious dialectic between Shiʿism and Sufism by examining a *maktūb* written in the Safavid *dār al-inshā* and despatched to the Uzbek royal camp in 915/1509.[156] This was led by Shaikh Muḥyī al-Dīn Aḥmad Shīrāzī, known as Shaikhzādah Lāhījī, a powerful protégé of Ismāʿīl's first vicegerent, or *vakīl*, Najm Masʿūd Rashtī, and "one of the most eminent and able men of his time."[157] In fact, Shaikhzādah Lāhījī was the son and successor to Shams al-Dīn Muḥammad Lāhījī, a Nūrbakhshiyyah shaikh and scholar of great repute (not to be confused with Ismaʿil's tutor in Gīlān, Shams al-Dīn Lāhījī). Shams al-Dīn Muḥammad Lāhījī was especially noted for his erudite commentary on Shabistārī's *Gulshan-i rāz*—the *Mafātīḥ al-iʿjāz fī sharḥ Gulshan-i rāz*.[158] His successor, Shaikhzādah Lāhījī, had fallen in with Ismāʿīl's camp in or around 1506 and quickly became one of the shah's boon companions.[159] He interacted closely with the different amirs (*arkān-i daulat*), specifically Najm Mas'ūd Rashtī, and in 915/1509 he was selected as the formal Safavid ambassador to Muḥammad Shībānī Khān. Despite his new Safavid colours, this study contends here that he was able to bring his training and heritage as a Shiʿite-minded Sufi shaikh to bear. Such Shiʿite-minded Sufi notables were routinely incorporated into the Safavid bureaucratic structure, as seen in the career of someone like `Abd al-Bāqī, the son of the eponymous founder of the Ni`matullāhī Order (Shāh Ni`mat Allāh Vālī Sānī). He replaced Qāḍī Shams al-Dīn Lāhījī as *ṣadr* and was later named to the highest office of *vakīl* in 1512.

The letter associated with Shaikhzādah Lāhījī charted new ground for the Safavid chancellery. The length and number of verses, Qur'ānic citations, and references to intricate systems of thought suggest an author with extensive training in both esoteric Sufi and exoteric Shi`ite doctrine. More importantly, this letter was the first official document to discuss Shāh Ismā`īl's promulgation of Shi`ism and provide a theological and doctrinal defence of that decision. Indeed, this letter stands as the first extant and contemporary declaration of Isma`il's new religious policy from the Safavid chancellery to the outside Islamic world,[160] and it is probably for this reason that Qāḍī Aḥmad chose to include the entire text in his *Khulāṣat al-tavārīkh.*[161] The *Khulāṣat al-tavārīkh* also records how Lāhījī made an attempt to win over Muḥammad Shībānī Khān to the Shi`ite *mazhab* during their meeting in the Uzbek *majlis.* The khan, after entering the council, pointedly turned the meeting into a religious debate by asking the *qāḍī*; "Why does this doctrine insist that the companions of the Prophet be reviled?" Lāhījī replied that he was astonished that the khan had not already accepted the unsullied truth of Shi`ism. Lāhījī pointed out how:

> Close to three to four hundred of your pious ones and religious scholars are part of this tradition, and they have written many books and volumes on the features of this doctrine. Your own forefather, Hulāgū Khān, was a follower of Khvājah Naṣīr al-Dīn Muḥammad Ṭūsī, who was a chronicler of the Shi`ite *`ulamā,* and [Hulāgū Khān] raised the Shi`ite *mazhab* [during his reign]. Moreover, Sulṭān Muḥammad Uljaitū, after one fleeting meeting with Shaikh Jamāl al-Dīn Mutahhar Ḥillī, who was one of the greatest proponents of this doctrine of truth, raised Shi`ism to a preeminent position.[162]

Acknowledging that the letter itself makes reference to his influential role and unique status ("Aḥmad, most learned dispenser of the rules of Islam, pillar of the scholars of religious sciences and knowledgeable ones, leader of the disciples of inspiration and knowledgeable ones, may God never stop giving him support"),[163]combined with the erudite and scholastic manner in which the letter uses mystical terminology and imagery to present its different doctrinal arguments, Shaikhzādah Lāhījī was almost certainly this letter's architect, either by way of formal authorship or as chancellery advisor.

Provocatively, Lāhījī begins his epistolary text with the first line of the Qur'ān (1: 1): "Praise be to God, Lord of the Worlds," which is then followed by Qur'ān 7: 128: "And the future is theirs who take heed for themselves." The *invocatio* is then concluded with Qur'ān 19: 54 and 19: 55: "Also mention in the Book of Ismā`īl: '[Ismā`īl] was strictly true to what he promised.... He used to enjoin on his people prayer and charity, and he was most acceptable in the sight of his Lord.'" This is an adroit manipulation of the term *kitāb-i Ismā`īl,* which concurrently referred to both the book of the Prophet Ismā`īl and the shah's diplomatic letter itself. In this sense, Ismā`īl's letter, or *kitāb*, is introduced structurally and metaphorically as a form of divine scripture. Lāhījī describes how a royal letter had arrived and made clear that the Uzbek had "revealed the reason for sincere ancestral desires" (*muṣarraḥ-i dalā'il-i irādat-i mūrūs̱ī-yi ṣamīmī*), and this in turn evoked a "stirring of the chains of old love and concord" (*muḥarrak-i salāsil-i muḥabbat va mavaddat-i qadīmī*).[164] While these two phrases show the *inshā* style of rhymed, structured prose (*tarṣī`*), *muḥarrak-i salāsil* implies rhetorically that Ismā`īl was the one who had mobilized the different, well-established Sufi orders. Shaikhzādah Lāhījī uses the subsequent section to explicate his notions of infallibility and pre-eternal essence. In doing so, he begins to narrate the emergence of Ismā`īl as a manifestation of the divine lights *(ẓuhūr-i ash`ah-yi Muḥammadī*). The premise of pre-eternal essence is "as clear as the sun in the sky" for those who are observant (*arbāb-i baṣā'ir va abṣār*), and Lāhījī supports this by citing the *ḥadīth-i qudsī* in which God said to the Prophet Muḥammad: "If it had not been for you, I would not have created the planets" (*laulāka mā khalaqtu al-aflāka*).[165] Accordingly, it was on account of the constant temporal and spiritual commands of the Imamate that Ismā`īl now enjoys the same authority in the physical and spiritual realms (*ayālat-i vilāyat-i ṣūrī va vilāyat-i mamālik-i ma`navī*).[166] The proofs and verification for Ismā`īl as the recipient of this most supreme of dominions and greatest of caliphates (*maẓhar-i salṭanat-i `uẓmā va khilāfat-i kubrā*), writes Lāhījī, are no different than those of the Prophet Muḥammad as he approached his throne in Heaven during the Ascension: "Then he drew near and drew closer, until a space of two bow arcs" (53: 9-10).

In describing Ismā`īl's period of hiding, quite tellingly we find a full elaboration of the aforementioned Sufi-Shi`ite syncretist discourse:

> Due to divine and temporal commands, friends [*wāris̱ān*] of that special community, as well as the most perfected of saints [*mukammal-i auliyā*] who were striving towards the hereditary rights [*ḥuqūq-i irs̱iyat*] offered by Ismā`īl, withdrew themselves from the hands of the lords of oppression and religious bigotry [*ayādī-yi arbāb-i ghaṣb va ta`aṣṣub*], and by refusing to associate [*ishtarāk*] with the worldly ones [*ahl-i dunyā*], they did not pronounce the names of dominion [*tasalluṭ*] and authority [*istīlā'*]. They would not bring themselves close to base people, and through hidden signs [*ishārāt-i ghaibiyyah*]and divine designs [*arādāt-i ilāhīyyah*], they showed their complete perfection.[167]

The amalgamation of traditional `Alid messianic rhetoric with Sufi Gnostic imagery continues. Lāhījī praises God that, thanks to `Alī's prescription, "All peoples have a reign, and our reign will be at the end of time" (*li-kull-i anās daulat wa daulatnā fī ākhir al-zamān*), and Ismā`īl has now raised his head from the meadow of the family of Prophecy and Imamate like a fertile young tree (*nahāl-i barūmand-i vujūd*). With hermetic language, Lāhījī adds that it is from "hiding" (*az makman*) that the world is now illuminated by this family of dominion (*dūdmān-i siyādat*) with the signs "for God wills to perfect His light" (9: 32), and "it is the fire kindled by God which penetrates the hearts" (104: 6–7).[168] After numerous other Qur'ānic citations of proof, Lāhījī again alludes to the predestined nature of Ismā`īl's rule by asserting that the angels had written "God mentioned in the Book of Ismā`īl" (19:55) on the "pages of the book" (*bar ṣafāyiḥ-i ṣaḥāyif*), a clear reference to the *lauḥ-i maḥfūẓ* as the pre-eternal recording of the destiny of men. With the recording of this illustrious name (*ism-i jalīl*), "the age of rule by the lords and dominion over the world and mankind has been made forever splendorous in the eyes of the people." Playing again on the themes of concealment and Shi`ite aspirations for justice, Lāhījī appends the *bait*: "The door to the treasury of mercy had been ordered closed/Our age has arrived and the door is now open."[169]

Having characterized Ismā`īl as an apocalyptic agent, who is manifested as a divine light from both the communities of the Prophets and the Imāms, Lāhījī shifts rhetorical gears by positing the superiority of the Imamate and its crucial importance to mankind. Again, we find an unprecedented methodical deliberation consistent with scholastic disputation, whereby scripture and well-vetted Prophetic proofs are cited regularly and fully. The rules and regulations of the Imamate have received the most careful attention (*ihtimām-i mazbūl*) from the Safavids, as revealed in *āyah* 23 of the Consultation: "Say: 'I ask no recompense of you for it other than obligations of relationship.'" The Qur'ānic verse here of 42: 23 was a favourite among Shi`ite and Sufi exegetes since the term *muwaddat* was translated as "love," while *al-qurbī* was understood as "kinfolk," implying that God prescribed humanity's love and respect for the kinfolk, or family, of the Prophet Muḥammad.[170] Lāhījī follows this Qur'ānic proof with a Prophetic one, namely the well-known Shi`ite Tradition of the Pool, or *ḥadīth-i ḥauḍ*: "Verily, I am leaving among you two objects of high estimation and of care: the Book of God, and my near kindred, my family. They are my vice-regents after me, and they will not part from each other until they meet at the pool on the Day of Judgment."[171] Thus, Lāhījī concludes, it is understood on the basis of that Prophetic tradition that this laudable method (*shīvah-yi raḍiyyah)* and agreeable habit (*shīmah-yi marḍiyyah)* were predetermined. In turn, the spiritial help (*amdādāt-i ma`naviyyah)* and religious guidances (*irshādāt-i dīniyyah)*, which have been commanded in the Book and are connected to Ismā`īl's noble ancestors, has now entered the physical world. With Ismā`īl's *ẓuhūr* placed squarely as the cumulative event in the pre-eternal history of the Imāms, Lāhījī writes that "it has been commanded the Truth and Twelver Imamism will be adopted and the commands of the noble Shari`ah in the pure ways of Muḥammad and `Alī, which [both] the Qur'ān and sound prophetical hadiths have justly proved the truth of those two, will be put into force."[172] At this juncture, Lāhījī turns to theological polemics and describes how the Uzbeks are narrowly confined prisoners of the slavish imitation and replications [found in the] fanciful stories told by their forefathers (*maḥbūsān-i maḍīq-i taqlīd va taqayyud bi afsānah-hā-yi abā'-i daulat*), as related in the Qur'ānic episode in 43: 22, whereby the disbelieving Meccans said to Muḥammad: "We found our fathers following a certain way, and are guided by their footprints." Shāh Ismā`īl, unlike the Uzbeks, is incapable of concealing this way of Truth (*rāh-i ḥaqq*) since it was commanded that "I follow the faith of my fathers, of Abraham" (12: 38), and "Say: 'Should I seek (the source of) of law elsewhere than God, when it is He who has revealed this Book to you?'" (6: 114).

Here we sense an interconnection between this letter and Lāhījī's ambassadorial mission. We recall that Lāhījī had pointed out the Mongol Shi`ite proclivities in person to the Uzbek *dargāh*, and the letter here also describes Shāh Ismā`īl's willingness to send sound religious scholars to the Uzbek court to present rational and logical proofs (*dalā'il-i `aqlī va naqlī*) of Twelver Shi`ism. These scholars will correspondingly corroborate the truth of Shi`ism according to God's command: "Ask them: 'Have you any knowledge? Then display it. You follow nothing but conjecture, and (you are nothing but liars)" (6: 148). The Safavid mandate of spreading the message of the Shi`ism in the face of Sunni antagonism is presented as a paradigmatic moment in the pre-eternal and historical experience of the Imamate. Lāhījī argues that it was part of God's original intention (*maqṣad-i aṣlī*) to introduce and spread the commands of that "saved community" (*firqah-yi nājiyyah)* to the earthly realm, despite the efforts of the Sunnis. In this sense, Sunnis are doorkeepers of oppression (*ḥujjāb-i ẓalām*), opponents of proper faith and state (*mukhalīfān-i dīn va daulat*), and defiers of kingship and religion (*mu`ānidān-i mulk va millat*) whose mandate is to conceal and hide those foundational and fundamental lights and secrets (*anvār va asrār-i uṣūl va furū`*).[173] The tone of the letter reverts, once again, to mystical moralizing when it describes how the Safavids and their supporters abhor and reject "dependency on earthly ways of the world and the trifling details of authority." Truly, Lāhījī writes, they "have not paid any attention on ignoble, worldly pageantries and impure, profane covetous ways."[174] This Sufi-Shi`ite discourse and its emphasis on asceticism and the inherent impurity of worldly ways intensify as Lāhījī remarks that opposing "hands of worldly attachment and dependency on this world and the immediate future" (*ayādī-yi tasalluṭ va ta`alluq-i dunyā va uqbā*) have been turned away from Shāh Ismā`īl, and those who protect the people of God (*ahl-i Allāh*) have accordingly saved themselves from defilement (*az lauṣ-i ālāyish*).

Lāhījī's style has an attractive symmetry, which manifests itself chiefly through the rhetorical device of *musajja`*, or rhymed prose, and *tarṣī`* (arrangements of corresponding, rhyming phrases). Moreover, while the introductory protocol of the letter begins with three Qur'ānic quotations, the concluding portion likewise consists of three scriptural quotations. The first, 4: 174, reads: "O Mankind! Verily there has come to you convincing proof from your Lord, for we have sent you a light that is manifest." This verse was popular among both Shi`ite and Sufi scholars in their respective treatises on the exigency of the Imamate and its manifestation through light, and it is clear that Lāhījī was referring here to his patron and *pīr*. This is followed by 6: 92: "And this is a book which we have sent down bringing blessing and confirming the revelations that have come before it." Again we find a continuation of seeing the term *kitāb* as a *tajnīs* for both the Qur'ān as well as the imperial missive in question. The letter finally comes to an end with 6: 115: "The word of your Lord finds fulfillment in truth and justice. None can change His words: for He is the one who hears and knows all." While the Shi`ite discourse for justice is signalled here, we cannot help but wonder if Lāhījī was deliberately concluding his epistolary text with the implication that, like the *kitāb-i Ismā`īl* once recited to the Prophet Ishamel, his own rendition of *kitāb-i Ismā`īl* was also infallible and enduring.

Lāhījī's epistolary text is significant for a number of reasons. Most importantly, it highlights the continuing influence of Shi`ite-oriented Sufi scholarship in the Safavid chancellery's earliest days. The consistent motifs of avoiding the "worldly ones" (*ahl-i dunyā*) and the inherent complications of embracing secular sovereignty also hint at what must have been a significant debate among the traditional anchorites who found themselves inextricably linked to this new, powerful imperial phenomenon. It is entirely possible that Shaikhzādah Lāhījī found himself at the heart of this debate, and his reluctance to embrace the rhetoric of violence and retribution that we see in other Safavid *fatḥ nāmah*s was rooted in his training and affiliation with the Nūrbakhshiyyah Order. Bashir has noted the strong similarities between Muḥammad Nūrbakhsh and Shāh Ismā`īl, who both advanced extreme religious claims and complex millenarian agendas. However, it would be Ismā`īl's "military adventurism" and a willingness to embrace the designation of "Sufi and Sultan" that would distinguish the Nūrbakhshiyyah from the Safavids so decisively.[175] Nonetheless, as someone who had been trained by and linked with Muḥammad Nūrbakhsh through Shams al-Dīn Muḥammad Lāhījī, Shaikhzādah Lāhījī was more than proficient at outlining the doctrinal underpinnings of Imami Shi`ism and providing their requisite Qu'rānic and Prophetic justifications. On the basis of such evidence, it is difficult to discount the impact of these scholastic groups of Sufis who had emerged in the doctrinal heterogeneity of the fifteenth century, such as the Nūrbakhshiyyah, and their role as important repositories for the development of Safavid Imami Shi`ism during a period when formal Sh`ite scholarship was relatively non-existent.[176]

The Safavid phenomenon had morphed considerably since Ismā`īl had first emerged from the Gīlānī periphery. Dynastic opponents had been vanquished, cities had been conquered, administrations had been incorporated, and religious communities had been coerced or expelled. A once parochial and religiously ambiguous millenarian movement that had depended heavily on the nomadic elements of the Anatolian and Āzarbāijānī environments now inherited the dynastic infrastructures of two well-established empires (the Āq Qoyūnlūs and Timurids) and annexed cities and territories from equally centralized polities, such as the Ottomans and the Mamluks. Assimilation of these different administrative, cultural, artistic, and scholastic features was by no means rapid or smooth. The Qizilbāsh military ethos, and the underlying millenarian agendas that motivated them, had far from dissipated. In fact, one could argue that this ethos continued to be embraced by Shāh Ismā`īl well after 1514 despite his new-found imperial pretensions and exposure to the rhetoric of kingship and state governance. The startling speed and success with which Shāh Ismā`īl marshalled support among the different Türkmen tribes and embarked on a decade-long campaign throughout `Irāq-i `Arab, the Iranian Plateau, Fārs, Khurāsān, and Transoxania was *not* a result of his ability to present himself as the logical imperial successor to the Āq Qoyūnlūs and the Timurids, but was largely in spite of it. Through his poetry, his proselytizing agents (*khalīfahs*), and lastly his epistolary correspondence, Ismā`īl embraced the metaphorical presentation of himself as a harbinger of the Apocalypse and instrument of God's wrath against the wicked. As this chapter has detailed, the rhetoric of millenarianism and social protest had a receptive audience in the late fifteenth- and early sixteenth-century Turco-Iranian world. There is little disputing that Ismā`īl's early success was contingent on the Safavid willingness to draw from and manipulate a corresponding corpus of stories, legends, fables, imagery, and motifs. The Safavid chancellery, in its early days, was an amorphous amalgamation of administrators, poets, storytellers, religious charismatics, and stylists who, for reasons of religious conviction or self-preservation, were willing to provide Shāh Ismā`īl with the rhetorical tools he needed.

Of central importance was the casting of Ismā`īl's ascension as the "rising of the Mahdī" (*qā'im al-Mahdī*) and his call-to-arms as, not the beginning of an enduring and centralized political state, but rather the start to an epoch of retribution for those who had wronged `Alī and the Imāms. In terms of the diplomatic correspondence examined here, *munshīs* made full use of the range of rhetorical exemplars (Noah, Abraham, `Alī, Ḥusain, Abū Muslim) to mould Ismā`īl's image to both the Safavid empire and the outside Islamic world. Ismā`īl's characterization as the divinely mandated judge and executioner and the martial exigency of the Safavid movement as a whole found a logical forum in the genre of the *fatḥ nāmah*, or victory letter. Lastly, while militancy and apocalyptic fervour were consistent themes in Ismā`īl's court and chancellery, we cannot forget the strong mystical orientation that pervaded the Safavids and the surrounding Turco-Iranian world. Elements of mysticism certainly manifested themselves in some of Safavid *fatḥ nāmah* literature, but we find the clearest and most consistent of such articulations in the letter presented by Shaikhzādah Lāhījī. This *maktūb* to Muḥammad Shībānī Khān of the Uzbeks was unprecedented in its doctrinal and theological anchoring and defence of Shāh Ismā`īl's "emergence." His *ẓuhūr* is contextualized in a Sufi cosmology, and strong distinctions are made between the perfect, spiritual world and its ignoble physical counterpart. This excellent example of Sufi-Shi`ite syncretist discourse is proof of not only the endurance of the Safavids' own roots as a *ṭarīqah* but also their absorption and utilization of Shi`ite-oriented mystical movements, such as the Nūrbakhshiyyah and the Ni`matullāhiyyah. In terms of daily administration and taxation, the Safavids clearly diluted the millenarian fervour found in diplomatic correspondence. In the documentary world of *farmāns*, *suyūrghāls*, and *raqams* we find a mélange of older Āq Qoyūnlū Turco-Mongol chancellery traditions with innovative genealogies and messianic slogans specific to the Safavid dynasty.

Recovery of Persian Bureaucratic Culture and the Imperializing of Epistolary Rhetoric, 1514–24

The period 1514–32—following Chāldirān but preceding the apogee of the chief Shi`ite hierocrat `Abd al-`Alī al-Karakī's influence—is highlighted by a resurgence of Persian administrative (*vizārat*) and clerical (*ṣadārat*) agency in the Safavid *dīvān-i a`lā*. Pivotal to this resurgence was the influx of Timurid-trained Persian administrators from Khurāsān and Transoxania after 1511. These new Safavid scholar-bureaucrats were moulded and framed by the wide-scale Persian literary and cultural renaissance, which emerged under Timurid sponsorship in the second half of the fifteenth century. The attenuation of heterogeneous Sufi-inspired millenarianism and a corresponding revival of interest in Persian poetry, literature, and pre-Islamic history, are best explained by this influx of scholars, bureaucrats, and saintly personalities from newly conquered centres in Āzarbāijān, the Central Iranian Plateau, Khurāsān, and western parts of Central Asia. From 1514 until 1524, we find a stark reversal in Ismā`īl's comportment, whereby aggressive campaigning was replaced by languid feasting and hunting. In this last decade of rule, the Safavids avoided any serious engagements with Ottoman, Mamluk, or Uzbek forces, and diplomatic activity became dilatory. From 1514 until 1532, which includes the last decade of Isma`il's reign and the beginning of Ṭahmāsp's lengthy rule, we indeed see an increasingly assertive agenda from a number of Persian administrators and a corresponding dilution of Qizilbāsh influence in the central administrative apparatus. A large part of this has its roots in 914/1508 and the appointment of Najm-i S̱ānī, whom Aubin described as "une tête politique," to the viceregency office of *vikālat*.

His ascension began in 1507, when he replaced Amīr Zakariyā and Maḥmūd Jān Daylamī in the *vizārat*—part of a larger administrative shuffle in which Mullā Shams al-Dīn Iṣfahānī was named *mustaufī-yi dīvān-i a`lā,*[177] and Qāḍī Muḥammad Kāshānī lost his post as *ṣadr* to Sayyid Sharīf al-Dīn `Alī Shīrāzī. As a native Iṣfahānī, Najm-i S̱ānī was far removed from the millenarian, Āzarbāijānī roots of the Safavid Order. The Khūzānī family, as discussed by Masashi Haneda, would continue to be involved in the upper echelons of Iṣfahānī administration long after Najm-i S̱ānī's death in 1512 at Ghijduvān, with his nephew Mīrzā Jān Beg serving as *dārūgha* for Iṣfahān in the 1530s and his grandson Mīrzā Hidāyat Allāh acting as the city's *nāẓir-i mu`āmalāt* (overseer of commercial taxes) in the 1580s.[178] In the span of a year, the *dīvān-i a`lā* had become more than just Persian in orientation and was now in fact an "Iṣfahānī administration."[179] Najm-i Sani enjoyed a remarkable degree of independence, which is confirmed by the historian Būdāq Munshī: "[Ismā`īl] was not current with his affairs—everything was in the hands of the *vakīl* and the *vazīrs*."[180] The historian Khvāndamīr narrates the meteoric rise of this Iṣfahānī urban notable, who bridged both worlds of bureaucracy and military power (*vizārat va imārat*): "[Ismā`īl] raised the banner of [Najm-i Sānī's] esteem and authority to the height of *farqadān* (the two stars near the pole of the Lesser Bear), made all the amirs, viziers, and men of the state obey him, entrusted the conduct of administrative and financial affairs to his unerring judgment, and treated him with the greatest favour and esteem."[181]

With bureaucratic and religious matters no longer wholly determined by Qizilbāsh Turkic amirs and now under the direction of arguably more moderate urban elements, the Safavid *dīvān-i a`lā* turned to the task of bringing order to an empire still reeling from the ravages of the Qizilbāsh. Appointments to the office of *ṣadārat*, which was responsible for the royal administration of pious endowments and religious conformity, suggest that this reinvigorated Persian urban elite was intent on marshalling and controlling the unruly Qizilbāsh proletariat. Qāḍī Muḥammad Kāshānī's replacement, Amīr Sharīf al-Dīn `Alī Shīrāzī, joined the imperial retinue shortly after the conquest of Shīrāz in 909/1504. He was one of the grandchildren of Sayyid Sharaf al-Dīn `Alī Jurjānī, who had been an urbane *`ālim* in Shīrāz during the reign of Shāh Shujā` and was later brought by Tīmūr to Samarqand.[182] Sharīf al-Dīn `Alī Shīrāzī's nomination to the *ṣadārat* was such a momentous occasion that the poet Khvājah Amīr Muḥammad Munshī Qummī wrote a *rubā'ī* with a chronogram commemorating this event.[183] Despite a hiatus in Najaf and Karbalā, Sharīf al-Dīn continued to occupy the office of *ṣadr* for some years, and anecdotal evidence seems to suggest that this station brought considerable administrative weight with it.[184] After the killing of Najm-i Sānī at Ghijduvān in 1512, there was a period of several months before Ismā`īl selected the Ni`matullāhī shaikh Amīr Niẓām al-Dīn `Abd al-Bāqī of Yazd as his new *vakīl*. `Abd al-Bāqī had served as the Safavid *ṣadr* between 1511 and 1512, and was considered a protégé of Najm-i Sānī's.[185] In fact, Ḥasan Beg Rūmlū commented how he was "distinguished for his letters and style above his fellows,"[186] and we see herein Ismā`īl's desire to keep the *vikālat* firmly in the hands of educated Persians. Jean Aubin commented on the nomination of this new *vakīl* as being a "ralliement de l'Iran central et méridional," which gave cohesion at a critical juncture.[187]

The invigorated networks of Persian Shi`ite and Sufi urban notables were undoubtedly buttressed by the formal adoption of doctrinal orthodox Twelver Shi`ism in the Safavid empire. While any nuanced appreciation for the scholastic and legalistic features of Twelver Shi`ism was notably absent, Safavid authorities were quick to manipulate a panoply of Shi`ite icons and slogans in a variety of public spaces. Meanwhile, *tabarrā'iyān*—state-sponsored Shi`ite zealots—were sent into the streets and markets to convert those who opposed the new religious order and force them to anathematize publicly the first three caliphs.[188] Ismā`īl purportedly spread the faith "in the manner that the Prophet Muḥammad, peace be upon him, had given the news,"[189] and "day by day, the rising sun of truth of *Ithnā `Asharī* Shi`ism was accepted, every area and part of the world was illuminated by the noble lights of this path of truth."[190] Ismā`īl commissioned the refurbishing of Imām Riḍā's shrine after the conquest of Mashhad in 916/1510, and the later *vakīl* Mīrzā Shāh Ḥusain Iṣfahānī built the *Hārūn-i Vilāyat* (in reference to the popular Shi`ite *ḥadīth-i Hārūn*) in Iṣfahān.[191] When we consider the timing of such shrine developments, along with the later appearance of seals on Safavid documents listing the Twelve Imāms[192] and letters discussing Ismā`īl's familial connection to the *ahl al-bait,*[193] we encounter a visual use of Shi`ite icons and slogans that, on the face of it, belied the lack of sophisticated appreciation of any legal and theological doctrines at these early dates.[194] As Ḥasan Beg Rūmlū remarked, "In those days men knew not of the Ja`farī faith and the rules of the 12 imāms."[195]

The influx after 1512 of Timurid-trained administrators, artists, and courtly elite into the upper Safavid echelons only intensified this reinvigorated Persian bureaucratic corporate culture. These emigré personalities were products of a courtly and cultural structure, which in numerous ways had been unsurpassed in the contemporary Islamic world. Many have noted the strong Timurid aegis of such structures in the fifteenth century and its sixteenth-century dissemination to the Iranian Plateau and the Indo-Gangetic Plain.[196] Under the supervision of Mīr `Alī Shīr, Sulṭān-Ḥusain Bāiqarā's confidant and principal minister, Timurid scribes and court functionaries would have enjoyed systematic training and exposure to an intricate bureaucratic literary tradition. As Maria Subtelny notes, Mīr `Alī Shīr "personally encouraged and financially supported the numerous poets, painters, musicians, calligraphers, architects, and historians who produced a breadth of cultural activity which some later Western scholars have called the 'Timurid Renaissance.'"[197] Originally an Uīghūr Turk, Mīr `Alī Shīr had been born in Herāt, was intricately acquainted with Persian belles lettres, and was more than comfortable working in the Perso-Islamic administrative culture.[198] In discussing the appeal of dislocated Timurid administrative elements, Khvāndamīr informs us that "most of the tax collectors, [who] were masters of [that] art, were secured by [Ismā`īl's] *ghāzī*s."[199] The speed and intensity with which Ismā`īl incorporated administrative luminaries like Bitikchī and Sāgharchī into the Safavid state is not surprising. The Bitikchī Khvājahs had distinguished themselves as the most important family of administrators in Astarābād and as such were a critical asset for whoever was in control of western Khurāsān.[200] According to Aubin, Bitikchī was "un bureaucrate expert en gestion financière, un emir versé dans les questions militaires ... et un gros propriétaire foncier."[201] Sāgharchī, on the other hand, was raised and trained in Herāt and had been in charge of "all matters of state and finance" for the Uzbeks.[202] Together, Bitikchī and Sāgharchī were the "monstres sacrés" of the Khurāsānī chancellery and a much-needed boost to this new program.

Given medieval Islamic patronage systems and court networks, it seems safe to suggest that both these viziers would have brought with them sizeable cadres of Timurid-trained *munshīyān* (chancellery stylists), *kātibān* (scribes), *nassākh* (copyists), *naqqāsh* (painters), *mustaufīyān* (financial auditors), and *`ummāl* (tax collectors). Khūrshāh ibn Qubād reports that the "sayyids, righteous ones, and lords [of Gurjān] proffered themselves to and were honoured by [Ismā`īl]" alongside Bitikchī.[203] The two sayyid brothers, Sayyid Ja`far and Shāh Qāsim Nūrbakhsh, who were prominent personalities in the Nūrbakhshiyya Order and eminent administrators in Dāmaghān under Sulṭān-Ḥusain Bāiqarā,[204] were appointed to serve as Safavid bureaucrats in `Arabistān and Rayy respectively.[205] Other prominent ex-Timurid legal functionaries who now served the Safavid court included: Amīr Abū al-Qāsim (*naqīb* of Nīshāpūr), Amīr Kāmal al-Dīn Ḥasan (*qāḍī* for Herāt), Amīr Muḥammad (*qāḍī* for Mashhad), Amīr Niẓām al-Dīn `Abd al-Ḥayy Astarābādī (a Timurid *naqīb* trained in Shi`ite jurisprudence serving in Herāt alongside Amīr Kamāl al-Dīn Ḥasan).[206] Other key scholar-bureaucrats who switched imperial patronage cloaks included Maulānā Nūr al-Dīn Muḥammad (a religio-legal official in Herāt), Amīr Niẓām al-Dīn Sidī-Aḥmad, and Amīr `Abd al-Ḥayy Rāzī (administrator under both Durmīsh Khān Shāmlū and Shāh Ismā`īl).[207] One of the most important landowning families of Sabzavār, and Khurāsān in general, the Bānū Mukhtār, had prospered under Sulṭān-Ḥusain Bāiqarā. Led by Mīr Shams al-Dīn `Alī, the *naqīb-i nuqabā*, this family joined ranks with the Safavids and helped administer the area.[208] The Safavids also gave refuge to Timurid political refugees, most notably Sulṭān-Ḥusain's eldest son Badī` al-Zamān, who was established in Tabrīz with a daily stipend of 1,000 *dīnār*s. Eventually he was given the governorship of Dāmaghān.[209] The ramifications of this arrival of the Timurid scholar-bureaucrats and the resurgence of Persian administrative consciousness emerged fairly quickly after 1514. The primacy of the Iṣfahānī networks was corroborated when Mīrzā Shāh Ḥusain Iṣfahānī was appointed to the *vikālat* to replace `Abd al-Bāqī (who was killed at Chāldirān). An architect and bureaucratic minister to Durmīsh Khān Shāmlū, the *dārūgha* of Iṣfahān, Mīrzā Shāh Ḥusain Iṣfahānī now controlled "all administrative and financial affairs" and an order was issued for him to run the affairs of the *salṭanat* independently with no interference from other viziers and high office-holders.[210]

How, then, can these changes and shifts among the Persian administrative and clerical elite inform our hope to map out the relationship between chancellery culture, dynastic legitimacy, and the art of rhetoric? If diplomatic correspondence was framed by the millenarian and mystical agenda of the Safavid movement between 1501 and 1514, did the aforementioned influx of Timurid scholar-bureaucrats then dictate a realignment? To best appreciate the role and influence of the Safavid chancellery, or *dār-i inshā*,[211] we are obliged to provide a prosopographic overview of the chancellery during this critical transition period of the 1510s and 1520s and the transition away from the Türkmen bureaucratic and courtly model. Admittedly, there is some confusion in the different conceptions of the *dīvān-i a`lā* and the *dīvān-i inshā*, which had been developed by earlier dynasties like the Khvārazmshāhs, the Ilkhāns, the Timurids, and the Qarā and Āq Qoyūnlū. In many ways, the Safavids seem to have syncretized Timurid and Türkmen bureaucratic ideologies since the *dīvān-i a`lā* acted both as a royal court of prominent amirs as well as a central government.[212] It was undoubtedly the Āq Qoyūnlū model that most directly influenced the Safavids, but their own administration was an amalgam of Turco-Mongolian traditions (with official acknowledgement of Turkic positions like *qūrchī, yasāvul, yūrtchī*)[213] and Perso-Islamic institutions, including the *dīvān-i parvānchī* and the *dīvān-i ṣadārat*.[214] John Woods describes the *dīvān-i a`lā* as "a supreme administrative council—a body regularly convened to direct the political, economic, and military affairs."[215] This definition nicely reflects early Safavid conceptions of the *dīvān-i a`lā*. In this sense, it had an overarching capacity as both a council for amirs as well as an administrative substructure; however, this also ensured that the *dīvān-i a`lā* and its appended offices of the *vikālat*, *vizārat*, and *ṣadārat* were loci of intense friction and rivalry between the Persian administrators and the Turkic Qizilbāsh tribal elite. Indeed, a review of how such key offices within the *dīvān-i a`lā*—the *muhrdār* (seal-bearer), *yasāvul* (usher), *īshīk āqāsī bāshī* (chamberlain), *tuvāchī bāshī* (troop inspector), and others—changed hands between different Türkmen tribes as well as Persian administrators in the first half of the sixteenth century underscores both the fluidity and ambiguity of the Safavid *dīvān-i a`lā*.[216]

This mutability is carried over into the nebulous institution of the Safavid *dīvān-i inshā*. As we observed with the transferred allegiances of Amīr Zakariyā Kukajī, Maḥmūd Daylamī Qazvīnī, and Qāḍī Ḍiyā al-Dīn Nūr Allāh Savājī, the *dīvān-i inshā* between 1501 and 1512 had been largely a continuation of its Āq Qoyūnlū counterpart. We also noted influence and input from eminent Sufi personalities—`Abd al-Bāqī Ni`matullāhī and Shaikhzāda Lāhījī Nūrbakhshī—in the *dīvān-i a`lā* and *dīvān-i inshā*. As a result, the epistolary style of the *dīvān-i inshā* employed a range of mystical and millenarian metaphors, images, and mythoi. Undoubtedly, these twin-pronged influences from the administrative culture of the Āq Qoyūnlū and the theosophical elements based in Āzarbāījān and western Iran were reinforced by the continued use of Tabrīz as an imperial capital. The influence of the Āq Qoyūnlū-trained Kukajī family of Tabrīz was attenuated considerably, however, with the appointments of two Iṣfahānīs (Najm-i Sānī, Mīrzā Shāh Ḥusain) to the *vikālat* and another Iṣfahānī (Maulānā Shams al-Dīn) to the office of *mustaufī al-mamālik*.[217]

The peripatetic nature of Ismā`il's court dictated a certain level of elasticity on the part of the central Safavid *dīvān-i inshā*. In certain instances, we know that *munshī*s would accompany the shah during summer sojourns and campaigns, but a number of chancellery officials were based permanently in Tabrīz's central palace complex and its appended library-atelier to attend to documenting tax assessments and remissions, canonical tax exemptions, notices of investiture, and various prohibitions and interdictions. The most recognizable was Khvājah `Atīq `Alī, whom the later compiler of the monumental *Munsha'āt al-Ṭūsī*—Ḥusain

Naṣīr al-Dīn al-Ṭūsī—hails as a paternal ancestor and one of the chief officials responsible for writing *inshā* for Shāh Ismā`īl.[218] Since Khvājah `Atīq `Alī is alleged to have designed Ismā`īl's *ṭughrā* as early as 1504, it seems likely that he left his native Urduābād and joined the Safavid movement in its infancy.[219] Generally, however, those chancellery stylists who served Ismā`īl in his early years were part of a familial network that had dominated Tabrīz since the days of the Ilkhāns.

The most recognizable *dīvānī* family was the Kukajī Tabrīzīs—best represented by Amīr Beg Zakariyā—and not surprisingly it was these Tabrīzīs who staffed the bulk of the chancellery positions.[220] One such individual was Khvājah Jalāl al-Dīn Muḥammad Tabrīzī, who would go on to assume the *vikālat* in the wake of Mīrzā Shāh Ḥusain Iṣfahānī's death in 930/1524. During his tenure in the chancellery, Jalāl al-Dīn Muḥammad Tabrīzī had been "unsurpassed" in his epistolary skills, and until his nomination as co-vizier with Qāḍī-yi Jahān Qazvīnī in 919/1514, he worked diligently in the chancellery.[221] Another local chancellery personality was Maulānā Niẓām al-Dīn `Alī, who had been based in Ardabīl and was famous for his calligraphic styles throughout Āzarbāījān. Other prominent chancellery officials, who were not part of the traditional Tabrīzī administrative elite, included Malik Maḥmūd Jān Daylamī (attained his position on account of the high status of his kinsman) and Sharaf al-Dīn Maḥmūd Daylamī Qazvīnī. Malik Maḥmūd is described by Sām Mīrzā as part of the "Daylamī group" and one of the great notables of Qazvīn (*akābir-i Qazvīn*), who had served Sulṭān Ya`qūb Bāyandur before switching allegiance to Shāh Ismā`īl.[222] Likewise, the two brothers Maulānā Anīs and Maulānā `Abd al-Karīm—originally from Khvārazm—had been in the employ of Sulṭān Ya`qūb Bāyandur but later joined Ismā`īl, writing calligraphy and *raqams* in a *nasta`līq* style reminiscent of the great calligrapher, Maulānā Sulṭān `Alī Mashhadī.[223] Not surprisingly, the growing prestige and influence of administrators from Iṣfahān in the *dīvān-i a`lā* also dictated a strong Iṣfahānī influence in the royal chancellery. The best example of this was Mīrzā `Aṭā Allāh Iṣfahānī. In addition to serving as Shāh Ismā`īl's provincial vizier to Āzarbāijān, Qarā Bāgh, and Shīrvān, he was the father of Mīrzā Aḥmad ibn `Aṭā Allāh, who became an eminent chief administrator during the reign of Shāh Ṭahmāsp. Indeed, when Shāh Ismā`īl passed away in 930/1524, Mīrzā `Aṭā Allāh Iṣfahānī was placed in charge of conveying Ismā`īl's last *farmān-i ḥukūmat* and royal robe of investiture to Shāh Ṭahmāsp's entourage. Iskander Beg Munshī lauded this administrator keenly,[224] and the poet `Abdī wrote a poem on the occasion of his death in the early 1560s.

After the annexation of the province of Khurāsān, the Safavid *dīvān-i inshā* began to assume cohesion. In terms of great Timurid epistolographic personalities who played a role in the newly articulated chancellery, we must mention Amīr Niẓām al-Dīn `Abd al-Ḥayy Munshī—whose father Amīr Abū Turāb had been one of the greatest Timurid men of the pen—and his appointment to the chief chancellery post (*ṣāḥib-i manṣab-i inshā*) under Muḥammad Shībānī Khān. He decided after 916/1510 to move to Safavid-controlled Astarābād and teach his skills in a madrasah setting.[225] Khvājah Muḥammad Mu'mīn—son of the great *munshī* and author of the *Sharaf nāmah*, `Abd Allāh Marvārīd—moved from Timurid Khurāsān to teach calligraphy to Ismā`īl and later personally tutored the shah's son, Sām Mīrzā.[226] The notable Mīrzā Qāsim—the son of a renowned Timurid astronomer and mathematician, Jalāl al-Dīn Mīrākī—had gone on to serve as vizier to the Timurid prince Badī` al-Zamān. Mīrzā Qāsim followed his liege to the Safavid court and was soon renowned for his contribution to administrative and fiscal matters as well as courtly calligraphy and epistolary style.[227] Lastly, we cannot overlook the epistolographic contribution of the great Timurid-Safavid-Mughal historian and scholar-bureaucrat, Khvāndamīr, who compiled his own collection of contemporary correspondence under Safavid auspices, the *Nāmah-yi nāmī,*[228] in 1519.[229] The *Tazkirah-yi tuḥfah-yi Sāmī* describes Khvāndamīr as one of the leading scholars in "*inshā*, eloquence, poetry, and rhetoric [*balāghat*]," who served the Safavid provincial administration in Herāt.[230] Other notable administrators who brought strong epistolary skills to the Safavid chancellery in the period 1514–32 include the Abrārī native, Maulānā Adham Munshī, who dominated the *dīvān-i inshā* under Shāh Ṭahmāsp.[231] A future chief chancellery stylist (*munshī al-mamālik*) for Shāh Ṭahmāsp, Khvājah Mīrāk cut his administrative teeth serving the provincial administration in Kirmān during the second half of the reign of Shāh Ismā`īl.[232]

Hence, there seems to be sufficient prosoprographic evidence to point to an infusion of Timurid aesthetics, style, and motifs into Safavid calligraphy and epistolary rhetoric after 1514. While Timurid chancellery luminaries, such as Khvājah Muḥammad Mu'mīn and Amīr Niẓām al-Dīn `Abd al-Ḥayy Munshī, were able to transmit their skills and acumen directly to the Safavid chancellery, edifying texts produced by Timurid emigré scholar-bureaucrats were also used to train the newly founded Safavid chancellery and calligraphic workshop based in Tabrīz. In addition to the aforementioned work of Khvāndamīr (*Nāmah-yi nāmī*), there were didactic calligraphic texts produced during 1514–32, which reflect Timurid influences, such as `Alī ibn Ḥasan Khūshmardān's *Ta`līm al-khuṭūṭ* and the *Adab-i khaṭṭ* by Majnūn ibn Maḥmūd Rafīqī Haravī Chap-nivīs ("the Left-handed").[233] In this period of remarkable transition, the question of Timurid influence and reorientation in the diplomatic material itself comes to the fore. If we see an extirpation of the images, motifs, and metaphors associated with pedestrian and popular millenarianism, what rhetorical devices do we see subsequently employed in this revamped chancellery after 1514? More pressing, perhaps, is the question of whether these Timurid-trained scholar-bureaucrats were able to work together with this newly empowered administration to effectively recharacterize Safavid claims to legitimacy at such a critical juncture.

A set of intriguing letters appears in Khvāndamīr's epistolary compilation, the *Nāmah-yi nāmī*.[234] Khvāndamīr had enjoyed Safavid patronage in Herāt during the governorship of Durmīsh Khān Shāmlū and vizierate of Karīm al-Dīn Khvājah Ḥabīb Allāh Sāvajī.[235] In this sense, it is probable that Khvāndamīr was ordered by Shāh Ismā`īl to write letters to the Uzbek ruler `Ubaid Allāh Khān and the Mughal fugitive Ẓahīr al-Dīn Bābur as well. The letter to `Ubaid Allāh Khān, probably written in 926/1520 during a protracted Uzbek siege,[236] is a relatively concise history of the Safavid position in the regions of Khurāsān and Transoxania in the last decade, which reflects a tone of conciliation and appeasement. The letter begins with a *rubā'ī* celebrating `Ubaid Allāh Khān's sovereignty, and here Khvāndamīr eschews any recognition of the Turkic nomadic background of the Uzbeks and looks to the pre-Islamic age of Persian kingship: "O Khusrau," the letter waxes poetic, "Bravo! He who has the gravity of Farīdūn/And the kingliness of Alexander and the power of Jamshīd." The overture towards peace is made clear from the beginning with the next *bait*: "Whomever shoots an arrow for the establishment of peace/Cannot shoot another in that manner into the valley of war."[237] The titulature for `Ubaid Allāh Khān is normally reserved for justice-wielding Persian monarchs, and we again find allusions to his likeness to Alexander and Jamshīd (*manqibat-i Iskandar martabat-i Jamjāh*). The pre-Islamic association between monarch and light is applied thoroughly as we read how `Ubaid Allāh Khān is "the light of the heavens of felicity and fortune, the sun of the sky of majesty and authority" (*mihr-i sipihr-i daulat va iqbāl āftāb-i āsmān-i ḥashamat va istiqlāl*). The metaphor of kingly sovereignty and divine light was a consistent feature of Achaemenid and Sasanian political rhetoric when discussing the Persian ruler and Ahura Mazda. While this language had been appropriated earlier by dynasties such as the `Abbasids, Mongols, and Timurids, its appearance here in Safavid epistolary rhetoric underscores the ongoing shift away from *ghuluww* millenarianism and the embracing of the language associated with ancient Persian ideals of kingship. After the subsequent section praises Muḥammad and his progeny, Khvāndamīr laments the forfeiture of security and safety in Khurāsān. He notes at this time that Shāh Ismā`īl is committed to reforging friendship and strengthening the affairs of religion and state (*umūr-i dīn va daulat*) and the important business of faith and kingship (*mahāmm-i millat va mulk*) according to the Qur'ānic verse: "If two groups of believers come to fight one another, promote peace between them" (49: 9).[238] God willing, Khvāndamīr hopes, `Ubaid Allāh, with ethical fingertips (*anāmil-i maḥāsin-i akhlāq*) that reflect the best qualities necessary for proper kingship (*aḥāsin-i auṣāf kih lāzimah-yi zāt-i mulkī*), will open the doors of peace and purity (*abvāb-i ṣulḥ va ṣafā*).[239] This strong impetus towards political ethics was a clear deviation from previous Safavid chancellery correspondence and its emphasis on violence, punition, and Shāh Ismā`īl's agency as harbinger of the Apocalypse.

Always the historian, Khvāndamīr shifts into a narrative style to describe Najm-i Sānī's 1512 Ghijduvān misadventure and how Salīm's subsequent invasion had prevented Shāh Ismā`īl from addressing the Khurāsānī front. With the accession of Sulṭān Sulaimān and his invasion of Europe, the shah concentrated on Transoxania and organized his forces to subdue the region. In a subtle shift of rhetoric—again using metaphors of earthly elements—Khvāndamīr predicts that if this undertaking happens, the conflagration of strife and disorder (*ishti`āl-i ātash-i fitnah va fasād*) will be prevented by the raindrops of caution from the advice of wise ones and a policy of peace of mind (*qaṭarāt-i ghammām-i andīsha va tadbīr-i ahl-i `aql va tadbīr-i taskīn*).[240] Stability, order, and management are integral to good monarchical government, and Khvāndamīr reminds his Uzbek audience that the courtyard of kingship and faith (*`arṣah-yi mulk va millat*) must be adorned with the lights of justice and merit (*anvār-i `adl va iḥsān*), and that the garden of religion and state (*rauḍah-yi dīn va daulat*) must be weeded of the thorn of injustice and sedition (*khār-i bīdād va ṭughyān*).[241] The admonitory quality of this letter and the explicit appeals to linking monarchy with justice are remniscent of the style and approach of the mirrors-for-princes genre (*akhlāq*). We can see the ontological interconnection between the epistolary sciences and political ethics/advice literature.

The second letter is a response (*javāb*) written to the political refugee and future founder of the Mughals in India, Ẓahīr al-Dīn Bābur. The absence of any reference or allusion to India, combined with the traditional compilation date of 1519 for the *Nāmah-yi nāmī*, suggests that this missive was written during the reign of Shāh Ismā`īl and not, as Riazul Islam suggested, during the reign of Shāh Ṭahmāsp.[242] Like Khvāndamīr's letter to `Ubaid Allāh Khān, this one begins with opening *rubā'ī* alluding to Bābur's original correspondence: "A *farmān* of victory, an exalted decree, an imperial mandate obeyed by all the world/Like a light from the summit of generosity, the need for goodwilled glory became clear."[243] He acknowledges an invitation from Bābur to join the Mughal court at Kābul, but in doing so he employs a number of interesting numinous metaphors. He presents his future arrival as comparable to the pilgrim (*ṭawwāf*) who arrives in the environs of Mecca (*iḥrām*) next to that "Ka`ba of security and desire."[244] Intriguingly, Khvāndamīr casts himself as the submissive bride and Bābur's court as the patriarchal household, but he adds an eschatological subtext, whereby his use of the term of *sadanah-yi sadah-yi sidrah* also alludes to the flaming lotus tree that stands at the entrance to Paradise. The iconography of the Paradisical setting of virgins, riches, and untold pleasures being guarded by this flaming bush (alluded to in 53: 14 and 56: 28 Qur'ān) was popular among contemporary Safavid painters.[245] Unable to come due to reasons that his ruler will explain in a future letter, Khvāndamīr informs Bābur that he is still sending along a collection of Prophetic hadiths, which he hopes will be to his liking.[246]

The epistles appearing in Khvāndamīr's compilation are worth noting for several reasons. Most importantly, we find a dearth of the Sufi-*ghuluww* tropes, which had characterized earlier Safavid correspondence. We encounter the introduction and recognition of a new set of rhetorical exemplars—Alexander, Khusrau, Jamshīd, Farīdūn, Darius—that initially supplanted the *ghuluww* and Imami personalities at the fore of earlier Safavid correspondence. This is not to imply that Khvāndamīr inserted a "secular" element to Safavid chancellery standards, but rather that he and other Timurid-trained bureaucrats insinuated yet another inventory of mythical and historical personalities, which Safavid scribes could use for metaphorical comparisons. The privation of Shi`ite slogans and dilution of panegyric poetry to the warrior figure of `Alī and their replacement by imperial-minded equivalents can be seen most starkly in Khvāndamīr's decision to open his letter with "O Khusrau!" while at the same time ignoring `Alī, who had been routinely and repeatedly evoked in a 916/1510 letter to Muḥammad Shībānī Khān. As other epistolary evidence from the royal chancellery centre in Tabrīz indicates, it would appear that the foregrounding of pre-Islamic Persian monarchs and heroic figures was not specific to Khvāndamīr, and chancellerists working in the central *dīvān-i inshā* were increasingly comfortable with such rhetorical models.

In this context, however, we have the introduction of a series of concepts and ideas that had long since characterized Timurid epistolary evidence[247] and as such represents an orientation of Safavid chancellery practice towards a Khurāsān style, or *sabk-i Khurāsānī,* if you will. Khvāndamīr is consistent in his use of binomials, such as *dīn va daulat* and *millat va mulk*, and represents a revival of medieval religio-political axioms associated with the eleventh and twelfth centuries. Sholeh Quinn commented on the introduction of the term *millat* in his *Ḥabīb al-siyar* as part of an overall trend to rewrite Safavid history and emphasize a sense of distinctive community.[248] This, in turn, gives us good reason to align closely medieval Persian epistolary sciences with mirrors-for-princes and political ethics literature. The mirrors-for-princes genre was best represented in the Perso-Islamic tradition by Khvājah Naṣīr al-Dīn al-Ṭūsī (d. 672/1274), whose *Akhlāq-i Nāṣirī* would serve as the authoritative model for successive generations of influential Persian philosophers, intellectuals, and literati, including Shihāb al-Dīn `Abd Allāh Vaṣṣāf, Jalāl al-Dīn al-Davānī, and Ḥusain Vā`iẓ Kāshifī.[249] In the Timurid period, we see impressive levels of production with regard to both *akhlāq* and *inshā* literature, while letters (*rasā'il*) and testaments (*waṣiyyāt*) had been dominant components of didactic court literature dating back to the `Abbasid era, if not earlier into the pre-Islamic age.[250] Finding such characterizations in the epistolary writings of Khvāndamīr is not at all surprising, given that he himself contributed an advice manual to this emerging corpus entitled the *Makārim al-akhlāq*. This work is essentially a compendium of Khvāndamīr's thoughts and ideas on a wide array of courtly subjects, but he does acknowledge the importance of epistolary sciences in chapter four (*dar zikr-i faḍīlat-i inshā va bayān-i afāḍil-i sukhan-ārā*).[251] In addition to noting a number of prominent Timurid epistolographers, he elaborates on how "*munshīs* have been responsible for honouring and revering the exalted sultans and kings of their age."[252]

Moving westwards to Tabriz and looking at the central newly constituted administration after Chāldirān, our next extant letter (ca. 921/1515) is a *ṣulḥ nāmah* sent to the Ottoman court. A Safavid embassy had been despatched earlier with a letter from Shāh Ismā`īl, but the ambassador, the Naqshbandī shaikh and *Shaikh al-Islām* Sayyid Nūr al-Dīn `Abd al-Vahhāb, had been imprisoned and the letter was lost.[253] The current document was sent following the Ottoman rebuff in an effort not only to effect some kind of lasting peace but also to entreat Salīm to release `Abd al-Vahhāb. While the original decision to send `Abd al-Wahhāb—who was described by the Ottomans themselves as "a saintly personage ... a sayyid of pure lineage and of erudite doctrine"[254]—was in all likelihood a deliberate attempt to gloss over doctrinal differences between the Safavids and the Ottomans, this appointment was also indicative of a new ecumenical dynamic in the Safavid court, which was now characterized partially by the Iṣfahānī administrative elite and the newly arrived Khurāsānī scholar-bureaucrats.[255]

The letter begins with an *intitulatio* section that continues the predominance of pre-Islamic Persian luminaries, whereby Salīm is described in astronomical metaphors as the living embodiment of Jamshīd, Farīdūn, and Darius.[256] While admittedly it was the Ottoman sultan who was the beneficiary of such similitudes, this letter demonstrates how the Safavid chancellery was actively accessing the corpus of motifs, tropes, and icons that had defined the central Islamic literary world since the New Persian renaissance. In the case of this letter, the scribe adds the encomium of *farr-i Iskandar,* or light of Alexander. On one level we see the Gnostic element of emanationist light at play (in a secular manner), while we are also reminded of how the Ottoman sultans made conscious attempts to draw direct genealogical links with Alexander the Great.[257] The Safavid scribe switches rhetorical gear substantially after these epitomaic comparisons to pre-Islamic Persian kings and begins extolling Salīm as the custodian and guardian of proper Islamic piety (*ḥāmī al-islām wa al-Muslimīn, mu'aiyid min `and al-mulk al-Allāh*).[258] This would become a fairly consistent feature in Perso-Islamic epistolography of the Safavid period, whereby rulers would first be acclaimed for their kingship—primarily in metaphorical Persian terms (e.g, *Jamshīd-dastgāh, Kai-Khusrau va Dārā Jāh `ālam-panāh*)—and then hailed primarily in Arabic as an orthodox and pious Muslim ruler who governed according to the principles of the Sharī`ah.[259]

The letter continues to propitiate as the Safavid *munshī* laments how the jealousy of neighbouring sultans and the envy of regional kings (*maḥsūd-i salāṭīn-i iqṭār va maghbūṣ-i khvavāqīn-i amṣār*) has torn asunder the bonds of friendship and concord between the Ottoman and Safavid courts, which had been established in the days of Salīm's predecessor, Bayāzīd II.[260] We find here again the rhetorical *balāghat* device of *tarṣī`*, whereby repetitive rhymed phrases are "strung like a necklace" throughout the *matn*, or main text, of the epistle.[261] Shāh Ismā`īl, the scribe writes, is committed to extirpating and removing these lords of deviation and rancour (*daf` va raf`-i arbāb-i zaigh va `udvān*) and tearing out and hammering the lords of disobedience and rebellion (*qal` va qam`-i aṣḥāb-i `iṣyān-i va ṭughyān*).[262] The theme here of chaos and disorder is contraposed in a subsequent *tarṣī`* in which Ismā`īl asks the sultan to "resurrect the customs of ancestral, sincere love" (*iḥyā-yi marāsim-i muḥabbat-i mūrūṣī-yi ṣamīmī*) and "the elevation of the signposts of ancient absolute honesty between [we] children of noble sovereignty" (*va i`lā-i ma`ālim-i ṣadāqat-i yaqīnī-yi qadīmī* *fī-mā bain-i aulād-i amjād salṭanat*).[263] The strong contraposition between Ismā`īl and Salīm and those lords of sedition is clearly intended as a literary antithesis (*muṭābaqah*), and we can see an extension of poetic practices where such antithetical pairs are used liberally.[264] The motif of promising and maintaining social order and stability intensifies as the scribe relates how "stately affairs and kingly matters" (*umūr-i salṭanat va mahāmm-i mamlakat*) were at one time enforced by benedictions of justice and equity of both their ancestors. We find the echoes of Khvāndamīr's emphasis on *millat va mulk* as the scribe explains the implications for such cordial relations on the "kingly and religious events and sacred and worldly developments" (*vaqāyi`-i mulkiyyah va milliyah va ḥavādis̱-i dīniyyah va dunyaviyyah*).[265]

Interestingly, the Safavid scribe employs a number of pecuniary metaphors in portraying these Safavid overtures to the Ottomans. This particular prose again works within the rhetorical medium of dual metaphors, and we read how thanks to Ismā`īl's initiatives the protection of the boundaries of Islam was "stored in the treasury of intention and [now] living in the coffer of desire."[266] This sense of pecuniary concern continues when the Safavid letter reminds Salīm the Grim that "arrangements for general mankind" (*maṣālaḥ-i `umūm-i anām*) and "the arrangement of affairs for the multitude of Muslims" (*intiẓām-i manāẓim-i umūr-i jumhūr-i Islām*) has allowed the "opening up of the doors of affluence" (*fatḥ-i abvāb-i rakhā*) and "the spreading of the accoutrement of friendship" (*nashr-i asbāb-i valā*).[267] This materialistic motif continues when Ismā`īl's letter declares that on the basis of such developments, a permit will be issued for the coming and going of caravans and pack animals (*tayvīz-i amad shud-i qavāful va ravāḥul khvāhand farmūd*), presumably a hint at the possibility of restoring the trade routes that had been severed by Sultan Salīm.[268] "It is the truth of the matter," the letter concludes, that the despatching of ambassadors (*irsāl-i rusul*) and the conveying of correspondence (*iblāgh-i murāsalat*), has been nothing other than the security and safety of the peasantry.[269]

The evanescing of mystical and millenarian tropes in this post-1514 chancellery and their replacement with the twinned motifs of kingship and orthodoxy (*mulk va millat*) continue in a subsequent 928/1522 letter to the Ottoman sultanate. This particular missive is indeed a *julūs nāmah* (or congratulatory letter to a newly enthroned ruler) addressed to the young Sulaimān, which was sent after a series of ambassadors had been exchanged in 1521 and 1522 at the behest of *vakīl* Mīrzā Shāh Ḥusain Iṣfahānī.[270] This particular embassy was led by a prominent Persian notable, Tāj al-Dīn Ḥasan Chalabī, the former *ṣadr* for the province of Khurāsān and very likely an ecclesiastic with strong Sufi leanings.[271] The *julūs nāmah* begins with a lengthy *du`ā* extolling the young sultan as a vigorous defender of Islam and punisher of infidelity—probably a recognition of Sulaimān's decision to inagurate his reign in 1521 with an invasion of Hapsburg Hungary.[272]

We find here a continuance of the Perso-Islamic concept of "shadow of God" (*ẓill-i Allāh*), and the message of divine umbrage is later repeated: "It is established that every victory and conquest of Islam over impiety (which casts its shadow on the right path), with divine assistance and help, uncovers the veil of doubt from the face of mankind."[273] In terms of the historical and mythical exemplars used by the Safavid *munshī* in the sultan's *intitulatio*, we find a rich repository of pre-Islamic Irano-Mediterranean personalities: Jamshīd, Alexander, Solomon, Darius, Khusrau, and Caesar.[274] The addition of Solomon and Caesar here to the Safavid repertoire is not necessarily surprising, given both the appellative appeal of Solomon in a letter to Sulaimān as well as the Ottoman penchant for appropriating Roman legacies. Despite the rhetorical appeal of such Sasanian, Jewish, and Christian kings and prophets, the letter adopts a clear polemical tone and argues for both the pre-eternal and ultimate nature of Islam as a divine message for humanity:

> No new types of existences will emerge from hidden places for did not Allāh say to the Prophet: 'If it had not been for you [Muḥammad], I would not have created the planets' [*laulāka mā khalaqtu al-aflāka*], and was it not revealed that 'I have created the jinns and men but to worship Me (51: 56)?'[275]

The predestined dominance of Islam and its unveiling become particularly poignant here, and the long-established poetic device, *ḥusn al-ibtidā'āt,* of introducing a theme through metaphors and similes of countenance and facial features becomes manifest. Discussing how the victory of Islam over impiety will "uncover the veil of doubt from the face of mankind," the letter goes on to relate a *ḥadīth-i qudsī*: "I have prepared for my righteous slaves (such excellent things) as no eye has ever seen, no ear has ever heard, and no human heart can even think of anything like it."[276] In past eras and epochs, observant ones (*al-abṣār*), wise men (*khiradmandān*), and those with right thoughts (*ḍamīrān-i ṣā'ib afkār*) would see nothing, hear nothing, and think nothing until God the Creator chose to enact and bring life to the spirits of the prophets, the Imāms, and the remainder of saints (*kāfah-yi awliyā'*) and those of purity (*zumrah-yi aṣfiyā*).[277] The letter concludes by praying for the eternal happiness of Sulaimān's predecessor and mentions how this letter is being born by Tāj al-Dīn Ḥasan Khalīfah to that "*qiblah* of fortune" in an act of pilgrimage that will lead to the "Ka`bah of security and safety" (*Ka`bah-i amānī va āmāl*).[278]

Early Years of Shāh Ṭahmāsp and the Persian-Turk Paradigm, 1524–32

The period of 1514–32 was, of course, marked by a dynastic transition, when Abū al-Fatḥ Ṭahmāsp Mīrzā assumed the throne at the age of ten in Rajab 930/May 1524. His birth in 918/1513, along with those of his later siblings (Sām, Alqāṣ, Bahrām) had no small effect on the nexus of relations between the central court and the provincial governorships. Until Ismā`īl's royal decree in 922/1516, announcing that the province of Khurāsān was henceforth a fief of Ṭahmāsp Mīrzā, *vilāyāt*s of the Safavid empire had been entrusted to the closest confidants of Ismā`īl, the *ahl-i ikhtiṣāṣ*, and other prominent supporters of the *ṭarīqah-yi Ṣafavīyyah*. The birth of Ṭahmāsp Mīrzā and his nomination as *ḥākim* of Khurāsān three years later signalled the continued transition towards an "imperializing" of the Safavid Order along Timurid lines. The appointment of a ruler's eldest son to a prominent province like Khurāsān had been a key fixture in the evolving sense of political tradition that had characterized medieval Persia under the Saljūqs, Mongols, and Timurids.[279] Ismā`īl's decision to put Khurāsān specifically in the hands of his three-year-old son, Ṭahmāsp, was a careful acknowledgement of the long-standing Turco-Mongolian practice of appointing a male heir to this particular province.[280] Herāt would go on to be the city where Safavid crown princes were raised, trained, and educated throughout the sixteenth century.[281]

It is not clear from the sources where and under whose care Ṭahmāsp was when Ismā`īl passed away.[282] Khūrshāh ibn Qubād and Būdāq Munshī only mention Ṭahmāsp's reappearance at his coronation and, in doing so, relate how the Qizilbāsh amir Dīv Sulṭān Rūmlū was made *amīr al-umarā*.[283] Dīv Sulṭān Rūmlū, nonetheless, emerged as the de facto ruler of the Safavid empire. It became clear he realized the importance of proximity to the royal body in Safavid court dynamics. Babayan remarked, "The belief that charisma was transmitted to all collateral members of the Safavid house allowed the Qizilbāsh to unite around different members of the Safavid family to express their political aspirations."[284] Köpek Sulṭān Ustājlū, the brother of the former *amīr-i dīvān* Chāyān Sulṭān, clearly did not see Dīv Sulṭān Rūmlū's political manoeuvring in such a positive light, while the Takkalū tribe and its leader, Chūha Sulṭān, were likewise ill-disposed to a Rūmlū ascendancy.[285] Despite an initial attempt at corporate rule between the Rūmlūs, Takkalūs, and Ustājlūs (often styled as a "junta" in earlier scholarship), tensions turned acrimonious and violent, the Ustājlūs were politically and militarily marginalized,[286] and Dīv Sulṭān Rūmlū himself was ultimately executed on 5 Shawwāl 933/July 5, 1527 as a result of Takkalū machinations.

Domestic discord was temporarily put aside with the arrival of a besieging Uzbek force at the city of Herāt in the summer of 934/1528, and Ṭahmāsp, along with Chūha Sulṭān Takkalū and other Safavid notables, struck out eastwards. The Uzbek and Safavid armies met near Jām, where Ṭahmāsp was able to win a victory over a larger force led by Jānī Beg Sulṭān (the epistolographic aspects of these events will be discussed shortly).[287] The then governor of Herāt and tutor to Ṭahmāsp's brother Sām Mīrzā, Ḥusain Khān Shāmlū, acquitted himself admirably during the battle and earned respect in the eyes of the shah. For the next year, Ḥusain Khān Shāmlū tenaciously defended Herāt against the encroaching Uzbeks but was forced to give up the city and head westwards.[288] Having two politically ambitious amirs like Ḥusain Khān Shāmlū and Chūha Sulṭān Takkalū in such proximity to the shah could promise only violence, and in 937/1531 the royal court was torn asunder as Takkalūs and Shāmlūs clashed in the presence of the shah. By then aged seventeen and tired of the tribal anarchy, Shāh Ṭahmāsp symbolically disentangled himself from this political debacle by ordering the wholesale execution of the Takkalū tribe, dubbed "the Takkalū disaster" (*āfat-i Takkalū*) in contemporary Persian chronicles and later scholarship.[289] Even though Ḥusain Khān Shāmlū was the shah's *vakīl*, Ṭahmāsp was no longer of an age where the office of *lala* was necessary. Ḥusain Khān Shāmlū circumvented this challenge by having himself named as the steward to Ṭahmāsp's newborn son, Muḥammad Mīrzā. Aggressive court behaviour combined with rumours of Ḥusain Khān's intention to depose Ṭahmāsp and place his brother Sām Mīrzā on the throne convinced Shāh Ṭahmāsp to rid himself of the powerful Shāmlū amir. With Ḥusain Khān Shāmlū's execution in 939/1532, the Qizilbāsh interlude officially came to an end.

The changing climate at the Safavid court between 1524 and 1532 understandably had a direct impact on the Safavid *dīvān-i a`lā*. With the ascendancy of the Rūmlū and the Shāmlū to the political centre, Qizilbāsh officers were able to reposition themselves into such *dīvān* offices as *amīr al-umarā* and the *amīr-i dīvān*, while inner court rivalries resulted in six *ṣadr*s being appointed in nine years. At the administrative level, there was a flurry of appointments, dismissals, arrests, and executions, thus introducing a period of unprecedented administrative decentralization. A new generation of functionaries had been trained in the last two decades, but this generation would face formidable political obstacles between 1524 and 1532. Viziers and *mustaufī*s would be appointed to the central *dīvān-i a`lā* by a powerful amir, only to be dismissed when a new vicegerent came to power. Likewise, appointments to crucial positions such as *muhrdār*, *īshīk āqāsī bāshī*, and *yasāvul* became especially contentious during this Türkmen rivalry.

Qāḍī-yi Jahān, from the line of Saifī sayyids based in Qazvīn, had originally acted as a *qāḍī* in his home city and was later made vizier to Mīrzā Shāh Ḥusain Iṣfahānī in the last years of Shāh Ismā`īl's reign. After Khvājah Jalāl al-Dīn Muḥammad Tabrīzī Kukajī and his protégé Maulānā Adham Qazvīnī were executed by Dīv Sulṭān Rūmlū, Qāḍī-yi Jahān was named vizier of the *dīvān-i a`lā*.[290]Almost immediately, Qāḍī-yi Jahān found himself caught in the power struggle between Dīv Sulṭān Rūmlū, Köpek Sulṭān Ustājlū, and Chūha Sulṭān Takkalū. There were almost certainly allegations of Qāḍī-yi Jahān having Ustājlū sympathies since his daughter had been married to the son of Köpek Sulṭān, and charges of crypto-Sunnism did not help.[291] Qāḍī-yi Jahān was imprisoned in the castle of Lūrī (*qil`ah-yi Lūrī*) but was soon released by a local Ustājlū notable, `Abd Allāh Khān. From there, he joined the remnants of the Ustājlū tribe that had hid in the forests of Gīlān, but he was ultimately discovered and placed for a decade in a nearby prison controlled by a local tributary elite, Muẓaffar Sulṭān Amīr Dubbāj.[292] The political machinations of the Qizilbāsh had deprived the Safavids of an administrative prodigy at a critical juncture.

With the administrative supremacy of the Kukajī Tabrīzīs and the Khūzānī Iṣfahānīs, the position of vizier had been monopolized by two administrative families. With the arrest and confinement of Qāḍī-yi Jahān and the execution of the leading Kujajī Tabrīzī (Khvājah Jalāl al-Dīn Muḥammad), after 1525 the Sāvajī family was able to assert partially its role in the Safavid administration.[293] Amīr Qavām al-Dīn Ja`far Sāvajī was ordered to the court to assume his post as the new vizier of the *dīvān-i a`lā,* but the internecine nature of court dynamics made this appointment unfeasible.[294] Realizing that control of the bureaucracy could also result in changes to the allocation of land assignments and tax exemptions (*tiyūl*s and *suyūrghāls*), the Qizilbāsh amirs insisted that their own personal viziers have equal rank in the *dīvān-i a`lā*. Interestingly, Dīv Sulṭān Rūmlū's vizier, Āqā Mullā, also belonged to the Sāvajī family as did Chūha Sulṭān Takkalū's, Khvājah Ārūḥ Sāvajī. Thus, the fractured nature in the *dīvān-i amīr* was replicated in the bureaucracy.[295] This arrangement continued unchanged for the next five to six years, until Ḥusain Khān Shāmlū's assassination of Chūha Sulṭān Takkalū in 937/1531 and the ensuing Takkalū debacle. Ḥusain Khān Shāmlū cleaned house during his tenure as *vakīl* and had his former Herātī vizier, Amīr Qavām al-Dīn Ja`far Sāvajī, as well as Khvājah Ārūḥ, arrested. Khvājah Ārūḥ Sāvajī was tortured to death, and Amīr Qivam al-Dīn Ja`far Sāvajī was summarily executed.[296] Moreover, Khvājah Shah Ḥusain Sārūqī, the *mustaufī al-mamālik*, was killed along with all his brothers.[297] With the liquidation of the Sāvajī administration, the *dīvān-i a`lā* was promptly staffed again by Iṣfahānīs, led by Aḥmad Beg Nūr Kamāl al-Dīn Iṣfahānī who had been Ḥusain Khān Shāmlū's personal vizier in Khurāsān.[298] Predictably, Nūr Kamāl al-Dīn Iṣfahānī only remained vizier as long as his patron was able to continue as the chief Qizilbāsh amir, and when Ḥusain Khān Shāmlū was killed in 939/1532, Nūr Kamāl al-Dīn was arrested and tortured, his possessions confiscated.[299]

Epistolographic style in these early years of Ṭahmāsp's reign suggests that Timurid models had established roots, despite the attenuation of Persian administrative influence during this Qizilbāsh interlude between 1524 and 1532. This is most apparent with the *fatḥ nāmah* (recorded by Qāḍī Aḥmad al-Qummī in his *Khulāṣat al-tavārīkh*[300]), which was sent to Tabrīz following the Safavid defeat of the Uzbeks at Jām.[301] The form and mode of expression of this *fatḥ nāmah* underscores the degree to which the Safavid dynasty had distanced itself from its parochial, millenarian roots. Previous religious iconography and literary devices—heralding the shah as an instrument of divine justice, citing popular Shi`ite slogans, showcasing genealogical connections with the *ahl al-bait*—had lost currency and became notably absent. In their place, we see highlighted the role of the Safavid shah as protector and guarantor of security while railing against the Uzbeks as raptorial miscreants and harbingers of social disorder. Previously, *fatḥ nāmah*s narrating the respective defeats of Muḥammad-Shibānī Khān, `Alā al-Daula, and Ḥusain Kiyā were generally consistent in their use of Near Eastern and Qur'ānic motifs to portray the Safavid forces as divinely sanctioned punishers of the wicked and sinful. We have here a new cluster of rhetorical motifs that look to the Safavid kings as martial champions and exemplars of bravery, honesty, and manliness. In turn, the Uzbeks are denigrated as cowards and "womanly" masters of deceit.

Following the battle of Jām, *munshīs* in the royal camp were ordered to write victory letters (*fatḥ nāmajāt*) that, in turn, were to be delivered to Tājlū Begum in Qumm and then relayed with a *yusāvul* to the city of Tabrīz.[302] While other letters were likely despatched to other prominent Safavid centres, the letter in question here is specifically addressed to the sayyids, *qāḍīs*, functionaries, notables, soldiers, and inhabitants of Tabrīz. The *munshī* narrates briefly how `Ubaid Allāh Khān—styled as "being of corrupt convictions" (*fāsid al-i`tiqād*)—set out to wage war and kill as part of a coalition of khans, sultans, and governors from Turkestān and Transoxania.[303] Seriously outnumbered and facing annihilation, Shāh Ṭahmāsp and his ability to overcome superior forces are presented by the *munshī* as both providence and a testimony to the heroism and intrepidity of the Safavid army. These qualities are rhetorically juxtaposed to those of the poltroonish and foppish Uzbeks. Trusting in the prayer, "Everything is in Your hand, you are the Almighty, and blessed by the spirits of Muḥammad, `Alī, and the Innocent Imāms," the "warriors who fight lions" (*ghāziyān-i shīr-shikār*) and "heroes of the battlefield" (*shīr-mardān-i ma`arik-i kārzar*) met those "cowardly outsiders" (*khārijiyān-i gamrāh*) and battled "that perfidious, wicked, and cowardly group" (*ān ṭā'ifah-yi ghadr va ashrār va nā-ba-kār*).[304] Previous Safavid correspondence had featured "standards of good government" and "banners of divine victory," this *fatḥ nāmah* instead describes how "the flags of manliness and virility were held up" (*a`lām-i mardī va mardānagī bar afrāshtah*), which "showed themselves to be soldiers and ready for self-sacrifice" (*iẓhār-i sar-bāzī va jān-sipārī namūdah*).[305] Thus, the image of the Safavid troops as dauntless stalwarts is cemented. The accomplishment of the outnumbered Safavids besting the Uzbeks is signalled by 2: 249: "Many a time has a small band defeated a large horde by the will of God," an allusion to David's victory over Goliath. After exhorting his audience to properly thank God and to never forget the battle of Jām, the *munshī* concludes by contrasting the Uzbeks with Shāh Ṭahmāsp and the Safavid dynasty as active patrons and sponsors of agricultural prosperity: "regarding the promotion of agriculture and cultivation, which is the current agenda of the policies of this conquering state, it is hoped that the men of [Khurāsān] will pull their reins in that direction."[306]

Hostilities, however, were not concluded at Jām. In less than a year, the Uzbeks and their allies recovered and reconstituteed another invasion force, which marched from Marv in 935/spring of 1529. As the Safavid force neared the Uzbek invading army, Shāh Ṭahmāsp heard that `Ubaid Allāh Khān had assembled 170, 000 soldiers of the peoples of Tatar, Qalmāq, Turkestān, Tūrān, and Khvārazm. He immediately ordered that "the gifted and magical *munshīs* write a letter to `Ubaid Allāh Khān."[307] It is probable that the author here is part of the same itinerant chancellery that had drafted the earlier Jām *fatḥ nāmah*, and likewise this correspondence was preserved by Qāḍī Aḥmad al-Qummī.[308] In light of Ṭahmāsp's victory at Jām and the acerbic tone of the *munshī*, clearly this particular letter was designed to goad the Uzbek court. Continuing the earlier theme of the Uzbeks as rapacious miscreants, the *munshī* questions their particular *mazhhab,* given that they "allow the plundering of women and children, imprisoning and raping them, and torturing them with bars and racks."[309] In contrast, Shāh Ṭahmāsp's justice gives rise to the "tranquility of the nobles and masses of this land [i.e., Khurāsān], which is a piece of Paradise."[310] The depth of Uzbek ignominy knows no bounds: undignified (*bī-vaqār*) and disgraceful (*bad-nām*) khans sanction theft (*duzdī*) and burning of crops (*ghalla sūkhtan*), as is read in the Qur'ān 2: 205: "(his aim is to) destroy crops and cattle." The theme of the Uzbek as the craven cheat and pusillanimous trickster—juxtaposed with the lion-hearted Safavid hero—is clearly a continuation of the thematic impulses established in the earlier *fatḥ nāmah* about Jām. The terrorizing of the population indicates how "the affairs of this Devil, full of deceit, are based on plotting, duplicity, deception, and fraud" (*banā-yi umūr ān Iblīs pur-talbīs bar makr va farīb va ḥīlah va tazvīr-ast*). The *munshī* cleverly extrapolates this theme of ignobility to subtly castigate `Ubaid Allāh Khān's masculinity, describing how he "constantly dresses with a [woman's] upper garment of strategem and the undergarment of impotency."[311]

The letter continues the narration of events leading to the battle of Jām and makes note of how Safavid forces were redirected from the Ottoman frontier to engage this new Uzbek threat in Khurāsān. While en route to Jām, the Safavid forces were intent on pushing the Uzbeks to the edge of the Āmū Daryā River, until they had no place to stand, and in doing so, they would "flee the province of Khurāsān like an ass loaded with the weight of defeat, as was revealed 'as if they were frightened asses escaping from a lion'" (74: 53). Surrounded by this assembly of khans and sultans from Transoxania, Qipchāq, and Turkestān but having complete trust in God, Ṭahmāsp "raised our celestial-like, pure umbrella in the battlements of Jām" (*chatr-i falāk-i sā-rā dar alang-i Jām bar afrākhtīm*). The *nāmah* does not replicate the earlier victory letter to Tabrīz and its graphic description of the slaughter of Uzbek khans and sultans. Instead, it tacitly proclaims that "we made a great pavilion as an encampment at the battlefield of Jām" (*hamān jang-gāh-i Jām-rā maḍrab-i surādiqāt-i jalāl sākhtīm*). Like the previous *fatḥ nāmah*, the missive is concluded with a short poem that praises Safavid martial skill and bravery while acerbicly denegrating the masculinity and pedigree of the Uzbek dynasty. The appeal of pre-Islamic Persian kingly personalities from the *Shāh nāmah* is apparent as the poem begins: "Oh Khān son of Khān of the tribes of Khāqāns/You bow to Kai Khusrau and Kai Qubād." The choice of two legendary monarchs such as Kai Khusrau and Kai Qubād, whose campaigns and exploits against Afrāsiyāb and the Tūrānians are some of the most celebrated sections of the *Shāh nāmah,* was no accident. As Robert Hillenbrand noted in his study of the *Shāh nāmah-yi Shāh Ṭahmāsp*, the Safavid library-atelier consciously profiled those sections of the *Shāh nāmah* that recounted the Iranian subjugation of Tūrān to celebrate Shāh Ṭahmāsp's victory over the Uzbeks in Khurāsān. It should not be overly surprising to find similar trends in the *dīvān-i inshā*.[312]

Typical of the syncretist trends we see in titulature and ideology in this early period, Shāh Ṭahmāsp uses this verse to cater to a wide range of Islamic and pre-Islamic exemplary figures. He connects himself to Alī and his heroic status in one *bait* ("I am the son of Alī/I am the lion-hearted shah, I am a brave champion"), while in a subsequent line he writes, "You are a worldy khan, and I am a king/You are the insignificant ant and I am Sulaimān." This latter rhetorical punch refers of course to the Qur'ānic surah of "The Ant" and King Solomon's amassing of an army of men, jinns, and birds and his encounter with a lowly massing of ants. Interestingly, this is also the verse that recounts Sulaimān's confrontation with Queen Sheba, and we come across the possibility of a subtle and deliberate juxtaposition of `Ubaid Allāh Khān—already epistographically emasculated—with one of the most recognized Qu'rānic female archetypes of seduction, wealth, and polytheism. Given that the relationship between Sulaimān and Queen Sheba is conducted primarily through diplomacy and the exchange of letters in 27: 33–44, we cannot help but wonder if the Safavid scribe was casting the current Safavid-Uzbek exchange within this particular Qur'ānic narrative framework. Just as in 27: 26: "Now when (the embassy of Queen Sheba) came to Sulaimān, he said 'Will ye give me abundance in wealth? But that which Allāh has given me is better than that which He has given you! Nay it is you who rejoice in your gift!'", the Safavid scribe pens a line: "I did not covet your belongings and revenue/there was no need for silver or gold," while admonishing as Sulaimān did the polytheistic Queen, "Your religion has become negligent/my religion has not deviated in any way."[313]

These propagandistic portrayals of the Safavid-Uzbek hostilities at Jām in 1529 inform our inquiry regarding shifts in epistolographic styles, motifs, and imagery. Since 1514, and after the rise of the native Persian administrative and clerical class, there appears to be a concerted effort to highlight themes of older pre-Islamic notions of divine rights of sovereignty, societal stability, and responsible government. The stylistic motifs of these latest letters point to the addition of yet another layer of medieval Perso-Islamic socio-cultural constructs: affinities for and admiration of virility (*mardānagī*) and heroic chivalry (*javānmardī*). The canonical text for such constructs, of course, is Firdausī's *Shāh nāmah*, and as we noted earlier, the library-atelier was dominated during the 1520s and 1530s by the ongoing project of the majestic *Shāh nāmah-yi Shāh Ṭahmāsp*.[314] In addition to Firdausī, other well-known texts, such as the twelfth-century romance *Samak-i `Ayyār* or the advice manual *Qābūs nāmah*, reflect both the currency and appeal of bravery, honesty, and courage in heroic figures.[315] Particularly, the icon of the *`ayyār* was, for many, a paragon of truth, honesty, moral rectitude, and incorruption, and these values were often celebrated in those very texts that were recited publicly in Safavid courts and markets: the *Shāh nāmah*, the *Abū Muslim nāmah*, the *Ḥamzah nāmah*, and so on.[316] This intertextuality between epistolary rhetoric and epic Persian literature is especially clear when we consider the thematic juxtaposition of the Safavid troops as "warriors who fight lions" (*ghāziyān-i shīr-shikār*) and "heroes" (*shīr-mardān*) with the Uzbek warriors who are depicted as avatars of plotting (*makr*), duplicity (*farīb*), deception (*ḥīlah*), and fraud (*tazvīr*). Such literary juxtaposition moves in concert with prominent themes of medieval Persian romance texts, including the Iranian/Tūrānian contraposition in the *Shāh nāmah*.[317] Lying, fraud, and trickery were more often aligned with the image of the Turk, while Persian heroes and military generals stood as avatars of nobility, gallantry, and honesty.[318] Stock terms appearing in these letters—*mardānagī* (virility), *mardī* (manliness), *shīr-mardī* (heroism), *nā-ba-kār* (idleness), *farīb* (duplicity)—are commonly used by Firdausī, particularly in those sections discussing the epic conflicts of Kai Khusrau, Bizhān, Farīdūn, and Rustam with their Turkic arch-enemies of Tūrān.[319]

The epistolographic context of these Safavid/Uzbek characterizations is likewise intriguing since the narrative element of popular romances (the *Samak-i `Ayyār*, the *Fīrūz shāh nāmah*, the *Darab nāmah*) was also often presented through the exchange of letters between kings, princes, nobility, and heroes.[320] We have already alluded to the exchange of embassies between Sulaimān and Queen Sheba, and we likewise find a possible allusion to an exchange of letters between Khusrau Parvīz (Sasanian Khusrau II, r. 591–628) and his rebellious brother Bahrām Chūbīnah. The aforementioned description of how Shāh Ṭahmāsp "ripped the [Uzbek] robe of fortune" (*jāmah-yi `āfīyat-i īshān-rā chāk kardah*) and his "pouring of dust over the hopes [of the Uzbeks]" (*bar sar-i umīd-shān khāk rīkhta*) looks to be borrowed from the story surrounding Khusrau Parvīz's despatching of embassies to the region of Khurāsān and the subsequent campaign in that province against Bahrām Chūbīnah and his allies, the Khāqān of China.[321] Like Shāh Ṭahmāsp's reporting of the events at Jām to `Ubaid Allāh Khān, this particular story involves the arrival of a letter/*farmān* from Khusrau Parvīz that proclaims him shah of Iran and narrates his battle with Bahrām. Intriguingly, those images associated with various stories involving Khusrau Parvīz were particularly popular in the royal atelier.[322]

Perhaps the most evocative representation of these epic literary themes appears with the diplomatic narrative that followed the delivery of the second missive to the Uzbek court. This ambassadorial privilege was extended to one Kabah Khalīfah Zū al-Qadar who had been nominated recently by Shāh Ṭahmāsp as the *muhrdār* (seal-holder). Kabah Khalīfah is described by Qāḍī Aḥmad al-Qummī as "firm in his resolve, brave, and famous for his Shi`ite and Sufi [convictions]."[323] He "was unique in his size and imposing nature" and no amir could match him in "size of body, coarseness, and power."[324] He was ordered to proceed as a diplomat (*bi īlchīgarī*) to the Uzbeks camped at Marv, and he brought with him the required correspondence, a mace (*shishparī*), and a woman's veil (*mi`jarī*). Before leaving he declared, "If `Ubaid Allāh Khān is confused about sovereignty and imperial rule, here is a mace! If he is contemplating flight, strategem, or deceit, here is a woman's veil!"[325] In a clearly dramatic tone, Qummī writes how Kabah Khalīfah entered the Uzbek council of sultans and, in observing his comportment (*raftār*), his gravity (*vaqār*), his dignity (*ṣalābat*), and his greatness (*mahābat*), they commented how he had the pride of Rustam and the power of Afrāsiyāb.[326] In watching his intrepidity (*tahavvur*) and his arrogance (*takabbur*), the sultans in council felt their hands start to tremble.[327] Kabah Khalīfah then produced the mace and woman's veil and placed them both in front of `Ubaid Allāh Khān. Kabah Khalīfah Muhrdār declared: "Oh Khān! In coming here I have separated myself from the [Safavid] host, and placed myself amongst 170,000 Uzbeks, yet you are terrified of killing me. My *pādshāh* and *murshid* has 120,000 men like me of whom the lowliest cannot be compared to me!"[328] Kabah Khalīfah was apparently "so inflamed with the fire of Sufism, he then said some very rough words to `Ubaid Allāh Khān."[329] Abū Sa`īd Khān intervened between *īlchī* and sultan, dismissed the council, ordered that Kabah Khalīfah Muhrdār be honoured with robes and gifts and sent back to Shāh Ṭahmāsp with a response.[330] This episode caters clearly to the classic medieval Persian idea of the heroic yet outspoken *`ayyār* who is undaunted by the presence of imperial sovereignty and speaks his mind truthfully, if not brazenly. His exemplary behaviour as a paragon of virility, and his denegration of the Uzbeks as epicene fops, are clearly meant as a metaphoric reference to Rustam. Indeed, Kabah Khalīfah's brandishing of a mace, which was the weapon best associated with the Iranian hero, only cements this literary association. The victory at Jām—Safavid Persian over Uzbek Turk—provided the secretaries and court chroniclers with a treasure-trove of popular metaphors, similes, and long-standing tropes, which had been developing in medieval Persian literature since the tenth century.

The years between 1501 and 1532 were hardly the most impressive years of Safavid imperial rule. Initial Safavid expansion was marked by retributive and large-scale organized violence against Sunnis and other communities of Muslims, and empire-building was arguably stalled after the 1514 Battle of Chaldirān. Never able to fully recover militarily and psychologically from Chaldirān, the Safavid empire under Ismā`īl entered a distinct phase of stasis and indolence. Between 1524 and 1532, a young and impressionable ruler, myriad ambitious personalities, warring factions, and two bordering, hostile Sunni empires all conspired to push the Safavids towards the brink of annihilation. It was precisely the ability and willingness to soften the pre-existing apocalyptic edge, however, that allowed the administrative and clerical Persian elite to assume bureaucratic and, to some extent, ideological custodianship of the Safavid empire. This incorporation in turn allowed for the emergence of a robust yet malleable dynastic legitimacy and imperial cult of personality, which could withstand the aforementioned pressures and strains. Discussions of ancient pre-Islamic Persian concepts of hierarchy, stability, and justice framed almost all of the Safavid letters after 1514, along with a new spectrum of legendary and historical iconographic figures from an array of deeper, more established traditions: Achaemenian, Sassanian, Roman, Qur'ānic, Talmudic. *Munshī*s were not especially motivated to confine themselves to historical exemplars, and we found that epic romance texts also served as a repository of themes, motifs, images, and terminology for chancellery officials to embellish their own epistolary narratives. One thing should remain clear: it would be a mistake to suggest that Safavid dynastic ideology was now fixed. This would certainly prove to be the case when we consider the career of `Alī ibn al-Ḥusain al-Karakī. He would be responsible for introducing a discernible Twelver Shi`ite juridical identity into the Safavid court, and chancellery production was indelibly changed as a result. In this sense, Safavid *inshā* continued to function dialectically, whereby pre-existing traditions from Āzarbāijān, Khurāsān, and `Irāq were fused together in the literary and cultural crucible of the Safavid chancellery.

2

COMPETING COSMOLOGIES, 1532–55

A watershed for the key issue of Safavid legitimation stands as 938/1532. From the very beginning, Türkmen families had exerted a strong influence in both civil and military affairs. Although this relationship was altered after the resurgence of Persian bureaucratic agency, they continued to play a critical role displayed in the power struggles that characterized the first years of Ṭahmāsp's reign in the 1520s. After 938/1532, we see an era of "personal rule" by Shāh Ṭahmāsp, who sought to contain and control these overbearing Qizilbāsh influences. A key illustration of this was his decision to release the former *vazīr* Qāḍī-yi Jahān Qazvīnī and reappoint him to the *dīvān-i a`lā* in 1535.[1] During the reign of Shāh Ismā`īl, Qāḍī-yi Jahān Qazvīnī had served a number of bureaucratic tenures under Qāḍī Muḥammad Kāshī, Khvājah Jalāl al-Dīn Muḥammad Tabrīzī, and Mīrzā Shāh Ḥusain Iṣfahānī. Qāḍī-yi Jahān, an exemplary Persian scholar-bureaucrat with two decades of administrative experience, had been educated by the great philosopher and intellectual Jalāl al-Dīn Davvānī, and he considered himself a product of the Shīrāzī philosophical tradition. His reappointment by Shāh Ṭahmāsp was clearly meant to bring stability to a bureaucracy that had been scandalized by rivalry and machinations and to realign the Safavid government towards some semblance of coherence. Under Qāḍī-yi Jahān's stewardship, diplomatic initiatives extended well beyond the Iranian theatre, and Shāh Ṭahmāsp began rhetorical dialogues with Muslim and non-Muslim polities, such as the Portuguese, the Venetians, the Mughals, and the Shi`ite kingdoms of the Deccan. The very symbolic execution of Ḥusain Khān Shāmlū and the rise to eminence of Qāḍī-yi Jahān two years later positions 938/1532 as the beginning of a crucial transition period, whereby the Safavids were distancing themselves—sometimes gently, sometimes less so—from the *ghuluww* parochialism of their Qizilbāsh adherents. Hans Robert Roemer once asked if the Safavids had built an Iranian kingdom with a Turkish region on the upper Euphrates across from the Ottoman border or if they had developed a Turkish kingdom with an Iranian zone in the east.[2] The question is valid, and it would appear that by 938/1532, with such events as the recent Takkalū debacle and the rise in Qizilbāsh defections to the Ottoman empire, the apogee of Türkmen power in the early Safavid empire (what Minorsky termed "the Türkmen third-phase"[3]) was beginning to dissipate.

The year 938/1532 is also important in the Safavid ideological narrative because of the growing influence of the conservative, sedentary *`ulamā* and their ability to lay the groundwork for a transition from popular shi`ism to doctrinal shi`ism.[4] Officially speaking, the appropriate steps were being taken to "Shi`itize" the dynasty itself: Ismā`īl's *Dīvān* was cleansed of blasphemous verses and the Safavid genealogy *Ṣafwat al-ṣafā'* was rearranged to concretize the Safavid claim to the seventh Imām Mūsā al-Kāẓim.[5] By 938/1532, the Safavid ruler had become more than just a millenarian *mahdī*; he would emerge as the "spiritual leader of the *shī`a* movement which the entire Muslim community of the world could come forward and accept."[6] In 938/1532 Shāh Ṭahmāsp made his public proclamation of repentance, and we find the first documentary evidence, a royal *farmān*, indicating the unrivalled religious power of `Alī ibn al-Ḥusain al-Karakī, known by his twin *laqab*s of al-Muḥaqqiq al-S̲ānī ("the second bearer of Truth") and Mujtahid al-Zamān ("interpreter of the Age").[7] This text has been translated by Said Arjomand and constitutes Ṭahmāsp's "key endorsement" of the clerical authority of the Shi`ite scholars.[8] Kathryn Babayan has likewise seized upon this period of the early 1530s as a significant shift with respect to Shāh Ṭahmāsp's dynastic self-view. In her estimation, Ṭahmāsp's endorsement of the Imami Shi`ites and the deprecation of popular Sufism through such things as public bans on alcohol point to a period wherein the martial, chiliastic tenor of Shāh Ismā`īl's empire was being realigned. In her discussion of Ṭahmāsp's memoirs, the *Tazkirah-yi Ṭahmāsp*, she observes that "a particular Alid lineage (Musavi) and narrative continue to be appropriated in Tahmasb's story of his reign. But Alid ghulat loyalty is reserved for Ali alone. In Tahmasb's newly adopted cosmology, there is no room for new revelations and prophetic experiences."[9]

After 938/1532, Shāh Ṭahmāsp initiated a new phase for Safavid legitimation, which was no longer framed exclusively by Qizilbāsh Türkmen concerns. In this context, such dilution was concurrent with an amelioration for the Persian administrative elite, but it is clear that orthodox Shi`ite theologians looked to this transitory stage as an opportunity to provide the state with what they deemed were the necessary doctrinal and juridical tools for a redefinition of authority in the Safavid Iranian context. Hitherto, subscribing to disparate trends of Āzarbāijānī *ghuluww* apocalypticism and pre-Islamic Persian divine absolutism, Safavid dynastic legitimation would become increasingly brass-bound by formal Shi`ite polemics and rhetoric. Al-Karakī, his various pupils, as well as other immigrant Arab theologians were custodians of long-standing Imami traditions. They infused an already heterogeneous Safavid chancellery with yet another aggregation of rhetorical exemplars, archetypes, symbols, and leitmotifs. Many of al-Karakī's treatises were popular, in the original Arabic as well as in Persian translation, and his *Risālah al-Ja`fariyya fī al-ṣalāt* (translated by Sayyid al-Amīr Abū Al-Ma`ālī Astarābādī) enjoyed wide circulation in sixteenth-century Iran.[10] Ṭahmāsp's 938/1532 proclomation for moral rectitude and abstention is logically twinned with al-Karakī's new degree of power and influence in the Safavid state. This in turn created a political and courtly environment that encouraged migration to Tabrīz and Qazvīn by not only Shi`ite juridicals from the Arab world but also Shi`ite notables and sayyids from `Alid centres like Qumm, Mashhad, and Astarābād.

At the same time, however, al-Karakī and his legacy interacted with an indissoluble Persian administrative legacy that championed a hierarchical model of authority based on absolutism and divine kingship. After 938/1532, these approaches were personified by Qāḍī-yi Jahān Qazvīnī, one of the most successful and celebrated *vazīrs* and *vakīls* of the Safavid empire. As a result, we see the emergence of a dichotomous administrative environment, whereby two sets of *Weltanschauungs* were orbiting around the resolute and charismatic personalities of al-Karakī and Qāḍī-yi Jahān. When al-Karakī passed away in 940/1534 in Najaf, his legacy was secure in the capable hands of an increasingly established clerical elite: Ḥusain ibn `Abd al-Ṣamad al-`Āmilī, Shams al-Dīn Muḥammad al-`Āmilī al-Ḥayyānī, Ḥasan ibn `Alī ibn `Abd al-`Alī al-Karakī, to name a few.[11] Roughly concurrent with al-Karakī's death was Qāḍī-yi Jahān's promotion to both the *vikālat* and *vizārat*, positions he would hold until his retirement and death in 960/1553. This chapter contends that al-Karakī moulded a courtly environment, which encouraged the chancellery to employ a model of discursive rhetoric. This rhetoric echoed if not mirrored those formalistic Shi`ite-Sunni apologetics that had defined the Islamic world since the ninth century. At the same time, however, Persian scholar-bureaucrats successfully retrenched themselves and remained faithful to a vision of the Safavid dynasty that bridged the pre-Islamic and Islamic worlds in terms of exemplars and historical imagination. This bifurcation among the Safavid intelligentsia is likewise reflected in the division between orthodox Shi`ite elements who followed al-Karakī and the Uṣūlī tradition and those who opposed Persian "clerical-notables" and sayyids who were in general devotees of philosophy, hermeneutics, and devotional mysticism. On occasion, the interests of the Persian administrative elite overlapped with the landowning sayyid class of "clerical-notables," but many groups, like the Askūya branch of Tabrīz for instance, discovered to their frustration that Qāḍī-yi Jahān was dedicated to reducing the entrenched political and socio-economic power of *both* the immigrant Arab clerics and the indigenous Persian hierocrats.[12] Although these networks were entangled and shifting constantly, it would be reasonable to suggest that sixteenth-century Safavid epistemology was defined roughly by two broad intellectual camps: the juridically minded Shi`ite émigrés and their Iranian supporters, and those Neoplatonic-influenced Persian scholastics who focused on logic, mathematics, and theosophy.[13] Some have argued that these can be binarized surgically along Uṣūlī and Akhbārī juridical lines; however, the religious and doctrinal landscape is far too nuanced and sophisticated to think in such dichotomous terms.[14]

Invective Rhetoric: al-Karakī and Models of Shi`ite Apologetic Discourse

Al-Karakī had joined the Safavid cause in the early days of Shāh Ismā`īl and was present with the young ruler during the conquests of Kāshān, Iṣfahān, Baghdad, and Herāt.[15] Al-Karakī was most noted for his extreme anti-Sunnism, exemplified in his 916/1511 treatise on the legality of anathematizing the Rightly Guided Caliphs, *Nafaḥāt al-lāhūt fī la`n al-jibt wa al-ṭāghūt*.[16] For much of Ismā`īl's reign, al-Karakī was based in the holy city of Najaf, where he was in administrative control of a sizeable territory in the province of `Irāq-i `Arab. His militant anti-Sunnism, his tacit approval of the shah's claims to the Imamate, as well as his acceptance of gifts and land grants from Ismā`īl, made al-Karakī the object of several written attacks by non-Safavid Shi`ite theologians.[17] Al-Karakī broke new ground in 916/1510 regarding the formulation of the role of the clerical elite in a Shi`ite state, when he wrote *Qāta'at al-lajāj fī ḥill al-kharāj* ("'The Annihilator of Obstinacy' on the Legality of Land Tax") as a rationalization for his accruing taxes from land given to him by Ismā`īl. Another work, the *Risālah al-Ja`fariyya fī al-ṣalāt*, was an exposition on the necessity, specifically the legality, of his leading the Friday congregational prayer as the *nā'ib al-imām* or deputy of the Imām. Al-Karakī's writings and the responses they elicited from his detractors were essentially focused on the issue of the Occultation and the extent to which Shi`ites in Safavid Iran could claim to be acting on behalf of the Imamate.[18] According to Akhbārī critics, these claims to be *nā'ib al-imām* were untenable. Nevertheless, Al-Karakī's Uṣūlī-based arguments stipulated that his support of a secular ruler was in no way illegal. On the contrary, his receipt of *kharāj* taxes from landholdings was indeed *ḥalāl* since "the *faqīh* [theologian] who possessed *ṣifāt al-niyāba* [the qualities of deputyship], by virtue of the principle of *niyāba `āmma* [general deputyship]—the general authority possessed on the Imām's behalf during the Occultation—was permitted to accept *al-kharāj*."[19] For al-Karakī, it was only logical in this period of the Great Occultation for Shāh Ismā`īl to act in the interests of the Imamate by collecting *kharāj* taxes on his behalf.[20] Debating such mundane matters in the Shi`ite community was by no means novel, and there is evidence to indicate that al-Karakī based some of his arguments on earlier writings produced during the Buyid period of the tenth and eleventh centuries.[21]

From 1524 until 1533, al-Karakī worked discreetly in the Safavid court, influencing whichever vicegerent was in power and avoiding pitfalls set up by his opponents. Despite his lack of formal status, al-Karakī saw to it in 935/1528 that one of his own students, Ni`mat Allāh al-Ḥillī, was appointed as co-*ṣadr* to Qavām al-Dīn al-Iṣfahānī.[22] When Qavām al-Dīn al-Iṣfahānī died a short time later, his half of the *ṣadārat* was given to Mīr Ghiyāṣ al-Dīn Manṣūr Shīrāzī,[23] a sayyid and former student of the Sunni theologian/jurist al-Davvānī.[24] Elements of the moderate theological community were clearly uncomfortable with al-Karakī's interpretation of Uṣūlī doctrine, since it translated into considerable power for the *mujtahid*.[25] Al-Ḥillī disputed al-Karakī's defence of leading congregational prayer, and in 936/1530 he was accused of defaming al-Karakī and was forced to leave Safavid territory for the region of Ḥilla.[26] When Ghiyās al-Dīn Manṣūr Shīrāzī likewise disputed al-Karakī's calculations on the *qiblah* a year later, he too was dismissed from the office of *ṣadr*. At that time, Mu`izz al-Dīn Muḥammad al-Iṣfahānī, another former student of al-Karakī, was appointed as the new *ṣadr*.[27] In 939/1532, a *farmān* was issued stipulating that, henceforth, all religious matters were to be controlled by al-Karakī.[28]

In light of the shah's celebrated public repentance one year later, the timing of this *farmān* was no accident. Invested with this new power, al-Karakī embarked on a program of imposing doctrinal uniformity and ensuring that Safavid cities and villages alike received instruction by the local religious elite in the tenets of Ja`farī Shi`ism.[29] In the late 1520s, he authored a concise legal manual with the *Jāmi` al-maqāṣid*—ostensibly a commentary on the *Qawā'id al-aḥkām* by `Allāmah al-Ḥillī[30]—which enjoyed circulation among theologians and religious judges throughout Iran.[31] On the basis of this, Sunnis were formally banished, and *miḥrāb*s of every mosque were reconfigured to match al-Karakī's personal calculations of the *qiblah*.[32] There is a *farmān*—inscribed on the wall of the Mīr `Imād *masjid* in Kāshān and dated 7 Rabī` I 941/16 September 1534—that orders the closure of public spaces associated with licentiousness and irreligious behaviour: taverns (*sharāb-khānah*), drug dens (*bang-khānah*), wine cellars (*būza-khānah*), public theatres (*qavāl-khānah*), brothels (*bait al-luṭf*), gaming rooms (*qumār-khānah*), and pigeon contests (*kabūtar-bāzī*).[33] Babayan has correctly seen this as part of a greater anti-Sufi program to challenge those who opposed this Arab-inspired wave of juridical orthopraxy, including the networks of intellectual theosophists in major urban centres.[34]

Using the accession of a young successor and the lack of consistent leadership in the office of *vakīl* between 1524 and 1534, al-Karakī personally controlled the nominations to the office of the *ṣadr* and secured a number of sizeable territories in the form of *suyūrghāl*s, while at the same he time positioned himself as the sole religious authority with respect to doctrinal and legal interpretation.[35] As will become clear, al-Karakī was opposed tacitly by elements among the Persian clerical elite who not only resented his new status but who also were alarmed by the staunch anti-Sunnism found in texts like the *Nafaḥāt al-lāhūt*. This prejudice against Sunnis, not surprisingly, earned al-Karakī a certain degree of support from the Qizilbāsh, and it seems clear that al-Karakī was tapping into the militant *ghuluww* ethos of the Qizilbāsh. Al-Karakī's willingness to accommodate the Qizilbāsh had its limits, however, and he was soon issuing *fatwā*s encouraging the public anathematization of Abū Muslim, the charismatic leader of the eighth-century `Abbasid revolution. He subsequently ordered a ban on any public recitations of the *Abū Muslim nāmah*, the heroic epic of Abū Muslim's exploits, which had enjoyed such popularity among the Qizilbāsh in the late fifteenth and early sixteenth centuries.[36] With respect to traditional Qizilbāsh reverence for the shah as *murshid-i kāmil*, al-Karakī attempted to provide a substitute. Shāh Ṭahmāsp was still their political and spiritual leader, but a new language based on Shi`ite veneration and reverence for the Imām had replaced the pre-existing set of Sufi paradigms. As Babayan put it, "Tahmasb, thus, altered the font of Isma`il's sufism."[37]

The first extant letter written in this hierocratic milieu is a response (*javāb nāmah*) in 939/1532 to a letter sent by `Ubaid Allāh Khān in the aftermath of the Uzbek-Safavid wars of the late 1520s.[38] Qāḍī Aḥmad refers to Shāh Ṭahmāsp despatching a number of poetic texts from the city of Herāt to the Uzbek ruler in 939/1532, and the verses he replicates are found in this *javāb nāmah,* which was preserved in the well-known Safavid collection of correspondence, the *Munsha'āt al-Ṭūsī.*[39] The most striking feature of this lengthy letter is its extensive and complex discussion of Imami doctrine. Its timing certainly coincides with al-Karakī's ascension in the Safavid court. The letter addresses recent Uzbek attempts to annex the region of Khurāsān, but the scribe uses apologetic discourse to place this conflict in a larger doctrinal battleground. Ṭahmāsp acknowledges his receipt of a letter from "those lost in the desert of deviation and ignorance" (*sar-gashtagān-i bādiya`-i ḍalālat va jahālat*) and "those wanderers in the valleys of misery and desperation [*gum-gashtagān-i audiyah-yi shaqāvat va ghavāyat*]," and we find here an application of the literary device of *tarṣī`*, whereby prose phrases are paralleled in terms of rhyming patterns.[40] Ṭahmāsp impugns the character of `Ubaid Allāh Khān by suggesting that he knowingly "concealed how that traitorous unlawful group had sullied and stained that sweet land of Khurāsān with its impure presence and defiling armies,"[41] describing how women and children were raped and slaughtered by that "odious group" (*gurūh-i makrūh*) who then went on to sack and plunder the Shi`ite community.[42]

The original Uzbek letter,[43] which challenged the Shi`ite claim that `Alī was predestined to hold the caliphate and cast aspersions on various Shi`ite doctrinal points, was sufficiently sophisticated to motivate the Safavids to respond with a detailed, point-by-point refutation of the Uzbeks' charges. The letter censures the "never-ending foolishness and limitless villainy" (*safāhat-i ghāyat va nahāyat-i shaqāvat*) of the Uzbek chancellery, and how they have portrayed the rules and customs of the `Alid tradition "as falsely adorned and blackly seductive" (*ārā-yi bāṭilah va ahvā-yi fāsidah*).[44] The letter is generally modelled on traditional methods of polemic disputation (*munāẓarah*), whereby a position is defended and rationalized in a rhetorical debate with an imaginary interlocutor. The points are supported/discounted by Qur'ānic quotations and Prophetic traditions and occasionally elaborated upon by appropriate Persian or Arabic verse. The manipulation of particular revelatory verses by Shi`ite theologians and scholars as esoteric evidence of God's support of the Imami community has a long and detailed history, and the Safavid chancellery had recourse to a sizeable canon.[45] This *munāẓarah* approach of presenting an argument through questions and answers (*su'āl va javāb*) was employed regularly in confessional polemics. In this way, the letter's point-by-point refutation of the Sunni Uzbeks shares a remarkable similarity with the methodology profiled by seminal Shi`ite apologetic work, *Kitāb al-naqḍ*, by Ibn Abī al-Ḥusain ibn Abī al-Faḍl al-Qazvīnī al-Rāzī.[46]

The scribe continues, noting how `Ubaid Allāh Khān and his followers "with [their] delirious, absurd words, and false and confused speeches, have steered their ship of weak and foolish beliefs towards that terrible whirlpool of infidelity and wickedness." The nautical theme continues, again expressed with the repetitive rhyming device of *tarṣī`*: "They remain in the whirlpool of impiety and barbarism, in the chaos of idolatry and strange aberration."[47] The allegorical use of ships and water is reminiscent of the popular Shi`ite motif of the *ahl al-bait* (Muḥammad, `Alī, Ḥusain, and Ḥasan) navigating their ship in a rough sea as the seventy other ships representing the world's different faiths capsize left and right, which in turn is based on the aforementioned *ḥadīth-i Safīna* ("Behold! My Family is like the Ark of Noah, whoever embarked in it was saved, and whoever turned away from it was drowned").[48] While this image had enjoyed millenarian resonances during the early reign of Ismā`īl, it was celebrated for its message of `Alid predestination in a Persian miniature, titled the "Ship of Shi`ism," in the famous copy of Firdausī's *Shāh nāmah,* completed in the early 1540s under Shāh Ṭahmāsp. This miniature matched a portion of Firdausī's foreword, which described how `Alī's ship was the only recourse in the stormy sea of eternity.[49] Knowing of the popularity of the *Shāh nāmah* in the court of Shāh Ṭahmāsp, we cannot help but wonder if this particular motif enjoyed a renewed popularity among the literati, calligraphers, and artists in the 1520s and 1530s.[50] Shani recently pointed out how a surge in pictorial representation of this tradition was part of "propagating and defending the Twelver Shi`ite doctrine which was professed by the Safavids."[51]

The scribe turns to Qur'ānic proof texts to continue this doctrinal attack. Indeed, it would appear that Safavid *munshī*s saw the epistolary genre as an appropriate and successful forum to profile evidentiary texts that had long been used by Shi`ite scholars in defence of their doctrinal positions. The *munāẓarah* style continues: "[In your last letter] there were some words which were strung together with writing by the pen of hypocrisy, stating that 'I belong to the community of forefathers and ancestors.'... Know that your argument does not follow and, regarding those eloquently filled sections which [you quoted] from the Qur'ān, they were improperly and carelessly used."[52] Continuing, the Shi`ite author then makes interesting use of two verses (23 and 24) from the Sura al-Zukhruf ("Ornaments of Gold") to substantiate his point. In this chapter, the Meccans doubted Muḥammad's message by stating, "We found our fathers following a certain way, and are guided by their footprints." The Prophet replied: "'Even if I bring you a better guidance,' he rejoined, 'than the one you found your fathers on?' Still they said: 'We do not believe in what you have brought.' Then we punished them. So look at the fate of those who denied!"

These revelatory verses are, in fact, the cornerstone to the Muslim rejection of blind imitation (*taqlīd*) of others in matters of religion. While this served well in a Meccan and Medinan context, *taqlīd*, or acquiescence to authoritarianism, in fact became the expected norm after the door closed on *ijtihād* (personal interpretation) in `Abbasid times.[53] In the Twelver Shi`ite world, however, *taqlīd* and the issue of *ijtihād* took on added significance and were a serious point of doctrinal and scholastic contention between Akhbārīs and Uṣūlīs. The more conservative Akhbārī school of thought holds that all Shi`ites must accept, or be *muqallid* to, the rulings and teachings of the Imām; *ijtihād*, or personal investigation, is rejected outright by this tradition.[54] Uṣūlī teachings, however, contend that *mujtahids*, in addition to the Imām, are indeed required for the Shi`ite community and *taqlīd* was considered anathema to personal faith and independent reason.[55] The Safavid letter closes the door of *taqlīd* by quoting the following lines of poetry:

> You raised the flag of *taqlīd* and covered the house of Truth with it
> Know and avoid the temptation of falseness and do not be so *muqallid*
> Do not follow in the footsteps of the forefathers with such zeal
> May the curse of God be upon you and *taqlīd*.[56]

Noting the degree of conviction regarding this rejection of *taqlīd*, we realize how the Safavid disdain for *taqlīd* is clearly rooted in the Uṣūlī doctrine formulated earlier by al-Karakī. Although addressed to a Sunni audience, this letter is intriguingly reflective of the debate in the larger Shi`ite intellectual community, and we have herein possibly the first public documentary evidence of Ṭahmāsp's sponsorship of al-Karakī and his Uṣūlī program.

The author cleverly transplants the issue of blind imitation, especially of distant forefathers, to the Sunni-Shi`ite debate by introducing the Uzbeks' vacuous acceptance of the much-hated Abū Bakr, `Umar, and `Uthmān. Again, this is apparently in response to barbed comments from `Ubaid Allāh Khān, since Ṭahmāsp writes: "You alleged, with a confused pen, that you are a follower of the Rightly-Guided Caliphs, and their path is the path of the Prophet Muḥammad—may God pray for him and his family." Abū Bakr, `Umar, and `Uthmān are "perfidious infidels and wicked idolaters," and to illustrate this point, the Safavid scribe turns to the traditional Shi`ite polemical arsenal and focuses on `Umar's alleged discontinuance of a number of practices sanctioned by the Prophet. The first and most controversial is the tradition of *mut`at al-nisā*, or custom of temporary marriage,[57] while another was *mut`at al-ḥajj*, which varied in meaning but usually referred to the performance of *`umra* (non-obligatory pilgrimage) during the *ḥajj* months. The Safavid *munshī* relates the tradition popular among Shi`ite theologians and jurists, whereby `Umar stood at a *minbar* and declared: "I am prohibiting the two *mut`a*s which were at the time of the Prophet of God and I will punish anyone who performs them, the *mut`at* of *ḥajj* and the *mut`at* of women, and [the saying of] 'hasten to the best of acts' during the time of prayer."[58] This particular quote was in all likelihood borrowed from the arguments of Ṣadr al-Dīn Muḥammad Dashtakī (d. 903/1497), who had discussed these matters in a supracommentary on `Alā al-Dīn Qushjī's own earlier commentary on al-Ṭūsī's *Tajrīd al-kalām*.[59] The debate over *muṭ`at* and the criticism from Shi`ite apologists that `Umar's actions were contrary to the Prophet's *sunnah* date back to the ninth century, and its tenacity as a source of Sunni-Shi`ite acrimony throughout the medieval period only underscores its value as a vehicle for confessional apologetics.[60]

The letter turns to the recent conquest of Herāt and the subjugation of Khurāsān by the Uzbeks. "God willing," the scribe writes, "those dogs of subterfuge and cheating will be hastened to the deepest pits of hell by the blows of [our] soul-melting swords."[61] To underscore the scale of `Ubaid Allāh Khān's impiety, the scribe parallels him with one of the most villainous characters in early Islamic history—Abū Lahāb—by quoting the poet Jāmī, who is "considered an infamous poet" (*hadaf-tīr-i bad-nāmī*): "Oh Abū Lahāb, there was nothing but hatred from you towards the Prophet, known as the shah of Yathrib/ There was no impiety, idolatry, or misery like yours in `Ajam or in `Arab."[62] This malicious slight of Jāmī was not at all surprising, given his decision to have the shrine of this famous Timurid poet Jāmī destroyed. The *munāẓarah* style of the letter surfaces again when the *munshī* refers to `Ubaid Allāh Khān's boasting of his construction of mosques and *khanāqāhs*. The scribe sarcastically comments that it is "useful and advantageous" (*mufīd va nāfi`*) to practise the proper laws of the Prophet's community in these mosques, but "what advantage is there in the falsely adorned and blackly seductive ways of Satan and the Damned?" In the eyes of the Safavid chancellery, such claims are spurious since the construction of these mosques comes from the money of "crime and sin" (*jināyat va khiyānat*), which is neither productive nor a good reward.[63] To illustrate his point, the Safavid scribe deploys an Arabo-Persian prooftext from the poetry of `Alī, specifically an admonition against Mu`āwiyah:

> I heard that you are building a mosque from collected taxes and you—thank God—are not successful
> Like the one who provides pomegranates by fornicating, damn you, do not fornicate and be charitable [with the proceeds] In the way that I saw you, oh infidel, what do you know about the endowment for your mosque and what do you know of God?[64]

In appropriating this particular verse and deploying it in this specific context, the scribe was depending on the exemplars of the infallible `Alī and the corrupt Mu`āwiyah to assemble a binary construct to understand the relationship between Shāh Ṭahmāsp and `Ubaid Allāh Khān. Citing the Arabic poetry of `Alī enjoyed a certain popularity among Safavid chancellery scribes. This development is likely explained by the distribution of commentaries such as Muḥammad ibn al-Ḥusain ibn al-Ḥasan Baihaqī's *Dīvān-i Imām `Alī* (c. 554/1160) and Qāḍī Mu`īn al-Dīn Maibudī's *Sharḥ-i dīvān mansūb bih Amīr al-Mu'minīn `Alī ibn Abī Ṭālib* (c. 890/1485).[65]

The issue of authority and leadership in the Muslim community is clearly the heart of the Sunni-Shi`ite divide, and `Alī's status as the true successor to the Prophet is clear. "Let it be known," Ṭahmāsp retorts, "that it is clear and indisputable to all of God's creatures that `Alī is the teacher and leader." The author alludes to `Alī's pre-eternal existence and death (*az mabdā'-i fiṭrat tā vaqt-i riḥlat*) and how the hem of his sinlessness (*dāman-i `iṣmat*) and countenance of sovereignty (*chihrah-yi khilāfat*) were never once "stained with the dust of sin or crime."[66] After describing how there is no shortage of verses and hadiths extolling the virtues of `Alī, he then simply quotes "*innā-mā.*" These are the beginning words of verse 55 of "The Feast," also known as "The Verse of Trusteeship [*Wilāyat*]" among the Shi`ite community, which is a cornerstone to the Imami concept of authority.[67] Such approaches form the basis for Shi`ite exegetical scholarship, which subscribes to the belief that hidden meanings in the Qur'ān can be flushed out with the appropriate hermeneutical tools. *Innā mā* is immediately followed by *wa hal atā* ("was there not ..."), the beginning words of Surat al-Dahr: "Was there not a time in the life of a man when he was not even a mentionable thing?" This verse is consistent with others in the Qur'ān, which Shi`ites interpret as evidence of `Alī's uncreatedness and how the Prophet, Fāṭima, and the Imāms were divinely conceived before the creation of the material world.[68] By simply quoting the first words of 5: 55 (*innā mā*) and 76: 1 (*wa hal atā*), the author employs the rhetorical device of *iqtibās,* whereby words or partial verses of the Qur'ān appear in prose without any formal introductory formula (e.g., *qāla Allāhu tabārak wa ta`āla*). This often works in conjunction with *talmīḥ*—allusion to famous passages of the Qur'ān or the Prophetic Traditions—but it should be noted that both these practices were fiercely debated by the different schools of interpretation of Islamic law.[69]

The epistolary author also demonstrates his skill as a *muḥaddis̱* by quoting a number of traditions, some that are accepted by the Sunni community and others that are not, which indicate both God and Muḥammad's preference for `Alī as caliph and Imām. The proof of `Alī's predestined *khilāfat* and Imamate begin with a brief narration of the *ḥadīth-i Ghadīr Khumm.*[70] Shi`ites believe that divine inspiration had already convinced Muḥammad of `Alī's predetermined caliphate and that Muḥammad chose to make his announcement at Ghadīr Khumm: "Whomsoever's master I am, this `Alī is also his master;" Shi`ite traditionalists contend that a *naṣṣ,* or a divine light, was passed from the Prophet to `Alī.[71] The letter also invokes the *ḥadīth-i Manzilat Hārūn,* whereby Muḥammad says: "You [`Alī] are to me as Aaron was to Moses. You are my brother, my successor, my caliph, and imām after me."[72]

Anti-Sunnism and sectarian polemics are especially vociferous with respect to the memory of the first three caliphs, and the Safavid scribe holds little back in this regard: "Abū Bakr, `Umar, and `Uthmān, may they be cursed, who before the revelation of Islam, were liars and hypocrites both on the inside and the outside, and drowning in a sea of error."[73] The author details, section by section, the crimes (*qabāyiḥ*) of the first three caliphs against `Alī and his wife, Fāṭima. He alludes to Abū Bakr's alleged theft of Fadak, a small town and estate near

Khaibar that purportedly belonged to the Prophet, and how `Umar maliciously tore up a contract between Fāṭima and Abū Bakr regarding this property.[74] In all probability, this was an exaggeration of `Umar's decision to retain these estates of Khaibar and Fadak on the basis that they should be at the disposal of the ruler of the Muslims.[75] The letter invokes the contentious hadith that stipulates how `Umar admitted publicly, "The oath of allegiance for Abū Bakr [made after Muḥammad's death by the Muḥājirūn and Anṣār at the Saqīfa Banī Sā`ida][76] was in fact a *falta* ['error'],[77] but that God had warded off its evil. Whosoever makes such an oath of allegiance will be killed."[78] As Madelung has noted, `Umar's admission that the election of Abū Bakr was an error "was obviously hard to accept for Sunnite supporters of the caliphate." Later traditionalists like al-Balādhurī insisted that `Umar declared Abū Bakr's election, in fact, to be no *falta*.[79] Despite his purported denial of Abū Bakr's caliphate, `Umar's crimes are "equally without limit," and we read how he forbade payment of the *khums* tax owed to the Prophet's family.[80] Whatever crimes might have been perpetrated against the *ahl al-bait* by the first three caliphs and "the followers of those cursed devils" pales in comparison to the usurping of the caliphate:

> At the time when the Prophet was preparing to leave this world to enter heaven, he demanded writing materials so that he could write something, after which [the *ummah*] would not be led into error, and it was the intention of both God and Muḥammad to transfer the Caliphate and Imamate to `Alī. And that cursed one [`Umar] interrupted and said "We have the Book of God and that is sufficient for us."[81]

We also have in this letter a contemporary justification by the Safavids of the practice of *la`n*, or anathematization, which clearly had been popularized in Safavid Iran thanks in part to al-Karakī's treatise on ritual cursing, the *Nafaḥāt al-lāhūt fī la`n al-jibt wa al-ṭāghūt*. In addition to using prose and citations from scripture in his attack on `Umar, `Uthmān, and Abū Bakr, the scribe also quotes several lines of vociferous anti-Sunni poetry:

> It is `Alī who is above scrutiny, and it is `Alī who is the king and prince
> It is `Alī who plants the meadow with the seedling of "*lā fatā*'[82] and he is the one who killed those violent hypocrites at Khaibar
> It is `Alī who, with a fiery blow from Zū al-Faqār, takes revenge on all infidels
> It is `Alī who is the guide to Truth and brings generosity to every corner
> And whoever has become a supporter of Abū Bakr deserves limitless anathematization
> The guide to Truth is `Alī, and those who do not know this have left the path of Muḥammad
> And the warlike infidels who know only evil oppression, may God curse those uncivilized ones.[83]

There is little doubt that this Safavid missive to the Uzbeks bears the mark of al-Karakī's influence on the chancellery. The hermeneutical defence of `Alī's claim to the Imamate, the deployment of Prophetic traditions to extol `Alī and the infallible Imāms, the justification of innovative approaches to juridical practices on the basis of *ijtihād* and the rejection of *taqlīd*, and above all else the corrosive treatment of Abū Bakr, `Umar, and `Uthmān all point to a realignment of the Safavid chancellery along lines prescribed and preached by al-Karakī.[84] The method of disputation combined with the complexity and detail of the arguments therein suggest a new phase, whereby officials were increasingly adept at accessing time-honoured tools and mechanisms of argumentation. Particularly noteworthy is the degree to which the Safavid chancellery was able to write confidently about poignant Shi`ite traditions and early Islamic history. In the theatre of Sunni-Shi`ite rivalry, this scholarly theological exchange suggests an ability and willingness on the part of the Safavid bureaucracy to defend and support a core part of its dynastic rationale with reasonable applications of rhetoric, scripture, and historiography. Theological emphases clearly have been substituted for those theosophical ones employed in earlier Safavid letters, while representation of the Safavid shahs through allegory to the historical exemplars of pre-Islamic Persian kingly figures, such as Jamshīd or Anūshīrvān, has been relegated—at least temporarily—to `Alid iconographic figures, such as `Alī and Ḥusain. We also acknowledge that anti-Sunni polemics constituted its own genre of literature within the Shi`ite traditions—arguably best represented by `Abd al-Jalīl al-Qazvīnī's twelfth-century *Kitāb al-naqḍ*—and the emphasis in this letter on the crimes of Abū Bakr, `Umar, and `Uthmān is certainly consistent with the tone, tenor, and argumentative style of such polemics.[85] Courtly diplomatic correspondence and the genre of *inshā* conveyed invective rhetoric along Shi`ite doctrinal lines in the 1530s and beyond. As more itinerant Shi`ite scholars arrived from outside of Iran, and more indigenous Persian Shi`ite scholars flocked to the central court, the Safavid *dīvān-i inshā* broadened its rhetorical capabilities significantly. This invective style of epistolography of the Shi`ite orthodox elements served an important purpose for the Safavid imperial apparatus, and in appropriate circumstances, the Safavid chancellery then had access to a standardized model of apologetic discourse that could be adapted to the "Sunni-Shi`i bimodality," which had characterized Muslim polemics since the ninth and tenth centuries.[86]

We see a strong continuity between this letter and a later missive from the early 1550s regarding the defection and subsequent invasion of Shāh Tahmāsp's brother, Alqāṣ Mīrzā.[87] The defection of Alqāṣ Mīrzā and his promise to "restore" Sunnism to Iran was a serious chink in the armour of Safavid Shi`ite legitimacy. This was likely the impetus for the next phase of doctrinal scrimmage and a series of pseudo-scholastic epistles written to the Ottomans throughout the 1550s. While the later missive is broadly consistent with *inshā* style (Arabic and Persian poetry and prose, Qur'ānic verses and hadiths, blessing and admonitions, narrative and aphorisms), there is nonetheless a scholastic and methodical structure to it that again evokes the *munāẓarah* style used in the aforementioned letter to the Uzbeks. Finished with a lengthy preamble of praise for God and Muhammad, the *munshī* presents a series of formulary invocations—primarily in Arabic—to `Alī and his family: "`Alī is [Muḥammad's] brother, the son of his uncle, and his legatee," and he is an Imām "whose pages of praise and leafs of qualities" (*ṣafāyiḥ-i madāyiḥ va ṣaḥāyif-i manāqib-ash*) are inscribed with the meritorious phrases 'O `Alī! You are the First Sayyid' and 'the angels have raised you high, Amīr Mu'minīn.'"[88] Interestingly, the Safavid scribe avails himself of the rich body of poetic literature dedicated to `Alī and the `Alid traditions and presents a number of verses in this particular section. One quatrain reads: "`Alī was the exalted Hashimi imām/Whose qualities on the page are most beautiful to behold/An imām for all Muslims, a friend of God/May the flame of his fortune grow with the lamented sighs [of the believers]!"[89] The theme of ineffability is particularly strong here as `Alī ranks with both God and Muḥammad with respect to the innumerability of his merits, and the scribe writes in Arabic how "even great scholars experience the futility of understanding his qualities." To illustrate this point, a line of poetry is quoted from the great scholar and jurist, Muḥammad ibn Idris Imām al-Shāfi`ī: "The doubt in him being God himself is sufficient enough [to speak] of his virtues."[90] The sheer number of exclusive Arabic formularies used in this section highlight a chancellery that boasted access to a variety of medieval Shi`ite texts on doctrinal polemics as well as `Alid *manāqib/faḍā'il* literature. It is no surprise that the scribe turns to the issue of the *ahl al-bait* and *wilāyat*, suggesting that `Alī's preferred status in the eyes of God is clear proof of his temporal dominion. "Therefore," the letter continues in Arabic, "the *wilāyat* of the people of earth is upon [`Alī's] family among the designated, innocent Imāms. It is they who have been designated with the authority in a necessary and right fashion with the command which stipulated to them: Say: 'I ask no recompense of you for it other than obligations of friendship.'" (42: 23).

After introducing the addressee (Sultān Sulaimān) in typical Perso-Islamic fashion and a short narration of the events surrounding Alqāṣ Mīrzā's catastrophe, the *munshī* maintains a relatively provocative epistolary stance and uses the issue of shrine visitation in `Irāq-i `Arab to expound upon the status of the Safavids as Shi`ite rulers. We read how Shāh Ṭahmāsp laments the inability of the three to four hundred thousand Muslims who live in this kingdom to practise *ziyārat* and visit their ancestors and progenitors in `Irāq-i `Arab, adding personally that he was unhappy with the prospect of being unable to send a caravan to the holy shrines. Using the popular Shi`ite metaphors of desert and thirst and combining them in a very appropriate allegorical fashion, the *munshī* writes how "a river had been brought to the shrine of Najaf by Shāh Ismā`īl" and a trusteeship (*taulīyat*) had been endowed which was now lost. Ṭahmāsp had issued several admonitions (*nazarī chand*) regarding the use of *vaqf*s to ornament the cupolas and walls of the shrines of the Imāms but to no avail.[91] The sententious and polemical tone here intensifies as the *munshī* uses the conclusion of this letter to present the eschatological implications for those who accept the Safavid message and the primacy of the Imamate: "On that day when kings and beggars are one and everyone is resolved to their fate, they will not be ashamed to appear before he who drinks from the Kauṡar river—`Alī, the friend of God—and her Excellency Fāṭima (*sayyidah al-nisā*), and the Innocent Imāms.... And for that earthly kingdom [i.e., the Ottomans] which rejects the hand of [Ṭahmāsp], they will say and know nothing of the mercy, grace, and beneficence of `Alī."[92]

While this letter manoeuvres adroitly within the *inshā* genre to present a convivial tone to Sultan Sulaimān, there is no mistaking that Ṭahmāsp and his chancellery were intent on incorporating components into Safavid correspondence that challenged—sometimes subtly, sometimes less so—the Sunni rationale of the Ottoman state. This model of the invective Shi`ite rhetoric was inspired by al-Karakī, and it demonstrated its most articulate yet apoplectic articulation with a letter despatched from Tabrīz to Istanbul in 1554, during the height of Safavid-Ottoman hostilities. Sunni-Shi`ite sensibilities had become particularly inflamed during a phase of renewed Safavid-Ottoman conflict in the early 1550s. At this time, we read of the return of Amīr Shams al-Dīn Dīljānī, who had been sent as an ambassador to the Ottoman court in the previous year as "one of the most excellent sayyids of Dīljān."[93] Ḥasan Beg Rūmlū tells us that he bore a letter from Sulaimān "that lacked respect" and cast aspersions on the caliphate of `Alī and dismissed Shāh Ṭahmāsp's claim to the Imamate. Likewise, the famous governor Iskandar Pāshā made "disparaging comments on the subject of Shāh Ṭahmāsp's *nisbah*,"[94] and when the local governor, Ḥusain Khān Sulṭān Rūmlū, sent some men of credentials (*martabah-yi mardum-i i`tibārī*)—possibly sayyids—Iskandar Pāshā detained them, explained how they were sons of infidels, cursed the family of the Prophet, and made unpleasant remarks about the Safavid connection to the Imamate.[95] To date, both sides had generally eschewed the use of overtly hostile religious polemic in their diplomatic correspondence with one another, but henceforth Safavid-Ottoman rhetoric clearly was running along stark, communalized lines.

In the case of this 1554 "Belt" Letter—dubbed thus because Shāh Ṭahmāsp repeatedly describes his faith in terms of girding the belt of love for `Alī and his family around his heart[96]—we have further proof of Shāh Ṭahmāsp transitioning his court towards an orthodox, historically developed grasp of Twelver Shi`ite doctrine. Similar to the 1532 response to the Uzbeks, this letter is a point-by-point rebuttal to an earlier theological and doctrinal attack by the Ottoman chancellery.[97] The "Belt" Letter is unsurpassed on many levels. For one, the tone and tenor of this letter are uncompromisingly disparaging and are unparalleled in sixteenth-century Safavid diplomatics. Ranging from a description of Istanbul as the "abode of infidelity" to a description of all Sunni religious scholars as idol-worshipping sodomites, this letter addresses a Safavid state that had embraced an uncompromising sectarian identity. Second, the "Belt Letter" manipulates a much wider range of divine scripture and Prophetic traditions. In this vein, we find vital additions from the larger corpus of Shi`ite apologetic writing—particular debates on `Alī's *waṣāyat* and quotes from the *Nahj al-Balāgha*, for instance—that had hitherto been absent. Third, we also discover a new feature of Safavid self-expression, wherein a strong sense of historical continuity is fashioned between the Safavids and the original Imamate. Here, we find Ṭahmāsp envisaging his war with Sulaimān as a discursive reconstruction of the early struggles of `Alī's "shī`a," or party, against the caliphal oppressors, or *ẓālimūn*: Mu`āwīya, Yazīd, and Marwān.

The "Belt" Letter's preamble, normally reserved for introducing the addressee and his *alqāb*, is one large Arabic *invocatio*, or *taḥmīdīyya*, praising Allāh, the Prophet, `Alī, and the Imāms. No mention is made here of Sulṭān Sulaimān and his qualities as an Islamic ruler, as we have come to expect in normative Perso-Islamic *inshā*. God is not lauded necessarily for His greatness (*`uẓm*) or His power (*jabr*), as we have seen in other letters, but for His gift of knowledge. With their exclusive claim to practise the "right religion" (*dīn-i ḥaqq*) and have access to "inner meaning" (*`ilm-i bāṭin*), we can see why the Safavids chose to praise Allāh as "He who is free of defects, blunders, and contradictions."[98] `Alī and the *ahl al-bait* are accordingly described as those who have been provided with "the [real] text of the Qur'ān" (*bi naṣṣ al-Qur'ān*).

Ṭahmāsp obviously conceived of his mandate as a divine one, and there is no reason to doubt the Safavid ruler's conviction that his state was destined to protect and spread the "true" Imami doctrine among Muslims and non-Muslims alike:

> Boundless praise and innumerable thanks for God's esteem for this court, whose banners of justice, power, government, and flags of dominion, rule, and conquest, have been raised to the highest possible point, as in 24: 54: 'God has promised to make those of you who believe and do the right, leaders in the land, as He had made those before them and will establish their faith which He has chosen for them and change their fear into security.'"[99]

Ṭahmāsp addresses the Qur'ānic reference to "leaders in the land" and claims that "the most high and lofty sayyids, who are descendents of Muḥammad and the best of all creatures, the pious *maulānas*, those who love the family of the Prophet, Shi`ites, and supporters of the imāms have been integrated into this never-ending excellent state."[100] The Qur'ānic reference here to fear and security (*khauf va amn*) is, again, hermeneutically emphasized: "The unfortunate world has now been made safe and secure from fear of the wicked hypocrites [*munāfiqān*] and the lowly dissenting Sunnis [*sunniyān-i khārijiyān-i khāksar*]."[101] A rhetorical construct of the Safavid state as a paradisical safe haven for "true" Muslims is presented and thus a *terra sacra* in which the rules and guidelines of the Imamate are enforced by a ruler claiming a genealogical connection with the Imamate through Mūsā al-Kāẓim, the seventh Imām. For the Safavid chancellery, this *terra shī`a* is neither ambiguous nor ephemeral: "The permanence of this fortunate state is like the Alburz Mountains and the exalted people of that place will remain there until the Day of Resurrection."[102]

We also begin to see evidence of the new appreciation for early Islamic history and the powerful allegories it provided for sixteenth-century Shi`ite propagandists. According to the letter, it is on account of diabolic advice that the security of the world is threatened by Sulṭān Sulaimān, who is reviving the customs of the faithless families of Ziyād,[103] Marwān,[104] and `Uthmān.[105] Inflated by arrogance, imperial fantasies, and regal vanity, Sulaimān believes he can conquer Iran, the best of all lands and the image of heaven itself (*nishānah-yi khuld-i barīn*).[106] For Ṭahmāsp and his court, however, "the foundation and duration of [your] state is [based] on Satan, [complete] with lies, trickery, fraud, and deceit."[107] Here, we sense the Shi`ite outrage towards the Sunni community—past and present—which has been documented and codified by generations of Shi`ite historians, hagiographers, and religious scholars. Ṭahmāsp provides a lengthy list of pejorative terms and descriptions for Sulaimān personally: he is the "*qiblah* for the wicked" (*qiblah-yi fujjār*), the "buyer of state and the seller of faith" (*daulatkhar va dīn-furūsh*), and "the most evil of the greatest of the Damned" (*badtarīn aulād-i buzurgtarīn-i ahl-i jahannum*).[108] Here, arrangements of parallel rhymed prose (*tarṣī`*) are cleverly employed: the sultan is "the liar [who leads] the state of trickery" (*muzauvir-i kishvar-i talbīs*) and "he who makes notations in the ledger of the devil" (*muzakkir-i daftar-i Iblīs*). The polemic reaches a shrill pitch as the scribe relates how: "[Sulaimān] is the chief priest of the idol temple, Istanbul [*sar-kishīsh-i butkadah-i Istānbūl*], may the curse of God be upon it and the groups of heretics and hypocrites [in it]!"[109] Ṭahmāsp informs the Ottoman sultan: "I have adorned myself in the way of proper religion … and according to 42: 23: 'Say, I ask no recompense of you for it other than love among kin,' [our heart] has been girded with the belt of love and respect for `Alī's family and guiding the imāms."[110] In referring to Safavid religious consciousness in terms of girding one's heart with "love and respect for `Alī's family," we encounter a subtle and interesting amalgamation of typical Sufi imagery with `Alid piety.[111] Girding took on specific `Alid connotations when Shi`ite traditionalists wrote how the Prophet had girded `Alī at Ghadīr Khumm and that `Alī in turn had girded a number of his supporters, including Salmān the Pure (al-Fārisī).[112]

In accordance with the legacy of al-Karakī's staunch support of anathematization, the Safavid "Belt" Letter illustrates how Shāh Ṭahmāsp had commanded that Shi`ite agents (*tabarrā'iyān*), antinomian preachers (*qalandarān*), and others be sent across Iran to publicly and secretly (*khafī va jalī*) defame the enemies of the Prophet's family.[113] Henceforth, Shāh Ṭahmāsp promised, the name of the sultan and the families of Umayya, Marwān, Barmakah,[114] and `Abbās would be included in this ritual cursing in every neighbourhood, market, *masjid*, and school and would be heard from every pulpit across Āzarbāījān, Khurāsān, and `Irāq.[115] The spread of Shi`ism at the pedestrian level is given further anecdotal proof when the scribe discusses how the population of Āzarbāījān and western

Iran repulsed Sulaimān's 1535 incursion. As a result, shaikhs and other religious personalities were narrating the tale of the Prophet's family and the *ḥadīth-i Safīna* to the Shi`ite community of Iran as a propagandist allegory to the Safavid empire's ability to survive military invasions by Sulaimān.[116] As a result of this divine sponsorship, close to one hundred thousand families have "girded their hearts with the [belt of Shi`ism]" and "have sent gifts and presents to the royal court."[117]

The cornerstone issue of Abū Bakr's usurping the caliphate with the consensus of the community (*bi ijmā`-i ummah*) predictably looms large: "If you have supposed that the *umma* agreed to [Abū Bakr], it is clear that something else took place according to the scholars."[118] "Why did the people of one city say yes to him, and [the people] of another did not agree?" the letter asks, referring to the debate at Saqīfa following the death of the Prophet.[119] This particular Sunni application of "consensus" (*ijma`*) has been a doctrinal sore point for Shi`ite scholars for many centuries, and the Safavid response to this particular argument is culled from standard orthodox Twelver Shi`ite presentations.[120] The letter subsequently defends `Alī's status as successor (*waṣī*) and *khalīfah* to Muḥammad: "From the creation of Adam to Muḥammad, there have been several ordinances and decrees from each of the prophets who have left this world which have commanded that `Alī was appointed as the caliph and successor."[121] `Alī was the most excellent of the successors and prophets among "ourselves and yourselves" (*anfusanā wa anfusakum*), and we see an application of *iqtibās* (hermeneutical allusion) to the *āyah Mubāhala*.[122] For Shi`ites, the story of *mubāhala* is proof of `Alī's pre-eternal right to succeed Muḥammad and the cornerstone to the Imami principle of legitimacy.[123] This tradition along with that of the *ḥadīth-i Safīna* have been depicted in illustrated manuscripts from the fifteenth century, and their appearance here only underscores their popularity in discursive polemics.[124]

Those who defy `Alī's succession "have seen no books of history and *tafsīr*, nor have stories or traditions come to their attention, and they have not studied books of theology which are outside convention and restriction."[125] The scribe then quotes a portion of the hadith associated with Ghadīr Khumm, and he notes how this tradition had been discussed by the *Shaikh al-Islām* of Herāt in a treatise written in the name of Mīr `Alī Shīr.[126] Texts written by `Alī Shīr Navā'ī's enjoyed popularity in Safavid Iran—for example, a copy of his Chaghatā'ī work on poets, the *Majālis al- nafā'is*, was translated into Persian in the late 1520s in Herāt[127]—and the reference here to a work on hadith in the name of Navā'ī[128] only underscores the sense of Timurid legacy to the Safavids. In this regard, Jamāl al-Ḥusainī `Aṭā Allāh ibn Faḍl Allāh's *Rauḍat al-Aḥbāb fī siyar al-nabī wa al-aṣḥāb* and Jāmī's *Shawāhid al-nubuwwat* are also cited by the Safavid *munshī*.[129] The Safavid *munshī* continues to make calculated use of Sunni traditions, stating how "it is mentioned in your collections of hadiths that when the Prophet was about to die, he commanded 'I have left you two weighty matters, the Book of God and my family. If you cling to them, you will not be led astray after me. These two shall not be parted until they return to the pool of [Paradise].'"[130] This tradition, the letter argues, is just like the *āyah al-Ṭathīr* (33: 33) of the Qur'ān, which states: "God desires to remove impurities from you, and to cleanse and bring out the best in you."[131] The *āyah al-Ṭathīr*, also known in Shi`ite circles as the "Purification Verse," is, next to the *āyah al-Mubāhala*, one of the pivotal revelations for the Ja`farī community. The Safavid scribe quotes yet another hadith, "There are 12 Imāms and they are all from the Quraish [tribe]," and he takes pain to mention how this is specifically from "your *Baina al-Ṣiḥāḥ* which is written by Muḥammad Ḥaidar."[132]

The Safavid letter continues to use a common corpus of hermeneutical tools to fashion its argument and points to another famous Prophetic tradition, "which the Sunni community relates" (*ki ahl-i sunnat naql kardah-and*): "He who wants to behold Adam in his knowledge, Noah in his piety, Abraham in his ethics, Moses in his gravity, and Jesus in his religious devotion, should look at `Alī."[133] Notably absent in this list is Abū Bakr, and the letter rhetorically challenges its Ottoman audience: "Can you still say that Abū Bakr, the cloth-seller, who is the most vile of the community, is the imām, *khalīfah*, and successor to the Prophet?"[134] The "Belt" Letter finalizes its castigation of Abū Bakr's election by narrating the confusion and disarray among the Quraish, Khazraj, Anṣārī, and Aws tribes that took place at Saqīfa following the death of the Prophet.[135] These traditions and events would have been well known to the "Belt" Letter's Ottoman audience. Ṭahmāsp's repetition of "and this is mentioned in your books" (*va dar kutub-i shumā mazkūr ast*) after each hadith reinforces Afsaruddin's argument that much of the Shi`ite-Sunni debate regarding leadership and legitimacy was based on "mutual tools" in terms of hermeneutics and prooftexts.[136]

Indeed, the particular dynamic of citing Sunni texts towards the defence of a Shi`ite polemic argument is consistently evident in al-Qazvīnī's own approach in the foundational *Kitāb al-naqḍ* of the twelfth century.[137] The Safavid scribe also looked to an exclusively Shi`ite canon to sustain this polemical discourse. He begins with the *Nahj al-Balāgha*, a compendium of sermons and letters ascribed to `Alī, which is "just below the Uncreated Qur'ān and [high] above the Created word (i.e., human speech)."[138] Ṭahmāsp informs Sulaimān that "many complaints, in clearly miraculous language, flow from that most holy lord [`Alī] regarding the oppression and cruelty of those wicked oppressors which have not been seen or heard [by you] and that can be found through studying the *Nahj al-Balāgha*."[139] If his *khilāfat* and *waṣāyat* were divinely determined, it was also clear that persecution of `Alī and his community had also been predestined, and here the letter profiles the one hundred fixty-sixth sermon of `Alī (translated in Persian).[140]

After extolling the virtues of patience (*ṣabr*) and dissimulation (*taqiyyah*), the letter goes on to itemize all the different abominations (*qabāyiḥ*) perpetrated against `Alī and the Twelve Imāms by the three *ẓālim*s (Abū Bakr, `Umar, `Uthmān) and their descendants in the Umayyad and `Abbasid families. It narrates the killing of al-Ḥusain, the massacre at Karbalā, the destruction of

Medina, the use of siege equipment against the Ka`bah during the First Civil War, and the assassination of the majority of Imāms.[141] Ultimately, the "Belt" Letter argues the persecution and annihilation of the Shi`ite community was in fact motivated by the Sunni caliphs' desire to suppress the proper truth and propagate their own versions. The *ahl al-bait* carried this secret narrative with them, and the Imāms disseminated this knowledge everywhere they could.[142] The Sunni program of suppression and disinformation was clear:

> And in every place where they were seen and heard, [the *ahl al-bait*] were killed. And every place where they had been, their books were burned. And they took refuge from the *`ālims*. And in the time of the Ummāyads, the Marwānids, and the `Abbāsids, books [full] of reasonings were made, and [these], replete with false claims and lies, are deceitful and fraudulent. And they hoodwinked everyone, [saying] that so-and-so, with the agreement of so-and-so, became *khalīfah* and amir, and that so-and-so in the [I] mamate had agreed [to this]. Then, they are to become the most excellent of the *`ālim*s, and likenesses of these ill-founded stores and cursed traditions are made acceptable in the science of revelation and prophecy, they are given the proof of verification by pure, clean, and holy angels. [But] these are in the language of men. And men have fallen 10,000 *farsakh*s way from knowing God, the Prophet, and the Imāms! Most of your stories and traditions are the opinions of the oppressors of the family of the Prophet.[143]

The outrage here at the "ill-founded stories" and "cursed traditions" of the Ottomans, which in turn are based on spurious *isnād*s compiled in the formative period of the `Abbasids, suggests that the Safavid chancellery was accessing a greater Shi`ite scholarly tradition that scrutinized intensely this foundational period of development in hadith and *akhbār*.[144] Indeed, the Shi`ite emphasis on historical revisionism shares some of the same impulses that characterize recent trends in early Islamic historiography and debates regarding when exactly the nominal corpus of mainstream Muslim religious traditions came into existence.[145] As the *`ulamā* and religious intelligentsia became increasingly interconnected with the political framework of both the Umayyad and `Abbasid dynasties, their compilation and interpretation of hadiths were in no small way influenced by sectarianism and other religio-political threats.[146] In response to the `Abbasid program of self-legitimizing and the emergence of an *`ulamā*-dominated scholarly tradition, the Shi`ites advanced reinterpretative histories that supported the `Alid cause. This epistolary text is an interesting manifestation of the Shi`ite historical consciousness and its well-developed suspicion regarding Sunni attempts to redact early Islamic history. The letter easily extrapolates the nefarious behaviour of the eighth and ninth centuries to the sixteenth century: "They cast about hearsay that they heard such-and-such hadith according to such-and-such shaikh, and that [this] shaikh is a master *muḥaddis̱* and a writer of Qur'ānic *tafsīr*.... They construct their knowledge, law, and ways according to dreams, fantasy, imagination, and superstitions."[147] "Most of your army," Ṭahmāsp continues, "come[s] from European kingdoms [*aks̱ar-i `asākir-i shumā ki az mamālik-i farangī āmadah*]," while Ottoman religious scholars fraternized openly with Europeans, Jews, Christians, and heretics.[148] On the subject of sectarian onomastics, Ṭahmāsp defends the terms "shi`a" according to a hadith: "Abraham, the friend of God, was informed by God of the high rank and excellence of `Alī, and Abraham prayed: 'I declare myself one of the *shī`a* of `Alī.'"[149] Ṭahmāsp rebukes Sulaimān by claiming that "you have created only one name for me, and you think that it is detestable, but, in my opinion, it is a laudable name." More profoundly, the Safavids know the Ottomans as "enemies of `Alī, Khārijites, Yazīdites,[150] [Nestorian?] Christians, Qadaris,[151] Marwānids, hypocrites, oppressors of the family of Muḥammad, and enemies of the *ahl al-bait*."[152]

The articulation of Shi`ite identity in discernible spatial terms was also important, and this was clearly linked with a program of proselytism. In this way, Ṭahmāsp was committed to promoting a growing community of Twelver Shi`ites—*a dār al-shī`a*, if you will—with the Safavid court as its centre: "Before this time there were not 500 Shi`ites in Anatolia, Central Asia, and India. Now, in the year 961, they have long surpassed 500 in every region.... Soon, God willing, all of the people of the world will be wholly devoted to this path and *maz̤hab*."[153] Ṭahmāsp waxes poetic on the spread of Safavid Shi`ism: "In the west, east, south, and north, the most exalted sayyids are ascending like the stars. This group is now in easy circumstances, with money, space, sustenance, and affluence."[154] The Safavid territorial ambitions are such that they hope to assume control of the Islamic lodestars of Mecca and Medina: "And from the roof of the great Ka`bah, the cries of 'Allāh! Allāh!' against enemies of the Prophet's family and supporters of that family will soon ring high."[155] The scribe realigns the conclusion—often reserved for a final set of encomiums for the addressee—and predicts "how [Sulaimān] and his amirs will be sent to burn in the lowest of hells [*asfal al-sāfilīn*] according to the divine revelation 4: 145: 'the Hypocrites will be in the lowest depths of the fire.'" Ṭahmāsp clearly sees himself as the harbinger of Ottoman perdition and promises: "You will suffer a hundred humiliations and indignities, such as what Yildirīm Bāyazīd suffered when he was captured by Amīr Tīmūr Gūrgān—may God illuminate his legacies—when you become a prisoner of my *ghāzīs*."[156] The Safavid predilection for shifting constantly between various historical exemplars is at work, and here we find a juxtaposition of Ṭahmāsp and Tīmūr on one side and Bāyazīd I and Sulaimān the Magnificent on the other.[157]

Under the custodianship of al-Karakī, the Safavid dynasty had been committed to introducing basic and complex features of Imami Shi`ism to the intellectual elite of Iranian society, and to some extent this letter bears the fruit of his efforts. These endeavours were supplemented with a translation initiative, whereby al-Karakī's treatises, as well as those by past master scholars of Imami

Twelver Shi`ism, were rendered into Persian and distributed. One of the most prolific translators during the mid-sixteenth century was in fact a former student, `Alī ibn al-Ḥasan al-Zawari, who translated seminal Shi`ite works—Al-Faḍl ibn al-Ḥasan al-Ṭabarsī's (d. 548/1153) *Al-Iḥtijāj* and Muḥammad ibn `Alī ibn Babūya al-Qummī's (d. 351/992) *Al-I`tiqād*—from Arabic into Persian.[158] Based on recent work by Rasūl Ja`fariyān, we know that al-Karakī's teachings and writings were circulated throughout Iran by the end of the sixteenth century.[159] Many of the features of the epistolary material examined thus far reflect these trends, whereby we can discern a quasi-scholastic approach that adopted disputational methods like *munāẓarah* and systematically invoked authoritative prooftexts like the *Nahj al-balagha* and various Prophetic traditions.

Qāḍī-yi Jahān Qazvīnī and the "Men of the Pen"

The confidence with which Safavid chancellery functionaries were able to articulate and defend the doctrinal and legal underpinnings to Shāh Ṭahmāsp's religio-political prerogatives suggests that the Safavid *dargāh* was increasingly familiar with generations of Shi`ite scholarship and its historical mandate to defend itself against Sunni chauvinism. However provocative such reorientations might be, we cannot forget that the Safavid *dār al-inshā* was first and foremost the domain of Persian scholar-bureaucrats. These individuals were beneficiaries to a corporate identity, which had been passed down for centuries since the advent of the `Abbasids. The careers of men like Niẓām al-Mulk, Naṣīr al-Dīn al-Ṭūsī, and Faḍl Allāh Rashīd al-Dīn loomed large in the collective memory of the Persian bureaucratic class. In the case of the Safavids, the waning of millenarian excitement and ongoing restrictions on the Qizilbāsh by both Shah Ismā`īl and Shāh Ṭahmāsp allowed the "men of the pen" to revive and consolidate their corporate identity. Moreover, the earlier power struggles, which had so badly splintered the vizierate in the late 1520s and 1530s, had passed. After 941/1535, we find the bureaucracy firmly in the capable hands of Qāḍī-yi Jahān, a moderate Persian *vazīr* who ushered in an era of centralized bureaucracy that had been conspicuously absent since 930/1524.

Qāḍī-yi Jahān, whose full name was Mīr Sharaf al-Dīn Muḥammad, was the scion of a well-established family of sayyids based in the city of Qazvīn. Born in Muḥarram 888/February 1483, he later became a student of the great philosopher Jalāl al-Dīn al-Davvānī at the Madrasah-yi Manṣūriyya and received extensive instruction in philosophy, logic, astronomy, calligraphy, and *inshā*.[160] Indeed, this madrasah, which was founded in 1477 by the great philosopher Ṣadr al-Dīn Muḥammad Dashtakī, would be a lodestar of philosophy and Gnostic thought for the next two centuries.[161] This relationship appears to have made a lasting impression in his family as Mīrzā Sharaf Jahān, the son of Qāḍī-yi Jahān, continued well into his career to praise al-Davvānī and the Shīrāzī tradition through panegyric poetry.[162] Qāḍī Aḥmad, in a short commemorative passage of Mīrzā Sharaf Jahān after his death in Zū al-Qi`da 968/August 1561, discusses the import of this family and how his father Qāḍī-yi Jahān had served in the "vicegerency" (*vikālat*) and "deputyship" (*niyābat*) of the shah. Ṭahmāsp's administration was undoubtedly stabilized by the return of Qāḍī-yi Jahān in 941/1535 from his citadel prison in Lūrī. At this point, Ṭahmāsp was intent on purging the *dīvān-i a`lā* of Qizilbāsh elements. He named Qāḍī-yi Jahān as the new co-*vazīr* alongside Mīr `Ināyat Allāh Khūzānī Iṣfahānī.[163] Qāḍī-yi Jahān's nomination as co-*vazīr*, to be shortly followed by a promotion to the office of *vakīl*, is a continuation of those policies that had been effected since the 1508 "palace revolution," keeping administrative power out of the hands of the Qizilbāsh. Mīr `Ināyat Allāh Khūzānī and Qāḍī-yi Jahān were unable to work together, and the former was executed some months later. Qāḍī-yi Jahān would go on to enjoy complete independence as *vazīr* for the next fifteen years.

Qāḍī-yi Jahān was an active patron and supporter of Persian administrators and men of letters throughout the remainder of his career. To some extent, this patronage was motivated by his proximity to al-Davvānī and the Shīrāzī tradition. His ecumenical stance—which some have signalled as evidence of crypto-Sunnism—permitted the incorporation of cosmopolitan scholar-bureaucrats who did not necessarily share the vision of al-Karakī and his cohort. Qāḍī-yi Jahān's catholic world view is perhaps best seen in the tradition whereby he prevented the public immolation of Jāmī's *Dīvān* and facilitated the reconstruction of his shrine at Herāt.[164] Likewise, during the Mughal ruler Humāyūn's exile in the Safavid court, he successfully moderated a tense dispute in which Shāh Ṭahmāsp had wanted to publicly execute the Mughal for refusing to convert to Twelver Shi`ism.

There is good evidence to suggest that, concomitant with Qāḍī-yi Jahān's appointment to the office of *vazīr*, subtle changes took place in the chancellery and the *dīvān-i a`lā*. In 942/1536, there is a reference to the death of Khvājah Mīrak bin Sharaf al-Dīn Kirmān, who had worked for years writing *inshā* in the *dīvān-i a`lā*. This position was then apparently given to Muḥammad Beg, the nephew of Mīr Zakariyā Kujajī.[165] Būdāq Munshī discusses how Muḥammad (or Muḥammadī) Beg had had an active career as a *munshī* prior to this appointment, when he had served for years as Prince Bahrām Mīrzā's private secretary.[166] Muḥammad Beg Kujajī would ultimately be replaced by a Herātī, Khvājah `Alā al-Dīn Manṣūr Haravī Karahrūdī, further underscoring the contribution of displaced Timurid-trained bureaucrats to the Safavid state.[167] In fact, Khvājah `Alā al-Dīn, in addition to being a master calligrapher, had also served as one of the local mayors in the region of Karahrūd.[168] Another prominent staff member included in Qāḍī-yi Jahān's circle was Sharaf al-Dīn Ḥusainī Qummī (*laqab*: Mīr Munshī), the father of the celebrated historian and calligrapher, Qāḍī Aḥmad. Mīr Munshī was a product of the Shīrāzī philosophical school—having studied with Ghiyāṣ al-Dīn Manṣūr Dashtakī—who then went on to serve as a ranking *munshī* within Ṭahmāsp's chancellery.[169] He is described as particularly active in the late 1520s and early 1530s as a *munshī* for both Sām Mīrzā and Shāh Ṭahmāsp, and he would continue to be known as the "sayyid-secretary" until his death in 1582.[170] The Khurāsānī association with the science of *inshā* is again borne out when we hear of how Mīrzā Akāfī al-Ṭūsī (his connection with other "al-Ṭūsī" bureaucrats is not clear) was acting as *munshī al-mamālik* in or about 942/1536.[171] The absorption of Timurid Khursāsān continued to be a great boon as it provided model administrative institutions and the qualified men to operate them.

Qāḍī-yi Jahān, himself well trained in *inshā* and the science of rhetoric, penned a number of *maktūbs*. These are helpful for appreciating this invigorated corporate identity and their use of epistolary sciences as an effective means of political discourse. Letters produced by Qāḍī-yi Jahān differ substantially from the chancellery materials discussed earlier in this chapter and suggest that the *dār al-inshā* was reflective of this greater dichotomy between `Arab jurist and Persian scholar-bureaucrat. There is a notable absence of the earlier Shi`ite invective, and in its place, we detect an emphasis on pre-Islamic Iranian notions of imperium, statehood, and justice. The first example is seen with a pair of letters, dated 946/1540, which were sent to the Doge of Venice, and as such are the first extant Safavid letters to a European power.[172] As a small city-state, Venice was in no position to offer any serious resistance to this pressure, and typical of its capriciousness in fifteenth- and sixteenth-century European politics and diplomacy, Venice began making overtures to non-European powers in an attempt to slow Ottoman expansion.[173] In 943/1537, Michel Membré was commissioned by the Doge and the city council to visit the Safavid court. In Rabī` I 947/August 1540 he reached Shāh Ṭahmāsp's royal encampment at Marand, near Tabrīz.[174] His ambassadorial mission to Ṭahmāsp lasted three years, during which he wrote his *Relazione di Persia*, one of the few European sources that describes the court of Shāh Ṭahmāsp.[175]

Shāh Ṭahmāsp was obviously intrigued by the possibilities of a Venetian-Safavid alliance, since two letters—one from Shāh Ṭahmāsp and the other from Qāḍī-yi Jahān—were drafted in response and sent back to Venice with Michel Membré. These letters are interesting in both their form and content. The first is ostensibly from the shah himself and is prefaced with the *invocatio*: *Huwa mālik al-mulk al-muta`āl, yā Muḥammad yā `Alī*![176] While the invocations to Muḥammad and `Alī are consistent with previous Safavid documents, the expression, "He is the Lord of Dominion, Most High," is a new addition to the Safavid repertoire. The letter then begins with the *intitulatio*: *asbāb-i `aẓamat va jahāndārī va as̱ār ubahhat va kāmkārī-yi khāqān-i khavāqīn-i nāmdār*.[177] Interestingly, this exact *intitulatio* is used in the second letter ascribed to Qāḍī-yi Jahān,[178] suggesting that the *vakīl* in fact wrote both letters. Qāḍī-yi Jahān must have accessed a copy of Ḥusain Vā`iẓ Kāshifī's *Makhzan al-inshā*, as the above *inscriptio* appears in the chart of *alqāb* listed under the rubric "introductory felicitations" for "the highest rank of sultans and kings."[179] As such this constitutes significant proof that Qāḍī-yi Jahān invested in and regularly employed Timurid chancellery standards.

Descriptions of Shāh Ṭahmāsp as well of Mikā'īl's (Michel's) arrival also appear in the second letter written by Qāḍī-yi Jahān.[180] In this initial *invocatio* portion, Ṭahmāsp's court is described as "that refuge of the lote-tree of Paradise, which is the real *qiblah* of people's needs and the *ka`bah* for men's prayers."[181] The shah also extols the Christian infidel to convert to Islam: "May God, most High, illuminate [the Doge's] heart with the light of the purification of Islam ... and expand his bosom with the augustness of Islam."[182] After this initial instance of religious imagery, the letter assumes more of a secular tone, and we realize how the shah must have been aware of the recent Holy League (formed by Spain, Venice, and the Papacy). He inquires "about the course of affairs in [Europe], in particular the happy union of the famous sultans to eradicate and smite the seditious" and predicts how "with the arrival of that alliance of powerful kings, the banners of my heaven-assisted armies have turned to the [Ottoman] area."[183] The letter promises how, together, the Safavids and the Holy League will "cleanse the earth of [Ottoman] wickedness" and "make apparent the perfection of boundless kingship and the infinite imperial compassion to those great [Ottoman] governors."[184]

The proposed alliance never came to fruition, but these letters nonetheless shed more light on the issue of Safavid ideological sensibilities. From a practical perspective, Shāh Ṭahmāsp's willingness to act in concert with a non-Muslim, Christian alliance only punctuates the precarious state of affairs in the Safavid state in the 1530s. This correspondence cautiously avoids overtly hostile religious rhetoric and deviates altogether from the polemical tone adopted by documents such as the "Belt" Letter sent to the Ottomans. Downplaying the inherent religious divisions between the Catholic Europeans and the Safavids, Qāḍī-yi Jahān focuses on the larger issues of legitimate sovereignty and bringing more responsible government to areas presently under Ottoman control.

Another unprecedented diplomatic situation emerged in 1544, when the Mughal Emperor Humāyūn and a small retinue arrived on the periphery of the Safavid empire to seek royal sanctuary in the court of Shāh Ṭahmāsp. The Safavids agreed to allow Humāyūn's entry, and he was sumptuously entertained at Herāt (see below). Later, as the Mughal entourage made its way westwards to Qazvīn, Humāyūn received a Safavid royal communiqué and decided to send ahead to the central court his chief notable, the Shi`ite Bairām Khān. Humāyūn's chronicler, Jauhar Āftābchī [the royal parasol bearer?], describes how Shāh Ṭahmāsp received Bairām Khān and then ordered him to cut his hair and don a Safavid cap (*tāj-i Ḥaidarī*). Bairām Khān replied that he was in fact the servant of another king and unable to accommodate such a request.[185] Angered, Ṭahmāsp ordered the wholesale execution of a number of prisoners (possibly Georgians from a recent invasion) to impress and frighten the Mughal envoy. This would be the first of two instances in which Qāḍī-yi Jahān was obliged to mediate Ṭahmāsp's bigoted communalism and use his rhetorical skills as a courtier and *adīb* to mollify the Mughal camp.[186]

The resulting letter of conciliation to Humāyūn was written by Qāḍī-yi Jahān, and we find a suitably extensive and encomiastic *intitulatio* on behalf of Humāyūn. Similar to his previous letters to the Doge of Venice, it appears that

Qāḍī-yi Jahān again makes use of Kāshifī's epistolographic manual, specifically the section on "Qualities of Children of Kings" (*ṣifāt-i aulād-i mulūk*), when listing the honorifics and titulature for the Mughal ruler.[187] While Humāyūn is styled as *mīrzā* (prince), he nonetheless is "the defender of the Caliphate," "the sultanic balance of justice and fairness," and "he who raises the banner of justice and equity."[188] The letter is remarkably muted in its presentation of the Safavid state and its newly earned role as the bulwark of orthodox Shi`ism, and we find many hallmark features of the classical *inshā* style. Employing the literary device of *tarṣī`*, Qāḍī-yi Jahān writes that "since earlier ages and events of the past until now" (*az savābiq-i zamān va savālif-i al-avān īlā al-ān*), Humāyūn has energetically dedicated himself to establishing a friendship with "the family who secures the caliphate" (*dūdmān-i khilāfat-i amān*) who is the embodiment of Qur'ān 14: 24: "a healthy tree whose roots are firm and branches in the sky."[189]

Qāḍī-yi Jahān is much more concerned with presenting the current status of relations between the two imperial households of Ṭahmāsp and Humāyūn and little is mentioned in the way of formal Twelver Shi`ite doctrine. Qāḍī-yi Jahān narrates how "eloquent speech and clear exposition" (*manṭiq-i faṣīḥ va bayān-i ṣarīḥ*) allowed a "very realitistic explanation" (*sharḥ-i kumāhī*) between Humāyūn's representatives (*vukalā*) and himself. Here, Qāḍī-yi Jahān's letter adopts a gnomic tone, and we are reminded of the intertextuality between such imperial *inshā* and princely advice manuals. The Safavid vizier advises Humāyūn that such friendships benefit all of humanity since they presently "burn with the fires [resulting] due to a lack of disagreement in the burning bush" (*bi ishti`āl-i navāyir-i `adam-i ittifāq dar būtah-yi iḥtirāq-and*). If the maintenance of the rules of friendship is suspended, it is well known that kingship (*mulk*) is permanently separated from dominion (*salṭanat*), and such a balance brings about the "rest and relaxation in the hearts of all people" (*rafāhiyyat va iṭiminān-i qulūb-i qāṭibah-yi `ālimiyān ast*).[190] Not a complete naïf, Qāḍī-yi Jahān nonetheless reminds Humāyūn that the successful emergence of these conditions are contingent upon requisite actions from Humāyūn himself, namely the suppression of dissidence and opposition in the Mughal camp, whereby they might "agree to disagree, and disagree to agree" (*muvāfiq-i khilāf va khilāf-i muvāfiqat*). From their perspective, the Safavids are committed to this objective of good will, and "in no way, will this be neglected or ignored."[191] Ever the literary stylist, he concludes his epistle with rhymed prose and a *tajnis* playing on the Mughal ruler's name: "May the shadows of that auspicious bird Humāyūn—the omen of fortune—be preserved from the stain of extinction and confusion!" (*ẓilāl-i humā-yi Humāyūn-i fāl-i iqbāl az vaṣmat-i zavāl va ikhtilāl maṣūn bād!*).[192]

Themes of pan-imperialism and Perso-Islamic notions of justice combined with an absence of acrimonious Shi`ite rhetoric and Qur'ānic text appear to be consistent characteristics of Qāḍī-yi Jahān's imperial *inshā*. An examination of extant bureaucratic *farmāns* and *raqams* produced by the Safavid chancellery during the period of Qāḍī-yi Jahān's stewardship (1535–53) points to a notable absence of Shi`ite motifs and imagery with the exception of two decrees—a 1533 *suyūrghāl* to one Zainal Beg and a 1549 investiture for Rustam Khān—in which we see a simple invocation to `Alī alongside one to Muḥammad.[193] Perhaps the best example of this ecumenical dynamic in the Safavid chancellery can be seen with a lengthy *farmān* that was drafted and despatched to a number of Safavid provincial centres on the eve of Humāyūn's aforementioned 1544 arrival in Khurāsān. Ostensibly, this *farmān* was addressed to the governor of Herāt, Muḥammad Khān Sharaf al-Dīn-Ūghlī Takkalū, who would be the first to formally host the Mughal ruler, but we know that copies of this text were despatched to other cities, including Sabzavār, Dāmaghān, Karraqān, Simnān, and Iṣfahān. This *farmān* was a document designed for internal circulation, and as such it functioned as an effective propagandistic tool.[194] It is also testimony to the degree to which Shāh Ṭahmāsp understood the reception and hosting of the Mughal Emperor Humāyūn as a monumental political event. Not unlike the correspondence with the Venetians, the reception of Humāyūn at Herāt and other Iranian centres went well beyond anything the Safavids had hitherto organized for diplomatic purposes. The contention here is that the prevalent appreciation for imperial hosting (*mihmānī*) contained in this *farmān* was yet another legacy of the Timurid empire. Although exterior neighbourhoods of Herāt underwent some change in their function,[195] the Safavids nonetheless continued to see Herāt—specifically the garden centres of the Bāgh-i Shahr and the Bāgh-i Zāghān—as imperial space. We see this with the intermittent ceremonies of investiture in such gardens for members of the royal Safavid family—Ṭahmāsp, Sām, Bahrām, Sulṭān-Muḥammad, `Abbās, to name a few—who were appointed over the years as the province's governor. On another level, the festivities in Herāt on Humāyūn's behalf were designed to convey an important message to the Mughal ruler: the former Timurid centre of Herāt was prospering under Safavid rule.

After describing Humāyūn in a long series of *alqāb*, the document informs Muḥammad Khān that he is to send his overseer (*dārūghah*) and financial officer (*vazīr*) to the city of Sabzavār so that they, along with a large number of court functionaries, can put together a royal procession.[196] A retinue of horses with ornamental tack was to be presented along with four hundred robes of velvet and European and Yazdi satin, as well as dynastic heirlooms, including a jewelled royal dagger belt (*kamar-i khanjar-i khāṣṣah-yi sharīf*), which had originally belonged to Shāh Ismā`īl.[197] Ṭahmāsp was impressively specific in his orders regarding how Humāyūn and his entourage were to be treated.[198] This *farmān* authorized Muḥammad Khān to pass on these instructions to the outlying governors of Khurāsān, the *ḥākim*s of Ghūrīyān, Fūshang, Karshūdar, Bākhirz, Khvāf, Tarshīz, and Zāva, and Sarā-yi Farhād. Knowing that Herāt was once the Timurid nucleus, it should not be surprising that such facilities would have already been in place.[199] Ṭahmāsp's demand for *qirmiz*, a variety of plush red velvet, to be presented to Humāyūn is particularly interesting in this Khurāsānī context since *qirmiz* was manufactured and distributed solely in the city of Samarqand and had in fact often been used by the Timurids as a gift for visiting royal personalities.[200] We have access to Timurid accounts of excessive assemblies of nobles, complete with banquets, music, wine drinking, and recitations in Herāt and the surrounding suburbs.[201]

It would be appear that the Safavid chancellery's drafting of this *farmān* was a deliberate initiative to emulate the Timurid culture of royal festivities and reception of foreign dignitaries. While on one level, the bestowal of gifts was designed to reinforce the power and prosperity of the bestower, on another level such gifts were construed as symbols of subordination and suzerainty.[202] Here, we turn to the richly embroidered and bejewelled robes, which were to be given to Humāyūn and his retinue. In the medieval Islamic context, the acceptance and donning of such robes of honour (*khil`at*) were symbolic gestures of obeisance and submission.[203] The Safavid willingness to embrace the importance of this institution of gift giving and the opportunity to demonstrate such imperial comportment during Humāyūn's visit are yet further indicators of the dedication of Qāḍī-yi Jahān and others to enforcing medieval Perso-Islamic political standards. Indeed, numerous medieval manuals and treatises, including Niẓām al-Mulk's *Siyāsat nāmah*, discuss the importance of gifting as an allegory for exchanging vows of obedience and authority.[204]

It is perhaps the *farmān*'s specific instructions regarding music, dancing, and other forms of entertainment that we see the best proof of how the Safavid chancellery was still capable of operating outside of hierocratic influences. "It is mandatory," the text decrees, "that the *ḥāfiẓ* Ṣābir Burqāq, Maulānā Qāsim Qānūnī ['the *qānūn* player'], Ustād Shāh Muḥammad Sar-nā'ī ['the flute player'], the *ḥāfiẓ* Dūst Muḥammad Khvāfī, Ustād Yūsuf Maudūd, and other famous reciters and singers who may be in the city, be constantly present."[205] Singers and musicians had not enjoyed healthy patronage after the shah's public repentance because Ṭahmāsp had dismissed most musicians in the early 1530s, thinking "that perhaps the royal princes, by associating with [musicians], might begin to pay too much attention to music, and that they might corrupt the amirs who were their moral tutors and guardians and thus generate a general demand at court for such forbidden pleasures."[206] Ibn Khvāndamīr gives a description of the later Herāti festivities, and it is clear that Ṭahmāsp's earlier abjuration had had little impact in Khurāsān:

> Fair women, amiable and meek, expert in rendering service, stood in every corner like virgins of paradise in that assembly of heavenly dignity. On account of their spirit-stimulating beauty the thought of life and the next world vanished. On account of the pleasure-exciting songs of singers the Venus was concealed (in shame) in the sheet of the sky and on account of the music of musicians grieved hearts became gladdened; and on account of the palatable foods and nice drinks the uneasy appetite in the hearts of beggars vanished like the desire for food in the hearts of rich persons. After the attainment of these materials of sensual pleasures and material

> delicacies, cash money in gold and silver was submitted to the king as presents.[207]

Such lavish, ribald court activity was hardly out of place in a medieval Persian imperial setting. In the case of Herāt and the Timurids, we know they were especially fond of such gatherings (*majālis*); the proliferation of garden suburbs (*bāghs*) from the reign of Shāh Rukh onwards was reflective of such affinities. Small buildings and pavilions were established in these Timurid *bāghs* for such wine parties and music performances, and these were often named as such (e.g., the Ṭarābkhānah or "House of Joy").[208]

Mystical Impulses and the Safavid *Inshā* Tradition

Qāḍī-yi Jahān, a religious moderate, clearly did not reflect the stringent Shi`ite atmosphere first inculcated by al-Karakī. Another indication of this *Weltanschauung* is seen in his relationship with various theosophic personalities and intellectuals, and chancellery material exists to point out that Qāḍī-yi Jahān maintained a discursive interaction with various notable Sufi scholar-bureaucrats. We also have evidence from this period that points to a continued role by Nūrbakhshiyyah shaikhs in the Safavid government. In chapter one, we posited that Nūrbakhshiyyah intellectual elements like Shaikhzādah Lāhījī had served influential roles in the Safavid chancellery during the reign of Ismā`īl. Clearly, this feature was diluted by the increasing role of formal Shi`ite doctrinal elements during the 1530s and 1540s; nonetheless, intellectually inclined Nūrbakhshiyyah continued to use the chancellery as a vehicle of interaction with the Safavid state. Acknowledging Qāḍī-yi Jahān's career and his relationship with Sufi personalities like Shāh Ṭahir and his connection with graduates of the Shīrāzī school like Mīr Ghiyāṣ al-Dīn Manṣūr Shīrāzī, this is not altogether surprising. Excellent proof of the Safavid connection with a Nūrbakhshiyyah chancellery element is seen with the hitherto unexplored *Inshā-yi `ālam ārā* ("The World-Adorning Inshā") written by Muḥammad al-Ḥusainī ibn Nāṣir al-Ḥaqq Nūrbakhshī (*takhalluṣ*: Sayyid).[209]

This is a didactic text dedicated to explaining the principles, rules, and guidelines of *inshā* as a rhetorical art. Nūrbakhshī provides little in the way of the typical methodology of quoting exemplary correspondence or epistolary writing. It differs even further from other *inshā* works in that it is not nearly as segmented and regimented in terms of its internal structure; periodically, we do come across *faṣls*, *qisms*, and other terms denoting sections, but generally this work treats the art of *inshā* and its use of poetic devices and techniques in a circuitous and meandering fashion. To be expected, the introductory section of dedications to God, Muḥammad, `Alī, and his family is rife with Qur'ānic quotations, Prophetic hadiths, sayings from `Alī, as well as poetry which all underscore the importance of God's creation of the universe and His gift of speech and reason to humanity. These invocations are in turn interspersed with a number of encomiastic verses that use the metaphors of paper (*ṣaḥā'if*), inkpots (*madād*), and pens (*aqlām*) to describe the divine act of creation and the importance of Muḥammad's family to humanity. In particular, one *rubā`ī* manipulates a famous hadith in which the Prophet Muḥammad said to `Alī: "If all the oceans were ink, all the trees were pens, all the world was pages, and all human beings were writers, even then your virtues could not be numbered!"[210] In another section of praise for `Alī, Nūrbakhshī describes how, "If every atom of my being was committed to speech [*nuṭq*] and expression [*bayān*], I would be an orator [*khwānum s̱anā*] of your glory until the end of time."[211]

After extolling the Twelve Imāms, Nūrbakhshī introduces the dedicatee of this treatise, Shāh Ṭahmāsp, who boasted genealogical connections with the Imamate through Mūsā al-Kāẓim, the seventh Imām. Typical of Perso-Islamic titulature, we find a fascinating amalgamation here of pre-Islamic and Islamic traditions, whereby Ṭahmāsp is heralded as the one who combines the statehood of Solomon with the justice of Anū Shīrvān (*paivastah-yi mamlakat-i Sulaimānī va mamlakat-i mu`adalat-i Nū-Shīrvānī*), while at the same time he is the embodiment of the Imamate itself: Ṭahmāsp has the essence of `Alī (*ẕāt-i `Alī*), the qualities of Ḥasan (*ṣifāt-i Ḥasan*), the countenance of Ḥusain (*ṣūrat-i Ḥusain*), the temperament of Zain al-`Ābidī (*sīrat-i `Ābidī*), the piety of al-Bāqir (*`ibādat-i Bāqirī*), the pedigree of Ja`far (*ḥasāb-i Ja`farī*), the right conduct of Mūsā (*maẕhab-i Mūsāvī*), the familial stock of Riḍā (*nasab-i Riḍavī*), the acquiescence of Muḥammad al-Taqī (*riḍā'yi Taqavī*), the piety of `Alī al-Naqī (*taqavī-yi Naqī*), the beauty of `Askar (*sīmā-yi `Askarī*), and lastly he holds the banner of the Mahdī (*rāyat-i Mahdī*).[212] There is no shortage here of traditions and verses extolling Shāh Ṭahmāsp, for example, as the "deputy of the Imāms" (*nā'ib al-a'immah*), as well as the plenipotentiary (*vakīl*) of the Hidden Imām (or the *Mahdī Ṣāhib al-zamān*). Indeed, Nūrbakhshī celebrates the fact that Ṭahmāsp's month of birth (Zū al-Ḥijja) is the same month in which Muḥammad's *waṣī*, or nomination, of `Alī is reputed to have taken place at Ghadīr Khumm![213]

The scope and purpose of the *Inshā-yi `ālam-ārā* are presented when Nūrbakhshī describes how he had been commissioned by Mīr Faḍl Allāh Mīr Mīrān,[214] who wanted "an all-inclusive treatise which gathers together the finer sentences of phrases and provides an intelligent and useful text on the customs, crafts, and beautiful features of this art of rhetoric."[215] Nūrbakhshī narrates how this commission from Faḍl Allāh was "from the most honourable of ministers" (*az jānib-i khuddām-i zū'l-iḥtirām*), who is "the most sublime paragon of dominion, the most regal epitome of the vizierate (*siyādat-panāh-i rafī` va vizārat-dastgāh-i shahryārī*). The ontological purpose of this work and its sponsorship by Mīr Faḍl Allāh are extrapolated to a general discussion of the fundamental importance of administrative prose writing towards the establishment and preservation of security and justice in an Islamic state. Here, Nūrbakhshī invokes the age-old Perso-Islamic tradition of exalting the office of the *vizārat*; several folios ensue with prose and poetry commendations specifically for Mīr Faḍl Allāh, and generally for bureaucrats and administrators. Particularly noteworthy is the author's reliance on the *Nahj al-balāghat,* a collection of `Alī's reputed sermons and letters, to demonstrate themes of justice, equity, and societal egalitarianism. In praising Mīr Faḍl Allāh's responsible government in Iṣfahān, Nūrbakhshī notes how it complied consistently with `Alī's admonition: "Behave justly with the people, and act in accordance with their needs, because you are treasurers of the people, representatives of the community, and ambassadors of the Imām."[216] Likewise, he quotes other `Alid maxims, such as "justice puts things in their places" and "the worst minister for you is he who has been a minister for mischievous persons before you because they are abettors of sinners and brothers of the oppressors."[217]

The bulk of the remainder of the *Inshā-yi `ālam-ārā* (ff. 22a–138a) comprises a detailed and nuanced exploration of *inshā* from a variety of theoretical, methodological, technical, rhetorical, and linguistic perspectives, of which only a few can be addressed with any substance here. The first section on the history of *inshā*, which is styled with a deliberate paronomasia in Sufi terms as "the path of *inshā*" (*ṭarīq-i inshā*), begins with a discussion of the different kinds of collecting and gathering by secretaries in the past. Returning to the provenance of the *inshā* tradition, Nūrbakhshī writes about those past masters of (*qudamā-yi arbāb-i inshā*) who established "the customs of this art of eloquence" (*ādāb īn fann-i faṣāḥat*) with pure remnants of Arabic and other foreign languages. With every passing era, contemporary masters had recorded the language of the day for posterity in the form of *munsha'āt* and *tarassulāt*; however, they used contemporaneous metaphors, similes, and other rhetoric idioms, which reflected their immediate cultural context.[218] In Nūrbakhshī's estimation, not one of these "esteemed books" (*muṣannafāt-i multafit*) had succeeded in explaining the craft and miracle of this "art of rhetoric" (*fann-i balāghat*).

At this juncture in the manuscript, the tone and technique of exposition become explicitly theosophical, and we sense Nūrbakhshī's fascination with a genre that promises so much in the way of hidden truth and esoteric knowledge. When this *mabdā`ī* ("young disciple," i.e., Nūrbakhshī) became aware of these antecedent works and began focusing on the issues with respect to perception and knowledge (*iṭillā` barīn muhtamimāt-i baṣīrat va vuqūfī*)—which in itself indicates a mystical understanding of this art (*bi ma`ārifat-i īn fann*)—he became preoccupied with mastering it. In this sense, Nūrbakhshī promises that this treatise will act as a "revealer" (*kāshif*), wherein every one of the customs, features, crafts, and miracles will be described and understood and thus accomplish what others could not.[219] Having outlined his rationale, he succinctly provides his table of contents (*fihrist*) within a clear mystical milieu: the sections are "flashes" (*lam`ah*), while the introduction (*fātiḥah*) will comprise a "revealing of *inshā*" (*ifshā-yi inshā*).[220]

For Nūrbakhshī, the art of *inshā* and the skill of the *munshī* are metaphors for God's ability to create light and meaning in the universe. With respect to language, *inshā* is synonymous with creation (*khalq*), production (*ījād*), and origination (*āfradan*), as in 36: 79: "He who has created you the first time, He has knowledge of every creation." In this way, the *munshī* must be understood as an inventor (*mūjid*), originator (*mubdi`*), and creator (*khāliq*).[221] In fact, it is in the "bridal-hall of thoughts" that the *munshī* adorns the exquisite brides of sublime realities with the jewels of eloquent metaphors and pearls of ornate tropes. In Nūrbakhshī's estimation, it is the *munshīyān-i divān* (the stylists of the chancellery)—in the spirit of the Qur'ānic admonition "*kun fa-ya-kūn*" ("Be and they were")—who in the darkness of the night sky employ the pen of craftsmanship to adorn the pages of light with the sunlike, golden lines of the hidden Truth.[222] The allegory of the creation of the world as orthography has a rich history in the mystical, Perso-Islamic traditions; as al-Suhravardī put it in reference to the letter *bā'* which opens the Qur'ān (e.g., *bism Allāh*): "O Master of the Supreme Circle from which issue all circles, with which terminate all lines, and from which is manifested the First Point which is Thy Exalted World cast upon Thy Universal Form."[223]

In an ensuing subsection entitled the "Customs of *Inshā*" (*ādāb-i inshā*), the author relates how the issue of conveying meaning and intention has no temporal or spatial limits (*har zamān va har makān*). People at all times and in all places communicate in societies through idioms and common language (*muṣṭaliḥ va muta`ārif*), and it is due to eloquent writing that cities of (mystical) truth and knowledge (*madā'īn-i ḥaqā'iq va `irfān*) are able to exist. In this indulgent spirit, Nūrbakhshī observes how in every group of humans (*har gurūhī az ādamiyān*) there are celestial texts (*kutub-i samāvī*), which contain ineffable decrees and commandments bestowed on them in their own language (*bi-zabān-i īshān bar īshān nāzil kardānīdah*), as commanded in 14: 4: "We sent not an apostle except [to teach] in the language of his [own] people, in order to make things clear."[224] It is the duty of the *munshī*s and orators to make these texts clear by using metaphors, similes, and other tools so that the message is readily understood by elite and plebeians alike (*jumhūr-i khvāṣṣ va `avāmm*). True to his Perso-Islamic orientation, Nūrbakhshī points out that many of these terms used in the past are "Persian, Arabic, and Old Persian."[225] However, those who are with Gnostic knowledge (*`ārifān*) work best in the milieu of *inshā*, and the *`arifān*—through the use of metaphors and other literary devices—are able to provide the keys to unlock the doors of truth (*abvāb-i taḥqīq*) which otherwise would remain closed for the ages. According to Nūrbakhshī, one notable key who had opened such treasuries of secrets (*khazā'in-i asrār*) was Maulānā Amīr Ḥusain Nīshāpūrī Mu`ammā'ī (d. 1498), a well-known poet and specialist of literary riddles and acrostics from late fifteenth-century Herāt.[226] Nūrbakhshī provides a short description of Mu`ammā'ī and his contribution to the epistolary sciences. We know that Amīr Ḥusain Mu`ammā'ī was in many ways responsible for the popularizing of *mu`ammās* during the late Timurid period, whereby verses were in fact elaborate constructions of chronograms and formal names.[227]

While there is a cursory overview of Persian rhetorical devices and tools of embellishments,[228] Nūrbakhshī presents an intense and exclusive analysis of *mu`ammā*s (poetic riddles and acrostics), which clearly had grown in popularity among litterateurs by the sixteenth century. *Mu`ammā*s ("things made obscure, hidden") were usually found in distichs or pairs of distichs, in which the object was to unveil hidden references to various letters. Upon reading a *bait* of *mu`ammā*, a reader could conceivably assemble a formal name.[229] We know that this was an especially popular literary device in the fifteenth and sixteenth centuries, and Nūrbakhshī's emphasis here is not at all surprising.[230] The Chaghatā'id poet and statesman Mīr `Alī Shīr Navā'ī, under the Timurid ruler Sulṭān-Ḥusain Bāiqarā, discusses this specific literary phenomenon and identifies several masters: Ḥāfiẓ Sa`d, Ḥājjī Abū al-Ḥasan, Qāḍī `Abd al-Vahhāb Mashhadī, Khvājah Faḍl Allāh Abū al-Laiṣī, the historian Sharaf al-Dīn Yazdī, Maulānā `Alā Shāshī, Maulānā Mīr Arghūn, and Maulānā Ni`matābādī.[231] Nūrbakhshī acknowledges the superlative work of the aforementioned Amīr Ḥusain Nīshāpūrī (Mu`ammā'ī) in this regard and in fact quotes how a particular verse of Amīr Ḥusain could be disassembled and partly rebuilt to form the name Ḥabīb.[232] This lengthy section on *mu`ammā* concludes with a deconstruction and reassembly of poetic elements to form the name Shāh Ṭahmāsp and his brother Sām Mīrzā, author of the *Tuḥfah-yi Sāmī* and well-known patron of poetry and the arts.[233] Interestingly, the only section where we see discernible discussion of missives and letters from a chancellery perspective is appended hurriedly and haphazardly at the end of the *Inshā-yi `ālam-ārā* in the last ten folios.

In many ways, Nūrbakhshī's exposition is unique and singular. First and foremost, this is a treatise that fuses unflinchingly the epistolary art of *inshā* with the intimidating edifice of rhetorical devices and embellishments (*badī`*) associated with the genre of Persian prosody. The *Inshā-yi `ālam-ārā* is similar in general structure to seminal works like the *Tarjuman al-balāghat* and *al-Mu`jam fī ma`āyir ash`ār al-`ajam;* however, it does not actively imitate Rādūyānī, Vaṭvāṭ, and Shams-i Qais in the same manner as later scholars did, such as Kāshifī demonstrated in his own fifteenth-century contribution, the *Badāyi` al-afkār.*[234] With respect to his analysis of prosody, certain rhetorical topics are ignored or overlooked. For example, nothing is said about popular devices like *radīf* (determination of key rhyming words in *ghazāl*s), *talmīḥ* (allusions), and *ījāz* (principles of concision). Nūrbakhshī, on the other hand, does provide fairly nuanced and substantive analyses of embellishments like *tajnīs* and *mu`ammā*s. This sense of authorial singularity is also seen in how the majority of the *mu`ammā*s he provides (over sixty) are not borrowed from any of the well-known poets who produced *mu`ammā*s in the fifteenth and sixteenth centuries.[235]

The *Inshā-yi `ālam-ārā* also stands as a distinctive text on rhetoric because Nūrbakhshī moves beyond simple discussions of certain literary devices, such as *taḍmīn* (quotations from religious and ethical literature), *tamṣīl* (use of proverbs), and *iqtibās* (partial Qur'ānic quotations). Rather, the *Inshā-yi `ālam-ārā* pursues—at least intermittently—a hermeneutical agenda by using these very tools to analyze a number of textual quotes and tropes from the Twelver Shi`ite tradition. Moreover, Nūrbakhshī's use of specific motifs and imagery in his discussion of the provenance of *inshā* (*ṭarīq-i inshā*) and its esoteric rationale (*ifshā-yi inshā*) suggests strong Sufi inclinations; needless to say, such theosophical threads are not found in normative accounts of rhetoric and epistolography. The most significant implication we can draw from this fascinating source is that it was produced by an individual who shared some kind of connection with the beleaguered Nūrbakhshiyyah Order. His own name, textual references to other Nūrbakhshiyyah personalities, as well as repeated instances of theosophic concepts, terms, and imagery all combine to suggest that this was indeed a bureaucratic manual produced by a Nūrbakhshiyyah scholar-bureaucrat. Thanks to the efficient work of Shahzad Bashir, we know that the Nūrbakhshiyyah had been effectively marginalized as a Sufi brotherhood by the 1520s, after the execution of Shaikh Qavām al-Dīn Ḥusain Nūrbakhsh. Nonetheless, in many ways the Nūrbakhshiyyah shared a similar cosmology and sense of millenarianism with the Safavid movement out of Ardabīl.[236]

This parallel, as we saw in chapter one, was initially productive for the Safavids as various members of the Nūrbakhshiyyah Order were able to position themselves accordingly in the nascent Safavid state. In the context of the 1550s, this relationship was deemed anathema by the Safavids, and the Nūrbakhshiyyah found themselves pushed coercively to the margin. The case of the *Inshā-yi `ālam ārā* and the information it brings to bear—the lively dedication to Shāh Ṭahmāsp, the spirited defence of the need for government and responsible taxation, plus an enthusiasm for the role of *munshī*s and *inshā*—suggests that there was at least some kind of Nūrbakhshiyyah representation during the reign of the orthodox Ṭahmāsp. The ability of urbane Sufi elements such as Nūrbakhshī to maintain some kind of relationship with the Safavid state is clearly a result of Qāḍī-yi Jahān's relatively ecumenical outlook and the existence of a relatively well-established Persian bureaucratic class. Chapter one discussed the arrival of such elements in the Safavid empire after the collapse of the Timurids. By examining the writings of bureaucrats such as Khvāndamīr, we were able to identify an infusion of Timurid chancellery styles, standards, and motifs, which were not especially concomitant with later trends of Shi`ite apologetic rhetoric and discourse. With Nūrbakhshī and his treatise on *inshā*, it would appear that this continuum between Timurid and Safavid literary cultures was still alive and that poetic and literary discourses of Mīr `Alī Shīr Navā'ī and Jāmī continued to be popular among Safavid provincial chancelleries. While Nūrbakhshī clearly operates well within a Shi`ite context, there is no mistaking his inspiration comes not from staunch personalities like al-Karakī but from broad-minded individuals like Qāḍī-yi Jahān.

The year 962/1555 marks another watershed for the Safavid dynasty and its juvenile empire. Geopolitically, this was the year of the negotiation and signing (18 Jumāda II/10 May) of the Treaty of Amāsiya by the Safavid envoy Farrukhzādah Beg and the cessation of three decades of intermittent Safavid-Ottoman warfare.[237] More importantly, at least for this study, this year signalled the end of an era in which Qāḍī-yi Jahān had in many ways defined the composition and comportment of the Safavid *dīvān-i a`lā*. This great Persian administrator had passed away a year earlier, and a subsequent period of flux and retrenchment would follow for the Safavid administration. It is no coincidence that the 1554 "Belt" Letter to the Ottomans—a text defined by its unsurpassed Shi`ite bigotry and jingoism—was written only months after Qāḍī-yi Jahān's death.

From the period 962/1555 onwards, we witness continued arrivals to Iran by Arab Shi`ite notables and the ongoing inculcation of formal Twelver Shi`ite doctrine in the court. In this sense, the mid-1550s and the death of Qāḍī-yi Jahān also led to a turn in fortune for intellectual Sufi urbanites. While some were killed or fled during the initial wave of Safavid expansion under Ismā`īl, other groups (Ni`matullāhiyyah, Nūrbakhshiyyah, Mar`ashi sayyids, Musha`sha` sayyids) managed to negotiate their inclusion into the Safavid state but were effectively marginalized by the 1550s.[238] To be sure, al-Karakī was preoccupied with eliminating "popular" Sufism, while his apprentices would later go on to also target "aristocratic" Sufi scholar-bureaucrats (*`ārifān*) who had escaped earlier purges. These doctrinal attacks, such as those by al-Karakī's son, Ḥasan ibn `Alī ibn `Abd al-`Alī al-Karakī in his *`Umdat al-maqāl fī kufr ahl al-dalāl* ("Best of Arguments Regarding the Infidelity of the Misguided"), moved beyond such external issues of dancing, music, and public behaviour to attack the very principles of Gnostic philosophy.[239] While we have good evidence of a minimal Nūrbakhshiyyah presence in the Safavid state until at least the early 1550s, it is clear that after 962/1555 the Nūrbakhshiyyah elected to remove themselves entirely from Iran and concentrate their *ṭarīqah* activity in Badakhsān, Kashmir, and Baltistān.[240] As Ishrāqī has argued, the Nuqṭavī movement could be understood as a rearticulation of the organization and aspirations of the Nūrbakhshiyyah Order.[241] The Nuqṭaviyyah would likewise find itself under the imperial microscope, and when the Nuqṭavī poet Abū al-Qāsim Amrī was blinded in 962/1555, a relentless campaign of ruthless suppression by the Safavid authorities was in full swing; indeed, many Sufi groups suffered as Shāh Ṭahmāsp's inspired religious convictions attained an elevated fervour during the 1550s.[242]

Between 938/1532 and 962/1555, then, we find profound development with respect to the issue of legitimacy and the Safavid religio-political empire. By the early 1530s, Shāh Ṭahmāsp had ultimately disentangled himself from Qizilbāsh rivalries and machinations, and the program of establishing Safavid rule in accordance with Twelver Shi`ite Imami doctrine was well on its way. His administration and chancellery were now partially staffed by functionaries who were not only familiar with imagery and tropes associated with Twelver Shi`ism, but also were in fact well-versed in Shi`ite doctrine and Qur'ānic exegesis. This initiative towards orthodox Shi`ism came unmistakably at the expense of institutional Sufism, as a result of the inculcation of anti-Sufi sentiment begun by al-Karakī in 937/1530, when he wrote *Maṭa`in al-mujrimiyyah fī radd al-*

ṣūfiyyah ("Criminal Reproachments Regarding the Refutation of Sufism").[243] On the other hand, we find traditional elements of the *dīvān-i a`lā* personified in Qāḍī-yi Jahān Qazvīnī, who sought out and maintained relationships with intellectuals and scholars trained in the theosophic Shīrāzī tradition. It is clear from the *munsha'āt* material reviewed thus far that these constituencies and their respective ideologies were both well represented in the Safavid chancellery.

Questions of the Imamate and its representation during the Occultation were especially debated during this period, and Shāh Ṭahmāsp associated himself with al-Karakī and a group scholars who advocated innovative interpretation (*ijtihād*) regarding authority and deputyship of the Imamate. With al-Karakī's legal apologia in hand, Ṭahmāsp embraced the role *al-sulṭān al-`ādil*, "The Just Ruler," who serves in the absence of the Hidden Imām but cannot act as a religious authority. As Sachedina remarks, "No government can become legitimate if it is not headed *by al-sulṭān al-`ādil*, who is explicitly appointed by a legitimate authority like the Prophet."[244] We find elaborate expression of such pretensions—Ṭahmāsp's genealogical connection to the seventh Imām, his *laqab* as *al-sulṭān al-`ādil*—and it is clear there was a program afoot to expand and reshape normative Perso-Islamic conceptions of authority. Orthodox Shi`ite elements within the chancellery also promoted an elaborate cosmology, whereby the Safavids hoped to restore the "true" Muslim state some eight hundred years after its suppression by opponents of the Imamate. They sought to promote Ṭahmāsp's image as the political and spiritual protector of Shi`ites both within and without Iran. As Shāh Ṭahmāsp predicted in a 1544 letter to Humāyūn, "The garden of the court of that love of the family of the Prophet [i.e., the Safavid court] will have an expanse which is as 'wide as that of the heavens and the earth'—which originally blossomed from the young shoot of purity and distinguished rosebush [i.e., the Safavid family]."

Having said all this, we must still recognize that political legitimacy in the medieval Perso-Islamic world was defined by deeply rooted notions of kingship, imperium, and absolutism. Whether it was earlier litterateur célèbres, such as Ibn al-Muqaffā' or Ibn Qutaibah, or later scholars, such as Niẓām al-Mulk or Ibn Khaldūn, there was agreement regarding the maintenance of a "relentless form" of absolutism, whereby kingship was conceived in its ideal model through princely advice manuals.[245] While imported Shi`ite scholars did their best to infuse new orthodox elements to this ideology, the Persian bureaucratic tradition was committed to defending this conception of authority on the basis of personal absolutism, royal genealogy, and divine investiture. In addition to the popularity of near-contemporary princely advice manuals like Jalāl al-Dīn Davvānī's *Akhlāq-i jalālī* and Ḥusain Vā`iẓ Kāshifī's *Akhlāq-i muḥsinī*, there was also Muẓaffar al-Ḥusainī al-Ṭabīb al-Kāshānī, who dedicated his own *Akhlāq -i shifā'ī* to Shāh Ṭahmāsp. These manuals were more or less elaborate recensions of Khvājah Naṣīr al-Dīn al-Ṭūsī's own foundational text, the *Akhlāq-i nāṣirī*.[246] As a result, we see a prominent foregrounding of the institution of kingship and its importance to maintaining equilibrium and societal stability in Safavid courtly and epistolary material.

To some degree, we see a mirroring here of two conceptions of authority, with both advocating unyielding loyalty and support for a charismatic ruler. What was particularly divisive in this arrangement, however, was determining which corporate institution (juridical or bureaucratic) was responsible for mediating that authority to the subjects at large. For men like Qāḍī-yi Jahān, al-Karakī and his cohort used their exalted religio-legal position as *mujtahid*s to usurp the traditional role of Persian administrators as advisors, intermediaries, and political plenipotentiaries[247] The concerns of Qāḍī-yi Jahān *et alia* overlapped with those of the Shīrāzī School under the stewardship of Ghiyās̱ al-Dīn Manṣūr Dashtakī.[248] To some degree, the opposition of these Shīrāzī elements to the Uṣūlī tradition was a response to al-Karakī's bigoted attacks on Sufis and mystical philosophers (*`ārifān*), which culminated in 937/1530-31 with *Maṭa`in al-mujrimiyya fī radd al-ṣūfiyya*. While Qāḍī-yi Jahān negotiated an uneasy coexistence with al-Karakī and his coterie, other theosophists, most notably Ghiyās̱ al-Dīn Manṣūr Dashtakī, were vociferously opposed to the Uṣūlīs, and "like several Persian aristocrats rejected al-Karakī's claims to authoritative leadership."[249]

3

SECOND REPENTANCE, 1555–76

Reorientation to Qazvīn and the East

Most scholarly narrative accounts tend to truncate the major events and developments of Ṭahmāsp's fifty-two-year reign. Thus we are likely to read more and know more about the first half of his rule: wars against the Uzbeks, Safavid-Ottoman hostilities, the Takkalū debacle, revolts by `Ulāma Beg Takkalū and Alqāṣ Mīrzā, the rise of al-Karakī, the asylum of Humāyūn, and so on. The subsequent period of 1555 to 1576 is rationalized as a time of relative calm and stability—the Amāsya Treaty had ended the Ottoman threat—while the "Shi`itization" of Iran continued unabated due largely to Shāh Ṭahmāsp's new-found piety and religious introspection. Such a Manichean presentation is problematic for those who see in this period 1555–76 a series of innovative developments in the Safavid court, administration, and chancellery. These reorientations and the emergence of new constituencies moved in lockstep with an unprecedented exercising and public articulation of power. Arguably the most provocative move during this period was the 1557 relocation of the royal court (*dargāh*) and its ancillary administration from Tabrīz to Qazvīn. Most historians see this move in a broader geopolitical light, suggesting that the decision to set up in Qazvīn was rooted in anxiety regarding the looming Ottoman frontier in Āzarbāijān. To see this decision through strictly Ottoman-coloured glasses does an injustice to the contemporary appeal of Qazvīn as an historical centre of administration, orthodoxy, and commerce. With roots dating to the Sasanian period, Qazvīn had emerged as a prominent frontier of expansion for the `Abbasids against the intractable Dailamītes of the Elburz Mountains. Later Mongol rule saw this region develop commercially as inter-regional trade routes between Āzarbāijān and Khurāsān crossed through Qazvīn.[1]

The decision by Ṭahmāsp to reorient his empire towards the Iranian Plateau is better understood in light of his objective to extend state control and disseminate the Imami Shi`ite message to points east. The appeal of Qazvīn indeed lay in its location, but it was not the Ottoman frontier that solely inspired Ṭahmāsp.

Its relative proximity to regions that to date had resisted formal inclusion into the greater Safavid Twelver Shi`ite project—Gīlān, Khvārazm, Māzandarān, Fārs, and Khūzistān—also held appeal. The decision to move to Qazvīn came within a decade after formal subjugation of the Caspian littoral—highlighted by the defeat of regional nobles like Amīr Dubbāj in Rasht and Amīr Shāhī in Māzandarān—and the expulsion of the Uzbeks from the province of Khurāsān. This move also allowed a greater degree of centralization, whereby peripheral provinces like Sīstān, Shīrvān, and Georgia were brought within the Safavid fold. As Ehsan Eshraqi commented: "[Qazvīn] était située sur l'ancienne route principale du Khurāsān, qui reliait la Transoxiane et le Khurāsān à l'Asie Mineure et à Constantinople ... elle reliat par ailleurs le Gīlān et le Māzandarān par les passages montagneux d'Alamut et de Taliqan."[2]

Qazvīn was earmarked in the early 1540s as a logical ceremonial and administrative centre, and planning initiatives were put in play accordingly.[3] A provincial palace (*daulat-khānah*) had been used during Ismā`īl's time, if not earlier during Āq Qoyūnlū times, and it would appear that Qāḍī-yi Jahān had exerted considerable pressure on the shah to consider adopting his own native city as a viable alternative to the Turk-dominated, Mongol-defined city of Tabrīz. In 952/1545, Ṭahmāsp began developing plans for an elaborate royal garden and residential complex in the suburb of Zangiābād, an expanse of property that had belonged to the Qāḍī-yi Jahān's family, the Saifī sayyids of Qazvīn. Būdāq Munshī describes the planting of trees and the construction of buildings with a chronogram (953) to celebrate the profusion of such "paradisical" gardens.[4] This "projet de grand envergure" would take fifteen years of engineering and construction and culminated with the royal gardens of Sa`ādatābād, which housed the Safavid palace (Chihil Sutūn) as well as other important courtly centres.[5] There was also considerable hydrographic engineering as *qanāt* systems were developed to access local rivers like the Dizāj and the Aranzak with the aim of sustaining not only the shah's new complex but also the various residential quarters being established by amirs, viziers, royal guardsmen (*qūrchīyān*), courtiers (*muqarrabān*), and others.[6] Qazvīn also appealed to Shāh Ṭahmāsp on the basis of its status as a centre of orthodoxy, a status it had earned beginning in the ninth century, when the `Abbasids developed the city as a bulwark of Sunni catholicism against the heretical Dailamītes to the north.[7]

There was an active patronage program based in twelfth- and thirteenth-century Qazvīn with Saljuq sultans and governors erecting a number of prominent mosques,[8] madrasahs, and mausoleums.[9] While there was a small `Alid residential quarter dating back to the medieval period, Ṭahmāsp embarked on a wide-scale urban program designed to reinvent the city of Qazvīn as a centre of Shi`ite piety and orthodoxy. Accounts discuss in detail how well-known calligraphers and artisans, like Maulānā Mālik Dailamī, Qāḍī `Aṭā Allāh Rāzī, Maulānā Muẓaffar `Alī, and Maulānā `Abd al-Jabbār Astarābādī, were engaged to decorate all manner of imperial, municipal, and religious spaces with poetic epigraphs exalting `Alī, Ḥusain, the family of the Prophet, as well as the *nasab* of the Safavid family to the Imamate.[10] A new neighbourhood was constructed in the environs of Qazvīn and named Ja`farābād—an acknowledgement of the sixth Imām—but it was popularly known as *Bāb al-Janna* (Heaven's Door). A new bazaar, mosque, and bathhouse were erected on the periphery of Qazvīn, while *tauḥīd-khānas* proliferated across the city.[11] The poet and administrator, `Abdī Beg Shīrāzī, spent the better part of two and a half years producing his monumental *Jannat-i `Adan*, a poetic collection of encomiastic verses designed to lionize the shah and these new municipal initiatives.[12]

Perhaps the boldest initiative was the renovation and expansion of the shrine of Ḥusain, son of the eighth Imām Riḍā, near the new imperial palace of Chihil Sutūn. Starting in the late 1520s, this shrine of Imāmzādah Ḥusain received regular, healthy *vaqf* endowments as well as the proceeds from religious taxes and private donations.[13] Recorded instances of Safavid support for the shrine in the form of charitable grants and the like are available for much of Shāh Ṭahmāsp's reign.[14] This development is not altogether surprising given that two of the most important Safavid shrines—Imām Riḍā's mausoleum in Mashhad and the familial sanctuary in Ardabīl—were routinely threatened throughout the 1530s by the Uzbeks and Ottomans respectively. The establishment and development of alternative *terra sacra* within Shāh Ṭahmāsp's central dominion is altogether understandable. Moreover, the extension and elaboration of the Astānah-yi Shāhzādah Ḥusain in Qazvīn was concomitant with Shāh Ṭahmāsp's sponsorship of al-Karakī, the propagation of his new Mūsāvī/Ḥusainī pedigree through the redacted *Ṣafwat al-ṣafā,* and an equally ambitious renovation program for the Safavid shrine in Ardabīl.[15] Ṭahmāsp narrates that around 940/1534 he had been visited by `Alī during a dream while he slept in the provincial *daulat-khānah* of Qazvīn. Such miracles occurred usually during visits by Ṭahmāsp to Imām Riḍā's shrine in Mashhad or the Safavid shrine in Ardabīl.[16] While Qazvīn emerged as a viable imperial replacement for Tabrīz in the 1540s, resources and support were directed increasingly towards the development of the Astānah-yi Shāhzādah Ḥusain.

Such changes had profound implications for the Safavid state and the remainder of Shāh Ṭahmāsp's reign. The relocation of the capital to north-central Iran signalled a new phase in the shah's program of assimilating semi-autonomous regions on the periphery. Consistent with medieval strategies and policies, local networks of political and religious elite were sponsored and co-opted by the Safavids through official nominations, diplomatic marriages, tax immunities, charitable endowments, and other administrative-state mechanisms. While the Arab theologians of Jabal `Āmil were integral to the shah's program, Eshraqi and others have also noted the importance of the Iranian *sādāt,* who suddenly became recipients of considerable political and financial support.[17] The one region, however, that emerged to assume a new profile after the transfer from Tabrīz to Qazvīn was the province of Māzandarān. Initially conquered by Shāh Ismā`īl in 1509, the *vilāyat-i Māzandarān* was a source of constant insurgency and civil war. The Safavid rulers allied themselves at first with local potentates, but Shāh Ṭahmāsp finally intervened and subdued the fractious region in the mid-1540s.[18] During the late 1540s and 1550s, nomadic Türkmen tribes tried repeatedly to conquer and control Māzandarānī cities like Bārfrūs, Sārī, Āmul, and Astarābād.[19] The new proximity of the Safavid royal court in Qazvīn was effective, and military support for Safavid governors in Astarābād was sufficient and regular. We hear of the last serious Māzandarānī Türkmen insurrection in 972/1564-65.[20]

Iskander Beg Munshī's detailed sectioning of Safavid elite during Ṭahmāsp's reign takes special notice of the sayyids as a class of landed elite that enjoyed considerable power. Traditionally, the Uskūya sayyids of Tabrīz had dominated the Safavid household during the 1530s and 1540s, and Iskander Beg observes archly how "any wish of theirs was translated into reality almost before it was uttered ... although they were guilty of unlawful practices."[21] Qāḍī-yi Jahān himself grappled with these Tabrīzī sayyids—best identified with men like Mīr Ṣadr al-Dīn Muḥammad and Amīr Niẓām al-Dīn Aḥmad—and their power and influence were attenuated considerably as a result. With the reorientation towards Qazvīn in the 1550s, a new network of sayyids, primarily from Māzandarān, came to the political and administrative forefront. As Māzandarān was increasingly subsumed into the Safavid state, Shāh Ṭahmāsp and his administration redoubled their efforts to co-opt elite political and religious elements. An ample number of official documents, such as tax exemptions (*suyūrghāl*s), diplomas of investiture, and others regarding the province of Astarābād in the 1540s and 1550s corroborate this state policy.[22] The growing role of the Māzandarānī religious elite in the Safavid state has been overshadowed by traditional emphases on another immigrant group, the Jabal `Āmilī theologians;[23] however, recent scholarship has endeavoured to also point out how a disproportionate number of sayyids and theologians from Astarābād and other Māzandarānī centres came to dominate the Safavid state in the 1550s and 1560s.[24] Not only did these individuals hold powerful posts like the *ṣadārat* and act as custodians (*mutavallī*s) for shrines, but also they supplemented the larger Safavid theological and judicial program by producing a number of extensive works on exegesis, hagiography, and law. The reorientation towards Qazvīn then prefaced another profound reorientation: the promotion of the Māzandarānīs as a powerful new constituency within the Safavid state.

One particular group from Māzandarān benefited especially from this development: the Mar`ashī sayyids. The origins of the Mar`ashī sayyids are not unlike those of the Safavids with their "founder" Amīr Qavām al-Dīn Mar`ashī (*laqab*: Mīr-i Buzurg), a local Sufi shaikh who managed to establish a political state in and around the city of Āmul in the mid-fourteenth century.[25] Thereafter, the Mar`ashī sayyids operated as de facto political rulers until the collapse of the region's stability in the early sixteenth century and its later incorporation by Shāh Ṭahmāsp.[26] Similar to his father's use of diplomatic marriage with the Ni`matullāhīs, Shāh Ṭahmāsp arranged to have his son, the future Muḥammad Khudābandah, marry the daughter (Khair al-Nisā, *laqab*: Mahd-i `Ulyā) of the chief Mar`ashī notable.[27] While the origins of the Mar`ashīs were distinctly Māzandarānī, there appears to have been a diffusion of Mar`ashī sayyids across Iran in the late fifteenth and sixteenth centuries.

By the period of Shāh Ṭahmāsp's reign, several "branches" of Mar`ashīs existed in Shushtar, Herāt, Tabrīz, Iṣfahān, and Qazvīn.[28] In Iṣfahān, we hear of the "Khalīfa" sayyids who boasted of a Mar`ashī genealogy back to Mīr-i Buzurg. Mīr Maḥmūd Iṣfahānī was one notable, while his relation Mīr Abū al-Qāsim was named the warden of Imām Riḍā's shrine in the 1570s.[29] The chief Mar`ashī notable of Shushtar, Asad Allāh Shushtarī, had held the post of *ṣadr* for nearly twenty years in the 1540s and 1550s. The Qazvīnī branch of the Mar`ashīs enjoyed the greatest political support and royal largesse of these different branches. Modaressī-Ṭabāṭabā'ī has reproduced various *farmāns* and *vaqf-namās* in his *Bargī az tārīkh-i Qazvīn* to demonstrate the rise of this sayyid family to religious and political power under the Safavids and well into the eighteenth and nineteenth centuries.[30] The Mar`ashī sayyids of Qazvīn had been chief local notables (*nuqabā*) since the fifteenth century, but it was not until the reign of Shāh Ṭahmāsp that the political fortunes of the Mar`ashī Qazvīnīs rose dramatically.[31] Earlier, in 937/1530, the Mar`ashī sayyids had been named the official superintendents of the Astānah-yi Shāhzādah Ḥusain in Qazvīn, and they oversaw its renovation and expansion in the 1530s and onwards.[32] Official confirmations of their custodianship (*taulīyat*) of the shrine appeared again in 938/1531, 943/1536, 946/1539, and 983/1575. By the time of the official transfer to Qazvīn, the Mar`ashī sayyids had positioned themselves as the local religious and administrative elite; it was evident that they had benefited most considerably from Shāh Ṭahmāsp's program to reinvent and "Shi`itize" this political and religious landscape.[33] There was of course a group of Mar`ashī sayyids in their lodestar of Astarābād, and official tax exemptions in 947/1541, 950/1544, and 954/1547 for the chief sayyid and *naqīb al-nuqabā* (local Shi`ite custodian) Kamāl al-Dīn Maḥmūd and his brothers `Imād al-Dīn Mas`ūd and Amīr Ibrāhīm hint at extensive landowning and continued political power in Māzandarān.[34]

In addition to the Mar`ashī sayyids, we see a disproportionate number of Māzandarānī sayyids, scholars, and theologians dominating the Safavid narrative in the second half of Ṭahmāsp's reign.[35] While he had been active in the 1530s and 1540s, the sayyid Mīr Fakhr al-Dīn Sammākī was in many ways responsible for establishing the genealogical and scholarly prestige of his family in the Safavid household. Fakhr al-Dīn is atypical in terms of what is arguably a period of intense conservative orthodoxy, given his instructorship at the hands of Ghiyās̱ al-Dīn Manṣūr Dashtakī and his own tutelage of future philosopher Mīr Dāmād.[36] Nonetheless, he contributed to the growing corpus of Shi`ite exegetical and legal works by producing commentaries and glosses on al-Ṭūsī's *Illāhiyat-i tajrid* and the *Ḥidāyah al-ḥikmat*.[37] His nephew `Imād al-Dīn `Alī Qārī Astarābādī, also known as Mīr Kālān, had initially lived in Mashhad but was summoned to Qazvīn, where he grew to be very close to Shāh Ṭahmāsp while serving as tutor to Ṭahmāsp's sister Shāhzādah Sulṭānum.[38] In addition to managing property bequeathed to the Fourteen Innocent Ones (the *ahl al-bait*) by Shāhzādah Sulṭānum herself, he developed a popular following because of his Qur'ānic recitations and ritual chanting.[39]

The office of *ṣadr* was likewise strongly influenced by this surge of Māzandarānī activity. After two successive Mar`ashī sayyids from Shushtar held this post between 941/1534-35 and 963/1556, Mīr Muḥammad Yūsuf Astarābādī, an intimate and tutor within the shah's court, was named jointly to this post with Mīr Sayyid `Alī, son of the previous *ṣadr* Asad Allāh Shushtarī, for a brief period starting in Shawwāl 970/June 1563. Described as one of the most eloquent sayyids of Astarābād, Mīr Muḥammad Yūsuf is also known to have taught and preached in the Masjid-i Panjah-i `Alī in Qazvīn.[40] Among the courtly and bureaucratic elite based in Qazvīn, the Māzandarānī hierocrats included Mīr Sayyid `Alī Khaṭīb Astarābādī who held the post of *khaṭīb* (preacher) and *muḥtasib al-mamālik* (chief regulator). Iskander Beg Munshī recalls that Sayyid `Alī was a domineering individual who controlled the thoughts and actions of two other important sayyid-bureaucrats, Mīr Ṭāhir Kāshī and Mīr Zain al-`Ābidīn (the *muḥtasib* for the city of Qazvīn).[41] Three other prominent Astarābādī sayyids include Mīr Muḥammad Mu'min Astarābādī (tutor to Ḥaidar Mīrzā before fleeing to one of the Deccanī kingdoms where he served as *vakīl*); Maulānā Mu`īn Astarābādī (an eloquent vizier to the Safavid prince, Sulṭān Ibrāhīm Mīrzā); and Mīr Muḥammad Ashraf.[42] The latter is described as one of the "long-haired" sayyids of Astarābād who functioned as the legal plenipotenary (*vakīl*) of Shāh Ṭahmāsp during his official visits to the shrine of Imām Riḍā in Mashhad.[43] Moreover, he was quite involved in the 1560s with collecting and collating the juridical and theological works of al-Karakī.[44]

If the 1530s and 1540s were periods of conflicting cosmologies between the indigenous Persian bureaucratic/philosophical elite and interloping Arab theologians and jurists, the second half of Shāh Ṭahmāsp's reign saw the advent of a new political and courtly agency in the sayyids and their various networks intersecting cities like Tabrīz, Qazvīn, Iṣfahān, as well as the recently incorporated centres of Rasht, Astarābād, and Āmul. Indeed, the developments during this period support the contention that one particular coterie of sayyids—those hailing from Māzandarān and the east—carried significant impact for the duration of Shāh Ṭahmāsp's reign. More compelling has been the suggestion that the Māzandarānī sayyids—specifically those from Astarābād—were integral to the dispersing, preaching, and popularizing of al-Karakī's interpretations of Shi`ism across Safavid dominions.[45] Sayyid al-Amīr Abū Al-Ma`ālī Astarābādī had translated one of his main works, *Risālah al-Ja`fariyya,* from Arabic into Persian, while we know of at least one other Arabic work by al-Karakī that had been translated by Amīr Faḍl Allāh Astarābādī, entitled *Masā'il-i mutaffariqah.*[46] These and other sayyid networks intermingled and intermarried with Jabal `Āmil contingents, of which the most prominent example is al-Karakī's marriage into a prominent Astarābādī sayyid family.[47] These marriage alliances created a distinctive and new generation of Shi`ite philosophers and scholars within Iran, including the philosophical luminaries of Mīr Dāmād, Shaikh Bahā'ī, and Mullā Ṣadrā.

This serves as context to the lesser-known "second repentance" of Ṭahmāsp in 963/1556, in which he had "decrees and orders" (*aḥkām va parvānijāt*) regarding new standards of public morality and piety issued by the chancellery and distributed to functionaries throughout the land.[48] Said Arjomand has examined an undated decree ("most likely issued in the middle part of the sixteenth century"), which contains numerous articles prohibiting homosexuality, alcohol, and music as well as enjoining citizens to lead moral, upright lifestyles.[49] Like much of Ṭahmāsp's policies, the inspiration for his decrees was a dream in which he was visited by `Alī. Kathryn Babayan has interpreted these prohibitions as a "public break" with the bon vivant Turco-Mongol culture enjoyed in his father's day, and as such they constituted a reaffirmation of the earlier decrees of 1532 under the influence of al-Karakī.[50] In the same year, we hear of Mīr Sayyid `Alī, of Shushtarī Mar`ashī fame, and his nomination to the *ṣadārat*. We cannot help but link this second repentance of Ṭahmāsp's to his fraternization with these reinvigorated sayyid networks.[51] Due in many ways to the rise of the Māzandarānī hierocratic element, al-Karakī's vision of a homogeneous Shi`ite state would come a long way, and this was certainly facilitated by the large-scale emigration to India and elsewhere of scribes, bureaucrats, painters, calligraphers, doctors, poets, bookbinders, and scholars. Anthony Welch describes the cumulative loss to Iran as "awesome," with "staggering" numbers of literati and scholars who emigrated to Mughal India and the various Deccanī kingdoms.[52] The Safavid chancellery was especially affected by these trends, and we find the *dār al-inshā* under conservative and inexperienced stewardship with the new chief vizier and *vakīl*, Ma`ṣūm Beg Ṣafavī.[53] The Persian bureaucratic/theosophic elite would be in a state of attenuation after the retirement and death of Qāḍī-yi Jahān. Chancellery output in the 1560s and 1570s reflects a period of uncertainty for Iranian courtly elite and intelligentsia. After the death of Ma`ṣūm Beg Ṣafavī in 1568, the office of chief vizier (*vazīr-i dīvān-i a`lā*) was in abeyance and would remain so until the rise of Mīrzā Salmān Jābirī fifteen years later. Iskander Beg Munshī remarks on the lack of direction in the Persian administration between 1568 and 1578, noting that no vizier was appointed with "independent authority" after Ma`ṣūm Beg Ṣafavī.[54] Būdāq Munshī describes how Ma`ṣūm Beg's successors, Jamāl al-Dīn `Alī Tabrīzī and Sayyid Ḥasan Farāḥānī, were completely ineffectual, and Shāh Ṭahmāsp once remarked caustically that Jamāl al-Dīn `Alī's speech resembled a cooing pigeon. In Būdāq Munshī's estimation, "they both became a laughing stock" (*har dū maḍḥakah shudand*).[55]

Decentralization best characterizes the Safavid administration and chancellery after 1555 and as such belied some of the greater objectives involved in transferring the capital to Qazvīn. While many poets and literati fled to South Asia, some relocated to provincial centres in an effort to escape the abstemious climate of Qazvīn. The best-known example of such active provincial patronage was Ibrāhīm Mīrzā's court in Mashhad during the late 1560s and 1570s. Ibrāhīm

Mīrzā and his court would cultivate a second generation of Safavid painters, calligraphers, and illuminators—Āqa Mīrāk and Muẓaffar `Alī, as well as younger protégés like Rustam `Alī (nephew of Bihzād), Muḥibb `Alī, and Sulṭān Maḥmūd Nīshāpūrī—who transformed Ibrāhīm's Mashhad atelier into a substantial cultural entrepôt. Prominent calligraphers like Maulānā Mālik Dailamī, Ayshī ibn `Ushratī, and Muḥammad Khāndan were summoned to Mashhad to contribute to this climate.[56] Much of the chancellery was similarly dispersed to the periphery, and some of the best *munshīs* and scribes found employment not in Qazvīn but in parochial urban centres.[57] Qāḍī Aḥmad al-Qummī's father, Mīr Munshī, had originally served in the *dīvān-i a`lā* in Qazvīn but later transferred to Mashhad, where this particular family did well as administrators under the patronage of Ibrāhīm Mīrzā.[58] Māzandarān and Gīlān would be two of the principal recipients of this "brain-drain" from Qazvīn, and the semi-autonomous courts became rich sources of patronage for artists, poets, and scribes.[59]

The most significant *munshī* to keep his distance from the imperial capital at Qazvīn but still remain within the Safavid fold was `Aṭā Allāh Iṣfahānī. `Aṭā Allāh spent the better part of thirty years in service to Shāh Ṭahmāsp; indeed, as *vazīr-i muhr* (vizier of the seal), he had been charged with the mission of carrying a *farmān* and robe of honour (*khil`at*) to the Shīrvānshāh court after the accession of Shāh Ṭahmāsp in 931/1524. He subsequently served as vizier to Āzarbāijān, Qarābāgh, and Shirvān but remained in Tabrīz after the capital was transferred to Qazvīn in 964/1557. When the fugitive Ottoman Prince Bāyazīd arrived in Armenia seeking refuge in 965/1558, `Aṭā Allāh escorted him to the royal court in Qazvīn.[60] Iskander Beg Munshī states that the work of `Aṭā Allāh Iṣfahānī, as well as Āqā Kamāl al-Dīn Zain al-`Ibād Kirmānī, was so impressive that "the administrative practices they instituted are still the rule and model in those provinces."[61] Likewise, Khvājah Ikhtiyār, a Herāti native, eschewed the imperial centre and spent his thirty-year career serving as the chief *munshī* for the Safavid provincial court of Herāt and was also responsible for tutoring the future Shāh Khudābandah in calligraphy and composition.[62]

In this new conservative climate, we see the relative displacement of those cosmopolitan bureaucrats who had excelled during Qāḍī-yi Jahān's stewardship and the genesis of a new class of stylists and scribes that reflected the previously discussed trends taking place in Safavid Iran between 1555 and 1576. Two key deaths in 969/1561 signalled the final stage of this transition: the first was Qāḍī-yi Jahān's own son, Mīrzā Sharaf-i Jahān, who was recognized for his *inshā* and poetry but had served in the royal camp (*urdū-yi humāyūn*) of Mīrzā Muḥammad (Khudābandah) in Herāt;[63] the other was Mīrzā Kāfī Urdūbādī who had been a central chancellery functionary since the days of Shāh Ismā`īl.[64] A descendant of Khvājah Naṣīr al-Dīn al-Tūsī, Mīrzā Kāfī was unequalled in the epistolary arts, and he had been an esteemed companion (*muṣāḥib*) of Shāh Ṭahmāsp while serving as *munshī al-mamālik* until his death in 969/1561.[65] His replacement, Muḥammadī Beg Kukajī, made little impact during the next thirteen years, despite his status as grandson of the Āq Qoyūnlū/early Safavid vizier

Amīr Zakariyya.[66] Likewise, the *munshī al-mamālik* between 1574 and 1576, Khvājah `Alā al-Dīn Manṣūr Karāhrūdī, appears to have been less than inspiring to the Safavid historians. Qāḍī Aḥmad points out that he was simply "admitted to assembly of the court" to trace *ṭughrā*s with gold ink.[67]

These substantive gaps were filled by scholastics who, in addition to demonstrating skill with epistolography, were also well noted for their orthodox contributions to the emerging Safavid Shi`ite canon. One such individual was Maulānā Mīrzā `Alī Sulṭānavī who was not only a master of calligraphy but also was "a peerless *munshī*" and rhetorician of the highest degree. His knowledge of Arabic syntax and grammar (*naḥw wa ṣarf*) were particularly refined as was his ability to analyze choice sentences and turns of phrases (*faqarāt*) in Arabic. He served as *qāḍī* for provinces in proximity to Qazvīn—Ṭārum and Zanjān—but he worked intimately with the royal court and produced purchase deeds and legal decisions (*qabalāt va amsilah*) for the central *ṣadārat*.[68] Another legalist-cum-stylist who emerged during this period was Qāḍī Ulugh Beg Urdūbādī (d. 972/1565). He is described as having openly emulated the *munshī* par excellence Khvājah `Abd al-Ḥayy. According to Qāḍī Aḥmad, there were few stylists who "possessed his taste in the epistolary art and phraseology," and he worked on behalf of Ṭahmāsp's family in the writing of *vaqf* documents for the estates of the *ahl al-bait*. He was well versed in *fiqh*, and Shāh Ṭahmāsp himself lionized Ulugh Beg in this verse: "A solid man is the judge of Urdūbād/A man like unto some tree."[69]

This policy of incorporating jurists into the central chancellery is best demonstrated with the career of Qāḍī `Abd Allāh of Khūy. Qāḍī `Abd Allāh, almost certainly an Azeri Turk, had originally served as judge for the regions of Khūy and Salmās but was brought to Qazvīn on account of his unsurpassed talent for writing *inshā* in both Persian and Turkish. He was "entrusted with correspondence in the paradisiacal court assembly" of Shāh Ṭahmāsp for a short time—possibly during the same time (1574–76) that Khvājah `Alā al-Dīn Manṣūr Karāhrūdī was providing the formulaic duties of *munshī al-mamālik*—while concurrently writing and despatching formal letters to the Ottoman and Mughal empires. Qāḍī `Abd Allāh took advantage of his proximity and compiled a treatise on religious duties, which he dedicated to his patron Shāh Ṭahmāsp.[70] "One of the greatest [Mūsāvī] sayyids," Mīr Niẓām al-Dīn Ashraf (d. 1586) fulfilled his legal duties as Shaikh al-Islām and *qāḍī* for Abarqūh, but he later joined the shah's retinue to provide both spiritual guidance and "good taste in epistolary art."[71] We also see evidence of the energized Māzandarānī elite in the chancellery with individuals like Maulānā Ibrāhīm Astarābādī and Mīr Qāsim Astarābādī. Mīr Qāsim, a sayyid in good standing, had been an intimate part of Ṭahmāsp's assembly and was noted for his innovative approaches to *inshā*. Maulānā Ibrāhīm was well connected with the Safavid court in a number of capacities. While visiting Damascus after a pilgrimage to Mecca and Medina, Ibrāhīm Astarābādī had discovered an Arabic text that defended the prerogatives of `Alī and the *ahl al-bait*. He translated it into Persian as *Risālah-yi Ḥusainiyyah,* and it was reportedly read with great delight by Shāh Ṭahmāsp.[72] He was named the official *munshī* for the shrine of Imām Riḍā in Mashhad. He had worked earlier in Qumm, and his panegyrics and epigraphs for the Prophet's family were celebrated among contemporaries.[73]

In 963/1556, Sultan Sulaimān inaugurated the majestic Masjid-i Suleimaniye, which had been six years in the making under the directorship of the Ottoman imperial architect Sinān Pāshā. As Necipoghlu has argued, the Suleimaniye mosque was much more than a testimony to Ottoman piety, and it is reasonable to accept that "the multilayered architectural discourse of the Suleymaniye complex operated within a specific social context, and [how] structures of signification were mobilized to communicate a political statement."[74] In that same year, 963/1556, Shāh Ṭahmāsp had himself undertaken his own massive ceremonial and imperial project in developing the royal complex at Sa`ādatābād. Like the Masjid-i Suleimaniye, the Maidan-i Sa`ādatābād was ultimately an articulation of imperial ideology. Ṭahmāsp's decision to instruct the Safavid chancellery to send a congratulatory letter to commemorate the inauguration of this ideological space is striking. Sulaimān's agenda of expressing his legitimacy through a mosque complex that clearly reflected the cultural and religious legacy of the Prophet Solomon seems clear: references in *vaqfiyyah* documents, the design of Sulaimān's mausoleum being derivative of the Dome of the Rock where the Temple of Solomon lay, and the alleged use of massive pillars from Solomon's palace.[75] It is perhaps for this reason that Ṭahmāsp decided to appoint a *munshī* who felt comfortable conveying a message that was imperially competitive and sufficiently grandiose without necessarily indulging in confessional polemics and exegetical disputation. We know that the letter's author was Mīrzā Kāfī Urdūbādī, described as one of the "noble descendants of the sultan of the seekers of Truth, teacher of the oceanic sages, Naṣīr al-Ḥaqq wal-millat wad-dīn Muḥammad al-Ṭūsī," and thus was more than likely part of a bureaucratic, scholarly culture, which embraced mysticism, theosophy, and philosophy.[76]

With this in mind, we discover that this "mosque" letter has none of the standard, introductory invocations to God, Muḥammad, `Alī, and the Imamate, but rather a lengthy rhymed prose (*saj`*) *intitulatio* for the benefit of the Ottoman sultan; in one section Sulaimān is profiled as "powerful as the imperial ruler Farīdūn and has the wise Cyrus-like manner of King Darius."[77] The *munshī* demonstrates his technical dexterity as well as his creative impulse by incorporating a partial Qur'ānic quote within this rhymed prose, whereby Sulaimān is "the manifestation of the lights of eternal assistances/ and the manifestation of the secrets contained in 'Give me such a dominion as none will merit after me' (38: 35)" (*maẓhar-i anvār-i ta'yīdāt-i abadī/maẓhar-i asrār-i waḥab lī-mulkān lā yanbagha li-aḥadin min ba`dī*).[78] Poems and rhymed prose form the bulk of not only the introduction but also the letter itself, and there are many instances of the Ottoman sultan sharing the same rhetorical space as exemplars like Darius, Cyrus, Jamshīd, Farīdūn, Anū Shīrvān, Alexander, and of course Solomon. Again, as with other correspondence written in earlier phases of the

Safavid chancellery, we have in this never-ending series of *alqāb* an amalgamation of qualities and virtues that spans the mythic, pre-Islamic, and Islamic eras. While Sulaimān is the one who guarantees justice and equity in the way of Anū Shīrvān, he is also a leader of the *ghāzī*s and *mujāhidīn*; at the same time that he bears the signature of Alexander the Great, his kingly aura is connected to Tīmūr.[79]

Ṭahmāsp turns to the matter at hand and writes that for years he had been hearing from travellers that Sulaimān's focus was dedicated to erecting mosques (*mu`āmar-i buyūt-i Allāh*). The sultan had clearly listened to the Qur'ānic imperatives of "the mosques of God shall be visited" (9: 18) and "the man who lays the foundations of his sanctum" (9: 109), and he had built a second Masjid al-Aqṣā for the Muslim world to admire.[80] To celebrate this auspicious event, Ṭahmāsp describes how he is sending this letter in the care of one of his servants, Kamāl al-Dīn Tibbat Āqā, with three illuminated Qur'āns (*sih jild-i maṣḥaf-i a`lā*) as diplomatic offerings since they were the best possible gift (*aḥsān-i tuḥaf*) and most appropriate for this context.[81] The *munshī* writes that Ṭahmāsp—for obvious reasons—would be unable to perform prayer in that mosque, but he does quote the Prophetic hadith: "Pointing out a good [task] is as good as having done it" (*al-dāl `alā al-khair ka-fā`iluhu*), and marvels at the good rewards yielded by reading the Qur'ān in such a majestic space. Keen to further demonstrate his largesse, Ṭahmāsp notes how a beautiful carpet could be woven in the shah's workshop and delivered to Istanbul should the sultan furnish the requisite dimensions (*`adad-i ṭūl va `arḍ*) and the colours needed for the centre and margins (*rang-i matn va ḥāshiyah*).[82] This letter, the presentation of illuminated Qur'āns, and the offer of intricate prayer carpets were all designed to celebrate Sulaimān's program of patronage and religious dedication; however, Ṭahmāsp was no stranger to issues of legitimacy and ideology, and in particular the writing of this letter was contemporary with his own ongoing orchestration of spectacle and space in Sa`ādatābād, the Astānah-yi Shāhzādah Ḥusain, and the surrounding city of Qazvīn. After his initial congratulations to Sulaimān regarding the Masjid-i Suleimāniye, the *munshī* presents an elaborated version of a poem first penned by the great medieval Indian poet Amīr Khusrau (d. 725/1324). This appears to have been a popular verse since Khvāndamīr cites it in his discussion of the construction of a mosque in Herāt by the Ghūrid sultan Abu al-Fatḥ Ghiyāṣ al-Dīn Muḥammad ibn Sām.[83]

> The shah's mosque[84] the congregation of God's bounty/makes the whisper of recitation reach the moon
> [Bounty] has come down to it from the blue sphere/By one recitation of the Qur'ān
> The noise of prayer beads within the cupola/has reached beyond the nine vaults of the sky
> Whomever has *sa`ādat* [fortune] as his guide/will eagerly prostrate at its door.[85]

What is particularly fascinating about this poem is that the fourth distich—the notion that prosperity and fortune (*sa`ādat*) are reserved for those who attend this mosque—is indeed extra-textual and was added by the Safavid *munshī* using the device of *iltizām* (amalgamating old verse with new *baits*) to qualify Amīr Khusrau's original poem. *Sa`ādat* here alluded to Ṭahmāsp's own ceremonial complex in Sa`databad and the elaborate Masjid-i Shāh therein. This combined with the fact that "shah" was inserted by the *munshī* as a descriptor in Amir Khusrau's first distich, so that we read *masjid-i shāh* instead of simply *masjid*, means that the *munshī* was manipulating parts of this letter in an attempt to self-reference his own patron and liege. This text was deliberately profiled to highlight Ṭahmāsp's own restoration and elevation of Qazvīn as an imperial and religious centre. While one level of interpretation suggests an obsequious, non-confrontational tenor to this letter, subtle rearrangements and realignments within the text reveal an anticipated rivalry and sense of imperial competition. Thus, this letter and others like it can be understood as competitive, rhetorical texts in which meaning, audience, and delivery were not necessarily the domain of either the addressee or the author. This reaffirms the contention that audiences for such texts were often multi-situated, whereby *munsha'āt* material was often produced and distributed in the "home" chancellery and court before being copied in *inshā* manuals and collections for posterity and the education of future generations of Safavid scribes.

An interesting episode that brought together the Safavid chancellery with Shi`ite conversion and proselytism occurred in Jumāda I 967/February 1560 when `Īsā Khān, a crown prince from one of the Georgian principalities and son of the ruler Lavand (Lū'and) Khān, arrived at the shah's camp based at Qil`ah-yi Almūtash. He apparently came of his own volition in search of Safavid sponsorship but set things astir with his formal gift presentation of a "cross and a painting of Jesus" (*kāj va ṣūrat-i but*).[86] `Īsā Khān was exalted as a son by Ṭahmāsp during the court ceremony and placed in the "old palace" (*daulat-khānah-yi qādīm*) along with Prince Bāyazīd, the refugee Ottoman prince who was seeking asylum with the Safavids (to be discussed shortly).[87] Qāḍī Aḥmad discusses this development and mentions how central chancellery *munshīs* were ordered to write a letter to Sulṭān Ibrāhīm in Mashhad and narrate this auspicious event. The epistolary text in question begins by listing the various addressees in Mashhad other than Sulṭān Mīrzā Ibrāhīm, Qanbar Beg Ustājlū, Sulaimān Beg Zū al-Qadar, and Aḥmad Beg Afshār, but the introduction is dominated less by political matters and more by eschatological concerns.

The *munshī* announces the good news regarding the imminent appearance of the Twelfth Imām who is the "seal of the pious Imāms" and "the redresser of wrongs against the family of Muḥammad."[88] His emergence from Occultation will be "rising of the lights" (*ṭulū`-i anvār*) in "all corners of the earth" (*dar aṭrāf va aknāf-i `ālam*), and the explosion of light from the Imām will be such that "all vestiges of the oppression of idolatry and wickedness will be annihilated and dispersed from the pages of the world."[89] The *munshī* introduces `Īsā

Khān, how he had arrived at the court of Shāh Ṭahmāsp, and his decision to place himself under the shadow of the Safavid shah on account of the display of purity and trust. Consistent with the saying, "all which is born according to its nature" (*kullu maulūdin yūladu `alā al-fiṭrahu*), the young prince turned away from Christianity and dedicated himself to Islam.

This episode of conversion is presented as a cumulative miracle, whereby the young prince—in Georgia and surrounded by Christian preachers—had once heard the words, "Invite all to the way of your God with wisdom and beautiful preaching" (16: 125). These verses were translated from Arabic, and he was inspired to hear "fortune" (*daulat*) and "felicity" (*iqbāl*) in his own language. He later heard verses again, telling him to turn towards the throne of God, but when he arrived at the Safavid court (*daulat-i majlis*) and heard the auspicious speech of Ṭahmāsp (*sa`ādat-i suḥbat-i humāyūn*), he was overcome. The letter reminds its Mashhadī audience that his conversion is the same day and month as when `Alī inflicted his great victory over Aisha at the Battle of the Camel (36/656), and it coincides with the birthday of the fourth Imām, Zain al-`Ābidīn, (38/659). To celebrate, twenty reciters were invited to the Safavid court who would recite to the newly converted `Īsā Khān various sayings, including: "His ancestors are Jews and Christians" (*abawāhu yahūdānahu wa naṣrānahu*); "[blasphemers say] 'God is one of three in a Trinity'" (5: 73); and the *shahāda*: "Know that there is no god but God."[90] On account of his conversion, the letter to Mashhad continues to narrate, `Īsā Khān was exalted by Shāh Ṭahmāsp as one of his own sons, and "his rank was not unlike the rank of his Excellency, our Prophet `Īsā, may peace be upon him." Now styled as *khān*, `Īsā Khān was given the *ulkā* of Shakkī and various dependencies in the form of a *tīyūl*.[91] Numerous kindnesses and favours were conferred on the young prince by Ṭahmāsp. In order to ensure a foundational education for this new Safavid client, the shah would endeavour to educate him so that "works from pages from the books of historians [would] become the guidelines of sultans" (*āsār az ṣaḥāyif-i kutub-i muvarrikhān-i dastūr al-`amal-i salāṭīn*).[92]

This epistolary narrative of `Īsā Khān's conversion and nomination as *khān* within the Safavid state is interesting for a number of reasons. First, it underscores the Safavid strategy of assimilating local and regional rulers along the periphery through alternate strategies of negotiation and incorporation. Second, we learn that high-profile converts such as `Īsā Khān were furnished with the requisite texts for their new tenures as semi-autonomous governors and rulers within a Perso-Islamic Shi`ite state. Last, in addition to emphasizing and celebrating the miraculous nature of `Īsā Khān's conversion, this letter to Sulṭān Mīrzā Ibrāhīm and his coteries was also pointedly eschatological and millenarian in its prefatory remarks about the Mahdī. Why, the question presents itself, would the central chancellery be so committed to sending a Shi`ite-framed text to Sulṭān Ibrāhīm that narrated `Īsā Khān's conversion and his elevation as one of Ṭahmāsp's sons? Given our earlier characterization of Ibrāhīm's court as a relative sanctuary for artists, calligraphers, poets, and administrators, perhaps this particular epistolary text was designed as an admonition to Mīrzā Ibrāhīm—by then twenty years of age—to forgo his passion for music, dancing, painting, and poetry and to emulate the piety and zealotry of his metaphorical brother in the Caucasus.[93] We know that he had been enjoined to enforce religious edicts in Mashhad by his uncle when he was first posted to Khurāsān four years earlier.[94]

The suggestion that Shāh Ṭahmāsp looked to his own official chancellery as a vehicle by which he could reify and profile his political and familial relationship with the Divine is borne out by a unique *farmān* (decree), which was produced and disseminated in Safavid Iran in the summer of 972/1565.[95] Interestingly, the text of this *farmān* was inscribed by a well-known calligrapher, Ustād `Alā al-Dīn Muḥammad Tabrīzī, on the wall of the Jāmi`-i Masjid in Tabrīz.[96] Indeed, some *farmāns* of import regarding local taxes and the like were inscribed on mosques and other public buildings.[97] This *farmān* discusses Shāh Ṭahmāsp's abrogation of certain taxes and appears to be a confirmation of an earlier *la`nat nāmah*, or "cursing text," which had called for God's punishment on all those who transgressed the command of the shah.[98] The uniqueness of this document lies in its hybridity. While ostensibly a decree regarding the abolition of extraordinary taxes, this sui generis text and its narrative style also borrow strongly from hagiographical and eschatological traditions and as such exemplify the degree to which the Safavid chancellery could operate within a framework of `Alid piety.

The text begins by showcasing the piety and religious dedication of Shāh Ṭahmāsp. While he is the "star of the army" (*satārah-yi sipāh*), he is also the "dust at the threshold of `Alī" (*khāk-i āstānah-yi khair al-bashar*), and this last *alqāb* in fact refers to part of the cursing formula—"`Alī is the best of all mankind"—used by Safavid *tabarrā'iyān*.[99] Continuing this urban dynamic and introducing a monetary motif, Ṭahmāsp is also presented as "he who promotes the *mazhab* of the Twelve Imāms" (*murauvij-i mazhab-i a'imma ithnā `asharī*).[100] The *farmān* adopts a first-person narrative stance and relates how Shāh Ṭahmāsp had a pious dream where the Twelfth Imām, Muḥammad al-Mahdī, appeared to him on 12 Sha`bān 972/15 March 1565. After a fairly detailed description of his appearance—tall, foreboding, beautiful countenance, attractive moustache and beard, impressive eyebrows, red turban, embroidered white robe, yellow shoes[101]—the *farmān* narrates a conversation between the Safavid ruler and the Twelfth Imām in which *tamghā-hā* (non-canonical taxes dating back to the Mongol period) are castigated, and Shāh Ṭahmāsp accedes to the Mahdi's command that remaining supraobligatory taxes (*tatimmat-i tamghā-hā*) should indeed be cancelled. Convinced of Ṭahmāsp's dedication to this matter, the Twelfth Imām promptly disappears (*ān ḥaḍrat ghā'ib shudand*).

The *farmān* in turn declares that the Twelfth Imām commanded the cessation of the collection of these supplemental taxes throughout the kingdom, including Āzarbāijān, `Irāq, Fārs, Khurāsān, Shīrvān, and Gīlān.[102] The governor and notables of Tabrīz are dedicated to the enforcement of this *La`nat nāmah*, and anyone who transgresses these orders will be punished; those who agree to it publicly and then ignore it will be especially penalized. This document, admittedly fascinating in its profiling of an eschatological figure such as the Hidden Imām for the good of civil service, is likewise compelling in its characterization as a public *la`nat nāmah*. The notoriety of the inscription in the Jāmi`-i Masjid and its tale of the saintly visitation became significant enough in the Safavid public discourse that the historian Būdāq Munshī discusses this occult episode and its subsequent documentation.[103]

This document and its dissemination highlight the degree to which chancellery material was increasingly influenced by a newly empowered hierocratic class of sayyids. Indeed, their aspiration to regulate and monitor public piety during this period is particularly manifest in a 1567 decree (*manshūr*) to Khān Aḥmad Khān of Gīlān. With Ṭahmāsp's blessing, Khān Aḥmad had been ruler of Gīlān since the late 1530s; however, his rule was diluted in the 1560s when the Safavid shah placed his own grandson, Jamshīd Khān, as governor of Pīapas. Khān Aḥmad Khān rebelled against the Safavid state and had executed Ṭahmāsp's envoy and intermediary Yūl Qulī Beg Zū al-Qadar.[104] This *manshūr*, an admonition and warning to Khān Aḥmad, was written and despatched on 27 Ṣafar 975/1 September 1567 in the hope of avoiding a formal Safavid invasion. Inspired by Muḥammad, `Alī, and the Twelve Imāms, the Safavids had founded their empire on the statutes of faith and state (*umūr-i dīn va dunyā*), and on the basis of these statutes "no mighty lord has shone brighter than the auspicious light of this fortunate [state]."[105] Several lines of poetry in honour of `Alī and the Twelfth Imām are included before the *munshī* introduces the main text (*matn*) of the *manshūr*.[106]

Ṭahmāsp provides a short narrative of Khān Aḥmad's incumbency in Gīlān, lamenting the past, when taxes were remitted regularly and Ja`farī Shi`ism was propogated with energy.[107] It is clear, Ṭahmāsp's *manshūr* reads, that Khān Aḥmad had started fraternizing with troublemakers (*ajāmirah*), ruffians (*aubāsh*), and wretched ones (*ajlāf*). The Safavid shah, motivated by the spirit of 16: 125—"Invite all to the way of your God with wisdom and beautiful preaching"—had counselled and informed him of his erroneous ways but with little success. Khān Aḥmad had been "seduced by a group of heretics like the youths who constantly play and jest."[108] Interestingly, the *manshūr* enumerates the various classes of people and professions allegedly encouraged by Khān Aḥmad. An informal taxonomy emerges of regulations and statutes against the *personae non gratae* in a model Shi`ite Safavid society: balladeer (*ṣarf-gūyanda*), innovators (*sāzanda*), street performers (*ma`rakah-gīr*), wrestlers (*kushtī-gīr*), athletes (*zūr-gar*), dancers (*raqqāṣ*), antinomian Sufis (*qalandar*), fencers (*shamshīr-bāz*), cockfighters (*khurūs-bāz*), ram-baiters (*qūch-bāz*), ox-baiters (*gāv-bāz*), wolf-baiters (*gurg-bāz*), illusionists (*ḥuqqah-bāz*), conjurors (*shu`bada-bāz*), gypsies (*shāṭirān*), minstrels (*muṭribān*), professional storytellers (*qiṣṣah-khvānān*), as well as as catamites (*ḥīzān*), clowns (*maskhari-gān*), and infidels (*muliḥidān*).[109]

In narrating the arrival and killing of Yūl Qulī Beg Zū al-Qadar, the *munshī* relates how Khān Aḥmad's army, consisting of jackals (*shughālān*) and foxes (*rūbāhān*), had cut off the Safavid envoy's head and sent it along with this *bait* of poetry:

> When the gnat goes up, he defeats the elephant with all his ferocity and speed
> And the ants which are allied together, then they can tear away the skin of the wild lion.[110]

While the zoological motif is interesting, perhaps more noteworthy is that a very similar poem had been cited in the 1506 *fatḥ nāmah* of Shāh Ismā`īl to Sulṭān Ḥusain Bāiqarā while narrating his defeat of Ḥusain Kiyā Chulāvī.[111] Ḥusain Kiyā Chulāvī, one of the Kār Kiyās who had based himself in the region of Rayy, had rebelled against Safavid rule and was ultimately defeated after a lengthy siege of his mountain citadel at Astā. It is entirely possible that Khān Aḥmad Khān, himself a scion of the Kār Kiyā family, had seen or heard of Ismā`īl's *fatḥ nāmah* and seized upon this as an opportunity to avenge the brutalities inflicted on his kinsman a half-century earlier by referencing the same poem cited by Ismā`īl's chancellery.

The *manshūr* likewise suggests that the aforementioned tasteless pursuits had insinuated themselves into the upper echelons of Khān Aḥmad's court, pointing out how the *ṣadr* of Gīlān, one Mullā `Abd al-Razzāq, was practising fraud and gambling (*sāz va qamār*) in his very own mosque. The *manshūr* admonishes, "These and other practices which are contrary to Islamic Shari`ah can be found everywhere in [your] kingdom."[112] The *farmān* continues by insisting on proper religious behaviour and sustained submission to the Safavid state; nonetheless, Ṭahmāsp writes that he is prepared to forgive him, and again will bring him in alignment with the Sufis, literally: "the path of those who practice hidden arts" (*silk-i manẓūrān-i nazar-i kīmīyā āsār*), which is like the other "road of those exalted sayyids of the state" (*ṭarīq-i sā'ir-i sādāt `alā darajāt-i mamālik-i maḥrūsah*).[113] In the same way that these sayyids are given *suyūrghāl*s for the propagation of the faith in places such as `Irāq, Khurāsān, Fārs, and Kirmān, likewise it is decreed that Khān Aḥmad will receive a *suyūrghāl* of 100-150-200 *tūmān*s as a salary. If Khān Aḥmad insists on defying these commands and orders, he should know that a Safavid army will arrive to apprehend him in the spirit of 17: 81: "And say: 'Truth has now arrived, and falsehood has perished, for falsehood is bound to perish.'"[114]

Khān Aḥmad did little to heed these warnings, and the situation in Gīlān deteriorated sufficiently that Ṭahmāsp ordered a formal invasion and occupation. Khān Aḥmad's forces were defeated, and the Gīlānī ruler was arrested and imprisoned in the Qahqaha fortress along with Mīrzā Ismā`īl.[115] Ṭahmāsp's 1567 *manshūr* to Khān Aḥmad sheds light on a number of important issues, not the least of which is the issue of how state-sponsored Ja`farī Shi`ism was still in a transitional stage in regions like Gīlān until the late 1560s. What is particularly noteworthy is how we see the Safavid imperial chancellery representing far more than the imperial, administrative interests of the Safavid throne. According to the *dār al-inshā*, Khān Aḥmad's program of autonomy was clearly rooted in irreligious behaviour and his fraternization with individuals and groups who were anathema to the Safavid religious elite. The text avoids any discussion of the historical sovereignty of the Kār Kiyā dynasty in Gīlān and the sponsorship of Shāh Ismā`īl during his Occultation. Neither do we see any reference to roughly four decades of provincial resistance on the part of the Gīlānīs.

Perhaps uncomfortable with confronting the Kār Kiyās on the basis of imperial sovereignty, the Safavid *munshī*s focus on the perceived societal contagions—gambling, homosexuality, blood-sports—that result from improper religious standards. The allegations and charges of these conservative *munshī*s are thus consistent with centuries of polemical literature produced by elite Sunni society about Sufis, Shi`ites, and other heretical threats. Kathryn Babayan noted how Ṭahmāsp's spiritual repentances and their censure of antinomian behaviour, such as wine-drinking, dancing, singing, and fraternization, were part of the general anti-Sufi tone and tenor of the Safavid court in the mid-sixteenth century.[116] As such, this decree and other epistolary material produced after 1557 are ironic testimonies to the rise of the sayyid class, the importation of scholastic jurists from the Arab lands, and the reorientation of the Safavid court towards the policing and enforcing of Ja`farī Shi`ism in Iran and outlying areas. The momentum that dictated the shah's public repentance in 1556 had been clearly sustained. Twelve years later, `Abdī Beg Shīrāzī describes how the shah sent out orders (*aḥkām-i muṭā`ah*) to the *`ulāma* that they were to organize compulsory "sessions of sermonizing" (*majālis-i va`ẓ*) throughout the kingdom; indeed, everyone was to know that attendance at these sessions would be mandatory.[117] The chancellery and its production of epistolary and documentary material—for external and internal audiences—were clearly a reflection of these impulses and imperatives in the Safavid state after 962/1555.

Solomonic Tropes

While the previous developments are important, there were two historical events between 1555 and 1576 that profoundly influenced the Safavid chancellery and its production of *inshā* texts. The first was the fraternal civil war of 966/1559 in the Ottoman empire between Sulaimān and his son Bāyazīd, as well as Ṭahmāsp's subsequent decision to provide safe haven for the dissenting prince. The second was the death of the greatest Ottoman sultan ever known and the accession of his son Salīm II in 974/1566. These events dictated a level and scope of diplomatic and chancellery activity that were unparalleled for the Safavid empire. Between Bāyazīd's initial mortification by his brother Salīm at the Battle of Konya and his execution two years later, nine letters—written in Persian, Ottoman Turkish, and Arabic—were despatched by the Safavid chancellery to various Ottoman personalities, including Sulṭān Sulaimān, Prince Bāyazīd, and Prince Salīm. In no other period of Safavid diplomatic history can such an intense and lively production of chancellery material be found for such a short period of time.

With respect to the death of Sulaimān five years later, the formal *ta`ziyyah nāmah* (condolence letter) despatched by Ṭahmāsp's *dār al-inshā* is easily the longest letter ever produced by the Safavid chancellery. It allegedly took eight months to complete, boasts over eleven hundred lines of verse, and contemporaries measured the length of the manuscript at 70 cubits (more than 100 feet).[118] This embassy, consisting of three hundred twenty notables and four hundred merchants, also presented the matchless *Shāh nāmah-yi Shāh Ṭahmāsp* (a.k.a. *Houghton Shāh nāmah*), as well as illuminated Qur'āns, carpets, brocaded cloths and silks, various jewelled baubles, and thousands of horses, camels, and donkeys. Safavid and Ottoman sources alike describe the singularity of this Safavid mission to officially mourn the departure of Sulaimān.[119] This was the largest and most ambitious entourage ever assembled by the Safavid court, and the accompanying letter reflected a new scope of imperial pretension and grandiosity.

Before we examine the details of these diplomatic and chancellery developments, one consistent feature of correspondence produced in the 1560s requires elaboration here: the historical exemplar of King Solomon. Evoked constantly in rhymed prose and profiled frequently in verse, Solomon is without a doubt the dominant iconographic personality in epistolary prose; although Alexander, Darius, Khusrau, and Jamshīd certainly merit invocation. Motifs, images, and references to Solomon abound in these texts, and we find therein a religio-cultural familiarity and textual dexterity among the Safavid *munshīs*. Of course, such tendencies in epistolary texts regarding the onomastic relationship between this ancient prophet and the Ottoman sultan are not altogether surprising. There are features, some subtle, others less so, that suggest Shāh Ṭahmāsp and his *munshīs* also understood Solomon as a powerful icon of Safavid sovereignty. In this way, the onomastic proximity between the Ottoman sultan and Solomon afforded the Safavid chancellery the opportunity to introduce a supplementary body of evocative tropes and devices to buttress and profile Shāh Ṭahmāsp as the perfect sovereign ruler who enjoyed a divine mandate to rule on earth.

Why we would encounter Solomon as such a powerful rhetorical apotheosis in Safavid epistolary texts is an interesting question. Many scholars have noted how Solomon enjoyed notable prestige in medieval Iran and Perso-Islamic traditions. While the Qur'ān, hadiths, and medieval Prophetic narratives (*qiṣāṣ al-anbiyā*) formed the basis for the popularity of such Near Eastern figures as Noah (Nūḥ), Joseph (Yūsuf), Jonah (Yūnus), and Ṣāliḥ, there is little mistaking that Solomon was accorded a unique status within Iranian culture. In addition to being a paragon of wisdom and mystical knowledge, Solomon was popularly acknowledged for his municipal patronage of gardens and construction of palatial complexes. Likewise, his instant creation and ornamentation of his own throne has connected Solomon with intricate craftsmanship, alchemy, gemology, and mining.[120] In Islamic lore, Solomon is named as the principal builder of the

Temple at the Dome of the Rock, the Baalbek Temple of Jupiter, and a palace in Alexandria; however, his connection to Persepolis and Takht-i Jamshīd is what interests us here.

With respect to medieval Iranian perceptions, we know that the philosopher Jalāl al-Dīn Muḥammad al-Davvānī wrote an account (*arḍ nāmah*) of a military parade by the governor of Fārs, Sulṭān Khalil, to the ruins of the Achaemenian complex in 881/1476. In this account, he relates how Persepolis was built in the time of mythical King Jamshīd but comments that Jamshīd was often understood to be the master-builder himself, King Solomon. We read how "he had caused a golden throne, studded with shining jewels, to be placed on the columns and sat on it in state."[121] While Fārs was associated as "Solomon's kingdom" by al-Davvānī, this in fact had been the rhetorical norm since Saljuq times.[122] Priscilla Soucek has qualified this phenomenon in her own treatments of Islamic Solomonic traditions, pointing out that Iranian literary traditions conflated Jamshīd and Solomon to the degree that "the two appear to be different aspects of the same persona."[123] In Melikian-Chirvani's analysis of thirteenth- and fifteenth-century inscriptions at Pasargadae and Persepolis, we find consistent invocations of King Solomon/Jamshīd as an exemplary ruler and leader in Iran.[124] These in turn can be combined with the popularizing of the Pasargadade complex as Takht-i Sulaimān and the circulated myth that Cyrus's mausoleum was in fact the tomb of Solomon's mother. The Mongols likewise understood the legitimizing-conferring appeal of Solomon in Iran and turned to the pre-Islamic site of Takht-i Sulaimān near Sūghūrlūq as the location of their new summer palace in the fourteenth century.[125]

The iconographic status of Solomon as ruler, prophet, builder, and mystic continued into the Safavid period. In his analysis of Safavid frontispieces produced in Shīrāz in the sixteenth century, Serpil Bagçi introduces the compelling suggestion that both Solomon and Queen Sheba were popular personalities among Iranian, specifically Shīrāzī, atelier workmen, artists, painters, and calligraphers from the late fifteenth century until the 1600s.[126] Given the predominance of the Shīrāzī miniature tradition in the sixteenth century, it is reasonable to assume that such Solomonic tropes—specifically the relationship between Solomon and Queen Sheba (Bilqīs)—were disseminated at least partially across chancelleries and ateliers alike during the reign of Shāh Ṭahmāsp and Shāh Muḥammad Khudābandah. One of the more famous Islamic depictions of Queen Sheba, in which she reclines by a river as she reads a letter delivered by Solomon's Hoopoe bird, was produced by Safavid artists in Qazvīn in the late sixteenth century. In one of Ṭahmāsp's earlier letters to Sulaimān, as well as a later letter sent by Khudābandah to Murād III, scribes copied two "Solomonic" distichs from the fourteenth-century epigraphs engraved at Persepolis by Shaikh Abū Isḥāq ibn Maḥmūd Injū.[127] In his collection of panegyric poetry, Muḥtasham Kāshānī describes Pārī Khān Khānum, the daughter of Shāh Ṭahmāsp, as the "Bilqīs of the Age" and includes several references to Sheban lore in his poetry.[128] Similarly, `Abdī Beg Shīrāzī quotes a *qiṭ`ah* first penned by one *faqīr*

Jārī in commemoration of the death of Ṭahmāsp's sister, Shāhzādah Sulṭānum (Māhīn Banū), in 969/1562: "When Mahd, the Bilqīs of the Age, passed away/ she joined the throne of Solomon which flies in the air."[129] The Safavid historian Natanzī describes Shīrāz as *Dār al-Mulk-i Sulaimānī* and how "with perfect power and grandeur, the Solominic throne-place was illuminated with the *farr* of Farīdūn and the pomp of Jamshīd."[130] Similarly, during the early reign of Shāh `Abbās, Safavid engineers, builders, and artisans built the Bāgh-i Fīn in the city of Kāshān. The aesthetic centrepiece of this garden, a quadrilateral (*chahār-bāgh*) water/*qanāt* system, was named the Sulaimāniya, and this pool was widely recognized for its restorative powers. Popular lore tells us that the springs at Bāgh-i Fīn were first struck by King Solomon/Jamshīd, and it is likely that the Sulaimāniya pool was an acknowledgement by Safavid artistans of the popularity of the mystical and literary traditions about Solomon and his bath complex.[131] The appeal of this Solomonic narrative and its various permutations across the medieval Near East has resulted in some interesting palatial innovations since as early as the eighth century, and it is almost certain that the Bāgh-i Fīn is part of a greater architectural and aesthetic continuity, which extended into the Qājār period.[132] In the court panegyric poetry of `Abdī Beg Shīrāzī, specifically the *Zīnat al-avrāq*, we see an extensive verse description (*vaṣf*) of a public bath in Qazvīn wherein Solomon is invoked as the ultimate bathhouse builder.[133] `Abd al-Ṣamad Shīrāzī, who had served Ṭahmāsp as an artist and calligrapher before entering the service of Humāyūn, was commissioned along with his son Muḥammad Sharīf to paint the interior vaults of Jahāngīr's palace in Lahore. The paintings there show Solomon and his motley entourage of birds, demons, and animals in what is clearly a representation of his temporary fall from God's grace after losing his signet ring of sovereignty and power.[134]

There are also good reasons to explain why Solomonic tropes might have been popular especially in the Safavid chancellery during the period of Ṭahmāsp's second repentance. Solomon is unique in Islamic prophetography on account of his dual status as king and prophet. Qur'ānic references are numerous with respect to his status as one of the prophets (6: 84; 4: 163), while at the same time we find scriptural references to Solomon as a divinely mandated king who engaged in diplomacy, war, and arbitration (21: 78–82; 28: 30–33; 27: 15–44). These traditions, combined with widely circulated Prophetic narratives about Solomon as a master builder of cities, palaces, gardens, and pavilions as well as a designer of elaborate thrones, crowns, and other regal paraphernalia present Solomon as one of the most complex yet appealing historical exemplars in medieval Perso-Islamic discourse.[135] This hybridity is exactly what was most appealing to the Safavid poets and scribes working in Ṭahmāsp's chancellery. On the one hand, Solomon was a paradigmatic figure for the Persian intelligentsia that subscribed to a cosmography defined by Illuminationist theosophy, Nasirean political ethics, and pre-Islamic Persian monarchical classicism. His mastery over construction and architecture; his control of the wind to navigate his majestic throne; his miraculous command over birds, animals, and demons; and his magical restoration of his seal became topics of debate and inquiry among Persian scholars and poets.[136] It is no mistake that Farīd al-Dīn `Aṭṭār seized upon Solomon's Hoopoe as the perfect guide (*murshid*) for the other birds to find the divine Sīmurgh in his *Manṭiq al-ṭair* ("Conference of the Birds").[137] On the other hand, the status of Solomon as a *nabī* who enjoyed equal footing with Abraham, Ismā`īl, and Noah made him equally palatable as an exemplar for orthodox circles in Ṭahmāsp's court and chancellery. The twelfth-century Shi`ite scholar Shaikh Faḍl ibn Ḥasan Tabarsī (d. 548/1153) had also written extensively about Solomon and his throne in his popular and well-known Shi`ite Qur'ānic commentary, the *Majma` al-bayān*.[138] A Shi`ite tradition about the Sixth Imām Ja`far al-Ṣādiq corroborates Solomon's prestigious status as both ruler and prophet in the eyes of the Imamate: "I have the sword and standard of the Apostle of God, as well as his breast-plate, his armor and his helmet. Indeed, the victorious standard of the Apostle of God is with me, as are the tablets and rod of Moses. I have the ring of Solomon, and the tray on which Moses used to offer sacrifice."[139]

The formal encomium of *Sulaimān-makān* in prose and poetry was often used to lionize rulers by comparing their mandate of rule to how Solomon occupied both temporal and spiritual space. Such twinning of kingship and religion was the hallmark of Perso-Islamic political thought.[140] There is, indeed, precedence for such constructions as we see in the `Abbasid milieu with contemporaneous depictions of Hārūn al-Rashīd as an "Islamicized Solomon."[141] Thinkers like Abū al-Ḥasan al-`Āmirī al-Nīshāpūrī (d. 381/991) reiterated the fundamental importance of prophecy and kingship: "There is no authority in learning and wisdom higher than prophecy. There is no higher authority in power and majesty than kingship."[142]

With respect to the Safavid context, we have then an intriguing parallelism between Solomon and Ṭahmāsp wherein both are worldly, secular kings who also enjoy a certain degree of propinquity to the divine. While Ṭahmāsp did not rank himself as a prophet, he was often venerated for his status as a shaikh and *murshid-i kāmil,* while at the same time he actively claimed a genealogical connection to the Imamate through the Seventh Imām Mūsā al-Kāẓim. Ṭahmāsp, by virtue of this genealogy, shared a relationship with the divine, and indeed many anecdotes appear in his memoirs, which point to his conviction that he was a recipient of divine knowledge.[143] This notion of a "prophet-king" was known among Islamic theorists and philosophers. Louise Marlow has noted how medieval scholars like al-Ḥasan ibn Abd Allāh al-`Abbāsī, who wrote his *Āthār al-uwal fī tartīb al-duwal* under Mamluk patronage in the early fourteenth century, liked to invoke those ancient kings that were also prophets.[144] Looking at al-`Abbāsī and other mirrors-for-princes authors, Marlow gives reasonable proof to suggest that medieval scholarly perceptions of kingship and prophecy were "closely linked" while at the same time "clearly ranked" in the same broad conception of authority.[145] For Ṭahmāsp and his courtiers, focusing on a "prophet-king" like Solomon as the ideal exemplar was an innovative way of rationalizing the Safavid amalgam of traditional kingship (*salṭanat*) and saintly authority (*walāyat*) derived from the Shi`ite and Sufi traditions.

Our first group of relevant texts was produced in the context of the Bāyazīd episode of 1559–61. The period leading up to this catastrophe was indeed troubling for the Ottoman royal household: Prince Muṣṭafā was executed in Shawwāl 960/October 1553, and Sulaimān's favourite wife, the famous Ukrainian-born Hurrem, passed away in Jumāda II 965/April 1558.[146] Salīm and Bāyazīd started to jockey ruthlessly against one another for sultanic preference and political advantage. Bāyazīd began fostering relationships with timariots, sharecroppers, and tribesmen who were alienated by and angry with Ottoman centralization policies and soaring price inflation across Anatolia.[147] In the spring of 966/1559, a motley army of twenty thousand marginalized Ottoman soldiers and peasants marched towards Salīm's bailiwick of Konya, but by this time Salīm had already adopted the role of dutiful son and had been guaranteed financial and military support by Sulaimān.[148] The fraternal civil war began and largely concluded in Rajab 966/May 1559, when Salīm emerged as the victor after a two-day battle near Konya. With family, retinue, and army in tow, Bāyazīd fled to the east while fighting a rearguard action against a pursuing Ottoman force. In Shawwāl 960/August 1559, the Safavid governor of Yerevan received news that "several tents had alighted" in the nearby region of Sa`d-Chukhūr.[149] Leading a small retinue of Ottoman personalities, Bāyazīd presented himself formally to Shāh Qulī Sulṭān Ustājlū and requested asylum in Safavid dominion.[150]

Bāyazīd formally entered the Safavid capital on 21 Muḥarram 967/23 October 1569, and his arrival was certainly reminiscent of Humāyūn's regal entrance into Herāt twenty-five years earlier. Streets, alleys, markets, shops, and various buildings were decorated lavishly, while sayyids, *naqībs* (headmen), *sharīfs* (noble ones), *bazārīs*, and guildsmen were organized for the reception. Shāh Ṭahmāsp's *vakīl* (plenipotentiary) Ma`ṣūm Beg Ṣafavī, as well as Sayyid Beg Kamūna, Sundūq Beg (the chief of the cavalry), and the seal keeper (*muhrdār*) `Alī Qulī Khalīfa met the Ottoman retinue outside the city environs and escorted it to the royal palatial gardens of Sa`ādatābād amid cheering and adulation from "massive crowds and throngs of people."[151] According to the *Tārīkh-i jahān-ārā,* these festivities lasted several days, and Ṭahmāsp concluded the formal reception by presenting Bāyazīd with 2,000 *tūmān*s in coins and kind (*dū hizār naqd va jins*). These were heaped on him by the crowd in a "huge tumult," but there was very little from the prince in the way of a friendly response.[152] As Iskander Beg Munshī noted, "The shah was prodigal in his royal favours [towards Bāyazīd]."[153] When exactly Shāh Ṭahmāsp decided to officially disband Bāyazīd's militia is unclear, but within months of the Ottoman prince's arrival, these forces had been dispersed. Qāḍī Aḥmad al-Qummī writes that hundreds were sent to Mashhad in the service of Ṭahmāsp's son, Ibrāhīm Mīrzā, while others found themselves in Qandahār.[154]

Bāyazīd was conveyed to the royal palace for safekeeping, and it had become clear that Ṭahmāsp no longer recognized Bāyazīd's claim to the Ottoman sultanate.[155] For the remaining year and a half, embassies would continue to journey back and forth between Istanbul and Qazvīn, and Sulaimān's patience with Ṭahmāsp regarding Bāyazīd's transfer to Ottoman control wore thin. On 14 Zū al-Qi`da 969/16 July 1562, the last of a series of Ottoman embassies arrived in Qazvīn, which was charged with the formal task of conveying the fugitive Prince Bāyazīd back to Istanbul. This entourage included Khusrau Pāshā (the governor of Vān), Sinān Pāshā, `Alī Āqā Chāvush Bāshī, and a retinue of two hundred individuals. In the accompanying letter, Sulaimān declared his readiness to renew the Treaty of Amāsya and begin a new era of Ottoman-Safavid relations.[156] Bāyazīd and his four sons were handed over to the Ottoman delegation, which then proceeded to the environs of Qazvīn. They promptly alighted and `Alī Āqā, a servant of Salīm, garrotted Bāyazīd and his four sons: Ūr Khān, Sulṭān Muḥammad, Sulṭān Maḥmūd, and Sulṭān `Abd Allāh.[157] A chronogram signalling this year, 969, is recorded in every single Safavid chronicle: "Five fewer Ottomans!"[158] Salīm ascended to the Ottoman throne unopposed four years later, and, as promised, honoured the Treaty of Amāsya until his own premature death in Sha`bān 982/December 1574.

During this diplomatic incident of 1559–61, a number of letters—twenty-one, to be precise—were exchanged between the Ottoman and Safavid chancelleries. The focus here will be on three particular letters: the first formal petition to Sulaimān from Ṭahmāsp on behalf of Bāyazīd, a response letter to Prince Salīm in the midst of the crisis, and a postmortem letter to Sulaimān lamenting the unfortunate turn of events in 969/1561. The preamble in each of these epistolary texts is framed by poetry or rhymed prose to hail the arrival of an august letter attached to the wing of a likewise auspicious bird. For instance, in Ṭahmāsp's 1559 petition to Sulaimān, the text begins with a *saj`* evoking the arrival of "the gold-winged bird of fortune" (*humā-yi zarrīn bāl-i humāyūn fāl*), "the musky-winged bird of dignity and glory" (*`anqā-yi mushkīn janāḥ-i `izzat va ijlāl*).[159] A similar device is used in a letter to Bāyazīd's brother, Prince Salīm, which was written by the Safavid *munshī al-mamālik* Mīrzā Kāfī Urdūbādī. Here, Mīrzā Kāfī begins with the *bait*: "The Hoopoe bird has come with *farr* and a dignified crown on his head/a letter of fortune and augustness tied to its wing."[160] In another letter sent to Sulaimān shortly after the unhappy end of the Bāyazīd episode, an introductory poem begins with "O! Happiness at the arrival of a bird of fortune/ Who has arrived from the sphere of power and grandeur.... Attached to his wing is a musky letter/An odiferous letter like a musk-bladder from China."[161] This metaphor of an auspicious bird bearing a royal epistle is clearly derived from the Qur'ānic tradition regarding Solomon and Sheba (Bilqīs).[162] This Qur'ānic tradition was elaborated considerably by the Prophetic stories that circulated the Near and Middle East in the classical and medieval periods.[163]

The Safavid *munshīs* elaborate on this particular allegory with some intensity. The first of our triad of letters discusses how the gold-winged bird (*humā-yi zarrīn bāl*) had descended from the "roomy sky of sultanic grace" (*az havā-yi faḍā-yi `āṭifat-i sulṭānī*) and the "tip of Mount Qāf which is the peak of Solomonic grandeur and power" (*qullah-yi Qāf-i shukūh va shaukat-i Sulaimānī*).[164] Likewise, we see the poem in the third letter describe how this royal bird (*ṭā'ir-i humāyūn*) came from "the sultanic court, the square of Solomonic imperium" (*ya`nī az bārgāh-i sulṭānī/sāḥat-i shaukat-i Sulaimānī*).[165] Of the three letters under review here, the third epistolary text is the most consistent in its use of and references to a wide range of Solomonic tropes and traditions. It continues to use Solomon as the exemplar in its poetic and prose honorifics, and a *maṡnavī* begins with the *bait*: "A king like Solomon has arrived/all of the earth is under his rule." Again, we find sustained references to this king-prophet in connection with palatial space and imperium: "The sky above his parasol is his canopy (*sāyabānī*)/Saturn stands guard on the roof of his palace."[166] Later, we read how he is "a king who with good judgement and prudence/it is he who laid down the foundation of kingship/the ordinances of Alexander are his craft/his bright innerself is a mirror."[167] After the very first poetic preamble, the Safavid *munshī* comments how these are miraculous times whereby the curtain of occultation (*tutuq-i ghaib*) has been drawn back from the bridal dais (*bar manṣah-i ẓuhūr jilwah namūd*). As a result, the beautiful face of the female object of desire—hitherto concealed in purdah—is now open. The letter continues to describe how the dewdrops of stability and hope blow in from the vent of sultanic munificence (*mahabb-i `āṭifat-i sulṭānī*) and flow in from the garden waterways of exalted Solomonic beneficence and mercy (*mauhibat va marḥamat-i a`lā haḍrat Sulaimānī*).[168] The latter image alludes clearly to the close connection in Islamic traditions regarding gardens, hydrography, and King Solomon, while the references to veiled, royal brides find their roots in the popularity of Queen Bilqīs in medieval Perso-Islamic culture. The phenomenon of the veil and Sheba seem to be intertwined at a semiotic level whereby Solomon is credited in some Islamic traditions as the first to introduce the royal canopy (*sayābān*) and the concept of prohibited quarters, or a harem, for privileged women. We can look to the near-contemporary Ḥusain Vā`iẓ Kāshifī and his ethico-religious treatise, the *Futuvvat-i nāmah-yi sulṭānī*, for further clarification on this. [169] The institution of *sarā-pardah* as well as the royal device of the courtly canopy have a Prophetic provenance. Kāshifī records how it was Solomon who devised the *sarā-pardah* and connects its appearance with when "Queen Bilqīs arrived, converted to Islam, and married King Solomon."[170] The invention of the canopy, itself a popular royal symbol from ancient Iran, is linked closely by Kāshifī to the Solomonic institution of the *sarā-pardah*.[171] After reiterating the unfortunate circumstances of Bāyazīd's fall from grace—but nonetheless affirming the survival of the Safavid-Ottoman peace—the letter concludes with an evocative *saj`*: "May the pleasant air of the spacious grounds of the Solomonic courtyard be kept pure and clear of the inauspicious dust of those who oppose us!"[172]

Solomon enjoyed a special distinction: medieval Perso-Islamic rulers and their courtly literati used oral traditions, miraculous Prophetic narratives, and poetic discourse to establish an indissoluble bond between this historical icon and Iran. Is it possible that the strong Solomonic dynamic in these letters was meant to address two different audiences on two different cognitive levels? In a more provocative sense, it is possible that Safavid *munshī*s used these epistolary texts to lay rhetorical claim to a powerful Judeo-Islamic icon that best represented the Safavid ideological program of investing secular and religious power in the institution of kingship? The consistency with which the Safavid *munshī*s frame the prologue of their own epistolary texts by invoking the tradition of Solomon despatching letters via the Hoopoe to the pagan Queen Bilqīs certainly points in this direction. Using the poetic devices of metonymy (*kināya*) and simile (*tashbīh*), the Safavid letter and its bearer become recreations of the Hoopoe and its delivery of Solomon's proselytizing missive. To follow the metaphor to its logical conclusion, Ṭahmāsp is understood here as King Solomon while Sulaimān is inverted rhetorically and assumes the role of Bilqīs, the pagan queen, rather than the role of his namesake.

Given that the Qur'ānic tale of Solomon and Bilqīs is essentially a tradition about diplomatic evangelism and conversion between two belligerent powers, its regular appearance here in correspondence from an established Shi`ite polity to a rival Sunni state is intriguing on doctrinal and soteriological grounds. Solomon's exhortation to the sun-worshipping Bilqīs to submit and adopt Islam was a topic of exegetical interest in medieval Islam, and various scholars have used this tradition in contemporary debates to justify a variety of theological positions.[173] While there are none of the same technical and sustained arguments in these Safavid letters, nonetheless Solomon's letter of admonition to the pagan Queen was understood as one of the first and most evocative conversions to the pre-eternal message of Islam prior to the lifetime of the Prophet Muḥammad. Its appearance here in such an oblique and veiled capacity underscores the rhetorical ability of the Safavid *munshī*s to operate on two very different levels of discourse.

The rhetorical metempsychosis of Solomon in the form of Ṭahmāsp and the ensuing corpus of symbols and motifs is best represented in the unparalleled *tahniyyah nāmah* (congratulatory letter), which was written and sent to Salīm II following the death of his father and his own accession to the Ottoman throne in 974/1566. This letter, included by Qāḍī Aḥmad al-Qummī in his *Khulāṣat al-tavārīkh* and numbering seventy printed pages, is an epistolary leviathan. After hearing of Sulaimān's death, Ṭahmāsp ordered that "all Tājīk functionaries, confidants, eloquent ones, and poets" be brought together for eight months to recite their verse and prose to the shah for possible inclusion into this monumental epistle.[174] It is no surprise that Qāḍī Aḥmad decided to include the entirety of the letter since he assembled the text, which included excerpts from a model *inshā* text (*nuskhah*) produced by his father, Mīr Munshī Qummī.[175] There is little doubt that this letter bears the imprint of individuals whose training and education were defined by an enduring notion of Perso-Islamic classicism tinged with a respect for mysticism. The staggering number of *ma̱snavī*s, *qaṣīdah*s, and *ghazal*s from a wide spectrum of classical poets (Ḥāfiẓ, Sa`dī, Jāmī, Niẓāmī) as well as contemporary, anonymous Safavid poets celebrating kingship, imperium, and statehood easily overwhelm the paucity of poetic elegies in honour of `Alī, Ḥusain, and the Twelve Imāms. All of the prose and most of the poetry is in Persian, while the chancellery chose to mollify the Ottomans by including the occasional excerpt of poetry in Turkish. Moreover, a large part of this letter (thirteen printed pages) consists of a versified account of Sulaimān's last campaign in Muḥarram 974/August 1566, when he besieged the town of Szigetvár in southern Hungary held by the Croatian *ban*, Nicola Zrinski.[176] This letter along with the *Shāh nāmah-yi Shāh Ṭahmāsp* were presented by Shāh Qulī Sulṭān Ustājlū to Salīm II at Edirne in Rajab 975/February 1568.[177] Other presented gifts included a copy of the Qur'ān allegedly copied by `Alī, a Badakshān ruby equal to the size of a pear, twenty large silk carpets, and extravagant textiles worth thousands of gold ducats.[178] The presentation of this unsurpassed *Shāh nāmah* reinforced clearly the profile of the Safavid ruler as a cultural patron par excellence to the young ascending sultan.[179]

The previously discussed Solomonic motifs are profiled boldly in this monumental diplomatic text. Before presenting the epistolary text itself, Qāḍī Aḥmad provides a brief introduction to the composition and mandate of the Safavid embassy under Shāh Qulī Sulṭān Ustājlū. With respect to the list of proffered gifts, Qāḍī Aḥmad makes no reference to the delivery of the celebrated *Shāh nāmah-yi Shāh Ṭahmāsp* or any of the other gifted items. He does, however, make specific mention of an elaborate canopy (*sayābān*) with images woven on the interior and adorned on the exterior by Qāḍī Kūchak Musharraf, a student of the calligraphic master Maulānā Mālik Dailamī.[180] This was evocative of the Prophetic tradition whereby Solomon proffered his own adorned *sayābān* to Bilqīs, and indeed the scribe chose to begin the letter with a suitable *ghazal* (no. 410) from Ḥāfiẓ.

> Although the sun of the sky is the light and the sight of the world,
> The dust under your feet is the illuminer of its sight
> Wherever the birds which make up your sky-high canopy cast a shade
> There becomes the landscape of the bird of happiness
> Of thousands of different laws of religion and wisdom
> Not a single point was lost from your learned heart.[181]

The introductory protocol of the letter is a seemingly never-ending tautology of praise and benediction, which makes repeated references to the exemplarity of Solomon (*Sulaimān-nishān*, *Sulaimān-makān*, *Sulaimān-nagīn*, *Sulaimān-zamān*, *waṣīyat-i ṣaulat-Sulaimān*, *Sulaimān-jāh*). We are given reason to suspect that the Safavid chancellery was using this epistolary text as a means of self-referencing the glory and grandeur of their own sovereign, Ṭahmāsp. From one perspective, it is difficult to accept that the Safavid chancellery would present such an effusive and lengthy proem—consisting of over two hundred fifty lines of poetry as well as large segments of rhymed prose—in recognition of a middle-aged sultan whose sole claim to fame prior to his enthronement had been the notorious murder of his brother and his family, not to mention two decades of sybaritism and licentiousness. Babayan has suggested that this diplomatic event and the gifting of the unsurpassed *Shāh nāmah-yi Shāh Ṭahmāsp* were an expression of Ṭahmāsp's paternalistic attitude towards Salim II.[182] This study would qualify her point by suggesting that the unbridled enthusiasm expressed for Salīm's accession might very well be understood better as a Safavid acknowledgement and celebration of a new era with Shāh Ṭahmāsp enjoying the status of pre-eminent ruler of the central Islamic world; in a sense, he was the *new* Sulaimān of the age. We read in the letter of the shah's great pleasure at hearing of Salīm's assumption of power and how "[Ṭahmāsp] had been waiting for a long time for this fortune [*sa`ādat*]."[183] This "indescribable happiness" spread throughout the Safavid court and was inscribed with the "double-tounged pen" (*qalam-i dū-zabān*) on the "*īvān* whose foundation is fortune" (*īvān-i sa`ādat-i bunyān*) and "the forty-pillared [palace of] Iram" (*chihil-sutūn-i Iram*). Colourful festivals and elaborate feasts were subsequently organized throughout Qazvīn, and a lengthy section describing these festivities appears in prose and poetry.[184]

This commemoration of divine absolutism and regal augustness is to such an extent that one cannot help but see this as a testimony to Safavid conceptions of legitimacy and ideology. Again we look to evidence of rhetorical devices for support. In one preamble, we read in prose that "he has the status of the emperor Jamshīd (Solomon) who is accompanied by augustness, [whose fortune] occupies the place of the Pleiades" (*pādshāh-i jam-jāh-i ṣāḥib-qirān-i sa`ādat-qarīn-i s̱uraiyyā-makān*).[185] The emphasis here and elsewhere regarding the proximity between the royal body and the personification of *sa`ādat*, or fortune, is no coincidence. Safavid *munshī*s focused or accented their prose and verse to highlight the term *sa`ādat* in recognition of Shāh Ṭahmāsp and his imperial garden-complex, Sa`ādatābād. We read how the exalted station of kingship is where the "royal falcon of fortune" (*shāhīn-i sa`ādat-qarīn*) flies,[186] while soon after the "addressee" is considered "the sultan of exalted fortune" (*sulṭān-i ṣāḥib-sa`ādat-i `ālā*).[187] In a later *mas̱navī* celebrating accessions and corroboration of divine kingship, we read:

> When the name of the king is struck on the gold coin/The gold received additional beauty because of his name
> The just king of kings who has a good opinion/he is filled with God's bounty from head to toe
> He is above all kings in his good fortune/Solomon gave the ring to him
> On account of God's favours, he is supported strongly/he wears the ring of fortune [*nagīn-i sa`ādat*] on his finger
> The goodness of fate is due to his fortune [*sa`ādat*]/Throne and crown are proud because of his fortune.

Later in the text, following an interminable *intitulatio* in both prose and poety and an equally drawn-out narration of the Battle of Szigetvár, the Safavid *munshīs* discuss the inauguration of a new age with the death of Sulaimān and the accession of Salīm II. They write how the "exalted Solomonic throne" (*masnad-i `ālā-yi Sulaimānī*) had been beautified by his auspicious arrival, while the "crown of dominion and kingship" (*afsar-i salṭanat va shāhriyār*) had been made pure and honourable.[188] The celebration of new imperium through Solomonic motifs continues in a short verse that describes, among other things, how "when he was placed on the throne of Solomon/the throne of power assumed a new type of beauty." The poem personifies the heavenly bodies and how they responded to his accession: "When the king sat on the throne, out of glory/and the heavens said: 'Congratulations! Be seated.'" Interestingly, the poem also includes a distich that describes how fortune (*sa`ādat*) took pains to congratulate the new ruler personally on his inheritance of power.[189] In a later lengthy encomium, ostensibly presented to Sulṭān Salīm, the Safavid letter reads how the "courtyard of the world was illuminated by the light of the appearing eternal fortune" (*sāḥat-i zamīn az nūr-i ẓuhūr-i daulat abad*), which is corroborated by 39: 69: "And the earth will shine with the light of its Lord."[190] This Qur'ānic verse and the preceding prose are borrowed from a corpus of Sufi-Shi`ite aphorisms and tropes, which had been cultivated in the chancellery to describe the miraculous nature of the Safavid shah and as such only reinforce the degree to which this diplomatic text was addressing two distinct audiences. The letter elaborates upon how this "state" enjoyed conspicuous divine sanction: "The angels [literally: *munshīyān-i `ālam-i bālā*] write out the decree of universal dominion [*manshūr-i salṭanat-i haft-kishvār*] in the sublime name of his sultanic Excellency, the shadow of God." Moreover, the caliphal fiat of the world (*nishān-i khilāfat-i rub`i maskūn*) has been exalted with the titulature (*alqāb*): "Humāyūn, his Excellency, shah of shahs, he who has the dignity of Alexander."[191]

These allusions, in turn, are reinforced by a number of unambiguous references to and descriptions of the paradisical qualities of Sa`ādatābād itself. The characterization here of the status, beauty, and significance of Ṭahmāsp's imperial centre by the Safavid *munshīs* also signal the transition of this epistolary text from coy allusion to blatant self-promotion. Ṭahmāsp's development of the Qazvīn complex is thus understood as a noble act, whereby "construction of the exalted buildings and the lofty, gilded palaces" elevated Sa`ādatābād to the ancient capital of Iram, "whose lofty pillars the like of which were not produced in all the land (89: 8)."[192] While many poetic references to Iram are also references to the paradisical gardens of Heaven, the allusion here is to a perceived historical space, the legendary ancient capital of King Shaddad and the tribe of `Ād in Yemen.[193] The imagery turns more paradisical as we read how the "sweet waters" (*jūy-hā-yi shīrīn*) and "sugary fruits" (*mīv-hā-yi shukrīn*) make Sa`ādatābād "representative of the gardens of Heaven" (*namūnah-yi rauḍat-i khuld-i barīn*). The *munshīs* discuss at length—primarily through verse—the abundant yield of the Sa`ādatābād gardens with respect to grapes, oranges, peaches, and other fruit. This productive capacity, however, allows a rhetorical fertility towards loftier comparisons: "What can I say about the garden of *Sa`ādat*?/*Sa`ādat* turns fortune towards me/It is adorned like the garden of Heaven/in it are fruits of every kind you may wish." The poem continues intermittently along these themes: "The water [of Sa`ādatābād] is made from the water of Khiḍr/when there is the water of Khiḍr the body's juices are ashamed in its presence," adding how "the taste of [those fruits], the pleasure provided by the sugary water/is like the water of Khiḍr which extends all life." Lastly, the scribe adds how, "You still have not brought it to your mouth/and it disappears on account of its delicateness/ And because this odiferous garden is like paradise/ its water is from the streams of Heaven."[194] The relationship between the mysterious Qur'ānic personality Khiḍr and miraculous water has been a favourite subject among Sufi commentators and poets. Based on the Qur'ānic/Prophetic traditions that relate how Moses and Joshua sought out the "confluence of the two oceans" (*majma` al-baḥrain*), Sufis are fond of opining on the relationship between Moses and the mysterious Khiḍr. Besides emerging as the perfect spiritual guide who is able to show a series of hidden meanings to the orthopraxic Prophet Moses, Khiḍr is also associated with the fountain of immortality (*mā al-ḥayāt*). This tradition is especially celebrated in the popular medieval genre of *Iskandar nāma*s, the epitome of which is the poetic work of Niẓāmī and his narrative of Alexander the Great meeting Khiḍr in his quest for the fountain of immortality.

Openly hailed as a second paradise (*bihisht-i s̱ānī*), Sa`ādatābād is lauded for much more than its seraphic setting, and we find its denizens cast in a distinctly eschatological light. In discussing the celebrations that resulted after hearing of Sulaimān's death and Salīm's accession, female singers (*mughanniyān*), minstrels (*muṭribān*), and rosy-cheeked ones with their light moustaches and moles (*gulrukhān ba khaṭṭ va khāl*) performed in "Sa`ādatābād which is equal to the rose-garden of Iram and the garden of Paradise" (*Sa`ādatābād ki namūnah-yi gulshan-i Iram va rauḍah-yi riḍwān*) and is also "similar to heavenly gardens and the flower gardens in the hereafter" (*mis̱ālī az riyāḍ-i firdaus va būstān-i jinnān ast*).[195] The soteriological implications of Ṭahmāsp's imperial garden indeed border on self-indulgence as we read, "In those paradisical fields, where the sun and moon meet, flasks of silver and goblets of gold are filled with liquor mixed with cloves and cinnamon" in commemoration of 76: 17: "And they will be given [in Heaven] a cup of wine mixed with Zanjabīl."[196] Similarly, the following poetry, despite working within a paradisical framework, instills a distinct sense of *bon vivre* in the Safavid court: "The moon-faced cup-bearers held/gilded porcelain decanters/The decanter was happy of its fortune/because the hands of the rosy-cheeked ones were on its neck/And the goblet's mouth has stayed open out of happiness/because it has kissed the lips of the coquettish ones."[197] The description of Sa`ādatābād in such opulent yet utopian terms is finished by the observation that "from every direction, the youthful ones who are like the servants of heaven—who have girded themselves with the belt of submission—carry porcelain dishes full of fruits [in accordance with 56: 32–33], 'and fruit in abundance whose season is not limited, nor its supply forbidden.'"[198]

The letter provides a lengthy verse description (*vaṣf*) of the environs of Sa`ādatābād and how the various walls, *īvāns*, and squares were constructed and ornamented. This is indeed reminiscent of `Abdī Beg Shīrāzī's use of his 1560 text, the *Jannat-i `Adan*, to provide an ekphrastic tour of the gardens of Sa`ādatābād in Qazvīn. We certainly can glean the centrality of this architectural refurbishing among the *adībs*, poets, artists, and chancellery officials of the day.[199] The first section of this poem discusses exclusively the work of craftsmen and jewellers.[200] Parts of this poem also allude to the presentation of the majestic *Shāh nāmah-yi Shāh Ṭahmāsp* and include a short adulatory narrative of its formation in the Safavid atelier. Herein, we read of the unrivalled status of their atelier in terms of Persian miniature production and the dedication of calligraphers and illuminators alike to the calligraphic and artistic traditions introduced and developed in the medieval period by Yāqūt al-Musta`ṣimī, Zarīn-Qalam, Bihzād, and Sulṭān `Alī Mashhadī.[201] Following the characterization of the artisans, the *munshīs* use verse to describe the singularity of the Safavid workshop (*dukkān*) and its mandate to produce the *Shāh nāmah* in the latter days of Shāh Ismā`īl's reign under the directorship of Bihzād.

> When the atelier of bookbinding was prepared/a great rise arose from the city
> The atelier is like a cypress in the garden/it is a new rose from a rose garden
> From that atelier—that good-natured cypress/the rose garden of paradise is ashamed
> What an atelier! Which was the envy of the abode of faeries/From the image [of the atelier], reason was stupefied
> This youth [i.e., book] sitting in the atelier/who is [such] an image that reason is perplexed by it
> The face of this youth [i.e., book] is so unique/that Bihzād went into a trance by its image
> When the dust of the down [on his lip] turns black [i.e., when his script is Written]/no one will care anymore about the calligraphy of Yāqūt
> In every ornament and beauty, in every way and manner/piled up a hundred sections [of the book]
> From the poems of the well-known Firdausī/who had done justice to the word in the age
> A *shāh nāmah* was proffered/ and his atelier was beautified by this gift
> It was gilded and illuminated most gloriously/it was bound with a hundred ornaments
> Its script was written by the master all over/its writing is illuminated like the light of the eye
> From the work of the pupils who have trained with Zarin-qalam/Each page had a design sketched on it
> One painting was done by Bihzād/But he departed and left behind regret

The organization and adornment [of this *Shāh nāmah*] was such that/reason and understanding were perplexed by it
The cover was jewel-studded like the celestial spheres/And it was on par with the moon in the sky
From the painting from the golden pen of Bihzād/who used to paint for kings
It was unique in this world/it was very much approved by the people of perfection
Many fragments of Khafī and great works/in the writing style of Yāqūt and Sulṭān `Alī
Were placed in the atelier of that beautiful youth [i.e., book]/All these writings—like the down of the beautiful ones—were life-consuming.[202]

The commissioning and arrangement of the *Shāh nāmah-yi Shāh Ṭahmāsp* had been conducted initially in Tabrīz under the stewardship of the prominent artist of the day, Sulṭān Muḥammad, while Bihzād was the director of the library-atelier and all its various projects after his arrival from Herāt in 928/1522. Fifteen painters and various teams of binders, calligraphers, illuminators, and paper-burnishers were dedicated to this project. Prominent artists who worked on this copy included Dūst Muḥammad, Mīr Muṣavvir, and Sulṭān Muḥammad. The Safavid *munshīs* also take pains to highlight Bihzād's involvement with this particular project and emphasize how this famous artist was himself amazed and stupefied by the final production. In particular, the reference above to "organization and adornment" (*tartīb va azyīn*) of the album were indeed key principles in a dizzying array of tasks associated with such projects. As Roxburgh noted, such "organizing" saw to "illumination, rulings, coloured grounds, the repair of damaged and abraded surfaces … the removal of interlinear strips of unused paper in calligraphies, the trimming, resizing, and reshaping of paintings, calligraphies and drawings."[203] Nonetheless, scholars concur that Bihzād contributed a number of illustrations to this commissioned copy and that he exerted a discernible influence on the prevalent Tabrīzī style of the day.[204]

The ensuing part of this poetic narrative—a discussion of how the Safavid elite responded to this majestic work—is interesting in that it parallels a number of contemporary texts, such as Dūst Muḥammad's preface to the Bahrām Mīrzā album, which commented on and analyzed the aesthetic link between medieval Iran and China by juxtaposing Bihzād and Mānī.[205] The poem also discusses the detail and ornamentation of various carpets, brocaded cloths, and silks; one notes the strong emphasis in this particular section on aesthetics, the exaltation of imagery and painting, as well as the profiling of artists such as Bihzād.[206]

The clear dearth of academic Shi`ite discourse and traditional `Alid elegies combined with the prevalence of motifs often associated with Timurid litterateurs situates this particular epistolary text squarely within the camp of the Persian bureaucratic elite. This is to some extent evident in the proffering of the reputed *Shāh nāmah,* which Babayan has interpreted as significant: "Beyond the artistic splendor of this generous gift, the choice of the text, the 'Epic of Kings,' is symbolic of the self-image Shah Tahmasp wished to transmit."[207] While we know that Qāḍī Aḥmad al-Qummī was the principal architect of this epistle, it is worth noting that this letter was an assembly of various poetic submissions from across a broad swath of "Tājīk" poets, rhetoricians, and scholars. In reviewing the formal *intitulatio* portion of this letter, whereby the invoking of Salīm II as the addressee is prefaced by extensive Perso-Arabic encomiums, we learn that the Safavid chancellery consulted the late Timurid chancellery manual par excellence, the *Makhzan al-inshā* by Ḥusain Vā`iẓ Kāshifī. When we read how "[he] is the refuge of the greatest of sultans in all quarters of the world" (*malādhu a`āẓimi al-salāṭīni fī al-āfāq*) as well as "the bearer of banners of clear victory, he who exalts the standards of honour" (*nāṣibu a`lāmi al-fatḥi al-mubīn, rāfi`u alwiyati al-`izzi wa al-tamkīn*), it is clear that these phrases were directly copied or slightly modified from exemplary phrases provided by al-Kāshifī in his section (ff. 27a–b) on "Qualities and Speeches for People of the Greatest Rank—Kings, Sultans and Caliphs" (*al-ṣifāt wa al-nuṭq lī-ahl al-ṭabaqa al-a`lā al-mulūk wa al-salāṭīn wa al-khulafā*).[208] This section of Kāshifī's appears to have been popular; the phrase, "He is the king [who] guards the people, master of the kings of Central Asia, `Irāq and Iran" (*māliku riqābi al-umami maulā mulūki al-turki wa al-`arabi wa al-`ajami*), is replicated in the same *intitulatio* by the Safavid scribes.[209] Likewise, the accolade of the ruler as "the defender of the kingdom of Islam, the effacer of the traces of infidelity" (*ḥāmī ḥauzati al-Islāmi, māḥī āthāri al-kufr*) is a nice rhetorical flourish—formally designated as a *muṭabaqa*, or antithesis, as the term *ḥāmī* (defender) is contraposed in meaning and spelling with *māḥī* (effacer)—which was extracted from fol. 38b of Kāshifī's manual.[210] The sponsorship by the Safavid stylists of such "classical" articulations as Kāshifī's of Perso-Islamic authority throughout this text, with a concomitant disavowal of overtly Shi`ite rhetoric, points to the indefatigability of the "men of the pen" when it came to articulating their vision of Safavid legitimacy.

The subject of the Amāsya Peace Treaty and its ratification by the new sultan is signalled by the phrase: "Thanks be to God that security and stability have arrived for the people of the region."[211] Interestingly, the epistolary text softens any pointed discussion of the Amāsya Treaty by steering the dialogue towards theosophical waters with an explication of how "friendship" and "love" in the corporeal world are understood as reflections of the pre-eternal love infused by God in humanity and all creatures. This is indeed signalled by the hadith, "spirits are like conscripted soldiers; those whom they recognize, they get along with, and those whom they do not recognize, they will not get along with."[212] Commentary in the letter states that this is understood (*mustafād mī shavad*) to mean physical relationships are derived from these preconceived spiritual orientations.[213] The Safavid scribes relate how "manifest love" (*muḥabbat-i ẓāhirī*) is thus a "product of spiritual love" (*natījah-yi mavaddat-i ma`navī*), and this relationship stems from God's decree at the beginning of creation (*dar* *badāyat-i fiṭrat*).[214] In this way, the letter suggests, friendship among societies such as those of the Ottomans and the Safavids is a condition that "was established at the very beginning of creation" (*dar āghāz-i ījād va khilqat muqarrar gashtah*). The continued care and maintenance of this divine gift of friendship is incumbent upon secular kings and sultans. The Safavids are fulfilling their religious duties by celebrating Salīm's day of accession and describe how Shāh Ṭahmāsp is now "tasting the wine of spirit-increasing love for he who has Solomonic majesty from the goblet of intimacy" (*rāḥ-i rūḥ-i afzā-yi muḥabbat-i `alā-ḥadrat-i Sulaimān-makān az sāghar-i mu'ālifat chishīdah*) while also sipping from the festive cup (*sāqī-yi bazm*) of friendship for "this mirror-image of Alexander."[215] The deposition for this supplication—which is corroborated by the Prophetic hadith, "One's honorific is a window to his heart" (*lī-laqab min al-qalb rauzana*)—means that peace between "real friends" (*dūstān-i ḥaqīqī*) and "sincere, like-minded companions" (*yik-jahatān-i taḥqīqī*) is now manifest on account of its original establishment "in the invisible world" (*bar mirāt-i khāṭir-i `āṭir-i malakūt*).[216]

The text goes on to describe how the "fortunate *munshīs*" (*munshīyān-i sa`ādat*) had inscribed the Arabic phrase "love is inherited" (*al-ḥubb yutāwarathu*)—alluding to the pre-existing peace between Sulaimān and the Safavids—and in doing so strengthened this ancient friendship and concord.[217] With hyperbole, the Safavid chancellery embraces the "winds of friendship" that are blowing into the court of Qazvīn, applauding "that king of kings" for his never-ending generosity and praying that "his dominion and kingship be extended by God until the Day of the Herafter."[218] Thanks to this unnamed ruler, the "rosebud of hope and security" (*ghunchah-yi umīd va amān*) flourishes, and this development is important with respect to those sultans of the region, especially in India and Central Asia, who have been arrogant as of late.[219] Understanding that the Peace Treaty of Amāsya will be ratified, the Safavid scribes write, "With the help of that pure one who is the king of kings and majestic ruler, the exalted banner has been fixed in place," and on the basis of this, "a copy of the royal order to be obeyed in all the lands has been written and despatched to all corners of the world."[220] The letter continues for some length, describing the mutual benefits of a lasting peace for stability of the region and its inhabitants.[221]

If this were an era of spiritual recovery and moral realignment, complete with a newly ascended sayyid class in the central *dargāh* of Shāh Ṭahmāsp, how can we explain the production of an epistolary text that so clearly eschews Shi`ite discourse in favour of a corporate perspective defined by ostentation, sumptuousness, epicurism, and esoteric elements? By Qāḍī Aḥmad al-Qummī's own admission, this text was in part based on an original *nuskhah* written by his father, Sharaf al-Dīn Ḥusainī Qummī (d. 990/1582), who had been a central pivot of the *dīvān-i inshā* for much of the reign of Ṭahmāsp. Moreover, Mīr Munshī (his *laqab*) and his exposure to ecumenical elements had begun early during his Shīrāzī education with the philosopher Mīr Ghiyās̱ al-Dīn Manṣūr. As well, he worked early on in the Herātī chancellery for the prince-cum-poet

Sām Mīrzā and later developed close connections with Qāḍī-yi Jahān Qazvīnī in the 1540s.[222] The arguably profane nature of this letter can also be attributed to Shāh Ṭahmāsp's general summons across the land to all Persian "eloquent ones and poets" (*fuḍalā va shu`arā*) to collaborate on this epistolary project.[223] Undoubtedly, the central *dīvān-i inshā* would have played a role by means of compiling and collating the different contributions, but it appears that the tone and content of this letter were strongly influenced by those "provincial" scholar-bureaucrats and litterateurs who had left Qazvīn to seek patronage in less conservative environments in Mashhad, Shīrāz, and Herāt. A case in point would be the strong possibility that those sections of Ṭahmāsp's commiseration letter—namely the enthusiastic depictions (*vaṣf*) in prose and verse of the Sa`ādatābād gardens in Qazvīn, as well as poignantly detailed descriptions of the atelier and its production of the *Shāh nāmah,* which was presented as a gift to the Ottoman court—were influenced by the elaborate paeans produced by `Abdī Beg Shīrāzī, who had in fact been one of those marginalized literary elements to leave Qazvīn to live in Ardabīl between 1565 and 1573. His *Jannat-i `Adan,* forty-one hundred verses appearing as a Niẓāmī-inspired quintet construct, has been described as "one of the longest and richest works of descriptive-encomiastic poetry in the medieval Near Eastern literary tradition," and it is difficult to imagine such a literary colossus did not exercise some influence on the court and chancellery in the 1560s.[224] Part of his encomiastic quintet, the *Zīnat al-avrāq* (967/1560), is remarkably consistent with respect to the tone and imagery in intermittent sections of this 1568 letter. It remains probable that `Abdī Beg Shīrāzī, or admirers of his, relied on this ekphrasistic text or the others appended to it (the *Rauḍat al-ṣifāt, Dauhat al-aẓhār, Jannat al-asmār, Saḥīfat al-ikhlāṣ*) for inspiration. As we learn more about `Abdī Beg Shīrāzī, it becomes evident that he was an avatar of the principles and ethos defining the Safavid state and chancellery in the second half of the sixteenth century.

Polychromatic Impulses: `Abdī Beg Shīrāzī and the Chancellery

The contribution of this bureaucrat-cum-litterateur to both epistolographic stylistics and the entire elite cultural discourse of the 1560s and 1570s requires more attention. A scion of an administrative family from Shīrāz, Khvājah `Abdī Beg Shīrāzī was born in Tabrīz on 9 Rajab 921/19 August 1515 and would spend much of his life in the administrative service of the Safavid family.[225] In many ways, he was the perfect *adīb*, who performed his administrative duties while producing histories (*Takmilat al-akhbār*), poetry, and epistolary *inshā*.[226] Paul Losensky recently noted the need to acknowledge `Abdī Beg Shīrāzī's work alongside that of his contemporaries Muḥtasham Kāshānī and Vaḥshī Bāfqī.[227] Not only did he bring an impressive skill set with respect to poetic genres and familiarity with rhetorical literary devices, but also he was well-trained in Shi`ite theology, jurisprudence, and exegesis due to his training in the famous *madrasah* established by Shaikh `Alī ibn `Abd al-`Alī al-Karakī.[228] He initially had served in the *vizārat* under Ḥusain Khān Shāmlū, but after the amir's execution in

940/1533-34, `Abdī Beg Shīrāzī found himself transferred to the central *dīvān-i a`lā* and working as a comptroller (*mustaufī*) and accountant (*avārijah-nivīs*) in the imperial registry (*daftar-i khānah-yi humāyūn*). He appears to have spent the better part of thirty years in Tabrīz and Qazvīn as an accountant; nonetheless, he earned a reputation as a court poet and elegist (with the *laqab* of Navīdī) by producing a voluminous corpus of *masnavī*s and *marsīyas*. His poetic celebration of Ṭahmāsp's urban renewal program in Qazvīn with the *Jannat-i `Adan* earned him widespread recognition amongst his peers and colleagues.[229] In 975/1565, he found himself suddenly dismissed from his post and forced to adopt the life of a "darvīsh."[230] He went to Ardabīl, where his grandfather Khvājah Niẓām al-Dīn Muḥammad had lived and worked as a bureaucrat under Shāh Ismā`īl, and spent the next seven years connected with the Safavid mausoleum complex.

During this period, he worked assiduously on the *Sarīḥ al-Milk* (a text dealing with *vaqf* properties and the Ardabīl shrine) and *Takmilat al-akhbār*, completing these in 977/1570 and 979/1571 respectively.[231] In 981/1573, he returned to the Safavid capital of Qazvīn for a number of years before returning to Ardabīl, where he passed away in 988/1580.[232] `Abdī Beg's unceremonial exile to Ardabīl was possibly a result of a clash with the Astarābādī clique that had come to dominate imperial and administrative life in Qazvīn in the second half of Shāh Ṭahmāsp's reign. He very well might have run afoul of Mīr Sayyid `Alī Khaṭīb Astarābādī, a key civil and religious official in Qazvīn, who had formed a minor Astarābādī cabal along with Mīr Ṭāhir Kāshī and Mīr Zain al-`Ābidīn.[233] Later restored to status of courtier, he presented Shāh Ṭahmāsp with his *Takmilat al-akhbār* (dedicated to his daughter, Parī Khān Khānum). `Abdī Beg's position would likely have been helped by the recent death of the *munshī al-mamālik* Muḥammadī Beg and the sudden dearth of well-trained and venerable *adīb*s in Qazvīn.

`Abdī Beg Shīrāzī is named as the author of an epistle sent to the Ottoman court in 982/1575 after the death of Salīm II and the accession of Sulṭān Murād III.[234] Tellingly, a number of verses that appear in this letter also appear in one of his poetic collections, the *Maẓhar al-asrār*, while there are certain similarities in the epistolary verse with another poetic collection, the *`Ain-i Iskandarī*.[235] More convincing proof comes with the quotation of a lengthy encomium to Murād III, which originally appeared in one of Shīrāzī's many eulogies to Shāh Ṭahmāsp profiled in *Jannat al-asmār* entitled "Praise to the Prince, Sayyid of Sultans, the King who Guards the Royal Women, May His Reign Endure." We are inspired again to see how such epistolary praise functioned beyond simple binaries of interlocutor and addressee towards a subtler program of self-referencing.[236] Further on in the letter, `Abdī Beg Shīrāzī manipulates 13: 35 of the Qur'ān, "[the likeness] of Paradise promised to the pious"—by adding "Eden" to Paradise (e.g., *Jinnāt-i `Adan*) to self-reference his own magnum opus in a coquettish application of *iqtibās*.[237] Thus, we find `Abdī Beg Shīrāzī repositioned in an arguably dominant role in the Safavid chancellery after his return from exile in 1574—an unsurprising development given that he was receiving patronage from two future political players, Shāh Ismā`īl II and Parī Khān Khānum.[238]

The letter we are focusing on here, an epistle of consolation (*ta`ziyyah nāmah*) sent to Murād III immediately after the death of his father, stands apart as an innovative text with regard to contemporaneous Safavid chancellery standards and practices. While previous correspondence from the period of Ṭahmāsp's second repentance had been influenced momentously by both newly imported Arab jurists and resurgent Māzandarānī sayyid classes, there were still chancellery elements that remained true to the Perso-Islamic models. They implicitly supported theosophic, cultural, and even profane discourse in the manner that had been popularized by Qāḍī-yi Jahān and others associated the Shīrāzī tradition. In this regard, `Abdī Beg's *inshā* functioned in a syncretic capacity, bringing together many of these disparate and divided traditions to present a discourse that functioned on a number of religious, ideological, ethnic, and linguistic levels. `Abdī Beg Shīrāzī stands as an example of the variegation and complexity that had come to characterize Safavid *adab* culture by the mid-sixteenth century: fluent in Arabic, Persian, and Turkish; proficient in the exacting technicalities of poetry and prosody; credentialed in accounting and comptrolling (*`ilm-i siyāq*); intimately familiar with the machinery of taxes and land-tenuring; rigorously trained in the exegetical and juridical sciences of Ithnā `Asharī Shi`ism; and percipient in his view of both Iranian and world history.

The *invocatio* is presented in typical Safavid epistolary fashion as a triad—praise of God, Muḥammad, and the Imamate. The eulogy for God is introduced by a Qur'ānic quote and a short poem celebrating His creation of the world. This is then followed by an acrobatic display of rhymed prose, which is intersected by no less than thirteen partial Qur'ānic quotations, ranging from 30: 11 ("For every age there is a book") to 36: 73 ("So all glory to Him who holds all power over every thing, to whom you will go back in the end").[239] In much the same structure as God's invocation, Muḥammad's mandate as a divine prophet is introduced by a Qur'ānic quote (21: 107: "We have sent you [a message] as a benevolence to the creatures of the world"), which is then followed by a short poem.

> He is the seal of prophets, the light of paths, king of all/ /He is the sultan of prophets [*sulṭān-i anbiyā*] and the king of saints [*shāhinshāh-i auliyā*]
> He is the chief and leader of the major prophets/And both the employer and master of the lords of power and knowledge
> The hand of his prophethood was empowered by the hand of God/[In the same way], Moses was strengthened when he took the staff with a pure hand
> The pilgrims of the gate of the city of his knowledge/are familiar with the guards of the dome of the throne [i.e., angels].[240]

As `Abdī Beg Shīrāzī's encomium to the Prophet continues, we encounter a style onsistent with theosophic, Perso-Islamic conceptions of Muḥammad as a divine and pre-eternal agent. The imagery of the cloak, or mantle, which has enjoyed great symbolic cache among Sufi poets and exegetes, is employed fully here. He is the "light of the glorious eye," who wears a cloak just as Joseph wore his amazing coat (*Yūsuf-i pīrhan*) and was revealed in verse 1 of "The Enfolded" ("O You, enfolded your mantle") and verse 1 of "The Enwrapped" ("O You, enwrapped in the cloak [of prophethood]").[241] The metaphors and similes of light and luminescence continue in subsequent poetic encomiums (*na`t*), but we find here a peculiar arrangement of verse that organizes deftly a number of Qur'ānic euphemisms for the Prophet with a number of other less orthodox metaphors and similes popular among literary Sufi circles. We read how "the light of the sun is from the emanation of Muḥammad's face/the sweet odour of the *houris* is from the dust of his abode."[242] Continuing this motif of light and urban landscape, we read how "the pinnacle of the vault of his stature [is evident with] 'Yā wa Sīn'/ the light of his perfect rank [is seen with] 'Tā wa Sīn.'" The citation here of the "mysterious letters" (*ḥurūf-i nūrānī*), which appear at the beginning of the Surah of Yāsīn ("Yā Sīn, I call to witness the Qur'ān") and al-Naml ("Tā Sīn, these are the verses of the Qur'ān"), are not entirely surprising given the popularity of Yāsīn and Tāsīn as euphemisms for the Prophet Muḥammad among Sufi thinkers, poets, and litterateurs.[243]

This device continues in the next *bait*, but with the subtle realignment of metaphors to include references to chancelleries and text: "The rank and Excellency of 'Ṭā wa Hā' is [recorded] in the registry [*ṭumār*] /The praise of 'Ṭā wa sīn' is sung by the peacock [*ṭā'ūs*] of the garden."[244] `Abdī Beg Shīrāzī continues these subtle Qur'ānic allusions by writing: "The surah of '*wa al-shams*' (91: 1) [describes] the lightness of his face/while the copy (*nuskha*) of '*wa al-lail*' (91: 4)[245] refers to [the darkness of] his hair," and carries on with this chancelleric motif: "The preamble [*dībācha*] of his eminence and glory [is visible] in his forehead/while his hair is a partial reflection of his excellence and perfection" (*jabḥah-ash dībāchah-yi jāh va jalāl/gīsū-yash sar-rashtah-yi faḍl va kamāl*). This use of Qur'ānic *iqtibās* with *wa al-shams* and *wa al-lail* is derivative of Sanā'ī's mystical poetry; indeed, this was a dominant device in later medieval panegyric poetry to Muḥammad.[246] The Solomonic motif is incorporated by Shīrāzī into his allusive Qur'ānic style at the end of this poem: "Like Solomon who was given a kingdom by God [according to the Qur'ānic phrase] *habb-lī*[247]/[Muḥammad] has the seal of prophecy in his hand."[248] This embedding of partial Qur'ānic allusions in Persian verse was consistent with a "mystico-didactic nature" that permeated such panegyric poetry on behalf of the Prophet,[249] while Rasūl Ja`fariyān has noted the strong impulse towards mystical philosophy (*`irfān*), which characterizes much of Shīrāzī's work.[250] True to his Shi`ite convictions, `Abdī Beg Shīrāzī provides a Persian *qaṣīdah* to `Alī that avoids inflamed sectarian anxieties by adopting classical theosophical imagery and stressing the interconnected and preternal relationship between Muḥammad and `Alī.

Whatever praise I give for [`Alī] is praise of the Prophet/Because the light

of both essences is from one shining essence
The One Light called himself Muṣṭafā and Murtaẓā/O! What a light, whose beam is a guide for creation
A light came from the divine light and shone/on two holy niches [i.e., Muḥammad and `Alī] in such a way that the sky is their servant
From that one [niche] the candle of prophethood lights up the congregation/ while the other [niche] is the glory of the crown of the king of *vilāyat*
Since there is nothing to be distinguished from the praise of the Prophet/ praise for each one of these no doubt is praise for the other one as well.[251]

This duality, in which Muḥammad is the vehicle of divine revelation and `Alī is responsible for its earthly establishment and dissemination, is seen again in one of Shīrāzī's many poetic collections, in this case the *Jannat al-amṣār*. For `Abdī Beg Shīrāzī, it is clear that the Imamate can be understood with stark imperial metaphors, and there is little doubt that such twinning between kingship and sacred served Shāh Ṭahmāsp's program of legitimacy very well. In his introductory praise of the Imams, `Abdī Beg Shīrāzī writes how "[`Alī] is the king of all kings of saintly authority, the ruler who provides divine guidance." The motif of the provenance of Muḥammad and `Alī as divine flourescence is reiterated with: "[`Alī's] nature is made of divine essence, and with the Prophet, he comes from One Light." The earthly mandate is evident in the following lines of poetry: "After the Prophet, he plants knowledge which springs forth like a fruit in place of the flower [of Muḥammad's prophecy]/On account of `Alī, best of the Imams, religion was established with his existence."[252]

Returning to the missive, we reach the third station of invocation with a series of verse and prose encomiums to the addressee, Murād III. Six sets of verses are presented here, divided by short, formulaic acclamations in Arabic. What makes this profane *invocatio* so interesting is `Abdī Beg Shīrāzī's decision to present these benedictions in macaronic verse. In this way, the first *bait* of poetry in Arabic is followed by subsequent lines of verse in Persian and Ottoman Turkish. Both bilingual and trilingual macaronic verses (*mumalla`āt*) were rare in medieval Arabic literature; however, the juxtaposition of Arabic and Persian verses in medieval Persian literature and the combination of Persian poetry with Urdu verse (*rikhtā*) were not uncommon.[253] The classical Persian prosodists Rādūyānī and Vaṭvāṭ discuss the use of *mulamma`āts*, but there appears to be a distinction between *mulamma`-i makshūf* and *mulamma`-i maḥjūb*, whereby the former identified a poem in which each hemistich was in Arabic and Persian, while the latter saw alternating lines of verse in Arabic and Persian.[254] This literary hybridity flourished in the Iranian and South Asian contexts, and macaronic verse, often employed in cultural and religious milieux, was characterized by a degree of cultural syncretism. In the context of `Abdī Beg Shīrāzī's use of macaronic verse, we see a presentation of *mulamma`-i maḥjūb*:

His deeds have exalted him/His generosity pointed to his good reputation

[in Arabic]
O! The new moon is following you obediently in the retinue/[where] the shadow of the parasol is a shield of the sun [in Persian]
God made his epoch on the world/His shadow is you, O King of the realm of the refuge of protection [in Ottoman Turkish].[255]

`Abdī Beg Shīrāzī interrupts this macaronic verse with a fragmented stylized Arabic phrase, "He is the arranger of the ornaments of dominion and compassion [*ḥāwī mafākhira al-salṭanat wa al-rā'fat*]; he is the possessor of the glories of kingship and caliphal rule" (*ḥā'iz ma'āthira al-mamlakat wa al-khilāfat*), before continuing with yet another trilingual panegyric to Murād.[256] Interestingly, by the 1570s the *intitulatio*s of Safavid letters had become oppressively lengthy and tautological, whereby such standard Arabic phrases used by chancelleries (e.g., *nāṣibu a`lāmi al-mulki wa al-dīn, ḥāfiẓu thughūri al-Islāmi wa al-muslimīn*) could run for several folios. `Abdī Beg Shīrāzī's decision to shorten these by breaking them up and reconstituting them throughout a series of macaronic sections only underscores his sense of innovation and ingenuity.

The next macaronic verse is prefaced by the Arabic phrase, "He is a sign of God's bounty among humanity, he is the beginning and end for generosity among all human beings." Then the macaronic verse:

Kingship has become glorious with his arrival/God has made his rule prosperous because of his good deeds [in Arabic]
He is the shadow of God, the king around whom all the kingdoms revolve/
The sea and land is overloaded from his generosity [in Persian]
The appearance of kingship and the meaning of kingship is his way/his banner is the sign of the shadow of God [in Ottoman Turkish].[257]

Murād is then lionized in staunch martial terms as the "defender of the battlefield of Islam against the heretical oppression and crimes" (*ḥāmī ḥaumata al-Islām `ain ẓalām al-bida` wa al-aṣām*) and subsequently praised in Arabic, Persian, and Ottoman Turkish.

He has created victory for his standards/God has made him one of His signs [in Arabic]
He is the defender of Islam with great effort and endeavour/The obliterator of infidels in the manner that is pleasing [in Persian]
He ruined the state and city/wherever there were places of idolatry [in Ottoman Turkish].[258]

This pattern of shifting symmetrically between Arabic panegyric prose and macaronic verse continues for several lines, until `Abdī Beg Shīrāzī presents a *qaṣīdah* that invokes a number of historical icons who intersect not only pre-Islamic and Islamic history but also Persian and Turkish iconography. Again, we have to wonder if the Safavid chancellery was not self-identifying as `Abdī Beg Shīrāzī writes about the supremacy of the shah and king (*khusrau*) over the caesars and kings of Cathay, while describing how the shah's courts are adorned with rows of Saljuq commanders (*sipah-dārān-i Saljūqī*) and Sasanian generals (*sar-afrāzān-i Sāsānī*). "He has no equal," one hemistich reads, "but the First Intellect [`*aql-i avval*] has become his encomiast [*s̱anā-khvān-ash*]," with the second hemistich adding, "With this in mind, what is wrong if the First Intellect is his praiser?"[259] The unparalleled nature of this epistolary text is further demonstrated by the range and scope of historical exemplars `Abdī Beg Shīrāzī uses to inspire comparison: "The curtain of his royal power is protected by the chamberlains Ṭughril and Arsalān, while the court tapestry of his grandeur is watched by the porters, Kai-Khusrau and Kai-Qubād."[260] Likewise, we read that the Roman King Heraclius (*Hirqil*) and the first-century German war chief Arminius (*Armānūs*) serve this ruler as brotherly chamberlains, while Emperor Constantine (*Qusṭanṭīn*) and the Macedonian Emperor Phillip II (*Failaqūs*) are generals (*mujannadah*) who lead his retinue.[261] The irregular list of kingly personages—Persian, Roman, Byzantine, Greek, Teutonic, Turkish—reflect the depth of `Abdī Beg Shīrāzī's imagination, scholastic training, and sense of innovation.

After a continued *intitulatio* dedicated to Murād III, `Abdī Beg Shīrāzī comes to the occasion for this particular diplomatic overture—the sudden death of Salīm II—and how Ṭahmāsp had decided to despatch a *ta`ziyyah nāmah* upon hearing the news. The text and style shift predictably towards Qur'ānic excerpts (*iqtibās*) and allusions (*talmīḥ*), thereby buttressing the soteriological and eschatological tenor of the text. Not content with conventional, formulaic lamentations, `Abdī Beg Shīrāzī turns to a lengthy prose eulogy, which employs a number of rhetorical devices as well as a broad brand of metaphors. The threnody soon reaches its climax, and we cannot help but detect some explicitly Shi`ite resonances

> And the gates of sighing and lamenting [*ta'assuf va talahhuf*] have been opened, and moans and groans [*āh va anīn*] from your friends have come to pass. And this is the second calamity after the regal death of that Sulaimān of the age—in this way, calamity builds on calamity [*ghamm bar ghamm*] and anguish builds on anguish [*alam bar alam*].[262]

`Abdī Beg Shīrāzī's rhetorical malleability is further demonstrated as he describes how the disparaging soul is soothed by the existence of "that protector of the kingship of Kai-Khusrau" and "that guardian of Khusrau's chain of justice" (*silsilah-yi `adl-i Kisrā*).[263] The Ottoman reader is informed how the banners of *al-Fātiḥa* (opening verse of the Qu'rān) have been raised according to the royal *farmān* (*al-amr-i jahān muṭā`*) of: "Say: 'My Lord, forgive and have mercy. You are the best of the merciful.'"[264] In this way, "the hand pleading mercy and pardon" (*dast-i istirḥām va istighfār*) has been firmly placed "on the skirt of hope" (*bar dāman-i rajā*). Here, `Abdī Beg Shīrāzī employs the device of *tadmīn* (i.e., the use of quotations from religious and ethical literature) whereby the image of the penitent Shi`ite throwing his hand on the skirt of `Alī was a popular one in `Alid traditions. Again we see the invocation of language and symbolism, which are better conveyed for and understood by a Safavid audience.[265] Deftly showing his macaronic skills, Shīrāzī describes how contrite Muslims have sought pardon from that "merciful, royal court" (*dargāh-i marḥamat va parvardgārī*) through self-abasement and crying (*taḍarru` va zārī*) and self-deprecation and humility (*tashaffu` va khāksarī*). The subtle Shi`ite motif is continued by Shīrāzī when he notes that the recently departed Salīm II (*ghufrān-dastgāh*) is in a dirt grave; however, the terms used here, *dar niqāb-i turāb,* can also be read as a *tajnis,* suggesting a rapprochement with Abū Turāb, or `Alī.[266] Ṭahmāsp and Murād should be in agreement that someone exists to take the place of a ruler when he abjures the throne, a sentiment Shīrāzī rearticulates coquettishly with this rhymed prose: "In the event that a moon sets on the sultanate, thank God that there is a sun to arise to take its place."[267] The letter concludes with further benedictions for Murād III and the hope that the manner of condolence (*rasm-i ta`azī*) and the way for congratulation (*aslūbī-yi tahanī*) have been properly observed.[268]

`Abdī Beg Shīrāzī and his work in the Safavid chancellery stand in many ways as the culmination of more than three decades of changes and realignments within the Safavid ruling infrastructure. His pedigree and training were such that Shīrāzī was able to stand at the centre of a complicated nexus in the *dīvān* where ideological, philosophical, and epistemological strands were intersecting and overlapping perpetually. It would be too ambitious to suggest a chauvinist Arab-rooted Shi`ism had supplanted the multi-faceted Perso-Islamic *adab* culture that had been established earlier by Persian intelligentsia like Qāḍī-yi Jahān Qazvīnī.[269] Nonetheless, the shah's attempt to extend political control over quasi-autonomous regions and cities was clear and manifest by reinforcing the Shi`ite orientation of the court and *dīvān* while concurrently extending sayyid networks, provincial courts, and *madrasah* systems. `Abdī Beg Shīrāzī and others were able to influence if not directly control the production of ideological discourse in the form of epistolary and documentary texts to reflect these different and often conflicted dynamics.

4

REX REDUX, 1576–98

Shāh Ismā`īl II's Challenge to the Hierocrats

The discomposed nature of Iranian court politics following the death of the longest reigning monarch in Safavid history resulted from panoplies of interest groups that had emerged since the early 1560s. The intention here is not to present the minutiae of Mīrzā Sulṭān Ḥaidar's tenuous bid for power in Ṣafar 984/May 1576 and the resulting putsch organized by the Afshār tribe in support of Ṭahmāsp's incarcerated son, Mīrzā Ismā`īl. Ismā`īl had been incarcerated since 1556 for allegedly conspiring to rebel against Ṭahmāsp. Savory adds that this may have indirectly come about thanks to the influence of Ma`ṣūm Beg Ṣafavī, the *lala* and handler of Mīrzā Sulṭān Ḥaidar.[1] Suffice it to say, when amirs and notables welcomed the forty-one-year old Ismā`īl II as the new ruler, Safavid politics were inexorably changed. The historiography of Shāh Ismā`īl II's reign has been defined by two broad characteristics: his policy of reviving Sunnism as state doctrine and a deranged paranoia that resulted in the massacre of most of the royal family. These characteristics are largely rooted in an older Orientalist historiographical framework typified by scholars like Sir John Malcolm and E. G. Browne.[2] Nonetheless, these blunt castigations of the nineteenth century were carried over into the twentieth century thanks to Walter Hinz, the first Western scholar to study Ismā`īl II's reign with any serious depth.[3] A generation of later scholars, such as Hans Robert Roemer and Roger Savory, provided more nuance to the period; however, these core perceptions of Ismā`īl as deranged and sociopathic were perpetuated.[4] Generally, explanations for Ismā`īl's aberrant behaviour lie in his lengthy incarceration in Qahqaha Prison in Gīlān, but it was also Hinz who helped to establish the western historiographical foothold regarding Ismā`īl II's Sunni sensibilities.[5] In this regard, Ismā`īl II has often been understood as having unleashed a lurking "crypto-Sunnism" among various Persian intelligentsia, most notably Mīrzā Makhdūm Sharīfī, in an attempt to reverse the Shi`ite policies of his predecessors.[6] While Abisaab acknowledges the problem of bias in official Safavid sources, she nonetheless sees Ismā`īl's religious policies as an attempt to "normalize" Sunnism in Iran.[7] Newman has recently suggested that Ismā`īl II's pro-Sunni policies were rooted in attempts to moderate "the exclusionist tendencies" of the Safavids and to placate the Ottoman empire to the west.[8]

A number of scholars are flushing out the historiographical nuances of this period and its significance for understanding Safavid court dynamics in the late sixteenth century. Shohreh Gholsorkhi examined Mīrzā Makhdūm Sharīfī's semi-autobiographical work, *al-Nawāqiḍ fī al-radd `alā al-rawāfiḍ*, to suggest that "Ismā`īl's course of action appears to be more of a political maneuver to thwart the powerful Shi`i scholars than a bona fide commitment to Sunni tenets."[9] More profoundly, Devin Stewart has looked at the writings of Muẓaffar `Alī and his biographical narration of Shaikh Bahā`ī's relationship with Ismā`īl to suggest the period of 1577–78 was indeed monumental in that Ismā`īl's policies rallied a broad brand of hierocrats—Arab jurists and Persian sayyids and judges—which in turn resulted in a "lasting marriage between the Safavid government and the Shi`ite religious establishment."[10] The underlying mechanics of Stewart's argument focus on how Ismā`īl II's decrees brought together two strands of Arab scholarship that had been historically hostile to one another: the respective families of Zain al-Dīn al-`Āmilī (*al-Shahīd al-Thānī*) and `Alī al-Karakī (*al-Muḥaqqiq al-Thānī*).[11] Manūchihr Pārsādūst, in his recent biography of the Safavid ruler, raised the pointed question of whether Ismā`īl II was a Sunni. Likewise this Iranian scholar sees much of Ismā`īl's religious policies guided by imperial, absolutist motivations.[12] There is little mistaking that the official sources for this period are uniformly hostile towards Ismā`īl II and arguably with good reason. He decimated the royal family and alienated Arab and Persian Shi`ite personalities alike with his challenges to the religious establishment. It would appear, however, that many of Ismā`īl's more antagonistic policies were not necessarily rooted in issues of Sunni-Shi`ite communalism and can be better understood as part of a greater campaign to realign the centrality and importance of Persian absolute monarchy. In this way, we can see contemporary characterizations like Afūshtah-ī Natanzī's—"the Qizilbāsh lived in fear of the Shah's invincible wrath and the results of his imperial ire and violence" (*qahr-i shāhī va āsār-i sukhuṭ va ghaṣbah-yi pādshāhī*)—as more consistent with an autocrat frustrated by anti-court and anti-imperial elements rather than a sociopath who manifested his pathology by flirting openly with Sunni policies.[13] Nonetheless, the extent to which Ismā`īl's policies were "communalized" is evident in Muẓaffar `Alī's fascinating depiction of Mīr Sayyid Ḥusain al-Karakī and Shāh Ismā`īl II as the "Ḥusain" and "Yazīd" of the age, sentiments that were arguably echoed in later court chronicles from the reign of `Abbās the Great and beyond.[14] Indeed, as Devin Stewart remarked, the complicated nexus of different factors in Ismā`īl II's court—Qizilbāsh, Persian administrators, Arab *faqīh*s, sayyids—are often reduced to "a simple conflict between Sunnism and Shi`ism."[15]

Ismā`īl's early behaviour indicates a personality intent on reversing the astonishing inroads made by various interest groups, including networks of Arab Shi`ite jurists and Qizilbāsh tribes. The ten-day interregnum in Ṣafar 984/May 1576 was dramatic, and chronicles concur that order and authority collapsed in Qazvīn after the murder of Ḥaidar; vendettas were fixed, grudges were carried out, and above all, pro-Ḥaidar Ustājlū Qizilbāsh were purged by pro-Ismā`īl elements.[16] Ismā`īl was initially reluctant to quit his Qahqaha Prison, and he strategically waited until profiled opposition in Qazvīn had been eliminated by his supporters.[17] Thus, the status and size of the assembly (five thousand by Būdāq Munshī's reckoning), which proceeded from Qazvīn to meet Ismā`īl II, point to a general acclamation of his rule by elite Safavid society, including princes (most notably Mīrzā Ibrāhīm), *qūrchī*s, amirs, administrators, sayyids, *faqīh*s, *`ulamā,* and functionaries. Despite the popular acclamation at Qahqaha and Zanjān, Ismā`īl was deeply concerned about a number of groups and individuals that had cultivated considerable power bases in the final years of Shāh Ṭahmāsp's reign. In this way, the summer of 984/1576 was marked by continued suppression of Ustājlūs and other dissenting Qizilbāsh in Qazvīn and provincial centres like Herāt.[18]

Soon after his arrival in Qazvīn, Ismā`īl chose to focus his energies on Ḥusain Qulī Rūmlū, the *khalīfa al-khulafā*, and arranged to have this powerful Qizilbāsh evicted from his residence. The shah and his retinue assumed ownership until the appropriate celestial moment for the shah's coronation—decided upon by Maulānā Aḥmad Ardabīlī, the court astrologer of Shāh Ṭahmāsp—at which point he would move into Sa`ādatābād.[19] Mindful of how this charismatic *khalīfa al-khulafā* commanded the direct loyalty of ten thousand Qizilbāsh Sufis, Ismā`īl II decided to co-opt Ḥusain Qulī Rūmlū by appointing him to the courtly position of *vakīl-i dīvān-i a`lā*. When Ḥusain Qulī Rūmlū refused, he was chastised in front of his Rūmlū brethren and kept waiting outside the gates of his own house in a display of ritual humiliation before later being named as *qūrchī bāshī* for the city of Mashhad.[20] Ismā`īl couched much of his public abasement of Ḥusain Qulī Rūmlū by invoking the pre-eminence and sanctity of his status not as king or sultan but as the *murshid-i kāmil.*[21] Construction was begun on new buildings and edifices, including a *daulat-khānah* in the Sa`ādatābād complex, while Muḥtasham Kāshānī produced a thirty-two-line poetic chronogram to celebrate the impending accession ceremony.[22]

Shāh Ismā`īl's coronation was held in the Chihil Sutūn on 27 Jumāda I 984/22 August 1576 amidst great pomp and circumstance. Invited attendees included royal family members, principal officers of state, and suzerain tributaries like the Georgian princes `Isā Khān and Samā`ūn Khān along with emissaries from Ibrāhīm Khān of Lār, Mīrzā Khān of Māzandarān and Shaikh Saḥḥar of `Arabistān. Ambassadorial missions and gifts from the Ottoman empire, the Deccanī kingdom of the Niẓāmshāhs, and the Portuguese also arrived for the ceremony.[23] The contemporary observer Būdāq Munshī commented how Ismā`īl's enthronement assembly (*majlis*) was comparable to the one assembled by Timur in Samarqand with the arrangement of five *farsakh*s (20 kilometres) of tents and canopies for festivities, which lasted three months.[24] Within days of Ismā`īl's enthronement, Mīrzā Shukr Allāh Iṣfahānī (previously chief accountant under Shāh Ṭahmāsp[25]) was named chief vizier (*manṣab-i `ālā-yi vizārat*); the date is commemorated in the chronogram "Āṣaf Barkhīya" in reference to the Solomonic minister.[26] The office of *ṣadr* was divided between two Persian notables, Mīrzā Makhdūm Sharīfi Shīrāzī and Shāh `Ināyat Allāh Iṣfahānī, the latter serving both as a *naqīb* as well as *qāḍī-yi mu`askir* during the reign of Shāh Ṭahmāsp. These appointments were concluded with formal ceremonies whereby Mīrzā Shukr Allāh, Mīrzā Makhdūm Sharīfi, and Shāh `Ināyat Allāh were girded with gold-adorned belts (*kamar-i ṭalā-yi muraṣṣa`*) and given ornamented ceremonial pens and inkpots and ceremonial robes.[27]

Of course, the elevation of Mīrzā Makhdūm Sharīfi is not at all surprising given that he was a grandson of Qāḍī-yi Jahān. His nomination and promotion are almost certainly results of Mīrzā Makhdūm Sharīfi's genealogical connection to this administrative giant of the 1530s and 1540s and had little to do with any Sunni proclivities he may or may not have had. As this study has argued in Chapter two, the family of Qāḍī-yi Jahān was part of an urban, ecumenical network of Persian intellectual theosophists based in cities like Shīrāz and Qazvīn. The poetry of Mīrzā Makhdūm Sharīfi's father, Mīrzā Sharaf Jahān, invokes the memory of the philosopher al-Davvānī while concurrently praising the qualities of `Alī and the Imamate; moreover, he had been educated in Shīrāz under Ghiyāṣ al-Dīn Manṣūr.[28] Recently, Gholsorkhi has challenged the degree to which we can confidently see Mīrzā Makhdūm Sharīfi as a staunch Sunni, especially in light of his career as a chief judge in Fārs and a popular preacher at the Ḥaidariyyah mosque in Qazvīn before the death of Shāh Ṭahmāsp. The subsequent autobiographical narrative detailed in *al-Nawāqiḍ fī al-radd `alā al-rawāfiḍ*—presented to Murād III after his flight to the Ottoman empire in 985/1577—is predictably pro-Sunni given that he was keen to project himself as a propagandistic asset to his new patrons.[29] His familial background and his request to be interred according to Imami Shi`ite rites before dying in 994/1586 suggest that Mīrzā Makhdūm Sharīfi was not the unrelenting Sunni he claimed to be.

Two months later, beginning in early Sha`bān, 984/late October 1576, Ismā`īl II decided to eliminate any royal familial threats to his rule by having a number of Safavid princes murdered, including the well-known cultural patron, miniaturist, and musician Ibrāhīm Mīrzā.[30] In some cases—namely the murder of Badī` al-Zamān Mīrzā (son of Bahrām Mīrzā) and other familial members in periphery centres like Sīstān—their removal was considered "the necessities of state affairs" (*daf`-i īshān az lavāzam-i umūr-i salṭanat ast*).[31] Ḥasan Beg Rūmlū remarked how the beloved Ibrāhīm Mīrzā "often times had shown treachery [and] received his punishment," while Iskander Beg Munshī states that Ismā`īl offered Ibrāhīm Mīrzā the position of *muhrdār* shortly before his coronation in Jumāda I 984/August 1576 "so he could always keep an eye on him."[32] Other royal family members, such as Sulṭān-Muḥammad Mīrzā in Shīrāz and Mīrzā

`Abbās in Herāt, were spared, likely because their *lala*s and local governors were part of the Zū al-Qadar and Shāmlū tribes. In fact, one year later Ismā`īl II installed `Abbās Mīrzā and his *lala* (`Alī Qulī Khān Shāmlū) as the new governor in the historical princely capital of Herāt with a troop increase of several thousand men.[33] At roughly the same time, Ismā`īl II installed his newborn son, Shujā` al-Dīn (b. 12 Rajab 985/25 September 1577), as nominal governor of the city of Shīrāz's influential centre. Sulṭān-Muḥammad Mīrzā and his coterie of Zū al-Qadar Qizilbāsh were openly contemptuous of the new prince and his handlers. Rather than order the elimination of these dissenting royal elements, Ismā`īl deferred and his son was installed elsewhere.[34]

Undoubtedly, the murders of the Safavid princes and princelings posed a shocking turn of events, however, the continued approval of `Abbās Mīrzā and Sulṭān-Muḥammad Mīrzā suggest that Ismā`īl II's fratricides might have been responses to shifts in the immediate political context of Qazvīn and a reflection of the shah's increasing conviction that the Qizilbāsh Sufis were looking to remove him and place Ibrāhīm Mīrzā or another Safavid prince on the throne. There is good reason to believe that Isma`il's suspicions were not unwarranted. Shortly before Ismā`īl's purge, thousands of Sufi Qizilbāsh from the region of Diyār Bakr had entered Qazvīn on the pretext of a local dispute with the city's *darūghah*. Alarmingly, they camped on the city outskirts, near the house of their spiritual intermediary (*khalīfa al-khulafā*), the recently humiliated Ḥusain Qulī Rūmlū. This Sufi Qizilbāsh contingent was construed as a direct and explicit threat because of their combative history; Ḥasan Beg Rūmlū commented how they "smote every man with whom they had a contention" during Ṭahmāsp's reign.[35] Orders were subsequently drawn up by Musīb Khān Takkalū and Murtaḍā Qulī Khān Purnāk for their dispersal and elimination.[36]

Ismā`īl II spent the early part of 985/winter 1577 finishing his program of eliminating potential rivals and suppressing regional dissidences, but the Shi`ite hierocratic elements that had flourished in the 1560s and 1570s remained largely untouched. Later historians have interpreted Ismā`īl's harassment of Shi`ite clerics, such as Sayyid Ḥusain al-Karakī, and the cessation of ritualized cursing among the *tabarrā'iyān* as evidence of his program to formally reintroduce Sunnism to Safavid Iran—undoubtedly an interpretation reinforced by later, prejudicial official Safavid sources. To look to lurking Sunni proclivities as a motive for such policies is problematic, and we cannot help but wonder if Ismā`īl II was hoping to suppress a *particular* class of Shi`ite juridical scholars, namely the progenitors of `Abd al-`Alī al-Karakī, who were in alignment with the Qizilbāsh and the public anathematization of the first three caliphs, Aisha, and a host of early "Sunni" personalities. From a broader vantage point, it is also reasonable to concur with Rula Abisaab who noted how "high-ranking leaders [of the Qizilbāsh] became gradually more open to mainstream Shi`ism even when the general tribal populace expressed diverse anti-clerical sentiments."[37] More profoundly, it was the Uṣūlī al-Karakīs who championed a privileged role for Shi`ite jurists in the new Safavid state, insisting that Friday prayer could be led in the absence of an Imam, *khums* and *ṣadaqat* taxes could be collected during the Occultation, and all religious matters should be approved or vetted by a Shi`ite *mujtahid*. In this light, Ismā`īl II emerges first and foremost as an imperial autocrat envisioning a polity defined by a general Shi`ite cultural framework, but he did not necessarily privilege Shi`ite clerical power. B. S. Amoretti would agree that Ismā`īl's religious program was "a weapon which would enable him to undermine the power of the Shī`ī *`ulamā*" and also a means of "combating the obscurantist tendencies of Ṭahmāsp's last years."[38]

Shāh Ismā`īl sought out individuals who could help disassemble this hegemonic structure, which had emerged under Shāh Ṭahmāsp. It is not surprising to see him turning to Persian notables, scholastics, and theologians from Shīrāz and Iṣfahān, such as Mīrzā Makhdūm Sharīfi, Maulānā Jān Shīrāzī, Shāh `Ināyat Allāh Iṣfahānī, and Mīr Makhdūm Lala.[39] The principal target was Mīr Sayyid Ḥusain al-Karakī, but others included Mīr Sayyid `Alī Khaṭīb, the new *qāḍī-yi mu`askir* Khvājah Afḍal Tarīkah, and other "militant Shi`ites" of the Astarābādī clique, which had come to dominate religious politics in Qazvīn and elsewhere since the 1540s.[40] According to Ḥasan Beg Rūmlū, Ismā`īl focused his energies on "the doctors of the religious law and especially the likes of those sayyid jurists." We read that some in this faction were expelled from court and that Mīr Sayyid Ḥusain al-Karakī's books were confiscated and locked away.[41] Ismā`īl II organized his own throng of *qūrchīs* to counter-intimidate al-Karakī and the *tabarrā'iyān*, indicating that the shah was clearly willing to do his part with respect to the "alliance" between the al-Karakīs, the Astarābādī coterie, and the Qizilbāsh.[42] Indeed, Ḥasan Beg Rūmlū comments how Ismā`īl II "paid the *qūrchīs*, whom [Ṭahmāsp] had not paid for fourteen years." One wonders if the shah seized upon this abeyant institution in the hope of organizing a martial force capable of countering these anti-imperial forces.[43] The new *khalīfa al-khulafā*, Bulgār Khalīfa, did not see eye to eye on this issue of anathematization, so the shah had him beaten and publicly shamed (not unlike his predecessor) before replacing him with Dada Khalīfa of the recently humbled Ustājlū tribe.[44] Bulgār Khalīfa's son Nūr `Alī Khalīfa was arrested on 6 Zū al-Ḥijja 984/24 February 1577, and shortly afterwards he was executed along with a number of other high-profile Sufi Qizilbāsh.[45] Ritual cursing by *`ulamā*-sponsored *tabarrā'iyān* was banned, while at the same time invective Shi`ite slogans were erased from mosques and palace walls in Qazvīn.[46] The ritualized cursing practised by such Qizilbāsh elements had been clearly endorsed by the Uṣūlī hierocratic elements since the halcyon days of `Abd al-`Alī al-Karakī, and it is here that Ismā`īl II chose to apply specific royal pressure. Mīr Sayyid Ḥusain had standardized and legitimated much of Safavid cursing in the 1570s and produced tracts that discussed the particulars of why and how to curse `Umar ibn al-Khaṭṭāb.[47] By heeling such militant Qizilbāsh elements, Ismā`īl II was indirectly undermining a popular source of support for the Uṣūlī Shi`ite clerics who had accrued so much influence and power. Afūshtah-ī Natanzī has noted, "[Ismā`īl] commanded that a number of measures be taken with the aim of humbling them."[48]

There is sufficient chancellery evidence from this period to support the assertion that Ismā`īl II was committed to maintaining Safavid sovereignty in its Shi`ite ideological framework while seeking to undermine the power and scope of the Shi`ite clerical structure. This in turn reflected a multivalent legitimacy championed by Shāh Ismā`īl II that sought to rediscover and rhetoricize the power and status of ancient Iranian monarchy and infallible Sufi directorship, while at the same time invoking generic Shi`ite tropes and imagery. In this way, Ismā`īl was not unlike his earlier sixteenth-century namesake who embraced his role of *shāhinshāh*-cum-*murshid* while similarly relying on the Persian intelligentsia and administrative class to counterbalance the corrosive effects of his Qizilbāsh supporters. Within weeks of Ismā`īl II's accession ceremony in Ṣafar 984/May 1576, grandees and notables of every region assembled in the court of Qazvīn for the purpose of hearing a new law (*qānūnī*). Afūshtah-ī Natanzī discusses the content of this new law by providing an approximate version of a decree, or *ḥukm*, written on Jumāda II 984/September 1576.[49] The *ḥukm* outlines the combined efforts of the *qāḍīs*, amirs, viziers, and others who sit in the council (*dīvān*) and how they had been commanded to ensure proper enforcement of Islamic law and customs.[50] The *ḥukm* narrates how a "regulatory programme" (*dastūr al-`amal*) will be produced by the amirs of the *dīvān* upon the arrival of one Shāh Rukh Khān Zū al-Qadar to the court. The *ḥukm* also notes the participation in this circulated regulation by Amīr `Ināyat Allāh, Mīrzā Makhdūm Sharīfī, Pīra Muḥammad Khān Ustājlū, Mīrzā Shukr Allāh Iṣfahānī, Muḥammadī Sulṭān, Ḥaidar Sulṭān Turkhān, and Qūrkhamas Beg Amīr.[51] This regulation—written by Mīrzā Muḥammad Munshī and certified by Ḥusain Beg Lala and Muḥammad Mu'min Mīrzā (*davāt-dār*)—was principally designed to address issues of mint and recoinage and publicly declared that no Turks or Tajiks were to henceforth accept old *dinārs* or gifts and salaries paid in coins.[52] Afūshtah-ī Natanzī added to this document by describing how "after this *qānūn* was established, [Ismā`īl II] ascertained and guaranteed the weight of the dirhams and *dinārs*. He then commanded that pure gold and silver be used, and gold coins be uniformly inscribed with the verse of `Aṭṭār: 'From the east to the west, if there is an Imam/`Alī and his family are everything to us!'"[53]

There are a number of interesting features worthy of comment here. First, the reference to regulations such as *qānūnī* and *dastūr al-`amal* appears to be documentary corroboration of the establishment of the renowned supplemental "court of justice" (*dīvān-i `adl*) by Ismā`īl II. Iskander Beg Munshī describes the mandate of this new legal institution.

> To give judgment both in individual cases involving financial problems and in matters affecting the welfare of the realm as a whole. Their judgments and mandates were to be embellished with the endorsement 'ratified by the supreme *dīvān*', and were to bear the imprint of the *mihr-āṡār* seal, which Shāh Ismā`īl had allocated for this purpose, and on which had been engraved the formula 'the seal of the supreme *dīvān*.'[54]

This court of law was under the directorship of the vizier Mīrzā Shukr Allāh Iṣfahānī and was assembled in tandem with the announcement that Mīrzā Makhdūm Sharīfī and Shāh `Ināyat Allāh Iṣfahānī were to jointly hold the office of *ṣadr*.[55] The only evidence of this *dīvān-i `adl* at work is found in a legal document issued to the governor of Chukhūr-i Sa`d regarding the payment of non-canonical taxes by a regional Armenian community.[56] Given that the *dīvān-i `adl* was charged with largely secular matters and that the joint *ṣadr*s were "empowered to make judicial decisions in accordance with the canon law,"[57] it is probable that Ismā`īl II was seeking to invest exclusive legal power—both sacred and profane—within the Persian administrative class. In the context of Ismā`īl's program to disarm the powerful Shi`ite juridical scholars, this attempt by the shah to create a substitutive judiciary looms large. Contemporary and later Shi`ite jurists seized upon Ismā`īl's abhorrent "crypto-Sunnism" to rationalize such alarming administrative developments. We can see the historiographical implications of this until today. It is more logical, however, to look to these kinds of institutional rearrangements and their implicit threat to the nascent juridical system developed by the `Arab *faqīh*s and Persian sayyids to make better sense of why Shi`ite notables like Mīr Sayyid Ḥusain al-Karakī were so vehemently opposed to the current rulership of the Safavid state.

This *ḥukm* is also valuable in that it defines who, exactly, was operating the rearticulated *dīvān-i a`lā* in 984/summer of 1576. Here we note not only the prominence of Mīrzā Makhdūm Sharīfī, Mīrzā `Ināyat Allāh Iṣfahānī, and Mīrzā Shukr Allāh Iṣfahānī but also the corresponding absence of key hierocrats who had dominated court politics in the 1560s and early 1570s. While some have looked to the elevation of the "crypto-Sunni" Mīrzā Makhdūm Sharīfī as proof of Ismā`īl's anti-Shi`ite agenda, the continued sponsorship and promotion of Mīrzā Shukr Allāh Iṣfahānī (former *mustaufī al-mamālik* and key functionary under Shāh Ṭahmāsp) points to a policy of continuity rather than variance. We are also introduced in this document to a key administrative player in Mīrzā Muḥammad Munshī, who would intermittently dominate the *dār al-inshā* and *dār al-istifā* until 996/1588 when `Abbās assumed power.[58] A grandson of Khvājah Mīrāk Munshī who had been the *munshī al-mamālik* and a featured calligrapher in the early reign of Shāh Ṭahmāsp, Mīrzā Muḥammad Munshī boasted a solid *dīvānī* pedigree.[59] Willem Floor has noted how he was conferred in his position by Ismā`īl II and that he was obliged to trace *ṭughrā*s (introductory formulas) for the new special judicial tribunal.[60]

Another notable mentioned in this *ḥukm* is Shāh Rukh Khān Zū al-Qadar, who would be promoted from *sifrahchī bāshī* to the official *muhrdār* (seal-bearer) and *dīvān-begī* (chief amir in the council) for Ismā`īl II. He had been incarcerated with Ismā`īl Mīrzā in Qahqaha, and it is not entirely surprising to see the new shah nominate and exalt those who had stood by his side (literally) during his detention. In a fascinating turn of events, Ismā`īl II named Shāh Rukh Khān as his *muhrdār* but refused to release him from Qahqaha. The phrasing in this official decree regarding how the "regulatory code" *will* be enacted ("when

Shāh Rukh Khān arrives, God willing" (*inshā Allāh ta`ālā chūn ayālat-panāh ḥukūmat-dastgāh Shāh Rukh Khān bi-dargāh-i jahān-panāh āyad*)) corroborates his continued incarceration.[61] Qāḍī Aḥmad describes how it was in fact Mīrzā Luṭf Allāh Shīrāzī, vizier of Shāh Rukh Khān, who stamped the official seal on all Safavid documents.[62] Mīrzā Luṭf Allāh Shīrāzī—a chief sayyid who had served five years in the holy city of Mashhad and two years in Astarābād as vizier on behalf of Shāh Valī Sulṭān Tātī-ūghlī, Shāh Rukh's brother—would later be part of a resurgent Shīrāzī elite that would control much of the *dīvān-i a`lā* during the reign of Shāh Khudābandah.[63] It is difficult to conceive of a more effective way of preserving a semblance of traditional Turkic Qizilbāsh corporate power structures than by acknowledging the tradition of naming Zū al-Qadars to the office of *muhrdārī*. Shāh Ismā`īl II ensured that the seal itself and the mechanisms of power that it enabled remained firmly in the hands of a Persian notable, namely Mīrzā Luṭf Allāh Shīrāzī. These rearrangements of the *dīvān* were clearly constituent elements in a greater program designed to check Qizilbāsh elements and their Shi`ite hierocratic sponsors.[64]

Also intriguing is this document's discussion of Shāh Ismā`īl II's decision to mint his inaugural currency with `Aṭṭār's famous encomium to `Alī: "'From the east to the west, if there is an Imam/`Alī and his family are everything to us!" This *bait* of poetry appeared sixty-five years earlier in a *fatḥ nāmah* (victory letter) sent to the Uzbek ruler Muḥammad Shībānī Khān, and it is clear that this was considered one of the many jingoistic slogans made popular among Persian literati and chancellery scribes in the medieval period. Nonetheless, Hinz regarded the appearance of this particular Shi`ite *bait* on Safavid coinage as evidence of Ismā`īl II's Sunni proclivities.[65] He suggested Ismā`īl removed the traditional Shi`ite testimonial (*lā illāha īlā allāh wa Muḥammad rasūl Allāhi wa `Alī walī Allāhi*) because the particular phrase "and `Alī is a Friend of God" was abhorrent to Ismā`īl's Sunni sensibilities.[66] Contending that Ismā`īl seized upon the aforementioned distich by `Aṭṭār because the embracing of `Alī and his family was contingent on a subjunctive element ("*if* there is an Imam"), Hinz argues sophistically that this *bait*'s conditional dynamic effectively neutered the validity of the apodosis ("`Alī and his family are everything to us") and thus made this verse theologically palatable to Ismā`īl II.[67] The popularity of this verse and its appearance in chancellery and numismatic materials before and after the reign of Ismā`īl II—for example, it appeared in a letter from Ismā`īl I to Muḥammad Shībānī Khān—renders Hinz's explanation somewhat unlikely.[68] The substitution of this literate and uniquely Perso-Islamic line of poetry celebrating the pre-eminence of the `Alids allowed Ismā`īl II and his coterie of Persian administrative class to maintain a Shi`ite tenor while avoiding formulaic expressions often associated with ritual, divisive *tabarrā'iyān* slogans.

This accenting of Persian administrative sensibilities is evident in two additional chancellery documents, which have received little attention until now. The first is a *dastūr*, or decree, announcing the appointment of the soon-to-be-great Mīrzā Salmān Jābirī to the office of *vizārat-i dīvān-i a`lā*. The second is the concurrent demotion of Mīrzā Shukr Allāh Iṣfahānī from vizier to *mustaufī al-mamālik*. Both appear in Abū al-Qāsim Īvūghlī's *Nuskhah-yi jāmi`a-i al-murāsalāt-i ulul albāb* but were not included by Navā'ī in his edited collection of documents pertaining to the reign of Shāh Ṭahmāsp.[69] Starting with the appointment of Mīrzā Salmān Jābirī, we find a unique document describing the beginning ascent of one of the dominant bureaucratic personalities of the second half of the sixteenth century. More intriguingly, this is a rare opportunity to learn how the Persian administrative culture—long accustomed to discoursing about kingly institutions—used the genre of epistolography to reflect on their own institutional bearing and ethos in a period of ideological and confessional ambiguity. The appearance of this decree is compared in the beginning of the text to God's own *creatio ex nihilo* by citing the Arabic aphorism "the Pen was created by God" (*mā khalaqa alaihi al-qalam*).[70] The Safavid scribe in turn reflects on the nature of Ismā`īl II's kingship, describing how "our praiseworthy qualities" (*zāt-i ḥamīdah-yi ṣifāt-i mā*) are evidenced by justice and goodness according to the "miraculous saying" (*mu`jiz-i kalām*): "If God wants to make a subject prosperous, he provides a merciful sultan, who in turn receives a [good] subject" (*idhā arādaha Allāhu ra`iyyata khairin ja`ala laha sulṭānan raḥīman wa fayyaḍa lahu ra`iyyatan*).

It is because Ismā`īl II's reign is defined by triumph (*pīrūzī*), gratitude (*ḥaqq-shināsī-yi shād*), security (*imānat*), and worthiness (*istiḥqāq*) that a group of viziers and notables have prospered and are responsible for carrying out the wishes of the shah. This sentiment is denoted in another Arabic aphorism: "If God wants to make a kingship prosperous, he gives it a sound vizier" (*idhā arāda Allāhu bi-mulkin ja`ala lahu wazīran ṣāliḥan*).[71] The *dastūr* orders how "the illustrious office of the vizarate of the central bureaucracy" (*manṣab-i jalīl al-qadr-i vizārat-i dīvān-i a`lā*), dedicated to "affairs of state" (*mahāmm-i kār-khānah-yi salṭanat*), had been conferred to Mīrzā Salmān. The Safavid scribe deliberates on the function of the vizier and discusses how Mīrzā Salmān was responsible for the "loosing and tying of the reins" (*ḥall va `adq*) of state matters, and the king had placed "absolute authority and dominion" (*min ḥaith al-infirād wa al-istiqlāl*) into his capable and knowledgeable hands (*bi kaff-i kifāyat va qabḍat-i dirāyat*).[72] Mīrzā Salmān would spend every minute of the day (*daqīqah az daqā'iq*) dispensing justice and ensuring the prosperity of the subjects in accordance with the praiseworthy maxim: "One hour of justice is better than seventy years of prayer" (*`adlu sā`atin khairun min `ibādati sab`īna sanatin*).[73] This particular Arabic phrase—often cited as a Prophetic adage—was popular in medieval Islamic mirrors-for-princes.[74]

The use of these quoted Arabic maxims in this document appear to be inspired by the seminal advice manuals of pseudo al-Ghazālī (*Naṣīḥat al-mulūk*) and Niẓām al-Mulk (*Siyar al-mulūk*), and as such texts like this emerge as truncated, epistolary versions of the *akhlāq* genre.[75] The Safavid bureaucrat goes on to demonstrate how this Persian vizier had fulfilled this requirement by demonstrating charity and sincerity towards the "affairs of men and those wretched ones in need" (*mahāmm-i barāyā va `ūzī-yi `ajzah*). The efforts of Mīrzā Salmān in turn had buttressed Ismā`īl II's mandate to address the "condition of the oppressed" (*ḥāl-i maẓlūmān*) and "secure the hopes of those who had been preyed upon" (*ḥuṣūl-i āmāl-i mulhūmān*). Continuing the device of rhymed parallel phrases (*tarṣī`*), the scribe relates how it was to become "clear and manifest in place and time" (*dar maḥālī-yi ẓuhūr va marātī-yi ṣudūr*) that virtuous efforts (*masā`ī-yi jamīla*) were to be expended wherever this order was enacted. God had established such rules of governance, and their fulfillments by administrators like Mīrzā Salmān were the beautiful objectives (*mashbūbāt*) of this Safavid state.

Given that the second document under consideration here is a decree demoting Mīrzā Shukr Allāh Iṣfahānī from vizier to *mustaufī al-mamālik*, it is reasonable to conclude that it was not only contemporaneous with the aforementioned *dastūr* but also that it was written by the same Safavid scribe.[76] Mīrzā Shukr Allāh had indeed been promoted from *mustaufī al-mamālik* (imperial accountant) to chief vizier by Ismā`īl II after his accession, but within months the shah had lost confidence in the Persian administrator and had him replaced by Mīrzā Salmān. The document begins with a series of Qur'ānic quotes that underscore the power of Ismā`īl to appoint and dismiss as he chose according to 126: 3: "You give power to whom you please"; 17: 70: "We have conferred on them special favours above a great part of Our creation"; and 74: 39: "[When Joseph attained his full manhood], We gave him power". The motif changes slightly as the decree blends benedictions with bureaucratic imagery, and the Safavid scribe writes how "the prologue of His great registry" (*dībāchah-yi daftar-i `uẓmat-ash*, e.g., the Qur'ān) was set down and arranged with the beautiful decree of 1: 68: "Nūn. By the pen and the [record] which [men] write."[77] Moreover, "the index of [Muḥammad's] prophecy" (*fihrist-i nuskhah-yi nubavvat-ash*) was illustrated with 68: 3: "There is surely an unending rewarding for you."[78] Praise is given to the Imamate (*āl-i abrār va `ishrat-i aṭhār*) who "will have an easy reckoning" (84: 8) according to the "accountants" (*muḥāsibān*); their fate is clear as the "scribes" (*kātibān*) have alluded to in 82: 10–11: "But verily over you [are appointed angels] to protect you, writing down [your deeds]." The *munshī* introduces the subject by noting the shah's interest in "contemplating and hastening the affairs of nobility and plebeians."[79]

Consistent with the previous document, the Safavid chancellery uses this decree as a vehicle to present the importance of the Persian administrative class to establishing and maintaining the equilibrium of justice and stability in a medieval Islamic state. Shāh Ismā`īl II's objective is to see the world and its inhabitants (*jahān va jahāniyān*) sitting in the shadow of security and safety (*amn va imān*) cast by the Safavid standard of victory (*rayāt-i nuṣrat-i ayāt-i humāyūn mā*).[80] With the advent of this particular reign, certain royal slaves (*ghulāmān-i ṣādiq al-ikhtiṣāṣ*) have been distinguished, and the Safavid state is as firm and established "as the foundation of the sky of the world and the light of the varying sky."[81] The *munshī* notes how the shah had privileged one particular group of slaves who were adept and skilfull. The wisdom of this sponsorship is endorsed in a quoted Persian maxim extolling the virtues of accounting (*`ilm-i siyāq*) and comptrolling (*fann-i ḥisāb*). The author evocatively summarizes the virtues of the administrative class: "With the tip of the pen of rhetoric, they draw the state decree themselves, illustrate the *ṭughrā*, and apply their signatures to caliphal *farmāns*. With the tip of [this] odiferous pen, they solve the difficulties of worldly affairs."[82] Having profiled this "ennobled group" (*zumrah-yi sharīfah*), the scribe introduces Mīrzā Shukr Allāh, who, as mentioned, had been dismissed in Rabī` I 985/June 1577 as *vazīr-i dīvān-i a`lā* for his inefficiency.[83] His subsequent reappointment here as *mustaufī al-mamālik* suggests he was not entirely *persona non grata* in the eyes of the shah. Perhaps Mīrzā Shukr Allāh's status as a long-time administrator under Shāh Ṭahmāsp earned him a reprieve. Nonetheless, the detail and stridency of the document's endorsement suggests Mīrzā Shukr Allāh had been a subject of scrutiny in the Safavid court. He is presented as neither having once placed his diligent fingers on the margin of forgetfulness and relaxation (*ḥarf-i sulū va nasiyān*), nor do his daily account books (*rūz-nāmachīh-yi a`māl-ū*) suggest any wrongdoing. The Safavid *munshī* records how "scrutinizers had seen nothing in those orders issued during his tenure to suggest anything other than the arranging of day-to-day affairs and seeing to the needs of all classes."[84] In a final gesture of legitimation, the Safavid scribe relates how Ismā`īl's decree was in accordance "with an order issued during the time of [Shāh Ṭahmāsp]."[85] The remainder of the text prescribes both the administration and court to recognize the conferral of this "illustrious office of state accountancy" (*manṣab-i jalīl al-qadr istifā al-mamālik*) on Mīrzā Shukr Allāh. Moreover, the decree applauds his performance in this office during the reign of Shāh Ṭahmāsp: "He was dedicated to a close and detailed examination of the proper arrangement of administrative affairs [*muhimmāt-i dīvānī*], taxes [*maḥṣūlāt*], gifts [*pīshkash]*, bribes [*nuzūrāt*], revenues [*taḥṣīlāt*], and organized receptions [*taqabbulāt*]."[86] The document concludes confidently, and we read how Shukr Allāh has supported Shāh Ismā`īl's program to make his land prosperous and to have his army organized (*ma`mūrī-yi kishvar va jam`iyat-i lashkar*); the decrees and orders to this effect have been stamped by him with the official seal (*muhr-i mihr-āsār*).[87]

In terms of diplomatic correspondence to other sovereign states, the reign of Shāh Ismā`īl II is not especially well represented. The only letter worth attention is a missive sent by Ismā`īl II to Khān Aḥmad Gīlān. Like other Safavid letters to the Kār Kiyā dynasty in Gīlān, this missive is not presented as brotherly (*ikhvānī*) imperial correspondence but rather as a decree (*manshūr*). Following formulaic titulature for Khān Aḥmad Gīlān, the *inscriptio* reads bluntly, *sharaf ikhtiṣāṣ yāft ki* ("it has been specially decreed").[88] The requisite invocation to God explains how the "hand of divine entreaty" (*dast-i tavassul*) seeks out the "greatest mountain of divine generosity" (*jabal al-matīn-i `ināyat Allāhī*) so as to plant the banner of "Say: 'God's is his bounty'" (3: 73). This is nicely paralleled where the literary device of bodily metaphors (*isti`ārah*) is used: "Those who place their foot of divine trust" (*pā-yi tavakkul*) on the "skirt of long-sufferance" (*dāman-i shakībā'ī*) reach their final destination of increased rank and august desires with the help: "If anyone puts his trust in God then [God] is sufficient for them" (65:3).[89]

Referring to Ismā`īl's twenty-year incarceration, the Safavid scribe relates how the "sun of our conquering dynasty" (*aftāb-i daulat-i qāhirah-yi mā*) was hidden by the concealing veil (*niqāb-i ḥujjāb*), while "our moon of manifest power" (*māh-i shaukat-i bāhirah-yi mā*) could not show its face.[90] This previous stage of occultation (*ghaibah*) and Ismā`īl II's subsequent release and coronation are presented as monumental events similar to his namesake's parousia seventy-five years earlier. For this reason, the scribe writes, this peerless and skilful ruler is mandated by 3: 25: "You give power to whom You wish," and 6: 128: "For the earth is God's to give as a heritage to whomever he pleases."[91] Thus, the metaphor of occultation and unveiling continues as Ismā`īl II informs Khān Aḥmad Khān that he has opened the "gates" (*abvāb*) of this world and the Hereafter to reveal (*aẓhār*) perfect power and unveil (*ẓuhūr*) unending dominion. These august events ensured that the Qur'ānic phrase 19: 55, "mention in the Book of Ismā`īl," had been corroborated. We found Safavid *munshīs* adroitly using this particular Qur'ānic verse in earlier correspondence from the reign of Shāh Ismā`īl, and its appearance here underscores the link between Ismā`īl II's program of legitimacy and that of his grandfather. Indeed, Sholeh Quinn noted how Ismā`īl I and Ismā`īl II were consciously twinned and juxtaposed by the historian Qāḍī Aḥmad with counterparts in the Mongol and Timurid dynasties.[92]

Ismā`īl II alludes to the once great relationship between the Kār Kiyās and the Safavids and how he remembered Khān Aḥmad Gīlān's sincere companionship at Qahqaha. Khān Aḥmad had since been transferred to Isṭakhr, but it was Ismā`īl II's intention to honour their pact and see him properly installed in Gīlān (*mamlakat-i Gīlān*).[93] This dynamic of Ismā`īl II looking to the Safavid past and invoking the imminent precedence of his namesake grandfather appears in another short letter sent to Mīrzā Muḥammad Ḥākim, the governor of Kābul and brother of the Mughal ruler Akbar.[94] In particular, the Safavid scribe delineates the historical amity between the two ruling houses, pointing out how Ismā`īl II's great ancestor Ismā`īl I (*jadd-i buzurgvāram*) had provided Ḥākim's own exalted grandfather (*jadd-i a`lā*), Ẓahīr al-Dīn Bābur Pādshāh, with assistance in the form of a victorious army (*amdād va mu`āvanat-i lashkar-i fīrūzī*) after the Timurid ruler was forced from the Farghana Valley.[95] The Safavid author of this letter also accessed the increasingly popular chancellery compendium, the *Makhzan al-inshā*, by Ḥusain Vā`iẓ Kāshifī. The formal blessing (*du`ā*), which appears after Mīrzā Muḥammad Ḥākim's name—"May God adorn the throne of his state with the properties of His essence, and may He illuminate the eyes of his state with the shimmering lights of His qualities"—was borrowed from the section "Arabic Prose Blessings for People of the First Rank."[96] Such propinquity to the administrative legacy of Timurid polymaths like Kāshifī is not altogether surprising given the strength and depth of these new administrative impulses in Shāh Ismā`īl II's court.

While there is little doubt that Ismā`īl's reign was short and intermittently bloody, we also have to acknowledge existing chancellery and documentary evidence that point to a surprisingly assertive administrative culture. Newman has likewise observed how "there was a greater degree of continuity of service among the Tajiks in the central and provincial administration" during this period.[97] In his larger ideological program of repositioning the very unique Safavid amalgam of pre-Islamic divine absolutism and Sufi notions of perfect spiritual authority, Shāh Ismā`īl II faced resistance and dissent early on from disenfranchised Qizilbāsh elements and entrenched clerical forces. Ismā`īl II built alliances with co-opted tribes, such as the Ustājlū and the Zū al-Qadar, but his most important partnership was undoubtedly with the Persian administrative class. Chancellery documents reviewed here—the *ḥukm* announcing the composition of Ismā`īl's administration and the newly articulated *dīvān-i `adl* along with appointments and reappointments of key Persian bureaucratic possibilities—highlight Ismā`īl II's reign, however short, as a period of regeneration for the "men of the pen." Although Ismā`īl's reign has been neatly packaged by Safavid historians as a period defined by Sunni intransigence and borderline mayhem and it is commonly referred to as the beginning of the "second Civil War," his reign in fact stands as an attempt to reverse an impressive scale of clerical influence and power in the Safavid court. By attempting to halt the trajectory of jurist notables like Mīr Sayyid Ḥusain al-Karakī and instead privilege networks of scribes, accountants, *adībs*, and scholar-bureaucrats, Ismā`īl II established a dynamic that characterized Safavid court and chancellery politics for the next two decades. As Klaus-Michael Röhrborn remarked: "In light of the career of [Mīrzā Muḥammad Munshī] under Isma`īl II, it would appear that that the chancery reform of `Abbās I is not so shocking."[98]

The Emergence of a New Esprit de Corps under Khudābandah

In many ways, Muḥammad Khudābandah has been as much a victim as his brother Ismā`īl II with respect to historiographical vilification. On account of the predatory nature of court politics in the 1570s and 1580s, the rule of Muḥammad Khudābandah has been signalled as a nadir in the timeline of sixteenth-century Safavid history. Disturbingly, some historians have pointed to the indirect rule of royal women like Parī Khān Khānum and Khair al-Nisā (Mahd-i `Ulyā) as evidence of the rapacious nature of Safavid politics in the 1570s; the assumption is that this volatility was driven by the desire of competing wives and concubines to secure the throne for their respective sons.[99] The inability to marshal such divisive trends is laid at the feet of Muḥammad Khudābandah himself, the only one of Ṭahmāsp's sons to survive Ismā`īl's ruthless purge the previous year. Khudābandah had spent most of his adulthood enjoying a *bon vivant* lifestyle in Herāt and Shīrāz before ascending the Safavid throne on 5 Zū al-Ḥijja 985/13 February 1578. His inability to control his sister (Parī Khān Khānum), his wife (Mahd-i `Ulyā), and his Qizilbāsh amirs combined with a debilitating ophthalmic condition have encouraged historians to consign Khudābandah to that ever-popular category of regal dupe.

Effectively blind and politically witless, Muḥammad Khudābandah is presented as the head of a court rife with debauchery, murder, intrigue, sex scandals, avarice, and ineptitude. Such historiographical extremes are undoubtedly rooted in the Safavid sources themselves, namely those chronicles like the *Khulāṣat al-tavārīkh* and the *Tārīkh-i `ālam-ārā-yi `Abbāsī,* that were commissioned during the period of Shāh `Abbās the Great, and these endeavoured to accentuate the unpleasant political conditions of Iran immediately prior to the accession of the greatest of Safavid rulers in 996/1588.[100] Moreover, it is clear that the authors of these sources needed to underscore the volatility and misdirection of Khudābandah's rule to better rationalize `Abbās's numerous rebellions in Khurāsān during the 1580s and the ultimate removal of his own father from power. The modern articulation of these prejudices is rooted in the work of one of the pioneers of Safavid political history, Hans Robert Roemer, who set the tenor for Khudābandah's reign with the 1939 work *Die Niedergang Irans nach dem Tode Ismā`īls der Grausamen (1577–1581).* At that time, he wrote of a shah who spent most of his time in the *ḥaram* and whose reign was a "departure" (*Abkehrung*) from normal kingly rule. [101] Roemer's misgivings about this period were reiterated years later when he typified Khudābandah's reign as one of "weakness, indifference, and incompetence."[102] In his later *Persien auf dem Weg*, he further castigates Khudābandah's reign as "being on the edge of chaos," adding that there were no benefits brought to Iran during his decade of rule.[103] This historiographical trend has continued among a variety of works until very recently.[104] Perhaps the problems we associate with the reign of Khudābandah were more a reflection of systemic difficulties in the Safavid empire than anything overtly specific to his personality or style of rule.[105] Since the mid-sixteenth century, the sanctity of the Safavid royal body had been diluted considerably, as we saw in the systematic elimination of Safavid princes and princelings during Ismā`īl II's reign. This was a particularly mercenary period in terms of Qizilbāsh brinkmanship, and Shāh Khudābandah's invertebrate ways were designed to placate this unruly element. At the same time, this was clearly a canny individual who had benefited from a thorough courtly education. It seems likely that Khudābandah had agency in his self-preservation and was not a passive recipient of intermittent Qizilbāsh goodwill and succour. Despite its status as a historiographical *bête noire* for scholars of Safavid Iranian history, this period of rule saw the continued momentum of a resurgent Perso-Islamic bureaucratic class in the chancellery.[106] An analysis of Muḥammad Khudābandah and his relationship with different sets of Persian administrators and religious personalities in cities such as Herāt, Shīrāz, and Qazvīn will give us good reason to reconsider how we understand this particular ruler. More importantly, this cadre of Persian scholar-bureaucrats was integral to maintaining the momentum established during the reign of Ismā`īl II, whereby key elements of Perso-Islamic concepts of authority, justice, and religion were resuscitated and moulded to the peculiar Safavid hybrid of kingship, Imami Shi`ism, and charismatic ideals of Sufism.

Sulṭān-Muḥammad Mīrzā, son of Shāh Ṭahmāsp and his Türkmen wife Sulṭānum Begum, was born in 937/1531 in Tabrīz. Little is known about his youth, but we do know that he was named the nominal governor of Herāt at the age of four, after the reconquest of that city from the Uzbeks in Shawwāl 943/ March 1537.[107] In reality, the city was under the governance of the powerful Muḥammad Sharaf al-Dīn Oghlī Takkalū, *lala* (tutor) to Sulṭān-Muḥammad Mīrzā.[108] In addition to receiving his training and education from one of the most powerful and talented Qizilbāsh amirs of the mid-sixteenth century, Sulṭān-Muḥammad Mīrzā was the ostensible overseer of an unprecedented urban renewal programme in Herāt: residential gardens, public edifices, shrines, and irrigation complexes were built or restored. A positive by-product of this reconstruction in the 1540s and 1550s was an influx of poets, litterateurs, artists, and calligraphers. It is certain that the young Sulṭān-Muḥammad Mīrzā would have been exposed to a rich array of cultural, bureaucratic, and scholarly influences in Herāt. Indeed, it was during his first tenure as governor of Khurāsān that he married the granddaughter of the great Persian vizier and *vakīl* Mīrzā Sharaf Qāḍī-yi Jahān in Ramaḍān 956/September 1549.[109]

Herāt was able to recover much of its Timurid glory thanks to the administrative efforts of Muḥammad Sharaf al-Dīn. During the period of Sulṭān-Muḥammad Mīrzā's nominal governorship, "the court of Herāt broadcasted manifestations of its splendour: festivals were organized, festivals which functioned effectively as propaganda for the regime."[110] Shāh Ṭahmāsp was pleased with the progress of this former Timurid capital and its newly invigorated imperial profile, and Sulṭān-Muḥammad Mīrzā was reappointed to this important appanage in 963/1555–56, after a very brief stint in which his brother Ismā`īl had taken over the governorship.[111] Other brothers were named to more peripheral governorships in Mashhad, Sīstān, and Qandahār.[112] In Sha`bān 974/February 1567, a larger administrative shuffle was ordered for Herāt after the revolt of Qazāq Khān in 971/1564. Yakān Shāh Qulī Ustājlū was named (honorary) tutor to the prince, while the chief religious position of *Shaikh al-Islām* was granted to Shaikh Ḥusain `Abd al-Ṣamād al-Ḥārithī al-`Āmilī, father of Shaikh Bahā'ī and exemplar of the `Āmilī Shi`ite clerical emigration to Iran in the mid-sixteenth century.[113]

Sulṭān-Muḥammad Mīrzā continued as *vālī* of Khurāsān for another six years, until he was named governor to Shīrāz in 979/1572.[114] During this time, he continued to develop and nurture a lively coterie of supporters in the form of poets, artists, and courtiers in Herāt Here he earned his reputation as a talented poet with the *takhalluṣ* of Fahmī, who participated energetically in poetry gatherings (*mash`arat*).[115] Sām Mīrzā notes in his biography of poets, *Tazkirah-yi tuḥfah-yi Sāmī*, that Sulṭān-Muḥammad was well noted for his education and cognitive acuity.[116] When he moved to Shīrāz, he was accompanied by a number of individuals from his Herātī retinue, the most recognizable of which was the *sayyid* Shāh Muẓaffar al-Dīn `Alī Injū, who would serve in Shīrāz as a judge to the local military (*qāḍī-yi `askar*).[117] From 981/1573 until his accession to the throne in 985/1578, Sulṭān-Muḥammad Mīrzā served as the nominal *vālī* of Fārs, while in reality the governorship was held by Vālī Sulṭān Qalmānchī Ughlī Zū al-Qadar.[118] Shīrāz was an important centre of philosophy and intellectual thought, and as discussed earlier, a Shīrāzī school of philosophy had been quite active there since the late fifteenth century due to the work of Jalāl al-Dīn al-Davvānī (d. 908/1502) and Ṣadr al-Dīn Muḥammad Dashtakī (d. 903/1497).[119] During Sulṭān-Muḥammad's tenure, key luminaries such as Fakhr al-Dīn Muḥammad ibn Ḥusain Samākī Astarābādī and Mullā Mīrzā Jān were producing work regarding various aspects of Perso-Islamic philosophy, with a focus on writing commentaries on Naṣīr al-Dīn al-Ṭūsī's seminal text on logic, the *Tajrīd al-manṭiq*.[120] It would also appear that Shīrāz continued its emergence as a centre of illustrated manuscript production during Sulṭān-Muḥammad's administration; throughout much of the 1570s and 1580s, Shīrāz began its ascent as a lodestar for manuscript illumination and binding.[121] Considerable political support for such initiatives also came from the local governor, Vālī Sulṭān Qalmānchī Ughlī Zū al-Qadar. He had publicly shown his ecumenical stripes by intervening on behalf of Makhdūm Sharīfī, who had been thrown into a pit by *tabarrā'iyān* because of his role in Ismā`īl II's campaign against the al-Karakī family of Shi`ite hierocrats.[122]

When Ismā`īl II died mysteriously on 13 Ramaḍān 985/24 November 1577, the Persian administrator Mīrzā Salmān Jābirī realized that the Safavid court could not function without proximity to a male member of the Safavid family. After two months of de facto rule by Parī Khān Khānum, he managed to make his way to Shīrāz and convince Sulṭān-Muḥammad to assume the throne. Sulṭān-Muḥammad, his wife Khair al-Nisā Begum (Mahd-i `Ulyā), and the sizeable retinue he had accrued in Shīrāz proceeded to the Safavid capital of Qazvīn. Parī Khān Khānum, who had engineered a series of motley alliances with various Turkomān, Takkalū, and Circassian groups, was assassinated, and a purge of various posts and offices ensued. Given that Mīrzā Salmān Jābirī had been raised and trained as an administrator in Shīrāz (his father had been the chief provincial *vazīr*),[123] it is not surprising that a "Shīrāzī" bloc of bureaucrats, courtiers, and literary men grew prominent in Qazvīn after the accession of Sulṭān-Muḥammad (now styled as Shāh Muḥammad Sulṭān but known popularly as Muḥammad Khudābandah). Abū al-Valī Injū, who had served as *mutawallī* in Mashhad and Ardabīl and acted as *qāḍī-yi `askar* in Shīrāz, was brought to Qazvīn and nominated to the office of *ṣadr*.[124] While Ḥusain Beg ibn Khvājah Shujā` al-Dīn would assume the post of *vazīr* to Khudābandah's son, Ḥamza Mīrzā, Mīr Qavām al-Dīn Ḥusain also enjoyed considerable political goodwill in this new order.[125] He had been the *mustaufī* for the governor of Shīrāz, Vālī Sulṭān Zū al-Qadar, before Khudābandah's ascension. After 1577, he would be appointed *vazīr* to Khudābandah's wife Khair al-Nisā.[126] Mīrzā Luṭf Allāh Shīrāzī, *vazīr* to Khudābandah's sister Zainab Sulṭān, later (991/1583) transferred to Sulṭān Ḥamza Mīrzā and was ultimately promoted to the *dīvān-i a`lā* in 996/1587.[127] Shīrāzī women appear to have played an important role in this reconstituted political environment: Ḥamza Mīrzā's wet nurse, Khān Jān Khānum, was a daughter of a prominent Shīrāzī notable who had married the chief Shāmlū amir, Sulṭān Ḥusain Khān. Khān Jān Khānum, in turn, was married to `Alī Qulī Khān Shāmlū, who would serve as *lala* and custodian of `Abbās Mīrzā in Khurāsān.[128] Immediate members of the shah's family assumed crucial positions, and in an unprecedented move, Khudābandah's own son Ḥamza Mīrzā was named *vakīl-i dīvān-i a`lā*,[129] while Mahd-i `Ulyā exercised considerable influence over her husband in administrative and governmental matters between 1578 and 1579.[130] Shīrāz had historically been a lodestar of intellectual and cultural activity dating back to the fourteenth century, since the rule of the Injuyids and the Muẓaffarids and up to the Timurids; thus, the dependency of Khudābandah in the 1570s on this urbane Shīrāzī contingent is not surprising.

Facing antagonism from disaffected Qizilbāsh groupings as well as entrenched Circassian and Georgian ethnic elements in the court, Khudābandah relied increasingly on the Persian secretarial and bureaucratic class with whom he had developed a lively and symbiotic relationship in the last thirty years. Khudābandah's partnership with Mīrzā Salmān Jābirī and other Persian bureaucrats was supplemented by Mahd-i `Ulyā's patronage of her fellow Māzandarānīs, such as Mīr Qavām al-Dīn Ḥusain, and her continued relationship with her family who served as local rulers in Māzandarān.[131] A conspiracy against Mahd-i `Ulyā emerged against the backdrop of a number of invasions of the Caucasus in 986–87/1578–79 by Sulṭān Murād III, who had despatched Lala Muṣṭafā Pāshā to wrestle away Safavid satellite zones in Georgia and Armenia. The ensuing Ottoman alliance with the Tātār ruler of Crimea threatened Safavid interests in the Caucasus. After the Tatars attacked the port city of Darband, Khudābandah despatched a successful retaliatory force to Shīrvān under the leadership of Mīrzā Salmān Jābirī and Ḥamza Mīrzā, which managed to capture the Tātār field commander and brother of the reigning Tātār khan, `Ādil Girāy Khān, on 28 Ramaḍān 986/28 November 1578. The conveyance of `Ādil Girāy Khān to Qazvīn and his confinement in the royal apartments at Chihil Sutūn would provide the enemies of Mahd-i `Ulyā with the ammunition they needed. The conspirators circulated the rumour that the Queen and the Tātār were having an affair. After killing `Ādil Girāy Khān, they burst into the *ḥaram* and strangled the Queen.

Following the death of his wife, Khudābandah relied increasingly on his bureaucratic ally, Mīrzā Salmān Jābirī, who had positioned himself as both a "lord of the sword *and* the pen" (*ṣāḥib al-saif wa al-qalam*).[132] This ontological duality was best manifested in 989/1581, when he emerged as the principal architect of a significant diplomatic arrangement, wherein the Georgian Kartel and Khakheti dynasties—led by Simon Khān and Alexander Khān respectively—were subordinated to the Safavid household.[133] This new suzerain status, whereby each

Georgian ruler proffered a son and daughter to the Safavid court (the daughters were married to Ḥamza Mīrzā while the sons were held as hostages), was negotiated by Mīrzā Salmān, who personally presided over the ceremony in Georgia where robes of honour were exchanged and monies were remitted.[134] He secured himself further with the Safavid family by arranging to have his daughter marry the heir apparent, Ḥamza Mīrzā, in 988/1580. Much of the next year was spent consolidating his position at the expense of other Persian administrators and Qizilbāsh amirs.[135] During this period, Mīrzā Salmān reversed many of the Ottoman successes in the Caucasus—highlighted by a Safavid-Georgian force overwhelming the Ottoman garrisons in Tblisi and Shīrvān—but a surprising victory by `Uthmān Pāshā at Meshale prevented further progress.[136] Mīrzā Salmān's brinkmanship contributed to the coalescing of a conspiracy around the *qūrchī bāshī* Qulī Beg Afshār, the *muhrdār* Shāh Rukh Khān Zū al-Qadar, and Muḥammad Khān Turkomān. Assassins were despatched after Mīrzā Salmān on 19 Rabī` II 991/12 May 1583, when he left Herāt to organize a celebratory feast in Gāzargāh at the shrine of his ancestor `Abd Allāh Anṣārī; however, supporters alerted him to this threat.[137] He promptly returned to Herāt and sought asylum in the madrasah of Sulṭān-Ḥusain Bāiqarā, where Khudābandah and Ḥamza Mīrzā had based their royal apartments, to little avail.[138]

Shāh Khudābandah was further isolated three years later when, during a campaign against the Ottomans in Āzarbāijān, his son Ḥamza Mīrzā was murdered while drinking with boon companions in the tent of `Alī Qulī Khān Fatḥ Ughlī Ustājlū on 28 Zū al-Ḥijja 994/10 December 1586.[139] After Ḥamza Mīrzā's death, Muḥammad Khudābandah countermanded the Qizilbāsh demand for the rebellious `Abbās Mīrzā to be appointed the formal successor and instead named his twelve-year-old son Abū Ṭālib Mīrzā as his crown prince (*vālī `ahd*). During this period, Khudābandah elevated the powerful Persian bureaucrat and confidant of the shah (*muqarrab haḍrat*), Mīrzā Muḥammad Munshī, from chief of the *dīvān-i inshā* to the *vazīr-i dīvān-i a`lā*. Skeptical about Khudābandah's ability to rule at the best of times, Manūchihr Pārsādūst nonetheless admits that the shah involved himself diligently in such matters of state between 994/1586 and 996/1588.[140] During this time, Khudābandah ordered extensive siege operations against Ottoman-held Tabrīz but was forced to call off the campaign after the arrival of a relief force under Farhād Pāshā in early 1587.[141] Khudābandah's chief political ally, besides Mīrzā Muḥammad Munshī, was `Alī Qulī Khān Ustājlū who was committed to preventing a Shāmlū ascendancy through the candidacy of `Abbās Mīrzā. In the eastern theatre, these intra-Qizilbāsh intrigues culminated in Murshid Qulī Khān Ustājlū successfully securing physical control of the young `Abbās Mīrzā at the expense of his main political rival `Alī Qulī Khān Shāmlū. By 1587, Murshid Qulī Khān was committed to attempting yet another putsch (one had failed earlier in 1582), and in December of that year, he marched to Qazvīn with his imperial charge to demand Khudābandah's abdication on 14 Zū al-Qa`da 996/5 October 1588. Khudābandah and his son Abū Ṭālib Mīrzā were courteously treated and transferred, along with another son Ṭahmāsp Mīrzā, to the Alamut castle near Qazvīn. Khudābandah spent the next seven years there in quiet "retirement" with his family and died peacefully at the age of sixty-five.

There was considerable continuity between the administrations that materialized during the reigns of Shāh Ṭahmāsp, Shāh Ismā`īl II, and Khudābandah. We can identify a number of prominent individuals who came to dominate if not monopolize key positions in these successive administrations. Probably the most famous administrator of this particular period is the aforementioned Mīrzā Salmān Jābirī. Appointed as *vazīr-i dīvān-i a`lā* by Shāh Ismā`īl II, Mīrzā Salmān was able to secure his position after Khudābandah's accession in 985/1578 by removing rivals within the administration and working in proximity to Khudābandah's wife, Khair al-Nisā. He earned the epithet of *I`timād al-daulat* (Pillar of the State) and was seen as a personification of the historical exemplar Āṣaf ibn Barkhiya—the legendary vizier to King Solomon—by Qāḍī Aḥmad who praised him as *Āṣaf-i zamān*.[142] On the subject of historical exemplars, he apparently attempted to make the most of his genealogical connection to the "best of the [Prophet's] Companions" (*`umdat al-aṣḥāb*),[143] and contemporaries would refer to him as the "wonder of the age, the Salmān of the times" (*u`jūbah-yi al-āwān Salmān al-waqt al-zamān*), a clear reference to the much vaunted Persian convert and confidant of the Prophet, Salmān al-Fārisī.[144] Afūshtah-ī Natanzī is particularly approbatory in his depiction of Mīrzā Salmān and describes this administrator as unsurpassed in eloquence and rhetoric and more than diligent in his handling of civilian and military matters.[145] This is partly rationalized by the fact that Afūshtah-ī Natanzī lived and worked in Shīrāz and was more than probably intimate with Mīrzā Salmān during his time there. According to the later Safavid source the *Jāmi`-i Mufīdī* by Muḥammad Mufīd Mustaufī Bafqī: "The *vizārat* of Mīrzā Salmān Jābirī ranks with the *vizārat*s of Khvājah Niẓām al-Mulk, Juvainī, Rashīd al-Dīn, and Najm-i S̱ānī."[146]

After Mīrzā Salmān, however, little is known about the Safavid bureaucracy. Qāḍī Aḥmad notes how two prominent secretaries and poets, Mīrzā Sharaf-i Jahān and Mīr Rūḥ Allāh, were the son and grandson of the famous vizier Qāḍī-yi Jahān.[147] He also mentions specifically the son of `Aṭā Allāh Iṣfahānī, Mīrzā Aḥmad, who had served as a chief bureaucrat in the regions of Āzarbāijān, Qarābāgh, and Shīrvān in the latter years of Shāh Ṭahmāsp and who had gone on to serve Khudābandah.[148] Mīrzā Aḥmad had penned a number of letters to the Ottomans on behalf of Ṭahmāsp, and after Khudābandah's accession he was transferred to an important post in the chancellery of Murshid Qulī Khān Ustājlū in Herāt because of a disagreement with the all-powerful Mīrzā Salmān.[149] Mīrzā Aḥmad's son, Mīrzā Shāh Vālī Iṣfahānī, was named as the replacement *vazīr* for the province of Khurāsān after his father's death in 1582.[150] Moreover, Mīrzā Shāh Vālī's promotion to the rank of *I`timād al-daulat* would be one of the first central bureaucratic appointments made by Shāh `Abbās when he came to power in 996/1588. Qāḍī `Abd Allāh of Khuy, who had "been entrusted with correspondence in the paradisical court assembly of Shāh

Ṭahmāsp," continued to work for the *dār al-inshā* after Ṭahmāsp's death, until his own passing in 991/1583.[151] Mīrzā Hidāyat Allāh, grandson of Najm-i S̱ānī, served Khudābandah as *vazīr* in the province of Gīlān until his promotion to chief vizier after the murder of Mīrzā Salmān in 991/1583.[152] Soon displaced by Mīrzā Muḥammad Munshī, he was made chief functionary (*nāẓir-i mu`āmalāt*) of Iṣfahān in 995/1586–87.[153] During the reign of Shāh `Abbās, we learn that Mīrzā Hidāyat Allāh was in charge of *tiyūl* dispersals in the royal camp.[154]

One particularly powerful administrator who bridged both reigns was Mīrzā Muḥammad Munshī, the son of `Alī Beg Surkh and grandson of Khvājah Mīrākī (a prominent *munshī* in the Safavid chancellery between 1524 and 1536).[155] Mīrzā Muḥammad Munshī began as a scribe (*kātib*) in the chancellery under Shāh Ṭahmāsp and was later promoted as head of correspondence during the reign of Ismā`īl II.[156] He was transferred to the accountancy as *mustaufī al-mamālik* in 991/1583 after the death of Mīrzā Salmān.[157] In 994/1586, he was promoted to chief vizier of the *dīvān-i a`lā,* pushing aside the aforementioned Mīrzā Hidāyat Allāh and earning the honorary designation of confindant to the shah (*muqarrab al-haḍrat*) as well as *I`timād al-daulat.*[158] In 996/1588 he was arrested after the arrival of Murshid Qulī Khān and `Abbās Mīrzā but managed to avoid the wholesale purge that took place soon after.[159] He was demoted as vizier to Khudābandah's surviving son Abū Ṭālib Mīrzā but managed to quickly recover his status and was reappointed as grand vizier in 996/1588. Unable to restrain his ambitions, he was arrested and executed six months later for being "overbearing and seditious."[160] Another battle-hardened administrator, of course, was Mīrzā Luṭf Allāh Shīrāzī who had shone briefly during the reign of Ismā`īl II but was consigned to a series of vizierships on behalf of members of the royal family (Zainab Sulṭān, Sulṭān Ḥamza Mīrzā) for much of the 1580s. He managed to recover with the accession of Shāh `Abbās, and in 998/1590 he was named *vazīr-i dīvān-i a`lā* for a very short period before he was replaced by Ḥātim Beg Urdūbādī.[161] Maulānā Muḥammad Amīn was another Persian bureaucrat who successfully bridged this critical transition between Khudābandah and `Abbās. Muḥammad Amīn had been entrusted under Shāh Ṭahmāsp and Khudābandah with the greater part of correspondence in Turkish and Persian. After 996/1588 he was promoted to the post of *munshī al-mamālik* and was in charge of all imperial correspondence (*inshā al-mamālik*) under Shāh `Abbās until his death in 1000/1591–92. Once again, the dynamic of generations of Persian *dīvāniyān* at work is evident in the fact that Muḥammad Amīn was the grandson of Maulānā Adham, who had been a key chancellery official during the latter years of Shāh Ismā`īl I's and the beginning of Shāh Ṭahmāsp's respective reigns.[162]

In terms of this dynamic of bureaucratic continuity, many of the future luminaries who served Shāh `Abbās cut their administrative teeth training and working under Khudābandah. One of the first administrators to come to mind in this regard is the famous court chronicler Iskander Beg Munshī. Iskander Beg had been an underling to Mīrzā `Aṭā Allāh, the governor of Āzarbāijān, in the early

1570s, but he made his way to the accountancy (*dār al-istifā*) and eventually found himself in the royal chancery (*daftar-i khānah-yi humāyūn*).[163] From there, he began working in the *dār al-inshā* in 996/1588 under the aforementioned *munshī al-mamālik* Maulānā Muḥammad Amīn, and during this time he was entrusted with correspondence and writing orders (*parvānas*) and missives to sultans.[164] Similarly, the historian Qāḍī Aḥmad had a long and illustrious career in the pre-`Abbās days, beginning with study and work in the famous atelier of Ibrāhīm Mīrzā in Mashhad during the mid-1550s. Eventually, he was named as *vazīr* to Ibrāhīm Mīrzā, a post he held for quite some time before working ultimately on behalf of the state accountant (*mustaufī al-mamālik*) Mīr Khān Ghāzī. In 989/1581, Qāḍī Aḥmad was appointed by Khudābandah to the lucrative position of administrator of pious foundations (*mustaufī-yi mauqufāt*), a position that no doubt afforded him the time to work on his magnum opus the *Khulāṣat al-tavārīkh*.[165] The third in this powerful troika was Ḥātim Beg Urdūbādī, who had served as the chief vizier for Shāh `Abbās until Rabī` I 1019/May 1610, when he died on campaign near Ūrumiyyah.[166] Ḥātim Beg hailed from one of the best-represented administrative families in Iran that traced their lineage back to the great bureaucrat/philosopher Khvājah Naṣīr al-Dīn al-Ṭūsī.[167] He was the son of Malik Bahrām, the local ruler of Urdūbād, who had received his appointment as *kalāntar* of Urdūbād in the Aras Valley from Shāh Ismā`īl. He had assumed this post after the death of his father, but during the reign of Khudābandah he moved directly into the provincial and central administration.[168] He had been named as *vazīr* to the governor of Kirmān, Vālī Beg Yūz Bāshī Afshār, in the 1570s and was later nominated to the post of *mustaufī al-mamālik* in Yazd.[169] In 999/1591, three years after `Abbās's accession, Ḥātim Beg Urdūbādī was appointed as *mustaufī al-mamālik* for all of Iran. Six months after this, he was named the grand *vazīr* and honoured with the *laqab* of *I`timād al-daulat*. He would be the architect of many of the administrative reforms instituted by Shāh `Abbās in the late 1590s, and he dominated the Safavid chancellery until 1621.[170]

Turning to the epistolary evidence, the most complicated yet fascinating document produced between 1577 and 1588 was a lengthy royal letter from Khudābandah to the Ottoman Sultan Murād III. [171] There are a number of features to this letter—very probably written soon after Ottoman hostilities broke out in 986/1578–79–requiring commentary, and in doing so informs our quest to understand the multitude of discourses that characterized this newly invigorated chancellery. The Perso-Arabic syncretist style of the *munshī* is profiled quickly as he begins the letter with a macaronic *rubā`ī* (bilingual quatrain). The first distich is, in fact, an Arabic Qur'ānic quote 2:32: "Glory to you (O Lord), knowledge we have none except what You have given us," and this is followed by a stylized Persian encomiastic to God's dominion and knowledge: "Earth and Heaven belong to you/What we have, we have only in name."[172] This linguistic dualism is in many ways framed by a larger binary whereby religious language and subject matter are interspersed regularly with "secular" motifs and tropes. This is especially evident in the introductory invocations to God and

Prophet Muḥammad. The Prophet and his family have been blessed by the unparalleled Artificer (*ṣāni`-i bīchūn*), who has "adorned [Muḥammad's] flaming crown of authority (*tāj-i vahhāj-i ayālat*) with the jewel, "We have appointed you caliphs in the land" (10:14). The exalted throne of the Prophet, the scribe writes, has flourished with the beauty of "We gave him authority in the land" (18:84), while the highly placed pulpits of his fortune (*manābir-i buland-pāyah-yi daulat-ash*) have been lit with "I have to place a trustee on earth" (2:30). Lastly, Muḥammad's sovereignty has been stamped by His bountiful mint (*dār al-ḍarb-i `ināyat*) on a coin that reads, "We have favoured some over the others" (2: 253).[173]

The proximity between the Prophet and such kingly, profane emblems of authority (crown, throne, *khuṭbah*, mint) is not something regularly demonstrated in normative Islamic discourse. This decidedly secular invocation to God and Muḥammad is unique in terms of epistolary standards to date, and we are immediately struck by its less-than-subtle argumentation that the descendants of Muḥammad have been divinely appointed as legatees and caliphs on earth. The inimitability of God is subsequently discussed, and we find a deliberate decision to frame this presentation in strict chancellery terms. God is the adorner of kingship (*mulk-i ārā'ī*) who defies description "even if the arrangers of the pearls of rhetoric came together and worked for centuries."[174] This presentation of God's power with epistolary motifs continues: "God, using his hand of decree [*dast-i qaḍā*] with the pen of power [*qalam-i qudrat*], has written the perfect words *huwā al-murād* [Thus, it is done] and the universe was created."[175] In self-aggrandizing style, the chancellery official writes, "God, like a chancellery stylist [*munshī-yi dār al-inshā*], uses His perfect power to create with a simple nod of his head."[176]

Provocatively, the letter introduces the addressee Murād III by observing blithely how an emperor, in the vigour of adolescence and the prime of youth (*dar `unfuvān-i javānī va ray`ān-i shabāb*), should avoid "carnal desires and illicit things" (*maḥẓūrāt va malāhī*) and withdraw his hand from "illegal and improper matters" (*munkarāt va manāhī*).[177] In a disappointed and avuncular tone, Khudābandah observes how the Arabic phrase, "Youth do not love the appeal of pious tranquility," had been inscribed on the forehead of Murād III's affairs (*nāṣiyyah-yi aḥvāl ash*), while the Qur'ānic phrase 19:57, "And We raised him to an exalted station," had appeared on the page of his hopes and desires (*ṣafḥah-yi āmāl ash*). These are rhetorical allusions to Sulṭān Murād's well-known harem antics, to which the scribe appends a number of verses by Sa`dī regarding the dangers of youthful exuberance. It is only at this point that the scribe acknowledges Perso-Islamic epistolary structure and introduces a lengthy *intitulatio* section in Arabo-Persian, which exalts the addressee through encomiums and epideictic language. Interestingly, this formulaic section appears to be a composite of Arabic phrases taken from earlier letters. Large sections of this *intitulatio*, wherein Murād III is described as "he who sets up the balance of good and kindness" (*wāḍi`u mīzāni al-birri wa al-iḥsān*), "he who pours the running waters of kindness on all of Islam" (*mufīḍu zawārifi al-`awārif `alā qāṭibat al-islām*), "the defender of kings and protector of rulers" (*mu`īnu al-mulūki wa ẓahīru al-khawāqīni*), as well as the "servant of the holy cities of Mecca and Medina" (*khādimu al-ḥaramaini al-sharīfain*),[178] are borrowed from the *intitulatio* of an earlier letter written by the Safavid chancellery to Sulaimān the Magnificent in the 1560s. Moreover, sections of verse also appear to have been recycled from this particular missive.[179] This replication is made further evident by the fact that the entire Arabic *elevatio*—that signal text designed to (finally) introduce the name of the addressee of an epistle's *intitulatio* and appears separate in the upper corner of the original missive—is the same *elevatio* used in Ṭahmāsp's letter to Sulaimān. Indeed, we find no less than thirteen poetic verses, some appearing as single *bait*s and some appearing as quatrains, which are quoted from earlier correspondence penned during the reign of Shāh Ṭahmāsp.

A number of classical Persian poets were singularly in vogue in Khudābandah's chancellery, and this study asserts that the choice of certain poems by these Safavid scribes yields some intriguing observations. After the formulaic *intitulatio*, the secretary is adamant in illustrating how vanity mixed with kingship is a dangerous concoction and as such is not a surprising theme, given Murād III's recent attack on Safavid territories. To this point, the scribe looks to three lines of poetry from Niẓāmī's panegyric to Shāh Muẓaffar al-Dīn Qizil Arsalān, which prefaces his great epic poem *Khusrau va Shirīn*.[180] In particular, the scribe rhetorically twists the line, "The Shah of the west is also penultimate in the east/ Qizil whose crown is higher than the moon," and replaces the name Qizil with the name Sulaimān.[181] We see further evidence of these literary dalliances with this term "Qizil" in a number of quotations from the first chapter of Sa`dī's *Būstān*, in which kingly virtues of justice and education are addressed. Sa`dī discusses many legends and fables in this chapter, but the Safavid scribe chooses to quote verses from a story about a meeting between Qizil Arsalān and a scholar (*ḥikāyat-i Qizil Arslan bā dānishmand*).[182] The didactic thrust of this story is Qizil Arsalān's realization that kingship is inherently fleeting, and there will always be a ruler prepared to sit in the place of another. Thus, the Safavid scribe drives his point home by quoting the scholar's advice to Qizil Arsalān: "A frantic one thus spoke in Persia to Anūshīrvān: 'O heir to the country of Jamshīd! If country and fortune remained with Jamshīd, when would crown and throne become available to you?'"[183] In other work, this study has suggested that Persian scholar-bureaucrats looked to the discursive practice of epistolography to enhance their own political status and fortune, while at the same time impeding if not denigrating the traditional warrior class (*ahl-i saif*) of the Turks.[184] In this particular instance, we have a frame narrative wherein traditional Persian sages (*dānishmand*) counsel an archetypal medieval Turkish ruler. While this particular textual episode can certainly be read allegorically as the Safavid Persian chancellery exhorting the Turkish Ottoman ruler against tyranny, we cannot help but wonder whether the selection of this particular *ḥikāyat*—wherein the principal antagonist (named "Qizil" on the basis of his red hair) shares an onomastic relationship with the unruly "redheads" (*Qizilbāsh*)—was not deliberately selected for edification. The manipulation of such moralistic poetry from the classical Persian canon to suit a particular historical context is not surprising. Julie Scott Meisami has likewise pointed how the twelfth-century scholar Muḥammad `Alī Ravandī quoted very selectively from Niẓāmī in his court panegyric (*Rāḥat al-ṣudūr*) to Kai Khusrau ibn Qilij Arslān of Konya.[185]

This motif of vanity undoing responsible rule is further underscored by a line from Rūmī's *Ma̱snavī*: "How Adam, upon whom be peace, marvelled at the perdition of Iblis and showed vanity. Everything except Allāh is vain."[186] Later in the letter, when discussing Murād III's recent breaking of the Amāsya Treaty, the scribe quotes Sanā'ī's poetic admonition that those who break their oaths will be left searching for unattainable truths and realities.[187] While we see occasional quotations from Niẓāmī, Rūmī, and Sanā'ī,[188] it is clear that this chancellery official is particularly enamoured with Sa`dī, citing the *Būstān* in a number of sequences: "Be careful! Sympathize with [your] vassals, and be wary of the supremacy of Fate,"[189] is followed by, "The hearts of kings become burdened when they see thorn-bearing donkeys mired in the mud," and, "Don't harm the peasants even a little for the ruler is the shepherd and his subjects are the flock."[190] This secretary's attraction to this particular poetic masterpiece suggests an affinity among Safavid chancery notables for the ethical reflections and maxims of worldly wisdom that characterize Sa`dī's poetry.

The theme of how the mutual relationship between king and subject supersedes all other concerns, specifically religious ones, is strongly represented in this particular epistolary text. Indeed, references to and discussion of pre-Islamic Iranian virtues of kingship emerge as potential challenges to normative Islamic discourse. The scribe observes that logical proofs (*barāhīn-i `aqliyyah*) and traditional evidences (*shavāhid-i naqliyyah*) demonstrate the ontological function of rulers is to distribute justice and equity. Here, the scribe brandishes the exemplary figure of Anūshīrvān, who stands as the classical embodiment of justice despite his status as a non-Muslim (*az dīn bīgānah būd dar `adl va dād yagānah būd*).[191] The secretary quotes a tradition from the Prophet whereby he purportedly said, "I was born at the time of [Anūshīrvān] [*waladatu ana fī zamān al-sulṭān al-`ādil*]." This, in turn, is followed by a quatrain: "The Prophet, who came to illuminate the world during the reign of Anūshīrvān/Always said that I am without guile regarding sedition because I was born in the age of Anūshīrvān."[192] The text relates how several histories testify that the Gabarān—meaning the pre-Islamic Persian kings—ruled for five thousand years, and they had always treated the peasantry with justice. Moreover, the Prophet/King David had commanded that the Persian rulers were not to be reviled or castigated because they had cultivated the world with justice in order that his descendants may live in this world (*īshān jahān-rā bi `adl ābādān karda-and tā bandagān-i man dar viy zindagānī kunand*).[193]

This is borrowed directly from pseudo al-Ghazālī, who described how the

Magians (*moghān*) dominated the world for four thousand years because they ruled over people with justice.[194] Moreover, it was pseudo al-Ghazālī who first related the tradition that God instructed David to treat the people of Iran (*ahl-i `Ajam*) well, and the Safavid scribe copied pseudo al-Ghazālī's exact phraseology regarding the cultivation of justice by the Persian kings (*ān kisānī būdand ki jahān ābādān kardand tā bandagān-i man dar viy zandagānī mī-kunand*).[195] Khudābandah's letter continues to echo pseudo-Ghazālī's advice manual, provocatively arguing that justice supercedes the role of religion: "Justice and fairness, not belief or disbelief, are what protect a kingdom/Justice without religion will exalt the world better than a religious king."[196] The scribe elaborates on this point, employing classical rhetorical tropes of natural elements and agriculture: "It is clear as the sun in the middle of the sky [*ka'l-shams fī wasaṭ al-samā' ast*] that the fruit of the tree of justice is the welfare of the subjects [*ra`āyā*], nothing else." It is incumbent upon the peasantry (*`āmmah-yi ra`āyat*) to plant the "seed of prayer" (*tukhm-i du`ā*) in the "field of worship" *(kasht-zār-i `ibādat)* and pray constantly (*lail-an va nahār-an*) to see these prayers deposited "in the constructed treasury of the ruler's life and fortune" (*khazānah-yi `āmirah-yi `umr va daulat*).[197] The hydrological/agricultural metaphor associated with kingship—a trope arguably made popular in the twelfth century by Khāqāni Shirvāni—is concluded with this poem:

> Kingship is a field and justice is a cloud full of water/God gave you a kingdom; hasten [and establish] justice
> You planted the seed, [now] endeavour to irrigate [your field]/Do not let it be thirsty and become a field of thorns
> This field, without water, will yield nothing/just as a dry tree bears no fruit.[198]

The preponderance of mystical references combined with quotations from theosophically inclined poets (Sanā'ī, Niẓāmī, Sa`dī) point to a cosmopolitan, urbane chancellery official with at least some level of affinity for Sufi concepts, tropes, and terminology. Notably, there are only the briefest references to traditional Shi`ite polemic as the secretary offhandedly mentions the sanctity of the Imamate by hurriedly citing 33:33: "God desires to remove impurities from you, O members of this house, and to cleanse and bring out the best in you"; 42:23: "Say: 'I ask no recompense of you for it other than obligations of relationship'"; and 12:18: "I seek the help of God alone."[199] The scribe is far more concerned with addressing the implications of Murād III's breaking of the Amāsya Treaty, the resulting ruin and trauma for the peasants at large, and how these in turn will have dire soteriological consequences for the Ottoman sultan: "The fleetingness of this world is evident, and the non-existence of fidelity in there is clear" (*fanā-yi dunyā shai'-i vāḍiḥ ast wa `adam-i vafā-yi u amrī lāyiḥ*). The scribe assumes a sententious tone and, using partial Qur'ānic allusions, warns Murād III of the ephemerality of his own existence, while at the same time including some like-minded Persian verses from Niẓāmī and Sa`dī.[200]

These are interspersed with lines of distinctive Arabic poetry, which reaffirm long-held mystical perceptions of this current existence as illusory and transient. "If anyone in the world could exist forever/Certainly the messenger of Allāh would have lived eternally in it" (*Wa lau kāna bi al-dunyā baqā' bi sākin/La kāna rasūlu Allāhi fīhā mukhalladan*), reads a line of poetry by Ḥassān ibn Thābit, the famous panegyrist, poet laureate, and Companion to the Prophet.[201] Indeed, this verse was identified as having `Alid connections by Qāḍī Mīr Ḥusain Maibudī in the late fifteenth century.[202] Thābit's verse, in turn, is followed by one verse from Labīd ibn Rabīa's famous *qaṣīdah*: "Know that everything is null and void except God/And without a doubt all riches come to an end" (*Alā kull shai'in mā khalā Allāhu bāṭil/Wa kull na`īmin lā muḥālatat zā'il*).[203] This cluster of moralizing Arabic verse continues with a quatrain allegedly penned by Imām `Alī himself and is placed immediately after Labīd's *qaṣīdah* to form an *iltizām* composite: "Your happiness in this world is deceptive and foolish/And your joy in this world is impossible and void/The world is like a caravanserai/Where you and your camels sleep during the night and continue travelling in the morning."[204] The metaphor of the world as a way station or battered caravanserai was a favourite among Persian classical poets such as `Umar Khayyām, Ḥāfiẓ, and Ibn Yamīn. The Safavid secretary brings this remonstrance to an end by hoping that "God forbid that there be a spilling of blood," and "the light of this message will shine on the blessed heart of that Anūshīrvān of the age [i.e., Murād III]." It would be in Murād III's best interests to observe the Qur'ānic 8:1, "So fulfill your duty to God and keep the peace among you," since, on the Day of Judgement (*rūz-i jazā*), "kings and beggars will be counted as one and all will see the wretchedness of their condition in the presence of both Muḥammad and `Alī."[205]

This letter is illustrative of what appears to be a complex and literary-minded chancellery working under Muḥammad Khudābandah. Particularly noteworthy is a cosmology that operates outside of traditional, orthodox Shi`ite models and instead embraces dictums and axioms that emphasize the importance of proper modes of conduct among rulers and kings. The lauding of Anūshīrvān and the pre-Islamic age of the Persian kings combined with the consistent use of rhetorical exemplars and classical Persian poetic verses associated with the Achaemenid and Sasanian ages, suggest a Safavid scribe whose *Weltanschauung* was not confined to a normative Shi`ite framework. Indeed, a good example of this non-compliance was the author's quotation of the Companion Ḥasan Thābit, who had actively opposed the candidacy of Imām `Alī in support of the Shi`ite antagonist par excellence Mu`āwiya.[206] His inclusion here is probably more a result of his appeal as an Arabic literary icon and the contribution of his poetry towards mysticism than anything else.[207] Consistent quoting of Sa`dī and Sanā'ī, the ease with which the text shifts back and forth between religious Arabic and secular Persian, and the dominant themes of temporal and spatial vacuity in this universe all combine to suggest a theosophically inclined scholar-bureaucrat.

While this study has argued thus far that this chancery was in many ways a continuity of what had existed in the latter years of Shāh Ṭahmāsp's reign, we nonetheless need to acknowledge the arrival of a strong, distinctive Shīrāzī element after Khudābandah's accession in 985/1578. Is it possible that the mystical undertones here combined with strong literary dynamics reflect such a shift in the chancellery?

It is probable that heterogeneous inclinations such as these were encouraged by Khudābandah himself. As mentioned, he had been developing links and partnerships with the Persian bureaucratic class and literati since his youthful governorship in Herāt, where he himself had written mystically inspired poetry under the pen name Fahmī and participated actively in poetry gatherings. The likelihood that Khudabāndah might have continued or even intensified such connections during his gubernatorial career in Shīrāz between 981/1573 and 1578 appears to be the case. Here, we turn to our last chancellery item: a short letter from Muḥammad Khudābandah to the well-reputed *sayyid* and respected scholar Mīr Fatḥ Allāh Shīrāzī.[208] After a short career in Shīrāz during the 1570s and 1580s, Fatḥ Allāh Shīrāzī left Iran to pursue a career in India, first under the `Ādilshāhs in Bījāpūr and later under Akbar the Great.[209] Mughal texts like the *Akbar nāmah*, the *Ā'in-i Akbarī*, and the *Ṭabaqāt-i Akbarī* all agree he was highly respected and admired by his peers in terms of his mastery of Qur'ānic exegesis (*tafsīr*), Prophetic hadiths, Arabic grammar and syntax, rhetoric, as well as astrology, astronomy, and philosophy.[210] Moreover, on the basis of this letter, we know that Fatḥ Allāh Shīrāzī and Muḥammad Khudābandah shared a close relationship during his governorship in Shīrāz, and it seems likely that Fatḥ Allāh left Iran during Ismā`īl II's chaotic rule to seek greener if not more soothing pastures on the Indian subcontinent.

The letter eschews invocations to God, Prophet Muḥammad, and the Imamate and begins instead with a series of laudatory Persian and Arabic epithets for Fatḥ Allāh Shīrāzī: "Most learned of the Imami religious scholars" (*`allāmat al-`ulamā' al-imāmiyyah*), "exemplar of the great *sayyids* and nobles" (*qudwat a`āẓim al-sādāt wa al-ashrāf*), and "master of mankind" (*ustād al-bashar*).[211] The letter makes it manifestly clear that Muḥammad Khudābandah considered himself, as one-time governor and patron of Shīrāzī, responsible for the creation, formation, and training of this future Sufi polymath and celebrity. In a clever use of Qur'ānic allusions, we read how such royal beneficence is akin to 20:50: "[We] gave to each created thing its form and nature, and further gave it guidance." Likewise, we read 6:165: "It is He who has made you [His] agents, inheritors of the earth. He has raised you in ranks, some above others"; 17:70: "We have conferred on them special favours, above a great part of [Our] creation"; and 12:22: "We gave him power and knowledge."[212] Khudābandah informs Fatḥ Allāh Shīrāzī that he was turning his royal attention to the memory of those pure times (*khulāṣah-yi auqāt*) when that most exalted group (*zumrah-yi `ālī al-sha'n*), that is the most perfect kind of humanity (*khulāṣah-yi anvā`-i insān ast*), would assemble and debate in this court.

The questions arise: who was in this "most sublime group" (*ṭā'ifah-yi rafī` al-makān*), and when were these "flawless times" (*nuqāvat-i sā`āt*) that Khudābandah idealizes so enthusiastically? Discussed earlier, there was a Shīrāzī school of philosophy since the late fifteenth century, which loosely coalesced around the Madrasah-yi Manṣūriyya founded by Ṣadr al-Dīn Muḥammad Dashtakī. This school was given concrete moorings in the 1530s with the writings and teachings of the prominent thinker Ghiyāṣ al-Dīn Manṣūr Dashtakī. Khudābandah was governor of Shīrāz during one of its more energetic phases, and the enthusiastic discussion of this esteemed group here suggests a social and intellectual nexus between Fatḥ Allāh Shīrāzī, this coterie of scholars based in the Madrasah-yi Manṣūriyya, and Mīrzā Muḥammad Khudābandah. Before leaving for India, Fatḥ Allāh Shīrāzī had been a disciple of a notable Sufi *shaikh* Mīrzā Mīr Takiya Shīrāzī and studied actively with noted philosophers like Khvājah Jamāl al-Dīn Maḥmūd Kamāl al-Dīn Shīrvānī. The later intellectual accomplishments and the resurgence of *ishrāqī* philosophy under the banner of Mīr Dāmād and Mullā Ṣadrā would appear to owe its roots, at least partly, to Khudābandah's gubernatorial sponsorship and support of this "most exalted group." Particularly intriguing is Mohamad Tavakoli-Targhi's recent observation that Fatḥ Allāh Shīrāzī had been a disciple at one point of the Zoroastrian mystic Āzar Kaivān.[213] According to Corbin, this individual would hold sessions and discussions in the environs of Iṣṭakhr (not far from Shīrāz) and discuss the connections between Sufism and *ishrāqī* elements in Zoroastrianism. This Zoroastrian illuminative school "was dominated by *Eshraqi* doctrine and terminology," borrowed from the writings of Shihāb al-Dīn Suhravardī.[214] Accordingly, key features of Āzar Kaivān's teachings were an emphasis on the glory of the pre-Islamic age and a veneration of the miraculous behaviour of select Achaemenian and Sasanian monarchs.[215] While Āzar Kaivān left for India before Khudābandah's appointment to Shīrāz, there is still debate among scholars as to the degree of influence this mystic/visionary exerted on this coterie of mystics and philosophers based in Shīrāz and the Madrasah-yi Manṣūriyya.[216]

Returning to the letter in question, we read that two disciples of Fatḥ Allāh Shīrāzī, Maulānā Luṭfī and Aḥmad Qulī Āqā, had recently arrived at the Safavid court.[217] Khudābandah implores the Sufi mystic to return to the Safavid court by describing how royal monies had already been sent to India and taxes accrued from Shīrāzī's property were to be henceforth protected by a royal *suyūrghāl*. God willing, after all this, he will come and "we will distinguish him with renewed kindnesses" (*tafaqqundāt-i tāzah*) and "immeasurable courtesies" (*nivāzishāt-i bī-andāzah*).[218] Khudābandah's relationship with this particular Sufi personality, who in turn boasted friendships, contacts, and tutelages with some of the most heterogeneous religious and mystical elements of the time, depicts a ruler who belies those reductive characterizations—lazy, uninspiring, and naïve—offered by scholars such as Hans Roemer, Manūchihr Pārsādūst, and others. To the contrary, we are presented with a ruler who actively sought to staff his religious administrative positions with dynamic individuals responsible for laying the groundwork for some of the most profound and exciting discussions to take place among future medieval Iranian philosophers and intellectuals.

These letters demonstrate innovative chancellery at work during the period of Muḥammad Khudābandah's rule, and this in turn was a reflection of intellectual trends and currents that had been encouraged if not sponsored by Khudābandah and his surrounding coterie from Herāt and Shīrāz. The uniqueness and vitality of the letters produced after 984/1577 point to a chancellery that no longer felt especially obliged to adhere strictly to a normative Shi`ite agenda. This is no clearer than in the strong profile accorded to axioms and gnomic expressions from the nucleus of the mirrors-for-princes genre: pseudo al-Ghazālī's *Naṣīḥat al-mulūk*. For instance, these *munshī*s began at least three chancellery texts with Qur'ānic quotes and Arabic aphorisms, which invoke the image of "the Pen" (*al-qalam*) as an allegory for God's creative power and augustness (e.g., *mā khalaqa alaihi al-qalam, qalam-i qudrat*). In at least one noted example, God was rhetorically presented as "the stylist of the chancellery" (*munshī-yi dār al-inshā*) who created the universe with a stroke of his pen. While one could concede the obvious regarding the use of Qur'ānic imagery for self-aggrandizing, pseudo al-Ghazālī nonetheless foregrounded his entire sixth chapter on secretaries and their art (*andar zikr-i dabīrān va hunarmandī-yi īshān*) with these very same quotations and references. Pseudo Al-Ghazālī writes how all scholars concede that "nothing is bigger than the pen," and these are corroborated with Qur'ānic verses such as 1: 68: "Nūn. By the pen and the [record] which [men] write," and 96: 3: "Read, for your Lord is most beneficent, Who taught by the pen and taught men that what he did not know." Moreover, the Prophet is reported to have said: "The first thing that God created was the Pen."[219] The stylistic and thematic proximity of pseudo al-Ghazālī and other medieval Perso-Islamic luminaries to this chancellery material supports one of the overarching contentions of this study: *inshā* material functioned as a tool for abstract political discourse. In some cases, namely the 1577 appointment decrees associated with Mīrzā Salmān and Mīrzā Shukr Allāh, the authors focused considerable attention and detail were on the importance and centrality of administrative offices like the *vazīr-i dīvān-i a`lā* and the *mustaufī al-mamālik.* We discern here a corporate identity among the Persian administrators, bureaucrats, literati, and scholar-bureaucrats. More importantly, many of these themes, imageries, motifs, and topics have an admonitory quality, which further underlines the intertextuality between these epistolary documents and the gnomic genre of *akhlāq*.

As a source of contemporary political thought, the chancellery material of this period invokes a Perso-Islamic model of authority, which clearly challenges theocratic structures that privileged the position of the jurist and as such is very much in line with the patterns established during the short rule by Shāh Ismā`īl II. The reigns of Shāh Ismā`īl II and Khudābandah were critical with regard to the roles and functions of Shi`ite clerics in a government during the Occultation, and one could reasonably argue that queries into such issues during the "height" of Safavid power under Shāh `Abbās are pointless unless we appreciate these earlier debates of the 1570s and 1580s. As we saw during the 1530s and 1540s, the theoretical implications of a secular kingship ruling a Shi`ite community had already become entangled, and the debate among scholars turned acrimonious for much of the mid-sixteenth century. We only need to look to the careers of Shaikh Ḥusain `Abd al-Ṣamād al-Ḥārithī al-`Āmilī and Mīr Sayyid Ḥusain al-Karakī in the second half of Shāh Ṭahmāsp's reign to understand the acerbity that characterized the debate about the role of juridical representatives and deputies during the Occultation.

Thanks to the work of Devin Stewart, we know there was considerable division between two sets of hierocrats: those who championed a rearticulation of the power of the Safavid shah and those orthodox Shi`ite clerics who insisted that secular deputyship in a Shi`ite state was an anathema. In particular, Stewart examined the career of Shaikh Ḥusain `Abd al-Ṣamād, previously *Shaikh al-Islām* for both Qazvīn and Herāt during the reign of Shāh Ṭahmāsp, to highlight this fracture among the religious intelligentsia.[220] In his writings, Shaikh Ḥusain `Abd al-Ṣamād argued that it was acceptable for Shi`ite scholars to receive patronage from a secular ruler, while in his famous *`Iqd al-Ḥusainī* he asserted that it was permissible to perform prostration (*sijdah*) to the shah—an incendiary proposal among Shi`ite hierocrats, to say the least.[221] This propinquity between God and the secular institution of kingship—highlighted in the preamble of Khudābandah's letter to Murād III wherein blessings and benedictions to God and Muhammad were allegories to "state" institutions like crowns, thrones, mints—would have been endorsed by Shaikh Ḥusain `Abd al-Ṣamād; Stewart noted this dynamic on numerous occasions in the *`Iqd al-Ḥusainī*.[222] Despite his `Āmilī geneaology, `Abd al-Ṣamād stood slightly apart from the juridical orientation of his Arab colleagues with "extracurricular" interests in literature, ethics, and theosophy.[223] His seemingly contradictory stance with respect to Uṣūlīsm and Akhbarism is also noted by Abisaab: "Curiously, at times Husayn upheld traditionist arguments and at other times rationalist ones in order to support new opinions and verdicts that arose not from hypothetical discussions of an isolated community of theologians but rather from a new realignment of ideology and class interest."[224]

Of course, Shaikh Ḥusain `Abd al-Ṣamād would ultimately fall into disfavour with the increasingly orthopraxic Shāh Ṭahmāsp, and he would leave Iran. It is telling that this same Shaikh Ḥusain `Abd al-Ṣamād had previously been responsible for the religious and scholarly tutelage of Muḥammad Khudābandah while serving as governor of Herāt from 975/1567 to 979/1572. Moreover, it would be `Abd al-Ṣamād's son Shaikh Bahā' al-Dīn `Āmili, also known as Shaikh Bahā'ī, who would play such a central role in the rise of *ishrāqī* Gnostic philosophy along with others from the Shīrāzī school at the turn of the sixteenth century. Newman noted how Shaikh Ḥusain `Abd al-Ṣamād was responsible for "teaching his interpretations to a new generation of scholars who, in turn, continued the process of establishing Imami doctrine in Safawid territory."[225] This study contends that the resurgence of royal authority characterizing the 1570s and later is rooted in these early formative relationships among Khudābandah and the Persian intelligentsia and singular individuals like `Abd al-Ṣamād while in Herāt and Shīrāz. In particular, `Abd al-Ṣamād was a vociferous critic of those Uṣūlī jurists like al-Karakī who championed broader mandates of power and wrote frequently against the permissibility of accepting rulings from dead jurists—in his own words: "No *mujtahid* is safe from a critic, nor a person from a deficiency."[226] Regarding the issue of Friday prayer, `Abd al-Ṣamād relegated the role of the jurist as imam, and instead promoted the shah in his place.[227] In many ways, Khudābandah's partnerships with mystics and scholar-bureaucrats in the chancellery and elsewhere were symbiotic. Sufis and intelligentsia (often these were one and the same) looked to Khudābandah and the sanctity of his royal station as a means of protection and support against the twin threats of Shi`ite jurists and Qizilbāsh Turks. We know, for instance, that the Ni`matullāhīs prospered considerably in their home city of Yazd during this period. The Ni`matullāhī *murshid* Mīr Ghiyas̱ al-Dīn Muḥammad Mīr-Mīrān oversaw significant urban renewal in Yazd such that this city "was virtually a principality in its own right."[228] To maintain the sanctity and strength of the Safavid throne, these Persian elements championed—often through the vehicle of state correspondence and *inshā*—the rule of the shah as inviolable and all-embracing. In some instances, this epistolary discourse was buttressed by the legal efforts of individuals like `Abd al-Ṣamād who were fearful of an unchecked clerical class. The Safavid chancellery protected and fostered this mandate of promoting imperial absolutism, while at the same time operating within a Shi`ite political framework. Future scribes and stylists like Iskander Beg Munshī and Ḥātim Beg Urdūbādī would come to play a crucial role in constructing a discourse that articulated and defended the absolutist and uncompromising rule of Shāh `Abbās the Great.

Narrating and Mapping a New Safavid Dominion, 1588–98

Shāh `Abbās's reign (996–1038/1588–1629) saw dramatic reform in Safavid government and society. Bureaucracies were standardized, trade and mercantile systems were centralized, military cultures became innovated and systemized, ethnic populations were socially engineered; by the end of `Abbās's reign, an expanded Safavid Iran was playing an integral role in regional and global dynamics. While much of this reached fruition in the 1610s and 1620s, there is no doubt that the seeds of this reform were planted in his first decade of rule. With unflagging energy and determination, Shāh `Abbās established his formidable dominion, while at the same time he fashioned a new and innovative dynastic ethos during these early years. His peripatetic style of rule and his intense interest in the day-to-day governance of the empire were largely based on a need to subdue and control competing arenas of authority. In this sense `Abbās was the greatest autocrat that Safavid Iran would ever know. Whether the objective was to subdue a rebellious governor in Māzandarān, extricate the Uzbeks from Khurāsān, or disarm the charismatic appeal of millenarian Nuqṭavī

Sufis, `Abbās's approach was swift and uncompromising. Interwoven into this aggressive dynastic rationale were more tactical and subtle issues of minimizing the power of traditional, internal Safavid institutions such as the Qizilbāsh Türkmen, the Imami jurists, the *sayyid* networks, and the Persian *ahl al-qalam*.

Shāh `Abbās, borrowing from the theosophical principles of the Perfect Man, endeavoured to present himself as an infallible imperator, whose empire functioned on principles of paternalism and personal loyalty in a way that would have been impossible for his progenitors. Of course, this was presented in symbolic terms, and the mechanisms of state power under `Abbās were guided by a principle of negotiating the distribution of power among Persian, Türkmen, Arab, and Caucasian nobles, notables, and jurists.[229] In terms of legitimacy, the distinctiveness of this image was bolstered by new articulations of imperial space, which operated with deliberate temporal and spatial boundaries. We find Shāh `Abbās turning to the chancellery and diplomatic correspondence as a means of historicizing the Safavids and profiling their long-standing imperial sensibilities. Concurrently, the mandate of Shāh `Abbās and his ancestors was explicitly fused with the historical, pre-Islamic legacy of Iran as a distinct political space. Thus, there is contiguity to `Abbās's correspondence between "the Safavid dynasty" (*dūdmān-i Ṣafavī*) and "the empire of Iran" (*mamlakat-i Īrān*) not discussed in earlier *inshā* material.

The first three years of this decade were critical for the young shah as he sought to balance a sense of administrative continuity and stability while forging a new, bold dynastic path. On 1 Jumāda I 997/28 April 1588, `Abbās named Murshid Qulī Khān as his *vakīl*, while giving the office of *muhrdār* to `Alī Qulī Sulṭān Zū al-Qadar. We have an intriguing reference to a *vazīr-i muhr* (Mīr Ṣafī Ardastānī) in Munajjim Yazdī's *Tārīkh-i `Abbāsī*, suggesting that `Abbās continued his predecessor Shāh Ismā`īl II's policy of having a Persian administrator and a Türkmen amir share the responsibility of the royal seal.[230] The *vizārat-i kull* was promised initially to Mīrzā Salmān's son, Mīrzā `Abd Allāh; however, Murshid Qulī Khān intervened and secured this powerful office for Mīrzā Shāh Vālī, who had been his own *vazīr* in Herāt and was the grandson of Shāh Ṭahmāsp's eminent administrator `Aṭā Allāh Iṣfahānī.[231] The ensuing coup against Murshid Qulī Khān was orchestrated by disgruntled bureaucratic elements, namely the former chief vizier Mīrzā Muḥammad Munshī and the aforementioned Mīrzā `Abd Allāh.[232] This agency and determination underscores the degree to which such bureaucratic and chancellery elements had emerged as concrete political actors during the 1570s and 1580s. The Qizilbāsh were further marginalized when `Alī Qulī Sulṭān Zū al-Qadar was dismissed as *muhrdār,* and `Abbās took the unprecedented step of naming a Persian notable, Sayyid Beg Kamūna, as his replacement.[233] A new, albeit temporary, bureaucratic lineup was arranged with two *dīvānī* personalities from the reigns of Shāh Ismā`īl II and Khudābandah in control. Mīrzā Muḥammad Munshī was reappointed as the *vazīr-i dīvān-i a`lā*, Mīrzā Luṭf Allāh Shīrāzī was named as *mustaufī al-mamālik*, and each was allocated 12,000 *tūmāns* (Qāḍī Aḥmad mentions 20,000 *tūmāns*).[234] The office of *niẓārat-i kull* was given to Mīrzā Sayyid `Alī Luṭf, while the post of *munshī al-mamālik* was bestowed on Mīrzā Muḥammad's nephew, Mīr Muḥammad Qāsim, who had served a few years earlier as vizier to Amīr Khān Mauṣillū, the governor of Āzarbāījān.[235]

The vizierate of Mīrzā Muḥammad Munshī only lasted sixty-seven days, and on 12 Rabī` I 997/29 January 1589 he was executed on the shah's orders along with `Alī Āqā Arbatan.[236] This was characterized as a response to Mīrzā Muḥammad's threat as a "seditious and ambitious man," and `Abbās turned to a cadre of older, trained bureaucrats. Mīrzā Luṭf Allāh Shīrāzī, who once wielded the seal in Ismā`īl II's "court of justice" (*dīvān-i `adl*), was promoted from the accountancy to the grand vizierate, and Shāh `Abbās decreed that Mīrzā Luṭf Allāh be regaled with all the standards and honours (jewelled sword belt, brocaded clock, horse with ornamented saddle and bridle) usually accorded to Türkmen amirs.[237] The chief accountancy, in turn, was given to Khvājah Shukr Allāh Iṣfahānī, very likely the same Shukr Allāh Iṣfahānī who had risen to power during the short reign of Ismā`īl II.[238] The post of *munshī al-mamālik* was transferred from the neophyte Mīr Muḥammad Qāsim to a bureaucrat whose career spanned no less than four Safavid shahs, Maulānā Muḥammad Amīn Munshī. Muḥammad Amīn had begun as a junior literary stylist and scribe during the reign of Shāh Ṭahmāsp, and he would continue to write royal correspondence for the next twenty years, until assuming this top chancellery position between 997/1589 and 999/1591.[239] Thus, the first two years of `Abbās's reign, admittedly fluid in terms of appointments and dismissals, were dominated by those Persian rainmakers who had defined Safavid politics for much of the 1570s and 1580s. One thing was becoming abundantly clear to the Persian *ahl al-qalam*: `Abbās was not a complacent ruler who would be easily dominated, and those who did not recognize this fact were unceremoniously removed from power.

These shifting dynamics were part and parcel of Shāh `Abbās's overall program to establish himself as the new Safavid sovereign. Between 1588 and 1591 he addressed a number of internal and external threats. The Uzbeks conquered much of eastern Khurāsān in these first three years; cities like Herāt, Mashhad, Isfrā'īn, and Jājarm would be the loci of repeated battles and sieges. `Abbās appreciated his vulnerability during these early days and entered into diplomatic negotiations with the Ottomans. The resulting Peace of Istanbul (14 Jumāda I 998/21 March 1590) saw sizeable loss of Safavid territory to the Ottomans: western Āzarbāījān, Qarābāgh, Shīrvān, Dāghistān, Baghdād, and parts of Kurdistān and Luristān.[240] This, in turn, accorded `Abbās the resources to concentrate on the Uzbeks and, above all else, to extinguish a number of rebellions that broke out in central Iran among Qizilbāsh tribal amirs between 996–98/1588–90. Chief among these was Ya`qūb Khān Zū al-Qadar, the governor of Shīrāz,[241] but other renegades included Biktāsh Khān in Yazd, Yulī Beg in Iṣfahān, and Yūsuf Khān Afshār in Kirmān.[242] As Charles Melville has shown, Shāh `Abbās's frenetic itinerary in these early years was more than a youthful sovereign responding to disparate challenges. This peripatetic intensity—which saw him travel 2,250 kilometers per annum between Ardabīl, Qazvīn, Shīrāz, and Mashhad in these first three years—was clearly designed to publicly profile his status as a sovereign of a newly centralized polity.[243]

The tide would turn for Shāh `Abbās in 999/1591. While this could be partly explained by the cessation of Ottoman-Safavid hostilities and the suppression of the various rebellions in central Iran, more profound perhaps was the arrival of Ḥātim Beg Urdūbādī to the royal central administration. Claiming descent from Khvājah Naṣīr al-Dīn al-Tūsī, Ḥātim Beg was a scion of a long-standing family of administrators and bureaucrats, and his father had served the Safavids as the *kalāntar* for the region of Urdūbād.[244] Ḥātim Beg first surfaced as Biktāsh Khān's vizier in Yazd, and Iskander Beg Munshī tells us that Urdūbādī worked tirelessly to bring Bektash Khān back into the Safavid fold after an initial flirtation with rebellion.[245] Munajjim Yazdī, however, records how he had been imprisoned for a short period in Shīrāz and was brought to Iṣfahān along with another prisoner, Mullā Aḥmad Ṭabasī.[246] Ḥātim Beg appears to have made a good impression on `Abbās, as he was exonerated and promoted in three quick successions within one year. Initially, he was named chief accountant for Yazd but was promoted to the chief accountancy (*mustaufī al-mamālik*) shortly afterwards, and in Jumāda I 999/March 1591, he was named the *vazīr-i dīvān-i a`lā* with the honorific of *I`timād al-daulat*.[247] At the same time, Khvājah Shāh `Alī Daulatābādī Iṣfahānī, formerly the *lashkar-i nivīs-i khāṣṣah-yi sharīfah* (chief bureaucrat to the military), was named the new *mustaufī al-mamālik*.[248]

These bureaucratic changes were concomitant with the launching of a new phase of territorial expansion. While the restoration of Khurāsān to Safavid control was an ongoing concern, in 1000/1592 Shāh `Abbās turned to the semi-independent state of Gīlān under the Kār Kiyā ruler, Khān Aḥmad Khān.[249] As we know, the indomitable Khān Aḥmad Khān had survived a number of wars as well as incarceration at the Safavids' hands, but he had built up a semi-autonomous fiefdom in Gīlān since his release in 986/1578. `Abbās had been frustrated by Khān Aḥmad's capricious diplomacy—for instance, refusing a marriage alliance between his daughter and `Abbās's son Ṣafī Mīrzā—but when Khān Aḥmad despatched an envoy to Istanbul to discuss a Gīlānī-Ottoman alliance, `Abbās seized upon this affront as an excuse to formally terminate the Kār Kiyā dynasty.[250] Farhād Khān Qarāmānlū and his brother Zū al-Faqār Khān were despatched to Gīlān with troops from Āzarbāījān and Tavālish, while Jamshīd Beg, the governor of Qazvīn, was ordered north via Daylam in 1000/1592.[251] Accounts suggest the Safavids were particularly ruthless in their subjugation of the region, and Khān Aḥmad escaped to seek asylum in Ottoman Istanbul. Shāh `Abbās arrived soon after and ordered the destruction of the Kār Kiyā palace. At the same time, he named Mahdī Qulī Khān Shāmlū as the new governor and reappointed Khān Aḥmad's minister, Khvājah Masīḥ Gīlānī, who had defected earlier to the Safavid cause.[252] During this period of 1000–02/1592–93, `Abbās redoubled his efforts to push the Uzbeks out of Khurāsān by entering into a mutual pact with the Khvārazmian khans of Urganj; however, most of this period saw limited skirmishes and failed sieges. In Ṣafar 1004/November 1595, a Safavid force of twenty thousand set out from Dāmaghān and routed the Uzbek army at Jājarm. The momentum from the success at Jājarm was propelled eastwards, and the city of Herāt was reconquered soon after.[253] The Uzbeks sued for peace, and a negotiated treaty saw the Safavids reclaim everything west of the Āmū Daryā river.[254] By the end of his first decade of rule, `Abbās had not only pacified much of the Iranian Plateau, but also he had annexed the long-standing independent principality of Gīlān and extended his dominion eastwards to include Khurāsān—a key lodestar of Iranian culture and historical identity.

Shāh `Abbās's program of centralizing and standardizing the administration of his new empire was promptly placed in the hands of the new *vazīr-i dīvān-i a`lā* and *I`timād al-daulat*, Ḥātim Beg Urdūbādī. Ḥātim Beg began instituting wide-ranging bureaucratic reforms in 1001/1593, when he initiated an intense audit of the *tīyūl* system in operation under the Qizilbāsh amirs.[255] It is almost certainly because of Ḥātim Beg's dissection of this traditional system that `Abbās put preliminary plans in place to assemble a regular, standing army of *ghulām* troops from the Caucasus. The new grand *vazīr* would be able to best demonstrate his financial and organizational acumen in the newest territorial addition to the Safavid state—the lucrative province of Gīlān. After completing his audit and assessment of Türkmen military finances and organizational principles, in 1003/1594–95 Ḥātim Beg was despatched along with a team of bureaucrats and comptrollers to Gīlān to overhaul the province's system of tax assessment and remittance. Ostensibly, this reform was at the behest of locals frustrated with Mahdī Qulī Khān's overbearing governorship, but it was the financial potential of this prosperous province—rich in silk production, tea, caviar, and lumber—that inspired Shāh `Abbās to send his most important bureaucrat "to fix the *dīvān* taxes and the dues in an equitable manner."[256]

Western and eastern regions of Gīlān were united as one province, and "the fiscal system they set up in that province is still in force and is used as the model."[257] Iskander Beg Munshī discusses how Ḥātim Beg had begun a "regulatory ledger" (*nuskhah-yi tashkhīṣ*) that recorded the total revenue and expenditure of the Safavid empire and how this ledger was consulted well into the seventeenth century as the pre-eminent model for the central administration.[258] Concurrent with these financial and organizational reforms was another "sovereignty tour" by Shāh `Abbās in 1002–03/1593–94, which saw the heeling of quasi-rebellious cities and regions such as Sulṭāniyyah, Abhār, Zanjān, Ṭārum, Ṭālish, eastern Āzarbāījān and Luristān, Kūh-i Gīlūyah and Khūzistān. These were subdued and placed under the jurisdiction of Safavid state functionaries, who saw that "matters [were] settled in accordance with the Shah's intent."[259] These centralizing policies were also moving in tandem with the shah's plans to relocate his royal palace from the city of Qazvīn to Iṣfahān. In this first decade of rule, he travelled between the two cities eighteen times to overlook the completion of the square and bazaar in Iṣfahān, which he had first commissioned in Ṣafar 1000/November 1591.[260]

The Safavid *dār al-inshā* was included in Ḥātim Beg Urdūbādī's mandate to centralize and standardize all pertinent departments and institutions of `Abbās's empire. Besides the nature and structure of the chancellery documents themselves (which will be discussed in more detail shortly), the impulse towards standardization is also seen in the relative marginalization of the position of *munshī al-mamālik* from the 1590s onwards. Specialized positions were created for new Safavid institutions, duties were redefined, and above all else the chancellery was stripped of any operational autonomy.[261] Qāḍī Aḥmad, who focuses in considerable detail in his *Gulistān-i hunar* on those key administrative personnel in the *dār al-inshā* during the reigns of Ṭahmāsp, Ismā`īl II, and Khudābandah, has almost nothing to say about key figures in the Safavid chancellery after the 1590s. On only one occasion does Iskander Beg Munshī, himself a long-time scribe who had worked in the *dār al-inshā* under Muḥammad Amīn, refer offhandedly to a *munshī al-mamālik* (`Abd al-Ḥusain al-Tūsī) during this period.[262] By the late seventeenth century, we know this office had been relegated to its counterpart, the *majlis nivīs,* and the duties of the *munshī al-mamālik* had been confined to ceremonial tracing of the heraldic device of the *ṭughrā*.[263]

Is it possible that the marginalization of this office saw its beginnings in Ḥātim Beg's tenure as *vazīr-i dīvān-i a`lā*? There is certainly good evidence to suggest this was the case. First, we learn from Faiḍī Iṣfahānī's *Afḍal al-tavārīkh* that Ḥātim Beg named his nephew Nāṣir Khān Beg as the *munshī al-mamālik* shortly after his own appointment to the *vizārat-i dīvān-i a`lā*.[264] In many ways, this appears to have been a deliberate move to disarm this office by having it posted to a minor figure with little or no chancellery experience. Second, there is no mistaking a consistent format was developed for Safavid correspondence in the chancellery after 999/1591. While there was still room for creativity and a certain degree of embellishment, Safavid letters during the first ten years of `Abbās's reign reflect a new professional ethos, which called for consistency and precision. The notion of *munshīs* as litterateurs who understood the epistolary and chancellery sciences as a means to profile their rhetorical dexterity and express their intimate grasp of courtly *adab* no longer defined the *dār al-inshā*. Third, we can accurately determine that the administrative *wunderkind* Ḥātim Beg assumed most of the responsibilities and duties of the chief *munshī* between 999/1591 and 1006–07/1598. No less than nine letters produced during this period have rubrics that name Ḥātim Beg Urdūbādī as their author; another nine are similar enough in language and style to suggest confidently that Ḥātim Beg was involved in some way. Knowing that he had installed his own nephew to this post, it is not surprising that Ḥātim Beg could so easily dominate the *dār al-inshā* during this critical period of territorial expansion and administrative centralization. One is tempted to see this as illustrative of a micromanaging compulsion. This study contends, however, that Ḥātim Beg had explicit ideas regarding the uses and applicability of Safavid epistolary texts at this juncture in `Abbās's imperial program, and that he simply wanted to carry out these ideas without interference from an overbearing *munshī al-mamālik*.

In the first ten years of `Abbās's reign, an impressive number of letters—approximately thirty—were written and despatched to outside Muslim and Christian courts. When we acknowledge this bureaucratic productivity with the shah's own frenetic state-building program in these crucial early years, we can sense the ongoing professionalization of the chancellery under Ḥātim Beg. While the thematic concerns will be discussed in more detail further on, patterns in this epistolary evidence include Safavid scribes repeatedly discussing explicit geographical parameters of the empire as well as providing short narratives about the historical successes of the Safavids as an imperial dynasty. Letters abroad to the Mughals, Uzbeks, Ottomans, and elsewhere were not so much exercises in hyperbolic rhetoric designed to intimidate the reader but rather functional texts that sought to profile a newly constituted Safavid Iranian empire with concrete spatial and temporal boundaries. If we then see the Safavid *dār al-inshā* as a state organ, it perhaps makes more sense to see these abbreviated, truncated letters and their consistent discourses about the state of the Safavid dominion in a style of a *rūz-namāchī* or "regular report."

The strongest evidence for this standardization, however, is in the diplomatic material itself, and an overall comparison of the correspondence reveals several traits worthy of mention. First and perhaps most obvious, Safavid letters during this period are considerably shorter. In terms of length, none of the letters produced by `Abbās's chancellery are comparable to many of the letters produced during the reigns of Shāh Ṭahmāsp and Khudābandah. Where we see the most radical editing is in the introductory preamble. Of the twenty-two letters surveyed, only three—one to the Ottoman religious official Sa`d al-Dīn, one to Meḥmed III, and one to Akbar—have systematic *invocatio*s in prose and poetry to God, the Prophet Muḥammad, and the Imamate. In the remainder, the letters are usually introduced by a brief but ornate reference to the sanctity of composition and then followed by an abbreviated *intitulatio* on behalf of the addressee, which includes Persian epitomic constructs (e.g., *salṭanat-dastgāh*) and Arabic superlative encomiums (e.g., *sulṭān al-salāṭīn*).

The forgoing of literary and documentary protocol does not mean that letters in this first decade of rule were stripped of religious discourse—to the contrary; however, it is clear that a deliberate policy had been mandated among the chancellery scribes: abstract deliberations and formulaic benedictions about God, prophecy, and the sanctity of `Alī were to be avoided. Second, we find that chancellery scribes wrote little or no poetry in roughly half of this diplomatic material. Interestingly, correspondence with the Ottoman sultans is substantially richer with respect to poetic arrangements within the text, and much of this verse appears in the introductory praise (*a`dīyah-yi iftitāḥiyyah*) on behalf of the addressee. In the case of those letters to Murād III and Meḥmed III, these poetic sections are invariably dedicated to discussing the qualities and virtues of kingship, sovereignty, religion, and justice. The dedication and consistency with which such "traditional" *inshā* were written to the Ottoman court—lengthy preambles, detailed encomiums to the ruler in prose and verse, observations on the primacy of kingship—suggest the Safavids could not entirely escape the imperative of cultural and literary competition that existed between the two courts. In the case of letters despatched to the Uzbeks, however, we find very little in the way of such effusive discussions, and addressees like `Abd Allāh Khān and `Abd al-Mu'min Khān are summarily hailed with no supracommentary on the success and endurance of their mandate to rule as Islamic sovereigns. While the hostilities between the two sides allows for some of this, it is clear that the Uzbeks could never share the same status and imperial station as the Ottomans or the Safavids because of their perceived benighted culture and Chingizid pedigree.

Within the material we can find specific examples of Ḥātim Beg's program to standardize and professionalize *inshā* writing. After the subject of the letter was addressed—which in many cases entailed short narratives about a recent diplomatic or military victory by Shāh `Abbās over another sovereign ruler—Safavid secretaries of this period were often fond of providing maxims on imperial qualities and kingly ethics. The security and wellbeing of the subject population, specifically the ability to perform *ḥajj* to places of pilgrimage in `Irāq and beyond, were profiled as mandates to which Ottoman sultans and Uzbek khans should aspire. In letters to Murād III and Meḥmed III, Ottoman sultans were encouraged to act, for instance, "regarding the noble kingly ethics and the compassionate laudable qualities of the shadow of God" (*az makārim-i akhlāq-i khāqānī va maḥāsin-i ishfāq-i ẓill-i subḥānī*).[265] Indeed, the term *makārim al-akhlāq* refers to an extensive body of advice literature first produced in classical and medieval times.[266] In our context, these admonitions were in principle designed as textual indicators that the letter was coming to a conclusion, in much the same way one might conclude a parable narrative with an explicit aphorism. In another letter to Murād III, its denouement closes with a maxim that references the "noble kingly ethics" (*makārim-i akhlāq-i khāqānī*): "the needy, citizens, merchants, and the disposed—who have been in the shadow of justice of that refuge of kings on tranquil and relaxed territory—have been preoccupied with prayers for the extension of this enduring dynasty and the justice of the royal sultanate."[267] Finally, the standardization of Safavid *inshā* is often seen in the regular inclusion of a concluding formula—a formal disavowal of embellishment—that reifies Ḥātim Beg's impulse to reform and trim epistolary composition. In many cases, such as `Abbās's letters to the Venetian Doges and the Uzbek khans, this phrase was short and to the point, such as: "Anything more than this would be to show prolixity!" (*ziyādah az īn chi iṭnāb namāyad*).[268] In a letter to Murād III, one scribe writes that "more hyperbole and prolixity is a violation of good *adab*" (*ziyād az iṭālat va iṭnāb khilāf-i adab ast*),[269] while in another we read, "more of this prolixity would be a forsaking of *adab* and custom" (*ziyād az īn iṭnāb sabab-i tark-i adab va gustākhī ast*).[270]

Perhaps the best indication of Ḥātim Beg's efforts towards standardization is his use of bureaucratic formulaic manuals like Ḥusain Vā`iẓ Kāshifī's *Makhzan al-inshā*. While there is evidence to suggest that Safavid secretaries had used this manual on occasion during the reigns of Shāh Ṭahmāsp and Khudābandah, letters produced after 996/1588 suggest the *Makhzan al-inshā* had become a permanent reference tool among the functionaries of the *dār al-inshā*. In an early letter (sometime between 996–999/1588–91) there are lines of poetry borrowed from Kāshifī's compendium of Arabic and Persian verses on "Qualities of Great Kings."[271] More consistent replication appears in a *ta`ziyyah* letter sent to Meḥmed III in 1003/1594–95, wherein poetry and prose encomiums are extracted from Kāshifī's early section (ff. 6b–7a) on honorifics for kings and sultans and sprinkled liberally throughout the *intitulatio* for the new sultan Meḥmed III.[272] Likewise, in a *tahniyyah* letter to the same ruler Meḥmed in 1004/1595–96, the Safavid scribe consulted fol. 81a of *Makhzan al-inshā* ("Concluding Poetry [for Letters] to Sultans and their Children") for model phrases.

The most prolific evidence for the use of Kāshifī's epistolographic manual comes in a Safavid letter written in 999/1590–91 to Akbar the Great. After the lengthy *invocatio* section to God, Muḥammad, and the Imamate, almost the entire *inscriptio* section appears to be a composite of model prose encomiums offered on fol. 22a and fol. 27a of *Makhzan al-inshā*. The epitomic Persian constructs and superlative Arabic eulogies[273] are borrowed from the columns of "Arabic prose arrangements" (*manṣūrah-yi arabiyyah*) and "Persian prose arrangements" (*manṣūrah-yi fārsiyyah*) that appear in Kāshifī's "Qualities and Expressions for People of the First Rank—Living Kings, Sultans, and Caliphs."[274] The lengthy *du`ā*[275] on behalf of Meḥmed III is likewise a composite of model benedictions copied from the first column of "Prose Arabic Benedictions for Exalted People."[276] While its appeal might lie in the simple and straightforward arrangement of verses and prose phrases in Arabic and Persian, the *Makhzan al-inshā* enjoyed its renaissance for its endorsement and showcasing of the Timurid model of kingly authority and imperium. Elsewhere, this study has argued that the *Makhzan al-inshā* provided a model schemata of Timurid society, wherein kings, sultans, and amirs were accorded the highest rank in society (*ṭabaqah-yi a`lā*) alongside the "men of the pen" (*ahl al-qalam*), while hierocratic and clerical elements were relegated to the second rank (*ṭabaqah-yi ashraf*). In this sense, Kāshifī's model society accorded less status for the religious functionaries and instead revolved around a strong imperial centre with a corresponding central role for the Persian bureaucratic tradition.[277] In a similar vein, Anthony Welch noted how the court artist Ṣādiqī Beg produced an illustrated manuscript of Kāshifī's *Anvār-i Suhailī* on 13 Ṣafar 1002/8 November 1593 on behalf of Shāh `Abbās: "Ṣādiqī was quite aware of `Abbās's developing predilection for Timurid models in his official architecture and manuscript painting."[278]

If there are enough formulaics and stock phrases to highlight a definite trend towards standardization and homogenization in the Safavid chancellery, the question remains whether the subject matter of these different letters can help us in the quest to understand the relationship between dynastic legitimacy and epistolary rhetoric. If the structure and form of these letters reflect Ḥātim Beg's mandate to centralize and professionalize the Safavid government, what can they tell us about `Abbās's ideological program of advocating a patrimonial, imperial state of Iran? Are there additional narratives and topoi in these letters that reinforce the presentation of Safavid Iran as a new political entity with definitive temporal and spatial boundaries? One discernible focus in `Abbās's correspondence is conquest and incorporation of new and old territories to Safavid dominion. Of the roughly twenty-five letters under review here, eight[279] include short narratives about `Abbās's conquest and incorporation of the province of Gīlān in 1000/1591–92. Another two were written to Khān Aḥmad Khān before and after the Safavid invasion. Of the six letters despatched to the Uzbeks during this decade, three include sustained reports about historical Safavid military successes in Khurāsān and elsewhere.

Ostensibly, these letters were presented as normative kingly correspondence; although, in reality their main texts consisted of victory narratives and as such classify them as informal *fatḥ nāmahs* ("victory letters"). In the case of the Safavid conquest of Gīlān, this correspondence to the loyal Kār Kiyā dynast Khān Aḥmad and the Ottoman ruler Murād III provided `Abbās with a discursive forum. It was clearly important to Shāh `Abbās that he present the invasion and incorporation of Gīlān within a historical framework, which could in turn permit a sustained, legal justification for this territorial expansion. In the letter to Khān Aḥmad, who had sought asylum with the Ottomans after the invasion, he explicitly pointed out "how we are a legatee of that exalted *khān*" (*navāb humāyūn-i mā vaṣī-yi ān khān `alā sha'n-and*) and that this legal claim was rooted in the time of `Abbās's father, Shāh Muḥammad Khudābandah.[280] To justify this, `Abbās presents a short history detailing the relationship between Khān Aḥmad and his aunt, Mahd-i `Ulyā, and specifically mentions that it was she who had released Khān Aḥmad from prison and organized his governorship of Bīya-Pīsh in Gīlān on the condition that he marry into the royal family.[281] From that point forward, the relationship of the Safavid family and Khān Aḥmad was defined by suzerainty: "The throne of dominion [of Gīlān] was subsequently adorned with our abundant and overflowing munificence."[282] To finalize this marriage alliance, the letter narrates how Mahd-i `Ulyā had arrived with her daughter to the region of Daylam, and with this "the Daylamis entered into royal service."[283]

This historical diplomatic development was critical to `Abbās's conception of Gīlān as a subsidiary province of the Safavids, and during the ensuing ceremony, "the group of officers and generals were honoured while paying their respects, and Gīlān was subsumed into the ownership of this saintly dynasty."[284] `Abbās's chancellery looked likewise to historical precedence to defend this annexation in a letter to the Ottoman sultan Murād III. After narrating the invasion, `Abbās writes that the "*ulkā* of Gīlān" had been in the Safavids' possession for nearly a century since the enthronement of Ismā`īl I, and the governors of this place had been remitting considerable taxes since the reign of Shāh Ṭahmāsp.[285] Moreover, when Khān Aḥmad had been imprisoned by Shāh Ṭahmāsp, the province of Gīlān had been consigned to his Qizilbāsh amirs (*ayālat-i Gīlān-rā* *bi umarā-yi Qizilbāsh rujū` farmūdah būdand*), but when `Abbās ascended to the throne, the *ulkā* had been reassigned to Khān Aḥmad. `Abbās had decided to revoke his appointment when the shah learned that the Kār Kiyā noble had become embroiled in plots and intrigues with the Ottomans.[286] In another letter sent to Murād III soon after, many of these arguments regarding Safavid incorporation of Gīlān were reiterated. "It is clear and obvious," the letter observes, "that governors of Gīlān have been appointed for a long time" (*ẓāhir va huvaidā ast ki ḥukkām-i Gīlān az qadīm nasb kardah*). The Safavid scribe relates how "continually [Safavid] coins and sermons, which are signs of imperium and dominion were in the names of [our] ancestors."[287] When `Abbās assumed the "reins of Iran's dominion" (*zimām-i salṭanat-i Īrān*), it was decreed that new coins and new sermons were to be affixed with his name along with new governors for the region of Gīlān.[288]

In many cases, these discussions regarding Gīlān and historical dynastic precedence were conjoined with explicit discussions of formal Safavid territory. Thus, the "narrating" of Safavid dominion was fused with a deliberate "mapping" of what then constituted Safavid Iran. In the first letter to Murād III, which had pointed out Safavid connection with Gīlān since the time of Ismā`īl I, the "victory narrative" of Gīlān is followed by a commentary on Ottoman-Safavid relations and how both sides were to respect the current peace accord and not enter one another's territory. The Ottomans should know that the Safavid royal court has determined the frontiers (*sinūr*), boundaries (*ḥudūd*), and straights (*s̱ughūr*) of the imperial provinces (*mamālik-maḥrūsah-yi pādshāhī*), and these now extend from Qarājah Dāgh on the edge of the Aras and Kar Rivers across to Māhī-Dasht, Ḥuvaizah, and `Arabistān.[289] The Safavid scribe adds how the proximity of Gīlān to the Safavid capital of Qazvīn necessitates its inclusion into the formal Safavid territories. In the second previously discussed letter to Murād III (about coins and sermons), the scribe likewise uses this opportunity to point out that Ottoman "officers and pashas" (*aminān va pāshān*), who are cognizant of the boundary and frontiers (*sar-ḥadd va sinūr*) of the two sides, should know that "Gīlān is within the boundaries of the [Safavid] kingdom."[290] Moreover, Murād III is informed that this *ulkā* of Gīlān is in `Abbās's possession and is run by functionaries and dependents of `Abbās's court.[291]

We find in many ways a mirroring of this discourse in those letters that present short historical narratives about Safavid military and diplomatic activity in the region of Khurāsān. Principally, Khurāsān had been a seat of royal Safavid power since its original conquest in 916/1510 by Shāh Ismā`īl. True to Turco-Mongol practice of the thirteenth and fourteenth centuries, the city of Herāt had been treated as a princely appanage with no less than nine *mīrzā*s holding this post in the sixteenth century.[292] Moreover, Herāt still maintained an elite status because of its Timurid pedigree, and the Safavids not surprisingly considered this province a cornerstone to their burgeoning empire. Thus, in a later letter (ca. 1004/1595–96) to `Abd al-Mu'min Khān, the Safavid scribe related how Shāh `Abbās was deeply connected to securing and guarding the kingdom of Khurāsān (*ḥirāsat va muḥāfaẓat-i mamlakat-i Khurāsān*) because "it is the caliphal capital and sultanic abode of [`Abbās's] great and beloved ancestors and forefathers."[293] In an earlier letter to `Abd al-Mu'min Khān, written approximately in the autumn of 1000/1592, during the height of the Safavid-Uzbek wars, `Abbās responded to a previous Uzbek letter that had invoked the historical legacy of a peace treaty in the region of Khurāsān between the Timurid Sulṭān-Ḥusain Mīrzā and the Āq Qoyūnlū Ūzūn Ḥasan as a possible model for the Uzbeks and the Safavids. The brusque rejoinder to `Abd al-Mu'min Khān leaves no doubt regarding Safavid dynastic sensibilities.

> With respect to establishing the same treaty between us that had been established between Sulṭān-Ḥusain Mīrzā and Ūzūn Ḥasan, it occurs to us that Sulṭān-Ḥusain Mīrzā—who is one of the Chaghatā'ī sultans—has no connection to you and Ūzūn Ḥasan—who is a Türkmen king—has no connection to us. If we were to establish a peace treaty, it should be according to the one established between my grandfather Shāh Ṭahmāsp and Kuskun [Kaskan?] Qarā Sulṭān and Pīr Muḥammad Khān, who were part of families which were close to that best of dynasties, the Chingīz Khāns.[294]

In one deft rhetorical manoeuvre, the Safavids deny the Ubzek claim to be the best Chingizid descendants, while at the same time they eschew any connection with the Türkmen Āq Qoyūnlū. The Safavid scribe subsequently moves from this topic to the specifics of territorial space and points out how the terms of that treaty had seen Khurāsān appended to the "kingly provinces" (*mamālik-maḥrūsah-yi shāhī*) of the Safavids, while Transoxania had been given to the Shaybanids ruling out of Bukhārā. If the Uzbeks had no interest in the terms of this kind of treaty, the Safavid chancellery points out the historical path of war taken by their ancestors—Ismā`īl versus Shaibak Khān and Ṭahmāsp versus `Ubaid Khān—and the Uzbek audience would understand the implicit references to the overwhelming Safavid victories at Marv and Jām in 916/1510 and 934/1528 respectively.[295] The scribe enjoins his Uzbek audience to heed the hadith in this matter whereby the Prophet Muḥammad warns: "Everything that doubles will triple" (*lā tathana shay'un īlā wa qad tathalatha*). He also refers to the "noble book" (probably the Qur'ān) that states help, assistance, and protection do not establish a dominion, neither is a small or large army necessarily an advantage. "From the first sunrise of matchless bounty of this caliphal family," waxes the letter, "until the time when the reins of state and dominion of this dynasty were in my grasp, not one of my concerns were dependent on the assistance of earthly sultans and kings, but rather solely based on the decree of God."[296] The Safavid chancellery scribe employs a device of contraposition (*muṭābaqah*) by subsequently explaining how this was the case because so many other Muslim dynasties had found themselves dependent on the Safavids: "Bābur, the children of Sulṭān-Ḥusain Mīrzā Bāiqarā, and the sultans of Shīrvān [have all] sought refuge with my ancestor [Shāh Ismā`īl] while Humāyūn Pādshāh and the sultans of Gurganj found asylum with my grandfather [Shāh Ṭahmāsp]."[297]

Of course, Khurāsān was also a topic of discussion in non-Uzbek letters, and in one of `Abbās's missives to Murād III (ca. 1001/1593), the Safavid scribe provides the Ottoman sultan with a sustained historical report of Safavid successes in the east. `Abbās admits frankly that he was unable to prevent the Uzbeks from invading Khurāsān early on in 995–96/1588 and describes how `Abd al-Mu'min Khān had recently assembled his entire army in Transoxania to annex Khurāsān.[298] Dynamics changed considerably, however, when the Uzbeks realized that `Abbās had concluded a peace treaty with the Ottomans, and as a result "they could not breach or damage those well-established lords in that region, and they were so incapable of opposing or resisting the wave of violence and attacks by [my] victorious army that they preferred flight to fight."[299] Consequently, "most places" (*akṣar-i maḥāl*) of Khurāsān were returned to the possession of Safavid commanders, and from place to place (*maḥal bi maḥal*), amirs and governors were duly appointed.[300] It was `Abbās's intention that summer to extricate the remaining Uzbeks from the cities of Herāt and Mashhad and to arrange to have Safavid amirs properly installed by the spring of the next year.[301]

Khurāsān was clearly as much a "contested space" in Uzbek correspondence as the province of Gīlān had been in letters to the Ottoman court. In much the same manner as the Safavid chancellery had presented Gīlānī-Safavid historical narratives in tandem with a textual map of sovereign Safavid territory, we see discussion of imperial space in tandem with these Khurāsānī narratives. In a later (1595/1003–04) missive to `Abd al-Mu'min Khān, `Abbās narrates how he is preoccupied with managing the affairs of princely provinces (*intiẓām-i mahāmm-i mamālik*) of `Irāq, Fārs, and Khūzistān. He also mentions the recent inclusion of Gīlān due to the successful ousting of Khān Aḥmad.[302] In the same spirit, `Abbās informs `Abd al-Mu'min Khān that he has despatched Farhād Khān Qarāmānlū to Khurāsān "in order to quickly restore ownership [of this province] to this saintly family."[303] After the conquest of that region, the affairs of Māzandarān, Bīsṭām, and Astarābād would be organized once commanders and functionaries have been properly despatched from the royal court.[304] Later, `Abbās discusses the historical relationship with the Chingizid families living in Central Asia and how Shāh Ṭahmāsp had secured their station and sovereignty as a regional, dynastic sponsor.[305] He iterates that he was faithful to this historical precedent: "I have fixed the Chingizid rulers on the royal, imperial throne of the provinces of Chingīz Khān."[306] Conditions had deteriorated to the point that `Abbās was forced to send in twenty thousand troops along with his two confederates, the Khvārazmian ruler Ḥājjī Muḥammad Khān and Nūr Muḥammad Khān who had been the ruler of Marv until recently.[307] This epistolary text culminates with `Abbās's dire prediction to `Abd al-Mu'min Khān, wherein he threatens the retaliatory strength of the entire Safavid empire: "The armies of `Irāq, Fārs, Kirmān, Khūzistān, Gīlān, Māzandarān, Astarābād, Āzarbāījān, Dāghistān, Kurdistān, Luristān, and Khurāsān will bring a level of killing, devastation, plundering, and depredation which will remain in infamy until the Day of Resurrection."[308] These letters constituted discursive forums, which allowed scribes to fuse the functionality of history (*tārīkh*) with the creativity of rhetoric (*inshā*) towards the ultimate goal of articulating dynastic precedence. Surpassing their *ḥijra*-century mark in 1006/1597, the Safavids had dominated much of southwest Asia for a hundred lunar years, and the chancellery material produced under `Abbās reflects this newly developed sense of historical and spatial self-awareness.

There were also attempts by the Safavid chancellery to buttress these new articulations with references to and discussions of older, traditional conceptions of identity within an ethnic Iranian space. Although we cannot see this as necessarily new and innovative, neither should we look to `Abbās's reign as a "golden period" of nascent, Iranian proto-nationalism. There is ample evidence pointing to `Abbās's program of incorporating and empowering a panoply of non-Iranian ethnic groups—Armenians, Georgians, Kurds, Turks, Arabs—during his reign to suggest the contrary. What is perhaps unique here is how Safavid scribes seized upon this body of imagery and topoi during a period when the royal court and bureaucracy seemed determined to define and project a centralized empire to the outside world. For instance, `Abbās's correspondence to `Abd Allāh Khān and `Abd al-Mu'min Khān would on occasion present Safavid-Uzbek relations within the popular Iranian-Turanian framework found in the epic poetic tradition of the *Shāh nāmah* and other legendary narratives. Safavid scribes in an early letter to `Abd Allāh Khān manipulated the Uzbek's titulature to profile his connection with historical and legendary exemplars associated with the "eastern" lands. Using an imperfect *tajnīs*, the scribe hails the Chingizid and Qarā Khitā'ī pedigree of `Abd Allāh Khān: he sits "on the beautiful throne of Chingīz Khān" (*zībandah-yi takht-i Chingīz Khānī*) and occupies the same "superior station of Gūr Khān" (*barāzandah-yi maqām-i Gūr Khānī*). At the same time, the Uzbek's rule is as "meritorious as the dominion of Afrasiyab's throne" (*mustaḥaqq-i istīlā-yi sarīr-i Afrāsiyāb*).[309] In one of the letters exchanged with `Abd al-Mu'min in the fall of 1000/1591, the Safavid scribe similarly describes the Uzbek addressee as sitting on "an equitable throne to the power and felicity and beauty of the throne of Farīdūn" (*barāzandah-yi sarīr-i salṭanat va kāmrān va zībandah-yi takht-i Farīdūn*), while sharing "the fortune of Chingīz Khān" (*bakht-i Chingīz Khānī*).[310] The Turanian-Iranian motif is explicitly profiled in `Abd al-Mu'min Khān's formal benediction (*du`ā*) in Arabic: "May the properties of his justice and goodness never cease [descending] on the heads of the people of Tūrān." The spirit of this benediction is continued with Persian prose: "Then [these properties] will have desire to unite the two sides which has been eagerly awaited for years by the people of Iran and Tūrān."[311]

Explicit use of legendary narrative frameworks appear at the end of yet another letter to `Abd al-Mu'min Khān. In this particular example, `Abbās invites `Abd al-Mu'min to do battle, arguing that whoever has superior qualities will emerge as the victor. Summing up the sentiment of "to the victor go the spoils,"

`Abbās promises the territory and army (*ulkā va lashkar*) of the vanquished will be claimed, and thousands of Muslims will be spared. The Safavid scribe concludes his letter with quotations from both Firdausī (*Shāh nāmah*) and Niẓāmī (*Sharaf nāmah*), and in both cases these verses are from scenarios where the principal protagonist and an antagonist are trading barbed remarks before an epic single combat. The first two lines are extracted from the belligerent dialogue between the hero Rustam and the hubristic Iranian King Isfandiyār,[312] while the last two are from Niẓāmī's account of Alexander's invasion of Zanzibar and his exchange with the Zanj King Palangar.[313]

> Let us see if Isfandiyar's horse returns rider-less to the stable
> Or if Rustam's horse will turn without a master towards his palace
>
> Come, so that I may display the battle of heroes/And we shall see the fighting of lions in this battlefield
> We shall see who will be on the summit/and as a result who will enjoy victory.

This device of presenting Safavid-Uzbek hostilities through the metaphorical lens of epic, legendary struggles between the Iranians and the Turanians was not surprising given the popularity of this Iran-Turan contraposition in medieval literature.[314] The profiling of Khurāsān as a space of epic struggle is also seen in a later letter (ca. 1004/1595–96) to `Abd al-Mu'min Khān. After discussing the cumulative carnage that had been inflicted on the province of Khurāsān in the last century, the Safavid scribe writes how "the battlefield has been emptied of whale-defeating heroes [*gardān-i nahang-afgan*] and elephant-bodied warriors [*shīrān-i fīl-tan*]." He points out that this is in accordance with a hadith (in Persian): "The battlefield remained empty of the brave, high-flying eagle [*`uqāb*] while the ignoble vulture [*kargas-i nā-kas*] circles in the air to strike."[315] In this way, Khurāsān is presented as a den of manlihood (*bīshah-yi mardī*), which has been emptied of champions who hunt lions (*hazhīrān-i shīr shikār*) and left to the perfidious foxes (*rubāh-i ghadār*).[316] As a result, the Uzbek leaders of Muḥammad Shibānī Khān and `Ubaid Allāh Khān descended onto Khurāsān and ruined it repeatedly with no remorse. The scribe casts these Uzbek khans as overindulged children in need of strong parental control and describes how the patriarchal figures of Shāh Ismā`īl and Shāh Ṭahmāsp rebuked Shibānī Khān and `Ubaid Allāh Khān with "a chastising box of the ear" (*sīlī-yi ta'dīb*) and a "punishing slap on the face" (*tapānchah-yi tanbiyyah*). In referring to these "children of Chingiz" (*aulād-i Chīngīz*), he adds how they had become penitent and ashamed. In conclusion, ` Abbās abjectly quotes this line of poetry: "This broken world is the one and the same that is seen with the *maidān* of Afrasiyāb."[317]

Mentioned earlier, we find a relative paucity of formal religious invocations in Safavid letters under Ḥātim Beg's tutelage. This is not to imply, however, that religious themes and apologetic discussions of Shi`ism and Sunnism were non-existent. For instance, in one of the letters to `Abd al-Mu'min Khān, `Abbās shifts his ongoing discussion to the Safavid status as protectors of Shi`ism with the introduction of an age-old `Alid axiom: "In the beginning of [this] scented letter ... it was ordered that the following be written: 'whoever falls on the family of `Alī will die.'" This ultimatum is in turn followed by invoking the *ḥadīth-i Safīna*: "My Family is like the Ark of Noah, whoever embarked in it was saved, and whoever turned away from it was drowned."[318] The scribe explains how the connection of the Safavid family to the Imamate (*khāndān-i ṭaibīn-i ṭāhirīn-i ma`ṣūmīn*) is obvious and manifest and warns: "Any earthly rulers who entered into a position of opposition and hatred with this family marked by *wilāyat* [i.e., the Safavids] has slowly found the dust of calamity sifted onto their head and the vapour of infirmity and despondency sprinkled on their face."[319] The Safavid scribes were also capable of framing contemporary enmity with classical sectarian exemplars. Again in a letter to `Abd al-Mu'min Khān, `Abbās describes how "I am the slave of `Alī and you are the slave of `Umar, Mu`āwiyah, and Abī Ṣufyān—may the curse of God be upon them." The historical memory of Sunni-Shi`ite enmity is charged on the basis of many early events and developments, but the Safavids look here to the historical battle of Ṣiffin (40/661) between `Alī and Mu`āwiyah and the resulting arbitration: "Just as in the battle of Ṣiffin—reflected in 2: 195: 'Fight in the way of God those who fight you, but do not transgress limits because God does not love transgressors'—where my Imam and master commanded to your Imam and master that 'let us do battle together.'"[320] Whoever is victorious on the battlefield, `Abbās predicts, will have God's blessing as in 57: 21: "That is the grace of God which He bestows on whom He pleases" and will take possession of both property and army. What is particularly intriguing is the language and style used here—invoking God's sense of preference and predestination, promising spoils to the victor—are the same as in the letter sent earlier, which had quoted Firdausī and Niẓāmī. In that letter, the identity of the Safavids was paralleled with two of the most popular exemplars of Iranian identity—Rustam and Alexander—while in this letter the chancellery instead focused on early Islamic exemplars, including `Alī, ` Umar, Mu`āwiyah, and Abī Ṣufyān.

While such acerbic Shi`ite rhetoric found its way very periodically into `Abbās's diplomatic material, the preponderance of religious discourse appears to be rooted in the theosophically inspired philosophical trends that were defining `Abbās's court as the sixteenth century was drawing to a close. By the early seventeenth century, key philosophers and theologians—Shaikh Bahā'ī, Mīr Muḥammad Bāqir Dāmād (*laqab*: Mīr Dāmād), Mullā Ṣadrā—had elevated Iṣfahān as a notable centre of doctrinal and philosophical inquiry. While Uṣūlī juridical elements still played a vital role with respect to religious law and enforcing orthopraxy across the empire, they no longer enjoyed the power they once had during the reign of Shāh Ṭahmāsp. Similar to other interest groups—such as confederations of Qizilbāsh Türkmen, various popular Sufi groups and confraternities, and the Persian bureaucratic and administrative elite—the juridical elements found themselves subverted and co-opted by this new absolutist shah.[321] `Abbās was careful to avoid any undue accruing of power by a particular hierocrat or group of clerics, and when the Shaikh al-Islām and pre-eminent Uṣūlī scholar Ḥusain ibn al-Ḥasan al-Karakī (Mīr Ḥusain Mujtahid) passed away at Qazvīn in 1001/1592–93 during an epidemic, an age of al-Karakī familial influence had come to a close. Moreover, jurist-sponsored *tabarrā'iyān* and the broadcasting of ritual curses among the Iranian populace were no longer the norm, and such behaviour was distinctly absent for the duration of Shāh `Abbās's reign.[322]

Nonetheless, Shāh `Abbās continued to fill the role of patron and protector to these orthodox Shi`ite elements and sought their opinions and rulings on various legal matters while at the same time disseminating their treatises throughout the Safavid empire.[323] Popular mysticism was declared anathema, and famous incidents of Sufi degradation and elimination include `Abbās's extirpation of a Nuqṭavī cabal, headed by Darvīsh Khusrau, within his own court.[324] More spectacular evidence is recorded by Munajjim Yazdī, who reports how Shāh `Abbās decreed that Ḥaidarī and Ni`matullāhī Sufis be pitted against one another as gladiators in the Maidan-i Sa`ādat of Qazvīn. The victors would be released during a ceremony which would also hold the public execution of disloyal Qizilbāsh amirs.[325] Popular, pedestrian Sufism suffered the full weight of official censure and harassment, while theosophical philosophers and theologians in the Neoplatonist tradition of Ibn Sinā and Suhravardī enjoyed relative patronage and support.[326] We know this class of philosopher/scholar-bureaucrat (and specifically those from Shīrāz) had overlapped with the Safavid chancellery during the reign of Khudābandah, and we see these same individuals, as well as their scions and students, enjoying a certain propinquity to the administration in the early years of Shāh `Abbās.

Shaikh Bahā'ī's relationship with Shāh `Abbās was volatile, but he appears to have been connected quite closely with the administration at times. He wrote official correspondence to his Ottoman counterparts and dedicated his treatise on the astrolabe to the chief vizier, Ḥātim Beg Urdūbādī.[327] Moreover, Shaikh Bahā'ī and Urdūbādī worked together to negotiate submissions by various regional amirs early on in `Abbās's reign, including an ultimately unsuccessful marriage alliance with Khān Aḥmad.[328] Shaikh Bahā'ī was also used on two different occasions in 998/1589–90 as a principal mediator in local rebellions, including the ones by Ya`qūb Khān Zū al-Qadar in Shīrāz,[329] Yulī Beg, the governor of Iṣfahān,[330] as well as Sayyid Mubārak of the Musha`sha`in Khūzistān.[331] Shaikh Bahā'ī's religious temperament has been a topic of some debate—Andrew Newman argues, for instance, that he was a conservative Uṣūlī Shi`ite scholar[332]—but his teachings and treatises are so varied that it seems more appropriate (and prudent) to see him rather as "a representative of the extensive stretch of middle ground between the two extremes [of fanatical Shi`ism and Ḥanbalī Sunnism]."[333]

Similarly, the philosopher Mīr Dāmād had a close relationship with Shāh `Abbās and the administration. He prepared a number of theological texts for the Safavid chancellery to send as official correspondence to the Ottoman court in the 1590s and also sent letters to the *`ulamā* of Baghdād.[334] During the Safavid invasion of `Irāq and attack on Baghdād in 1032/1623, Mīr Dāmād was asked by Shāh `Abbās to produce a *fatwā* stating that Safavid soldiers killed in battle were to be hailed as martyrs, while those who fled could be legally declared rebels.[335] Also similar to Shaikh Bahā'ī, Mīr Dāmād enjoyed a relationship with the administrative baron, Ḥātim Beg Urdūbādī. For instance, Shaikh Āqā Buzurgin (author of *Kalamāt al-shu`arā*) relates a story of how Ḥātim Beg acted as an intermediary for Mīr Dāmād when he presented one of his works on philosophy, *Khalsat al-malakūt*, to Shāh `Abbās.[336]

There is evidence to suggest that some of these theosophical impulses governed how the chancellery chose to introduce religion in their epistolary texts. Shāh `Abbās's support for avatars of the "high" philosophical tradition—namely Shaikh Bahā'ī and Mīr Dāmād, as well as the constructive relationship they shared with Ḥātim Beg Urdūbādī—played a role in how and why the Safavid scribes and *munshī*s approached religious rhetoric. In one of the earliest letters, to `Abd Allah Khān Uzbek, the Safavid author introduces the common Sufi refrain of the ephemeral nature of temporal dominion and poetically invokes Alexander the Great: "Iskander had the world in his hand/but in that moment he left and the world passed by."[337] This transitory dynamic continues as a focus of the letter as the scribe writes how "the endurance of a frail, worldly state—with its fleeting sense of covenant, fidelity, and dignity—is clear and obvious in the opinion of contemporaries and wise ones."[338] The genealogical pedigree of the Safavids endows them with special insight on this matter: "Our resplendent mind and noble-diffusing thought will become clear and manifest" thanks to their connection (*nisbat-i mā*) to the Imamate (*khāndān-i ṭaibīn-i ṭāhirīn*) and the Sufi masters and saints (*silsilah-yi auliyā va aṣafiyā*).[339] Such paralleling of the Imamate and the learned Sufi shaikhs of the past was a popular approach in Safavid official rhetoric, whereby their real and fabricated genealogies operate from within two very different realms of authority and legitimacy. This ecumenical dynamic is further seen in Shāh `Abbās's letter of congratulations to Meḥmed III upon his accession to the Ottoman throne in 1004/1595. Lamenting the death of Murād III, the scribe writes how `Abbās commanded that groups of pious ones (*ṣulaḥā*), eloquent ones (*fuḍalā*), religious scholars (*`ulamā*), and spiritual ones (*aṣḥāb-i zuhd va taqā*) along with the "pure-hearted Sufis of this dynasty" (*bā ṣūfiyān-i ṣāfī-nahād-i īn dūdmān*) place themselves in "our cell of sorrow" (*kulba'ih-yi iḥzān-i mā*) during the month of Ramaḍān. Having presented the dynasty in Sufi terms as a "cell of sorrow," the Safavid *munshī* describes how the Safavids are connected with Muḥammad (*mansūb bi āstān-i mulk-āsiyān-i Muṣṭafaviyyah*), bound to `Alī (*marbūṭ bi khāndān-i quds-nishān-i Murtaḍaviyyah*), and dependent on the shaikhs of Ardabīl (*manūṭ bi silsilah-yi rafī`ah-yi jalīlah-yi mashāyikh-i Ṣafavī*).[340]

The most manifest evidence for Sufi-inspired correspondence comes with Shāh `Abbās's 999/1591 letter to the Mughal ruler Akbar the Great. In fact, this letter stands slightly apart from the corpus of epistolary material produced under Urdūbādī's directorship for its embrace of poetry as well as traditional rhetorical structures and tools. For instance, in the beginning, the scribe includes the three-tiered religious invocation (God, Muḥammad, the Imamate) and parallels the appearance of this august letter with God's pre-eternal commands of "Be and it was" (*kun fayakūn*).[341] Much of the invocatory verse in this section is borrowed from various dedicatory sections found in Niẓāmī's *Khamsah*. For example, this letter's first versified praise of God is copied from Niẓāmī's dedication to the Divine at the beginning of *Laila va Majnūn*[342] and corresponding sections in the *Makhzan al-asrār*.[343] Not surprisingly, the Safavid scribe's exaltation of Muḥammad as the most perfect of God's creations relies heavily on the *Khamsah* for inspiration. The author focuses on the Prophet's Ascension (*mi`rāj*) as the best forum to highlight Muḥammad's singular superiority over all created creatures, including previous prophets, and a short prose narrative is provided of how the Prophet ascended and toured the different levels of Paradise (*malakūt, jabarūt*) on his legendary mount, Burāq.[344] The scribe provides a poem to celebrate this event, with the first line modified slightly from the praise section (*dar na`t-i payghambar-i akrām*) of the *Iqbāl nāmah* by Niẓāmī.[345] The scribe subsequently quotes three lines of poetry from the Mi`rāj section of Niẓāmī's *Makhzan al-asrār*, and we can now see how this account of the Ascension continued to be a source of great inspiration for poets, artists, and calligraphers throughout the sixteenth century.[346] The mystical appeal of Niẓāmī, especially with respect to the mythic presentation of the Prophet during the Mi`rāj, was a constant in Safavid Iran, but anecdotal evidence suggests this thirteenth-century poet's popularity grew during the reign of Shāh `Abbās.[347] We also know that on occasion `Abbās challenged many of his court poets (Awḥadī, Shifā'ī) to compose and recite poetry based on the quintuple structure of the *Khamsah*.[348] Returning to the epistle in question, `Alī appears in this ekphrastic tour, and consistent with previous correspondence, we find Muḥammad and `Alī presented as the twinned bearers of prophecy and kingship respectively. In this sense, `Alī enjoys the mandate to enforce the proper faith as Muḥammad's legatee (*farmān-farmā-yi kishvar-i vasāṣat va sharī`at gastarī*), and it is the mystical, royal documents (*manāshīr-i jabarūt-ash*) of this "king of kings" that appeared and were entitled with the *ṭughrā* of "I am making you an Imām of the People" (*anī jā`alaka li'l-nāssi imāman*).[349]

After this mystical presentation of Muḥammad and `Alī, the scribe adopts a metaphysical tenor and turns to the issue of multiplicity in ontology and epistemology. He is particularly drawn to explaining the hidden secrets (*asrār-i naḥānī*) that exist in this earthly layer of reality and how the physical world, specifically politics, is governed by what is determined on higher, more spiritual planes of existence. Here, he quotes the hadith: "Spirits are like conscripted soldiers; those whom they recognize, they get along with, and those whom they do not recognize, they will not get along with."[350] In this way, the scribe elaborates, "their blessed spirits" (*arvāḥ-i muqaddisah-yi īshān*) are forged with another by friendship, concord, and amity in the "spirit world" (*dar `ālam-i arvāḥ*) as essences before they assume the form of accidents in the world of physical forms (*dar `ālam-i ashbāh*) and are unduly influenced by worldly encounters (*malāqāt-i ẓāhirī*) and materialistic dialogues (*muwāṣalah-yi ṣūrī*).[351] The letter emphasizes the binary of physical and spiritual existence, pointing out that whatever was not revealed to kings in the physical world (*dīdah-yi ẓāhir dar `ālam-i nāsūt*) was certainly determined and known in the divine world (*`arṣah-yi lāhūt*).[352]

These distinctions between layers of existence in the physical and spiritual worlds (*malakūt, jabarūt, lāhūt, nāsūt*) and how they overlap with respect to articulations of prophecy and kingship are reflective of the contemporary intellectual milieu of the Safavid court. The strong sense of metaphysical stratification, the preponderance of light imagery, and the deliberate profiling of Niẓāmī's poetry all point to eschatological and soteriological viewpoints with distinct Illuminationist moorings.[353] It seems likely that Mīr Dāmād was in part responsible for the intellectual impulses expressed in this letter to Akbar the Great, since the cosmology discussed here reflects his adamant separation of essences and accidents, whereby the "the world is partly a manifestation of the archetypal superior realm and partly independent from it, being controlled by the emanation directly preceding it."[354] Boasting the *laqab* of "Third Master" (*al-Mu`allim al-Thālith*), Mīr Dāmād has been credited with borrowing and adapting many Suhravardian principles to the Safavid context.[355] The consistent use of Niẓāmī here might also be connected with Mīr Dāmād because of his affinity for the poetic stylings of this great mystical poet; indeed, the Safavid historian Muḥammad Yūsuf Vālih described how the poetic arrangements of Ishrāqī (Mīr Dāmād's *takhalluṣ*) were presented in the same poetic metre (*ham-vazn*) as the *Makhzan al-asrār*.[356] To find an individual so intimately defined by this Avicennan world view in proximity to the chancellery is not necessarily surprising given that the Safavid state's chief vizier, Ḥātim Beg Urdūbādī, claimed direct descent from one of the greatest Peripatetic philosophers of medieval Iran, Khvājah Naṣīr al-Dīn al-Ṭūsī.[357]

In conclusion, we come away with an impression of `Abbās's chancellery that stands apart from what we had encountered under previous Safavid shahs. Ḥātim Beg's mandate of streamlining and standardizing Safavid *inshā* had clearly been implemented soon after his appointment as chief vizier of the Safavid government. Excessive use of various rhetorical devices like lengthy rhymed parallelisms (*tarṣī`*) and intricate paronomasias (*tajnīs*) were restricted, while poetry was allowed on a much reduced scale. The new functionality of Safavid *inshā* is best seen in its rearticulation as a genre that favours reports, histories, and traditions about the Safavid family as an Iranian imperial dynasty. Of course, dynastic correspondence is inherently propagandistic, but the model under `Abbās appears to have been geared towards using such official texts as short, dynastic manifestoes, which were released to audiences at home and abroad with remarkable regularity. In no other previous period of Safavid history do we find such a prolific and industrious chancellery, and the letters produced in this decade would in turn be vastly outnumbered by what was produced between 1598 and 1629. In an era defined by centralization and state-building, these letters/reports to both the Safavid court and the outside world served a crucial function of establishing the temporal and spatial precedence of the Safavids in Iran and defending it rhetorically against dynastic competitors. Of course, such pretensions demanded more than words, and `Abbās spend his first decade "walking the talk," to use a popular catchphrase. It is no coincidence, then, that Qāḍī Aḥmad and Afūshtah-ī Natanzī chose to focus so intently on `Abbās's 998/1590 subjugation of the rebellious Ya`qūb Khān Zū al-Qadar in Shīrāz in their respective histories; this narrative was fundamental to `Abbās's burgeoning ideology as an uncompromising centralizer.[358] On the basis of this rhetorical and political programme built between 1588 and 1598, `Abbās was able to initiate in the early seventeenth century a series of political, tribal, military, economic, and religious reforms, which would substantially alter Safavid society. This early rhetorical programme in the chancellery was chiefly under the aegis of key bureaucratic elements like Ḥātim Beg Urdūbādī. As was pointed out previously, these enfranchised Persian bureaucrats had received a key dynastic impulse and momentum decades earlier, during the reigns of Ismā`īl II and Khudābandah. A similar counterpoint is seen when examining religio-legal scholarship. As Devin Stewart remarked when discussing the famous philosopher and jurist Shaikh Bahā'ī, "it is anachronistic to view al-Bahā'ī's achievements as exclusively linked to `Abbās's favor, for he was a reputed authority well before Shāh `Abbās ascended the throne."[359]

While `Abbās was adamant about establishing his reign as unique and unprecedented, he still looked to the Timurid dynasty as the exemplary model in terms of historical invocations. Sholeh Quinn has pointed out the extent to which "pro-Timurid" sentiments influenced Qāḍī Aḥmad's writing of the *Khulāṣat al-tavārīkh.*[360]Maria Szuppe has likewise pointed out how one of the court chroniclers, Siyāqī Niẓāmī, manipulated the *abjad* system in his *Futūḥāt-i Humāyūn* in 1598, to "establish a link between Shāh `Abbās and Tīmūr, with the latter being presented an imperial figure par excellence, and who has a sort of divine grace which guides him in the conduct of state affairs."[361] In the case of epistolary discourse, this Timurid model could be more than explicit, such as when `Abbās chided `Abd al-Mu'min in 1003/1594–95 for the lack of *adab*: if you wrote a letter to Tīmūr Khān who was one of the great kings, you would refer to him as "the glory of the Turkish sultans!" In the same prefatory poem, however, `Abbās describes how Timur Khān had patronized the sayyids and the construction of buildings in Najaf, and Shāh Rukh had built a *masjid* and *khānqāh* in Mashhad.[362] On the issue of religion and rhetoric, the Timurid model was also inspiring to `Abbās because of two characteristics. First, the Timurids were relatively accommodating with respect to amalgamating Sufi and Shi`ite principles within the general orthodoxy of the day and thus can be considered custodians of a certain degree of religious heterogeneity. Second, the Timurids had developed an ideological programme, which profiled the extent of political and religious power exercised by a divinely mandated king at the expense of traditional networks of orthodox *`ulamā*. On the first point, Shāh `Abbās was infamously capricious, and one could certainly debate the degree to which he adhered to the ecumenical model of the Timurids. Nonetheless, the exemplarity of Timurid latitudinarianism allowed the Safavid chancellery to operate with fairly broad mandates when necessary. The second point was much more appealing to `Abbās because of its applicability to his absolutism and centralizing policies. It also had a unique appeal in the Safavid context because the Timurid vision of the "divine king" shared a conspicuous complementarity with Shi`ite conceptions of the Imamate. As Babayan noted, the traditional Safavid political culture of the first half of the sixteenth century defied any centralization: "The particular blend of Turco-Mongol and sufi paradigms of authority was being overshadowed by a new synthesis in which notions of Iranian kingship merged with the Shi`i symbols to shape a new language of temporal authority."[363]

CONCLUSION

In his well-known study *The Calligraphic State*, Brinkley Messick sets out to navigate the relationship between texts and textual domination in medieval and modern Islamic societies, wherein he notes that any study of texts in a political context "requires a view of writing that stresses its cultural and historical variability rather than its universal characteristics, and its implications in relations of domination rather than its neutrality or transparency as a medium."[1] Admittedly, this current study cannot hope to match the scope and substance of *The Calligraphic State*; nonetheless, these issues of textual variability and textual domination resonate here. There is no denying that the historiography of Safavid Iran is defined by the limited corpus of sources and historical materials available to scholars. As the basis of political, religious, and social interaction and discourse in Safavid Iran became increasingly defined by official and juridical representatives of Imami Shi`ism in the seventeenth century, we see a corresponding truncation of textual production, which operated outside of this expanding normative framework. In the case of the sixteenth century, we find a remarkable degree of heterogeneity with respect to textual production, and we cannot help but be impressed by the degree to which Safavid Iran continued to reflect plurality and variety at both the popular and elite levels. Perhaps most impressive is that such diversity can be located in a milieu inherently defined by its status as a body of officials charged with representing the interests of the state: the *dār al-inshā*.

What allows us to approach the chancellery in such an innovative manner is our willingness to step outside traditional, scholarly perceptions of administrative texts, which are arguably bound by older, Western impulses of essentialism and categorization. Hitherto, chancellery material like *inshā* was consigned by traditional Western scholarship to the same epistemological space as other mundane administrative documents, with little appreciation for the strong interdependence of poetics and rhetoric that had emerged in the medieval Perso-Islamic world. Implicit in this older categorization was the understanding that *munshī*s and litterateurs were governed by a static, unyielding model of epistolography, which resulted in a derivative body of literature across the Islamic world from the fourteenth century onwards. The operating ethos of this current study rejects such assumptions and insists that chancellery *munsha'āt* occupied a unique space that intersected rhetoric, normative prose writing, and the world of poetics. If anything, it is impossible to categorize the *inshā* genre with such blunt epistemological tools, and we need to acknowledge that contemporary scholars of the medieval period could widely vary with respect to how they chose to define *inshā*. For instance, the *Manāẓir al-inshā* produced in the Deccani Bahmanid kingdom by Maḥmūd Gāvān Ṣadr-i Jahān presents a ponderous taxonomy of documents, letters, and decrees, complete with strict admonitions and interdictions about how to properly format letters.[2] This could not be further in design and presentation from something like the *Inshā-yi `ālam-ārā* by Nāṣir al-Ḥaqq Nūrbakhshī; categorization and systemization are disregarded here in favour of a meandering good-natured treatment of how to best employ metaphors, similes, paronomasia, and countless other rhetorical devices. This sense of variability is evident in sixteenth-century Safavid *munsha'āt* themselves as they navigate the genres of prose, rhymed prose, and poetry to present a loose aggregate of historical narratives, epic tales, legal traditions, exegetical scholarship, hagiographical anecdotes, Qur'ānic text, Prophetic traditions, and ethical maxims. These composites are not exclusively defined by the Iranian Twelver Shi`ite world as some might expect; rather, they are rooted in a nebulous religious and cultural space, which crosses all manner of temporal, religious, and ethnic boundaries—pre-Islamic and Islamic, Sufi and Sunni, Arab and Persian, to name a few.

Examining early Safavid bureaucratic standards is similar to a chemist analyzing a complex chemical compound to isolate its individual elements. The Safavids subscribed to a long-standing, highly developed body of Perso-Arabic literary and religious traditions; at the same time, they inherited a collection of Turco-Mongolian traditions with their own distinct diplomatic, judicial, and bureaucratic standards.[3] The conquests of Chingīz Khān and Tīmūr, along with the resulting suzerain states in eastern Anatolia, Iran, and Central Asia, had fused Chingīzid and Chaghatā'ī elements into the Persian bureaucratic culture as well as its use of terminology, seals, and symbols. While eastern Iran, notably Khurāsān, adhered to Timurid chancellery practices, Anatolian and western Iranian bureaucratic practices experienced further changes under the Tūrkmen dynasties of the Qarā Qoyūnlū and Āq Qoyūnlū. Certainly, we cannot discount the influence of the neighbouring and relatively more established Ottoman empire.[4] The Safavid dynasty, then, was not the recipient of a singular, linearly developed chancellery culture, but rather a complex and shifting nexus of different bureaucratic practices, which reflect the ethnically fragmented and politically decentralized history of the Turco-Mongolian world between 1300 and 1500.

Another objective of this book has been to locate and analyze the chancellery culture responsible for this discursive production. The binomial of "men of the sword" and "men of the pen" is a constant in studies of medieval Perso-Islamic culture, and it is safe to say that contemporary Safavid scholarship has invested considerably more time in mapping the political world of the sword-holders than their counterparts in the bureaucracy. Of course, there has always been interest in the intellectual Safavid world, but contemporary scholars are often motivated by the availability of sources; thus, we find a disproportionate representation of poetry, legal history, philosophy, and Twelver Shi`ite tradition in our field. By working intimately with this underexposed body of literature in conjunction with historical chronicles, it has been the hope here to shed light on this specific constituency among the "men of the pen" and their importance in defining and articulating the Safavid imperial project. Of course, we cannot succumb to the same pitfall of categorization and essentialism critiqued earlier; evidence exists to suggest this corporate identity was made up of a wide cross-section of poets, litterateurs, religious judges, sayyids, and theologians, who did not necessarily define themselves strictly with respect to confessional identity. If we could identify one common denominator, however, it would be the overlapping between chancellery official and court historian. Khvāndamīr, arguably the greatest historian of the early sixteenth century, produced his own *inshā* manual (*Namāh-yi nāmī*) and included commentary on the *`ilm-i inshā* in the compendium, the *Makārim al-akhlāq*.[5] Some of our most important sources for later Safavid history—the *Tārīkh-i `ālam ārā-yi `Abbāsī,* the *Khulāṣat al-tavārīkh*, the *Takmilat al-akhbār*—were written by men who had trained and worked in the *dār al-inshā* at some point in their career.

It is likely because of this close relationship between *tārīkh* and *inshā* that historians like Qāḍī Aḥmad and Iskander Beg Munshī chose to include epistolary texts (in part or in full) in their respective narratives. Iskander Beg Munshī replicated part of a letter from Humāyūn to Ṭahmāsp during his sojourn in Iran, a number of internal communiqués from Murshid Qulī Khān Ustājlu on the eve of `Abbās's rebellion, correspondence between the Safavids and the Uzbeks, and an exchange of letters with the Ottoman empire about the conquest of Baghdad by Shāh `Abbās in 1035/1625–26.[6] Qāḍī Aḥmad was more dedicated to replicating *inshā* material. The largest and most impressive was the massive *julūs nāmah* sent to Salīm II on his accession, but other epistolary texts include a letter sent to Muḥammad Shībānī Khān,[7] a response letter to Salīm II,[8] a short missive (borne by the ambassador Kabah Khalīfah from Ṭahmāsp to `Ubaid Allāh),[9] a *farmān* sent to Ibrāhīm Mīrzā,[10] as well as other royal decrees. Qāḍī Aḥmad admitted that he incorporated "state and official documents and writings" in the writing of the *Khulāṣat al-tavārīkh.*[11] Moreover, we know the epistolary letters themselves were capable of replicating prose sections or poetry from earlier incarnations. One of the best examples of this was Shāh Khudābandah's letter to Murād III, which drew heavily on poetry and prose *inscriptio*s that had appeared earlier in correspondence between Shāh Ṭahmāsp and Sulṭān Sulaimān. In the monumental letter sent to Salīm II, sections of its poetry were borrowed from earlier letters sent from Shāh Ṭahmāsp to Sulṭān Sulaimān and Khān Ahmad Khān.[12]

In one case, Qāḍī Aḥmad talks about a particular Safavid ambassadorial mission to the Uzbek court (ca. 939/1532), mentioning how several lines of poetry were sent to `Ubaid Allāh Khān, which he in turn presents for the reader.[13] These in fact were extracted from the much larger and highly polemical letter sent to the Uzbeks, but Qāḍī Aḥmad makes no reference to their provenance.[14] *Munshīs* were also not above disseminating their own poetry through the epistolary medium. As discussed in Chapter 4, `Abdī Beg Shīrāzī borrowed healthy sections of encomiastic poetry from his various poetic collections, including the *Maẓhar al-asrār*, the *`Ain-i Iskandarī*, and the *Jannat al-asmār*. Intertextuality between history and *inshā* could also move the other way, and there is evidence that *munshīs* drew upon historical chronicles to present specific narratives in their own epistolary settings. Probably the best example is the narration of the Battle of Jām (934/1528) between Shāh Ṭahmāsp and `Ubaid Allāh Khān, which appears in the famous "Belt Letter" sent to the Ottomans in 961/1554.[15] A number of poems, along with specific narratives of this monumental battle, are remarkably similar to sections of Qāḍī Aḥmad's narrative appearing in the *Khulāṣat al-tavārīkh*.[16] While Qāḍī Aḥmad's version is certainly more detailed, key expressions, phrases, and Qur'ānic quotations sustain this idea of an intertextual relationship. It is unlikely (although certainly intriguing!) that Qāḍī Aḥmad looked to the "Belt Letter" as a historical source, and it would appear that the two accounts are based on one of the historical chronicles produced in the 1530s and 1540s: the *Futuḥāt-i shāhī* (ca. 937/1531), the *Lubb al-tavārīkh* (948/1542), or the *Zail-i ḥabīb al-siyar* (957/1550).[17]

The *inshā* genre during the Safavid period was far from a monolithic discourse, and the most rewarding evidence of this is seen through the lens of legitimacy and constructs of authority. Depending on the milieu, chancellery *munsha'āt* were capable of impressive scope and diversity with respect to content, function, and form. Working within the context of ideological pretensions, a fundamental argument here has been that this inherent resourcefulness of *inshā* allowed for a wide range of religio-political articulations by the dynasty in the sixteenth century. The early Safavid chancellery reflected the confessional ambiguity of the day, and diplomatic correspondence was committed to "arguing" the millenarian agenda of Shāh Ismā`īl and his cohorts, while concurrently reflecting the multifarious Sufi environment of eastern Anatolia and Āzarbāijān. The dynasty continued to use Persian as a literary medium; however, in every other respect Ismā`īl and his cohorts were Turcophones, thus continuing the use of some Turkic expressions and terminology used under the earlier Qarā Qoyūnlū and Āq Qoyūnlū dynasties. The Safavid absorption of Timurid Khurāsān and the rise of Tajik-Türkmen rivalries in the royal court only add to the difficulty in trying to map out the relationship between Safavid bureaucratic standards and those of the Safavids' predecessors. The slow infusion of classical Perso-Islamic rhetoric of kingship and imperium allowed the Safavid dynasty to begin tacking towards the arguably more stable waters of divine absolutism in the 1520s and 1530s. This, in turn, was amalgamated by mid-century with a body of comprehensive Twelver Shi`ite scholarship, and for the remainder of the sixteenth century we find Safavid ideology framed increasingly by classical models of Imami authority. Traditional Perso-Islamic terminology and tropes found in early Safavid correspondence—references to Judeo-Christian tradition, pre-Islamic Iranian mythology, Turko-Mongolian concepts of patrimonial rule—would become intertwined with a corpus of traditions and writings associated with the Twelver Shi`ite historical experience. *Inshā* material would reconfigure itself again as the sixteenth century came to a close, when imperial prerogative became sacrosanct during the early rule of Shāh `Abbās the Great. As Kathryn Babayan remarks, "the dynastic household … encoded the complex interface of contemporaneous meanings and shapes of spiritual and temporal rule. The two-hundred-year dominion of the Safavi household offers a picture of the ways in which paradigms of authority shifted, reflecting in the process broader mystical, philosophical, and religio-legal tensions that had activated impulses toward change in Safavi society."[18]

As we have seen, the articulation of these shifting "paradigms of authority" at home and abroad constituted a healthy corpus of epistolary literature. This body of evidence was produced by a class of professionals that seized upon the genre of *inshā* as a means of articulating the religio-political ethics of the day, just as countless generations of Persian administrators had done before them. In the heyday of the Qizilbāsh, the millenarian ethos of the Safavid Sufis encouraged an apocalyptic tenor in the court and chancellery as a means of justifying their militant expansion against other nominal Muslim polities and "established" communities. The next significant shift took place mid-century, as Shi`ite hierocratic elements redirected the chancellery towards well-established and rehearsed confessional rhetoric in an effort to profile Safavid Iran as an "abode of Shi`ism" (*Dār al-Shī`ah*). This ideological colouration endorsed the historical enmity between Sunnis and Shi`ites and promoted "state" violence against non-Shi`ite populations. After 1588, however, we see a centralized effort towards promoting a "universalist" Safavid dynasty under Shāh `Abbās. Elements of millenarian and pedestrian Sufi rhetoric had been largely expunged, and Twelver Shi`ite discourse had lost its political dominance in the court; nonetheless, it was clear that chancellery correspondence after 1588 pointed to the Safavid dynasty as a custodian of a complex heritage, which on the one hand recognized ecumenicalism and on the other claimed exclusive divine absolutism and soteriological superiority. This Universalist emphasis was in part inherited from the Turco-Mongol world of the fourteenth and fifteenth centuries,[19] but we also cannot dismiss the importance of those ideal Universalist empires and world conquerors of the Achaemenian and Sasanian eras represented so faithfully as exemplars in medieval Perso-Islamic literature and art. The story of the Safavid chancellery during these shifts in ideology and legitimacy is no less dynamic; however, it remains clear they were the best equipped in terms of rhetorical tools to accommodate this unsurpassed political, religious, and cultural diversity.

NOTES

Introduction

1 For a good overview of this issue, see William Hanaway's entry on Iranian identity during the medieval Islamic period, forthcoming in *Encyclopedia Iranica.*

2 Aziz al-Azmeh, *Muslim Kingship: Power and the Sacred in Muslim, Christian, and Pagan Polities* (London: 1997), p. 9.

3 Mohamad Tavakoli-Targhi, *Refashioning Iran: Orientalism, Occidentalism, and Histioriography* (New York: 2001), p. 97.

4 Firoozeh Kashani-Sabet, *Frontier Fictions: Shaping the Iranian Nation, 1804–1946* (Princeton: 1999), pp. 30–37, pp. 75–80.

5 Quoted in Tavakoli-Targhi, *Refashioning Iran*, p. 102.

6 The shah's official titulature was *Shahinshah Arya-mehr*, or "shah of shahs, the light of Aryan-ness."

7 Colin Heywood, "Between Historical Myth and 'Mythohistory': The Limits of Ottoman History," in *Writing Ottoman History: Documents and Interpretations*, ed. C. Heywood (Aldershot: 2002), p. 318.

8 G. E. Von Grunebaum, "The Concept of Cultural Classicism," in *Modern Islam: The Search For Cultural Identity* (Berkeley: 1962), p. 91.

9 Allesandro Bausani discussed peripherally how the Safavids were the first to act in a "re-archaized" monarchical role since the Sasanian dynasty and the arrival of the Islam. Allesandro Bausani, "Muḥammad or Darius? The Elements and Basis of Iranian Culture," in *Islam and Cultural Change in the Middle Ages*, ed. S. Vryonis (Wiesbaden: 1975), p. 46.

10 Term used by W. H. McNeill in *Mythistory and other essays* (Chicago: 1986), p. 7.

11 Ann K. S. Lambton, "Justice in the Medieval Persian Theory of Kingship," *Studia Islamica*, vol. 17 (1962), pp. 91–119, *Theory and Practice in Medieavel Persian Government* (London: 1980). See also Louise Marlow, *Hierarchy and Egalitarianism in Islamic Thought* (Cambridge: 1997), pp. 66–90.

12 Kathryn Babayan, *Mystics, Monarchs, and Messiahs: Cultural Landscapes of Early Modern Iran* (Cambridge, Mass.: 2002), pp. 263–64.

13 Cornell Fleischer, "Mahdi and Millennium: Messianic Dimensions in the Development of Ottoman Imperial Ideology," in *The Great Ottoman-Turkish Civilization*, ed. K. Çiçek, vol. 3 (Philosophy, Science and Institutions), (Ankara: 2000), p. 43.

14 A Turkish term ("red head") referring to their distinctive head gear.

15 Walther Hinz, *Irans Aufstieg zum Nationalstaat im fünfzehnten Jahrhundert* (Berlin: 1936), Richard Cottam, *Nationalism in Iran* (Pittsburgh: 1964). Recently, Roger Savory wrote in his entry on the Safavids for the *Encyclopedia of Islam* that "the imposition of Ithna` Ashari uniformity throughout Persia had largely been achieved

by the end of the reign of Ismā`īl I." Roger Savory, "Safavids," *EI*[2], vol. 10, p. 769.

16 Sholeh Quinn, *Historical Writing During the Reign of Shāh `Abbās: Ideology, Imitation, and Legitimacy in Safavid Chronicles* (Salt Lake City: 2000).

17 Undoubtedly, the greatest contributor to our understanding of Safavid diplomatic material is `Abd al-Ḥusain Navā'ī. He has single-handedly collected and edited the bulk of manuscript materials that may contain such correspondence. See *Shāh Ismā`īl Ṣafavī: Majmū`ah-yi asnād va mukātibāt-i tārīkhī-yi hamrāh bā yāddāsht-hā-yi tafṣīl* (Tehran: 1969), *Shāh Ṭahmāsp Ṣafavī: Majmū`ah-yi asnād va mukātibāt-i tārīkhī-yi hamrāh bā yāddāsht-hā-yi tafṣīl* (Tehran: 1971), and *Shāh `Abbās: Majmū`ah-yi asnād va mukātibāt-i tārīkhī-yi hamrāh bā yāddāsht-hā-yi tafṣīl*, 3 vols. (Tehran: 1974).

18 Riazul Islam has provided synopses of letters exchanged between the Safavids and the Mughals but provides little by way of interpreting these documents in any larger sense of ideology. See Riazul Islam, *A Calendar of Documents on Indo-Persian Relations*, 2 vols. (Tehran: 1979).

19 C. E. Bosworth, "Administrative Literature," in *Religion, Learning and Science in the `Abbasid Period*, eds. M. J. L. Young, J. D. Latham, and R. B. Serjeant (Cambridge: 1990), p. 155.

20 For early administrative transitions between Sasanian and Arab rule, see Touraj Daryaee, "The Effect of the Arab Muslim Conquest on the Administrative Division of Sasanian Persia," *Iran: Journal of Persian Studies*, vol. 41 (2003), pp. 197–98.

21 See John Watt, "Eastward and Westward Transmission of Classical Rhetoric," in *Centres of Learning: Learning and Location in Pre-Modern Europe and the Near East*, eds. J. Drijvers and A. MacDonald (Leiden: 1995), pp. 63–75.

22 Deborah Black, *Logic and Aristotle's* Rhetoric *and* Poetics *in Medieval Arabic Philosophy* (Leiden: 1990), p. 1.

23 The unique Paris manuscript (*MS* Parisnus Arabe 2346, ancien fonds ar. 882a) contains an Arabic translation of the *Organon*. This has been edited and published with M. C. Lyons, *Aristotle's* Ars Rhetorica*: The Arabic Version* (Cambridge: 1982). See also John Watt, "Syriac Rhetorical Theory and the Syriac Tradition of Aristotle's Rhetoric," in *Peripatetic Rhetoric After Aristotle*, eds. W. Fortenbaugh and D. Mirhady, Rutgers University Studies in Classical Humanities, vol. 6 (New Brunswick: 1994), pp. 243–60, and Maroun Aouad, "Les fondements da la *Rhétorique* d'Aristote reconsidérés par Averroès dans l'abrégé de la rhétorique, ou le développement du concept du 'point de vue immediate,'' in *Peripatetic Rhetoric After Aristotle*, eds. W. Fortenbaugh and D. Mirhady, Rutgers University Studies in Classical Humanities, vol. 6 (New Brunswick: 1994), pp. 261–313.

24 Maround Aouad, arguably the leading scholar of the study of medieval Islamic philosophical approaches to rhetoric, provides a succinct summary of the different representations of the *Rhetoric* in "*La Rhéorique*. Tradition Syriaque et Arabe," *Dictionnaire des philosophes antiques*, vol. 1, ed. R. Goulet (Paris: 1989), pp. 455–472. See also "L'exégèse da la *Rhétorique* d'Aristote: recherches sur quelques commentateurs grecs, arabes et byzantins," *Medioevo. Rivista di storia della filosofia medievale,* vol. 25 (1999–2000), pp. 551–649, and "Commentateurs 'satisfaisants' et 'non-satisfaisants' de la *Rhétorique* selon Averroes," in *Averroes and the Aristotelian Tradition. Sources, Constitution and Reception of the Philosophy of Ibn Rushd (1126–1198). Proceedings of the Fourth Symposium Averroicum* (Cologne: 1996), eds. G. Endress and J. Aertsen (Leident: 1999), pp. 83–124.

25 See J. Langhade (trans. and ed.), "Le *Kitāb al-khaṭaba* d'al-Fārābī," critical Arabic text and French translation in *Mélanges de l'Université Saint-Joseph de Beyrouth*, vol. 43 (1968), pp. 61–177.

26 See M. S. Salem (ed.), *Kitāb al-majmū` wa al-ḥikma al-` arūḍiyya, fī ma`ānī kitāb*

Riṭūrīqā (Cairo: 1953).

27 See C. E. Butterworth (trans. and ed.), *Averroes' Three Short Commentaries on Aristotle's 'Topics', 'Rhetoric', and 'Poetics'* (Albany: 1977).

28 S. A. Bonebakker, "Aspects of the History of Literary Rhetoric and Poetics in Arabic Literature," *Viator*, vol. 1 (1970), pp. 75–95, William Smyth, "Rhetoric and *`Ilm al-Balāgha*: Christianity and Islam," *Muslim World*, vol. 82 (1992), nos. 3–4, pp. 242–55.

29 John Wansbrough, "A Note on Arabic Rhetoric," in *Lebende Antike: Symposion für Rudolf Sühnel*, eds. H. Meller and H. Zimmerman (Berlin: 1967), p. 55.

30 Bonebakker, "Aspects of the History of Literary Rhetoric and Poetics in Arabic Literature," p. 85.

31 Natalia Chalisova, "Persian Rhetoric: Elm-e Bayān," in *Introduction to Persian Literature*, vol. 1, eds. J.T.P. De Bruijn and Ehsan Yarshater (London: 2008), p. 141.

32 A German translation is available in H. Ritter, *Die Geheimnisse der Wortkunst* (Wiesbaden: 1959). See also Margaret Larkin, *The Theology of Meaning: `Abd al-Qahir al-Jurjani's Theory of Discourse* (New Haven: 1995).

33 See Udo Gerlad Simon, *Mittelalterische arabische Sprachbetrachtung zwischen Grammatik und Rhetoric:* `ilm al-ma`ani *as-Sakkaki* (Heidelberg: 1993).

34 The best treatment of al-Qazvīnī is available with Herbjorn Jenssen, *The Subtleties and Secrets of the Arabic Language: Preliminary Investigations into al-Qazwini's* Talkhis al-Miftāḥ (Bergen: 1998). See also Maria Subtelny and Anas Khalidov, "The Curriculum of Islamic Higher Learning in Timurid Iran in the Light of the Sunni Revival Under Shah Rukh," *Journal of the American Oriental Society*, vol. 115 (1995), no. 2, p. 226, and Francis Robinson, "Ottomans-Safavids-Mughals: Shared Knowledge and Connective Systems," *Journal of Islamic Studies*, vol. 8 (1997), no. 2, pp. 174–77.

35 Bosworth, "Administrative Literature," p. 156. For an exhaustive treatment of Buyid epistolary styles, see Klaus Hachmeier, "Private Letters, Official Correspondence: Buyid *Inshā* as a Historical Source," *Journal of Islamic Studies*, vol. 13 (2002), no. 2, pp. 125–54.

36 Chalisova, "Persian Rhetoric: Elm-e Badi` and Elm-e Bayān," p. 145.

37 See Muḥammad ibn `Umar Rādūyānī's *Tarjuman al-balāghat*, ed. `Alī Qavīm (Tehran: 1960), pp. 161–63. For the most up-to-date discussion on Rādūyānī, see Chalisova, "Persian Rhetoric: Elm-e Badi` and Elm-e Bayān," pp. 144–51. Some prominent devices include: rhymed prose (*tasjī`*), parallel rhymed phrases (*tarṣī`*), arrangement of numerous synonymous words in one sentence (*barā`at-i istihlāl*), partial Qur'ānic allusions (*iqtibās*), metaphors (*ista`ārah*), metonymy (*kināyat*), praise by apparent vilification (*tā'kīd al-madḥ bi-mā yushbihu al-ḍamm*), to arrange in poetry or prose numerous, varied qualities for a subject (*tasnīq al-ṣifāt*), amphibology (*īhām*), chiasmus (*laff va nashr*), [rhetorical] observances for particular conditions (*murā`āt-i munāsibāt*), ellipsis (*iḍmār*), palindromes (*maqlūb-i musṭavā*), rhetorical etymology (*ishtiqāq*), and the addition of rhymes and verses to existing *qaṣīdahs* and *masnavīs* (*iltizām*).

38 An Arabic edition is available with Rashīd al-Dīn Vaṭvāṭ, *Ḥadā'iq al-siḥr fī daqā'iq al-shi`r*, ed. Ibrāhīm Amīn al-Shūrābī (Cairo: 1945), pp. 133–50, 184–89. Chalisova, "Persian Rhetoric: Elm-e Badi` and Elm-e Bayān," pp. 151–58.

39 Shams al-Dīn Muḥammad ibn Qais al-Rāzī (Shams-i Qais), *Al-Mu`jam fī ma`āyir ash`ār al-`ajam*, ed. Muḥammad Qazvīnī (Tehran: 1959). Chalisova, "Persian Rhetoric: Elm-e Badi` and Elm-e Bayān," pp. 158–65.

40 Marta Simidchieva, "Imitation and Innovation in Timurid Poetics: Kāshifī's *Badāyi` al-afkār*, and its Predecessors, *al-Mu`jam* and *Ḥadā'iq al-siḥr*," *Iranian Studies*, vol.

36 (2003), no. 4, pp. 509–30.

41 A Turkish edition of Muḥammad Mayhānī is available with *Destūr-i debīrī*, ed. A. S. Erzi (Ankara: 1962). A Persian edition of *Chahār maqāla* has been published with Niẓāmī `Arūḍī Samarqandī, *Chahār maqālah*, ed. Muhammad Mu`in (Tehran: 1995), while the well-known English translation by E. G. Browne appeared as *Revised Translation of the* Chahār maqāla *("Four Discourses" of* Niẓāmī `Arūḍ*)* (London: 1921). An English translation of Kai Kāvūs is available with *A Mirror for Princes: the* Qābūs nāma, trans. R. Levy (London: 1951). See also Chalisova, "Persian Rhetoric: Elm-e Badi` and Elm-e Bayān," pp. 141–42.

42 Roemer, "Insha'," p. 1243, Roemer, *Staatsschreiben der Timüridenzeit*, p. 11. See also K. Allin Luther, "Islamic Rhetoric and the Persian Historians 1100–1300 A.D.," in *Studies in Near Eastern Culture and History in Memory of Ernest T. Abdel-Massih*, ed. J. A. Bellamy (Ann Arbor: 1990), pp. 92–94.

43 Muḥammad ibn Hindūshāh Nakhjuvānī, *Dastūr al-kātib fī'l ta`yīn al-marātib*, ed. `Abd al-Karīm `Alīzādah, vol. 1 (Moscow: 1964), p. 13.

44 Cemal Kafadar, *Between Two Worlds: The Construction of the Ottoman State* (Berkeley: 1995), p. 18.

45 H. R. Roemer, *Staatsschreiben der Timüridenzeit: des* Sharaf Nāma *des `Abdullah Marwarid im kritischer Auswertung* (Wiesbaden, 1952), Niẓām al-Dīn `Abd al-Vāsi` Niẓāmī, *Manshā al-inshā*, ed. Rukn al-Dīn Humāyūn Farrukh (Tehran: 1978), Ḥusain Vā'iẓ Kāshifī. *Makhzan al-inshā*, *MS*, Paris, Bibliothèque Nationale, Supplément persan, no. 73, London, British Library, Add. 25865, Ghiyāṡ al-Dīn ibn Humām al-Dīn Khvāndamīr, *Nāmah-yi nāmī*, *MS*, Paris, Bibliothèque Nationale, supplément persan, no. 1842.

46 Colin P. Mitchell, "Safavid Imperial *Tarassul* and the Persian *Inshā* Tradition," *Studia Iranica*, vol. 26 (1997), no. 2, p. 208.

47 The two most well-known and well-used works are: `Abd al-Ḥusain al-Naṣīr al-Ṭūsī, *Munsha'āt al-Ṭūsī*, *MS*, Paris, Bibliothèque Nationale, supplément persan, no. 1838, and Abū al-Qāsim Ḥaidar Beg Īvūghlī, *Nuskhah-yi jāmi`a-i al-murāsalāt-i ulul albāb*, *MS*, London, British Library, Add. 7688. See also Muḥammad Ṭāhir Vaḥīd Qazvīnī, *Munsha'āt-i Ṭāhir Vaḥīd*, *MS*, Cambridge: Cambridge University Library *MS* Or. 1070. Anonymous collections include *Inshā* Collection, *MS* Oxford, Bodleian Library, Pers. D. 84 and *Majmū`ah*, *MS*, London, British Library, I.O. Islamic 379. Other less known works are enumerated and discussed by Muḥammad Taqī Dāneshpazhūh, "Navīsandagī va dabīrī," in *Ḥadis-e `esq*, vol. 1, eds. N. Moṭṭalebī-Kāshānī and S. Moḥammad-Ḥossein Mar`ashī (Tehran: 2003), pp. 172–74.

48 Yūsuf b. Muḥammad Harātī, *Badā`i al-inshā*, *MS*, London, British Library, Add. 6608 and I. O. Islamic 1972 is a good example of a Timurid-style *inshā* work produced under the Mughals. Extensive lists of Indo-Persian *inshā* works are available with M. Mohiuddin, *The Chancellery and Persian Epistolography under the Mughals* (Calcutta: 1971), and Islam, *A Calendar of Documents on Indo-Persian Relations*.

49 Ottoman appreciation for *inshā* is profound as is contemporary interest in Ottoman scribal culture. Farīdūn Beg, *Munsha'āt al-salāṭīn*, 2 vols. (Istanbul: 1857–58) is one of the most well-known miscellanies of *inshā* materials, while lesser known examples include `Abd al-Ghaffār Ṣiddiqī Ḥusainī Haravī, *Ṣaḥīfa al-ikhlāṣ*, *MS*, Paris, Bibliothèque Nationale, no. 1061. See also Sinasi Tekin (ed.), *Menahicu'l-Insa: The Earliest Ottoman Chancellery Manual by Yahya bin Mehmed el-Katib from the 15th Century* (Cambridge: 1971).

50 Muhammad Taqi Daneshpazhuh, "Navisandagi va dabiri," pp. 135–229.

51 One recent definition rehabilitates rhetoric comprehensively as "a social practice of public, persuasive, constitutive, and socially constituted utterance; [rhetoric]

is a discipline located at the intersection of aesthetics, politics, and ethics; it is a method of inquiry whose object is to discover how audiences are moved or persuaded through the interplay of style, form, content, and context in texts both spoken and written." Stephen D. O'Leary *Arguing the Apocalypse: A Theory of Millennial Rhetoric* (Oxford: 1994), p. 4.

52 Overviews of Sasanian administrative practice can be seen in Richard Frye, *The Heritage of Persia* (Cleveland: 1963), pp. 206–08, Josef Wieshöfer, *Ancient Persia* (London: 1996), pp. 183–91.

53 Dimitri Gutas, *Greek Thought, Arabic Culture: The Graeco-Arabic Translation Movement in Baghdad and Early `Abbasid Society* (London: 1998), pp. 111–13.

54 For the continued use of certain middle Persian administrative terms (*`awāraj, rūznāmaj, jabbadh*), see C. E. Bosworth, "Al-Karazmi on the Technical Terms of the Secretary's Art," *Journal of the Economic and Social History of the Orient*, vol. 12 (1969), pp. 121–23. See also J. P. de Menasce, "Zoroastrian Pahlavī Writings," in *Cambridge History of Iran*, ed. E. Yarshater, vol. 3 (2), (Cambridge: 1983), pp. 1182–88.

55 Dimitri Gutas, "Classical Arabic Wisdom Literature: Nature and Scope," *Journal of the American Oriental Society*, vol. 101 (1981), no. 1, p. 61.

56 De Menasce, "Zoroastrian Pahlavī Writings," p. 1184. See *Nāmah-yi Tansar*, ed. M. Minovī (Tehran: 1932), and translation with Mary Boyce, *The Letter of Tansar* (Rome: 1968).

57 Marlow, *Hierarchy and Egalitarianism in Islamic Thought*, pp. 72–75.

58 Marlow, *Hierarchy and Egalitarianism in Islamic Thought*, p. 117.

59 `Alī ibn Abī Ṭālib, *al-Mu`jam al-mufahras lī alfāẓ Nahj al-balāgha*, ed. Muḥammad Dashtī (Tehran: 2001). An English translation is available with *Nahj al-balāghah: Selections from Sermons, Letters and Sayings of Amir al-Mu'minin, `Ali ibn Abi Talib*, ed. Sayyid Abū al-Ḥasan and trans. Sayyid `Alī Riḍā, 2 vols. (Karachi: 1955).

60 Joel Kraemer, "Humanism in the Renaissance of Islam: A Preliminary Study," *Journal of the American Oriental Society*, vol. 104 (1984), no. 1, p. 149.

61 Richard Walzer (ed.), *Al-Fārābī on the Perfect State: Abu Nasr al-Fārābī's* Mabadi' ara' ahl al-madina al-fadila (Oxford: 1985), p. 438.

62 Watt, "Eastward and Westward Transmission of Classical Rhetoric," p. 74.

63 Barilli, *Rhetoric*, p. 12.

64 *Rhetoric*, 1355b.

65 For a good and recent discussion of the differences between *balāghat* and *khaṭābat* and the ramifications of these differences on contemporary study of rhetoric in the Muslim world, see Philip Halldén, "What is Arab Islamic Rhetoric? Rethinking the History of Muslim Oratory Art and Homiletics," *International Journal of Middle East Studies,* vol. 37 (2005), no. 1, pp. 19–38.

66 Ann K. S. Lambton, *Continuity and Change in Medieval Persia: Aspects of Administrative, Economic and Social History, 11th–14th Century* (Albany: 1988), pp. 221–24, V.V. Bartold, *Turkestan Down to the Mongol Invasions*, ed. and trans. T. Minorsky (London: 1928), p. 227.

67 Kraemer details the changing definitions of *adab* from the original "habit" or "custom" to the later connoting of "values of urbane, civil, courteous, refined and elegant conduct." Kraemer, "Humanism in the Renaissance of Islam," pp. 151–56.

68 Joel Kraemer, "Humanism in the Renaissance of Islam," p. 152.

69 Quoted in Kraemer, "Humanism in the Renaissance of Islam," p. 154.

70 Bertrand Badie, "La Philosophie Politique de l'Héllénisme Musulman," *Revue Française de Science Politique*, vol. 28 (1977), no. 2, p. 291. See also C. Jambet, "Idéal du politique et politique idéale selon Naṣīr al-Dīn Ṭūsī," in *Naṣīr al-Dīn Ṭūsī:*

Philosophe et savant du XIIIe siècle, eds. N. Pourjavady and Z. Vesel (Tehran: 2000), pp. 31–58.

71 Naṣīr al-Dīn al-Ṭūsī, *Akhlāq-i Nāṣirī*, ed. and tr. G. M. Wickens as *The Nasirean Ethics* (London: 1964), pp. 215–16.

72 Naṣīr al-Dīn al-Ṭūsī, *Akhlāq-i Nāṣirī*, p. 216.

73 G. M. Wickens, "A<u>k</u>laq-e Jalali," *Encyclopedia Iranica*, vol. 1, p. 724, and "A<u>k</u>laq-e Mohseni," in *Encylopedia Iranica*, vol. 1, pp. 724–25, Al-Azmeh, *Muslim Kingship*, p. 95.

74 "The Books of greatest vogue, are those of *Corge Nessir Tussi* (*sic*) of the City *Tuss*, in the Province of *Korasam*, wrote Five hundred years ago; he, as it is credible, understood the Greek Language as well as others; from whence he has explained some Ancient Authors, as *Euclid, Ptolemy's* Alguma (*Algemist*) and Opticks, and has reduced them into a Compendium, as also the Works of Plato." John Fryer, *A New Account of East India and Persia Being Nine Years' Travels 1672–1681*, ed. William Crooke, vol. 3 (Nendeln: 1967), p. 70.

75 Roxborough, *Prefacing the Image*, pp. 124–25.

76 Jan Rypka writes in his authoritative account of the history of Persian literature: "The model letters can have been composed *ad hoc* or extracted from correspondence that had actually taken place, no matter from what section of society or of state politics. In the latter case, they are not without importance in connection with the biographical and historical aspects, although it must be admitted that their factual contents stand in inverse ratio to their verbosity." Jan Rypka, "History of Persian Literature Up to the Beginning of the 20th Century," in ed. K. Jahn, *History of Iranian Literature* (Dordrecht: 1968), pp. 315–16.

77 Deborah Black noted that "poetry developed alongside the development or after the development of the syllogistic art of rhetoric." Black, *Logic and Aristotle's* Rhetoric *and* Poetics *in Medieval Arabic Philosophy*, p. 213.

78 Moran, "Artifice and Persuasion," p. 391.

79 Kenneth Burke, *A Rhetoric of Motives* (Berkeley: 1969), p. 87.

80 Julie Scott Meisami, *Structure and Meaning in Medieval Arabic and Persian Poetry: Orient Pearls* (London: 2003), p. 345.

81 Babayan, *Mystics, Monarchs, and Messiahs*, p. xix.

82 John Renard, *Islam and the Heroic Image: Themes in Literature and the Visual Arts* (Columbia, S. C.: 1993), pp. 34–36.

83 Timothy Hampton, *Writing from History: The Rhetoric of Exemplarity in Renaissance Literature* (Ithaca: 1990), p. 19. See also Gian Biagio Conte, *The Rhetoric of Imitation: Genre and Poetic Memory in Virgil and Other Latin Poets*, trans. C. Segal (Ithaca: 1987).

84 Hampton, *Writing from History*, p. 21, p. 30.

85 Meisami, *Structure and Meaning in Medieval Arabic and Persian Poetry*, pp. 134–35.

86 Al-Azmeh, *Muslim Kingship*, p. 89.

87 Suzanne P. Stetkevych, *The Poetics of Islamic Legitimacy: Myth, Gender, and Ceremony in the Classical Arabic Ode* (Bloomington: 2002), pp. 26–27.

88 Al-Azmeh, *Muslim Kingship*, p. 89.

89 For details as to this process, see Willem Floor, *Safavid Government Institutions* (Costa Mesa, CA: 2001), pp. 40–63.

90 Quinn, *Historical Writing During the Reign of Shāh `Abbās*, Maria Szuppe, "L'évolution de l'image de Timour et des Timourides dans l'historiographie safavide du XVIe au XVIIIe siècle," in *L'Héritage timouride Iran – Asie centrale – Inde XVe-XVIIIe siècles*, ed. M. Szuppe (Aix-en-Provence: 1997), pp. 313–31.

91 For Mughal studies, see John F. Richards, *Document Forms for Official Orders of*

Appointment in the Mughal Empire (Cambridge: 1986), Mohiuddin, *The Chancellery and Persian Epistolography under the Mughals*, S. H. Askari, "Mahmud Gawan and his book Manazir-ul-insha," *Indo-Iranica*, vol. 6 (1952–53), no. 4, pp. 28–36, M. I. Dar, "Riyad al-insha—its literary and historical value," *Islamic Culture*, vol. 24 (1950), pp. 231–4. The Ottoman field is much richer historiographically: C. Ferrard, "The Development of an Ottoman Rhetoric Up to 1882 Part II," Josef Matuz, *Das Kanzleiwesen Sultan Suleymans des Prachtigen* (Weisbaden: 1974), Cornell Fleischer, "Between the Lines: Realities of Scribal Life in the Sixteenth Century," in *Studies in Ottoman History in Honour of Professor V. L. Ménage*, eds. Colin Heywood and Colin Imber (Istanbul: 1994), pp. 45–62, Christine Woodhead, "Ottoman insha and the Art of Letter-Writing: Influences Upon the Career of the Nishanchi and Prose Stylist Okccuzade (d. 1630)," *Osmanli arasstirmalari (Journal of Ottoman Studies),* vol. 7–8 (1988), pp. 143–159 and "From Scribe to Litterateur: The Career of a Sixteenth-Century Ottoman Katib," *British Society for Middle Eastern Studies*, vol. 9 (1982), no. 1, pp. 55–74, Joel Shinder, "Career Line Formation in the Ottoman Bureaucracy, 1648–1750: A New Perspective," *Journal of the Economic and Social History of the Orient*, vol. 16 (1973), nos. 2–3, pp. 217–237, and Jean-Louis Bacqué-Grammont, "Remarques sur quelques types de carrières et de functions dans l'administration ottomane au XVIe siècle," *Archivum Ottomanicum*, vol. 17 (1999), pp. 233–40.

92 Some exceptions do exist to this general trend, including the reference works of Renate Schimkoreit, *Registen publizierter safawidischer Herrscherurkunden* (Berlin: 1982), Bert Fragner, *Repertorium persicher Herrscherurkunden* (Freiburg: 1980). Bert Fragner has been especially influential with respect to Safavid chancellery. See "Shah Ismail's Fermans and Sanads: Tradition and Reform in Persophone Administration and Chancellery Affairs," *Journal of Azerbaijani Studies*, vol. 1 (1998), no. 1, pp. 35–46 and "Tradition, Legitimät und Abgrenzung: formale Symbolaussagen persischsprachiger Herrscherurkunden," in *Akten des Melzer Symposiums 1991: Veranstalted aus Anlass der Hundertjahrfeier indo-iranischer Forschung in Graz*, eds. W. Slaje and C. Zinko (Leykam: 1992), pp. 84–113. For older yet foundational work, see the work of K. M. Röhrborn in *Provinzen und Zentralgewalt Persiens im 16. und 17. Jahrhundert* (Berlin: 1966), "Regierung und Verwaltung Irans unter den Safawiden," *Handbuch der Orientalistik*, vol. 6 (1979), pp. 17–50, "Staatskanzlei und Absolutismus im safawidischen Persien," *Zeitschrift der Deutschen Morgenländischen Gesellschaft*, vol. 127 (1977), pp. 313–43. Specific documents are discussed in Gottfried Herrmann, "Zwei Erlasse Schah Ismā`īls I.," *Archaeologische Mitteilungen aus Iran*, vol. 19 (1986), pp, 289–306 and "Ein Erlaß Tahmasps I. von 934/1528," *Zeitschrift der Deutschen Morgenländischen Gesellschaft*, vol. 139 (1989), no. 1, pp. 104–19. See also A. H. Morton, "An Introductory Note on a Safavid Munshī's Manual in the Library of the School of Oriental and African Studies," *Bulletin of the School of Oriental and African Studies*, vol. 36 (1970), pp. 352–58 and Iraj Afshar, "*Maktub* and *Majmu`a*: Essential Sources for Safavid Research," in *Society and Culture in the Early Modern Middle East: Studies on Iran in the Safavid Period*, ed. A. J. Newman (Leiden: 2003), pp. 51–62.

Chapter One

1 Tourkhan Gandjei, "Isma`il I 2. His Poetry," *EI2*, vol. 4, pp. 187–88.

2 Jean Aubin, "L'avènement des Safavides reconsidéré," *Moyen Orient et océan Indien*, vol. 5 (1988), pp. 1-130.

3 The idea of Ismā`īl's reign representing a "third Türkmen phase" was first articulated by Vladimir Minorsky. See Vladimir Minorsky, *Tadhkirat al-muluk: A Manual*

of Safavid Administration (London: 1943), pp. 189–95.

4 Jean Calmard, "Les rituals shiites et le pouvoir: l'imposition du shiisme safavide: eulogies et malédictions canoniques," in *Études Safavides*, ed. J. Calmard (Paris: 1993), pp. 114–16.

5 Shahzad Bashir, "The Imam's Return: Messianic Leadership in Late Medieval Shi`ism," in *The Most Learned of the Shi`a: The Institution of the* Marja` Taqlid, ed. L. S. Walbridge (New York: 2001), p. 21.

6 Oktaj Efendiev, "Le rôle des tribus de langue Turque," *Turcica*, vol. 6 (1975), p. 27.

7 Hans Robert Roemer, *Persien auf dem Weg in die Neuzeit: iranische Geschichte von 1350–1750* (Beirut: 1989), p. 238; Hans Robert Roemer, "Das Türkmenische Intermezzo: Persische Geschichte zwischen Mongolen und Safawiden," *Archaeologische Mitteilungen aus Iran*, vol. 9 (1976), pp. 294–95.

8 See Minorsky's translation of Faḍl Allah ibn Rūzbīhān Khunjī in *Persia in A.D. 1478–1490: An Abridged Translation of Faḍlullāh b. Rūzbīhān Khunjī's* Tārīkh-i `ālam-ārā-yi Amīnī (London: 1957), p. 66.

9 Minorsky (ed.), *Persia in A.D. 1478–1490*, p. 73.

10 For the best historiographical treatment of the youth of Ismā`īl, see A. H. Morton, "The Early Years of Shāh Ismā`īl in the Afḍal al-tavārīkh and Elsewhere," in *Safavid Persia: The History and Politics of an Islamic Society*, ed. C. Melville (London: 1996), pp. 27–51.

11 Roger Savory, "The Struggle for Supremacy in Persia After the Death of Timur," *Der Islam*, vol. 40 (1964), No. 1, p. 57.

12 Būdāq Munshī Qazvīnī, *Javāhir al-akhbār*, ed. M. Bahramnezād (Tehran: 2000), p. 86.

13 Renard, *Islam and the Heroic Image*, pp. 75–76.

14 Būdāq Munshī, *Javāhir al-akhbār*, p. 86.

15 Efendiev, "Le rôle des tribus de langue Turque," p. 28; Ghulam Sarwar, *History of Shāh Ismā`īl Ṣafavī* (Aligarh: 1939), pp. 30–31.

16 John Woods, *The Aqquyunlu: Clan, Confederation, Empire*, new and rev. ed. (Salt Lake City: 1999), p. 157.

17 Roemer, *Persien auf dem Weg*, p. 245.

18 Wilferd Madelung (ed.), *Akhbār a'immat al-Zaidī fī Ṭabaristān wa Dailam wa Jīlān* (Beirut: 1987), pp. 11–12.

19 Sarwar, *History of Shāh Ismā`īl Ṣafavī*, p. 32.

20 Aubin, "L'avènement des Safavides reconsidéré," p. 5.

21 Sarwar, *History of Shāh Ismā`īl Ṣafavī*, p. 32.

22 Irène Mélikoff, "L'Islam Heterdodéxé en Anatolie," in *Sur les traces du soufisme Turc: Recherches sur l'Islam populaire en Anatolie* (Istanbul: 1992), pp. 64–65.

23 Poonawala, "Apocalyptic II. In Muslim Iran," *Encyclopadia Iranica*, ed. E. Yarshater, vol. 2, p. 158.

24 Muḥammad ibn Ya`qūb ibn Isḥāq al-Kulainī, *Kāfī al-uṣūl min al-kāfī*, ed. A. A. Ghaffārī, vol. 1 (Tehran: 1968), p. 168. Quoted in Abdulaziz Abdulhussein Sachedina, *Islamic Messianism: The Idea of the Mahdi in Twelver Shi`ism* (Albany: 1981), p. 173.

25 Allouche provides a brief overview of the different options discussed by the Qizilbāsh amirs. Adel Allouche, *The Origins and Development of the Ottoman-Safavid Conflict (906–962/1500–1555)* (Berlin: 1983), pp. 71–72.

26 Ghiyāṣ al-Dīn ibn Humām al-Dīn Khvāndamīr, *Ḥabīb al-siyar*, ed. Muḥammad Dabīr Siyāqī, vol. 4 (Tehran: 1983), pp. 453–54; Ḥasan Beg Rūmlū, *Aḥsan al-tavārīkh*, ed. C. Seddon, vol. 1 (Baroda: 1931), p. 47.

27 Iskander Beg Munshī, *History of Shah `Abbas the Great*, ed. and trans. R. Savory,

vol. 1 (Boulder: 1980), p. 41; for Persian, see Iskander Beg Munshī, *Tārīkh-i `ālam-ārā-yi `Abbāsī*, ed. I. Afshar, Vol. 1 (Tehran: 2003), p. 25.

28 Khūrshāh ibn Qubād al-Ḥusainī, *Tārīkh-i īlchī-yi Niẓāmshāh*, ed. M. R. Nāṣirī and K. Haneda (Tehran: 2000), p. 8.

29 Khūrshāh ibn Qubād, *Tārīkh-i īlchī-yi Niẓāmshāh*, p. 8; `Abdī Beg Shīrāzī, *Takmilat al-akhbār*, ed. Abd al-Ḥusain Navā'ī (Tehran: 1990), p. 37.

30 Khvāndamīr, *Ḥabīb al-siyar*, vol. 4, pp. 461–62.

31 Khvāndamīr, *Ḥabīb al-siyar*, vol. 4, p. 461.

32 `Abdī Beg Shīrāzī, *Takmilat al-akhbār*, p. 38.

33 Būdāq Munshī, *Javāhir al-akhbār*, p. 115.

34 Būdāq Munshī, *Javāhir al-akhbār*, p. 119.

35 This particular text uses *jaḥidu*, which I translate as the imperative for "fight," as opposed to other translations that interpret the root *ja-ḥa-da* as "striving," "struggle," "expending energy." This particular Qur'ānic verse appears in other instances associated with *ghazā*, or frontier warfare, suggesting *jiḥād* to be understood as militant struggle against non-Muslims.

36 `Abdī Beg Shīrāzī, *Takmilat al-akhbār*, p. 40.

37 Amir Said Arjomand, *The Shadow of God and the Hidden Imam* (Albany: 1980), p. 12.

38 Qāḍī Aḥmad, *Khulāṣat al-tavārīkh*, vol. 1, p. 74, Khvāndamīr, *Ḥabīb al-siyar*, vol. 4, p. 469.

39 Palmira Brummet, "The Myth of Shah Isma`il Safavi: Political Rehtoric and 'Divine' Kingship," in *Medieval Christian Perceptions of Islam*, ed. J. Tolan (New York: 1996), p. 337.

40 Brummet, "The Myth of Shah Isma`il Safavi," pp. 337–38.

41 Khvāndamīr, *Ḥabīb al-siyar*, vol. 4, p. 472.

42 Aubin, "Shāh Ismā`īl et les notables de l'Iraq persan," *Journal of the Economic and Social History of the Orient*. Vol. 2 (1959), p. 58; Qāḍī Aḥmad, *Khulāṣat al-tavārīkh*, vol. 1, p. 81.

43 Ḥāfiẓ Ḥusain Karbalā'ī Tabrīzī, *Rauḍāt al-jinān va jannāt al-jinān*, ed. J. Sulṭān al-Qurrā'ī, vol. 1 (Tehran: 1965), p. 490, p. 159.

44 Khvāndamīr, *Ḥabīb al-siyar*, vol. 4, p. 473.

45 `Abdī Beg Shīrāzī, *Takmilat al-akhbār*, p. 42.

46 `Abdī Beg Shīrāzī, *Takmilat al-akhbār*, p. 43; Būdāq Munshī, *Javāhir al-akhbār*, p. 122; Aubin, "L'avènement des Safavides reconsidéré," p. 45–46. Khūrshāh ibn Qubād gives an account of this infamous incident in *Tārīkh-i īlchī-yi Niẓāmshāh*, p. 26. This alleged cannibalism has been a recent focus of inquiry for Shahzad Bashir in "Shah Isma`il and the Qizilbash: Cannibalism in the Religious History of Early Safavid Iran," *History of Religions*, vol. 45 (2006), No. 3, pp. 239–41.

47 Khvāndamīr, *Ḥabīb al-siyar*, vol. 4, p. 476, p. 479.

48 Khvāndamīr, *Ḥabīb al-siyar*, vol. 4, pp. 480–1.

49 Aubin, "Revolution Chiite," p. 41.

50 `Abdī Beg Shīrāzī, *Takmilat al-akhbār*, p. 43.

51 Khvāndamīr, *Ḥabīb al-siyar*, vol. 4, p. 480; Muḥammad Yūsuf Vālih Iṣfahānī, *Khuld-i barīn*, ed. Mīr Hāshim Muḥaddis̱ (Tehran: 1993), pp. 148–49.

52 Qāḍī Aḥmad Ghaffārī Qazvīnī, *Tārīkh-i jahān-ārā*, ed. Mujtabī Minuvī (Tehran: 1964), p. 270.

53 Qāḍī Aḥmad Ghaffārī, *Tārīkh-i jahān-ārā*, p. 271; `Abdī Beg Shīrāzī, *Takmilat al-akhbār*, p. 46.

54 Roger Savory, "The Consolidation of Safavid Power in Persia," *Der Islam*, vol. 41 (1965), p. 76.

55 Aubin, "Revolution Chiite," p. 4.

56 Qāḍī Aḥmad, *Khulāṣat al-tavārīkh*, vol. 1, p. 94; Qāḍī Aḥmad Ghaffārī, *Tārīkh-i jahān-ārā*, p. 272; Khvāndamīr, *Ḥabīb al-siyar*, vol. 4, p. 498.
57 To date, few studies have surpassed the work of the great Central Asian historian, Wilhelm Barthold. For a clear introduction to the daunting Timurid political narrative, see his *Four Studies on the History of Central Asia*, ed. and trans. Vladimir Minorsky (Leiden: 1956). One exception would be Maria Subtelny's recent *Timurids in Transition: Turko-Persian Politics and Acculturation in Medieval Iran* (Leiden: 2007).
58 Thomas W. Lentz and Glenn D. Lowry, *Timur and the Princely Vision: Persian Art and Culture in the Fifteenth Century* (Washington: 1989), p. 160; Thomas Lentz, "Dynastic Imagery in Early Timurid Painting," *Muqarnas,* vol. 10 (1993), pp. 253–63; Paul Losensky, *Welcoming Fighani: Imitation and Poetic Individuality in the Safavid-Mughal Ghazal* (Costa Mesa, 1998), p. 135.
59 Khvāndamīr, *Ḥabīb al-siyar*, vol. 4, p. 507.
60 Khūrshāh ibn Qubād, *Tārīkh-i īlchī-yi Niẓāmshāhi*, p. 62.
61 `Abdī Beg Shīrāzī, *Takmilat al-akhbār*, p. 50; Maḥmūd ibn Khvāndamīr, *Tārīkh-i Shāh Ismā`īl va Shāh Ṭahmāsp*, ed. M. A. Jarāhī (Tehran: 1994), p. 68. It should be noted that this latter source is particularly valuable for information on Safavid-Uzbek relations. For a detailed description of this battle, see `Abbās Qulī Ghaffārī Fard, *Ravābiṭ-i Ṣafaviyyah va Uzbekān* (Tehran: 1997), pp. 109–21.
62 Khvāndamīr, *Ḥabīb al-siyar,* vol. 4, p. 514.
63 This included the Shaikh al-Islām Aḥmad al-Taftazānī, Amīr Niẓām al-Dīn `Abd al-Qādir Mashhadī, Sayyid Ghiyāṣ al-Dīn Muḥammad, Qāḍī Ṣadr al-Dīn Muḥammad al-Imāmī, and Qāḍī Ikhtiyār al-Dīn Ḥasan al-Turbatī. Khvāndamīr, *Ḥabīb al-siyar,* vol. 4, p. 514.
64 Khvāndamīr, *Ḥabīb al-siyar*, vol. 4, p. 515; Muḥammad Yūsuf Vālih, *Khuld-i barīn,* p. 186.
65 Ibn Khvāndamīr, *Tārīkh-i Shāh Ismā`īl va Shāh Ṭahmāsp*, p. 72; see also Calmard, "Les rituals shiites et le pouvoir," pp. 122–23.
66 Babayan, *Monarchs, Mystics, and Messiahs*, p. 131, p. 222.
67 Khūrshāh ibn Qubād, *Tārīkh-i īlchī-yi Niẓāmshāh*, p. 54.
68 Muḥammad Yūsuf Vālih, *Khuld-i barīn*, p. 199.
69 Khūrshāh ibn Qubād, *Tārīkh-i īlchī-yi Niẓāmshāhī,* p. 54. Ikhtiyār al-Dīn had been used mostly as a prison by Sulṭān-Ḥusain Bāiqarā. Barthold, *Herat unter Husein Baiqara*, ed. and trans. W. Hinz (Nendeln Kraus: 1966), p. 73. See also Maria E. Subtelny, "Ek̲tiar al-Dīn," *Encyclopædia Iranica*, vol. 7, pp. 290–91.
70 Khūrshāh ibn Qubād, *Tārīkh-i īlchī-yi Niẓāmshāhī,* p. 55.
71 Khvāndamīr, *Ḥabīb al-siyar*, vol. 4, p. 519, Muḥammad Yūsuf Vālih, *Khuld-i barīn*, p. 203; Ibn Khvāndamīr, *Tārīkh-i Shāh Ismā`īl va Shāh Ṭahmāsp*, pp. 70-73; Qāḍī Aḥmad, *Khulāṣat al-tavārīkh*, Vol 1., p. 115; Riazul Islam, *Indo-Persian Relations: A Study of Political and Diplomatic Relations Between the Mughal Empire and Iran* (Tehran: 1970), p. 7.
72 Būdāq Munshī, *Javāhir al-akhbār*, p. 130; `Abdī Beg Shīrāzī, *Takmilat al-akhbār*, p. 52; Muḥammad Yūsuf Vālih, *Khuld-i barīn*, pp. 311–12.
73 The battle itself will not be discussed here, but suffice to say that it was a disaster for the Safavid military and administration, which lost key figures like Ḥusain Beg Shāmlū, Muḥammad Khān Ustājlū, `Abd al-Bāqī, Sayyid Sharīf al-Dīn `Alī, and Sayyid Muḥammad Kamūna.
74 Aubin, "L'avènement des Safavides reconsidéré," p. 27.
75 Klaus-Michael Röhrborn, *Provinzen und Zentralgewalt Persiens im 16. und 17. Jahrhundert* (Berlin: 1966), p. 24.
76 Vladimir Minorsky, "A Civil and Military Review in Fars in 881/1476," *Bulletin of*

the School of Oriental and African Studies, Vol. 10 (1940–42), p. 170.

77 Aubin, "Shāh Ismā`īl et les notables de l'Iraq persan," pp. 61–62.

78 Qāḍī Aḥmad, *Khulāṣat al-tavārīkh*, vol. 1, p. 64; Qāḍī Aḥmad Ghaffārī, *Tārīkh-i jahān-ārā*, p. 265; `Abdī Beg Shīrāzī, *Takmilat al-akhbār*, p. 39.

79 Yaḥyā ibn Muḥammad ibn `Abd al-Laṭīf Qazvīnī. *Lubb al-tavārīkh*, partial ed. and trans. H. Braun as *Aḥvāl-i Shāh Ismā`īl: eine unerschlossene Darstellung des lebens des ersten Safawidenschahs*, unpublished Ph.D. dissertation (Göttingen: 1947), p. 17. Khvāndamīr describes his post as *rāyat-i vizārat*. *Ḥabīb al-siyar*, vol. 4, p. 66.

80 Aubin, "Shāh Ismā`īl et les notables de l'Iraq persan," p. 63.

81 One of his relatives—Shāh `Imād al-Dīn Salmān Daylamī—had served as *vazīr* to Khalīl Sulṭān, the son of Ūzūn Ḥasan. Shāh `Imād al-Dīn Salmān Daylamī had enjoyed a powerful career in Iṣfahān under the local governor, Ḥājjī Beg ibn Shaikh Ḥasan Beg, but was eventually executed for being overly ambitious. Aubin, "Shāh Ismā`īl et les notables de l'Iraq persan," p. 62; Minorsky, "A Civil and Military Review," p. 176.

82 Minorsky, "A Civil and Military Review," p. 176.

83 Aubin, "Shāh Ismā`īl et les notables de l'Iraq persan," p. 64.

84 Qāḍī Aḥmad, *Khulāṣat al-tavārīkh*, vol. 1, p. 79.

85 Yaḥyā ibn Muḥammad, *Lubb al-tavārīkh*, p. 79.

86 Heribert Busse, *Untersuchungen zum islamischen Kanzleiwesen an Hand türkmenischer und safawidischer Urkunden* (Cairo: 1959), p. 154.

87 Busse, *Untersuchungen zum islamischen Kanzleiwesen*, p. 162.

88 Hans Robert Roemer, "Le Dernier Firman de Rustam Bahadur Aq Qoyunlu?" *Bulletin de l'Institut Français d'archeologie orientale*, vol. 59 (1960), p. 284.

89 Gottfried Herrmann, "Zur Intitulatio timuridischer Herrscherurkunden," *Zeitschrift der Deutschen Morgenländischen Gesellschaft, Supplement II: XVIII. Deutscher Orientalistentag* (Weisbaden: 1974), pp. 498–521; Heribert Busse, "Persische Diplomatik im Überblick: Ergebnisse und Probleme," *Der Islam*, vol. 37 (1961), pp. 226–31.

90 Bert Fragner, "Tradition, Legitimät und Abgrenzung: formale Symbolaussagen persischsprachiger Herrscherurkunden," in *Akten des Melzer Symposiums 1991: Veranstalted aus Anlass der Hundertjahrfeier indo-iranischer Forschung in Graz*, eds. W. Slaje and C. Zinko (Leykam: 1992), p. 96.

91 Gottfried Herrmann, "Zwei Erlasse Schah Ismā`īls I.," *Archaeologische Mitteilungen aus Iran*, vol. 19 (1986), p. 300.

92 Renate Schimkoreit, *Regesten publizierter safawidischer Herrscherurkunden: Erlasse und Staatsschreiben der frühen Neuzeit Iran* (Berlin: 1982), p. 31.

93 Schimkoreit, *Regesten publizierter safawidischer Herrscherurkunden*, p. 38.

94 Schimkoreit, *Regesten publizierter safawidischer Herrscherurkunden*, p. 39.

95 Qāḍī Aḥmad, *Khulāṣat al-tavārīkh*, vol. 1, p. 77.

96 Norman Cohn, *The Pursuit of the Millennium: Revolutionary Millenarians and Mystical Anarchists of the Middle Ages*, rev. ed. (London: 1970).

97 Michael Barkun, *Disaster and the Millennnium* (Syracuse: 1974).

98 O'Leary, *Arguing the Apocalypse*, p. 13.

99 Jonathan Berkey has rehabilitated traditional depictions of storytelling and preaching in *Popular Preaching and Religious Authority in the Medieval Islamic Near East* (Seattle: 2001).

100 Jean Calmard, "Popular Literature Under the Safavids," in *Society and Culture in the Early Modern Middle East: Studies on Iran in the Safavid Period*, ed. A. J. Newman (Leiden: 2003), p. 317.

101 For notes on different manuscripts and dates of this *Dīvān*, see Wheeler Thackston, "The Diwan of Khata'i: Pictures for the Poetry of Shāh Ismā`īl I," *Asian Art* (Fall,

1988), pp. 38–39, and Vladmir Minorsky, "The Poetry of Shāh Ismā`īl I," *Bulletin of the School of Oriental and African Studies*, vol. 10 (1940–43), p. 1008a–1010a.

102 Babayan, *Mystics, Monarchs, and Messiahs*, p. 124.

103 Kathryn Babayan, "The Safavid Synthesis: From Qizilbash Islam to Imamite Shi`ism," *Iranian Studies*, vol. 27 (1994), p. 145. The *Abū Muslim nāmah* has been published recently. See Abū Ṭāhir Ṭarṭūsī, *Abū Muslim nāmah*, ed. Husain Ismā`īlī, 4 vols. (Tehran: 2001).

104 Sām Mīrza, *Tazkirah-yi tuḥfah-yi Sāmī*, ed. R. H. Farrukh (Tehran: 1970), p. 138, pp. 140–41, p. 367.

105 Babayan, *Mystics, Monarchs, and Messiahs*, p. 141.

106 Berkey, *Popular Preaching and Religious Authority*, p. 50.

107 This is no more clearer than in no. 103 of the *Dīvān*, in all likelihood written in 1506 or 1507, when he wrote: "Should he rise and sit down, the ordeal of the end of the world will burst out/Let all the people of Shīrvān rush to Tabrīz/The Persian kingdom will ask: when is the Last Day to come? ... Since in the Pre-Eternity, Khaṭā'ī has contemplated the certainty of this issue/The signs of Noah have appeared in him and the Flood is to burst out." Minorsky, "The Poetry of Shāh Ismā`īl," p. 1045a.

108 We see this best in no. 15: "I have recovered my father's blood from Yazīd. Be sure that I am of Ḥaidarian essence.... My sire is Ṣafī, my father Ḥaidar. Truly I am the Ja`far of the audacious." Minorsky, "The Poetry of Shāh Ismā`īl," p. 1042a.

109 Minorsky, "The Poetry of Shāh Ismā`īl," p. 1044a.

110 "Today I have come to the world as a Master. Know truly that I am Ḥaidar's son/I am Farīdūn, Khusrau, Jamshīd, and Zohāk. I am Zāl's son (Rustam) and Alexander/ The mystery of Anā'l-Ḥaqq is hidden in this my heart. I am the Absolute Truth and what I say is Truth." Minorsky, "The Poetry of Shāh Ismā`īl," p. 1047a.

111 In the anonymous *Munsha'āt*, this letter is introduced with the rubric *Kitābat-i `alā-ḥaḍrat ṣāḥib-qirānī bi Sulṭān Ḥusain Mīrzā Bāiqarā dar bāb-i sha`ārash-i Muḥammad Ḥusain Mīrzā va fatḥ-i qil`ah-yi Fīrūz Kūh*, located on ff. 102b–103b of Add. 7654 of the British Library. See also Īvūghlī, *Nuskhah-yi jāmi`a-i al-murāsalāt*, ff. 68a–68b. See also `Alī Akbar Vilāyatī, *Tārīkh-i ravābiṭ-i khārijī-yi Īrān dar `ahd-i Shāh Ismā`īl Ṣafavī* (Tehran: 1996), pp. 287–89.

112 Anon., *Munsha'āt*, *MS*, London, British Library, Add. 7654, fol. 102b.

113 Anon., *Munsha'āt*, fol. 103a.

114 Babayan, *Monarchs, Mystics, and Messiahs*, p. 138.

115 Anon., *Munsha'āt*, fol. 103a.

116 Khvāndamīr, *Ḥabīb al-siyar*, vol. 4, p. 477; Qāḍī Aḥmad, *Khulāṣat al-tavārīkh*, vol. 2, p. 83.

117 Anon., *Munsha'āt*, fol. 103b.

118 *qarīb bi-dah hazār kas misl-i Murād Jahān-Shāmlū va Aslamas va aqribah va muta`liqān-i Ḥusain Kiyā va tamāmat-i īshān-rā bi-siyāsat rasānīdand.* Anon., *Munsha'āt*, fol. 103b.

119 Chittick, "Eschatology," p. 394.

120 G. Awad, "Babil," *EI2*, vol. 1, p. 846.

121 Ismā`īl himself alludes to this tradition in no. 18 of his *Dīvān*: "I was on the gibbet with Manṣūr; with Abraham in the fire, and with Moses on Sinai." Minorsky, "The Poetry of Shāh Ismā`īl," p. 1043a.

122 *Ḥusain Kiyā-i pāy-yi āb-i dar-zada khāk nā-pāk-i u-rā bar bād va havā bar dādand.* Anon., *Munsha'āt*, fol. 103b.

123 On eschatological and theosophical interpretations of the garden in Perso-Islamic civilization, see Maria Subtelny, *Le monde est un jardin: aspects de l'histoire culturelle de l'Iran médiéval* (Paris: 2002), pp. 101–152.

124 *Gulzār-i an nāḥiyyah az khār-i ta`arruz-i ān gurūh-i bī shukūh pāk shud.* Anon.,

Munsha'āt, fol. 103b.

125 "Whoever of those who confuse the victory, bravery, opinion and rationale of their sovereignty/Throw the stone of vanity in the middle [for all to see]/In the primary school of [Ismā`īl's] eternal knowledge, the intellect of the *pīr*/Is just like a child thrown from the arms of the tablet and utterance [of the Qur'ān]." Īvūghlī, *Nuskhah-yi jāmi`a-i al-murāsalāt-i ulul albab*, 70b, Navā'ī (ed.), *Shāh Ismā`īl Ṣafavī*, p. 71.

126 Īvūghlī, *Nuskhah-yi jāmi`a-i al-murāsalāt-i ulul albab*, 70b; Navā'ī (ed.), *Shāh Ismā`īl Ṣafavī*, p. 71.

127 Īvūghlī, *Nuskhah-yi jāmi`a-i al-murāsalāt-i ulul albab*, 70b, Navā'ī (ed.), *Shāh Ismā`īl Ṣafavī*, p. 72.

128 Abū al-Qāsim Rādfar, *Manāqib-i `alavī dar āyīnah-i shi`r-i Fārsī* (Tehran: 2002), p. 32.

129 Īvūghlī, *Nuskhah-yi jāmi`a-i al-murāsalāt-i ulul albab*, 71a, Navā'ī (ed.), *Shāh Ismā`īl Ṣafavī*, p. 72. Interestingly, part of this poetry appears to have been inspired by a *rubā'ī* that first appeared in the heroic epic, *Abū Muslim nāmah*, and its narration of the attack on Qāsim ibn Kathīr in Baghdad by the Khiyātīn. The original line appears as "with broken armour and belt-less, he stood alone with no mail on his breast." The scribe, however, replaces *silāḥ* ("armour") with *ṣalāḥ* (virtue), and adds his own line (*nah yārā-yi dast va nah pārvā-yi sar*). See Abū Ṭāhir Ṭarṭūsī, *Abū Muslim nāmah*, vol. 4, p. 152.

130 Īvūghlī, *Nuskhah-yi jāmi`a-i al-murāsalāt-i ulul albab*, 70b, Navā'ī (ed.), *Shāh Ismā`īl Ṣafavī*, p. 72.

131 Īvūghlī, *Nuskhah-yi jāmi`a-i al-murāsalāt-i ulul albab*, 71a. Navā'ī (ed.), *Shāh Ismā`īl Ṣafavī*, p. 73.

132 Sayyid Muhammad Ziya `Abadi, *Hajj: The Islamic Pilgrimage*, trans. A. A. Ashtianī (Qumm: n.d.).

133 Īvūghlī, *Nuskhah-yi jāmi`a-i al-murāsalāt-i ulul albab*, 71a; Navā'ī (ed.), *Shāh Ismā`īl Ṣafavī*, p. 73.

134 Aḥmad ibn Ḥajjār al-Makkī, *al-Savā'iq al-Muḥriqa*, ed. `Abd al-Wahhāb `Abd al-Latif (Cairo: 1955), p. 150; al-Ḥākim al-Naisabūrī, *al-Mustadarak*, vol. 3 (Riyad: n.d.) pp. 150–51.

135 See Momen, *An Introduction to Shi`i Islam*, p. 16. H. Kindermann and C. E. Bosworth note that, despite the lack of biographical evidence of Muḥammad having been at sea, dramatic accounts of the ocean in Qur'ān and hadīth, suggest some familiarity. H. Kindermann and C. E. Bosworth, "Safīna: 1. In the Pre-Modern Period," *EI2*, vol. 8, p. 808.

136 See Raya Shani, "Noah's Ark and the Ship of Faith in Persian Painting: From the Fourteenth to the Sixteenth Century," *Jerusalem Studies in Arabic and Islam*, vol. 27 (2002), pp. 127–203. See also her "Illustrations to the Parable of the Ship of Faith in Firdausi's Prologue to the Shahnama," in *Shahnama Studies I (Pembroke Papers, 5)*, ed. Charles Melville (Cambridge: 2006), pp. 1–40.

137 Etan Kohlberg, "Some Shī`ī Views of the Antediluvian World," *Studia Islamica*, vol. 52 (1980), p. 53.

138 Shaikh Al-Mufīd, *Kitāb al-irshād (The Book of Guidance into the Lives of the Twelve Imams)*, p. 15, quoted in Heinz Halm, *Shi`a Islam: From Religion to Revolution*, trans. A. Brown (Princeton: 1997), p. 7.

139 Īvūghlī, *Nuskhah-yi jāmi`a-i al-murāsalāt-i ulul albab*, ff. 73b–74a, Navā'ī (ed.), *Shāh Ismā`īl Ṣafavī*, pp. 93–96.

140 Īvūghlī, *Nuskhah-yi jāmi`a-i al-murāsalāt-i ulul albab*, fol. 73b, Navā'ī (ed.), *Shāh Ismā`īl Ṣafavī*, p. 94.

141 Clifford, "Some Observations," pp. 264–65.

142 Īvūghlī, *Nuskhah-yi jāmi`a-i al-murāsalāt-i ulul albab*, fol. 73b, Navā'ī (ed.), *Shāh*

Ismā`īl Ṣafavī, p. 95.

143 Arjomand, "Origins and Development of Apocalypticism," p. 9.

144 Īvūghlī, *Nuskhah-yi jāmi`a-i al-murāsalāt-i ulul albab*, fol. 73b, Navā'ī (ed.), *Shāh Ismā`īl Ṣafavī*, p. 95.

145 Shams al-Dīn Muḥammad ibn Tūlūn, *Mufākahat al-khillān fī ḥawādith al-zamān*, ed. Muḥammad Muṣtafā, vol. 1 (Cairo: 1962), p. 357.

146 Navā'ī (ed.), *Asnad va mukātibāt-i tārīkhī-yi Īrān*, p. 611. This is possibly an expedition Sulṭān Ya`qūb organized in 887/1482 against Georgia. See Savory, "The Struggle for Supremacy," p. 55.

147 Quṭb al-Dīn Abū al-Ḥasan Muḥammad ibn al-Ḥusain ibn al-Ḥasan Baihaqī Nishāpūrī Kaidarī, *Dīvān-i Imām `Alī*, ed. Abū al-Qāsim Imāmī (Tehran: 1995), pp. 243–44.

148 I am grateful to Maria Subtelny for first alerting me to this tradition. For details, see Hellmut Ritter, *The Ocean of the Soul: Man, the World, and God in the Storiesof Farid al-Dīn `Attar*, trans. J. O'Kane (Leiden: 2003) p. 103.

149 Khvāndamīr, *Ḥabīb al-siyar*, vol. 4, p. 514, Khūrshāh ibn Qubād, *Tārīkh-i īlchī-yi Niẓāmshāh*, p. 54.

150 Claude Cahen, "La problème du Shi`isme dans l'Asie Mineure Turque preottomane," in *Le Shi`isme Imamite: Colloque de Strasbourg (6–9 mai 1968)*, eds. R. Brunschvig and T. Fahd (Paris: 1970), p. 126.

151 Babayan, *Mystics, Monarchs, and Messiahs*, p. 173.

152 See Shahzad Bashir, *Messianic Hopes and Mystical Visions: The Nurbakhshiyya Between Medieval and Modern Islam* (Columbia, South Carolina: 2003), pp. 161–97 for material on the Nūrbakhshiyyah. See Farhad Daftary, "Ismā`īlī-Sufi relations in early post-Alamut and Safavid Persia" in *The Heritage of Sufism*, vol. 3, eds. L. Lewisohn and D. Morgon (Oxford: 1999), pp. 275–89 for information on the Ismā`īlī community. See Irène Mélikoff, *Sur les traces du soufisme Turc: Recherches sur l'Islam populaire en Anatolie* (Istanbul: 1992), pp. 173–75 for observations on the Ḥurūfiyya. Regarding the Ni`matullāhis, see Leonard Lewisohn, "An Introduction to the history of modern Persian Sufism, part I: The Ni`matullahi Order: Persecution, Revival and Schism," *Bulletin of the School of Oriental and African Studies*, vol. 61 (1998), pp. 437–64.

153 Rula Abisaab, *Converting Persia: Religion and Power in the Safavid Empire, 1501–1736* (London: 2004) and "The `Ulama of Jabal `Amil in Safavid Iran, 1501–1736: Marginality, Migration, and Social Change," *Iranian Studies*, vol. 27 (1994), No. 1, pp. 103–22; Rasūl Ja`fariyān, *Dīn va siyāsat dar daurah-yi Ṣafavī* (Qumm: 1991), and "The Immigrant Manuscripts: A Study of the Migration of Shi`i Works from the Arab Regions to Iran in the Early Safavid Era," in *Society and Culture in the Early Modern Middle East: Studies on Iran in the Safavid Period*, ed. A. J. Newman (Leiden: 2003), pp. 351–69.

154 Richard Gramlich, *Die schiitischen derwischorden persiens*, vol. 2 (Wiesbaden: 1965), p. 101.

155 Bashir, *Messianic Hopes and Mystical Visions*, pp. 38–41.

156 Ghaffārī Fard, *Ravābiṭ-i Ṣafaviyyah va Uzbekān*, p. 102.

157 Iskander Beg Munshī, *History of Shah `Abbas the Great*, vol. 1, p. 60; for Persian, see *Tārīkh-i `ālam-ārā-yi `Abbāsī*, vol. 1, p. 37.

158 Gramlich, *Die schiitischen derwischorden persiens*, vol. 1, p. 14.

159 Sām Mīrzā, *Tazkirah-yi tuḥfah-yi Sāmī*, p. 109.

160 The earliest extant rationalization of Shāh Ismā`īl's decision to promulgate Shi`ism appears in Khvāndamīr: "And then all of the [shah's] designs were turned and focused towards the propagation of the `Alīd Imami school and the strengthening of all orthodox religious considerations. At the beginning of the royal enthronement, a *farmān* was publicly proclaimed that the preachers of the kingdoms of Āzarbāījān

read the *khuṭbah* in the name of the Twelve Imāms ('May the blessings of God be upon them until the Day of Resurrection') and all leaders of prayer in their [respective] places of worship and leaders of religious groups put an end to heretical, despicable practices. Also, the *muazzins* of *masjids* and [other] places of prayer were to add to the call to prayer the words: 'I testify that `Alī is God's deputy'. Moreover, faithful *ghāzīs* and *mujāhidīn*, who witnessed someone committing an act repugnant to Muḥammad's community, should cut [that person's] head from their body. Of course, the fame of the qualities of the most innocent Imāms, and an ongoing prayer for the fortune of [Ismā`īl] to be rightly guided were proclaimed from the pulpit. The currency was engraved with the exalted names of those guides on the path of truth, as well as the honorifics of [the shah]." Khvāndamīr, *Ḥabīb al-siyar*, vol. 4, pp. 576–77.

161 Qāḍī Aḥmad, *Khulāṣat al-tavārīkh*, vol. 1, pp. 102–8.

162 Qāḍī Aḥmad, *Khulāṣat al-tavārīkh*, vol. 1, p. 102.

163 Īvūghlī, *Nuskhah-yi jāmi`a-i al-murāsalāt-i ulul albab*, fol. 73b, Navā'ī (ed.), *Shāh Ismā`īl Ṣafavī*, p. 95.

164 `Abd al-Ḥusain al-Ṭūsī, *Munsha'āt al-Ṭūsī*, fol. 60b, Navā'ī (ed.), *Shāh Ismā`īl Ṣafavī*, p. 45.

165 Annemarie Schimmel, *Mystical Dimensions of Islam* (Chapel Hill: 1975), p. 215.

166 `Abd al-Ḥusain al-Ṭūsī, *Munsha'āt al-Ṭūsī*, fol. 61a, Navā'ī (ed.), *Shāh Ismā`īl Ṣafavī*, p. 46.

167 `Abd al-Ḥusain al-Ṭūsī, *Munsha'āt al-Ṭūsī*, fol. 61b, Navā'ī (ed.), *Shāh Ismā`īl Ṣafavī*, p. 46.

168 `Abd al-Ḥusain al-Ṭūsī, *Munsha'āt al-Ṭūsī*, fol. 62a, Navā'ī (ed.), *Shāh Ismā`īl Ṣafavī*, pp. 46-47.

169 *dar-i khazānah-yi raḥmat fī qufl-i ḥukmat būd/zamān-i daulat-i mā dar rasīd va dar vashīd.* `Abd al-Ḥusain al-Ṭūsī, *Munsha'āt al-Ṭūsī*, fol. 62a, Navā'ī (ed.), *Shāh Ismā`īl Ṣafavī*, pp. 46–47.

170 Moojan Momen, *An Introduction to Shi`i Islam: The History and Doctrines of Twelver Shi`ism* (New Haven: 1985), p. 151; Meir Bar-Asher, *Scripture and Exegesis in Early Imami-Shiism* (Leiden: 1999), p. 193; Muḥammad Nūrbakhsh cites this verse in his *Risālat al-hudā*, see Bashir, *Millenarian Hopes and Mystical Visions*, p. 79.

171 `Abd al-Ḥusain al-Ṭūsī, *Munsha'āt al-Ṭūsī*, fol. 62b, Navā'ī (ed.), *Shāh Ismā`īl Ṣafavī*, p. 48. See Sachedina, *Islamic Messianism*, p. 103.

172 `Abd al-Ḥusain al-Ṭūsī, *Munsha'āt al-Ṭūsī*, fol. 63a, Navā'ī (ed.), *Shāh Ismā`īl Ṣafavī*, p. 48.

173 `Abd al-Ḥusain al-Ṭūsī, *Munsha'āt al-Ṭūsī*, fol. 63b, Navā'ī (ed.), *Shāh Ismā`īl Ṣafavī*, p. 49.

174 `Abd al-Ḥusain al-Ṭūsī, *Munsha'āt al-Ṭūsī*, fol. 63b. It should be noted that Navā'ī reads *na-farmāyand* in the manuscript as *namāyad,* which renders an entirely different meaning. See Navā'ī (ed.), *Shāh Ismā`īl Ṣafavī*, p. 49.

175 Bashir, *Messianic Hopes and Mystical Visions*, pp. 72–74.

176 See the detailed presentation of how these Sufi groups profiled their exegesis, belief systems, and orthopraxy in Gramlich, *Die schiitischen derwischorden persiens*, vol. 2.

177 `Abdī Beg Shīrāzī, *Takmilat al-akhbār*, p. 47.

178 Masashi Haneda, "La famille Khūzānī d'Isfahan (15e–17e siècles)," *Studia Iranica*, vol. 18 (1989), pp. 82–83.

179 Aubin, "Sāh Ismā`īl et les notables de l'Iraq persan," p. 67.

180 Būdāq Munshī, *Javāhir al-akhbār*, p. 140.

181 Khvāndamīr, *Ḥabīb al-siyar*, vol. 4, p. 501.

182 Khvāndamīr, *Ḥabīb al-siyar*, vol. 4, p. 500; Qāḍī Aḥmad, *Khulāṣat al-tavārīkh*, vol. 1, p. 81; `Abdī Beg Shīrāzī, *Takmilat al-akhbār*, p. 48n.

183 Qāḍī Aḥmad, *Khulāṣat al-tavārīkh*, vol. 1, p. 100.

184 Khūrshāh ibn Qubād, *Tārīkh-i īlchī-yi Niẓāmshāh*, p. 62.

185 Khvāndamīr, *Ḥabīb al-siyar,* vol. 4, p. 540; Khūrshāh ibn Qubād, *Tārīkh-i īlchī-yi Niẓāmshāh*, p. 56.

186 Ḥasan Beg Rūmlū, *Aḥsan al-tavārīkh*, vol. 1, p. 72.

187 Aubin, "L'avènement des Safavides reconsidéré," p. 92.

188 Khūrshāh ibn Qubād, *Tārīkh-i īlchī-yi Niẓāmshāh*, p. 81; Qāḍī Aḥmad, *Khulāṣat al-tavārīkh*, p. 73.

189 `Abdī Beg Shīrāzī, *Takmilat al-akhbār*, p. 38.

190 Qāḍī Aḥmad, *Khulāṣat al-tavārīkh*, vol. 1, p. 73.

191 Newman, *Safavid Iran*, p. 19.

192 Discussed in the introduction, documents from 914/1508 and 918/1512 have a seal showing Ismā`īl's attempt to connect himself to the Imamate.

193 Elements of Ismā`īl's letter to Muḥammad Shībānī Khān in 914/1508 portray the shah as a descendant of the Imamate. See `Abd al-Ḥusain al-Ṭūsī, *Munsha'āt al-Ṭūsī*, ff.60b-65b. Three years later, Ismā`īl sent an embassy to the Mamlūk, which presented, among other things, a genealogy listing Ismā`īl as the inheritor of the Imamate.

194 Andrew Newman has suggested that elite and plebeian alike expressed only "a cursory interest" in formal Twelver Shi`ism. See Newman, *Safavid Iran*, p. 24. In a recent review essay, David Morgan explored the possibility that Shāh Ismā`īl downplayed his Twelver Shi`ite convictions—in effect, adopted *taqiyya*—to secure the continued support of the Qizilbāsh. See David Morgan, "Rethinking Safavid Shi`ism," in *The Heritage of Sufism*, vol. 3, eds. L. Lewisohn and D. Morgon (Oxford: 1999), pp. 25–26.

195 Ḥasan Beg Rūmlū, *Aḥsan al-tavārīkh*, p. 27.

196 Lentz and Lowry, *Timur and the Princely Vision*, Maria E. Subtelny, "The Timurid Legacy: A Reaffirmation and a Reassessment," *Cahiers d'Asie Centrale*, vols. 3–4 (1997), pp. 9–19; Losensky, *Welcoming Fighani*, p. 135; Stephen Dale, "The Legacy of the Timurids," *Journal of the Royal Asiatic Society*, vol. 8 (1998), No. 1, pp. 43–58.

197 Maria E. Subtelny, "`Alī Shīr Navā'ī: *Bakhshī* and *Beg*," *Harvard Ukranian Studies*, vol. 3–4 (1979–80), p. 797.

198 He compiled his own collection (*muraqqa`*) of correspondence between himself and various personalities in the Naqshbandiyya movement, most notably Khvājah `Ubaid Allāh Aḥrār. This has recently been published by Jo-Ann Gross and Asom Urunbaev. See Jo-Ann Gross and Asom Urunbaev, *The Letters of Khwāja `Ubayd Allāh Aḥrār and his Associates* (Leiden: 2002).

199 Khvāndamīr, *Ḥabīb al-siyar*, vol. 1, p. 513.

200 Aubin, "Revolution Chiite," p. 16; Röhrborn, *Provinzen und Zentralgewalt Persiens*, p. 99.

201 Aubin, "Revolution Chiite," p. 16.

202 Khvāndamīr, *Ḥabīb al-siyar*, vol. 4, p. 513.

203 Khūrshāh ibn Qubād, *Tārīkh-i īlchī-yi Niẓāmshāh*, p. 48.

204 There is, in fact, a letter from Sulṭān-Ḥusain Bāiqarā to Shāh Qāsim Nūrbakhsh in `Abd al-Ḥusain Navā'ī's edited work, *Asnād va mukātibāt-i tārīkhī-yi Īrān*, pp. 403–4.

205 Khūrshāh ibn Qubād mentions Sayyid Ja`far and Shāh Qalandar (possibly Shāh Qāsim?) as *a`ayān-i shahr-i Damaghān*. Khūrshāh ibn Qubād, *Tārīkh-i īlchī-yi Niẓāmshāhī*, p. 48; Muḥammad Yūsuf Vālih, *Khuld-i barīn*, p. 321

206 Khvāndamīr, *Ḥabīb al-siyar*, vol. 4, p.333, p. 584, p. 613–14.
207 Khvāndamīr, *Ḥabīb al-siyar*, vol. 4, p. 615.
208 Iskander Beg Munshī, *History of Shah `Abbas the Great*, vol. 1, pp. 242–43; for Persian, *Tārīkh-i `ālam-ārā-yi `Abbāsī*, vol. 1, p. 152.
209 Vilāyatī, *Tārīkh-i ravābiṭ-i khārijī-yi Īrān*, p. 66.
210 Khvāndamīr, *Ḥabīb al-siyar*, vol. 4, p. 549.
211 There are in fact numerous terms for the chancellery that appear in medieval Islamic history, including *dār al-inshā*, *dīvān al-rasā'il*, and *dīvān al-rasā'il wa al-sirr*. For the sake of consistency and simplicity, I use *dīvān-i inshā* and *dār-i inshā* interchangeably to refer to that group of individuals associated with the central administration who were responsible for drafting internal documents and foreign correspondence.
212 C. E. Bosworth, "Dīvān II. Government Office," *Encyclopedia Iranica*, ed. E. Yarshater, vol. 7, p. 436. See also Beatrice Manz's comments on the *dīvān* in her recent work on the Timurids, *Power, Politics and Religion in Timurid Iran* (Cambridge: 2007), pp. 79–83.
213 Shiro Ando, *Timuridische Emire nach dem Mu`izz al-ansāb: Untersuchung zur Stammesaristokratie Zentralasiens im 14. um 15. Jahrhundert* (Berlin: 1992), pp. 219–48.
214 Bosworth, "Dīvān II. Government Office," p. 435.
215 Woods, *The Aqquyunlu*, p. 17.
216 Sixteenth-century studies of the *dīvān-i a`lā* have not abounded as a rule in Safavid scholarship. See Savory's work on administration: "The Principal Offices of the Ṣafawid State During the Reign of Ismā`īl I," and "The Principal Offices of the Safawid State During the Reign of Tahmāsp I." For definitions and etymologies of particular terms, see the pertinent volume of Doerfer, *Turkische und mongolische Elemente im Neupersischen: Unter besonderer Berücksightigung Alterer neupersischer Geschichtsquellen, vor allem der Mongolen- und Timüriden-zeit.* For detailed analyses of Āq Qoyūnlū administrative structure, see Minorsky's seminal article "A Civil and Military Review," pp. 141–78, and Woods, *The Aqquyunlu*, pp. 15–17.
217 Another Iṣfahānī, Niẓām al-Dīn Aḥmad Beg, would be named chief *vazīr* for all of Khurāsān after 1512.See Khvāndamīr, *Ḥabīb al-siyar*, vol. 4, p. 588.
218 `Abd al-Ḥusain al-Ṭūsī, *Munsha'āt al-Ṭūsī*, ff. 8b–9a.
219 This *ṭughrā* appears in colour reproduction of a 1504 *farmān* in Priscilla Soucek, "Calligraphy in the Safavid Period 1501–1576," in *Hunt for Paradise: Court Arts of Safavid Iran, 1501–1576*, eds. J. Thompson and S. Canby (Milan: 2003), p. 48.
220 Christoph Werner noted recently (London, 2006) that the Kukajī family was in fact one of the competing Sufi groups in fourteenth-century Āzarbāijān before losing their mystical inclinations and turning to conventional political service. Christoph Werner, "A Rival to the Safavids? Sheikh Muhammad Kujuji, Mystic, Poet, and Politician of the Fourteenth Century," paper presented at Sixth Biennial of Iranian Studies, London, August, 2006.
221 Sām Mīrzā, *Tazkirah-yi tuḥfah-yi Sāmī*, p. 90; Roger Savory, "The Principal Offices of the Ṣafawid State During the Reign of Ismā`īl I (907–30/1501–24)," *Bulletin of the School of Oriental and African Studies*, vol. 23 (1960), p. 102.
222 Sām Mīrzā, *Tazkirah-yi tuḥfah-yi Sāmī*, p. 91; Mahdī Bayānī, *Aḥvāl va ās̱ār-i khūshnivīsān*, vol. 4 (Tehran: 1966), pp. 384–86.
223 Sām Mīrzā, *Tazkirah-yi tuḥfah-yi Sāmī*, p.134.
224 Iskander Beg Munshī, *History of Shah `Abbas the Great*, vol. 1, p. 259; for Persian, see *Tārīkh-i `ālam-ārā-yi `Abbāsī*, vol. 1, p. 165.
225 Khvāndamīr, *Ḥabīb al-siyar*, vol. 4, p. 617.
226 Khvāndamīr, *Ḥabīb al-siyar*, vol. 4, p. 616.

227 Khvāndamīr, *Ḥabīb al-siyar*, vol. 4, p. 617.
228 Two good *MSS* are available of Khvāndamīr's *Nāmah-yi nāmī.* See Paris, Bibliothèque Nationale, supplément persan, no. 1842, and London, British Library, I. O. Islamic, no. 2711.
229 Khvāndamīr writes in his preface that the *Nāmah-yi nāmī* did not consist of letters composed entirely by him but in fact was a collection of contemporaries' writings. Khvāndamīr, *Nāmah-yi nāmī*, Ms., Paris, fol. 4b.
230 Sām Mīrzā, *Tazkirah-yi tuḥfah-yi Sāmī*, p. 108.
231 Qāḍī Aḥmad, *Khulāṣat al-tavārīkh*, vol. 1, p. 156.
232 Qāḍī Aḥmad, *Khulāṣat al-tavārīkh*, vol. 1, pp. 262–63.
233 `Alī ibn Ḥasan Khūshmardān (Sayyid Bābā), *Ta`līm al-khuṭūṭ*, ed. Aḥsan Allāh Shukr Allāh Ṭalāqānī, *Bahāristān nāmah*, vol. 3 (2003), No. 2, pp. 317–23. See also Bayānī, *Aḥvāl va āṣār-i khūshnivīsān,* p. 455; Iraj Afshar, "Risālah-yi khaṭṭ-i Khalīl Tabrīzī," in *Pand-o Sokhan: mélanges offerts à Charles-Henri de Fouchécour*, eds. C. Balay, C. Kappler, Z. Vesel (Paris: 1995), p. 326. An extract of *Adab-i khaṭṭ* is available in *Risālah-yi khaṭṭ-i Majnūn Rafīqī Harāvī*, ed. Māyil-i Herāvī (Kabul: 1976), pp. 209–36. Roxburgh titles this work as *Rasm al-khaṭṭ*, David Roxburgh, *Prefacing the Image: The Writing of Art History in Sixteenth-Century Iran* (Leiden: 2001), p. 147.
234 A partial transcription and German translation is available in Gottfried Hermann, "Das historische Gehalt des 'Nāma-yi nāmī' von Ḫāndamīr," unpublished Ph.D. dissertation, 2 vols. (Göttingen: 1968).
235 Quinn, *Historical Writing During the Reign of Shah `Abbas*, p. 16.
236 This speculation is put forward by `Abd al-Ḥusain Navā'ī in the preface to this letter. `Abd al-Ḥusain Navā'ī (ed.), Shāh *Ismā`īl Ṣafavī*, p. 336.
237 Khvāndamīr, *Nāmah-yi nāmī*, fol. 17b, Navā'ī (ed.), *Shāh Ismā`īl Ṣafavī*, p. 339.
238 Khvāndamīr, *Nāmah-yi nāmī*, fol. 18a. Navā'ī (ed.), *Shāh Ismā`īl Ṣafavī*, p. 340.
239 Khvāndamīr, *Nāmah-yi nāmī*, fol. 18b, Navā'ī (ed.), *Shāh Ismā`īl Ṣafavī*, p. 340.
240 Khvāndamīr, *Nāmah-yi nāmī*, fol. 19a, Navā'ī (ed.), *Shāh Ismā`īl Ṣafavī*, p. 341.
241 Khvāndamīr, *Nāmah-yi nāmī*, ff. 19b–20a. Navā'ī (ed.), *Shāh Ismā`īl Ṣafavī*, pp. 342–43.
242 Islam, *A Calendar of Documents on Indo-Persian Relations*, vol. 1, p. 61.
243 Khvāndamīr, *Nāmah-yi nāmī*, fol. 20a, Navā'ī (ed.), *Shāh Ismā`īl Ṣafavī*, p. 383.
244 Khvāndamīr, *Nāmah-yi nāmī*, fol. 20b, Navā'ī (ed.), *Shāh Ismā`īl Ṣafavī*, p. 383.
245 Images from the Bahrām Mīrzā album, most notably from the *Mi`rāj nāmah*, depict several scenes of this *sidrah*. Roxburgh, *Prefacing the Image*, pp. 201–3.
246 Khvāndamīr, *Nāmah-yi nāmī*, fol. 20b; Navā'ī (ed.), *Shāh Ismā`īl Ṣafavī*, p. 384.
247 Letters from Sulṭān-Ḥusain Bāiqarā to Ismā`īl and Jahānshāh Qarā Qoyūnlū make mention of this notion of *millat va mulk*. Roemer, fol. 30a, Isfizārī, *Manshā al-inshā*, p. 88.
248 Quinn, *Historical Writing During the Reign of Shah `Abbas*, p. 78.
249 See Ann K. S. Lambton, "*Quis Custodiet Custodes?*: Some Reflections on the Persian Theory of Government (Part 1)," *Studia Islamica*, vol. 5 (1955), pp. 125–48.
250 Marlow, *Hierarchy and Egalitarianism in Islamic Thought*, pp. 118–28.
251 Ghiyāṣ al-Dīn ibn Humām al-Dīn Khvāndamīr, *Makārim al-akhlāq*, ed. Muḥammad Akbar `Ashīq (Tehran: 1999), pp. 81–86.
252 Khvāndamīr, *Makārim al-akhlāq*, p. 83.
253 Qāḍī Aḥmad, *Khulāṣat al-tavārīkh*, vol. 1, p. 142.
254 Jean-Louis Bacqué-Grammont, *Les Ottomans, les Safavides, et leurs voisins* (Leiden: 1987), p. 86.
255 Aubin, "L'avènement des Safavides reconsidéré," p. 100.
256 Farīdūn Beg, *Munsha'āt al-salāṭīn*, vol. 1, p. 413; Navā'ī (ed.), *Shāh Ismā`īl Ṣafavī*,

p. 235.

257 See Fatma Müge Göcek, "The Social Construction of an Empire: Ottoman State Under Suleyman the Magnificent," in *Suleyman the Second and His Time*, eds. H. Inalcik and C. Kafadar (Istanbul: 1993), pp. 93–108.

258 Farīdūn Beg, *Munsha'āt al-salāṭīn*, vol. 1, p. 413, Navā'ī (ed.), *Shāh Ismā`īl Ṣafavī*, p. 235.

259 Mitchell, "Safavid Imperial *Tarassul* and the Persian *Inshā'* Tradition," pp. 184–85.

260 Farīdūn Beg, *Munsha'āt al-salāṭīn*, vol. 1, p. 413; Navā'ī (ed.), *Shāh Ismā`īl Ṣafavī*, p. 235.

261 Meisami, *Structure and Meaning in Medieval Arabic and Persian Poetry*, p. 296.

262 Farīdūn Beg, *Munsha'āt al-salāṭīn*, vol. 1, p. 413; Navā'ī (ed.), *Shāh Ismā`īl Ṣafavī*, p. 236.

263 Farīdūn Beg, *Munsha'āt al-salāṭīn*, vol. 1, p. 413; Navā'ī (ed.), *Shāh Ismā`īl Ṣafavī*, p. 236.

264 Meisami, *Structure and Meaning in Medieval Arabic and Persian Poetry*, p. 253.

265 Farīdūn Beg, *Munsha'āt al-salāṭīn*, vol. 1, p. 413; Navā'ī (ed.), *Shāh Ismā`īl Ṣafavī*, p. 236.

266 *ḥamāyat-i ḥudūd-i Islām makhzūn khazīnah-yi niyat va maknūn-i ganchīnah-yi ṭuvait būd.* Farīdūn Beg, *Munsha'āt al-salāṭīn*, vol. 1, p. 414; Navā'ī (ed.), *Shāh Ismā`īl Ṣafavī*, p. 237.

267 Farīdūn Beg, *Munsha'āt al-salāṭīn*, vol. 1, p. 414; Navā'ī (ed.), *Shāh Ismā`īl Ṣafavī*, p. 238.

268 Jean-Louis Bacqué-Grammont, "Études sur blocus de commerce iranien par Selim Ier," *Turcica*, vol. 6 (1975), pp. 68–88.

269 Farīdūn Beg, *Munsha'āt al-salāṭīn*, vol. 1, p. 414; Navā'ī (ed.), *Shāh Ismā`īl Ṣafavī*, p. 238.

270 Bacqué-Grammont, *Les Ottomans, les Safavides, et leurs voisins*, pp. 337–42.

271 The epilogue of this letter refers to Tāj al-Dīn Ḥusain Chalabī as one of the "old-school" *khalīfas* (*az khulafā mu`timdadān-i qadīm īn khāndān ast*), suggesting his status as a senior mystical personality. Tāj al-Dīn Ḥasan Chalabī appears to be the first career diplomatic serving the Safavid dynasty since he had been despatched by Dūrmīsh Khān Shāmlū to Kābul in the summer of 928/1522 to reaffirm an earlier treaty with Bābur. Khvāndamīr, *Ḥabīb al-siyar*, vol. 4, p. 591.

272 "May God most high perpetuate the shadow of his rule among kings, assist his soldiers and forces, exterminate [any] remnants of the enemies of [Islam], eradicate those who practice polytheism, destroy the pulpits of infidelity and disbelievers, and may he grant victory to the military forces of Islam and Muslim soldiers until [that] Day when He will reward the most worthy of men." Farīdūn Beg, *Munsha'āt al-salāṭīn*, vol. 1, pp. 525–26; Navā'ī (ed.), *Shāh Ismā`īl Ṣafavī*, p. 329.

273 Farīdūn Beg, *Munsha'āt al-salāṭīn*, vol. 1, p. 526; Navā'ī (ed.), *Shāh Ismā`īl Ṣafavī*, p. 330.

274 Farīdūn Beg, *Munsha'āt al-salāṭīn*, vol. 1, p. 525; Navā'ī (ed.), *Shāh Ismā`īl Ṣafavī*, p. 329.

275 Farīdūn Beg, *Munsha'āt al-salāṭīn*, vol. 1, p. 525; Navā'ī (ed.), *Shāh Ismā`īl Ṣafavī*, p. 329.

276 Farīdūn Beg, *Munsha'āt al-salāṭīn*, vol. 1, p. 526; Navā'ī (ed.), *Shāh Ismā`īl Ṣafavī*, p. 330. The hadith is number 589, from Book 93 (*tauḥīd*) of Bukhārī, *Ṣaḥīḥ*, vol. 9.

277 Farīdūn Beg, *Munsha'āt al-salāṭīn*, vol. 1, p. 526; Navā'ī (ed.), *Shāh Ismā`īl Ṣafavī*, p. 330.

278 Farīdūn Beg, *Munsha'āt al-salāṭīn*, vol. 1, p. 526; Navā'ī (ed.), *Shāh Ismā`īl Ṣafavī*, p. 330.

279 Lambton, *Continuity and Change in Medieval Persia*, pp. 225–29. See also my forthcoming entry on Shāh Ṭahmāsp for the *Encyclopedia Iranica.*

280 For details of this transition, see Maria Szuppe, *Entre Timourides, Uzbeks et Safavides: Questions d'histoire politique et sociale de Hérat dans la première moitié du XVIe siècle* (Paris: 1992).

281 A series of Safavid princes grew up in Herāt in the sixteenth century—Ṭahmāsp, Sām Mīrzā, Ibrāhīm Mīrzā, Muḥammad Khudābanda, and `Abbās.

282 Martin Dickson, *The Duel for Khurasan: Shāh Ṭahmāsp and the Özbeks*, unpublished Ph.D. dissertation, Princeton University, 1958, p. 12.

283 Khūrshāh ibn Qubād, *Tārīkh-i īlchī-yi Niẓāmshāh*, p. 87; Būdāq Munshī, *Javāhir al-akhbār*, p. 147.

284 Babayan, "The Safavid Synthesis," p. 141.

285 Dickson, *Shāh Ṭahmāsp and the Uzbeks*, p. 13.

286 Shāh Ṭahmāsp, *Tazkirah-yi Shāh Ṭahmāsp*, p. 579; Roemer, *Persien auf dem Weg*, p. 275; Savory, *Iran Under the Safavids*, p. 52.

287 Savory, *Iran Under the Safavids*, p. 53.

288 Savory, *Iran Under the Safavids*, p. 54.

289 Shāh Ṭahmāsp, *Tazkirah-yi Shāh Ṭahmāsp*, p. 586; Savory, *Iran Under the Safavids*, p. 55.

290 The exact title of Qāḍī-yi Jahān's office is unclear. Khūrshāh ibn Qubād describes him as the *vakīl*. Khūrshāh ibn Qubād, *Tārīkh-i īlchī-yi Niẓāmshāh*, p. 85. Qāḍī Aḥmad used *vazīr-i dīvān-i a`lā*, while Ṭahmāsp used *vazīr* and *ṣāḥib dīvānī*. Qāḍī Aḥmad, *Khulāṣat al-tavārīkh*, vol. 1, p. 156; Shāh Ṭahmāsp, *Tazkirah-yi Shāh Ṭahmāsp*, p. 576. Muḥammad Yūsuf Vālih used *nāẓir-i dīvān-i a`lā*. Muḥammad Yūsuf Vālih, *Khuld-i barīn*, p. 226.

291 Michele Membré, *Mission to the Lord Sophy of Persia (1539–1542)*, ed. and trans. A. H. Morton (London: 1993), p. 74; Khūrshāh ibn Qubād, *Tārīkh-i īlchī-yi Niẓāmshāh*, p. 85.

292 Qāḍī Aḥmad, *Khulāṣat al-tavārīkh*, vol. 1, p. 254.

293 Qāḍī Ḍiyā al-Dīn Nūr Allāh Sāvajī had served as Ismā`īl's ambassador to Muḥammad Shībānī Khān in 916/1510, while his brother Qāḍī Nūr al-Dīn `Abd al-Raḥmān was the *qāḍī al-quḍāt* for Tabrīz until 929/1523. Moreover, the *qāḍī* for Rayy, Qāḍī Muḥammad, was a distant Sāvajīī cousin. It would appear that the Sāvajī family enjoyed prominence in the Khurāsānī provinces. Khvājah Karīm al-Dīn Ḥabīb Allāh Sāvajī had served as vizier to Durmīsh Khān in Herāt from 928-32/1522–26. Amīr Qavām al-Dīn Ja`far Sāvajī had likewise served as a Khurāsānī vizier, specifically for the city of Astarābād and its governor, Zain al-Dīn Sulṭān Shāmlū.

294 Qāḍī Aḥmad, *Khulāṣat al-tavārīkh*, vol. 1, p.160; Shāh Ṭahmāsp, *Tazkirah-yi Shāh Ṭahmāsp*, p. 578; Ḥasan Beg Rūmlū, *Aḥsan al-tavārīkh*, vol. 1, p.189.

295 Būdāq Munshī, *Javāhir al-akhbār*, p. 150.

296 Roger Savory, "The Principal Offices of the Ṣafawid State During the Reign of Ṭahmāsp (930–84/1524–76)," *Bulletin of the School of Oriental and African Studies*, vol. 24 (1961), p. 74.

297 Qāḍī Aḥmad, *Khulāṣat al-tavārīkh*, vol. 1, p. 218.

298 Qāḍī Aḥmad, *Khulāṣat al-tavārīkh*, vol. 1, p. 218; and Ḥasan Beg Rūmlū, *Aḥsan al-tavārīkh*, vol. 1, p. 244.

299 Khūrshāh ibn Qubād, *Tārīkh-i īlchī-yi Niẓāmshāh*, p. 125. He was ultimately released and allowed to retire in his home city of Iṣfahān. Savory, "The Principal Offices of the Ṣafawid State During the Reign of Ṭahmāsp I," p. 74.

300 Qāḍī Aḥmad, *Khulāṣat al-tavārīkh*, vol. 1, pp. 186–87.

301 For details of this monumental battle, see Ghaffārī Fard, *Ravābiṭ-i Ṣafaviyya va Uzbekān*, pp. 163–69, or Dickson, *Shah Tahmasb*, pp. 127–42.

302 Qāḍī Aḥmad, *Khulāṣat al-tavārīkh*, vol. 1, p. 186.
303 Qāḍī Aḥmad, *Khulāṣat al-tavārīkh*, vol. 1, p. 187.
304 Qāḍī Aḥmad, *Khulāṣat al-tavārīkh*, vol. 1, p. 187.
305 Qāḍī Aḥmad, *Khulāṣat al-tavārīkh*, vol. 1, p. 187.
306 Qāḍī Aḥmad, *Khulāṣat al-tavārīkh*, vol. 1, p. 188.
307 Qāḍī Aḥmad, *Khulāṣat al-tavārīkh*, vol. 1, p. 206.
308 Qāḍī Aḥmad, *Khulāṣat al-tavārīkh*, vol. 1, pp. 206–8.
309 *fasād bā zanān va farzandān-i muslimānān kardan va ān jamā`at-rā ghārat va asīr kardan va dar zīr-fīn va shikanjah kashtan tajvīz kardah-and.* Qāḍī Aḥmad, *Khulāṣat al-tavārīkh*, vol. 1, p. 206.
310 Qāḍī Aḥmad, *Khulāṣat al-tavārīkh*, vol. 1, p. 206.
311 Qāḍī Aḥmad, *Khulāṣat al-tavārīkh*, vol. 1, p. 207.
312 Robert Hillenbrand, "The Iconography of the Shah-nama-yi Shahi," in *Safavid Persia: The History and Politics of an Islamic Society*, ed. C. Melville (London: 1996), p. 63.
313 Qāḍī Aḥmad, *Khulāṣat al-tavārīkh*, vol. 1, p. 208.
314 M. B. Dickson, and S. C. Welch, *The Houghton Shahnameh*, 2 vols. (London: 1981) and S. C. Welch, *A King's Book of Kings. The Shah-Nameh of Shah Tahmasp* (London: 1972).
315 Renard, *Islam and the Heroic Image*, pp. 56–57.
316 Deborah Tor, "Toward A Revised Understanding of the `Ayyār Phenomenon," in *Iran: questions et conaissances (Actes du IVe congrès Européen des études Iraniennes organisé par la Societas Iranologica Europaea, Paris, 6–10 Septembre 1999)*, vol. 2 (Périodes médiévale et moderne) (Paris: 2002), pp. 231–54; William Hanaway, "`Ayyār II. `Ayyār in Persian Sources," *Encyclopedia Iranica*, vol. 1, pp. 159–63; Calmard, "Popular Literature Under the Safavids," p. 332.
317 William Hanaway, "Formal Elements in the Persian Popular Romances," *Review of National Literatures*, vol. 2 (1971), p. 151.
318 As Kai Kāvūs remonstrated: "Ensure that you will never attempt to avenge the past or act treacherously, for treachery is not consistent with gallantry and nobility" (*khiyānat kardan dar sharṭ-i javānmardī nīst*) Kai Kāvūs, *Guzīdah-yi Qābūs nāmah*, p. 326. See a slightly variant English translation in Kai Kāvūs, *A Mirror for Princes*, p. 258.
319 Jerome Clinton, "The Uses of Guile in the *Shahnama*," *Iranian Studies*, vol. 32 (1999), No. 2, pp. 223–30.
320 Hanaway, "Formal Elements in the Persian Popular Romances," p. 150.
321 See section on "the kingship of Khusrau Parvīz" in Abū al-Qāsim Firdausī, *Shāh nāmah*, Sa`īd Ḥamīdiyān (Tehran: 2002), p. 1288.
322 Welch, *A King's Book of Kings*, pp. 196–97.
323 *matānat-i i`tiqād va bahādurī va dar tashayyu` va ṣūfī-garī kih mashūr būd.* Qāḍī Aḥmad, *Khulāṣat al-tavārīkh*, vol. 1, p. 208.
324 Qāḍī Aḥmad, *Khulāṣat al-tavārīkh*, vol. 1, p. 208.
325 Qāḍī Aḥmad, *Khulāṣat al-tavārīkh*, vol. 1, p. 208.
326 Qāḍī Aḥmad, *Khulāṣat al-tavārīkh*, vol. 1, p. 210.
327 Qāḍī Aḥmad, *Khulāṣat al-tavārīkh*, vol. 1, p. 210.
328 Qāḍī Aḥmad, *Khulāṣat al-tavārīkh*, vol. 1, p. 210.
329 Qāḍī Aḥmad, *Khulāṣat al-tavārīkh*, vol. 1, p. 210.
330 Qāḍī Aḥmad, *Khulāṣat al-tavārīkh*, vol. 1, p. 210.

Chapter Two

1 Qāḍī Aḥmad, *Khulāṣat al-tavārīkh*, vol. 1, p. 254.
2 "...ob sich seine Staatsgründung, deren Grenze gegenüber den Osmanen der

Oberlauf des Euphrats bildete, zu einem iranischen Reich mit einem türkischen Galcis im Westen oder zu einem türkischen mit einem iranischen Vorfeld im Osten entwickeln werde." Roemer, *Persien auf dem Weg*, p. 267.

3 Minorsky, *Tadhkirat al-mulūk*, pp. 189–95.

4 Heinz Halm, *Die Schia* (Darmstadt: 1988), p. 109.

5 Halm, *Die Schia*, p. 109. See also Michel Mazzaoui, "A 'New' Edition of the Safvat al-safa," *History and Historiography of Post-Mongol Central Asia and the Middle East. Studies in Honor of John E. Woods*, eds. J. Pfeiffer and S. Quinn (Wiesbaden: 2006), pp. 303–10.

6 Halm, *Die Schia*, p. 109.

7 Khūrshāh ibn Qubād, *Tārīkh-i īlchī-yi Niẓāmshāh*, p. 108.

8 Said Amir Arjomand, "Two Decrees of Shāh Ṭahmāsp Concerning Statecraft and the Authority of Shaykh `Alī al-Karakī," *Authority and Political Culture in Shi`ism*, ed. S. A. Arjomand (Albany: 1988), p. 250.

9 Babayan, *Mystics, Monarchs, and Messiahs*, p. 312.

10 Wilferd Madelung, "al-Karakī," *EI²*, vol. 4, p. 610. See also Rasūl Ja`fariyān, "Astarābād dar qarn-i nukhast-i ḥukūmat-i Ṣafavī," p. 14. This was an offprint circulated by Dr. Ja`fariyān at the Fourth Roundtable of Safavid Studies in Bamberg in July 2003.

11 For a good summary of these immigrant clerics, see Appendix I, Abisaab, *Converting Persia*, p. 147.

12 Ḥasan Beg Rūmlū, *Aḥsan al-tavārīkh*, vol. 1, p. 136; Iskander Beg Munshī, *History of Shah `Abbas the Great*, vol. 1, pp. 229–30; for Persian, see *Tārīkh-i `ālam-ārā-yi `Abbāsī*, vol. 1, pp. 143–44.

13 Abisaab, *Converting Persia*, p. 14.

14 The juxtaposition of Uṣūlī and Akhbārī camps was formalized by Said Arjomand and later reiterated by Leonard Lewisohn. See Arjomand, *The Shadow of God and the Hidden Imam*, pp. 132–37; Leonard Lewisohn, "Sufism and the School of Iṣfahān: *Taṣawwuf* and *`Irfān* in Late Safavid Iran (`Abd al-Razzāq Lāhījī and Fayḍ-i Kāshānī on the Relation of *Taṣawwuf*, *Ḥikmat* and *`Irfān*)," in *The Heritage of Sufism vol. III: Late Classical Persianate Sufism (1501–1750) The Safavid & Mughal Period*, eds. L. Lewisohn and D. Morgan (London: 1999), pp. 79–80. Likewise, John Cooper in "Some Observations on the Religious Intellectual Milieu of Safawid Persia," pp. 152–53. Andrew Newman has countered much of Arjomand's arguments in "The Role of the Sādāt in Safavid Iran: Confrontation or Accommodation?" in *Oriente Moderno*, vol. 18 (1999), pp. 577–96.

15 Newman, "The Myth of the Clerical Migration to Safavid Iran: Arab Shiite Opposition to `Alī al-Karakī and Safawid Shiism," *Die Welt des Islams*, vol. 33 (1993), no. 1, p. 79.

16 Abisaab, *Converting Persia*, p. 27.

17 Newman, "The Myth of Clerical Migration to Ṣafawid Iran," p. 83.

18 Andrew Newman, "Fayd al-Kashani and the Rejection of the Clergy/State Alliance: Friday Prayer as Politics in the Safavid Period," *The Most Learned of the Shi`a: The Institution of the* Marja` Taqlid, ed. L. S. Walbridge (New York: 2001), pp. 34–52.

19 Newman, "The Myth of Clerical Migration to Ṣafawid Iran," p. 85; Halm, *Die Schia*, p. 112. See also Madelung, "Al-Karakī," p. 610.

20 Rasūl Ja`fariyān, *Dīn va siyāsat dar daurah-yi Ṣafavī* (Tehran: 1991), pp. 191–93.

21 Heinz Halm describes how Sharīf al-Ṭāhir al-Mūsavī, a descendant of the seventh Imām, Mūsā, served as the superintendent of the sayyid community in tenth century Būyid Baghdad. Part of Sharīf al-Ṭāhir's responsibilities was to collect taxes due to the descendants of the Prophet. His son, Sharīf al-Murtaḍā (d. 435/1044), in fact, wrote a treatise defending such Shi`ite secular participation in "The Problem of

Participating in the Government." Halm, *Shi`a Islam*, p. 108, p. 96. See also W. Madelung, "A Treatise of the Sharīf al-Murtaḍā on the Legality of Working for the Government (*Mas'ala fī'l-`ammal ma`a al-Sulṭān*)," *Bulletin of the School of Oriental and African Studies*, vol. 6 (1979), pp. 18–31.

22 Shāh Ṭahmāsp, *Tazkirah-yi Shāh Ṭahmāsp*, p. 584.

23 Shāh Ṭahmāsp, *Tazkirah-yi Shāh Ṭahmāsp*, p. 585.

24 Abisaab, *Converting Persia*, p. 18.

25 Rasūl Ja`fariyān has provided a list of the various works on prayer (*namāz*) that were produced by al-Karakī and contemporaries. See Ja`fariyān, *Dīn va siyāsat dar daurah-yi Ṣafavī*, pp. 126–45.

26 Khūrshāh ibn Qubād, *Tārīkh-i īlchī-yi Niẓāmshāh*, p. 108.

27 Khūrshāh ibn Qubād, *Tārīkh-i īlchī-yi Niẓāmshāh*, pp. 111–12; Halm, *Die Schia*, p. 112; Abisaab, *Converting Persia*, p. 18.

28 "Heir to the sciences of the Lord of the Messengers, Protector of the Religion of the Commander of the Faithful, the *qiblah* of the pious faithful, the Exemplar of expert *`ulamā*, the Proof of Islam (*ḥujjat al-islām*) and of the Muslims who directs the people onto the clear path, Erector of the banners of the indelible Law who is obeyed by the great governors of the times, and Guide (*muqtadā*) of all people of the time, the Clarifier of the permissible and the forbidden, the Deputy of the Imam (*nā'ib al-imām*)—peace be upon him—who has clarified the difficulties of the rules of the community of believers and the rightful laws; may he not come to an end, like his elevated victorious namesake, `Alī." Arjomand, "Two Decrees of Shāh Ṭahmāsp Concerning Statecraft and the Authority of Shaykh `Alī al-Karakī," pp. 250–62.

29 Newman, "The Myth of Clerical Migration to Ṣafawid Iran," p. 101; Halm, *Shi`a Islam*, p. 108.

30 Aspects of al-Karakī's legal deliberations can be found in `Alī ibn `Abd al-`Alī al-Karakī (trans. Muḥammad Bāqir Anṣārī and `Alī Qulī Qarā'ī), "Ṭarīq Istinbāṭ al-Aḥkām (The Method of Derivation of the Rules of the Sharī`ah," *al-Tawḥīd*, vol. 2 (1985), no. 3, pp. 42–55.

31 Abisaab, *Converting Persia*, p. 28; Newman, "Fayd al-Kashani and the Rejection of the Clergy/State Alliance," p. 36.

32 Newman, "The Myth of Clerical Migration to Ṣafawid Iran," p. 101.

33 Navā'ī (ed.), *Shāh Ṭahmāsp Ṣafavī*, p. 513.

34 Babayan, *Mystics, Monarchs, and Messiahs*, pp. 319–21.

35 Newman, "The Myth of Clerical Migration to Ṣafawid Iran," p. 100, Abisaab, *Converting Persia*, p. 17. For a good discussion of al-Karakī's political reasoning, see Said Arjomand, "Conceptions of Authority and the Transition of Shi`ism from Sectarian to National Religion in Iran," *Culture and Memory in Medieval Islam: Essays in Honour of Wilferd Madelung*, eds. F. Daftary and J. Meri (London: 2003), pp. 393–94.

36 Babayan, "The Safavid Synthesis," p. 144.

37 Babayan, *Mystics, Monarchs, and Messiahs*, p. 321.

38 This letter originally appears in al-Ṭūsī's *Munsha'āt al-Ṭūsī*, ff. 194b–204a. An edited version appears in Navā'ī (ed.), *Shāh Ṭahmāsp Ṣafavī*, pp. 35–44.

39 Qāḍī Aḥmad, *Khulāṣat al-tavārīkh*, vol. 1, pp. 227–28.

40 `Abd al-Ḥusain al-Ṭūsī, *Munsha'āt al-Ṭūsī*, fol. 194b; Navā'ī (ed.), *Shāh Ṭahmāsp Ṣafavī*, p. 35.

41 `Abd al-Ḥusain al-Ṭūsī, *Munsha'āt al-Ṭūsī*, fol. 194b; Navā'ī (ed.), *Shāh Ṭahmāsp Ṣafavī*, p. 35.

42 `Abd al-Ḥusain al-Ṭūsī, *Munsha'āt al-Ṭūsī*, fol. 195a; Navā'ī (ed.), *Shāh Ṭahmāsp Ṣafavī*, p. 36.

43 `Abd al-Ḥusain al-Ṭūsī, *Munsha'āt al-Ṭūsī*, ff. 188b-194a; Navā'ī (ed.), *Shāh Ṭahmāsp Ṣafavī*, pp. 28–33.

44 `Abd al-Ḥusain al-Ṭūsī, *Munsha'āt al-Ṭūsī*, fol. 195a; Navā'ī (ed.), *Shāh Ṭahmāsp Ṣafavī*, p. 36.

45 Etan Kohlberg has dominated this particular field. See "Some Imāmī Shī`ī Views on the Ṣaḥāba," *Jersusalem Studies in Arabic and Islam*, vol. 5 (1984), pp. 143–75,"The Term 'Rāfiḍa' in Imāmī Shī`ī Usage," *Journal of the American Oriental Society*, vol. 99 (1976), pp. 1–9; "Imam and Community in the Pre-Ghayba Period," *Authority and Poltical Culture in Shī`ism*, ed. Said Amir Arjomand (New York: 1988), pp. 25–53; "Some Imāmī Shī`ī Interpretations of Umayyad History," *Studies on the First Century of Islamic Society*, ed. G. H. A. Juynboll (Illionois: 1982), pp. 145–49; "Description of the Corpus of Shī`ī Ḥadīth," *Arabic Literature to the End of the Umayyad Period*, eds. A. F. L. Beeston, T. M. Johnstone, R. B. Serjeant, and G. R. Smith (Cambridge: 1983), pp. 299–307. See also Meir M. Bar-Asher, *Scripture and Exegesis in Early Imami-Shi`ism* (Leiden: 1999), and Moojan Momen, *An Introduction to Shi`i Islam* (New Haven: 1985).

46 `Abd al-Jalīl Ibn Abī al-Ḥusain ibn Abī al-Faḍl al-Qazvīnī al-Rāzī, *Kitāb al-naqḍ*, ed. Sayyid Jalāl al-Dīn Muḥaddiṣ (Tehran: 1952).

47 *dar varṭah-yi kufr va jahālat-i sar-gardarān va dar ẓulmat-i shirk va ḍalālat ḥairān māndah.* `Abd al-Ḥusain al-Ṭūsī, *Munsha'āt al-Ṭūsī*, fol. 195b–96a; Navā'ī (ed.), *Shāh Ṭahmāsp Ṣafavī*, p. 37.

48 *Mathalu ahli baitī mathalu safīnati Nūḥin man rakibahā najā wa man takhallafa `anhā ghariqa.* Aḥmad ibn Ḥajār al-Makkī, *al-Ṣawā'iq al-Muḥrīqa*, ed. `Abd al-Wahhāb `Abd al-Laṭīf (Cairo: 1955), p. 150; al-Ḥākim al-Naisābūrī, *al-Mustadarak*, vol. 3 (Riyad: n.d.) pp. 150–51. See Momen, *An Introduction to Shi`i Islam*, p. 16. H. Kindermann and C. E. Bosworth note that, despite the lack of biographical evidence of Muḥammad having been at sea, dramatic accounts of the ocean in Qur'ān and hadith, suggest some familiarity. H. Kindermann and C. E. Bosworth, "Safīna: 1. In the Pre-Modern Period," *EI*[2], vol. 8, p. 808.

49 Firdausī, *Shāh nāmah*, p. 4.

50 Welch, *A King's Book of Kings*, p. 84.

51 Shani, "Noah's Ark and the Ship of Faith in Persian Painting," p. 181.

52 `Abd al-Ḥusain al-Ṭūsī, *Munsha'āt al-Ṭūsī*, fol. 196b; Navā'ī (ed.), *Shāh Ṭahmāsp Ṣafavī*, p. 37.

53 Noel Coulson, *Conflicts and Tensions in Islamic Jurisprudence* (Chicago: 1969), p. 43.

54 Halm, *Shi`a Islam*, pp. 104–6.

55 Momen, *An Introduction to Shi`i Islam*, pp. 223–24; Noel Coulson, *Conflicts and Tensions in Islamic Jurisprudence*, p. 43, p. 96.

56 *Khānah-yi taḥqīq bar andākhtī/rāyat-i taqlīd bar arākhtī*
Tābi` ijdād bi-dīn jadd ma-bāsh/bi-shinū va bisyār muqallid ma-bāsh
Hast bih taqlīd chū taqyīd-i tū/li`nat-i ḥaqq bar tū va taqlīd
Abd al-Ḥusain al-Ṭūsī, *Munsha'āt al-Ṭūsī*, fol. 197a; Navā'ī (ed.), *Shāh Ṭahmāsp Ṣafavī*, p. 37.

57 `Umar's prohibition of temporary marriage is ascribed to a celebrated hadith, which narrates how the second caliph had discovered his younger sister `Afra nursing a baby that had been conceived through this practice of *muta`t al-nisā*. Infuriated, `Umar seized the child, brought it to the mosque, and declared that henceforth this paritucular practice was abrogated. Those who disobeyed would be beaten. See Arthur Gribetz, *Strange Bedfellows:* Mut`at al-nisā' and Mut`at al-ḥajj (Berlin, Klaus Schwarz Verlag, 1994), pp. 56–57. This tradition has been translated and made available in Dwight Donaldson, "Temporary Marriage in Iran," *Muslim*

World, vol. 26 (1936), pp. 361–62.

58 *Thalāthun kunna ḥalālan fī `ahdi rasūli Allāhi wa anā uḥarrimuhunna `alaikum wa u`āqibu `alaihunna: mut`atu al-ḥajj wa mut`atu al-nisā' wa ḥayā `alā khair al-`amal.* `Abd al-Ḥusain al-Ṭūsī, *Munsha'āt al-Ṭūsī*, fol. 197b; Navā'ī (ed.), *Shāh Ṭahmāsp Ṣafavī*, p. 38.

59 Muḥammad Barakat, *Kitāb-shināsī-yi maktab-i falsafī-yi Shīrāz* (Shiraz: 2004), p. 23.

60 W. Heffening, "Mut`a," *EI*[2], vol. 7, p. 757; Momen, *An Introduction to Shi`i Islam*, p. 182.

61 *ān sagān-i ruhbāh-bāz ḥilat-sāz bih ḍarb-i khanjar-i jān-gudāz bi qa`r-i jahhanam khvāhand shitāft.* `Abd al-Ḥusain al-Ṭūsī, *Munsha'āt al-Ṭūsī*, fol. 199b; Navā'ī (ed.), *Shāh Ṭahmāsp Ṣafavī*, p. 40.

62 `Abd al-Ḥusain al-Ṭūsī, *Munsha'āt al-Ṭūsī*, fol. 200a; Navā'ī (ed.), *Shāh Ṭahmāsp Ṣafavī*, p. 40.

63 `Abd al-Ḥusain al-Ṭūsī, *Munsha'āt al-Ṭūsī*, fol. 200a; Navā'ī (ed.), *Shāh Ṭahmāsp Ṣafavī*, p. 40.

64 `Abd al-Ḥusain al-Ṭūsī, *Munsha'āt al-Ṭūsī*, fol. 200a; Navā'ī (ed.), *Shāh Ṭahmāsp Ṣafavī*, pp. 40–41. In the original letter, the verse appears as a macaronic arrangement with Arabic and Persian: *Sami`tuka tabnī masjidān min jibāyatin wa anta bi hamdi Allāhi ghairu muwaffaqin/Kamu`ṭiyati al-rummāni min kasbi farjihā laka al-wailu lā taznī wa lā tataṣaddaq/īn-ṭaur kih man dīdam-at ai kāfir-i kīsh masjid-i tu chih dānī va khudā chih shināsī.* However, the original poetry ascribed to `Alī reads as: "Like the one who feeds pomengranate [from the money of] adultery, she became an example of a traitor who is charitable/The wise and the pious ones said: 'Woe unto you! Do not fornicate, and [thus] give charity!'" (*Sami`tuka tabnī masjidān min jibāyatin wa anta bi hamdi Allāhi ghairu muwaffaqin/kamu`ṭiyati al-rummāni mimmā zanat bihi jarat mathalan li'l-khā'ini al-mutaṣaddiqi/faqāla laha ahlu al-basīrati wa al-tuqā laki al-wailu la taznī wa la tataṣaddaq*). See Quṭb al-Dīn Kaidarī's *Dīvān-i Imām `Alī*, p. 309.

65 Qāḍī Kamāl al-Dīn Mīr Ḥusain ibn Mu`īn al-Dīn Maibudī Yazdī, *Sharḥ-i dīvān mansūb bih Amīr al-Mu'minīn `Alī ibn Abī Ṭālib*, eds. H. Raḥmānī and S. E. A. Shirīn (Tehran: 2000).

66 `Abd al-Ḥusain al-Ṭūsī, *Munsha'āt al-Ṭūsī*, fol. 201b; Navā'ī (ed.), *Shāh Ṭahmāsp Ṣafavī*, p. 42.

67 *Wilāya* ("authority") also refers to the right of a properly trained Shi`ite scholar to act on behalf of the Imamate and was of critical importance at those times in Islamic history during which an Imamite dynasty found itself in power, such as the case of the Safavids. *Wilāya* also, according to Sachedina, serves as the underpinnings to the Prophet's religious and secular leadership of the Muslim community: "The sense in which the Qur'ān speaks about the *wilāya* of the Prophet is necessarily in conformity with the Qur'ānic view of the divine guidance regulating the whole of human life, not just a limited segment of it." Sachedina, *The Just Ruler*, p. 95.

68 Momen, *An Introduction to Shi`i Islam*, p. 149.

69 D. B. MacDonald and S. A. Bonebakker, "Iktibās," *EI*[2], vol. 3, pp. 1091–92. Stephan Dähne has recently argued that such methods were part of a collection of devices used in political speeches that made use of the Qur'ān, suggesting that "by alluding to the context of the revelation and communication of the Qur'ān by the Prophet Muḥammad also, the speech text was somehow given a notion of spiritual authority." Stephan Dähne, "Allusions to the Qur'ān: A Rehtorical Device in Political Speeches in Classical Arabic Literature," *Insights into Arabic Literature and Islam: Ideas, Concepts and Modes of Portrayal,* ed. S. Guenther (Leiden: 2005), p. 14.

70 `Abd al-Ḥusain al-Ṭūsī, *Munsha'āt al-Ṭūsī*, fol. 201b; Navā'ī (ed.), *Shāh Ṭahmāsp*

Ṣafavī, p. 41. The tradition states that Muḥammad was returning from his Farewell Pilgrimage when he stopped at Ghadīr Khumm (an oasis between Mecca and Medina) and gathered his followers around him. There, he asked his fellow pilgrims: "Am I not closer to the Believers than they were to themselves? And they said: Yes!" Taking `Alī by the hand, Muḥammad then stated: "Whomsoever's master I am, this `Alī is also his master" (*Man kuntu maulāhu fa-`Alī maulāhu*). This tradition appears in Aḥmad ibn Ḥanbal, *Musnad*, vol. 1 (Cairo: 1895), pp. 118–19. Unlike Sunni versions of this tradition, the Shi`ite hadith here also adds "Oh God! Love him who loves `Alī, and be the enemy of the enemy of `Alī, help him who helps `Alī, and forsake him who forsakes `Alī."

71 L. Vecca Vaglieri, "Ghadīr Khumm," *EI*[2], vol. 2, p. 993. There is, in fact, a Safavid copy of Mīr Khvānd's *Rauḍat al-Ṣafā* with a miniature depicting Muḥammad appointing `Alī as his successor at Ghadīr Khumm. See Momen, figure 2, *An Introduction to Shi`i Islam.*

72 *Anta minnī bimanzilati Hārūn min Mūsā.* `Abd al-Ḥusain al-Ṭūsī, *Munsha'āt al-Ṭūsī*, fol. 202a; Navā'ī (ed.), *Shāh Ṭahmāsp Ṣafavī*, p. 43.

73 `Abd al-Ḥusain al-Ṭūsī, *Munsha'āt al-Ṭūsī*, ff. 202a-b; Navā'ī (ed.), *Shāh Ṭahmāsp Ṣafavī*, p. 43.

74 `Abd al-Ḥusain al-Ṭūsī, *Munsha'āt al-Ṭūsī*, fol. 202b; Navā'ī (ed.), *Shāh Ṭahmāsp Ṣafavī*, p. 43. In one of the first divisive issues between the *ahl al-bait*, Fāṭima claimed ownership to Fadak, as per her right as the closest surviving family member of the Prophet, but Abū Bakr denied her claim stating that the property belonged to the entire Muslim community as a *ṣadaqa* (public property used for benevolent purposes). In doing so, he quoted the Prophet's wishes: "No one shall inherit from me, but what I leave for alms." L. Veccia Vaglieri, "Fadak," *EI*[2], vol. 2, p. 725, Wilferd Madelung, *The Succession to Muḥammad: A Study of the Early Caliphate* (Cambridge: 1997), p. 50, pp. 360–63; Momen, *An Introduction to Shi`i Islam*, p. 20.

75 Madelung, *The Succession to Muḥammad*, p. 62.

76 G. Lecomte, "Saqīfa," *EI*[2], vol. 8, pp. 889–90; Momen, *An Introduction to Shi`i Islam*, pp. 18–22; Madelung, *The Succession to Muḥammad*, pp. 29–31.

77 Navā'ī mistakenly transcribes this as *fitna*, or sedition. See Navā'ī (ed.), *Shāh Ṭahmāsp Ṣafavī*, p. 43; `Abd al-Ḥusain al-Ṭūsī, *Munsha'āt al-Ṭūsī*, fol. 202b.

78 `Abd al-Ḥusain al-Ṭūsī, *Munsha'āt al-Ṭūsī*, fol. 202b; Navā'ī (ed.), *Shāh Ṭahmāsp Ṣafavī*, p. 43.

79 Al-Balādhurī, *Ansāb al-ashraf*, ed. Muḥammad Ḥamīd Allāh, vol. 1 (Cairo: 1959), p. 584. Quoted in Madelung, *The Succession to Muḥammad*, p. 30n. See also Jafri, *Origins and Early Development of Shi`a Islam* (Karachi: 2000), p. 43.

80 `Abd al-Ḥusain al-Ṭūsī, *Munsha'āt al-Ṭūsī*, fol. 202b; Navā'ī (ed.), *Shāh Ṭahmāsp Ṣafavī*, p. 43.

81 `Abd al-Ḥusain al-Ṭūsī, *Munsha'āt al-Ṭūsī*, fol. 203a–203b; Navā'ī (ed.), *Shāh Ṭahmāsp Ṣafavī*, p. 44; Al-Bukhārī, *Ṣaḥīḥ*, vol. 1, p. 41.

82 *Lā fatā* refers to the popular Shi`ite saying: *lā fatā ilā `Alī la saif ailla Zū al-Faqār* ("There is no youth braver than `Alī and there is no sword except the unfailing sword, *Zū al-Faqār*").

83 `Abd al-Ḥusain al-Ṭūsī, *Munsha'āt al-Ṭūsī*, fol. 202a; Navā'ī (ed.), *Shāh Ṭahmāsp Ṣafavī*, p. 42–43.

84 Calmard noted that sections of Ṭahmāsp's letter were clearly based on al-Karakī's treatise on the legality of cursing the Companions of the Prophet. Unfortunately, a copy of this treatise in Arabic was not available for consultation and comparison. Calmard, "Les rituals shiites et le pouvoir," p. 126.

85 Calmard, "Les rituals shiites et le pouvoir," p. 121.

86 Afsaruddin, *Excellence and Precedence*, p. 283.

87 After a defeat in Ṣafar 954/March 1547, Alqāṣ Mīrzā and sixty followers sought asylum in the Ottoman court of Sulaimān. Promising extensive Qizilbāsh support, Alqāṣ was able to convince the Ottoman sultan to launch an invasion, but the campaign (begun in Jumāda I 955/July 1548) was a logistical disaster and the Ottomans disentagled themselves quickly. Cornell Fleischer, "Alqāṣ Mirzā," *Encyclopaedia Iranica*, vol. 1, p. 907.

88 Īvūghlī, *Nuskhah-yi jāmi`a-i al-murāsalāt*, fol. 130a; Navā'ī (ed.), *Shāh Ṭahmāsp Ṣafavī*, p. 290.

89 Īvūghlī, *Nuskhah-yi jāmi`a-i al-murāsalāt*, fol. 130a; Navā'ī (ed.), *Shāh Ṭahmāsp Ṣafavī*, p. 290.

90 *Kafā fī faḍli Maulānā `Alī/wuqū `u al-shakki fīhi annahu Allāhu*. Īvūghlī, *Nuskhah-yi jāmi`a-i al-murāsalāt*, fol. 130b; Navā'ī (ed.), *Shāh Ṭahmāsp Ṣafavī*, p. 290. See also Qāḍī Kamāl al-Dīn Maibudī, *Sharḥ-i dīvān*, p. 185.

91 Īvūghlī, *Nuskhah-yi jāmi`a-i al-murāsalāt*, fol. 104b; Navā'ī (ed.), *Shāh Ṭahmāsp Ṣafavī*, p. 295.

92 Īvūghlī, *Nuskhah-yi jāmi`a-i al-murāsalāt*, fol. 105a; Navā'ī (ed.), *Shāh Ṭahmāsp Ṣafavī*, p. 296.

93 Qāḍī Aḥmad, *Khulāṣat al-tavārīkh*, vol. 1, p. 363.

94 Khūrshāh ibn Qubād, *Tārīkh-i īlchī-yi Niẓāmshāh*, p. 177.

95 Khūrshāh ibn Qubād, *Tārīkh-i īlchī-yi Niẓāmshāh*, p. 178.

96 *Kamar-i muḥabbat-i ahl al-bait bar miyān bastah.*

97 A slightly abridged version of this letter appears in Īvūghlī, *Nuskhah-yi jāmi`a-i al-murāsalāt-i ulul albāb*, ff. 74b–82b. The lengthier version, with specific discussions of the battle of Jām and the Ottoman campaign in Yemen, is available with Navā'ī's edited text, see Navā'ī (ed.), *Shāh Ṭahmāsp Ṣafavī*, pp. 203–37.

98 Īvūghlī, *Nuskhah-yi jāmi`a-i al-murāsalāt*, fol. 74b; Navā'ī (ed.), *Shāh Ṭahmāsp Ṣafavī*, p. 203.

99 Īvūghlī, *Nuskhah-yi jāmi`a-i al-murāsalāt*, fol. 74b; Navā'ī (ed.), *Shāh Ṭahmāsp Ṣafavī*, p. 204.

100 Īvūghlī, *Nuskhah-yi jāmi`a-i al-murāsalāt*, fol. 75a; Navā'ī (ed.), *Shāh Ṭahmāsp Ṣafavī*, p. 204.

101 Īvūghlī, *Nuskhah-yi jāmi`a-i al-murāsalāt*, fol. 75a; Navā'ī (ed.), *Shāh Ṭahmāsp Ṣafavī*, p. 204.

102 Īvūghlī, *Nuskhah-yi jāmi`a-i al-murāsalāt*, fol. 75a; Navā'ī (ed.), *Shāh Ṭahmāsp Ṣafavī*, p. 204.

103 The family of Ziyād is a reference to `Ubaid Allāh ibn Ziyād, who was the governor of Kūfa during the time of al-Ḥusain, the third Imām. It was he who ordered `Umar ibn Sa`d to prevent al-Ḥusain and his entourage from safely reaching Kūfa, leading to the massacre at Karbalā. S. Ḥusain M. Jafri, *Origins and Early Development of Shi`a Islam*, pp. 183–85.

104 Marwān ibn al-Ḥasan was the Umayyad caliphal successor to Yazīd. In addition to being the governor of Egypt and Syria at the time of Karbalā, his reign was primarily focused on the revolt of `Abd Allāh ibn al-Zubair. Jafri, *Origins and Early Development of Shi`a Islam*, p. 227.

105 `Uthmān, of course, was the third caliph and listed among the companions who deprived `Alī of his succession. The *munshī* is clearly drawing a connection between this family and the later Ottomans.

106 Īvūghlī, *Nuskhah-yi jāmi`a-i al-murāsalāt*, fol. 75a; Navā'ī (ed.), *Shāh Ṭahmāsp Ṣafavī*, p. 204.

107 This particular section is not copied in the Īvūghlī text. Navā'ī (ed.), *Shāh Ṭahmāsp Ṣafavī*, p. 206.

108 Navā'ī (ed.), *Shāh Ṭahmāsp Ṣafavī,* p. 207.
109 Navā'ī (ed.), *Shāh Ṭahmāsp Ṣafavī,* p. 207.
110 Navā'ī (ed.), *Shāh Ṭahmāsp Ṣafavī,* p. 208.
111 Girding one's waist has had a number of meanings in the ancient Near East, including the Zoroastrian custom where one wore a girdle (*kustīk*) as an expression of their devotion to Ahura Mazda. In the social and political context of the Sasanians, sashes and belts were associated with submission and expression of loyalty to one's master. In the later Persian medieval world, girding one's waist or, more technically, to have a disciple girded by his master, was a necessary initiation rite in Sufi *futuwwat* ceremonies. Mohsen Zakari, *Sasānīd Soldiers in Early Muslim Society: The Origins of the `Ayyārān and Futuwwa* (Wiesbaden: 1995), p. 74, p. 309. See also Arley Loewen, *The Concept of Jawānmardī (manliness) in Persian Literature and Society*, unpublished Ph.D. dissertation (Toronto: 2001), pp. 179–80.
112 Loewen, *The Concept of Jawānmardī*, pp. 187–88.
113 Navā'ī (ed.), *Shāh Ṭahmāsp Ṣafavī,* p. 214.
114 Yaḥyā ibn Khālid of the Barmakī family, *vazīr* to the caliph Hārūn al-Rashīd, had plotted the murder of the seventh Imam, Mūsā al-Kāẓim. Momen, *An Introduction to Shi`i Islam*, p. 40.
115 Navā'ī (ed.), *Shāh Ṭahmāsp Ṣafavī,* p. 214.
116 Īvūghlī, *Nuskhah-yi jāmi`a-i al-murāsalāt*, ff. 75a–75b; Navā'ī (ed.), *Shāh Ṭahmāsp Ṣafavī*, p. 216.
117 Īvūghlī, *Nuskhah-yi jāmi`a-i al-murāsalāt*, fol. 75b; Navā'ī (ed.), *Shāh Ṭahmāsp Ṣafavī*, p. 217.
118 Īvūghlī, *Nuskhah-yi jāmi`a-i al-murāsalāt*, fol. 75b; Navā'ī (ed.), *Shāh Ṭahmāsp Ṣafavī*, p. 217.
119 The Anṣārī tribe, denizens of Medina, supported the claim of Sa`d ibn `Ubāda of the Khazraj, while the Muḥājirūn (originally from Mecca) supported the claim of Abū Bakr and the Quraish. For a detailed discussion of the events at Saqīfa and their interpretation, see chapter two ("Saqifa: The First Manifestations") of S. H. M. Jafri, *The Origins and Early Development of Shi`a Islam.*
120 "And if it is argued that there was a consensus among the nobles of the community with the agreement of the entire community, [but] `Alī, al-Ḥasan, al-Ḥusain, `Abbās, `Abd Allāh`Abbās, Ṭalḥa, Zubair, Salmān, Abū Zarr, Miqdād, `Umār, `Abd Allāh bin Mas`ūd, Abū Ayūb Anṣārī, Abī Ka`b, Mālik Ashtar, Mālik ibn Zuhair, along with 10,000 others of that tribe, as well as Sa`d ibn `Ubāda, Qays ibn Sa`d and 10,000 people of the Khazraj tribe, disagreed with Abū Bakr and did not give their oath—and this is explicitly stated in your collection of books." Īvūghlī, *Nuskhah-yi jāmi`a-i al-murāsalāt*, fol. 75b, Navā'ī (ed.), *Shāh Ṭahmāsp Ṣafavī*, p. 217.
121 Īvūghlī, *Nuskhah-yi jāmi`a-i al-murāsalāt*, fol. 76a; Navā'ī (ed.), *Shāh Ṭahmāsp Ṣafavī*, p. 218.
122 The event of Mubāhala took place in 9/630 when a number of Christian theologians from Nājrān had been sent to Medina to debate Muḥammad's prophecy. After some contention, it was agreed they should mutually curse (*mubāhala*) one another, thus referring the matter to God and inviting God's condemnation on the lying party. When Muḥammad stepped forth to engage in the *mubāhala*, he brought with him `Alī, Fāṭima, Ḥasan, and Ḥusain and all stood under one cloak; the Christian delegation remembered a prophecy of theirs that Adam had once witnessed a great light, surrounded by four other lights, and how Adam had then been told by God that these five lights were his descendants. The Christians then accepted Muḥammad's claim to prophecy and agreed to pay tribute, and because Muḥammad and the *ahl al-bait* had used one cloak, they would become known as the *ahl al-kisā* ("the people of the cloak"). See Momen, *An Introduction to Shi`i Islam*, p. 14.

123 Sa`d Ibn Abi Waqqās relates a Prophetic tradition that states that "when [this] verse was revealed, the Prophet called `Alī, Fāṭima, al-Ḥasan, and al-Ḥusain. Then the Prophet said: 'O Lord! These are my family members." W. Schmucker, "Mubāhala," *EI*[2], vol. 7, p. 276. Sunni sources such as al-Ḥākim al-Naisābūrī accept this tradition. See al-Naisābūrī, *al-Mustadarak*, vol. 3, p. 150.
124 Shani, "Noah's Ark and the Ship of Faith in Persian Painting," p. 164.
125 Īvūghlī, *Nuskhah-yi jāmi`a-i al-murāsalāt*, fol. 76a; Navā'ī (ed.), *Shāh Ṭahmāsp Ṣafavī*, p. 218.
126 Īvūghlī, *Nuskhah-yi jāmi`a-i al-murāsalāt*, fol. 76b; Navā'ī (ed.), *Shāh Ṭahmāsp Ṣafavī*, p. 220.
127 Charles Rieu, *A Catalogue of the Persian MSS in the British Library*, vol. 1 (London: 1879), p. 366.
128 Although the title is transcribed by the Iranian scholar Navā'ī as *Risālah-yi wahīla*, it is almost certainly a reference to Ḥusain Vā'iz Kāshifī's hadith commentary, *Risālah-yi al-`alīyya*. Ḥusain Vā'iz Kāshifī, *Al-risālah-yi al-`aliyya fī'l-aḥādith al-nabawīyya*, ed. Sayyid Jalāl al-Din Muḥaddis̱ (Tehran: 1965).
129 Khwāndamīr tells us that first source, Jamāl al-Ḥusainī (d. 1520), was a teacher and historian based in Herāt who was unsurpassed in matters of hadith. His son, Mīrāk Shāh, was also noted as a *muḥaddis̱*, quite possibly under the Safavids. Jamāl al-Ḥusainī's work on the Prophet and his family was written at the request of Mīr `Alī Shīr in 900/1494. Khvāndamīr, *Ḥabīb al-siyar*, vol. 4, p. 360; Szuppe, *Entre Timourides, Uzbeks, et Safavides*, p. 134n; Roger Savory, "Djamāl al-Ḥusaynī," *EI*[2], vol. 2, p. 420.
130 *Innī tārikiun fī kum al-thaqalain kitāba Allāhi wa `itratī wa inna tamassakatum bi-hā lan taḍillu ba`dī wa lan tafariqqā ḥattā yaridā `alā al-hauḍa*. Īvūghlī, *Nuskhah-yi jāmi`a-i al-murāsalāt*, fol. 76b; Navā'ī (ed.), *Shāh Ṭahmāsp Ṣafavī*, p. 220. This report, the hadith of Two Weighty Matters (*al-thaqalain*), is a popular one among both Sunnis and Shi`ites and is included among Ibn Ḥanbal's Musnad. See Ibn Ḥanbal, *Musnad*, vol. 3, p. 59.
131 As the author of the "Belt" Letter goes on to explain, it was with this verse that God attested to the sinlessness (*`iṣmat*) and purity (*ṭahārat*) of the Prophet's family. Īvūghlī, *Nuskhah-yi jāmi`a-i al-murāsalāt*, fol. 76b; Navā'ī (ed.), *Shāh Ṭahmāsp Ṣafavī*, p. 220.
132 Īvūghlī, *Nuskhah-yi jāmi`a-i al-murāsalāt*, fol. 76b; Navā'ī (ed.), *Shāh Ṭahmāsp Ṣafavī*, p. 220. Possibly, this is a citation of Rāḍī al-Dīn al-Ḥasan ibn Muḥammad ibn al-Ḥasan ibn al-Ḥaidar al-Ṣaghānī, a thirteenth-century lexicographer and *muḥaddis̱* from the Ghārjistān region. His principal hadith work, *Mashārik al-anwār al-nabawīyya*, is essentially a culling of the two prominent works by the great Traditionalists, al-Bukhārī and Muslim. The title referred to here, *Jami`i Baina al-Siḥāḥ(ain)* ("Between the Two *Ṣaḥīḥ*s"), points intriguingly toward al-Saghānī. Ramzi Baalbaki, "Al-Saghani," *EI*[2], vol. 8, p. 821.
133 *Man arāda an yanẓura ilā Ādama fī `ilmihi wa ilā Nuḥa fī taqwāh wa ilā Ibrāhīma fī khuluqihi wa ilā Mūsā fī haibatihi wa ilā `Isā fī `ibādatihi falyanẓur ilā `Alī ibn Abī Ṭālib*. Īvūghlī, *Nuskhah-yi jāmi`a-i al-murāsalāt*, fol. 77a; Navā'ī (ed.), *Shāh Ṭahmāsp Ṣafavī*, p. 221.
134 Īvūghlī, *Nuskhah-yi jāmi`a-i al-murāsalāt*, fol. 77a; Navā'ī (ed.), *Shāh Ṭahmāsp Ṣafavī*, p. 221.
135 Īvūghlī, *Nuskhah-yi jāmi`a-i al-murāsalāt*, fol. 77a; Navā'ī (ed.), *Shāh Ṭahmāsp Ṣafavī*, p. 221–22.
136 Afsaruddin, *Excellence and Precedence*, pp. 283–84.
137 `Abd al-Jalīl al-Qazvīnī al-Rāzī, *Kitāb al-naqḍ*, pp. 11–12.
138 *taḥt-i kalām-i khāliq va fūq-i kalām-i makhlūq mī bāshad*. Īvūghlī, *Nuskhah-yi*

jāmi`a-i al-murāsalāt, fol. 77b; Navā'ī (ed.), *Shāh Ṭahmāsp Ṣafavī*, p. 222.

139 Īvūghlī, *Nuskhah-yi jāmi`a-i al-murāsalāt*, fol. 77b; Navā'ī (ed.), *Shāh Ṭahmāsp Ṣafavī*, p. 222–23.

140 "Muḥammad said to `Alī: `O `Alī! After me, there will be a plethora of plots against you. A group of my Companions will not accept my stipulation that, if they will oppress you, they will oppress me.' I replied: 'If you are afraid of me being killed, then I will prevent them.' He said: 'O `Alī! Excellent King, news has been given that, if you draw your sword, they will make war with you. Your friends from the Banū Hāshim and the great Companions, already a small number, will not grow in size. And they will entice your people away. [If you make war], Islām will be neglected, and the Qur'ān and the Traditions will be lost sight of. If you tolerate this [oppression], it is better." This specific tradition can be found under Sermon 156 of the *Nahj al-balāgha*. See Muḥammad Dashtī (ed.), *Al-Mu`jam al-mufahras lī alfāẓ Nahj al-balāgha*, p. 81. An approximate version of this also appears in `Abd al-Jalīl al-Qazvīnī al-Rāzī, *Kitāb al-naqḍ*, p. 8; Īvūghlī, *Nuskhah-yi jāmi`a-i al-murāsalāt*, fol. 77b; Navā'ī (ed.), *Shāh Ṭahmāsp Ṣafavī*, p. 223.

141 Īvūghlī, *Nuskhah-yi jāmi`a-i al-murāsalāt*, ff. 77b–78a; Navā'ī (ed.), *Shāh Ṭahmāsp Ṣafavī*, p. 223.

142 Īvūghlī, *Nuskhah-yi jāmi`a-i al-murāsalāt*, fol. 78a; Navā'ī (ed.), *Shāh Ṭahmāsp Ṣafavī*, p. 224.

143 Īvūghlī, *Nuskhah-yi jāmi`a-i al-murāsalāt*, fol. 78a; Navā'ī (ed.), *Shāh Ṭahmāsp Ṣafavī*, p. 224.

144 Although Khalidi was writing of certain circles of western scholarship in the last decade, he approximates how the Safavids appeared to have felt about the Ummāyad and `Abbasid complilation of Prophetic traditions: "[They have attempted] to show that no trust can be placed in the authenticity of any hadith or Hadith-like material before the third century, all such materials being essentially an imaginative reconstruction by later generations." Khalidi, *Arabic Historical Thought*, p. 25.

145 In a philological examination of early scriptural texts and traditions, John Wansborough suggested that the core of Muslim religious tradition came at a much later date. John Wansborough, *Quranic Studies* (London: 1977). This has been challenged, most recently by Tarif Khalidi in *Arabic Historical Thought in the Classical Period* (Cambridge: 1994). Khalidi argues: "Little doubt remains that a substantial corpus of written hadith existed by at least as early as the first half of the first century A.H." p. 20. See also J. Burton, *The Collection of the Qur'ān* (Cambridge: 1977), G. H. A. Juynboll, *Muslim Tradition* (Cambridge: 1983) and Stephen Humphreys, *Islamic History: A Framework for Inquiry* (Princeton: 1991), pp. 81–84.

146 As Khalidi has remarked, "The influence of sectarian polemics on the evolution of *isnād* and of historical thought cannot be overemphasized." Khalidi, *Arabic Historical Thought*, p. 40.

147 Īvūghlī, *Nuskhah-yi jāmi`a-i al-murāsalāt*, fol. 78a; Navā'ī (ed.), *Shāh Ṭahmāsp Ṣafavī*, p. 224.

148 Īvūghlī, *Nuskhah-yi jāmi`a-i al-murāsalāt*, fol. 79a; Navā'ī (ed.), *Shāh Ṭahmāsp Ṣafavī*, p. 226.

149 Īvūghlī, *Nuskhah-yi jāmi`a-i al-murāsalāt*, fol. 79b; Navā'ī (ed.), *Shāh Ṭahmāsp Ṣafavī*, p. 228.

150 Yazīdis grew in northern `Irāq under the influence of Mandean Christianity; they believed that the world was sustained not by God but by a hierarchy of ever-evolving subordinate beings.

151 Qadaris were proponents of a free-will doctrine and were ultimately persecuted as heretics in the eighth and ninth centuries.

152 Īvūghlī, *Nuskhah-yi jāmi`a-i al-murāsalāt*, fol. 79b; Navā'ī (ed.), *Shāh Ṭahmāsp Ṣafavī*, p. 228.
153 Īvūghlī, *Nuskhah-yi jāmi`a-i al-murāsalāt*, ff. 79b–80a; Navā'ī (ed.), *Shāh Ṭahmāsp Ṣafavī*, p. 229.
154 Īvūghlī, *Nuskhah-yi jāmi`a-i al-murāsalāt*, fol. 80a; Navā'ī (ed.), *Shāh Ṭahmāsp Ṣafavī*, p. 229.
155 Īvūghlī, *Nuskhah-yi jāmi`a-i al-murāsalāt*, fol. 81a; Navā'ī (ed.), *Shāh Ṭahmāsp Ṣafavī*, p. 232.
156 Īvūghlī, *Nuskhah-yi jāmi`a-i al-murāsalāt*, fol. 82b; Navā'ī (ed.), *Shāh Ṭahmāsp Ṣafavī*, p. 236.
157 This should serve as a slight corrective to Sholeh Quinn's work on Timurid models and the Safavid court, wherein she argues that the image of Tīmūr was cultivated particularly during the reign of Shāh `Abbās. See Quinn, *Historical Writing During the Reign of Shah `Abbas*, pp. 141–42.
158 Abisaab, *Converting Persia*, p. 28.
159 Ja`fariyan, "Astarābād dar qarn-i nukhast-i ḥukūmat-i Ṣafavī," pp. 14–33.
160 Mir Fazaluddin Ali Khan, *Life and Works of Mirza Sharaf Jahan Qazwini: A Poet of Shāh Ṭahmāsp Safawi's Regime* (Hyderabad: 1995), pp. 42–46.
161 An original document from 893/1488 discussing the foundation and funding of this madrasah is profiled in Vladimir Minosrky, "A 'Soyurghal' of Qasim b. Jahangir Aq-qoyunlu (903/1498)," *Bulletin of the School of African and Oriental Studies*, vol. 9 (1939), no. 4, p. 953.
162 Mir Fazaluddin Ali Khan, *Life and Works of Mirza Sharaf Jahan Qazwini*, p. 95. A manuscript copy of his poetry, *Dīvān-i Sharaf*, is located at the Malana Azad Library, Aligarh Muslim University, MC. no. 157/2 (Poetical Collection).
163 Khūrshāh ibn Qubād, *Tārīkh-i īlchī-yi Niẓāmshāh*, p. 141.
164 Emboldened by al-Karakī's bigotry and informed that Jāmī had been anti-`Alid, the shah had ordered the demolition of the great Timurid's shrine at Herāt. Ṭahmāsp was about to order the public immolation of all copies of Jāmī's *Dīvān* but was dissuaded by Qāḍī-yi Jahān. Qāḍī-yi Jahān, in turn, revealed a number of *qaṣīdahs* in honour of `Alī and the Imamate and successfully used one of them as an augury. Jāmī's tomb was subsequently rebuilt and revered henceforth by the Safavid family.
165 Qāḍī Aḥmad, *Khulāṣat al-tavārīkh*, vol. 1, p. 263.
166 Būdāq Munshī, *Javāhir al-akhbār*, p. 185.
167 Muḥammad Yūsuf Vālih, *Khuld-i barīn*, p. 427.
168 Muḥammad Yūsuf Vālih, *Khuld-i barīn*, p. 444.
169 Muḥammad Yūsuf Vālih, *Khuld-i barīn*, p. 641, p. 976.
170 B. N. Zakhoder, "Preface," in *Calligraphers and Painters: A Treatise by Qāḍī Aḥmad, Son of Mīr Munshī*, p. 2.
171 Whether or not this was *munshī al-mamālik* for the entire Safavid dominion, or just Khurāsān, is not clear.
172 There are references of letters being sent to Europe by Shāh Ismā`īl, specifically one sent in 1523 to the Holy Roman Emperor Charles V, but there are no surviving copies. Likewise, Palmira Brummet talks of a Safavid envoy named `Alī who had been sent in 1515 with a letter to the Hospitallers based on the island of Rhodes. Palmira Brummett, "The Overrated Adversary: Rhodes and Ottoman Naval Power," *The Historical Journal*, vol. 36 (1993), no. 3, p. 538.
173 The Āq Qoyūnlū ruler Ūzūn Ḥasan had once discussed an alliance with the Venetians against the Ottomans during an ambassadorial mission led by Caterino Zeno. Roemer, "Das Türkmenische Intermezzo," pp. 288–89. See also Paulo Preto, "Relations Between the Papacy, Venice and the Ottoman Empire in the Age of

Sūleymân the Magnificent," in *Süleymân the Second and His Time*, eds. H. Inalcik and C. Kafadar (Istanbul: 1993), pp. 195–202.

174 Morton, "Introduction," in Membré, *Mission to the Lord Sophy of Persia*, p. xiii.

175 We are grateful for Sandy Morton's painstaking translation of this valuable source. It was originally published in Italian by the Instituto Universitario Orientale in Naples in 1969.

176 Fekete, *Einführung in die persische Paläographie*, p. 384.

177 Fekete, *Einführung in die persische Paläographie*, p. 384.

178 Fekete, *Einführung in die persische Paläographie*, p. 390. This is also borne out by Morton, who in his appendix states; "The first, though representing Royal policy, was in fact a letter of the Minister Qāḍī-yi Jahān, whose large seal appears on its back." Morton, "Appendix," in Membré, *Mission to the Lord Sophy of Persia*, p. 59.

179 Kāshifī, *Makhzan al-inshā'*, fol. 6b.

180 Fekete, *Einführung in die persische Paläographie*, p. 384.

181 Fekete, *Einführung in die persische Paläographie*, p. 384.

182 Fekete, *Einführung in die persische Paläographie*, p. 384; Morton, "Appendix," p. 63. This reads identically in Qāḍī-yi Jahān's letter, except for the fact that the Doge is addressed in the second person plural.

183 Fekete, *Einführung in die persische Paläographie*, p. 384.

184 Fekete, *Einführung in die persische Paläographie*, p. 384.

185 Jauhar Āftābchī, *Tazkirat al-waqi`āt,* ed. and trans. C. Stewart (London: 1932), p. 62. For a general description of Humāyūn's exile, see Sukumar Ray, *Humayun in Persia* (Calcutta: 1948).

186 Later, Ṭahmāsp would threaten to burn Humāyūn alive for not converting to Shi`ism, and it was only thanks to Qāḍī-yi Jahān's diplomatic acrobatics that the situation was eventually resolved.

187 Īvūghlī, *Nuskhah-yi jāmi`a-i al-murāsalāt*, fol. 127a; Navā'ī (ed.), *Shāh Ṭahmāsp Ṣafavī*, p. 63. See the British copy (Add. 25,865) of Kāshifī, *Makhzan al-inshā'*, fol. 29b.

188 Īvūghlī, *Nuskhah-yi jāmi`a-i al-murāsalāt*, fol. 127a; Navā'ī (ed.), *Shāh Ṭahmāsp Ṣafavī*, p. 63.

189 Īvūghlī, *Nuskhah-yi jāmi`a-i al-murāsalāt*, fol. 127a; Navā'ī (ed.), *Shāh Ṭahmāsp Ṣafavī*, p. 63.

190 Īvūghlī, *Nuskhah-yi jāmi`a-i al-murāsalāt*, fol. 127b; Navā'ī (ed.), *Shāh Ṭahmāsp Ṣafavī*, p. 64.

191 Īvūghlī, *Nuskhah-yi jāmi`a-i al-murāsalāt*, fol. 127b; Navā'ī (ed.), *Shāh Ṭahmāsp Ṣafavī*, p. 64.

192 Īvūghlī, *Nuskhah-yi jāmi`a-i al-murāsalāt*, fol. 127b; Navā'ī (ed.), *Shāh Ṭahmāsp Ṣafavī*, p. 64.

193 Fekete, *Einführung in die persische Paläographie*, pp. 371–410.

194 Anonymous, *Majmū`ah, MS*, London, British Library, I. O. Islamic 379, ff. 95a–102b. Navā'ī provides an edited text, Navā'ī (ed.), *Shāh Ṭahmāsp Ṣafavī*, pp. 53–61. An older English translation is available in Abū al-Fazl `Allāmī, *Akbar nāmah*, ed. and trans. H. Beveridge, vol. 1, pp. 418–31.

195 Szuppe argues that the former Timurid imperial garden complex of Bāgh-i Jahān Ārā, located midway between the city centre and Gāzargāh, was increasingly used by the Safavids as a military post and staging area for counterattacks against encroaching Uzbeks. Szuppe, "Les residences princières de Herat," pp. 272–76.

196 Anonymous, *Majmū`ah, MS*, I. O. Islamic 379, ff. 95b–96a; Navā'ī (ed.), *Shāh Ṭahmāsp Ṣafavī*, p. 54.

197 Anonymous, *Majmū`ah*, ff. 96a–96b; Navā'ī (ed.), *Shāh Ṭahmāsp Ṣafavī*, p. 54.

198 We read that, en route to Herāt, the Mughals were to be met and served rose-watered sherbet and citron juice (*sharbat-i gulāb va āb-i līmū*), cooled by snow and ice. After this, candied apples from Mashhad (*murbāhā-yi sīb-i mushkin-i Mashhadī*), pumpkins (*hindūvāna*), and grapes (*angūr*) were to be presented with white breads (*nānhā-yi safīd*). Once in Herāt, the emperor was to be attended to in the royal quarters (*majlis-i `ālī*) with no less than twelve hundred plates of food suitable for a king's table. On the day of hosting (*rūz-i mihmānī*), when formal gifts were exchanged, the shah insisted that Bairām Khān, a fellow Shi`ite, be one of the four horses to be presented to the Mughal retinue. Humāyūn's men were to be given robes of honour made of satin, Damascus and Yazdi silk, as well as Mashhadī and Khvāfī finery, and each one of Humāyūn's soldiers and servants was also to receive a sum of two Tabrīzī *tūmāns*. Anonymous, *Majmū`ah, MS*, I. O. Islamic 379, fol. 96b–98b; Navā'ī (ed.), *Shāh Ṭahmāsp Ṣafavī*, p. 55–57.

199 Anonymous, *Majmū`ah, MS*, I. O. Islamic 379, fol. 99b; Navā'ī (ed.), *Shāh Ṭahmāsp Ṣafavī*, p. 54.

200 Ulugh Beg had ordered that *qirmiz* be presented to Shāh Rukh's visiting wife, Gawhar Shād, upon arrival in Samarqand. R. G. Mukminova, "Craftsmen and Guild Life in Samarqand," in *Timurid Art and Culture: Iran and Central Asia in the Fifteenth Century*, eds. L. Golombek and M. Subtelny (Leiden: 1992), p. 31.

201 In one such event, Majd al-Dīn Muḥammad, a leading *vazīr* of Sulṭān-Ḥusain Bāīqarā, spent nearly 100,000 *tamghas* hosting a garden feast outside of Herāt, complete with singers, musicians, and reciters; carpets and textiles were spread out, and a wide variety of iced drinks and meals were provided by one of Sulṭān-Ḥusain Bāīqarā's leading chefs. Lentz and Lowry, *Timur and the Princely Vision*, p. 258; Subtelny, *The Poetic Circle at the Court of the Timurid Sultan Ḥusain Baiqara, and Its Political Significance*. Unpublished Ph.D. Dissertation (Harvard: 1979). pp. 144–45.

202 F. Rosenthal, C. E. Bosworth, et alia, "Hiba," *EI*[2], vol. 3, p. 345.

203 N. A. Stillman, "Khil`a," *EI*[2], vol. 5, pp. 6–7. For more on such cultural aspects, see T. T. Allsen, *Commodity and Exchange in the Mongol Empire: A Cultural History of Islamic Textiles* (Cambridge: 1997).

204 Anonymous, *Books of Gifts and Rarities (Kitāb al-Hadāya wa al-Tuḥaf)*, trans. G. al-Qaddumi (Cambridge, M.A.: 1996), Hilāl al-Ṣābi`, *Rusūm Dar al-Khilāfah (The Rules and Regulations of the `Abbasid Court)*, trans. E. A. Salem (Beirut: 1977).

205 Anonymous, *Majmū`ah, MS*, I. O. Islamic 379, ff. 100a–100b; Navā'ī (ed.), *Shāh Ṭahmāsp Ṣafavī*, p. 59.

206 Iskander Beg Munshī, *History of Shah `Abbas the Great*, vol. 1, p. 281; for Persian, see *Tārīkh-i `ālam-ārā-yi `Abbāsī*, vol. 1, p. 190.

207 Ibn Khvāndamīr, *Tārīkh-i Shāh Ismā`īl va Shāh Ṭahmāsp*, p. 214.

208 Dominic Brookshaw, "Palaces, Pavilions and Pleasure-gardens: The Context and Setting of the Medieval *Majlis*," *Middle Eastern Literatures*, vol. 6 (2003), no. 2, p. 206.

209 Muḥammad al-Ḥusainī ibn Nasir al-Haqq Nūrbakhshī, *Inshā-yi `ālam ārā, MS*, Tehran, Kitābkhānah-yi Majlis-i shūrā-yi Islāmī, no. 13757.

210 Nūrbakhshī, *Inshā-yi `ālam ārā*, fol. 3a.

211 Nūrbakhshī, *Inshā-yi `ālam ārā*, fol. 5a.

212 Nūrbakhshī, *Inshā-yi `ālam ārā*, ff. 6a–6b.

213 Nūrbakhshī, *Inshā-yi `ālam ārā*, fol. 7b.

214 Although not explicitly named, he is alluded to with 5: 54 and 4: 133: "Such is the favour of God (*faḍl Allāh*) which He bestows on whomever He wills" and "Great have the blessings of God (*faḍl Allāh*) been on you."

215 *Risālah-yi jāmi`-i munṭavī bar fiqrāt-i munsha'āt va maqālah-yi nāfi`ah-yi*

mutabbinī bar ādāb va ṣanāyi` va muḥsanāt-i īn fann-i balāghat.* Nūrbakhshī, *Inshā-yi `ālam-ārā, f. 12b.

216 Nūrbakhshī, *Inshā-yi `ālam-ārā*, f. 14b. See Muḥammad Dashtī (ed.), *al-Mu`jam al-mufahras lī alfāẓ Nahj al-balāgha*, p. 171.

217 Nūrbakhshī, *Inshā-yi `ālam-ārā*, f. 15a–b; Dashtī (ed.), *al-Mu`jam al-mufahras lī alfāẓ Nahj al-balāgha*, p. 226, p. 173.

218 Nūrbakhshī, *Inshā-yi `ālam-ārā,* ff. 22b–23a.

219 Nūrbakhshī, *Inshā-yi `ālam-ārā,* f. 23b.

220 Nūrbakhshī, *Inshā-yi `ālam-ārā,* f. 24a.

221 Nūrbakhshī, *Inshā-yi `ālam-ārā,* f. 26a.

222 Nūrbakhshī, *Inshā-yi `ālam-ārā*, f. 26b.

223 Quoted in Seyyed Hossein Nasr, *Islamic Art and Spirituality* (Albany: 1987), p. 18.

224 Nūrbakhshī, *Inshā-yi `ālam-ārā*, ff. 27b–28a.

225 Nūrbakhshī, *Inshā-yi `ālam-ārā*, f. 28a.

226 Nūrbakhshī, *Inshā-yi `ālam-ārā*, f. 28b.

227 Indeed, his impact was such that a collection of commentaries of his work called the *Sharḥ-i dastūr-i mu`ammā-yi Nīshāpūrī* was produced in the early sixteenth century. Maria Subtelny, "A Taste for the Intricate: The Persian Poetry of the Late Timurid Period," *Zeitschrift der Deutschen Morgenländischen Gesellschaft*, vol. 136 (1986), no. 1, pp. 76–77; Francis Richard, "Quelques traités d'énigmes (*mo`ammâ*) en persan des XVe et XVIe siècles," *Pand-o Sokhan: Melanges offerts à Charles-Henri de Fouchécour*, eds. C. Balağ, C. Kappler, and Z. Vesel (Tehran: 1995), p. 241.

228 Some prominent devices include: rhymed prose (*tasjī`*), parallel rhymed phrases (*tarsī`*), arrangement of numerous synonymous words in one sentence (*barā`at-i istihlāl*), partial Qur'ānic allusions (*iqtibās*), metaphors (*ista`ārah*), metonymy (*kināyat*), praise by apparent vilification (*tākīd al-madh bi-mā yushbihu al-zamm*), poetic/prose arrangement of contradictory qualities (*tasnīq al-ṣifāt*), amphibology (*īhām*), chiasmus (*laff va nashr*), [rhetorical] observances for particular conditions (*murā`āt-i munāsabāt*), ellipsis (*iḍmār*), palindromes (*maqlūb-i musṭawā*), rhetorical etymology (*ishtiqāq*), and the addition of rhymes and verses to existing *qaṣīdah*s and *maṣnavī*s (*iltizām*).

229 Losensky gives a nice overview of Timurid and Safavid *mu`ammâs*. See Losensky, *Welcoming Fighani*, pp. 154–64.

230 Richard, "Quelques traités d'énigmes (*mo`ammâ*) en persan des XV[e] et XVI[e] siècles," pp. 233–34. For an excellent review of all *mu`ammā* sources produced in the medieval and early modern period, see Shams Anwari-Alhosseini, *Logaz und mo`ammā: eine Quellenstudie zur Kunstform des persische Rätsels* (Berlin: 1986).

231 Mīr `Alī Shīr Navā'ī, *Majālis al-nafā'is*, quoted in Ihsan Yarshater, *Shi`r-i fārs ī dar `ahd-i Shāh Rukh* (Tehran: 1956), p. 239.

232 Nūrbakhshī, *Inshā-yi `ālam-ārā*, f. 103a.

233 Nūrbakhshī, *Inshā-yi `ālam-ārā*, ff. 127b–130a.

234 Simidchieva, "Imitation and Innovation in Timurid Poetics," pp. 516–17.

235 In addition to Nīshāpūrī and Naṣrābādī, I consulted the relevant sections in the poetic works of Muḥtasham Kāshānī, Vaḥshī Bāfqī, and `Abd al-Raḥmān Jāmī and found no evidence of replication.

236 Bashir, *Messianic Hopes and Mystical Visions*, pp. 192–93.

237 M. Kohbach, "Amasya," *Encyclopedia Iranica*, ed. E. Yarshater, vol. 1, p. 928.

238 Lewisohn, "Sufism and the School of Iṣfahān," p. 80.

239 Abisaab, *Converting Persia*, p. 26.

240 Bashir, *Messianic Hopes and Mystical Visions*, pp. 198–243.

241 Ishrāqī, "Nuqtaviyyeh à l'époque Safavides," p. 349.
242 Said Amir Arjomand, "Religious Extremism, (*Ghuluww*), Sufism and Sunnism in Safavid Iran," *Journal of Asian History*, vol. 15 (1981), pp. 8-21.
243 Ja`fariyān, *Dīn va siyāsat dar daurah-yi Ṣafavī*, pp. 226–27, Abisaab, *Converting Persia*, p. 24.
244 Sachedina, *The Just Ruler*, p. 99.
245 Azmeh, *Muslim Kingship*, p. 124.
246 Ann K. S. Lambton, "*Quis Custodiet Custodes?*: Some Reflections on the Persian Theory of Government (Part 2)" in *Studia Islamica*, vol. 6 (1956), p. 126.
247 Arjomand, "Conceptions of Authority," p. 404.
248 Seyyid Hossein Nasr talks about the need to identify a "Shīrāz school" of philosophy, not unlike the "Iṣfahān school" that he and Henri Corbin had discussed. S. H. Nasr, "The Place of Iṣfahān in Islamic Philosophy and Sufism," p. 5 fn. 4. In this vein, a major philosophy conference on the *Maktab-i falsafī-yi Shīrāz* was held in the spring of 2004 in Shīrāz.
249 Abisaab, *Converting Persia*, p. 18.

Chapter Three

1 Ann K. Lambton, "Kazwin - i. Geography and History," *EI^2*, vol. 4, pp. 858–60. For excellent maps and a good introduction to the city layout of Qazvīn in Safavid and Qājār times, see also Eugen Wirth, "Qazvīn—Safavidische Stadtplanung und Qadjarischer Bazar," *Archäeologische Mitteilungen aus Iran und Turan*, vol. 29 (1997), pp. 464—69.
2 Ehsan Eshraqi, "Le *Dār al-salṭana* de Qazvīn," *Safavid Persia: The History and Politics of an Islamic Society*, ed. C. Melville (London: 1996), p. 107. See also Newman, *Safavid Iran*, pp. 30–31.
3 The best treatment of Qazvīn's development in the sixteenth century is available with Maria Szuppe's "Palais et jardins: le complexe royal des premiers Safavides à Qazvīn, milieu XVIe-début XVIIe siècles," *Sites et monuments disparu d'après les témoignages de voyageurs*, ed. R. Gyselen, in *Res Orientales*, vol. VIII (1996), pp. 143–77.
4 Būdāq Munshī, *Javāhir al-akhbār*, p. 203.
5 Eshraqi, "Le *Dār al-salṭana* de Qazvīn," p. 110.
6 Szuppe, "Palais et jardins," p. 147–50. See also Qāḍī Aḥmad, *Khulāṣat al-tavārīkh,* vol. 1, p. 401.
7 For a survey of Qazvīn's early history, see Ardavan Amirshah, "Le développement de la ville de Qazwin jusqu'au milieu du VIIIe/XIVe siècle," *Revue des Études Islamiques*, vol. 49 (1981), pp. 1–42.
8 See Haeedeh Laleh, "La maqsura monumentale de la mosquée du vendredi de Qazvīn à l'époque saljuqide," in *Bamberger Symposium: Rezeption in der islamischen Kunst vom 26.6.–28.6.1992*, eds. B. Finster, B. Fragner, H. Hafenrichter (Beirut: 1999), pp. 217–30, as well as D. N. Wilber, "Le masǧid-i ǧami` de Qazwin," *Revue des Études Islamiques*, vol. 41 (1973), pp. 199–229.
9 Ahmad Schafiyha, "Das Grab des Seyhu'l-Islam Magdu'd-Din Abu'l-Futuh Ahmad Gazzali in Qazwin," *Oriens*, vol. 34 (1994), pp. 348–53.
10 Qāḍī Aḥmad, *Khulāṣat al-tavārīkh*, vol. 1, pp. 399–401.
11 Ishrāqī, "Le *Dār al-salṭana* de Qazvīn," pp. 108–11.
12 Paul Losensky, "The Palace of Praise and the Melons of Time: Descriptive Patterns in `Abdi Bayk Shīrāzī's *Garden of Eden*," *Eurasian Studies: the Skilliter Center-Instiuto per l'Oriente Journal for Balkan, Eastern Mediterranean, Anatolian, Middle Eastern, Iranian, and Central Asian Studies*, vol. 2 (2003), no. 1, pp. 2–3.
13 Manṣūr Ṣifatgol, "Safavid Administration of Avqāf: Structure, Changes, and

Functions, 1077–1135/1666–1722," in *Society and Culture in the Early Modern Middle East: Studies on Iran in the Safavid Period*, ed. A. J. Newman (Leiden: 2003), p. 399.

14 Sayyid Ḥusain Modaressī-Ṭabāṭabā'ī, *Bargī az tārīkh-i Qazvīn* (Tehran: 1982), pp. 121–50.

15 Kishvar Rizvi, "'Its Mortar Mixed with the Sweetness of Life:' Architecture and Ceremonial at the Shrine of Ṣafī al-Dīn Isḥāq Ardabīlī During the Reign of Shāh Ṭahmāsb," *Muslim World*, vol. 90 (2000), nos. 3/4, p. 325.

16 Shāh Ṭahmāsp, *Tazkirah-yi Ṭahmāsp*, p. 592.

17 Ishrāqī, "Le *Dār al-salṭana* de Qazvīn," p. 112.

18 Roemer, *Provinzen und Zentralgewalt Persiens im 16. und 17. Jahrhundert*, p. 47.

19 Ja`fariyān, "Astarābād dar qarn-i nukhast ḥukūmat-i Ṣafavī," pp. 8–9.

20 Ja`fariyān, "Astarābād dar qarn-i nukhast ḥukūmat-i Ṣafavī," p. 9.

21 Iskander Beg Munshī, *History of Shah `Abbas the Great,* vol.1, p. 229; for Persian, see *Tārīkh-i `ālam-ārā-yi `Abbāsī*, vol. 1, p. 143.

22 Schimkoreit, *Regesten publizierter safawidischer Herrscherurkunden,* p. 135, p. 137, p. 138, p. 139, p. 140, p. 141, p. 155, p. 159, p. 160, p. 165.

23 Albert Hourani, "From Jabal `Amil to Persia," *Bulletin of the School of Oriental and African Studies*, vol. 49 (1986), pp. 133–40.

24 Ja`fariyān, "Astarābād dar qarn-i nukhast ḥukūmat-i Ṣafavī," pp. 13–19; Babayan, *Mystics, Monarchs, and Messiahs*, pp. 377–78.

25 Arjomand, *The Shadow of God and the Hidden Imām*, p. 67.

26 Momen, *An Introduction to Shi`i Islam*, p. 93; Yukako Goto, "Der Aufstieg zweier Sayyid-Familien am Kaspischen Meer: 'Volksislamische' Strömungen in Iran des 8/14. Und 9/15. Jahrhunderts," *Wiener Zeitschrift für die Kunde des Morgenlandes*, vol. 89 (1999), pp. 52–55. For a good genealogical chart, see Jean Calmard, "Mar`ashīs," *EI*[2], vol. 6, p. 511. See also Sulṭān Hāshim Mīrzā, *Zābūr-i āl-i Dāvūd: sharḥ-i irtibāṭ-i sādāt-i mar`ashī bā salāṭīn-i ṣafaviyyah* (Tehran: 2000).

27 Calmard, "Mar`ashīs," p. 515.

28 Sulṭān Hāshim Mīrzā, *Zābūr-i āl-i Dāvūd*, p. 24.

29 Muḥammad Yūsuf Vālih, *Khuld-i barīn*, p. 424.

30 Modaressī-Ṭabāṭabā'ī, *Bargī az tārīkh-i Qazvīn*, pp. 121–214.

31 The foundation for this relationship had been laid by Mīr `Alā al-Mulk, who had been appointed *ṣadr* for the province of Gīlān during the 1530s. His trajectory intensified with the transfer of the royal capital to Qazvīn, when he was then named military chaplain (*qāḍī-yi mu`askar*) for the royal court while at the same time acting as a chief sayyid functionary (*sar-i daftar-i arbāb-i faḍl va afḍāl*). Mīr `Alā al-Mulk is described as one of the "eloquent ones of the age" (*fuḍalā' ān `aṣr*), who managed to live and work until the reign of Shāh Ismā`īl II. Muḥammad Yūsuf Vālih, *Khuld-i barīn*, p. 415; Modaressī-Ṭabāṭabā'ī, *Bargī az tārīkh-i Qazvīn*, p. 64.

32 Modaressī-Ṭabāṭabā'ī, *Bargī az tārīkh-i Qazvīn*, p. 55; Babayan, *Mystics, Monarchs, and Messiahs*, p. 378.

33 Modaressī-Ṭabāṭabā'ī, *Bargī az tārīkh-i Qazvīn*, pp. 131–50.

34 Schimkoreit, *Regesten publizierter safawidischer Herrscherurkunden,* p. 135, p. 137, p. 138, p. 140.

35 See Ja`fariyān, "Astarābād dar qarn-i nukhast ḥukūmat-i Ṣafavī," pp. 28–34.

36 Iskander Beg Munshī, *History of Shah `Abbas the Great,* vol. 1, p. 233; for Persian, see *Tārīkh-i `ālam-ārā-yi `Abbāsī*, vol. 1, pp. 145–46.

37 Ja`fariyān, "Astarābād dar qarn-i nukhast ḥukūmat-i Ṣafavī," p. 29.

38 Muḥammad Yūsuf Vālih, *Khuld-i barīn*, p. 420.

39 Iskander Beg Munshī, *History of Shah `Abbas the Great,* vol. 1, p. 240; for Persian,

see *Tārīkh-i `ālam-ārā-yi `Abbāsī*, vol. 1, p. 150.

40 Qāḍī Aḥmad Ghaffārī, *Tārīkh-i jahān-ārā*, p. 308, Qāḍī Aḥmad, *Khulāṣat al-tavārīkh*, vol. 1, pp. 364–65.

41 Iskander Beg Munshī, *History of Shah `Abbas the Great,* vol. 1, pp. 240–41; for Persian, see *Tārīkh-i `ālam-ārā-yi `Abbāsī*, vol. 1, pp. 150–51.

42 Muḥammad Yūsuf Vālih, *Khuld-i barīn*, pp. 419–20; Ja`fariyān, "Astarābād dar qarn-i nukhast ḥukūmat-i Ṣafavī," p. 32.

43 Iskander Beg Munshī, *History of Shah `Abbas the Great,* vol. 1, p. 241; for Persian, see *Tārīkh-i `ālam-ārā-yi `Abbāsī*, vol. 1, p. 151.

44 Ja`fariyān, "Astarābād dar qarn-i nukhast ḥukūmat-i Ṣafavī," p. 28.

45 Ja`fariyān, "Astarābād dar qarn-i nukhast ḥukūmat-i Ṣafavī," pp. 13–14.

46 This source is discussed in the catalogue description of an anonymous *Majmū`ah*, *MS*, Yazd, Kitābkhānah-yi vazīrī-yi jāmi`i-i Yazdī, vol. 1 of the *Fihrist-i fīlm-i nuskhah-hā-yi khaṭṭī* (Tehran: 1970), p. 702.

47 Newman, *Safavid Iran*, p. 24.

48 This decree included the quatrain: "Ṭahmāsp the Just, ruler of the land of faith/ Has pledged an oath for the repentance of [himself and] his subjects/The date of this imposed repentance is 'Unrelapsing penitence'/It is God's will, may no one transgress this." Qāḍī Aḥmad, *Khulāṣat al-tavārīkh*, vol. 1, p. 386.

49 Arjomand, "Two Decrees Concerning Statecraft and the Authority of Shaykh `Alī al-Karakī," pp. 256–61.

50 Babayan, *Mystics, Monarchs, and Messiahs*, p. 319.

51 Būdāq Munshī, *Javāhir al-akhbār*, p. 213.

52 Anthony Welch, *Artists for the Shah: Late Sixteenth-Century Painting at the Imperial Court of Iran* (New Haven: 1976), pp. 5–10.

53 Ma`ṣūm Beg Ṣafavī could not be any more different than Qāḍī-yi Jahān. Linked genealogically with the Safavid family on account of the fact that his great-grandfather had been a brother of Haidar, Ma`ṣūm Beg Ṣafavī was a Qizilbāsh amir whose pedigree earned him the position of *mutavallī* for the shrine of Ardabīl during the 1530s and 1540s. He served as a ranking amir in the late 1540s and 1550s, most notably as Ismā`īl Mīrzā's warden during his transfer to Qahqaha prison, and he was later named as both chief vizier and *amīr-i dīvān* despite his relative lack of experience in the *dīvān-i `alā*. Dissatisfied with acting as a central administrator, Ma`ṣūm Beg retired eventually and returned to his Qizilbāsh roots by initiating a secret campaign of propaganda as a *khalīfah* in the Anatolian hinterland where he was later arrested and executed by Ottoman provincial agents. Bekir Sidki Kūtūkoglu, "Les rélations entre l'empire ottoman et l'Iran dans la seconde moitié du XVIe siècle," *Turcica*, vol. 6 (1975), pp. 129–30.

54 Iskander Beg Munshī, *History of Shah `Abbas the Great,* vol. 1, p. 254; for Persian, see *Tārīkh-i `ālam-ārā-yi `Abbāsī*, vol. 1, p. 162.

55 Būdāq Munshī, *Javāhir al-akhbār*, p. 234.

56 Welch, *Artists for the Shah*, pp. 153–58. See also Maria Shreve Simpson, *Sultan Ibrahim-Mirza's* Haft Awrang*: A Princely Manuscript from Sixteenth-century Iran* (New Haven: 1997).

57 Mīr Sayyid Aḥmad Mashhadī, for instance, had been a prominent chancellery *munshī* and calligrapher until 1550, but news of gatherings at his house of "beardless youths and tulip-cheeked ones" alienated the now moralistic Ṭahmāsp, and he was dismissed from imperial service. Mashhadī moved to join Ibrāhīm Mīrzā's court for six years and then sought patronage in the court of the regional ruler of Māzandarān, Murād Khān. Qāḍī Aḥmad, *Gulistān-i hunar*, pp. 139–44, p. 192.

58 Qāḍī Aḥmad, *Gulistān-i hunar*, p. 3.

59 Mīrzā Ḥidāyat Allāh, who would go on to be *mustaufī al-mamālik* and *vazīr-i*

dīvān-i a`lā during the reign of Muḥammad Khudābandah, spent the 1560s and early 1570s as the vizier of eastern Gīlān. The robustness of the Gīlānī chancellery, particularly the one associated with the court of Khān Aḥmad Khān of Bīa-pas, is attested to by its sustained production and dispatching of *munsha'āt* and *mukātibāt* to the Safavid court. See Fiyādūn Nawzād (ed.), *Nāma-hā-yi Khān Aḥmad Khān Gīlānī* (Tehran: 1994).

60 Būdāq Munshī, *Javāhir al-akhbār*, p. 217.

61 Iskander Beg Munshī, *History of Shah `Abbas the Great*, vol. 1, p. 259; for Persian, see *Tārīkh-i `ālam-ārā-yi `Abbāsī*, vol. 1, p. 165.

62 Qāḍī Aḥmad, *Gulistān-i hunar*, p. 91.

63 Qāḍī Aḥmad discusses his import at length, see Qāḍī Aḥmad, *Gulistān-i hunar*, pp. 421–29. See also his *Khulāṣat al-tavārīkh*, vol. 1, p. 421–22.

64 Sām Mīrzā, *Tazkirah-yi tuḥfah-yi Sāmī*, p. 115.

65 Qāḍī Aḥmad, *Gulistān-i hunar*, p. 93; Būdāq Munshī, *Javāhir al-akhbār*, p. 220. See also Floor, *Safavid Government Institutions*, p. 53.

66 Qāḍī Aḥmad, *Gulistān-i hunar*, p. 92.

67 Qāḍī Aḥmad, *Gulistān-i hunar*, p. 96; Floor, *Safavid Government Institutions*, p. 53.

68 Qāḍī Aḥmad, *Gulistān-i hunar*, p. 81.

69 Qāḍī Aḥmad, *Gulistān-i hunar*, p. 93.

70 Qāḍī Aḥmad, *Gulistān-i hunar*, pp. 94–95.

71 Qāḍī Aḥmad, *Gulistān-i hunar*, pp. 79–80.

72 Ibrāhīm ibn Valī Allāh Astarābādī, *Risālah-yi Ḥusainiyyah, MS*, London, British Library, Egerton 1020. See Rieu, *Catalogue of the Persian Manuscripts in the British Museum*, vol. 1 (London: 1879), p. 30.

73 Qāḍī Aḥmad, *Gulistān-i hunar*, pp. 89–90.

74 See Gülru Necipoghlu, "The Sūleymaniye Complex in Istanbul: An Interpretation," *Muqarnas*, vol. 3 (1985), p. 111. See also her section on the complex in *The Age of Sinan: Architectural Culture in the Ottoman Empire* (London: 2005), pp. 207–30.

75 Necipoghlu, "The Sūleymaniye Complex in Istanbul: An Interpretation," pp. 99–104.

76 Qāḍī Aḥmad, *Gulistān-i hunar*, p. 92. Ivughli identifies Mīrzā Kāfī Urdūbādī as the author in the rubric to this letter. See Īvūghlī, *Nuskhah-yi jāmi`a-i al-murāsalāt*, fol. 92a.

77 *Pādshāh-i Farīdūn-i jamjāh-i iqtidār/khaqān-i Dārā rāi-yi Kisrā shi`ār.*

78 Farīdūn Beg, *Munsha'āt al-salāṭīn*, vol. 2, p. 15; Navā'ī (ed.), *Shāh Ṭahmāsp Ṣafavī*, p. 330.

79 Farīdūn Beg, *Munsha'āt al-salāṭīn*, vol. 2, pp. 15–16; Navā'ī (ed.), *Shāh Ṭahmāsp Ṣafavī*, pp. 332–33.

80 Farīdūn Beg, *Munsha'āt al-salāṭīn*, vol. 2, p. 17; Navā'ī (ed.), *Shāh Ṭahmāsp Ṣafavī*, p. 335.

81 Farīdūn Beg, *Munsha'āt al-salāṭīn*, vol. 2, p. 17; Navā'ī (ed.), *Shāh Ṭahmāsp Ṣafavī*, p. 336.

82 Farīdūn Beg, *Munsha'āt al-salāṭīn*, vol. 2, p. 17; Navā'ī (ed.), *Shāh Ṭahmāsp Ṣafavī*, p. 336. J. M. Rogers noted this particular request in his study of Suleymaniye aesthetics and suggests that the Ottomans did indeed take Ṭahmāsp up on his offer, but the carpet would not be delivered until 1568 when a lavish Safavid entourage arrived in Istanbul to congratulate the newly enthroned Salīm II. See J. M. Rogers, "The State and the Arts in Ottoman Turkey, part 2: The Furniture and Decoration of Suleymaniye," *International Journal of Middle East Studies*, vol. 14 (1982), p. 308.

83 Ghiyāṣ al-Dīn Khvāndamīr, *Makāram al-akhlāq*, ed. Muḥammad Akbar `Ashīq

(Tehran: 1999), p. 97.

84 The first hemistich of the original reads *masjid-i jāmi` ki az faiḍ allāh*, meaning that the *munshī* added *masjid-i shāh*, or "the shah's mosque."

85 Farīdūn Beg, *Munsha'āt al-salāṭīn*, vol. 2, p. 17; Navā'ī (ed.), *Shāh Ṭahmāsp Ṣafavī*, p. 335.

86 Būdāq Munshī, *Javāhir al-akhbār*, p. 222.

87 Qāḍī Aḥmad, *Khulāṣat al-tavārīkh*, vol. 1, p. 410.

88 *Khātim al-a'immat al-bararat* and *qā'im ahl al-bait Muḥammad*. Qāḍī Aḥmad, *Khulāṣat al-tavārīkh*, vol. 1, p. 410.

89 *Āṣār-i ẓulmat-i shirk va taghiyān az ṣafaḥāt-i `ālam mutalāshī va parīshān khvāhad gasht* Qāḍī Aḥmad, *Khulāṣat al-tavārīkh*, vol. 1, p. 410.

90 Qāḍī Aḥmad, *Khulāṣat al-tavārīkh*, vol. 1, p. 411.

91 Qāḍī Aḥmad, *Khulāṣat al-tavārīkh*, vol. 1, p. 411.

92 Qāḍī Aḥmad, *Khulāṣat al-tavārīkh*, vol. 1, p. 412.

93 Mīrzā Sulṭān Ibrāhīm would be in and out of favour with his uncle Ṭahmāsp throughout the 1560s and 1570s. Marianna Simpson, "Ebrāhim Mirzā," *Encyclopedia Iranica*, vol. 8, pp. 74–75.

94 Newman, *Safavid Iran*, p. 32.

95 Navā'ī (ed.), *Shāh Ṭahmāsp Ṣafavī*, pp. 22–23.

96 A full text of this inscription, as well as a photo, is available in `Abd al-`Alī Karang, *Āsār-i bastān-i Āzarbāijān*, vol. 1 (Tehran: 1972), pp. 276–81.

97 A similar *farmān* to this one—undated—discusses how the "image of the decree being presented was to be inscribed on the wall of the Jāmi` masjid [in Tabrīz]. Navā'ī (ed.), *Shāh Ṭahmāsp Ṣafavī*, p. 21.

98 I'd like to thank Dr. Christoph Werner for his help with identifying this particular epigraph.

99 Rosemary Stanfield-Johnson, "The Tabarra'iyan and the Early Safavids," *Iranian Studies*, vol. 37 (2004), no. 1, p. 57.

100 Navā'ī (ed.), *Shāh Ṭahmāsp Ṣafavī*, p. 22.

101 All of these are consistent with Shi`ite *malāḥim* literature predicting his arrival. See Cook, *Studies in Muslim Apocalyptic*, pp. 157–58.

102 The *farmān* lists the collected taxes to date from Tabrīz to Erzerum and `Irāq at 3,875 *tūmān*s and 800 *dīnār*s under Ottoman control, and Ṭahmāsp suggests that "this evil innovation" has crept into Safavid administrative practice, but now state accountants do not record its collection, and "its name and custom has been erased from the registries." Navā'ī (ed.), *Shāh Ṭahmāsp Ṣafavī*, p. 23.

103 Būdāq Munshī, *Javāhir al-akhbār*, p. 225.

104 Manouchehr Kasheff, "Gilan – v. History under the Safavids," *Encyclopaedia Iranica*, vol. 10, p. 639.

105 *Hīch sāḥib daulatī az sipihr-i iqbāl bi-dīn sa`ādat ṭāli` na-shudah*. Navā'ī (ed.), *Shāh Ṭahmāsp Ṣafavī*, p. 118.

106 Navā'ī (ed.), *Shāh Ṭahmāsp Ṣafavī*, p. 119.

107 Navā'ī (ed.), *Shāh Ṭahmāsp Ṣafavī*, p. 120.

108 *Ighvā' -yi jami` ī az ahl-i ḍalāl bi ṭarīq-i aṭfal hamīsha bi lahv va la`ib ghuzarānidah*. Navā'ī (ed.), *Shāh Ṭahmāsp Ṣafavī*, p. 120.

109 Navā'ī (ed.), *Shāh Ṭahmāsp Ṣafavī*, p. 120.

110 Navā'ī (ed.), *Shāh Ṭahmāsp Ṣafavī*, p. 122.

111 Anonymous, *Munsha'āt, MS*, London, British Library, Add. 7654, fol. 103b.

112 Navā'ī (ed.), *Shāh Ṭahmāsp Ṣafavī*, p. 124.

113 Navā'ī (ed.), *Shāh Ṭahmāsp Ṣafavī*, p. 124.

114 Navā'ī (ed.), *Shāh Ṭahmāsp Ṣafavī*, p. 125.

115 He would ultimately be released with the accession of Ismā`īl II and returned to

power in Gīlān in 1578. Internecine conflict would dominate the remainder of his reign until Shāh `Abbās formally annexed Gilān in 1000/1592. Kasheff, "Gilan – v. History under the Safavids," p. 641.

116 Babayan, *Mystics, Monarchs, and Messiahs*, p. 319.

117 `Abdī Beg Shīrāzī, *Takmilat al-akhbār*, p. 131.

118 Qāḍī Aḥmad, *Khulāṣat al-tavārīkh*, vol. 1, p. 478.

119 See Appendix II "Shāh Ṭahmāsp's Gift of the Shahnameh to Sultan Selim II," in *The Houghton Shahnameh*, vol. 1, eds. M. Dickson and S. C. Welch, (Cambridge, Mass.: 1981), pp. 270–71.

120 See Priscilla Soucek, "The Temple of Solomon in Islamic Legend and Art," *The Temple of Solomon: Archaeological Fact and Medieval Tradition in Christian, Islamic and Jewish Art*, ed. J. Gutmann (Ann Arbor: 1976), pp. 73–123.

121 Minorsky, "A Civil and Military Review," pp. 150–51.

122 Minorsky, "A Civil and Military Review," p. 149, fn. 7.

123 Priscilla Soucek, "Solomon's Throne/Solomon's Bath: Model or Metaphor?", *Ars Orientalis*, vol. 23 (1993), p. 116.

124 It should be noted that Melikian-Chirvani reinterprets the "civil and military review" presented by Minorsky as a Sufi ceremony and procession. Assadullah Souren Melikian-Chirvani, "Le Royaume de Salomon: Les inscriptions persanes de sites Achéménides," in *Le monde Iranien et l'Islam: sociétés et cultures*, vol. 1 (Paris: 1971), pp. 1–41.

125 One of the more comprehensive treatments of this appeared in Tomoko Masuya, *The Ilkhanid Phase of Takht-i Sulaimān*, unpublished Ph.D. Dissertation, New York University, 1997. See also her article "Ilkhanid Courtly Life," in *The Legacy of Genghis Khan: Courtly Art and Culture in Western Asia, 1256–1353*, eds. L. Komaroff and S. Carboni, (New York: 2002), pp. 74–104. For early archaeological surveys, see Hans Henning von der Osten and Rudolf Naumann, *Takht-i-Suleiman: Vorläufiger Bericht uber die Ausgrabungen 1959* (Berlin: 1961).

126 Serpil Bagci, "A New Theme of the Shīrāzī Frontispeice Miniatures: the Dīvān of Solomon," *Muqarnas*, vol. 12 (1995), pp. 101–11.

127 Melikian-Chirvani, "Le Royaume de Salomon," pp. 20–21; Navā'ī (ed.), *Shāh Ṭahmāsp Ṣafavī*, p. 293; Navā'ī (ed.), *Shāh `Abbās*, vol. 1, p. 60.

128 Muḥtasham Kāshānī, *Dīvān-i Maulānā Muḥtasham Kāshānī*, ed. Mihr `Alī Kirmānī (Tehran: 1997), pp. 172–80.

129 `Abdī Beg Shīrāzī, *Takmilat al-akhbār*, p. 119.

130 Afūshtah-ī Natanzī, *Naqāvat al-āsār*, p. 351.

131 Classical Qur'ānic exegetical texts, as well as Prophetic narratives, discuss the tradition whereby Queen Sheba, mistaking the glass floor of Solomon's reception chamber as a pool of water, raised her skirts to bear her legs; realizing her error, she submits to the King/Prophet and converts from paganism to Islam. Muḥammad ibn `Abd Allāh al-Kisā'ī, *Tales of the Prophets (Qiṣaṣ al-anbiyā')*, ed. and trans. W. M. Thackston Jr. (Chicago: 1997), pp. 315–16.

132 Soucek examines various architectural settings to determine the influence of Solomon's bath tradition, including the eighth-century Umayyad complex of Khirbat al-Majfar and Fatḥ `Alī Shāh's patronage of the Takht-i Marmar in nineteenth-century Tehran. See Soucek, "Solomon's Throne/Solomon's Bath."

133 Losensky, "The Palace of Praise and the Melons of Time," p. 21.

134 Soucek, "Solomon's Throne/Solomon's Bath," pp. 121–22.

135 Al-Kisā'ī, *Tales of the Prophets* pp. 300–16.

136 Schimmel, *As Through a Veil*, p. 40, p. 75.

137 Seyyed Hossein Nasr, *Islamic Art and Spirituality* (Albany: 1987), pp. 101–02.

138 Soucek, "Solomon's Throne/Solomon's Bath," p. 114.

139 (Shaikh) al-Mufīd, *Kitāb al-irshad* (*Book of Guidance into the Lives of the Twelve Imāms*), p. 415.
140 Melikian-Chirvani, "Le Royaume de Salomon," p. 32.
141 Tayeb el-Hibri, "A Note on Biblical Narrative and `Abbasid History," *Views from the Edge: Essays in Honour of Richard W. Bulliet*, eds. N. Yavari, L. G. Potter, J. R. Oppenheim (New York: 2004), p. 67.
142 Abū al-Ḥasan al-`Āmirī al-Nīshāpūrī, *Al-I`lām bi-manāqib al-Islām*, ed. A. Ghurab (Cairo: 1967), p. 152, quoted in Said Arjomand, "Perso-Indian Statecraft, Greek Political Science and the Muslim Idea of Government," *International Sociology*, vol. 16 (2001), no. 3, p. 466.
143 After a long description of a number of dreams in the year 962/1554 in which he saw written or found himself spontaneously speaking the phrase *fa-sayakfikahum* "[and God] will suffice thee against them" (*iqtibās*, or partial quote, from 2: 137), Ṭahmāsp writes in his memoirs how he was astonished to find that this verse referred to God's promise that His Prophets will be victorious over their enemies. Ṭahmāsp writes "After realizing this, I was very anxious, and it occurred to me again then that the flash of light of His divine Excellency—may His name be exalted—had burst forth and made itself apparent." Ṭahmāsp relates how God has revealed himself through miraculous light to the Prophet Moses on Mount Sinai (*ṭaur-i Sinā*), and that He spoke to the Prophet Moōammad from behind a curtain during the night ascension (*mi`rāj*). Ṭahmāsp concludes how "it is known that I saw these types of miracles (*nau`-i `ajā'ibāt*) and in this way, the Qur'ānic verse [of 2: 137] had run off my tongue." Shāh Ṭahmāsp, *Tazkirah-yi Ṭahmāsp*, p. 637.
144 Lousie Marlow, "Kings, Prophets, and the `Ulamā in Mediaeval Islamic Advice Literature," *Studia Islamica*, vol. 81 (1995), no. 1, p. 107.
145 Marlow, "Kings, Prophets, and the `Ulamā," p. 109.
146 Colin Imber, *The Ottoman Empire, 1300–1650: The Structure of Power* (New York: 2002), p. 104.
147 Leslie Peirce, *The Imperial Harem: Women and Sovereignty in the Ottoman Empire* (New York: 1993), pp. 92–93.
148 Mindful of the growing popularity of Bāyazīd's cause among the lower classes at large, Sulaimān procured a *fatwā* from the Chief Muftī of Istanbul, Ebū's-Su`ūd, which stated that it was indeed legal from a formal Islamic juristic perspective for the sultan to fight and kill his own son. Imber, *The Ottoman Empire, 1300–1650*, p. 106.
149 Ḥasan Beg Rūmlū, *Aḥsan al-tavārīkh*, vol. 1, p. 178; Qāḍī Aḥmad Ghaffārī, *Tārīkh-i jahān-ārā*, p. 304.
150 Ḥasan Beg Rūmlū, *Aḥsan al-tavārīkh*, vol. 1, p. 178.
151 Iskander Beg Munshī, *History of Shah `Abbas the Great*, vol. 1, p. 168; for Persian, see *Tārīkh-i `ālam-ārā-yi `Abbāsī*, vol. 1, p. 102; Ḥasan Beg Rūmlū, *Aḥsan al-tavārīkh*, vol. 1, p. 179.
152 Qāḍī Aḥmad Ghaffārī, *Tārīkh-i jahān-ārā*, p. 305.
153 Iskander Beg Munshī, *History of Shah `Abbas the Great*, vol. 1, p. 168; for Persian, see *Tārīkh-i `ālam-ārā-yi `Abbāsī*, vol. 1, p. 102.
154 Qāḍī Aḥmad, *Khulāṣat al-tavārīkh*, vol. 1, p. 407. Interestingly, the incorporation of disaffected Ottoman elements would prove to be a future Safavid policy in the late sixteenth and seventeenth centuries as revolting "Jalālīs"—composites of armed peasants and disaffected timar-holders—fled eastward from Anatolia and found sanction in Safavid Iran. Richad Tapper, "Shahsevan in Safavid Persia," *Bulletin of the School of African and Oriental Studies*, vol. 37 (1974), p. 328.
155 In Rajab 967/April 1560, Safavid chroniclers describe how a plot was hatched by Bāyazīd and his immediate coterie to take over the Safavid court and invite

his father to invade the Ottoman territory; redeemed in Sulaimān's eyes, Bāyazīd would be restored to good graces and named as the governor of Iran. According to Iskander Beg Munshī, the elite of his retinue were seized and killed, and Bāyazīd was formally placed under house arrest. See Qāḍī Aḥmad Ghaffārī, *Tārīkh-i jahān-ārā*, p. 305 and Iskander Beg Munshī, *History of Shah `Abbas the Great*, vol. 1, p. 171; for Persian see *Tārīkh-i `ālam-ārā-yi `Abbāsī*, ed. I. Afshar, vol. 1, p. 103.

156 Qāḍī Aḥmad Ghaffārī, *Tārīkh-i jahān-ārā*, p. 307; Ḥasan Beg Rūmlū, *Aḥsan al-tavārīkh*, vol. 1, p. 182.

157 Ḥasan Beg Rūmlū, *Aḥsan al-tavārīkh*, vol. 1, p. 180, p. 182.

158 Qāḍī Aḥmad Ghaffārī, *Tārīkh-i jahān-ārā*, p. 307; Qāḍī Aḥmad, *Khulāṣat al-tavārīkh*, vol. 1, p. 433; Ḥasan Beg Rūmlū, *Aḥsan al-tavārīkh*, vol. 1, p. 182.

159 Īvūghlī, *Nuskhah-yi jāmi`a-i al-murāsalāt*, fol. 88a; Navā'ī (ed.), *Shāh Ṭahmāsp Ṣafavī*, p. 361.

160 Īvūghlī, *Nuskhah-yi jāmi`a-i al-murāsalāt*, fol. 91b; Navā'ī (ed.), *Shāh Ṭahmāsp Ṣafavī*, p. 387.

161 Farīdūn Beg, *Munsha'āt al-salāṭīn*, vol. 2, p. 46; Navā'ī (ed.), *Shāh Ṭahmāsp Ṣafavī*, p. 425.

162 The Qur'ān narrates in Surat al-Naml how one of King Solomon's prized birds, the Hoopoe, had flown to Saba and discovered a Queen named Sheba who ruled over a sun-worshipping people. True to his dual role as prophet and king, Solomon ordered the despatching of a diplomatic letter via the Hoopoe bird to Queen Sheba that exhorted her to submit to God and adopt the path of Islam. The Qur'ānic term for this aviary messenger is *hudhud*—the Safavid letters use respectively *humā*, *`anqā*, *hudhudī*, and *ṭā'ir*—while Verses 28–29 of Surat al-Naml discuss how Solomon ordered Hud-hud to deliver his letter (*izhabu bi-kitābī*) to Sheba, who reportedly said: "O nobles, a venerable letter has been delivered to me, it is from Solomon" (*qālat yā ayyuhā al-mala'u innī ulqiya ilayya kitābun karīmun. Innahu min Sulaimāna*).

163 With respect to the Hoopoe bird and its delivery of Solomon's letter, al-Kisā'ī embellishes the story and adds that the Solomonic text was written on a leaf of gold by Solomon's chief vizier, Āṣaf ibn Barkiyā, and perfumed in musk by the king's servants. Al-Kisā'ī, *Tales of the Prophets*, p. 314. See also Montgomery Watt, "The Queen of Sheba in Islamic Tradition," in *Solomon and Sheba*, ed. J. B. Pritchard (London: 1974), p. 97.

164 Īvūghlī, *Nuskhah-yi jāmi`a-i al-murāsalāt*, fol. 88a; Navā'ī (ed.), *Shāh Ṭahmāsp Ṣafavī*, p. 361.

165 Farīdūn Beg, *Munsha'āt al-salāṭīn*, vol. 2, p. 46; Navā'ī (ed.), *Shāh Ṭahmāsp Ṣafavī*, p. 425.

166 Farīdūn Beg, *Munsha'āt al-salāṭīn*, vol. 2, p. 47; Navā'ī (ed.), *Shāh Ṭahmāsp Ṣafavī*, p. 426.

167 Farīdūn Beg, *Munsha'āt al-salāṭīn*, vol. 2, p. 47; Navā'ī (ed.), *Shāh Ṭahmāsp Ṣafavī*, p. 426.

168 Farīdūn Beg, *Munsha'āt al-salāṭīn*, vol. 2, p. 46; Navā'ī (ed.), *Shāh Ṭahmāsp Ṣafavī*, p. 425.

169 In the seventh chapter ("Exposition on the People of Power and their Conditions"), Kāshifī discusses the point of origin and ontology of various kingly devices, institutions, and regalia. In one particular *faṣl* here ("Exposition on the Tuqmāq Tribe"), he makes note of how powerful Turkish tribes were privy to the "forbidden secrets of kings" (*muḥarram-i asrār-i mulūk*) and provides a short essay regarding the genesis of royal tents, canopies, lamps, and other courtly features. Ḥusain Vā`iẓ Kāshifī, *Futuvvat-i nāmah-yi sulṭānī*, ed. M. J. Maḥjūb (Tehran: 1971), p. 370–71.

170 Kāshifī notes sardonically how "she loved [Solomon] so much that he had no patience

for her company," and that she "followed him everywhere, sitting on Solomon's throne-carpet, which was carried by demons and mortals." He commanded that a veiled area (*sarā-pardah*) be created, whereby each corner of the majestic carpet (*shādirvān*) was raised up, and Bilqīs was kept inside with her servants so that no one could see her. Kāshifī, *Futuvvat-i nāmah-yi sulṭānī*, p. 371.

171 Kāshifī writes that Queen Sheba, in her carpet-walled quarters, was complaining to Solomon that she was suffering from the heat of the sun, and she pled to Solomon: "There are so many birds flying over you which are providing shelter from the sun. Can you not order a small group of them to fly over my head and provide [the same]?" Solomon replied that this miracle was a Prophetic privilege (*mu`jizat-i nubawwat ast*) but decided that he would build a substitute for Bilqīs. Thus, a *sāyabān*—a canopy (possibly held up on four staves in the corners)—was built over Queen Bilqīs, and many figures and images were painted on it (*naqsh-hā kardand ki bi ṣūrat-i khūbān-i shabīah būd*). Kāshifī, *Futuvvat-i nāmah-yi sulṭānī*, p. 371.

172 Farīdūn Beg, *Munsha'āt al-salāṭīn*, vol. 2, p. 48; Navā'ī (ed.), *Shāh Ṭahmāsp Ṣafavī*, p. 428.

173 Johns, "Solomon and the Queen of Sheba," pp. 74–75.

174 Qāḍī Aḥmad, *Khulāṣat al-tavārīkh*, vol. 1, pp. 477–78.

175 Qāḍī Aḥmad, *Khulāṣat al-tavārīkh*, vol. 1, p. 478.

176 Al-Qummi, *Khulāṣat al-tavārīkh*, vol. 1, pp. 494–507.

177 M. Dickson and S. C. Welch (eds.), *The Houghton Shahnameh*, vol. 1, p. 270.

178 M. Dickson and S. C. Welch (eds.), *The Houghton Shahnameh*, vol. 1, p. 270.

179 Hillenbrand, "The Iconography of the *Shah-namah-yi Shahi*," p. 69.

180 Qāḍī Aḥmad, *Khulāṣat al-tavārīkh*, vol. 1, p. 478.

181 Reza Saberi identifies this *ghazal* as no. 403, but other editions list this as no. 410. Ḥāfiẓ, *The Dīvān of Hafez*, trans. and ed. Reza Saberi (Lanham: 2002), p. 475.

182 Babayan, *Mystics, Monarchs, and Messiahs*, p. 326.

183 Qāḍī Aḥmad, *Khulāṣat al-tavārīkh*, vol. 1, p. 510.

184 Qāḍī Aḥmad, *Khulāṣat al-tavārīkh*, vol. 1, p. 511–14.

185 Qāḍī Aḥmad, *Khulāṣat al-tavārīkh*, vol. 1, p. 480.

186 Qāḍī Aḥmad, *Khulāṣat al-tavārīkh*, vol. 1, p. 481.

187 Qāḍī Aḥmad, *Khulāṣat al-tavārīkh*, vol. 1, p. 482.

188 Qāḍī Aḥmad, *Khulāṣat al-tavārīkh*, vol. 1, p. 508.

189 Qāḍī Aḥmad, *Khulāṣat al-tavārīkh*, vol. 1, p. 508.

190 Qāḍī Aḥmad, *Khulāṣat al-tavārīkh*, vol. 1, p. 539.

191 Qāḍī Aḥmad, *Khulāṣat al-tavārīkh*, vol. 1, p. 530.

192 Qāḍī Aḥmad, *Khulāṣat al-tavārīkh*, vol. 1, p. 519.

193 Iram possessed a rhetoric appeal in the medieval Islamic world as an architectural exemplar; its famed pillars and quarters appeared across Islamic literature, and Renard notes the popularity of this imagery in Timurid miniature painting. Renard, *Islam and the Heroic Image*, pp. 167–68.

194 Qāḍī Aḥmad, *Khulāṣat al-tavārīkh*, vol. 1, pp. 519–20.

195 Qāḍī Aḥmad, *Khulāṣat al-tavārīkh*, vol. 1, p. 520.

196 Qāḍī Aḥmad, *Khulāṣat al-tavārīkh*, vol. 1, p. 521.

197 Qāḍī Aḥmad, *Khulāṣat al-tavārīkh*, vol. 1, p. 521.

198 Qāḍī Aḥmad, *Khulāṣat al-tavārīkh*, vol. 1, p. 521.

199 Losensky, "The Palace of Praise and the Melons of Time," p. 5.

200 Men of craft and construction/divided the walls with glorious wall-carpets
Gem-sellers with hundred-fold beauty and ornamentation/scattered hundreds of jewels
They adorned all of them with royal gems/in every space, there were countless precious stones

Precious *Yāqūt-i rūmmānīs* and pure gems/ some were bored with holes and others were unbored
And the flashing arrangements of rows of gems/were such that these precious pearls presented a river
And with this virtuous and golden ornamentation/the flower garden became a quarry of gold
If the humble slave works with copper/an elixir of brilliance will spring forth.
Qāḍī Aḥmad, *Khulāṣat al-tavārīkh*, vol. 1, p. 515.

201 Qāḍī Aḥmad, *Khulāṣat al-tavārīkh*, vol. 1, pp. 515–16.
202 Qāḍī Aḥmad, *Khulāṣat al-tavārīkh*, vol. 1, pp. 515–16.
203 Roxburgh, *Prefacing the Image*, p. 54.
204 Canby, "Safavid Painting," p. 82.
205 There are many poetic sections whose meanings are secret and manifest/all of them are in the style of Yāqūt and Sulṭān `Alī
That beloved object [e.g., *Shāh nāmah*] was placed in the atelier/and those that saw it had their souls revived
From forms of Chinese and China/thousands of faces were made handsome
From every direction [they came] to that artistic atelier/and these handsome ones were arranged in rows
They sit now in that beloved object like fairies/as if Bihzād had given them form
Thus, these images came to be peerless/ and of which Mānī himelf would say a hundred praises
Qāḍī Aḥmad, *Khulāṣat al-tavārīkh*, vol. 1, p. 516.
206 Qāḍī Aḥmad, *Khulāṣat al-tavārīkh*, vol. 1, p. 517.
207 Babayan, *Mystics, Monarchs, and Messiahs*, p. 326.
208 Qāḍī Aḥmad, *Khulāṣat al-tavārīkh,* vol. 1, p. 490; Kāshifī, *Makhzan al-inshā*, ff. 27a–b.
209 Qāḍī Aḥmad, *Khulāṣat al-tavārīkh,* vol. 1, p. 490; Kāshifī, *Makhzan al-inshā*, fol. 27a.
210 Qāḍī Aḥmad, *Khulāṣat al-tavārīkh,* vol. 1, p. 490; Kāshifī, *Makhzan al-inshā*, fol. 38b.
211 Qāḍī Aḥmad, *Khulāṣat al-tavārīkh*, vol. 1, p. 541.
212 *Al-arwāḥ junūd mujannadah fa-mā tā`araf min-hā iytilāf wa mā tanākir min-hā ikhtilāf.* Saḥīḥ al-Bukharī, *Bāb-i aḥādith al-anbiyā, Bāb al-Arwāḥ junūd mujannadah.*
213 Qāḍī Aḥmad, *Khulāṣat al-tavārīkh*, vol. 1, p. 541.
214 Qāḍī Aḥmad, *Khulāṣat al-tavārīkh*, vol. 1, p. 541.
215 Qāḍī Aḥmad, *Khulāṣat al-tavārīkh*, vol. 1, p. 542.
216 Qāḍī Aḥmad, *Khulāṣat al-tavārīkh*, vol. 1, p. 542.
217 Qāḍī Aḥmad, *Khulāṣat al-tavārīkh*, vol. 1, p. 542.
218 *Khaladu Allāhu mulkahu va salṭanatahu īlā yaum al-qirār*. Qāḍī Aḥmad, *Khulāṣat al-tavārīkh*, vol. 1, pp. 542–43.
219 Qāḍī Aḥmad, *Khulāṣat al-tavārīkh*, vol. 1, p. 543.
220 Qāḍī Aḥmad, *Khulāṣat al-tavārīkh*, vol. 1, p. 543.
221 Qāḍī Aḥmad, *Khulāṣat al-tavārīkh*, vol. 1, pp. 543–44.
222 Qāḍī Aḥmad, *Gulistān-i hunar*, p. 76.
223 Qāḍī Aḥmad, *Khulāṣat al-tavārīkh,* vol. 1, pp. 477–78.
224 Losensky, "The Palace of Praise and the Melons of Time," p. 2.
225 M. Dabirsaqi and Bert Fragner, "`Abdī Shīrāzī," *Encyclopedia Iranica*, vol. 1, pp. 209–10; Quinn, *Historical Writing During the Reign of Shah `Abbas*, p. 18.
226 His most famous poetic work, the *Jannat-i `Adan*, is a *khamsah*-styled collection of encomiastic works, which included among others the *Rauḍat al-ṣifāt*, *Dauhat*

al-azhār, and the *Saḥīfat al-ikhlāṣ*. Other poetic texts of his include the *Maẓhar al-asrār*, *Jām-i Jamshīdī*, and the *`Ain-i Iskandarī*. See `Abd al-Ḥusain Navā'ī's introduction to Shirāzī, *Takmilat al-akhbār*, pp. 7–41, and Losensky, "The Palace of Praise and the Melons of Time," p. 6.

227 Losensky, "The Palace of Praise and the Melons of Time," p. 1.

228 See Navā'ī's introduction in Shirāzī, *Takmilat al-akhbār*, p. 17.

229 Tāj al-Dīn Kāshī, a contemporary poet, described him as matchless with respect to poetry and eloquence. Navā'ī's introduction in Shirāzī, *Takmilat al-akhbār*, p. 14; Sām Mīrzā, *Tazkirah-yi tuḥfah-yi Sāmī*, p. 95.

230 Navā'ī's introduction in Shirāzī, *Takmilat al-akhbār*, p. 20.

231 Abū al-Faḍl Hāshim-ūghlī Raḥīmov in his introduction to *Maẓhar al-asrār*, p. 8.

232 Navā'ī's introduction in Shirāzī, *Takmilat al-akhbār*, p. 21.

233 It cannot be a coincidence that `Abdī Beg's reversal of fortune and his return to Qazvīn in 1573 was the same year in which Mīr Sayyid `Alī Khaṭīb died.

234 Īvūghlī, *Nuskhah-yi jāmi`a-i al-murāsalāt*, fol. 102a; Navā'ī (ed.), *Shāh Ṭahmāsp Ṣafavī*, p. 486.

235 Specifically, lines 153 and 162 from his poetic eulogium (*s̱anā*) to Shāh Ṭahmāsp in `Abdī Beg Shīrāzī, *Maẓhar al-asrār*, p. 192. Likewise, parts of the poetic benedictions to the Prophet Muḥammad are similar to `Abdī Beg Shīrāzī's praise of the Prophet in *`Ain-i Iskandarī*. ` Abdī Beg Shīrāzī, *`Ain-i Iskandarī*, ed. Abū al-Faḍl Hāshim-ūghlī Raḥīmov (Moscow: 1977), pp. 8–9.

236 Īvūghlī, *Nuskhah-yi jāmi`a-i al-murāsalāt*, fol. 103a; Navā'ī (ed.), *Shāh Ṭahmāsp Ṣafavī*, p. 490; `Abdī Beg Shīrāzī, *Jannat al-as̱mār* in *Rauḍat al-ṣifāt*, ed. Abū al-Faḍl Hāshim-ūghlī Raḥīmov (Moscow: 1974), pp. 103–04.

237 Īvūghlī, *Nuskhah-yi jāmi`a-i al-murāsalāt*, fol. 103b; Navā'ī (ed.), *Shāh Ṭahmāsp Ṣafavī*, p. 493.

238 For instance, his poetic work on Alexander the Great was produced in 984/1575 and dedicated to Shāh Ismā`il II (even though he was in prison!). `Abdī Beg Shīrāzī, *`Ain-i Iskandarī*, pp. 8–9, pp. 136–37.

239 Īvūghlī, *Nuskhah-yi jāmi`a-i al-murāsalāt*, fol. 102a; Navā'ī (ed.), *Shāh Ṭahmāsp Ṣafavī*, pp. 486–87.

240 Īvūghlī, *Nuskhah-yi jāmi`a-i al-murāsalāt*, fol. 102a–102b; Navā'ī (ed.), *Shāh Ṭahmāsp Ṣafavī*, p. 487.

241 Īvūghlī, *Nuskhah-yi jāmi`a-i al-murāsalāt*, fol. 102b; Navā'ī (ed.), *Shāh Ṭahmāsp Ṣafavī*, p. 487.

242 Īvūghlī, *Nuskhah-yi jāmi`a-i al-murāsalāt*, fol. 102b; Navā'ī (ed.), *Shāh Ṭahmāsp Ṣafavī*, p. 487.

243 Annemarie Schimmel, *And Muhammad is His Messenger* (Chapel Hill: 1985), pp. 108–09.

244 Īvūghlī, *Nuskhah-yi jāmi`a-i al-murāsalāt*, fol. 102b; Navā'ī (ed.), *Shāh Ṭahmāsp Ṣafavī*, p. 488. Interestingly, the device of the garden peacock has been used in panegyric poetry on behalf of `Ali. See Kamāl al-Dīn Maḥmūd's poetry in Aḥmad Aḥmadī Birjandī, *Manāqib-i `alavī dar shi`r-i Fārsī* (Tehran: 1987), p. 29, as well as Rādfar, *Manāqib-i `alavī dar āyīnah-yi shi`r-i Fārsī*, p. 62.

245 Navā'ī mistakenly attributes this *iqtibās* to Surah 92 ("The Night").

246 Schimmel, *And Muhammad is His Messenger*, pp. 195–96.

247 This is an excerpt from Surah al-Ṣād.

248 Īvūghlī, *Nuskhah-yi jāmi`a-i al-murāsalāt*, fol. 102b; Navā'ī (ed.), *Shāh Ṭahmāsp Ṣafavī*, p. 488.

249 Schimmel, *A Two-Colored Brocade*, p. 42; Schimmel, *Mystical Dimensions of Islam*, p. 218; Nargis Virani, *"I am the Nightingale of the Merciful" Macaronic or Upside-Down: The* Mulamma`āt *of Jalāl al-Dīn Rūmī*, Unpublished Ph.D.

Dissertation (Cambridge, Mass.: 1999), p. 66.

250 Rasūl Ja`fariyān, "Dīdgāh-hā-yi siyāsī-yi `Abdī Beg Shīrāzī dar barā-yi Shāh Ṭahmāsp Ṣafavī," *Ṣafaviyyah dar `arṣah-yi dīn, farhang va siyāsat*, ed. R. Ja`fariyān, vol. 1 (Tehran: 2000), p. 494.

251 Īvūghlī, *Nuskhah-yi jāmi`a-i al-murāsalāt*, fol. 102b; Navā'ī (ed.), *Shāh Ṭahmāsp Ṣafavī*, p. 488.

252 `Abdī Beg Shīrāzī, *Jannat al-asmār*, pp. 3–4.

253 Virani, *"I am the Nightingale of the Merciful,"* pp. 51–52, pp. 55–56.

254 Virani, *"I am the Nightingale of the Merciful,"* p. 54.

255 Īvūghlī, *Nuskhah-yi jāmi`a-i al-murāsalāt*; Navā'ī (ed.), *Shāh Ṭahmāsp Ṣafavī*, p. 489.

256 Īvūghlī, *Nuskhah-yi jāmi`a-i al-murāsalāt*; Navā'ī (ed.), *Shāh Ṭahmāsp Ṣafavī*, p. 489.

257 Īvūghlī, *Nuskhah-yi jāmi`a-i al-murāsalāt*; Navā'ī (ed.), *Shāh Ṭahmāsp Ṣafavī*, p. 489.

258 Īvūghlī, *Nuskhah-yi jāmi`a-i al-murāsalāt*; Navā'ī (ed.), *Shāh Ṭahmāsp Ṣafavī*, p. 489.

259 Īvūghlī, *Nuskhah-yi jāmi`a-i al-murāsalāt*, fol. 103a; Navā'ī (ed.), *Shāh Ṭahmāsp Ṣafavī*, p. 490.

260 Īvūghlī, *Nuskhah-yi jāmi`a-i al-murāsalāt*, fol. 103a; Navā'ī (ed.), *Shāh Ṭahmāsp Ṣafavī*, p. 490.

261 Īvūghlī, *Nuskhah-yi jāmi`a-i al-murāsalāt*, fol. 103a; Navā'ī (ed.), *Shāh Ṭahmāsp Ṣafavī*, p. 490.

262 Īvūghlī, *Nuskhah-yi jāmi`a-i al-murāsalāt*, fol. 104a; Navā'ī (ed.), *Shāh Ṭahmāsp Ṣafavī*, p. 494.

263 Īvūghlī, *Nuskhah-yi jāmi`a-i al-murāsalāt*, fol. 104a; Navā'ī (ed.), *Shāh Ṭahmāsp Ṣafavī*, p. 495.

264 Īvūghlī, *Nuskhah-yi jāmi`a-i al-murāsalāt*, fol. 104a; Navā'ī (ed.), *Shāh Ṭahmāsp Ṣafavī*, p. 495.

265 A narrative is apparently recorded by al-Zamakhsharī in his *Rabi` al-abrār* whereby the Prophet said to `Alī: "Oh `Alī! On the Day of Judgement the skirt of God's mercy will be in my hand, and my skirt will be in your hand, and your skirt will be held by your descendents, and the Shi`as of your descendents will be hanging on to their skirt." See `Allāmah Muḥammad Ḥusain al-Kāshif al-Ghiṭā', *The Origin of Shi`ite Islam and its Principles* (Qumm: 1993), p. 27.

266 Īvūghlī, *Nuskhah-yi jāmi`a-i al-murāsalāt*, fol. 104a, Navā'ī (ed.), *Shāh Ṭahmāsp Ṣafavī*, p. 495.

267 Īvūghlī, *Nuskhah-yi jāmi`a-i al-murāsalāt*, fol. 104b; Navā'ī (ed.), *Shāh Ṭahmāsp Ṣafavī*, p. 495.

268 Īvūghlī, *Nuskhah-yi jāmi`a-i al-murāsalāt*, fol. 104b; Navā'ī (ed.), *Shāh Ṭahmāsp Ṣafavī*, p. 496.

269 While Rula Abissab presents a detailed account of the interplay between political policies and religious doctrine, her study *Converting Persia* privileges the role of the Arab émigrés. Particularly, her chapter on the reigns of Shāh Ṭahmāsp, Shāh Ismā`īl II, and Shāh Khudābandah ("The Mujtahids Navigate the Sovereignt's World") posits an unchallenged degree of power and influence for the al-Karakī and al-`Āmilī families. Abisaab, *Converting Persia*, pp. 31–52.

Chapter Four

1 Savory, *Iran Under the Safavids*, p. 68.

2 E. G. Browne, *A Literary History of Persia*, vol. 4, pp. 98–99; Sir John Malcolm, *The History of Persia*, vol. 2 (London: 1815), p. 515.

3 Walther Hinz, "Schah Esma`il II. Ein Beitrag zur Geschichte der Safaviden," *Mitteilungen des Seminars für orientalische Sprachen*, vol. 26 (1933), pp. 19–100.
4 Hans Robert Roemer set the tone with his publication of *Die Niedergang Irans nach dem Tode Isma`ils der Grausamen (1577–1581)* (Würzburg-Aumühle: 1939). Many of his arguments were later reiterated in Roemer, "The Safavid Period," pp. 250–53, and *Persien auf dem Weg*, pp. 295–98. Savory talks about his "pathological suspiciousness" in "The Office of Khalifat al-khulafa Under the Safawids," *Journal of the American Oriental Society*, vol. 85 (1965), p. 498; see also "Esmā`il II," *EI*², vol. 4, p. 188 and *Iran Under the Safavids*, p. 69.
5 Hinz, "Schah Esma`il II," pp. 76–85.
6 Stanfield-Johnson, "The Tabarra'iyan and the Early Safavids," p. 65; Arjomand, *The Shadow of God and the Hidden Imam*, p. 120.
7 Abisaab, *Converting Persia*, pp. 41–44.
8 Newman, *Safavid Iran*, p. 46.
9 Shohreh Gholsorkhi, "Ismail II and Mirza Makhdum Sharifi: An Interlude in Safavid History," *International Journal of Middle East Studies*, vol. 26 (1994), p. 485.
10 Devin Stewart, "The Lost Biography of Baha' al-Dīn al-Amili and the Reign of Shah Ismā`il II in Safavid Historiography," *Iranian Studies*, vol. 31 (1998), p. 203.
11 Stewart, "The Lost Biography of Baha' al-Dīn al-Amili," p. 193.
12 Manūchihr Pārsādūst, *Shāh Ismā`īl-i duvvum: Shujā` tabāh shudah* (Tehran: 2002), pp. 114–25.
13 Afūshtah-ī Natanzī, *Naqāvat al-āsār*, p. 58.
14 Stewart, "The Lost Biography of Baha' al-Dīn al-Amili," p. 198.
15 Stewart, "The Lost Biography of Baha' al-Dīn al-Amili," p. 201.
16 Iskander Beg Munshī, *History of Shah `Abbas the Great*, vol. 1, pp. 292–93; for Persian, see *Tārīkh-i `ālam-ārā-yi `Abbāsī*, vol. 1, pp. 197–98.
17 Afūshtah-ī Natanzī, *Naqāvat al-āsār*, p. 38.
18 Iskander Beg Munshī, *History of Shah `Abbas the Great*, vol. 1, pp. 302–03; for Persian, see *Tārīkh-i `ālam-ārā-yi `Abbāsī*, vol. 1, p. 204; Afūshtah-ī Natanzī, *Naqāvat al-āsār*, p. 38.
19 The shah would also stay in the residence of Yaqkān Shāh Qulī and Parī Khān Khānum. Qāḍī Aḥmad, *Khulāṣat al-tavārīkh*, vol. 2, p. 621.
20 Iskander Beg Munshī, *History of Shah `Abbas the Great*, vol. 1, pp. 300-01; for Persian, see *Tārīkh-i `ālam-ārā-yi `Abbāsī*, vol. 1, p. 202.
21 Iskander Beg Munshī, *History of Shah `Abbas the Great*, vol. 1, pp. 300-01; for Persian, see *Tārīkh-i `ālam-ārā-yi `Abbāsī*, vol. 1, p. 202.
22 Qāḍī Aḥmad, *Khulāṣat al-tavārīkh*, vol. 2, pp. 619–21.
23 Iskander Beg Munshī, *History of Shah `Abbas the Great*, vol. 1, pp. 307–08; for Persian, see *Tārīkh-i `ālam-ārā-yi `Abbāsī*, vol. 1, p. 207; Ḥasan Beg Rūmlū, *Aḥsan al-tavārīkh*, vol. 1, pp. 206–07.
24 Būdāq Munshī, *Javāhir al-akhbār*, p. 246.
25 Īvūghlī preserved a copy of a little-known *parvānchah* from Shāh Ṭahmāsp naming Mīrzā Shukr Allāh Iṣfahānī as *mustaufī al-mamālik*. See Īvūghlī, *Nuskhah-yi jāmi`a-i al-murāsalāt*, ff. 122b–124a.
26 Būdāq Munshī, *Javāhir al-akhbār*, p. 245.
27 Būdāq Munshī, *Javāhir al-akhbār*, p. 245.
28 Mir Fazaluddin Ali Khān, *Life and Works of Mirza Sharaf Jahan Qazwini*, p. 95.
29 Gholsorkhi, "Ismail II and Mirza Makhdum Sharifi," p. 484.
30 Qāḍī Aḥmad, *Khulāṣat al-tavārīkh*, vol. 2, pp. 629–30. Qāḍī Aḥmad also provided a brief biography, pp. 633–44.
31 Qāḍī Aḥmad, *Khulāṣat al-tavārīkh*, vol. 2, p. 644.

32 Ḥasan Beg Rūmlū, *Aḥsan al-tavārīkh*, vol. 1, p. 208; Iskander Beg Munshī, *History of Shah `Abbas the Great*, vol. 1, p. 306; for Persian, see *Tārīkh-i `ālam-ārā-yi `Abbāsī*, vol. 1, p. 206.

33 Qāḍī Aḥmad, *Khulāṣat al-tavārīkh*, vol. 2, p. 651. It should also be noted that the Qizilbāsh ranks of Herāt had demonstrated their loyalty to the shah in the summer of 1576, when a number of Qizilbāsh quashed a potential rebellion by Shāh Qulī Sulṭān Ustājlū, the *amīr al-umarā* of Khurāsān. Ḥasan Beg Rūmlū, *Aḥsan al-tavārīkh*, vol. 1, p. 207.

34 Iskander Beg Munshī, *History of Shah `Abbas the Great*, vol. 1, p. 316; for Persian, see *Tārīkh-i `ālam-ārā-yi `Abbāsī*, vol. 1, p. 213.

35 Ḥasan Beg Rūmlū, *Aḥsan al-tavārīkh*, vol. 1, p. 208.

36 Iskander Beg Munshī, *History of Shah `Abbas the Great*, vol. 1, p. 310; for Persian, see *Tārīkh-i `ālam-ārā-yi `Abbāsī*, vol. 1, p. 208; Qāḍī Aḥmad, *Khulāṣat al-tavārīkh*, vol. 2, p. 643.

37 Abisaab, *Converting Persia*, p. 20.

38 B. S. Amoretti, "Religion in the Timurid and Safavid Periods," in *Cambridge History of Iran*, ed. P. Jackson, vol. 6 (1986), p. 643.

39 Iskander Beg Munshī, *History of Shah `Abbas the Great*, vol. 1, p. 308, p. 319; for Persian, see *Tārīkh-i `ālam-ārā-yi `Abbāsī*, vol. 1, p. 206, p. 214.

40 Iskander Beg Munshī, *History of Shah `Abbas the Great*, vol. 1, p. 320; for Persian, see *Tārīkh-i `ālam-ārā-yi `Abbāsī*, vol. 1 p. 215; Stewart, "The Lost Biography of Baha' al-Dīn al-Amili," p. 200; Abisaab, *Converting Persia*, p. 46.

41 Michel Mazzaoui, "The Religious Policy of Shah Ismā`il II" in *Intellectual Studies on Islam: Essays Written in Honor of Martin B. Dickson*, eds. M. Mazzaoui and V. Moreen (Salt Lake City: 1990), p. 53; Iskander Beg Munshī, *History of Shah `Abbas the Great*, vol. 1, p. 320; for Persian, see *Tārīkh-i `ālam-ārā-yi `Abbāsī*, vol. 1, p. 215.

42 Stanfield-Johnson, "The Tabarra'iyan and the Early Safavids," p. 65; Gholsorkhi, "Ismail II and Mirza Makhdum Sharifi," p. 481.

43 Ḥasan Beg Rūmlū, *Aḥsan al-tavārīkh*, vol. 1, p. 205.

44 Iskander Beg Munshī, *History of Shah `Abbas the Great*, vol. 1, pp. 318–19; for Persian, see *Tārīkh-i `ālam-ārā-yi `Abbāsī*, vol. 1 (Tehran: 2003), p. 214.

45 Ḥasan Beg Rūmlū, *Aḥsan al-tavārīkh*, vol. 1, pp. 207–08.

46 Pārsādūst, *Shāh Ismā`īl-i duvvum*, pp. 110–12.

47 Abisaab, *Converting Persia*, p. 46.

48 Afūshtah-ī Natanzī, *Naqāvat al-āsār*, p. 41; Stewart, "The Lost Biography of Baha' al-Dīn al-Amili," pp. 202–03.

49 Afūshtah-ī Natanzī, *Naqāvat al-āsār*, pp. 39–40.

50 Afūshtah-ī Natanzī, *Naqāvat al-āsār*, p. 39.

51 Afūshtah-ī Natanzī, *Naqāvat al-āsār*, p. 40.

52 Afūshtah-ī Natanzī, *Naqāvat al-āsār*, p. 40.

53 Afūshtah-ī Natanzī, *Naqāvat al-āsār*, p. 40.

54 Iskander Beg Munshī, *History of Shah `Abbas the Great*, vol. 1, p. 308; for Persian, see *Tārīkh-i `ālam-ārā-yi `Abbāsī*, vol. 1, p. 207.

55 Muḥammad Yūsuf Vālih, *Khuld-i barīn*, p. 540.

56 Rather than the standardized and ubiquitous introductory formula of *farmān-i humāyūn shud*, this particular document (dated 12 Zū al-Qa`da 984/31 January 1577) reads *amr-i dīvān-i a`lā shud*, and this appears to conform to the protocol described by Iskander Beg Munshī regarding the new *dīvān-i `adl*. It is not entirely surprising that the governor of this particular province would be willing to enforce the dictates of this new legal body. The governor was Muḥammadī Khān Tuqmāq Ustājlū, a kinsman of Pīra Muḥammad Khān and an ally of Ismā`īl II. Schimkoreit,

Regesten publizierter safawidischer Herrscherurkunden, p. 162. Heribert Busse confirmed the significance of this in his seminal article on medieval Persian diplomatics. Busse, "Persische Diplomatik im Überblick," p. 231.

57 Iskander Beg Munshī, *History of Shah `Abbas the Great,* vol. 1, p. 308; for Persian, see *Tārīkh-i `ālam-ārā-yi `Abbāsī,* vol. 1, p. 207.

58 Röhrborn, "Staatskanzlei und Absolutismus im safawidischen Persien," p. 314.

59 Qāḍī Aḥmad, *Gulistān-i hunar,* p. 92.

60 Floor, *Safavid Government Institutions,* p. 52.

61 Qāḍī Aḥmad, *Khulāṣat al-tavārīkh,* vol. 2, p. 627.

62 Qāḍī Aḥmad, *Khulāṣat al-tavārīkh,* vol. 2, p. 627; Pārsādūst, *Shāh Ismā`īl-i duvvum,* p. 105.

63 Qāḍī Aḥmad, *Khulāṣat al-tavārīkh,* vol. 2, p. 627; Afūshtah-ī Natanzī, *Naqāvat al-āsār,* pp. 272–73.

64 This list of privileged personalities appearing in this *ḥukm* also makes mention of Pīra Muḥammad Khān Ustājlū, governor of Lāhījān and former custodian of Shāh Ṭahmāsp's son Imām Qulī Mīrzā. In light of the scope of anti-Ustājlū violence in the summer of 1576, the appearance here of Pīra Muḥammad Khān suggests that the Ustājlūs had been effectively heeled and fully co-opted by the shah. The marriage alliance between the families of Ismā`īl II and Pīra Muḥammad Khān in Sha`bān 984/October 1576 might very well have been a reward for Pīra Muḥammad Sulṭān's collusion in the recent murder of his former charge and brother of Ismā`īl, Imām Qulī Mīrzā. Pīra Muḥammad Ustājlū was thus confirmed in his post as governor of Gīlān, while his kinsmen Muḥammadī Khān Tuqmāq Ustājlū and Abū Turāb Beg Ustājlū were named governors of Chukhūr Sa`d and Shīrvān. Pārsādūst, *Shāh Ismā`īl-i duvvum,* p. 78, p. 81, p. 102.

65 Images of the coins in question are available in H. L. Rabino di Borgomale, *Coins, Medals, and Seals of the Shahs of Iran 1500–1941,* Hertford, U.K.: 1945, plate 6.

66 *...er nehme nur an dieser schiitischen Formel Anstoss.* Hinz, "Schah Esma`il II," p. 83.

67 Hinz, "Schah Esma`il II," p. 83.

68 `Abd al-Ḥusain al-Ṭūsī, *Munsha'āt al-Ṭūsī,* f. 63a; Navā'ī (ed.), *Shāh Ismā`īl Ṣafavī,* p. 48.

69 Īvūghlī, *Nuskhah-yi jāmi`a-i al-murāsalāt,* ff. 128b–129a.

70 Īvūghlī, *Nuskhah-yi jāmi`a-i al-murāsalāt,* fol. 128b.

71 Īvūghlī, *Nuskhah-yi jāmi`a-i al-murāsalāt,* fol. 128b.

72 Īvūghlī, *Nuskhah-yi jāmi`a-i al-murāsalāt,* fol. 128b.

73 Īvūghlī, *Nuskhah-yi jāmi`a-i al-murāsalāt,* fol. 129a.

74 The historian Khvāndamīr cites this tradition in his own advice manual, Khvāndamīr, *Makāram al-akhlāq,* p. 89. See also A. K. S. Lambton, "Changing Concepts of Justice and Injustice from the 5th/11th Century to the 8th/14th Century in Persia: The Saljuq Empire and the Ilkhanate," *Studia Islamica,* vol. 68 (1988), p. 39.

75 The original quote from al-Ghazālī reads, "one hour of justice is better than sixty years of prayer." See Muḥammad ibn Muḥammad ibn Ghazālī Ṭūsī, *Naṣīḥat al-mulūk,* ed. Jalāl al-Dīn Humā'ī (Tehran: 1972), p. 301. The use of seventy as opposed to sixty is not significant given that al-Ghazālī stated elsewhere that "one hour of justice is better than a hundred years of prayer." Lambton, "Changing Concepts of Justice and Injustice," p. 40. For Niẓām al-Mulk's discussion of the value of viziers to a Perso-Islamic state, see Khvājah Niẓām al-Mulk, *Siyar al-mulūk,* ed. H. Darke (Tehran: 1962), pp. 29–40.

76 A similar style of language and various phrases appear in both documents. Īvūghlī, *Nuskhah-yi jāmi`a-i al-murāsalāt,* fols. 129a–b.

77 Īvūghlī, *Nuskhah-yi jāmi`a-i al-murāsalāt,* fol. 129a.

78 Īvūghlī, *Nuskhah-yi jāmi`a-i al-murāsalāt*, fol. 129a.
79 *Murāqibāt-i ḥāl va mubādarāt-i aḥvāl-i khvāṣṣ va `avāmm.*
80 Īvūghlī, *Nuskhah-yi jāmi`a-i al-murāsalāt*, fol. 129a.
81 *Chūn asās-i ṭārum-nilgūn-i dunyāvī va sipihr-i būqalamūn.*
82 Īvūghlī, *Nuskhah-yi jāmi`a-i al-murāsalāt*, fol. 129b.
83 Iskander Beg Munshī, *History of Shah `Abbas the Great*, vol. 1, p. 315; for Persian, see *Tārīkh-i `ālam-ārā-yi `Abbāsī*, vol. 1, p. 212.
84 Īvūghlī, *Nuskhah-yi jāmi`a-i al-murāsalāt*, fol. 129b.
85 Īvūghlī, *Nuskhah-yi jāmi`a-i al-murāsalāt*, fol. 129b.
86 Īvūghlī, *Nuskhah-yi jāmi`a-i al-murāsalāt*, fol. 129b.
87 Īvūghlī, *Nuskhah-yi jāmi`a-i al-murāsalāt*, fol. 129b.
88 Navā'ī (ed.), *Shāh Ṭahmāsp Ṣafavī*, p. 135.
89 Navā'ī (ed.), *Shāh Ṭahmāsp Ṣafavī*, p. 135.
90 Navā'ī (ed.), *Shāh Ṭahmāsp Ṣafavī*, p. 135.
91 Navā'ī (ed.), *Shāh Ṭahmāsp Ṣafavī*, p. 135.
92 Quinn, *Historical Writing During the Reign of Shah Abbas*, p. 45.
93 Navā'ī (ed.), *Shāh Ṭahmāsp Ṣafavī*, p. 136.
94 Īvūghlī, *Nuskhah-yi jāmi`a-i al-murāsalāt*, fols. 128a–b, Navā'ī (ed.); *Shāh Ṭahmāsp Ṣafavī*, pp. 503–05.
95 Īvūghlī, *Nuskhah-yi jāmi`a-i al-murāsalāt*, fol. 128a; Navā'ī (ed.), *Shāh Ṭahmāsp Ṣafavī*, p. 504.
96 *Al-ad`iyya al-manthūra al-`arabiyya li-ahli al-ṭabaqa al-awwalī.* Ḥusain Vā`iẓ Kāshifī, *Makhzan al-inshā*, fol. 22a.
97 Newman, *Safavid Iran*, p. 44.
98 Röhrborn, "Staatskanzlei und Absolutismus im safawidischen Persien," p. 315.
99 Hans Robert Roemer describes how Khair al-Nisā Begum was an ambitious woman and "her enterprise and lust for power found undreamed-of opportunities" in the court of Khudābandah. It was in response to her autocratic ways that Türkmen leaders ultimately fell into a pattern of recrimination and violence that beset "the internal crisis of the Safavid empire, which had been simmer[ing] ever since Shāh Ṭahmāsp's death." See Roemer, "The Safavid Period," pp. 255–56. Similar depictions of Mahd-i `Ulyā are found in Roemer, *Persien auf dem Weg in die Neuzeit*, p. 300. Likewise, see Walther Hinz, "Schah Esma`il II," pp. 19–100.
100 Roger Savory notes some of these features with Iskander Beg Munshī in "'Very Dull and Arduous Reading': A Reappraisal of the *History of Shah `Abbas the Great* by Iskandar Beg Munshi," *Hamdard Islamicus*, vol. 3 (1980), no. 1, pp. 27–30.
101 Roemer, *Die Niedergang Irans*, p. 9.
102 Roemer, "The Safavid Period," p. 253.
103 Roemer, *Persien auf dem Weg in die Neuzeit*, p. 298.
104 In Iḥsan Ishrāqī's chapter on the Safavids, reign of Ismā`īl II and Khudābandah—styled as "A Decade of Upheavals (1576–87)—is situated between two sections entitled respectively "Shāh Ṭahmāsp I (1524–76): The Consolidation of the Empire" and "Shāh `Abbās the Great (1587–1629): The Rebirth of the Empire on a New Foundation." See Iḥsan Ishrāqī, "Persia During the Period of the Safavids, the Afshars and the Early Qajars," in *History of Civilizations of Central Asia,* eds. C. Adle, I. Habib, vol. 5 (*Development in Contrast: From the Sixteenth to the Mid-Nineteenth Century*), (Paris: 2003), pp. 247–71. In a similar vein, David Morgan suggests that Muḥammad Khudābandah "seems never to have taken much interest in the business of being ruler of Persia" and was content to remain in the background while Parī Khān Khānum *et alia* dominated the foreground. David Morgan, *Medieval Persia 1040–1797* (London: 1988), p. 130. For more recent reproving interpretations, see Manūchihr Pārsādūst, *Shāh Muḥammad: pādshāhi ki shāh na-*

būd (Tehran: 2002), pp. 221–23.

105 For a recent discussion on the problems associated with the Safavid notion of corporate sovereignty, see Sussan Babaie, Kathryn Babayan, Ina Baghdiantz-McCabe, and Massumeh Farhad, *Slaves of the Shah: New Elites of Safavid Iran* (London: 2004), pp. 25–30.

106 Newman, *Safavid Iran*, p. 44.

107 Szuppe, *Entre Timourides, Uzbeks et Safavides*, p. 31, p. 109.

108 For the best study of this individual, see Maria Szuppe, "Kinship Ties Between the Safavids and the Qizilbāsh Amirs in Late Sixteenth-Century Iran."

109 Szuppe, *Entre Timourides, Uzbeks, et Safavides*, p. 117; Aubin, "Shah Isma`il et les notables de l'Iraq persan," p. 74.

110 Szuppe, *Entre Timourides, Uzbeks, et Safavides*, p. 119.

111 Röhrborn, *Provinzen und Zentralgewalt Persiens*, p. 43; Pārsādūst, *Shāh Muḥammad* p. 18.

112 Babaie *et alia*, *Slaves of the Shah*, p. 26.

113 Devin Stewart, "The First Shaikh al-Islam of the Safavid Capital Qazvīn," *Journal of the American Oriental Society*, vol. 116 (1996), no. 3, pp. 393–94.

114 Röhrborn, *Provinzen und Zentralgewalt Persiens*, p. 41.

115 Iskander Beg Munshī, *History of Shah `Abbas the Great*, vol. 1, pp. 206–07; for Persian, see *Tārīkh-i `ālam-ārā-yi `Abbāsī*, vol. 1, p. 125.

116 Sām Mīrzā, *Tazkirah-yi tuḥfah-yi Sāmī*, pp. 12–13.

117 Qāḍī Aḥmad, *Khulāṣat al-tavārīkh*, vol. 2, p. 671.

118 Roemer, *Die Niedergang Irans*, p. 4.

119 Henri Corbin, *History of Islamic Philosophy*, trans. L. Sherrard (London: 1993), pp. 335–37.

120 Barakat, *Kitāb-shināsī-yi maktab-i falsafī-yi Shīrāz*, pp. 209–40.

121 Lale Uluç, "Selling to the Court: Late-Sixteenth-Century Manuscript Production in Shīrāz" in *Muqarnas*, vol. 17 (2000), pp. 73–96; and Babaie *et alia*, *Slaves of the Shah*, p. 115. For earlier instances of Shīrāzi manuscript production, see Francis Richard, "Nasr al-Soltani, Nasir al-Din Mozahheb et la bibliothèque d'Ebrahim Soltan à Shiraz." For a general discussion of sixteenth and seventeenth century bibliotist dynamics, see Maria Szuppe, "Circulation des lettrés et circles littéraires entre Asie centrale, Iran et Inde du nord XVe-XVIIIe siècle," *Annales (Histoire, Sciences Sociales)*, vol. 59 (2004), nos. 5–6, pp. 1000–05.

122 Stanfield-Johnson, "The Tabarra'iyan and the Early Safavids," p. 66.

123 Muḥammad Yūsuf Vālih, *Khuld-i barīn*, p. 449.

124 Qāḍī Aḥmad, *Khulāṣat al-tavārīkh*, vol. 2, p. 1078; Sayyid Ḥusain Modarresī-Ṭabāṭabā'ī, *Miṣāl-hā-yi ṣudūr-i Ṣafavī* (Qumm: 1975), p. 14.

125 Jalāl al-Dīn Munajjim Yazdī, *Tārīkh-i `Abbāsī*, *MS*, London, British Library, Or. 6263, fol. 17a.

126 Qāḍī Aḥmad, *Khulāṣat al-tavārīkh*, vol. 2, p. 696, p. 700.

127 Afūshtah-ī Natanzī, *Naqāvat al-āsār*, pp. 272–73; Munajjim Yazdī, *Tārīkh-i `Abbāsī*, fol. 23a.

128 Szuppe, "La participation des femmes da la famille royale," p. 69.

129 This nomination is mentioned in a *farmān* to Khān Aḥmad Gīlānī from Abū Ṭālib Mīrzā, son of Muḥammad Khudābandah. See Navā'ī (ed.), *Shāh Ṭahmāsp*, p. 116.

130 For aspects of this woman's impact on the Safavid court, see Szuppe, "Status, Knowledge, and Politics," pp. 158–60.

131 Szuppe, "La participation des femmes da la famille royale," pp. 90–91; Qāḍī Aḥmad, *Khulāṣat al-tavārīkh*, vol. 2, p. 695, p. 697.

132 Qāḍī Aḥmad *Khulāṣat al-tavārīkh*, vol. 2, p. 685.

133 Qāḍī Aḥmad, *Khulāṣat al-tavārīkh*, vol. 2, p. 715.

134 Qāḍī Aḥmad, *Khulāṣat al-tavārīkh*, vol. 2, p. 716; Muḥammad Yūsuf Vālih, *Khuld-i barīn*, p. 636. See also Hirotake Maeda, "On the Ethno-Social Background of Four Gholam Families From Georgia in Safavid Iran," *Studia Iranica*, vol. 32 (2003), no. 2, p. 257.
135 Roger Savory, "The Significance of the Political Murder of Mīrzā Salmān," *Islamic Studies*, vol. 3 (1964), p. 182.
136 Imber, *The Ottoman Empire*, p. 65.
137 Qāḍī Aḥmad, *Khulāṣat al-tavārīkh*, vol. 2, p. 743; Muḥammad Yūsuf Vālih, *Khuld-i barīn*, pp. 671–72.
138 Surrounded by Qizilbāsh amirs who argued that only strife and civil war would result from Salmān's continued presence, the shah conceded submissively to the conspirators' demands, and Qizilbāsh amirs killed the Persian vizier in the Bāgh-i Zāghān. Qāḍī Aḥmad, *Khulāṣat al-tavārīkh*, vol. 2, pp. 746–47.
139 Pārsādūst, *Shāh Muḥammad*, p. 179.
140 Pārsādūst, *Shāh Muḥammad*, p. 185.
141 Imber, *The Ottoman Empire*, p. 66.
142 Qāḍī Aḥmad, *Khulāṣat al-tavārīkh*, vol. 2, p. 702.
143 Afūshtah-ī Natanzī, *Naqāvat al-āsār*, p. 144.
144 Shāh Ṭāhir al-Ḥusainī, *Inshā-yi Shāh Ṭāhir*, ff. 15a–b. See also, Louis Massignon, "Salmān Pak et les premices spirituelles de l'Islam iranien," in *Opera Minora*, ed. Y. Moubarag, vol. 1 (Beirut: 1934), pp. 443–83.
145 Afūshtah-ī Natanzī, *Naqāvat al-āsār*, pp. 144–45.
146 Muḥammad Mufīd Mustaufī Bafqī, *Jāmi`i-i Mufīdī*, ed. I. Afshār (Tehran: 1961), p. 242.
147 Qāḍī Aḥmad, *Gulistān-i hunar*, p. 146.
148 Qāḍī Aḥmad, *Gulistān-i hunar*, p. 94.
149 Haneda, "La famille Huzani d'Iṣfahān," p. 86.
150 Haneda, "La famille Huzani d'Iṣfahān," p. 87.
151 Qāḍī Aḥmad, *Gulistān-i hunar*, pp. 94–95.
152 Munajjim Yazdī, *Tārīkh-i `Abbāsī*, fol. 23a.
153 Haneda, "La famille Huzani d'Iṣfahān," p. 83.
154 Munajjim Yazdī, *Tārīkh-i `Abbāsī*, fol. 40a.
155 Qāḍī Aḥmad, *Khulāṣat al-tavārīkh*, vol. 2, p. 847.
156 Afūshtah-ī Natanzī, *Naqāvat al-āsār*, pp. 29–30.
157 Munajjim Yazdī, *Tārīkh-i `Abbāsī*, fol. 23a.
158 Afūshtah-ī Natanzī, *Naqāvat al-āsār*, p. 272.
159 Afūshtah-ī Natanzī, *Naqāvat al-āsār*, pp. 272–73; Qāḍī Aḥmad, *Khulāṣat al-tavārīkh*, vol. 2, p. 889.
160 Munajjim Yazdī, *Tārīkh-i `Abbāsī*, fol. 32a; Iskander Beg Munshī, *History of Shah `Abbas the Great*, vol. 2, p. 581; for Persian, see *Tārīkh-i `ālam-ārā-yi `Abbāsī*, vol. 1, p. 404.
161 Iskander Beg Munshī, *History of Shah `Abbas the Great*, vol. 2, p. 606; for Persian, see *Tārīkh-i `ālam-ārā-yi `Abbāsī*, vol. 1, p. 430.
162 Qāḍī Aḥmad, *Gulistān-i hunar*, p. 96.
163 This is courtesy of the recently discovered third volume of Faḍlī ibn Zain al-`Ābidīn Khūzānī's *Afḍal al-tavārīkh*. See Charles Melville, "New Light on the Reign of Shāh `Abbās: Volume III of the *Afzal al-tavarikh*," in *Society and Culture in the Early Modern Middle East: Studies on Iran in the Safavid Period*, ed. A. Newman (Leiden: 2003), p. 86.
164 For a detailed biography, see Franz von Erdmann, "Iskender Munschi und sein Werk," *Zeitschrift der deutschen morgenländischen Gesellschaft*, vol. 15 (1861), pp. 457–501.

165 Qāḍī Aḥmad, *Gulistān-i hunar*, pp. 7–12.
166 Falsafī, *Zindagānī-yi Shāh `Abbās*, vol. 2, p. 400.
167 Melville, "New Light on the Reign of Shāh `Abbās," p. 71; A. H. Morton, "An Introductory Note on a Safawid Munshi's Manual," p. 355.
168 Babaie *et alia*, *Slaves of the Shah*, p. 160, fn. 92.
169 Qāḍī Aḥmad, *Khulāṣat al-tavārīkh*, vol. 2, p. 1018, p. 1081.
170 Röhrborn mentions that Urdūbādī, early on as *mustaufī al-mamālik*, had prepared a plan for organizing financial returns and expenditures for the entire kingdom. Röhrborn, *Provinzen und Zentralgewalt Persiens*, p. 57.
171 Īvūghlī, *Nuskhah-yi jāmi`a-i al-murāsalāt*, ff. 136b–140a. Edited text appears in `Abd al-Ḥusain Navā'ī (ed.), *Shāh `Abbās: majmū`ah-yi asnād va mukātabāt-i tārīkhī*, vol. 1 (Tehran: 1974), pp. 43–63.
172 Īvūghlī, *Nuskhah-yi jāmi`a-i al-murāsalāt*, fol. 136b; Navā'ī (ed.), *Shāh `Abbās*, vol. 1, p. 43.
173 Īvūghlī, *Nuskhah-yi jāmi`a-i al-murāsalāt*, fol. 136b; Navā'ī (ed.), *Shāh `Abbās*, vol. 1, p. 43.
174 *Agar nāẓiman-i durar-i balāghat-rā qarn-an ba`d qarn bā yakdīgar vifāq ḥāṣil āyad*. Īvūghlī, *Nuskhah-yi jāmi`a-i al-murāsalāt*, fol. 136b; Navā'ī (ed.), *Shāh `Abbās*, vol. 1, p. 43.
175 This is an allusion to the addressee of the letter itself: Sulṭān Murād III.
176 Īvūghlī, *Nuskhah-yi jāmi`a-i al-murāsalāt*, fol. 136b; Navā'ī (ed.), *Shāh `Abbās*, vol. 1, p. 44.
177 Īvūghlī, *Nuskhah-yi jāmi`a-i al-murāsalāt*, fol. 136b; Navā'ī (ed.), *Shāh `Abbās*, vol. 1, p. 45.
178 Īvūghlī, *Nuskhah-yi jāmi`a-i al-murāsalāt*, fol. 137a; Navā'ī (ed.), *Shāh `Abbās*, vol. 1, pp. 47–48.
179 Navā'ī (ed.), *Shāh Ṭahmāsp Ṣafavī*, pp. 330–37.
180 Ḥakīm Niẓāmī Ganjavī, *Kulliyāt-i Ḥakīm Niẓāmī Ganjavī*, ed. Vahīd Dastgirdī, vol. 1 (Tehran: reprint 2002), p. 91.
181 Īvūghlī, *Nuskhah-yi jāmi`a-i al-murāsalāt*, fol. 137; Navā'ī (ed.), *Shāh `Abbās*, vol. 1, p. 47.
182 Sa`dī Shīrāzī, *Kulliyāt-i Sa`dī*, Muḥammad `Alī Furūghī (Tehran: 2000), pp. 225–26.
183 Īvūghlī, *Nuskhah-yi jāmi`a-i al-murāsalāt*, fol. 139b; Navā'ī (ed.), *Shāh `Abbās*, vol. 1, p. 59.
184 Colin P. Mitchell, "To Preserve and Protect: Husayn Va`iz-i Kashfi and Perso-Islamic Chancellery Culture," *Iranian Studies*, vol. 36 (2003), no. 4, pp. 485-507.
185 Julie Scott Meisami, "The Historian and the Poet: Ravandi, Nizami, and the Rhetoric of History," in *The Poetry of Nizami Ganjavi: Knowledge, Love, and Rhetoric* (New York: 2000), pp. 102–06.
186 Īvūghlī, *Nuskhah-yi jāmi`a-i al-murāsalāt*, fol. 139b; Navā'ī (ed.), *Shāh `Abbās*, vol. 1, p. 59.
187 Īvūghlī, *Nuskhah-yi jāmi`a-i al-murāsalāt*, fol. 138b; Navā'ī (ed.), *Shāh `Abbās*, vol. 1, p. 54.
188 Īvūghlī, *Nuskhah-yi jāmi`a-i al-murāsalāt*, fols. 137a–b, 139a, 139b; Navā'ī (ed.), *Shāh `Abbās*, vol. 1, p. 46, p. 48, pp. 57–59.
189 Ḥusain Vā`iẓ Kāshifī quotes this poetry in his section discussing the role of sultans and amirs. See Kāshifī, *Makhzan al-inshā*, p. 246.
190 Īvūghlī, *Nuskhah-yi jāmi`a-i al-murāsalāt*, fol. 139a; Navā'ī (ed.), *Shāh `Abbās*, vol. 1, p. 58; Sa`dī, *Kulliyāt-i Sa`dī*, pp. 217–18, p. 223.
191 Īvūghlī, *Nuskhah-yi jāmi`a-i al-murāsalāt*, fol. 137b; Navā'ī (ed.), *Shāh `Abbās*, vol. 1, p. 49.

192 Īvūghlī, *Nuskhah-yi jāmi`a-i al-murāsalāt*, fol. 137b; Navā'ī (ed.), *Shāh `Abbās*, vol. 1, p. 49.
193 Īvūghlī, *Nuskhah-yi jāmi`a-i al-murāsalāt*, fol. 137b; Navā'ī (ed.), *Shāh `Abbās*, vol. 1, p. 50.
194 Al-Ghazālī, *Naṣīḥat al-mulūk*, p. 82. See also A. K. S. Lambton, "The Theory of Kingship in the *Nasihat-ul-Muluk* of al-Ghazali," *The Islamic Quarterly*, vol. 1 (1954), pp. 47–55.
195 Al-Ghazālī, *Naṣīḥat al-mulūk*, p. 83.
196 Īvūghlī, *Nuskhah-yi jāmi`a-i al-murāsalāt*, f. 137b; Navā'ī (ed.), *Shāh `Abbās*, vol. 1, p. 50.
197 Īvūghlī, *Nuskhah-yi jāmi`a-i al-murāsalāt*, f. 137b; Navā'ī (ed.), *Shāh `Abbās*, vol. 1, p. 50.
198 Īvūghlī, *Nuskhah-yi jāmi`a-i al-murāsalāt*, f. 137b; Navā'ī (ed.), *Shāh `Abbās*, vol. 1, p. 51.
199 Īvūghlī, *Nuskhah-yi jāmi`a-i al-murāsalāt*, f. 139a; Navā'ī (ed.), *Shāh `Abbās*, vol. 1, p. 50.
200 Qur'ān, 15:72, 39:30, 55:26, 3:185. Īvūghlī, *Nuskhah-yi jāmi`a-i al-murāsalāt*, f. 139a, Navā'ī (ed.), *Shāh `Abbās*, vol. 1, p. 58.
201 R. A. Nicholson, *A Literary History of the Arabs* (Cambridge: 1953), pp. 53–54.
202 Qāḍī Kamāl al-Dīn Maibudī, *Sharḥ-i dīvān*, p. 227.
203 Nicholson, *A Literary History of the Arabs*, p. 119.
204 Īvūghlī, *Nuskhah-yi jāmi`a-i al-murāsalāt*, fol.139a; Navā'ī (ed.), *Shāh `Abbās*, vol. 1, pp. 58–59; Muḥammad ibn al-Ḥusain ibn al-Ḥasan Baihaqī, *Dīvān-i Imām `Alī*, ed. Abū Al-Qāsim Imāmī (Tehran: 1996), p. 326.
205 Īvūghlī, *Nuskhah-yi jāmi`a-i al-murāsalāt*, fol.139b; Navā'ī (ed.), *Shāh `Abbās*, vol. 1, p. 60.
206 Madelung, *The Succession to Muhammad*, p. 148, p. 192.
207 Schimmel, *As Through a Veil*, pp. 173–77.
208 Īvūghlī, *Nuskhah-yi jāmi`a-i al-murāsalāt*, ff. 140a–140b; Navā'ī (ed.), *Shāh `Abbās*, pp. 113–16.
209 Abū al-Faḍl `Allāmī, *Ā'in-i Akbarī*, vol. 1, trans. E. Blochmann (New Delhi: 1927), p. 208.
210 Niẓām al-Dīn Aḥmad, *Ṭabaqāt-i Akbarī*, vol. 2, trans. B. De (Calcutta: 1936), pp. 624–25.
211 Īvūghlī, *Nuskhah-yi jāmi`a-i al-murāsalāt*, fol. 140a, Navā'ī (ed.), *Shāh `Abbās*, vol. 1, p. 113.
212 Īvūghlī, *Nuskhah-yi jāmi`a-i al-murāsalāt*, fol. 140a; Navā'ī (ed.), *Shāh `Abbās*, vol. 1, pp. 113–14.
213 Mohamed Tavakoli-Targhi, "Contested Memories: Narrative Structures and Allegorical Meanings of Iran's Pre-Islamic History," *Iranian Studies*, vol. 29 (1996), nos. 1–2, pp. 149–75. See also M. A. Alvi and A. Rahman, *Fathullah Shirazi: A Sixteenth-Century Indian Scientist* (New Delhi: 1968), pp. 29–30.
214 Henri Corbin, "Azar Kayyan," *Encyclopedia Iranica*, vol. 1, p. 183.
215 Babayan, *Monarchs, Mystics and Messiahs*, p. 493.
216 Corbin, "Azar Kayyan," pp. 184–85.
217 Īvūghlī, *Nuskhah-yi jāmi`a-i al-murāsalāt*, fol. 140b; Navā'ī (ed.), *Shāh `Abbās*, vol. 1, p. 115.
218 Īvūghlī, *Nuskhah-yi jāmi`a-i al-murāsalāt*, fol. 140b; Navā'ī (ed.), *Shāh `Abbās*, vol. 1, p. 116.
219 Al-Ghazālī, *Naṣīḥat al-mulūk*, p. 187.
220 Stewart, "The First Shaykh al-Islam," pp. 400–01.
221 Stewart, "The First Shaykh al-Islam," p. 399.

222 Stewart, "The First Shaykh al-Islam," p. 400.
223 Abisaab, *Converting Persia*, p. 29.
224 Abisaab, *Converting Persia*, p. 37.
225 Andrew Newman, "Towards a Reconsideration of the 'Iṣfahān School of Philosophy': Shaykh Bahā'ī and the Role of the Safawi," *Studia Iranica*, vol. 15 (1986), no. 2, p. 171.
226 Abisaab, *Converting Persia*, p. 33, p. 35.
227 Abisaab, *Converting Persia*, p. 38.
228 Terry Graham, "The Ni`matu'llahi Order Under Safavid Suppression and in Indian Exile," in *The Heritage of Sufism vol. III: Late Classical Persianate Sufism (1501–1750) The Safavid & Mughal Period*, eds. L. Lewisohn and D. Morgan (London: 1999), p. 192.
229 Rudolph Matthee, *The Politics of Trade in Safavid Iran* (London: 1999), pp. 8–9.
230 Munajjim Yazdī, *Tārīkh-i `Abbāsī*, fol. 30b.
231 Munajjim Yazdī, *Tārīkh-i `Abbāsī*, fol. 30b; Naṣr Allāh Falsafī, *Zindagānī-yi Shāh `Abbās*, vol. 2 (Tehran: 1974) p. 399.
232 Iskander Beg Munshī, *History of Shah `Abbas the Great*, vol. 2, p. 551; for Persian, see *Tārīkh-i `ālam-ārā-yi `Abbāsī*, vol. 1, pp. 381–82.
233 Sayyid Beg Kamūna had been the governor of Simnān during the reign of Muḥammad Khudābandah. Parsadūst, *Shāh Muḥammad*, p. 227. See also Iskander Beg Munshī, *History of Shah `Abbas the Great*, vol. 2, p. 555; for Persian, see *Tārīkh-i `ālam-ārā-yi `Abbāsī*, vol. 1, p. 385.
234 Falsafī, *Zindagānī-yi Shāh `Abbās*, vol. 2, p. 400; Afūshtah-ī Natanzī, *Naqāvat al-āsār*, p. 317; Qāḍī Aḥmad, *Khulāṣat al-tavārīkh*, vol. 2, p. 1081.
235 Munajjim Yazdī, *Tārīkh-i `Abbāsī*, fol. 32a; Qāḍī Aḥmad, *Khulāṣat al-tavārīkh*, vol. 2, p. 761, p. 769.
236 Munajjim Yazdī, *Tārīkh-i `Abbāsī*, fol. 35a; Afūshtah-ī Natanzī, *Naqāvat al-āsār*, p. 321.
237 Qāḍī Aḥmad, *Khulāṣat al-tavārīkh*, vol. 2, p. 1081; Iskander Beg Munshī, *History of Shah `Abbas the Great*, vol. 2, p. 606; for Persian, see *Tārīkh-i `ālam-ārā-yi `Abbāsī*, ed. vol. 1, p. 431.
238 Iskander Beg Munshī, *History of Shah `Abbas the Great*, vol. 2, p. 1321; for Persian, see *Tārīkh-i `ālam-ārā-yi `Abbāsī*, vol. 2, p. 1092.
239 Qāḍī Aḥmad, *Gulistān-i hunar*, p. 96.
240 Afūshtah-ī Natanzī, *Naqāvat al-āsār*, pp. 341–42.
241 Falsafī, *Zindagānī-yi Shāh `Abbās*, vol. 3, pp. 125–30.
242 Afūshtah-ī Natanzī, *Naqāvat al-āsār*, pp. 319–39; Iskander Beg Munshī, *History of Shah `Abbas the Great*, vol. 2, pp. 601–10; for Persian, see *Tārīkh-i `ālam-ārā-yi `Abbāsī*, vol. 1, pp. 426–34.
243 Charles Melville, "From Qars to Qandahar: The Itineraries of Shah `Abbas I (995–1038/1587–1629)," in *Études Safavides*, ed. J. Calmard (Paris: 1993), pp. 193–207.
244 Falsafī, *Zindagānī-yi Shāh `Abbās*, vol. 2, p. 400.
245 Iskander Beg Munshī, *History of Shah `Abbas the Great*, vol. 1, pp. 596-97; for Persian, see *Tārīkh-i `ālam-ārā-yi `Abbāsī*, vol. 1, pp. 419–20.
246 Munajjim Yazdī, *Tārīkh-i `Abbāsī*, fol. 43a–46a.
247 Munajjim Yazdī, *Tārīkh-i `Abbāsī*, fol. 54b; Qāḍī Aḥmad, *Khulāṣat al-tavārīkh*, vol. 2, p. 1081.
248 Qāḍī Aḥmad, *Khulāṣat al-tavārīkh*, vol. 2, p. 1082.
249 For an overview of `Abbās's relationship with Khān Aḥmad, see Falsafī, *Zindagānī-yi Shāh `Abbās*, vol. 1, p. 131–57.
250 Kasheff, "Gilan – v. History under the Safavids," p. 640.

251 Iskander Beg Munshī, *History of Shah `Abbas the Great*, vol. 2, p. 622; for Persian, see *Tārīkh-i `ālam-ārā-yi `Abbāsī*, vol. 1, p. 449.
252 Kasheff, "Gilan – v. History under the Safavids," p. 641.
253 Afūshtah-ī Natanzī, *Naqāvat al-āsār*, pp. 600–01.
254 Iskander Beg Munshī, *History of Shah `Abbas the Great*, vol. 2, p. 691; for Persian, see *Tārīkh-i `ālam-ārā-yi `Abbāsī*, vol. 1, p. 515.
255 Iskander Beg Munshī, *History of Shah `Abbas the Great*, vol. 2, p. 628; for Persian, see *Tārīkh-i `ālam-ārā-yi `Abbāsī*, vol. 1, p. 455.
256 Iskander Beg Munshī, *History of Shah `Abbas the Great*, vol. 2, p. 633; for Persian, see *Tārīkh-i `ālam-ārā-yi `Abbāsī*, vol. 1, p. 459.
257 Iskander Beg Munshī, *History of Shah `Abbas the Great*, vol. 2, p. 633; for Persian, see *Tārīkh-i `ālam-ārā-yi `Abbāsī*, vol. 1, p. 459.
258 Röhrborn, *Provinzen und Zentralgewalt Persiens*, p. 57.
259 Iskander Beg Munshī, *History of Shah `Abbas the Great*, vol. 2, p. 674; for Persian, see *Tārīkh-i `ālam-ārā-yi `Abbāsī*, vol. 1, p. 500.
260 Melville, "From Qars to Qandahar," pp. 200–01.
261 Busse, "Persische Diplomatik im Überblick," pp. 230–31.
262 Iskander Beg Munshī, *History of Shah `Abbas the Great*, vol. 2, p. 1007; for Persian, see *Tārīkh-i `ālam-ārā-yi `Abbāsī*, vol. 2, p. 805.
263 Minorsky (ed.), *Tazkirat al-muluk*, p. 61. See also Floor, *Safavid Government Institutions*, p. 54.
264 Melville, "New Light on the Reign of Shah `Abbās," p. 86.
265 Īvūghlī, *Nuskhah-yi jāmi`a-i al-murāsalāt*, fol. 153a; Navā'ī (ed.), *Shāh `Abbās*, vol. 2, p. 207. In one letter to Meḥmed III, the scribe uses *az makārim-i alṭāf va maḥāsin-i ashfāq-i khusravī*, while in another, *az makārim-i alṭāf-i balā-nahāyāt-i shāhānah va marjū az marāḥim-i i`tāf-i balāghāyāt-i khusrānah* is used. See Īvūghlī, *Nuskhah-yi jāmi`a-i al-murāsalāt*, fol. 155a; `Abd al-Ḥusain al-Ṭūsī, *Munsha'āt al-Ṭūsī*, ff. 105b. For edited versions, see Navā'ī (ed.), *Shāh `Abbās*, vol. 2, p. 247, p. 235,
266 James Bellamy, "The *Makārim al-Akhlāq* by Ibn Abi'l-Dunya," *Muslim World*, vol. 53 (1963), p. 107.
267 Īvūghlī, *Nuskhah-yi jāmi`a-i al-murāsalāt*, fol. 147b; Navā'ī (ed.), *Shāh `Abbās*, vol. 2, p. 160.
268 Fekete, *Einführung in die persische Paläographie*, p. 456, p. 460; `Abd al-Ḥusain al-Ṭūsī, *Munsha'āt al-Ṭūsī*, fol. 208b, fol. 259a, fol. 264a, fol. 268a; Navā'ī (ed.), *Shāh `Abbās*, vol. 1, p. 187, p. 228, p. 238, p. 254.
269 Navā'ī (ed.), *Shāh `Abbās*, vol. 2, p. 94; Farīdūn Beg, *Munsha'āt al-salāṭīn*, vol. 2, p. 320.
270 Navā'ī (ed.), *Shāh `Abbās*, vol. 2, p. 129. Navā'ī references this letter from Īvūghlī's collection, but I was unable to locate it.
271 Navā'ī (ed.), *Shāh `Abbās*, vol. 2, p. 88, p. 94; Farīdūn Beg, *Munsha'āt al-salāṭīn*, vol. 2, p. 317, p. 320; Kāshifī, *Makhzan al-inshā*, fol. 27b.
272 `Abd al-Ḥusain al-Ṭūsī, *Munsha'āt al-Ṭūsī*, ff. 103a–104b; Navā'ī (ed.), *Shāh `Abbās*, vol. 2, pp. 232–34. See the British Library copy (*MS* Add. 25, 865), Kāshifī, *Makhzan al-inshā*, ff. 6b–7a.
273 *Bāsiṭ-i bisāṭ-i amn va amān rāfi`-i lavā-yi birr va iḥsān ṣā`id-i maṣā`id al-salṭanat al-bāhirat `ārij-i ma`ārij al-khilāfat al-qāhirat ṭirāz-i kiswat-i salṭanat va farmān-ravāyī nigīn-khātam-i salṭanat va kishvar-gushā'ī murvad-i `āṭifat-i rabānnī, mahbaṭ-i `ināyat-i subḥānī al-sulṭān al-mu`ayid al-a`ẓam va al-khāqān al-mujaddid al-afkham jalāl al-salṭanat va al-khilāfat va al-`aẓamat va al-naṣafat va al-ra'fat va al-mulk va al-daulat va al-dunyā va al-dīn Abū al-Muẓaffar Muḥammad Akbar Pādshāh Ghāẓī*. Navā'ī (ed.), *Shāh `Abbās*, vol. 3, p. 338.

274 *Al-ṣifāt wa al-nuṭq lī-ahl al-ṭabaqat al-a`lā al-mulūk al-salāṭīn al-khulafā al-`arḍīn.* Kāshifī, *Makhzan al-inshā*, fol. 27a.
275 *madda Allāhu ta`ālā ẓalāla khilāfatahu al-kāmilat fī basīṭ al-ghabrā wa basaṭa jalāla mu`adalatahu al-shāmilat taḥt bisāṭ al-khaḍā wa zaina sarīra al-khilāfatahu al-uẓmī bi-miyāmana dhātahi wa nawara shu'ūna al-salṭanatahu al-kubrā bi-lawāma`i anwār-i ṣifātihi.* Navā'ī (ed.), *Shāh `Abbās*, vol. 3, p. 338.
276 *Al-a`dīya al-manthūrat al-`arabiyyat li-ahli al-awwalī.* Kāshifī, *Makhzan al-inshā*, fol. 22a.
277 Mitchell, "To Preserve and Protect," pp. 505–06.
278 Welch, *Artists for the Shah*, p. 129.
279 Seven are to the Ottoman court, with three letters to Murād III, one to the viziers of Murād III, and three to Mullā Sa`d al-Dīn Muḥammad. Another letter to the Uzbek `Abd al-Mu'min Khān also narrates the Gīlānī conquest.
280 Īvūghlī, *Nuskhah-yi jāmi`a-i al-murāsalāt*, fol. 244a; Navā'ī (ed.), *Shāh `Abbās*, vol. 2, p. 28.
281 Navā'ī (ed.), *Shāh `Abbās*, vol. 2, p. 30.
282 Navā'ī (ed.), *Shāh `Abbās*, vol. 2, p. 31.
283 Navā'ī (ed.), *Shāh `Abbās*, vol. 2, p. 32.
284 *Jamī`-i sardārān va sipahsālārān bi `izz bisāṭ būs sar-afrāz shudand va Gīlān bi taḥt-i taṣarruf-i auliyā-yi daulat-qāhirah dar āmad.* Navā'ī (ed.), *Shāh `Abbās*, vol. 2, p. 32.
285 Navā'ī (ed.), *Shāh `Abbās*, vol. 2, p. 126.
286 Navā'ī (ed.), *Shāh `Abbās*, vol. 2, p. 126.
287 *Hamīshah sakkah va khuṭbah-yi īshān ki `alāmat-i pādshāhī va salṭanat ast bi nām-i abā-yi kirām-i mukhliṣ būdah.* Īvūghlī, *Nuskhah-yi jāmi`a-i al-murāsalāt*, ff. 149a–149b; Navā'ī (ed.), *Shāh `Abbās*, vol. 2, p. 149.
288 Īvūghlī, *Nuskhah-yi jāmi`a-i al-murāsalāt*, fol. 149b; Navā'ī (ed.), *Shāh `Abbās*, vol. 2, p. 149.
289 Navā'ī (ed.), *Shāh `Abbās*, vol. 2, p. 127.
290 *Gīlān dākhil-i sinūr-i mamlakat-i mukhliṣ-i nīk-khvāh ast.* Īvūghlī, *Nuskhah-yi jāmi`a-i al-murāsalāt*, fol. 149b; Navā'ī (ed.), *Shāh `Abbās*, vol. 2, p. 149.
291 Īvūghlī, *Nuskhah-yi jāmi`a-i al-murāsalāt*, fol. 149b; Navā'ī (ed.), *Shāh `Abbās*, vol. 2, p. 149.
292 Röhrborn, *Provinzen und Zentralgewalt Persiens*, pp. 42–43.
293 *Muqarr-i khilāfat va mustaqarr-i salṭanat-i ābā va ajdād-i `iẓām-i girām-i navvāb-i kāmyāb ast.* Īvūghlī, *Nuskhah-yi jāmi`a-i al-murāsalāt*, fol. 232a; Navā'ī (ed.), *Shāh `Abbās*, vol. 1, p. 255.
294 `Abd al-Ḥusain al-Ṭūsī, *Munsha'āt al-Ṭūsī*, fol. 252a; Navā'ī (ed.), *Shāh `Abbās*, vol. 1, p. 217.
295 `Abd al-Ḥusain al-Ṭūsī, *Munsha'āt al-Ṭūsī*, fol. 252b; Navā'ī (ed.), *Shāh `Abbās*, vol. 1, p. 218.
296 `Abd al-Ḥusain al-Ṭūsī, *Munsha'āt al-Ṭūsī*, ff. 252b–53a; Navā'ī (ed.), *Shāh `Abbās*, vol. 1, p. 218.
297 `Abd al-Ḥusain al-Ṭūsī, *Munsha'āt al-Ṭūsī*, ff. 256b-257a; Navā'ī (ed.), *Shāh `Abbās*, vol. 1, pp. 224–25.
298 Īvūghlī, *Nuskhah-yi jāmi`a-i al-murāsalāt*, fol. 148b; Navā'ī (ed.), *Shāh `Abbās*, vol. 2, pp. 146–47.
299 Īvūghlī, *Nuskhah-yi jāmi`a-i al-murāsalāt*, fol. 149a; Navā'ī (ed.), *Shāh `Abbās*, vol. 2, p. 147.
300 Īvūghlī, *Nuskhah-yi jāmi`a-i al-murāsalāt*, fol. 149a Navā'ī (ed.), *Shāh `Abbās*, vol. 2, p. 147.
301 Īvūghlī, *Nuskhah-yi jāmi`a-i al-murāsalāt*, fol. 149a; Navā'ī (ed.), *Shāh `Abbās*,

vol. 2, p. 147.
302 Īvūghlī, *Nuskhah-yi jāmi`a-i al-murāsalāt*, fol. 154a; Navā'ī (ed.), *Shāh `Abbās*, vol. 1, p. 243.
303 *Tā bi andak-i zamān bi taṣarruf-i auliyā-yi daulat-qāhirah dar āvarad.* Īvūghlī, *Nuskhah-yi jāmi`a-i al-murāsalāt*, fol. 154a; Navā'ī (ed.), *Shāh `Abbās*, vol. 1, p. 243.
304 Īvūghlī, *Nuskhah-yi jāmi`a-i al-murāsalāt*, fol. 154a; Navā'ī (ed.), *Shāh `Abbās*, vol. 1, p. 243.
305 Īvūghlī, *Nuskhah-yi jāmi`a-i al-murāsalāt*, fol. 154a; Navā'ī (ed.), *Shāh `Abbās*, vol. 1, p. 243.
306 *Pādshāhān-i Chingīzī-rā bar sarīr-i khusravī va dārā'ī-yi mamālik-i Chingīz Khānī mutammakin sāzīm.* Īvūghlī, *Nuskhah-yi jāmi`a-i al-murāsalāt*, fol. 154b; Navā'ī (ed.), *Shāh `Abbās*, vol. 1, p. 246.
307 For a good overview of the military and diplomatic narrative during these years, see Nava'i's discussion of Uzbek-Safavid relations in Navā'ī (ed.), *Shāh `Abbās*, vol. 1, pp. 142–64. See also Falsafī, *Zindagānī-yi Shāh `Abbās*, vol. 4, pp. 119–42.
308 Īvūghlī, *Nuskhah-yi jāmi`a-i al-murāsalāt*, fol. 154b; Navā'ī (ed.), *Shāh `Abbās*, vol. 1, pp. 246–47.
309 `Abd al-Ḥusain al-Ṭūsī, *Munsha'āt al-Ṭūsī*, fol. 204b; Navā'ī (ed.), *Shāh `Abbās*, vol. 1, p. 181.
310 `Abd al-Ḥusain al-Ṭūsī, *Munsha'āt al-Ṭūsī*, fol. 260b; Navā'ī (ed.), *Shāh `Abbās*, vol. 1, p. 234.
311 `Abd al-Ḥusain al-Ṭūsī, *Munsha'āt al-Ṭūsī*, fol. 261a; Navā'ī (ed.), *Shāh `Abbās*, vol. 1, p. 234.
312 Firdausī. *Shāh nāmah*, p. 741.
313 Niẓāmī, *Sharaf nāmah* in *Kulliyāt-i Ḥakīm Niẓāmī Ganjavī* p. 635.
314 Renard, *Islam and the Heroic Image*, pp. 126–27.
315 Īvūghlī, *Nuskhah-yi jāmi`a-i al-murāsalāt*, fol. 232a; Navā'ī (ed.), *Shāh `Abbās*, vol. 1, p. 255. This particular hadith could not be identified.
316 Īvūghlī, *Nuskhah-yi jāmi`a-i al-murāsalāt*, fol. 232a; Navā'ī (ed.), *Shāh `Abbās*, vol. 1, p. 256.
317 Īvūghlī, *Nuskhah-yi jāmi`a-i al-murāsalāt*, fol. 232b; Navā'ī (ed.), *Shāh `Abbās*, vol. 1, p. 256.
318 `Abd al-Ḥusain al-Ṭūsī, *Munsha'āt al-Ṭūsī*, fol. 256a; Navā'ī (ed.), *Shāh `Abbās*, vol. 1, p. 224.
319 `Abd al-Ḥusain al-Ṭūsī, *Munsha'āt al-Ṭūsī*, fol. 256b; Navā'ī (ed.), *Shāh `Abbās*, vol. 1, p. 224.
320 `Abd al-Ḥusain al-Ṭūsī, *Munsha'āt al-Ṭūsī*, fol. 268a; Navā'ī (ed.), *Shāh `Abbās*, vol. 1, p. 253.
321 Abisaab, *Converting Persia*, pp. 55–56.
322 Stanfield-Johnson, "The Tabarra'iyan and the Early Safavids," p. 66.
323 Abisaab, *Converting Persia*, pp. 58–59.
324 Afūshtah-ī Natanzī, *Naqāvat al-āsār*, pp. 518–27. See also Babayan, *Monarchs, Mystics and Messiahs*, pp. 90-108.
325 Munajjim Yazdī, *Tārīkh-i `Abbāsī*, fol. 64a. Jean Calmard discusses these gladiator-style combats in "Shi`i Rituals and Power II," pp. 144–45.
326 Majid Fakhry, *A History of Islamic Philosophy* (New York: 1970), pp. 339–40; Babayan, *Monarchs, Mystics and Messiahs*, p. 407.
327 Newman, "Towards a Reconsideration of the 'Iṣfahān School of Philosophy,'" p. 179.
328 Stewart, "The Lost Biography of Baha' al-Din al-Amili" p. 190–91; Falsafī, *Zindagānī -yi Shāh `Abbās*, vol. 1, p. 141.

329 Falsafī, *Zindagānī -yi Shāh `Abbās*, vol. 3, p. 128.
330 Afūshtah-ī Natanzī, *Naqāvat al-āsār*, pp. 334–35.
331 Andrew Newman, "Towards a Reconsideration of the 'Iṣfahān School of Philosophy': Shaykh Bahā'ī and the Role of the Safawi," *Studia Iranica*, vol. 15 (1986), no. 2, p. 177.
332 Newman, "Towards a Reconsideration of the 'Iṣfahān School of Philosophy," p. 177.
333 C. E. Bosworth comes to this conclusion after reading Shaikh Bahā'ī's heterogenous compendium, the *Kashkūl*. See C. E. Bosworth, *Bahā' al-Dīn al-`Āmilī and His Literary Anthologies* (Manchester: 1989), p. 38. Part of this issue is complicated by Shaikh Bahā'ī's "Sunni profile" during his travels outside of Safavid Iran. See Devin Stewart, "*Taqiyyah* as Performance: The Travels of Bahā' al-Dīn al-`Āmilī in the Ottoman Empire (991–93/1583–85)," in *Law and Society in Islam* (Princeton: 1996), pp. 1–70.
334 Navā'ī (ed.), *Shāh `Abbās*, vol. 2, pp. 178–93;`Alī Aujabī, *Mīr Dāmād: Bunyān-guzār-i ḥikmat-i yamānī* (Tehran: 2002), p. 203.
335 Aujabī, *Mīr Dāmād*, p. 203.
336 Aujabī, *Mīr Dāmād*, p. 183.
337 `Abd al-Ḥusain al-Ṭūsī, *Munsha'āt al-Ṭūsī*, fol. 205b; Navā'ī (ed.), *Shāh `Abbās*, vol. 1, p. 183.
338 `Abd al-Ḥusain al-Ṭūsī, *Munsha'āt al-Ṭūsī*, fol. 205b; Navā'ī (ed.), *Shāh `Abbās*, vol. 1, p. 183.
339 `Abd al-Ḥusain al-Ṭūsī, *Munsha'āt al-Ṭūsī*, fol. 206a; Navā'ī (ed.), *Shāh `Abbās*, vol. 1, p. 183.
340 Īvūghlī, *Nuskhah-yi jāmi`a-i al-murāsalāt*, fol. 154b; Navā'ī (ed.), *Shāh `Abbās*, vol. 2, p. 246.
341 Īvūghlī, *Nuskhah-yi jāmi`a-i al-murāsalāt*, fol. 202b; Navā'ī (ed.), *Shāh `Abbās*, vol. 3, p. 331.
342 Lines 9, 10, 25, 28 of *Laila va Majnūn*, see Niẓāmī, *Kulliyāt-i Ḥakīm Niẓāmī Ganjavī*, vol. 1, pp. 295–96.
343 In one part, he quotes three lines (44–46) from the foreword (*āghāz-i sukhan*), and later amalgamates three lines from (4–5) *Manājāt-i avval* and (1) *Manājāt-i duvvum*. See Niẓāmī, *Kulliyāt-i Ḥakīm Niẓāmī Ganjavī*, vol. 1, p. 2, p. 3, p. 4.
344 Īvūghlī, *Nuskhah-yi jāmi`a-i al-murāsalāt*, fol. 203a; Navā'ī (ed.), *Shāh `Abbās*, vol. 3, p. 334.
345 "The Prophet is rightfully the king whose throne is the lote tree [in Heaven]/He was crowned while sitting on this throne
He is the intercessor for mankind, the seal of the prophets/The light of the message, king of the pure ones
He is the messenger of the Arabs and king of Yathrib/Mount Ṭafīl is the path for both the Arabs and the Persians.
Īvūghlī, *Nuskhah-yi jāmi`a-i al-murāsalāt*, fol. 203a–203b; Navā'ī (ed.), *Shāh `Abbās*, vol. 3, pp. 333–34. See Niẓāmī, *Kulliyāt-i Ḥakīm Niẓāmī Ganjavī*, vol. 1, p. 825.
346 Canby, "Safavid Painting," pp. 104–05, pp. 115–23; Laurence Binyon, J. V. S. Wilkonson and Basil Gray, *Persian Miniature Painting*, (New York: 1933), pp. 113–116; Renard, *Islam and the Heroic Image*, pp. 177–80.
347 In one famous incident, the poet Mullā Muḥammad Zamān Zamānī—described by Falsafī as a believer in *tanāsukh* (metempsychosis) but labelled by Babayan as a Nuqṭavī—confronted `Abbās with his poetic reply to Niẓāmī, which he intended to present "in person." `Abbās responded by asking, "And how are you going to respond to God?" Falsafī, *Zindagānī-yi Shāh `Abbās*, vol. 2, p. 27, fn. 3; Babayan,

Monarchs, Mystics and Messiahs, pp. 107–08.

348 Falsafī, *Zindagānī-yi Shāh `Abbās*, vol. 2, pp. 39–41.

349 Īvūghlī, *Nuskhah-yi jāmi`a-i al-murāsalāt*, fol. 203a; Navā'ī (ed.), *Shāh `Abbās*, vol. 3, p. 334.

350 *Al-arwāḥ junūd mujannadah fa-mā tā`araf min-hā iytilāf wa mā tanākir min-hā ikhtilāf.* Īvūghlī, *Nuskhah-yi jāmi`a-i al-murāsalāt*, fol. 203a; Navā'ī (ed.), *Shāh `Abbās*, vol. 3, p. 335.

351 Īvūghlī, *Nuskhah-yi jāmi`a-i al-murāsalāt*, fol. 203a; Navā'ī (ed.), *Shāh `Abbās*, vol. 3, p. 335.

352 Īvūghlī, *Nuskhah-yi jāmi`a-i al-murāsalāt*, fol. 204a; Navā'ī (ed.), *Shāh `Abbās*, vol. 3, p. 339.

353 Seyyed Hossein Nasr talked about the compatability of Niẓāmī's poetry with the Neoplatonist Illuminationst philosophy of his contemporary, Suhravardī. See S. H. Nasr, "The World View and Philosophical Perspective of Hakim Nizāmi Ganjawi," *The Muslim World*, vol. 82, pp. 191–200.

354 Abisaab, *Converting Persia*, p. 73.

355 Ian Richard Netton, "Suhrawardi's Heir? The Ishraqi Philosophy of Mir Damad," in *The Heritage of Sufism vol. III: Late Classical Persianate Sufism (1501–1750) The Safavid & Mughal Period*, eds. L. Lewisohn and D. Morgan (London: 1999), p. 226.

356 Muḥammad Yūsuf Vālih, *Khuld-i barīn*, p. 419.

357 Julie Scott Meisami has noted the strong similarities between Niẓāmī's *Haft Paykar* and Khvājah Naṣīr al-Dīn al-Ṭūsī's advice manual, the *Akhlāq-i Nāṣirī*. See Julie Scott Meisami, "Cosmic Numbers: The Symbolic Design of Nizami's *Haft Paykar*," in *Humanism, Culture, and Language in the Near East: Studies in Honor of George Krotkoff*, eds. A. Afsaruddin and A. H. M. Zahniser (Winona Lake: 1997), pp. 42–45.

358 See Sholeh Quinn's chapter on the Ya`qūb Khān rebellion in *Historical Writing During the Reign of Shah `Abbas*, pp. 95–124.

359 Devin Stewart, "A Biographical Notice on Bahā' al-Dīn al-`Āmilī (d. 1030/1621)," *Journal of the American Oriental Society*, vol. 113 (1991), no. 3, p. 569.

360 Quinn, *Historical Writing During the Reign of Shah `Abbas*, p. 99.

361 Szuppe, "L'évolution de l'image de Timour et des Timourides," p. 324.

362 Īvūghlī, *Nuskhah-yi jāmi`a-i al-murāsalāt*, ff. 234a–234b; Navā'ī (ed.), *Shāh `Abbās*, vol. 1, pp. 242–43.

363 Babayan, *Monarchs, Mystics and Messiahs*, p. 376.

Conclusion

1 Brinkley Messick, *The Calligraphic State: Textual Domination and History in a Muslim Society* (Berkeley, 1992), p. 2.

2 (Khvājah) `Imād al-Dīn Maḥmūd Gāvān Ṣadr-i Jahān. *Manāẓir al-inshā*. ed. Ma`ṣūmah Ma`dan-Kan (Tehran: 2002). See Riazul Islam's overview of this in *A Calendar of Documents on Indo-Persian Relations*, vol. 1, pp. 11–24.

3 Gottfried Hermann, *Persische Urkunden der Mongolenzeit* (Wiesbaden: 2004), pp. 9–42.

4 For a good overview, see Jan Reychman and Ananiasz Kajaczkowski, *Handbook of Ottoman-Turkish Diplomatics*, trans. A. Ehrenkreutz (The Hague: 1968).

5 Khvāndamīr, *Makārim al-akhlāq*, pp. 81–86.

6 Iskander Beg Munshī, *History of Shah `Abbas the Great,* vol. 1, p. 162, vol. 2, pp. 560–75, pp. 750–51, pp. 1274–80.

7 Qāḍī Aḥmad, *Khulāṣat al-tavārīkh*, vol. 1, pp. 102–08.

8 Written by the sons (Mīr `Abd al-Bāqī, Mīr `Īd al-Ghaffārī) and Mīr `Abd al-Razzāq

of the imprisoned Naqshbandī shaikh, Mīr `Abd al-Wahhāb. Qāḍī Aḥmad, *Khulāṣat al-tavārīkh*, vol. 1, pp. 145–46.

9 Qāḍī Aḥmad, *Khulāṣat al-tavārīkh*, vol. 1, pp. 206–08.

10 Qāḍī Aḥmad, *Khulāṣat al-tavārīkh*, vol. 1, pp. 410–11.

11 Quinn, *Historical Writing During the Reign of Shah `Abbas*, p. 19.

12 Compare, for instance, Qāḍī Aḥmad, *Khulāṣat al-tavārīkh*, vol. 1, p. 483 and p. 506 with Navā'ī (ed.), *Shāh Ṭahmāsp Ṣafavī*, pp. 118–20, p. 364, p. 426.

13 Qāḍī Aḥmad, *Khulāṣat al-tavārīkh*, vol. 1, pp. 226–27.

14 Navā'ī (ed.), *Shāh Ṭahmāsp Ṣafavī*, pp. 35–36.

15 Navā'ī (ed.), *Shāh Ṭahmāsp Ṣafavī*, pp. 210–12.

16 Qāḍī Aḥmad, *Khulāṣat al-tavārīkh*, vol. 1, pp. 179–89.

17 Quinn, *Historical Writing During the Reign of Shah `Abbas*, pp. 16–17.

18 Babayan, *Mystics, Monarchs, and Messiahs*, p. 306.

19 Quinn, *Historical Writing During the Reign of Shāh `Abbas*, pp. 142–43.

BIBLIOGRAPHY

I. Unpublished Primary Sources

Anonymous. "Inshā Collection." MS, Oxford, Bodleian Library, Pers. D. 84.

------. "Majmū`ah" (Inserted between volumes of *Tārīkh-i `ālam-ārā-yi `Abbāsī*). MS, London, British Library, Add. 7654.

------. "Majmū`ah." MS, Berlin, Staatsbibliothek zū Berlin Preussischer Kulturebesitz, Orientalabteilung, MS or. fol.1257.

------. "Majmū`ah." MS, London, British Library, I. O. Islamic 379.

------. "Maktūbāt." MS, London, British Library, no. 2067.

`Abd al-`Alī Tabrīzī. "Munsha'āt-i nāẓir al-mamālik al-sulṭāniyyah-yi Ḥājjī `Abd al-`Alī Tabrīzī." MS, London, British Library, Add. 6600.

`Abd al-Ghaffār Ṣiddiqī Ḥusainī Haravī. "Ṣaḥīfa al-ikhlāṣ." MS, Paris, Bibliothèque Nationale, no. 1061.

`Abd al-Ḥusain al-Naṣīr al-Ṭūsī. "Munsha'āt al-Ṭūsī." MS, Paris, Bibliothèque Nationale, supplément persan, no. 1838.

Abū al-Qāsim Ḥaidar Beg Īvūghlī. "Nuskhah-yi jāmi`a-i al-murāsalāt-i ulul albāb." MS, London, British Library, B. M. Add. 7688.

(Munshī) Būdāq Qazvīnī. "Javāhir al-akhbār." MS, St. Petersburg, Russian National Library, no. 288.

Ghiyās̱ al-Dīn ibn Humām al-Dīn Khvāndamīr. "Nāmah-yi nāmī." MS, Paris, Bibliothèque Nationale, supplément persan, no. 1842.

(Amīr) Ḥusain Nīshāpūrī (Mu`ammā'ī). "Risālah fī al-mu`ammā." MS Oxford, Bodleian Library, Ouseley no. 143.

Ḥusain Vā'iẓ Kāshifī. "Makhzan al-inshā." MS, Paris, Bibliothèque Nationale, supplément fonds persan, no. 73 and MS, London, British Library, Add. 25,865.

Jalāl al-Dīn Munajjim Yazdī. "Tārīkh-i `Abbāsī." MS, London, British Library, Or. 6263.

Muḥammad al-Ḥusainī ibn Nāṣir al-Ḥaqq Nūrbakhshī. "Inshā-yi `ālam-ārā." MS, Tehran, Kitābkhānah-yi Majlis-i shūrā-yi Islāmī, no. 13757.

Mu`īn al-Dīn Muḥammad Zamchī Isfizārī. "Risālah-yi qavānīn" (or "Inshā-yi Mu`īn Zamchī"). MS, Lahore, Punjab University Library, Pe II Li 2324/231.

Sharaf al-Dīn Ḥasan Shifā'ī. "Munsha'āt-i Shifā'i." This work is included on ff. 67–97 in Anonymous, "Majmū`a." MS, London, British Library, no. Or. 13215.

Yūsuf ibn Muḥammad Harātī. "Badā`i al-inshā." MS, London, British Library, Add. 6608 and I. O. Islamic 1972.

II. Published Primary Sources

Anononymous. *`Ālam-ārā-yi Shāh Ismā`īl*. Edited by Aṣghar Munaẓẓir Ṣāḥib. (Tehran:

1990).
`Abd al-`Alī Karang. *Āsār-i bastān-i Āzarbāijān.* 2 vols. (Tehran: 1972).
`Abd al-Ḥusain Navā'ī, ed. *Asnād va mukātabāt-i siyāsī-yi Īrān.* (Tehran: 1981).
------. *Asnād va mukātabāt-i tārīkhī-yi Īrān az Tīmūr tā Shāh Ismā`īl.* (Tehran: 1963).
------. *Shāh `Abbās: Majmū`ah-yi asnād va mukātabāt-i tārīkhī.* 3 vols. (Tehran: 1974).
------. *Shāh Ismā`īl Ṣafavī: Majmū`ah-yi asnād va mukātibāt-i tārīkhī-yi hamrāh bā yāddāsht-hā-yi tafṣīl.* (Tehran: 1969).
------. *Shāh Ṭahmāsp Ṣafavī: Majmū`ah-yi asnād va mukātibāt-i tārīkhī-yi hamrāh bā yāddāsht-hā-yi tafṣīl.* (Tehran: 1971).
`Abd al-Jalīl Ibn Abī al-Ḥusain ibn Abī al-Faḍl al-Qazvīnī al-Rāzī. *Kitāb al-naqḍ.* Edited by Sayyid Jalāl al-Dīn Muḥaddis. (Tehran: 1952).
`Abd Allāh Muḥammad bin Yazīd al-Qazvīnī ibn Mājda. *Sunan.* 2 vols. Edited by Muḥammad Fu'ād `Abd al-Bāqī. (Cairo: 1952).
`Abd al-Qādir al-Badā'ūnī. *Muntakhab al-tavārīkh.* Edited and translated by W. H. Lowe. 3 vols. (Calcutta: 1884–1925).
`Abd al-Qāhir al-Jurjānī. *Die Geheimnisse der Wortkunst (Asrār al-balāgha).* Edited and translated by H. Ritter. (Wiesbaden: 1959).
`Abd al-Raḥmān Aḥmad Jāmī. *Nāmah-hā va munsha'āt-i Jāmī.* Edited by Asom Urunbaev and Asrar Rahmanof (Tehran: 2002).
------. *The Precious Pearl: al-Jami's* al-Durrah al-Fakhirah *with the Commentary of `Abd al-Ghafur al-Lari.* Translated by N. Leer. (Albany: 1979).
------. *Shavāhid al-nubuvva.* (Istanbul: 1995).
`Abdī Beg Shīrāzī. *`Ain-i Iskandarī.* Edited by Abū al-Faḍl Hāshim-ūghlī Raḥīmov. (Moscow: 1977).
------. *Rauḍat al-ṣifāt.* Edited by Abū al-Faḍl Hāshim-Ūghlī Raḥīmov. (Moscow: 1974).
------. *Takmilat al-akhbār.* Edited by Abd al-Ḥusain Navā'ī. (Tehran: 1990).
Abū al-Faḍl `Allāmī. *Ā`īn-i Akbarī.* Edited and translated by H. Blochmann. 2 vols. (Calcutta: 1868–94).
------. *Akbar nāma.* Edited and translated by H. Beveridge. 3 vols. (Calcutta: 1897–1939).
Abū al-Ḥasan `Alī ibn Ismā`īl al-Ash`arī. *Maqālat al-islāmiyyīn wa ikhtilāf al-musallīn.* Edited by `Abd al-Hamīd. 2 vols. (Cairo: 1950).
Abū al-Qāsim Firdausī. *Shāh nāmah.* Ed. Sa`īd Ḥamīdiyān. (Tehran: 2002).
Abū al-Qāsim Rādfar. *Manāqib-i `alavī dar āyīnah-yi shi`r-i Fārsī.* (Tehran: 2002).
Abū Ṭāhir Ṭarṭūsī. *Abū Muslim nāmah.* Edited by Ḥusain Ismā`īlī. 4 vols. (Tehran: 2001).
Afshar, Iraj. "*Maktub* and *Majmu`a*: Essential Sources for Safavid Research." In *Society and Culture in the Early Modern Middle East: Studies on Iran in the Safavid Period.* Edited by A. J. Newman. (Leiden: 2003), pp. 51–62.
------. "Risāla-yi khaṭṭ-i Khalīl Tabrīzī." In *Pand-o Sokhan: mélanges offerts à Charles-Henri de Fouchécour.* Edited by C. Balay, C. Kappler, Z. Vesel. (Paris: 1995) pp. 307–28.
Aḥmad Aḥmadī Birjandī, ed. *Manāqib-i `alavī dar shi`r-i farsī.* (Tehran: 1987).
Ahmad, `Ali, ed. and trans. *Al-Quran: A Contemporary Translation.* (Princeton: 1984).
(Qāḍī) Aḥmad Ghaffārī Qazvīnī. *Tārīkh-i jahān-ārā.* Edited by Mujtabī Minuvī. (Tehran: 1964).
Aḥmad ibn Ḥanbal. *Musnad.* 6 vols. (Cairo: 1895). (Qāḍī) Aḥmad ibn Sharaf al-Dīn al-Ḥusain al-Ḥusainī al-Qummī. *Calligraphers and Painters: A Treatise by Qāḍī Aḥmad, Son of Mīr Munshī.* Edited and translated by V. Minorsky. (Washington: 1959).
------. *Khulāṣat al-tavārīkh.* Edited by I. Ishrāqī. 2 vols. (Tehran: 1980).
`Alī ibn `Abd al-`Alī al-Karakī."Ṭarīq Istinbāṭ al-Aḥkām (The Method of Derivation of

the Rules of the Sharī`ah).” In *Al-Tawḥīd*. Translated by Muḥammad Bāqir Anṣārī and `Alī Qulī Qarā'ī.Vol. 2. No. 3. (1985), pp. 42–55.

`Alī ibn Abī Ṭālib. *Al-Mu`jam al-mufahras lī alfāẓ-i Nahj al-balāgha*. Edited by Muḥammad Dashtī. (Tehran: 2001).

------. *Nahj al-balāghah: Selections from Sermons, Letters and Sayings of Amir al-Mu'minin, `Ali ibn Abi Talib*. Edited by Sayyid Abū al-Ḥasan and translated by Sayyid `Alī Riḍā. 2 vols. (Karachi: 1955).

`Alī ibn Ḥasan Khūshmardān (Sayyid Bābā). *Ta`līm al-khuṭūṭ*. Edited by Aḥsan Allāh Shukr Allāh Ṭalāqānī. In *Bahāristān nāmah*. Vol. 3. No. 2. (2003), pp. 317–23.

(Sayyid) `Alī Ṭabātabā'ī. *Burhān-i ma'āṣir*. Edited by Sa`īd Hāshimī. (Delhi: 1936).

Amīn Aḥmad Rāḍī. *Haft iqlīm*. Edited by M. Ishaque. 3 vols. (Calcutta: 1963).

Arjomand, Said Amir. “Two Decrees of Shāh Ṭahmāsp Concerning Statecraft and the Authority of Shaykh `Alī al-Karakī.” In *Authority and Political Culture in Shi`ism*. Edited by S. A. Arjomand. (Albany: 1988), pp. 250–62.

Bābur. *Bābur nāma*. Edited and translated by A. Beveridge. (London: 1921).

Bacqué-Grammont, Jean-Louis. “Deux rapports sur Shāh Ismā`īl et les Özbeks.” In *Quand le crible était dans la paille: hommage à Pertev Naili Boratov*. (Paris: 1978), pp. 65–82.

Browne, E. G., ed. and trans. *Revised Translation of the* Chahār maqāla *(“Four Discourses” of* Niẓāmī `Arūḍ*)*. (London: 1921).

Būdāq Munshī Qazvīnī. *Javāhir al-akhbār*. Edited by M. Bahrāmnezhād. (Tehran: 2000).

Busse, Heribert. *Untersuchungen zum islamischen Kanzleiwesen an Hand türkmenisches und safawidischer Urkunden*. (Cairo: 1959).

De Busbecq, Ogier Ghiselin. *The Turkish Letters of Ogier Ghiselin de Busbecq, Imperial Ambassador at Constantinople, 1554–1562*. (Baton Rouge: 2005).

Dickson, M. and Welch, S. C., eds. *The Houghton Shahnameh*. 2 vols. (Cambridge, Mass.: 1981).

Farīdūn Beg. *Munsha'āt al-salāṭīn*. 2 vols. (Istanbul: 1858).

Fekete, L. *Einführung in die persische Paläographie*. (Budapest: 1977).

Fiyādūn Nawzād, ed. *Nāma-hā-yi Khān Aḥmad Khān Gīlānī*. (Tehran: 1994).

Fragner, Bert. *Repertorium persicher Herrscherurkunden*. (Freiburg: 1980).

Fryer, John. *A New Account of East India and Persia Being Nine Years' Travels, 1672–1681*. Edited by William Crooke. 3 vols. (Nendeln: 1967).

Ghiyāṣ al-Dīn ibn Humām al-Dīn Khvāndamīr. *Ḥabīb al-siyar*. Edited by Muḥammad Dabīr Siyāqī. 3 vols. (Tehran: 1983).

------. *Humāyūn nāma* (or *Qānūn-i Humāyūn*). Edited and translated by B. Prasad. (Calcutta: 1940).

------. *Makārim al-akhlāq*. Edited by Muḥammad Akbar `Ashīq. (Tehran: 1999).

Gross, Jo-Ann and Asom Urunbaev. *The Letters of Khwāja `Ubayd Allāh Aḥrār and his Associates*. (Leiden: 2002).

Gul Badan Begam. *Humāyūn nāma*. Edited and translated by A. S. Beveridge. (London: 1902).

Ḥāfiẓ. *The Divan of Hafez*. Translated and edited by Reza Saberi. (Lanham: 2002).

Ḥāfiẓ Ḥusain Karbalā'ī Tabrīzī. *Rauḍāt al-jinān va jannāt al-jinān*. Edited by J. Sulṭān al-Qurrā'ī. 2 vols. (Tehran: 1965).

Al-Ḥākim al-Naisābūrī. *Al-Mustadarak*. 4 vols. (Riyad: n.d.).

Ḥakīm Niẓāmī Ganjavī. *Kulliyāt-i Ḥakīm Niẓāmī Ganjavī*. Edited by Vahīd Dastgirdī. 2 vols. (Tehran: reprint 2002).

Ḥasan Beg Rūmlū. *Aḥsan al-tavārīkh*. Edited and translated by C. Seddon. 2 vols. (Baroda: 1931).

Hermann, Gottfried. “Ein Erlaß Tahmasps I. von 934/1528.” *Zeitschrift der Deutschen*

Morgenländischen Gesellschaft. Vol. 139. No. 1. (1989), pp. 104–19.
------. "Das historische Gehalt des 'Nāma-y nāmī' von Khwāndamīr." Unpublished Ph.D. Dissertation. (University of Göttingen: 1968).
------. *Persische Urkunden der Mongolenzeit*. (Wiesbaden: 2004).
------. "Zwei Erlasse Schah Isma`ils I." *Archaeologische Mitteilungen aus Iran*. Vol. 19. (1986), pp. 289–306.
Hinz, Walther. *Die Risalā-yi Falakiyyā des `Abdullāh ibn Muḥammad ibn Kiyā al-Māzandarān: Ein persischer Leitfaden des staatlichen Rechnungswesens (um 1363)*. (Weisbaden: 1952).
Ḥusain Vā'iẓ Kāshifī. *Futuvvat-i nāmah-yi sulṭānī*. Edited by M. J. Maḥjūb. (Tehran: 1971).
------. *Rauḍat al-shuhadā*. Edited by M. Ramaḍānī. (Tehran: 1962).
------. *Al-Risāla al-`āliyya fī'l-aḥādith al-nabawiyya*. Edited by Sayyid Jalāl al-Dīn Muḥaddis̱. (Tehran: 1965).
------. *Ṣaḥīfa-i shāhī*. (Lithograph abridgement of *Makhzan al-inshā*). (Lucknow: 1844).
Ibn Khaldūn. *The Muqaddima*. Translated by F. Rosenzthal. 2 vols. (Princeton: 1967).
(Khvājah) `Imād al-Dīn Maḥmūd Gāvān Ṣadr-i Jahān. *Manāẓir al-inshā*. Edited by Ma`ṣūmah Ma`dan-Kan. (Tehran: 2002).
------. *Riyāḍ al-inshā*. (Hyderabad: 1948).
Ishaque, M. "Letter from Queen Elizabeth of England to Tahmasp I, Shah of Persia." *Indo-Iranica*. Vol. 2. No. 1. (1947–48), pp. 29–30.
Iskander Beg Munshī. *History of Shah `Abbas the Great)*. Edited and translated by R. Savory. 2 vols. (Boulder: 1978). Persian edition: *Tārīkh-i `ālam-ārā-yi `Abbāsī*. Edited by I. Afshar. 2 vols. (Tehran: 2003).
Islam, Riazul. *A Calendar of Documents on Indo-Persian Relations*. 2 vols. (Tehran: 1979).
Jahāngīr Qā'im Māqamī, ed. *Yakṣad va panjāh sanad-i tārīkhī*. (Tehran: 1970).
(Qāḍī) Kamāl al-Dīn Mīr Ḥusain ibn Mu`īn al-Dīn Maibodī Yazdī. *Sharḥ-i dīvān mansūb bih Amīr al-Mu'minīn `Alī ibn Abī Ṭālib*. Edited by H. Raḥmānī and S. E. A. Shirīn (Tehran: 2000).
Keçik, Mehmet Sefik. *Briefe und Urkunden aus der Kanzlei Uzun Hasans: Ein Beitrag zur Geschichte Ost-Anatoliens im 15. Jahrhundert*. (Freiburg: 1976).
Khāfī Khān. *Muntakhab al-lubāb*. Edited by Maḥmūd Aḥmad Fāruqī. 3 vols. (Karachi: 1963).
Khan, Mir Fazaluddin Ali. *Life and Works of Mirza Sharaf Jahan Qazwini: A Poet of Shah Tahmasp Safawi's Regime*. (Hyderabad: 1995).
Khūrshāh ibn Qubād al-Ḥusainī. *Tārīkh-i īlchī-yi Niẓāmshāh*. Edited by M. R. Nāṣirī and K. Haneda. (Tehran: 2000).
Langhade, J., trans. and ed. "Le Kitab al-khataba d'al-Farabi." Critical Arabic text and French translation. In *Mélanges de l'Université Saint-Joseph de Beyrouth*. Vol. 43. (1968), pp. 61–177.
Madelung, Wilferd, ed. *Akhbār a'immat al-Zaidī fī Ṭabaristān wa Dailam wa Jīlān*. (Beirut: 1987).
Maḥmūd ibn Ḥidāyat Allāh Afūshtah-ī Natanzī. *Naqāvat al-āsār fī zikr al-akhbār*. Edited by I. Ishrāqī. (Tehran: 1971).
Maḥmūd ibn Khvāndamīr. *Tārīkh-i Shāh Ismā`īl va Shāh Ṭahmāsp*. Edited by Muḥammad Alī Jarāḥī. (Tehran: 1994).
Martin, R. G. "Seven Safavid Documents from Azarbayjan." In *Documents from Islamic Chanceries*. Edited by S. M. Stern. Vol. 3. (Oxford: 1965), pp. 171–206.
Membré, Michele. *Mission to the Lord Sophy of Persia (1539–1542)*. Edited by A. H. Morton. (London: 1993).
Minorsky, Vladimir, trans. *Persia in A.D. 1478–1490: An Abridged Translation of*

Fadlullah b. Ruzbihan Khunji's Tārīkh-i ʿālam-ārā-yi Amīnī. (London: 1957).
------. "A Soyūrghāl of Qāsim b. Jahāngīr Āq-Qoyūnlū (903/1498)." *Bulletin of the School of Oriental and African Studies.* Vol. 9. (1937–39), pp. 927–60.
------, ed. and trans. *Tadhkirat al-mulūk: A Manual of Safavid Administration.* (London: 1943).
Mīr ʿAlī Haravī. *Muraqqaʿ-i nāy-nāmah-yi Jāmī.* Edited by Nasrullah Pourjavady. (Tehran: 2001).
Muḥammad ibn ʿAbd Allāh al-Kisāʾī. *Tales of the Prophets (Qiṣaṣ al-anbiyāʾ).* Edited and translated by W. M. Thackston Jr. (Chicago: 1997).
Muḥammad ibn Aḥmad Ibn Ilyās al-Hanafī. *Badāʿ al-ẓuhūr fī waqāʾiʿ al-duhūr.* Edited by Muḥammad Muṣṭafā. 4 vols. (Cairo: 1960).
Muḥammad Favād ʿAbd al-Bāqī, ed. *Al-Muʿjam al-mufahras.* (Tehran: 2000).
Muḥammad ibn Hindūshāh Nakhjuvānī. *Dastūr al-kātib fīʾl taʿyīn al-marātib.* Edited by ʿAbd al-Karīm ʿAlīzādah. 3 vols. (Moscow: 1964).
Muḥammad ibn Ibrāhīm ibn Jaʿfar Nuʿmanī. *Kitāb al-ghaibah.* Edited by A. A. al-Ghaffārī. (Tehran: 1977).
Muḥammad ibn Muḥammad ibn Ghazālī Ṭūsī. *Naṣīḥat al-mulūk.* Edited by Jalāl al-Dīn Humāʾī. (Tehran: 1972).
Muḥammad ibn Muḥammad al-Nuʿman al-Mufīd. *Kitāb al-irshād.* Translated by I. K. Howard. (Elmhurst: 1981).
Muḥammad ibn ʿUmar Rādūyānī. *Tarjuman al-balāghat.* Edited by ʿAlī Qavīm. (Tehran: 1960).
Muḥammad Mufīd Mustaufī Bafqī, *Jāmiʿi-i Mufīdī.* Edited by I. Afshār. (Tehran: 1961).
Muḥammad ibn Yaʿqūb ibn Isḥaq al-Kulainī. *Kāfī al-uṣūl min al-kāfī.* Edited by A. A. Ghaffārī. 2 vols. (Tehran: 1968).
Muḥammad Yūsuf Vālih Iṣfahānī. *Khuld-i barīn.* Edited by Mīr Hāshim Muḥaddis̱. (Tehran: 1993).
Muḥtasham Kāshānī. *Dīvān-i Maulānā Muḥtasham Kāshānī.* Edited by Mihr ʿAlī Kirmānī. (Tehran: 1997).
Niẓām al-Dīn ʿAbd al-Vāsiʿ Niẓāmī. *Manshā al-inshā.* Edited by Rukn al-Dīn Humāyūn Farrukh. (Tehran: 1978).
Niẓām al-Dīn Aḥmad Haravī. *Ṭabaqāt-i Akbarī.* Edited and translated by B. De and B. Prashad. 3 Vols. (Calcutta: 1913–40).
Niẓām al-Mulk. *Siyāsat nāma.* Edited and translated by H. Darke. (London: 1962).
Niẓāmī ʿArūḍī Samarqandī, *Chahār maqālah.* Ed. Muhammad Muḥammad Mūʿīn (Tehran: 1995).
Nūr Allāh Shūshtarī. *Majālis al-muʾminīn.* Lithograph edition. Edited by Mullā Amīn Tehrānī. (Tehran: 1881).
Papazian, A. D., ed. *Persidskie dokumenti Matenadarana.* 3 vols. (Yerevan: 1956).
Quṭb al-Dīn Abū al-Ḥasan Muḥammad ibn al-Ḥusain ibn al-Ḥasan Baihaqī Nīshāpūrī Kaidarī. *Dīvān-i Imām ʿAlī.* Edited by Abū al-Qāsim Imāmī. (Tehran: 1995).
Rashīd al-Dīn Vaṭvāṭ. *Ḥadāʾiq al-siḥr fī daqāʾiq al-shiʿr.* Arabic edition. Edited by Ibrāhīm Amīn al-Shūrābī. (Cairo: 1945).
Roemer, Hans Robert. "Le Dernier Firman de Rustam Bahadur Aq Qoyunlu?" In *Bulletin de l'Institut Français d'archeologie orientale.* Vol. 59. (1960), pp. 273–87.
------, ed. and trans. *Staatsschreiben der Timüridenzeit: das Sharaf Nāma des ʿAbdullāh Marwārīd im kritischer Auswertung.* (Weisbaden: 1952).
Röhrborn, Klaus Michael. "Staatskanzlei und Absolutismus im safawidischen Persien." *Zeitschrift der Deutschen Morgenländischen Gesellschaft.* Vol. 127. (1977), pp. 313–43.
Ṣābityān, J. *Asnād va nāmah-hā-yi tārīkhī-yi daurah-yi Ṣafaviyyah.* (Tehran: 1964).

Sa`dī Shīrāzī. *Kulliyāt-i Sa`dī*. Edited by Muḥammad `Alī Furūghī. (Tehran: 2000).
Ṣaḥīḥ al-Bukhārī. *Ṣaḥīḥ*. 8 Vols. (Beirut: 1992).
Sām Mīrzā. *Tazkirah-yi tuḥfah-yi Sāmī*. Edited by Rukn al-Dīn Humāyūn Farrukh (Tehran: 1936).
Schimkoreit, Renate. *Registen publizierter safawidischer Herrscherurkunden: Erlasse und Staatsschreiben der frühen Neuzeit Irans*. (Berlin: 1982).
Shams al-Dīn Muḥammad ibn Qais al-Rāzī (Shams-i Qais). *Al-Mu`jam fī ma`āyir ash`ār al-`ajam*. Edited by Muḥammad Qazvīnī. (Tehran: 1959).
Shams al-Dīn Muḥammad ibn Tūlūn. *Mufākahat al-khillān fī ḥawādith al-zamān*. Edited by Muḥammad Muṣṭafā. 2 Vols. (Cairo: 1962).
(Amīr) Sharaf al-Dīn Batlisī. *Sharaf nāmah*. Edited by Jamil Bandi Ruzhbayani. (Cairo: 1953).
Sulṭān Hāshim Mīrzā. *Zābūr-i āl-i Dāvūd: sharḥ-i irtibāṭ-i sādāt-i mar`ashī bā salāṭīn-i Ṣafaviyyah*. (Tehran: 2000).
(Shāh) Ṭahmāsp. *Tazkirah-yi Ṭahmāsp*. In Paul Horn, "Die Denkwürdigkeiten des Shāh Ṭahmāsp I von Persien." *Zeitschrift der Deutschen Morgenländischen Gesellschaft*. Vol. 44. (1890), pp. 563–649, and Vol. 45. (1891), pp. 241–95.
`Unsur al-Ma`ālī Kai Kāvūs ibn Iskandar. *A Mirror for Princes: the* Qābūs nāma. Edited and translated by Reuben Levy. (London: 1951).
------. *Guzīdah-yi Qābūs nāmah*. Edited by Ghulām Ḥusain Yusufī. (Tehran: 2002).
Walzer, Richard, ed. *Al-Farabi on the Perfect State: Abu Nasr al-Farabi's* Mabadi' ara' ahl al-madina al-fadila. (Oxford: 1985).
Wickens, G. M., ed. and trans. *The Nasirean Ethics (Akhlāq-i Nāṣirī)*. (London: 1964).
Woods, John, ed. and trans. *Fadlullah Kunji-Isfahani's* Tarikh-i Alam-ara-yi Amini. Persian text edited by John E. Woods with an English translation by Vladimir Minorsky, revised and augmented by John E. Woods. (London: 1992).
Yaḥyā ibn Muḥammad ibn `Abd al-Laṭīf Qazvīnī. *Lubb al-tavārīkh*. Partially edited and translated by H. Braun as "Aḥvāl-i Shāh Ismā`īl: eine unerschlossene Darstellung des lebens des ersten Safawidenschahs." Unpublished Ph.D. Dissertation. (University of Göttingen: 1947.)

III. Secondary Sources

Abisaab, Rula. *Converting Persia: Religion and Power in the Safavid Empire, 1501–1736*. (London: 2004).
------."The `Ulama of Jabal `Amil in Safavid Iran, 1501–1736: Marginality, Migration, and Social Change." *Iranian Studies*. Vol. 27. No. 1. (1994), pp. 103–122.
Afsaruddin, Asma. *Excellence and Precedence: Medieval Islamic Discourse on Legitimate Leadership*. (Leiden: 2002).
Ahmad, Aziz. "Safawid Poets and India." *Iran*. Vol. 14. (1976), pp. 117–32.
Alam, Muzaffar. "The Pursuit of Persian Language in Mughal Politics." *Modern Asian Studies*. Vol. 31. (1998), pp. 317–49.
Algar, Hamid. "Naqshbandis and Safavids: A Contribution to the Religious History of Iran and Her Neighbors." In *Safavid Iran and Her Neighbors*. Edited by M. Mazzaoui. (Salt Lake City: 2003), pp. 7–48.
Allen, Terry. *Timurid Herat*. (Wiesbaden: 1983).
Allouche, Adel. *The Origins and Development of the Ottoman-Safavid Diplomatic Conflict, 906–966/1500–1555*. (Berlin: 1983).
Allsen, T. T. *Commodity and Exchange in the Mongol Empire: A Cultural History of Islamic Textiles*. (Cambridge: 1997).
Amirshah, Ardavan. "Le développement de la ville de Qazwin jusqu'au milieu du VIIIe/XIVe siècle." *Revue des Études Islamiques*. Vol. 49. (1981), pp. 1–42.
Amirsoleimani, Soheila. "Of This World and the Next: Metaphors and Meanings in the

Qabus-nama." *Iranian Studies*. Vol. 35. Nos. 1–3. (2002), pp. 1–22.

Ando, Shiro. *Timuridische Emire nach dem* Mu`izz al-ansāb: *Untersuchung zur Stammesaristokratie Zentralasiens im 14. um 15. Jahrhundert.* (Berlin: 1992).

Aouad, Maroun. "Commentateurs 'satisfaisants' et 'non-satisfaisants' de la Rhétorique selon Averroes." In *Averroes and the Aristotelian Tradition: Sources, Constitution and Reception of the Philosophy of Ibn Rushd (1126–1198).* Proceedings of the Fourth Symposium Averroicum. (Cologne, 1996). Edited by G. Endress and J. Aertsen. (Leident: 1999), pp. 83–124.

------. "L'exégèse da la Rhétorique d'Aristote: recherches sur quelques commentateurs grecs, arabes et byzantins." In *Medioevo. Rivista di storia della filosofia medievale.* Vol. 25. (1999–2000), pp. 551–649.

------. "Les fondements da la Rhétorique d'Aristote reconsidérés par Averroès dans l'abrégé de la rhétorique, ou le développement du concept du 'point de vue immediate." In *Peripatetic Rhetoric After Aristotle.* Edited by W. Fortenbaugh and D. Mirhady. Rutgers University Studies in Classical Humanities. Vol. 6. (New Brunswick: 1994), pp. 261–313.

------. "La Rhéorique. Tradition Syriaque et Arabe." In *Dictionnaire des philosophes antiques.* Edited by R. Goulet. Vol. 1. (Paris: 1989), pp. 455–72.

Arjomand, Said Amir. "Conceptions of Authority and the Transition of Shi`ism from Sectarian to National Religion in Iran." In *Culture and Memory in Medieval Islam: Essays in Honour of Wilferd Madelung.* Edited by F. Daftary and J. Meri. (London: 2003), pp. 388–409.

------. "The Crisis of the Imamate and the Institution of Occultation in Twelver Shi`ism: a Sociohistorical Perspective." *International Journal of Middle East Studies.* Vol. 28. No. 4. (1996), pp. 491–515.

------. "Imam absconditus and the Beginnings of a Theology of Occultation: Imami Shi`ism circa 280–90 A.H./900 A.D." *Journal of the American Oriental Society.* Vol. 117. No. 1. (1997), pp. 1–12.

------. "Perso-Indian Statecraft, Greek Political Science and the Muslim Idea of Government." *International Sociology.* Vol. 16. No. 3. (2001), p. 455–73.

------. *The Shadow of God and the Hidden Imam.* (Albany: 1980).

------."Religious Extremism (guluww), Sufism, and Sunnism in Safavid Iran: 1501–1722." *Journal of Asian History.* Vol. 15. (1981), pp. 1–35.

Askari, S. H. "Mahmud Gawan and his book Manazir-ul-insha." *Indo-Iranica.* Vol. 6. No. 4. (1952–53), pp. 28–36.

Aubin, Jean. "L'avènement des Safavides reconsidéré." *Moyen Orient et océan Indien.* Vol. 5. (1988), pp. 1–130.

------. *Materiaux pour la biographie de Shah Ni`matollah Wali Kermani.* (Paris: 1956).

------. "Notes sur quelques documents Aq-Qoyunlu." In *Mélanges Louis Massignon.* Vol. 1. (Damascus: 1956), pp. 123–47.

------. "*Per viam portugalensem*: autour d'un projet diplomatique de Maximilien II." *Mare-Luso Indicum.* Vol. 4. (1980), pp. 45–73.

------. "La politique religieuse des Safavides." In *Le Shî`ism imâmite.* (Paris: 1970), pp. 235–44.

------. "Les rélations diplomatiques entre les Aq-qoyunlu et les Bahmanides." In *Iran and Islam: In Memory of the Late Vladimir Minorsky.* Edited by C. E. Bosworth. (Edinburgh: 1971).

------. "Révolution chiite et conservatisme: les soufis de Lahejan, 1500–1514." *Moyen Orient et océan Indien.* Vol. 1. (1984), pp. 1–40.

------. "Le royaume d'Ormuz au début du XVIe siècle." *Mare Luso-Indicum.* Vol. 2. (1972), pp. 77–179.

------. "Shah Isma`īl et les notables de l'Iraq persan." *Journal of the Economic and Social*

History of the Orient. Vol. 2. (1959), pp. 37–81.
Aujabī, `Alī. *Mīr Dāmād: Bunyān-guzār-i ḥikmat-i yamānī.* (Tehran: 2002).
Al-Azmeh, Aziz. "God's Chronography and Dissipative Time: Vaticinium ex Eventu in Classical and Medieval Muslim Apocalyptic Traditions." *Medieval History Journal*, Vol. 7. No. 2. (2004), pp. 199–225.
------. *Muslim Kingship: Power and the Sacred in Muslim, Christian, and Pagan Polities.* (London: 1997).
Babaie, Sussan, Kathryn Babayan, Ina Baghdiantz-McCabe, and Massumeh Farhad. *Slaves of the Shah: New Elites of Safavid Iran.* (London: 2004).
Babayan, Kathryn. *Mystics, Monarchs, and Messiahs: Cultural Landscapes of Early Modern Iran.* (Cambridge, Mass.: 2002).
------. "The Safavid Synthesis: From Qizilbash Islam to Imamite Shi`ism." *Iranian Studies*. Vol. 27. No. 4. (1994), pp. 135–61.
Bacqué-Grammont, Jean-Louis. "The Eastern Policy of Süleymân the Magnificent, 1520–1533." In *Süleymân the Second and His Time*. Edited by H. Inalcik and C. Kafadar. (Istanbul: 1993), pp. 219–28.
------. "Études sur blocus de commerce iranien par Selim Ier." *Turcica*. Vol. 6. (1975), pp. 68–88.
------. "Notes et documents sur les Ottomans, les Safavides et la Géorgie, 1516–1521." *Cahiers du monde russe et soviétique*. Vol. 20. (1979), pp. 239–72.
------. *Les Ottomans, les Safavides, et la Géorgie, 1516–1524.* (Istanbul: 1991).
------. *Les Ottomans, les Safavides, et leurs voisins.* (Leiden: 1987).
------. "Remarques sur quelques types de carrières et de functions dans l'administration ottomane au XVIe siécle." *Archivum Ottomanicum*. Vol. 17. (1999), pp. 233–40.
Badie, Bertrand. "La Philosophie Politique de l'Héllénisme Musulman." *Revue Française de Science Politique*. Vol. 28. No. 2. (1977), pp. 291–304.
Bagçi, Serpil. "A New Theme of the Shīrāzī Frontispeice Miniatures: the Dīvān of Solomon." *Muqarnas*. Vol. 12. (1995), pp. 101–11.
Bahari, Ebadollah. *Bihzad: Master of Persian Painting.* (London: 1996).
Barakat, Muḥammad. *Kitāb-shināsī-yi maktab-i falsafī-yi Shīrāz.* (Shiraz: 2004).
Bar-Asher, M. Meir. *Scripture and Exegesis in Early Imami-Shiism.* (Leiden: 1999).
Barilli, Renato. *Rhetoric*. Translated by G. Menozzi. Theory and History of Literature Series. Vol. 63. (Minneapolis: 1989).
Barkun, Michael. *Disaster and the Millennnium.* (Syracuse: 1974).
Barthes, Roland. *S/Z.* Translated by R. Miller. (New York: 1974).
Barthold, Wilehelm. *Four Studies on the History of Central Asia*. Edited and translated by Vladimir Minorsky. (Leiden: 1956).
------. *Herat unter Husein Baiqara*. Edited and translated by W. Hinz. (Nendeln Kraus: 1966).
------. *An Historical Geography of Iran*. Edited and translated by S. Soucek. (Princeton: 1984).
------. *Turkestan Down to the Mongol Invasion*. Edited and translated by T. Minorsky. (London: 1928).
Bashir, Shahzad. "Deciphering the Cosmos from Creation to Apocalypse: The Hurufiyya Movement and Medieval Islamic Esotericism." In *Imagining the End: Visions of Apocalypse from the Ancient Middle East to Modern America*. Edited by A. Amanat and M. Berhardsson. (London: 2002), pp. 168–84.
------. "Enshrining Divinity: The Death and Memorialization of Fazlallah Astarabadi in Hurufi Thought." *The Muslim World*. Vol. 90. (2000), pp. 293–301.
------. "The Imam's Return: Messianic Leadership in Late Medieval Shi`ism." In *The Most Learned of the Shi`a: The Institution of the* Marja` Taqlid. Edited by L. S. Walbridge. (New York: 2001), pp. 21–33.

------. *Messianic Hopes and Mystical Visions: The Nurbakhshiyya Between Medieval and Modern Islam.* (Columbia, South Carolina: 2003).

------. "Shah Isma`il and the Qizilbash: Cannibalism in the Religious History of Early Safavid Iran." *History of Religions.* Vol. 45. No. 3. (2006), pp. 234–56.

Bausani, Allesandro. "Muhammad or Darius? The Elements and Basis of Iranian Culture." In *Islam and Cultural Change in the Middle Ages.* Edited by S. Vryonis. (Wiesbaden: 1975), pp. 43–57.

Bāyanī, Khānbāba. *Les rélations d'Iran avec l'Europe occidentale à l'époque Safavide.* (Paris: 1939).

Bayānī, Mahdī. *Aḥvāl va āsār-i khūshnivīsān.* 4 vols. (Tehran: 1966).

Berkey, Jonathan. *Popular Preaching and Religious Authority in the Medieval Islamic Near East.* (Seattle: 2001).

Binyon, Laurence, J. V. S., Wilkonson, and Basil Gray. *Persian Miniature Painting.* (New York: 1933).

Black, Deborah. *Logic and Aristotle's* Rhetoric *and* Poetics *in Medieval Arabic Philosophy.* (Leiden: 1990).

Bonebakker, S. A. "Aspects of the History of Literary Rhetoric and Poetics in Arabic Literature." *Viator.* Vol. 1. (1970), pp. 75–95.

Bosworth, C. E. "Administrative Literature." In *Religion, Learning and Science in the `Abbasid Period.* Edited by M. J. L. Young, J. D. Latham, and R. B. Serjeant. (Cambridge: 1990), pp. 155–67.

------. *Bahā' al-Dīn al-`Āmilī and His Literary Anthologies.* (Manchester: 1989).

------. "Dīvān II. Government Office." *Encyclopaedia Iranica.* Vol. 7. pp. 432–38.

------. *The Ghaznavids, Their Empire in Afghanistan and Eastern Iran, 994–1040.* (Edinburgh: 1963).

------. "Al-Karazmi on the Technical Terms of the Secretary's Art." *Journal of the Economic and Social History of the Orient.* Vol. 12. (1969), pp. 113–64.

------. "Lāhīdjān ." *EI²*. Vol. 5. pp. 602–04.

Boyle, J. A. "The Evolution of Iran as a National State." *Belleten.* Vol. 39. (1975), pp. 633–44.

Brookshaw, Dominic. "Palaces, Pavilions and Pleasure-gardens: The Context and Setting of the Medieval *Majlis.*" *Middle Eastern Literatures.* Vol. 6. No. 2. (2003), pp. 199–223.

Browne, E. G. *Literary History of Persia.* 4 Vols. (Cambridge: 1958).

Brummet, Palmira. "The Myth of Shah Isma`il Safavi: Political Rehtoric and 'Divine' Kingship." In *Medieval Christian Perceptions of Islam.* Edited by J. Tolan. (New York: 1996), pp. 331–59.

Burke, Kenneth. *A Rhetoric of Motives.* (Berkeley: 1969).

Busse, Heribert. "Diplomatic—Persia." *EI²*. Vol. 2. pp. 308–13.

------."Persische Diplomatik im Überblick. Ergebnisse und Probleme." *Der Islam.* Vol. 37. (1961), pp. 202–45.

Cahen, Claude. "La problème du Shi`isme dans l'Asie Mineure Turque preottomane." In *Le Shi`isme Imamite: Colloque de Strasbourg (6–9 mai 1968).* Edited by R. Brunschvig and T. Fahd. (Paris: 1970), pp. 115–29.

Calder, Norman. "Khums in Imami Shi`i Jurisprudence from the Tenth to the Sixteenth Century A. D." *Bulletin of the School of Oriental and African Studies.* Vol. 45. (1982), pp. 39–47.

Calmard, Jean. "Mar`ashīs." *EI²*. Vol. 6. p. 510–18.

------. "Popular Literature Under the Safavids." In *Society and Culture in the Early Modern Middle East: Studies on Iran in the Safavid Period.* Edited by A. J. Newman. (Leiden: 2003), pp. 315–39.

------."Les rituals shiites et le pouvoir: l'imposition du shiisme safavide: eulogies et

malédictions canoniques." In *Études Safavides*. Edited by J. Calmard. (Paris: 1993), pp. 109–50.
------. "Shi`i Rituals and Power. II The Consolidation of Safavid Shi`ism: Folklore and Popular Religion." In *Safavid Persia: The History and Politics of an Islamic Society*. Edited by C. Melville. (London: 1996), pp. 139–90.
Canby, Sheila. "Safavid Painting." In *Hunt for Paradise: Court Arts of Safavid Iran, 1501–1576*. Edited by J. Thompson and S. Canby. (Milan: 2003), pp. 73–134.
Chalisova, Natalia. "Persian Rhetoric: Elm-e Badi` and Elm-e Bayān," In *Introduction to Persian Literature*. Vol. 1, Eds. J.T.P. De Bruijn and Ehsan Yarshater. (London: 2008), pp. 139-71.
Chittick, William. "Eschatology." In *Islamic Spirituality: Foundations*. Edited by S. H. Nasr. Vol. 1. (New York: 1987), pp. 378–409.
Clifford, W. W. "Some Observations on the Course of Mamluk-Safavi Relations (1502–1516/908-922)." *Der Islam*. Vol. 70. No. 2. (1993), pp. 245–78.
Clinton, Jerome. "The Uses of Guile in the Shahnama." *Iranian Studies*. Vol. 32. No. 2. (1999), pp. 223–30.
Cohn, Norman. *The Pursuit of the Millennium: Revolutionary Millenarians and Mystical Anarchists of the Middle Ages*. Revised edition. (London: 1970).
Conte, Gian Biagio. *The Rhetoric of Imitation: Genre and Poetic Memory in Virgil and Other Latin Poets*. Translated by C. Segal. (Ithaca: 1987).
Cook, David. *Studies in Muslim Apocalyptic*. (Princeton: 2002).
Cooper, John. "Some Observations on the Religious Intellectual Milieu of Safawid Persia." In *Intellectual Traditions in Islam*. Edited by F. Daftary. (London: 2001), pp. 146–59.
Corbin, Henri. *Spiritual Body and Celestial Earth: From Mazdean Iran to Shi`ite Iran*. Translated by N. Pearson. (Princeton: 1977).
Coulson, Noel. *Conflicts and Tensions in Islamic Jurisprudence*. (Chicago: 1969).
Crone, Patricia. *God's Rule: Six Centuries of Medieval Islamic Political Thought*. (New York: 2004).
Dabirsaqi, M. and Bert Fragner. "`Abdī Shīrāzī." *Encyclopaedia Iranica*. Vol. 1. pp. 209–10.
Daftary, Farhad. "Ismā`īlī-Sufi Relations in Early Post-Alamut and Safavid Persia." In *The Heritage of Sufism Vol. III: Late Classical Persianate Sufism (1501–1750) The Safavid & Mughal Period*. Edited by L. Lewisohn and D. Morgan. (London: 1999), pp. 275–89.
Dähne, Stephan. "Allusions to the Qur'ān: A Rhetorical Device in Political Speeches in Classical Arabic Literature." In *Insights into Arabic Literature and Islam: Ideas, Concepts, and Modes of Portrayal*. Edited by S. Guenther. (Leiden: 2005), pp. 1–20.
Dale, Stephen. "The Legacy of the Timurids." *Journal of the Royal Asiatic Society*. Vol. 8. No. 1. (1998), pp. 43–58.
Dāneshpazhūh, Muḥammad Taqī. "Navīsandagī va dabīrī." In *Ḥadīṡ-e `eshq*. Vol. 1. Edited by N. Moṭṭalebī-Kāshānī and S. Moḥammad-Ḥossein Mar`ashī. (Tehran: 2003), pp. 135–230.
Daryaee, Touraj. "The Effect of the Arab Muslim Conquest on the Administrative Division of Sasanian Persia." *Iran: Journal of Persian Studies*. Vol. 41. (2003), pp. 193–204.
Dickson, Martin. "The Duel for Khurasan: Shāh Ṭahmāsp and the Özbeks." Unpublished Ph.D. Dissertation. (Princeton University: 1958).
------ and S. C. Welch. *The Houghton Shahnameh*. 2 vols. (London: 1981).
Doerfer, Gerhard. *Turkische und mongolische Elemente im Neupersischen: Unter besonderer Berücksightigung Alterer neupersischer Geschichtsquellen, vor allem der*

Mongolen- und Timüriden-zeit. 4 Vols. (Weisbaden: 1963–67).
Edwards, C. C. "Calligraphers and Artists: A Persian Work of the Late 16th Century." *Bulletin of the School of Oriental and African Studies*. Vol. 1. (1939), pp. 199–211.
Efendiev, O. A. "Le rôle des tribus de langue turque dans la création de l'état safavide." *Turcica*. Vol. 7. (1975), pp. 24–33.
El-Hibri, Tayeb. "A Note on Biblical Narrative and `Abbasid History." In *Views from the Edge: Essays in Honour of Richard W. Bulliet*. Edited by N. Yavari, L. G. Potter, J. R. Oppenheim. (New York: 2004), pp. 63–69.
von Erdmann, Franz. "Iskender Munschi und sein Werk." *Zeitschrift der deutschen morgenländischen Gesellschaft*. Vol. 15. (1861), pp. 457–501.
Fakhry, Majid. *A History of Islamic Philosophy*. (New York: 1970).
Falsafī, Naṣr Allāh. *Zindagānī-yi Shāh `Abbās*. 5 Vols. (Tehran: 1966–74).
Fard, `Abbās Qulī Ghaffārī. *Ravābiṭ-i Ṣafaviyyah va Uzbekān*. (Tehran: 1997).
Ferrard, C. "The Development of an Ottoman Rhetoric up to 1882 Part II: Contributions from Outside the Medrese." *Osmanli Arasstirmalari (Journal of Ottoman Studies)*. Vol. 4. (1984), pp. 19–34.
Findley, Carter. *Bureaucratic Reform in the Ottoman Empire*. (Princeton: 1980).
Fishārakī, Muḥammad. "Īstā'ī va taqlīd va intiḥāl dar ta`līf-i kutub-i balāghī." *Ayandah*. Vol. 12. Nos. 9–10. (1986–87), pp. 570–78.
Fleischer, Cornell. "Alqās Mīrzā." *Encyclopaedia Iranica*. Vol. 1. pp. 907–09.
------. "Between the Lines: Realities of Scribal Life in the Sixteenth Century." In *Studies in Ottoman History in Honour of Professor V. L. Ménage*. Edited by C. Heywood and C. Imber. (Istanbul: 1994), pp. 45–62.
------. "Mahdi and Millennium: Messianic Dimensions in the Development of Ottoman Imperial Ideology." In *The Great Ottoman-Turkish Civilization*. Edited by K. Çiçek. Vol. 3 (Philosophy, Science and Institutions). (Ankara: 2000), pp. 42–54.
Floor, Willem. *Safavid Government Institutions*. (Costa Mesa, CA: 2001).
Fragner, Bert. "Das Ardabīl Heiligtum in den Urkunden." *Wiener Zeitschrift für die Kunde des Morgenlandes*. Vol. 67. (1975), pp. 169–215.
------."Katib. II: In Persia." *EI*[2]. Vol. 4. pp. 757–58.
------. "Shah Ismail's Fermans and Sanads: Tradition and Reform in Persophone Administration and Chancellery Affairs." *Journal of Azerbaijani Studies*. Vol. 1. No. 1. (1998), pp. 35–46.
------. "Social and Internal Economic Affairs." In *Cambridge History of Iran*. Edited by P. Jackson. Vol. 6. (Cambridge: 1986), pp. 491–567.
------. "Tradition, Legitimät und Abgrenzung: formale Symbolaussagen persischsprachiger Herrscherurkunden." In *Akten des Melzer Symposiums 1991: Veranstalted aus Anlass der Hundertjahrfeier indo-iranischer Forschung in Graz*. Edited by W. Slaje and C. Zinko. (Leykam: 1992), pp. 84–113.
Frye, Richard. *The Heritage of Persia*. (Cleveland: 1963).
Gandjei, Tourkhan. "Isma`il I 2. His Poetry." *EI*[2]. Vol. 4. pp. 187–88.
Al-Ghiṭā', `Allāmah Muḥammad Ḥusain al-Kāshif. *The Origin of Shi`ite Islam and its Principles*. (Qumm: 1993).
Gholsorkhi, Shohreh. "Ismail II and Mirza Makhdum Sharifi: An Interlude in Safavid History." *International Journal of Middle East Studies*, Vol. 26. (1994), pp. 477-88.
Göcek, Fatma Müge. "The Social Construction of an Empire: Ottoman State Under Suleyman the Magnificent." In *Süleymân the Second and His Time*. Edited by H. Inalcik and C. Kafadar. (Istanbul: 1993), pp. 93–108.
Golombek, Lisa. *The Timurid Shrine at Gazur Gah*. (Toronto: 1968).
Goto, Yukako. "Der Aufstieg zweier Sayyid-Familien am Kaspischen Meer:

'Volksislamische' Strömungen in Iran des 8/14. Und 9/15. Jahrhunderts." *Wiener Zeitschrift für die Kunde des Morgenlandes*. Vol. 89. (1999), pp. 45–84.
Graham, Terry. "The Ni`matu'llahi Order Under Safavid Suppression and in Indian Exile." In *The Heritage of Sufism Vol. III: Late Classical Persianate Sufism (1501–1750) The Safavid & Mughal Period*. Edited by L. Lewisohn and D. Morgan. (London: 1999), pp. 165–200.
Gramlich, Richard. *Die schiitischen derwischorden persiens*. 3 Vols. (Wiesbaden: 1965).
Gribetz, Arthur. *Strange Bedfellows*: Mut`at al-nisā' *and* Mut`at al-ḥajj. (Berlin: 1994).
Gronke, Monika. "The Persian Court Between Palace and Tent: From Timur to `Abbas I." In *Timurid Art and Culture: Iran and Central Asia in the Fifteenth Century*. Edited by L. Golombek and M. Subtelny. (Leiden: 1992), pp. 17–22.
von Grunebaum, G. E. "The Concept of Cultural Classicism." In *Modern Islam: The Search for Cultural Identity*. (Berkeley: 1962), pp. 73–96.
Gully, Adrian. "Epistles for Grammarians: Illustrations from the Insha' Literature." *British Journal of Middle Eastern Studies*. Vol. 23. No. 2. (1996), pp. 147–66.
Günther, Sebastian. "Der Shāfi`itische Traditionalist Abū Sulaimān al-Khaṭṭābī und die Situation der religiösen Wissenschaften im 10. Jahrhundert." *Zeitschrift der Deutschen Morgenländischen Gesellschaft*. Vol. 146. No. 1. (1996), pp. 61–91.
Gutas, Dimitri. "Classical Arabic Wisdom Literature: Nature and Scope." *Journal of the American Oriental Society*. Vol. 101. No. 1. (1981), pp. 49–86.
------. *Greek Thought, Arabic Culture: The Graeco-Arabic Translation Movement in Baghdad and Early `Abbasid Society*. (London: 1998).
Hachmeier, Klaus. "Private Letters, Official Correspondence: Buyid *Inshā* as a Historical Source." *Journal of Islamic Studies*. Vol. 13. No. 2. (2002), pp. 125–54.
Halldén, Philip. "What is Arab Islamic Rhetoric? Rethinking the History of Muslim Oratory Art and Homiletics." *International Journal of Middle East Studies*. Vol. 37. No. 1. (2005), pp. 19–38.
Halm, Heinz. *Die Schia*. (Darmstadt: 1988).
------. *Shi`a Islam: From Religion to Revolution*. Translated by A. Brown. (Princeton: 1997).
Hampton, Timothy. *Writing from History: The Rhetoric of Exemplarity in Renaissance Literature*. (Ithaca: 1990).
Hanaway, William. "`Ayyār II. `Ayyār in Persian Sources." *Encyclopaedia Iranica*. Vol. 1. pp. 159–63.
------. "Formal Elements in the Persian Popular Romances." *Review of National Literatures*. Vol. 2. (1971), pp. 139–60.
Haneda, Masashi. *Le chah et les qizilbash; le système militaire safavide*. (Berlin: 1987).
------. "The Evolution of the Safavid Royal Guard." *Iranian Studies*. Vol. 21. Nos. 2–3. (1989), pp. 57–85.
------. "La famille Khūzānī d'Isfahan (15e-17e siècles)." *Studia Iranica*. Vol. 18. (1989), pp. 77–92.
Hermann, Gottfried. "Zur Intitulatio timuridischer Herrscherurkunden." *Zeitschrift der Deutschen Morgenländischen Gesellschaft*. Supplement II: XVIII. Deutscher Orientalistentag. (Weisbaden: 1974), pp. 498–521.
Heywood, Colin. "Between Historical Myth and 'Mythohistory': The Limits of Ottoman History." In *Writing Ottoman History: Documents and Interpretations*. Edited by C. Heywood. (Aldershot: 2002), pp. 315–45.
Hillenbrand, Robert. "The Iconography of the *Shah-nama-yi Shahi*." In *Safavid Persia: The History and Politics of an Islamic Society*. Edited by C. Melville. (London: 1996), pp. 53–78.
Hinz, Walther. *Irans Aufstieg zum Nationaliststaat im fünfzehnten Jahrhundert*. (Berlin:

1936).
------. "Die persische Geheimkanzlei im Mittelalter." In *Westöstliche Abhandlungen Rudolf Tschudi zum siebzigsten Geburtstag überreicht von Freunden und Schūlern.* (Weisbaden: 1954), pp. 342–54.
------. "Schah Esma`il II. Ein Beitrag zur Geschichte der Safaviden." *Mitteilungen des Seminars für orientalische Sprachen.* Vol. 26. (1933), pp. 19–100.
Hodgson, Marshall. *The Venture of Islam.* 3 Vols. (Chicago: 1974).
Horst, Heribert. *Tīmūr und Hojä `Alī: ein Beitrag zur Geschichte der Safawiden.* (Wiesbaden: 1958).
Hourani, Albert. "From Jabal `Amil to Persia." *Bulletin of the School of Oriental and African Studies.* Vol. 49. (1986), pp. 133–40.
Humphreys, Stephen. *Islamic History: A Framework for Inquiry.* (Princeton: 1991).
Hunt, Everett Lee. "Plato and Aristotle on Rhetoric and Rhetoricians." In *Essays on the Rhetoric of the Western World.* Edited by E. Corbett, J. Golden, and G. Berquist. (Dubuque: 1990), pp. 129–61.
Imber, Colin. *The Ottoman Empire, 1300–1650: The Structure of Power.* (New York: 2002).
Ishrāqī, Iḥsan. "Le *Dār al-salṭana* de Qazvīn." In *Safavid Persia: The History and Politics of an Islamic Society.* Edited by C. Melville. (London: 1996), pp. 105–15.
------. "Nuqtaviyyeh à l'époque Safavides." In *Society and Culture in the Early Modern Middle East: Studies on Iran in the Safavid Period.* Edited by A. Newman. (Leiden: 2003), pp. 341–49.
------. "Persia During the Period of the Safavids, the Afshars and the Early Qajars." In *History of Civilizations of Central Asia.* Edited by C. Adle, I. Habib. Vol. 5 (*Development in Contrast: From the Sixteenth to the Mid-Nineteenth Century*). (Paris: 2003), pp. 247–71.
Islam, Riazul. *Indo-Persian Relations: A Study of Political and Diplomatic Relations Between the Mughal Empire and Iran.* (Tehran: 1970).
Jackson, Peter, ed. *Cambridge History of Iran.* Vol. 6. (Cambridge: 1986).
Ja`fariyān, Rasūl. "Astarābād dar qarn-i nukhast-i ḥukūmat-i Ṣafavī." (n.p.: n.d.).
------. "Dīdgāh-hā-yi siyāsī-yi `Abdī Beg Shīrāzī dar barā-yi Shāh Ṭahmāsp Ṣafavī." In *Ṣafaviyyah dar `arṣah-i dīn, farhang va siyāsat.* Edited by R. Ja`fariyān. Vol. 1. (Tehran: 2000), pp. 493–503.
------. *Dīn va siyāsat dar daurah-yi Ṣafavī.* (Tehran: 1991).
------. "The Immigrant Manuscripts: A Study of the Migration of Shi`i Works from Arab Regions to Iran in the Early Safavid Era." In *Society and Culture in the Early Modern Middle East: Studies on Iran in the Safavid Period.* Edited by A. Newman (Leiden: 2003), pp. 315–70.
Jafri, S. H. M. *Origins and Early Development of Shi`a Islam.* (Karachi: 2000).
Jambet, C. "Idéal du politique et politique idéale selon Nasir al-Din Tusi." In *Nasir al-Din Tusi: Philosophe et savant du XIII*[e] *siècle.* Edited by N. Pourjavady and Z. Vesel. (Tehran: 2000), pp. 31–58.
Jenssen, Herbjorn. *The Subtleties and Secrets of the Arabic Lanuage: Preliminary Investigations into al-Qazwini's* Talkhis al-Miftah. (Bergen: 1998).
Johns, A. H. "Solomon and the Queen of Sheba: Fakhr al-Din al-Razi's Treatment of the Qur'anic Telling of the Story." In *Abr Nahrain.* Vol. 24. (1986), pp. 58–82.
Juynboll, J. H. A. *Muslim Tradition.* (Cambridge: 1983).
Kafadar, Cemal. *Between Two Worlds: The Construction of the Ottoman State.* (Berkeley: 1995).
Karamustafa, Ahmet. "Esmā`īl Ṣafawī II. His Poetry." *Encyclopaedia Iranica.* Vol. 8. pp. 635–36.
Kashani-Sabet, Firoozeh. *Frontier Fictions: Shaping the Iranian Nation, 1804–1946*

(Princeton: 1999).
Kasheff, Manouchehr. "Gilan – v. History under the Safavids." *Encyclopaedia Iranica*. Vol. 10. pp. 635–42.
Katouzian, Homa. *State and Society in Iran: The Eclipse of the Qajars and the Emergence of the Pahlavis*. (London: 2000).
Khalidi, Tarif. *Arabic Historical Thought in the Classical Period*. (Cambridge: 1994).
Kippenberg, Hans G. "Die Geschichte der mittelpersischen apokalyptischen Traditionen." *Studia Iranica*. Vol. 7. (1978), pp. 49–80.
Kissling, H. J. "Sah Isma`il, la nouvelle route des Indes et les Ottomans." *Turcica*. Vol. 6. (1975), pp. 89–102.
Kohlberg, Etan. "Description of the Corpus of Shī`ī Ḥadīth." In *Arabic Literature to the End of the Umayyad Period*. Edited by A. F. L. Beeston, T. M. Johnstone, R. B. Serjeant, and G. R. Smith. (Cambridge: 1983), pp. 299–307.
------. "Imam and Community in the Pre-Ghayba Period." In *Authority and Political Culture in Shi`ism*. Edited by Said Amir Arjomand. (New York: 1988), pp. 25–53.
------. "Some Imāmī Shī`ī Interpretations of Umayyad History." In *Studies on the First Century of Islamic Society*. Edited by G. H. A. Juynboll. (Illionois: 1982), pp. 145–49.
------. "Some Imāmī Shī`ī Views on the Ṣaḥāba." *Jersusalem Studies in Arabic and Islam*. Vol. 5. (1984), pp. 143–75.
------. "Some Imami-Shī`ī Views on taqiyya." *Journal of the American Oriental Society*. Vol. 95. (1975), pp. 395–402.
------. "Some Shī`ī Views of the Antediluvian World." *Studia Islamica*. Vol. 52. (1980), pp. 41–66.
------. "The Term 'Rāfiḍa' in Imāmī Shī`ī Usage." *Journal of the American Oriental Society*. Vol. 99. (1976), pp. 1–9.
Kraemer, Joel. "Humanism in the Renaissance of Islam: A Preliminary Study." *Journal of the American Oriental Society*. Vol. 104. No. 1. (1984), pp. 135–59.
Kütükoglu, Bekir Sidki. "Les rélations entre l'Empire Ottoman et l'Iran dans la second moitié du XVIe siècle." *Turcica*. Vol. 6. (1975), pp. 128–45.
Laleh, Haeedeh. "La maqsura monumentale de la mosquée du vendredi de Qazvīn à l'époque saljuqide." In *Bamberger Symposium: Rezeption in der islamischen Kunst vom 26.6.–28.6.1992*. Edited by B. Finster, B. Fragner, H. Hafenrichter. (Beirut: 1999), pp. 217–30.
Lambton, Ann K. S. "The *Āthār wa aḥyā'* of Rashīd al-Dīn Faḍl Allāh Hamadānī and his Contribution as an Agronomist, Arboriculturist, and Horticulturalist." In *The Mongol Empire & Its Legacy*. Edited by R. Amitai-Preiss and D. Morgan. (Leiden: 2000), pp. 126–137.
------. "Changing Concepts of Justice and Injustice from the 5th/11th Century to the 8th/14th Century in Persia: The Saljuq Empire and the Ilkhanate." *Studia Islamica*. Vol. 68. (1988), pp. 27–60.
------. *Continuity and Change in Medieval Persia*. (Albany: 1988).
------. "The Dilemma of Government in Islamic Persia: The *Siyasat-Nama* of Nizam al-Mulk." *Iran*. Vol. 22. (1984), pp. 55–66.
------."Islamic Mirrors for Princes." In *Atti del convegno, internazionale sul tema, La Persia nel mediovo*. (Rome: 1971), pp. 419–42.
------. "Justice in the Medieval Persian Theory of Kingship." *Studia Islamica*. Vol. 17. (1962), pp. 91–119.
------. "Kazwin - i. Geography and History." *EI*². Vol. 4. pp. 858–60.
------. *Landlord and Peasant in Persia*. (London: 1953).
------. "*Quis Custodiet Custodes?*: Some Reflections on the Persian Theory of Government (Part 1)." *Studia Islamica*. Vol. 5. (1955), pp. 125–48.

------. "*Quis Custodiet Custodes?*: Some Reflections on the Persian Theory of Government (Part 2)." *Studia Islamica*. Vol. 6. (1956), pp. 125–46.

------. *Theory and Practice in Medieavel Persian Government*. (London: 1980).

------. "The Theory of Kingship in the *Nasihat-ul-Muluk* of al-Ghazali." *The Islamic Quarterly*. Vol. 1. (1954), pp. 47–55.

Larkin, Margaret. *The Theology of Meaning: `Abd al-Qahir al-Jurjani's Theory of Discourse*. (New Haven: 1995).

Lentz, Thomas. "Dynastic Imagery in Early Timurid Painting." *Muqarnas: An Annual on Islamic Art and Architecture*. Vol. 10. (1993), pp. 253–263.

Lentz, Thomas W. and Glenn D. Lowry. *Timur and the Princely Vision: Persian Art and Culture in the Fifteenth Century*. (Washington: 1989).

Lewisohn, Leonard. "An Introduction to the history of modern Persian Sufism, part I: The Ni`matullahi Order: Persecution, Revival and Schism." *Bulletin of the School of African and Oriental Studies*. Vol. 61. (1998), pp. 437–64.

------. "Sufism and the School of Iṣfahān: *Taṣawwuf* and *`Irfān* in Late Safavid Iran (`Abd al-Razzāq Lāhījī and Fayḍ-i Kāshānī on the Relation of *Taṣawwuf, Ḥikmat* and *`Irfān*)." In *The Heritage of Sufism Vol. III: Late Classical Persianate Sufism (1501–1750) The Safavid & Mughal Period*. Edited by L. Lewisohn and D. Morgan. (London: 1999), pp. 63–134.

Losensky, Paul. "The Palace of Praise and the Melons of Time: Descriptive Patterns in `Abdi Bayk Shirazi's *Garden of Eden*." *Eurasian Studies: the Skilliter Center-Instiuto per l'Oriente Journal for Balkan, Eastern Mediterranean, Anatolian, Middle Eastern, Iranian, and Central Asian Studies*. Vol. 2. No. 1. (2003), pp. 1–29.

------. *Welcoming Fighani: Imitation and Poetic Individuality in the Safavid-Mughal Ghazal*. (Costa Mesa: 1998).

Luther, K. Allin. "Islamic Rhetoric and the Persian Historians 1100–1300 A.D." In *Studies in Near Eastern Culture and History in Memory of Ernest T. Abdel-Massih*. Edited by J. A. Bellamy. (Ann Arbor: 1990), pp. 90–98.

Madelung, Wilferd. *The Succession to Muḥammad: A Study of the Early Caliphate*. (Cambridge: 1997).

------. "A Treatise of the Sharīf al-Murtaḍā on the Legality of Working for the Government (*Mas'ala fī'l-`ammal ma`a'l -Sulṭān*)." *Bulletin of the School of Oriental and African Studies*. Vol. 43. (1980), pp. 18–31.

Maeda, Hirotake. "On the Ethno-Social Background of Four Gholam Families From Georgia in Safavid Iran." *Studia Iranica*. Vol. 32. No. 2. (2003), pp. 243–78.

Manz, Beatrice. *Power, Politics and Religion in Timurid Iran*. (Cambridge: 2007).

------. *The Rise and Rule of Tamerlane*. (Cambridge: 1989).

Marlow, Louise. *Hierarchy and Egalitarianism in Islamic Thought*. (Cambridge: 1997).

------. "Kings, Prophets, and the `Ulamā in Mediaeval Islamic Advice Literature." *Studia Islamica*. Vol. 81. No. 1. (1995), pp. 101–20.

Masuya, Tomoko. "Ilkhanid Courtly Life." In *The Legacy of Genghis Khan: Courtly Art and Culture in Western Asia, 1256–1353*. Edited by L. Komaroff and S. Carboni, (New York: 2002), pp. 74–104.

------. "The Ilkhanid Phase of Takht-i Sulaiman," Unpublished Ph.D. Dissertation. (New York University: 1997).

Matthee, Rudolph. *The Politics of Trade in Safavid Iran: Silk for Silver, 1600–1730*. (Cambridge: 1999).

Matuz, Josef. *Das Kanzleiwesen Sultan Suleymans des Prachtigen*. (Weisbaden: 1974).

Mazzaoui, Michel. "The Ghazi Background of the Safavid State." *Iqbal Review*. Vol. 12. No. 3. (1971), pp. 79–90.

------. "A 'New' Edition of the Safvat al-safa." In *History and Historiography of Post-Mongol Central Asia and the Middle East. Studies in Honor of John E. Woods.*

Edited by J. Pfeiffer and S. Quinn. (Wiesbaden: 2006), pp. 303–10.
------. *The Origins of the Safavids: Shi`ism, Sufism, and the Gula.t* (Wiesbaden: 1972).
------. "The Religious Policy of Shah Isma`il II." In *Intellectual Studies on Islam: Essays Written in Honor of Martin B. Dickson*. Edited by M. Mazzaoui and V. Moreen. (Salt Lake City: 1990), pp. 49–56.
McChesney, Robert. "'Barrier of Heterodoxy'?: Rethinking the Ties Between Iran and Central Asia in the Seventeenth Century." In *Safavid Persia: The History and Politics of an Islamic Society*. Edited by C. Melville. (London: 1996), pp. 231–68.
------. "The Conquest of Herat 995–6/1587–8: Sources for the Study of Safavid/ Qizilbash-Shibanid/Uzbak Relations." In *Études Safavides*. Edited by J. Calmard. (Paris: 1993), pp. 69–107.
------. "Waqf and Public Policy: The Waqfs of Shah `Abbas, 1011–1023/1602–1614." *Asian and African Studies*. Vol. 15. (1981), pp. 165–190.
McNeill, W. H. *Mythistory and other essays*. (Chicago: 1986).
Meisami, Julie Scott. "Cosmic Numbers: The Symbolic Design of Nizami's *Haft Paykar*." In *Humanism, Culture, and Language in the Near East: Studies in Honor of George Krotkoff*. Edited by A. Afsaruddin and A. H. M. Zahniser. (Winona Lake: 1997), pp. 42–45.
------. "The Historian and the Poet: Ravandi, Nizami, and the Rhetoric of History." In *The Poetry of Nizami Ganjavi: Knowledge, Love, and Rhetoric*. Edited by K. Talattof and J. Clinton. (New York: 2000), pp. 97–128.
------. *Structure and Meaning in Medieval Arabic and Persian Poetry: Orient Pearls*. (London: 2003).
Melikian-Chirvani, Assadullah Souren. "Conscience du passé et résistance culturelle dans l'Iran Mongol." In *L'Iran face à la domination Mongole*. Edited by D. Aigle. (Tehran: 1997), pp. 135–77.
------. "Le Royaume de Salomon: Les inscriptions persanes de sites Achéménides." In *Le monde Iranien et l'Islam: sociétés et cultures*. Vol. 1. (Paris: 1971), pp. 1–41.
Mélikoff, Irène. *Sur les traces du soufisme Turc: Recherches sur l'Islam populaire en Anatolie*. (Istanbul: 1992).
Melville, Charles. "From Qars to Qandahar: The Itineraries of Shah `Abbas I (995–1038/1587–1629)." In *Études Safavides*. Edited by J. Calmard. (Paris: 1993), pp. 195–224.
------. "New Light on the Reign of Shāh `Abbās: Volume III of the *Afzal al-tavarikh*." In *Society and Culture in the Early Modern Middle East: Studies on Iran in the Safavid Period*. Edited by A. Newman. (Leiden: 2003), pp. 63–96.
Menasce, J. P. de. "Zoroastrian Pahlavi Writings." In *Cambridge History of Iran*. Edited by E. Yarshater. Vol. 3 (2). (Cambridge: 1983), pp. 1166–95.
Minorsky, Vladimir. "A Civil and Military Review in Fārs in 881/1476." *Bulletin of the School of Oriental and African Studies*. Vol. 10. (1940–42), pp. 141–78.
------. *Medieval Iran and Its Neighbours*. (London: 1982).
------. "The Poetry of Shāh Ismā`īl I." *Bulletin of the School of Oriental and African Studies*. Vol. 10. (1940–43), pp. 1006–53.
------. "The Qara-Qoyunlu and the Qutb-Shahs." *Bulletin of the School of Oriental and African Studies*. Vol. 17. (1947), pp. 50–73.
------. "A Soyūrghāl of Qāsim b. Jahāngīr Āq-Qoyūnlū (903/1498)." *Bulletin of the School of Oriental and African Studies*. Vol. 9. (1937–39), pp. 927–60.
------. *The Turks, Iran and the Caucasus in the Middle Ages*. (London: 1978).
Mitchell, Colin Paul. "Safavid Imperial Tarassul and the Persian Inshā' Tradition." *Studia Iranica*. Vol. 27. No. 2. (1997), pp. 173–209.
------. "To Preserve and Protect: Husayn Va`iz-i Kashifi and Perso-Islamic Chancellery Culture." *Iranian Studies*. Vol. 36. No. 4. (2003), pp. 485–507.

Modaressī-Ṭabāṭabā'ī, Sayyid Ḥusain. *Bargī az tārīkh-i Qazvīn*. (Tehran: 1982).
------. *Mis̱āl-hā-yi ṣudūr-i Ṣafavī*. (Qumm: 1975).
Mohiuddin, Momin. *The Chancellery and Perisan Epistolography under the Mughals*. (Calcutta: 1970).
Momen, Moojan. *An Introduction to Shi`i Islam*. (New Haven: 1985).
Moran, Richard. "Artifice and Persuasion: The Work of Metaphor in the Rhetoric." In *Essays on Aristotle's Rhetoric*. Edited by A. O. Rorty. (Berkeley: 1996), pp. 385–98.
Morgan, David. "The 'Great Yāsā of Chingiz Khān' and Mongol Law in the Īlkhānate." *Bulletin of the School of Oriental and African Studies*. Vol. 49. (1986), pp. 163–76.
------. *Medieval Persia, 1040–1797*. (London: 1988).
------. "Rethinking Safavid Shī`ism." In *The Heritage of Sufism: Vol. 3 Late Classical Persianate Sufism (1501–1750)*. Edited by L. Lewisohn and D. Morgan. Vol. 3. (Oxford: 1999), pp. 19–27.
Morton, A. H. "The chub-i tariq and Qizilbash Ritual in Safavid Persia." In *Études Safavides*. Edited by J. Calmard. (Paris: 1993), pp. 225–45.
------. "The Date and Attribution of the Ross Anonymous. Notes on a Persian History of Shāh Ismā`īl I." In *Pembroke Papers*. Edited by Charles Melville. Vol. 1. (1990), pp. 179–212.
------. "The Early Years of Shāh Ismā`īl in the *Afḍal al-tavārīkh* and Elsewhere." In *Safavid Persia: The History and Politics of an Islamic Society*. Edited by C. Melville. (London: 1996), pp. 27–51.
------. "An Introductory Note on a Safavid Munshī's Manual in the Library of the School of Oriental and African Studies." *Bulletin of the School of Oriental and African Studies*. Vol. 36. (1970), pp. 352–58.
------."The Letters of Rashid al-Din: Ilkhanid Fact or Timurid Fiction?" In *The Mongol Empire & its Legacy*. Edited by D. Morgon and R. Amitai-Preiss. (Leiden: 2000), pp. 155–99.
Mukminova, Rozija G. "Craftsmen and Guild Life in Samarqand." In *Timurid Art and Culture: Iran and Central Asia in the Fifteenth Century*. Edited by L. Golombek and M. Subtelny. (Leiden: 1992), pp. 29–35.
------. "Die Rolle der beiden Hauptrichtungen des Islam in der Politik der Kriege Shaibānī Khāns und Shāh Ismā`īls." In *Bamberger Zentralasienstudien: Konforenzakten ESCAS IV*. Edited by I. Baldauf and M. Friedrich (Berlin: 1994), pp. 249–56.
Murphey, Rhoads. "Süleyman's Eastern Policy." In *Süleymân the Second and His Time*. Edited by H. Inalcik and C. Kafadar. (Istanbul: 1993), pp. 229–48.
Murphy, James. *Rhetoric in the Middle Ages: A History of Rhetoric Theory from Saint Augustine to the Renaissance*. (Berkeley: 1974).
Nasr, Sayyid Hussein. *Islamic Art and Spirituality*. (Albany: 1987).
------. "The Place of Iṣfahān in Islamic Philosophy and Sufism." In *The Heritage of Sufism Vol. III: Late Classical Persianate Sufism (1501–1750) The Safavid & Mughal Period*. Edited by L. Lewisohn and D. Morgan. (London: 1999), pp. 3–15.
------. "Shi`ism and Sufism: Their Relationship in Essence and in History." In *Sufi Essays*. Edited by S. H. Nasr. (London: 1972), pp. 104–20.
------. "The World View and Philosophical Perspective of Hakīm Nizamī Ganjawī." *The Muslim World*. Vol. 82. pp. 191–200.
Naumann, Rudolf and Hans Henning von der Osten. *Takht-i-Suleiman: Vorläufiger Bericht uber die Ausgrabungen 1959*. (Berlin: 1961).
Navā'ī, `Abd al-Ḥusain. *Ravābiṭ-i siyāsī-yi Īrān va Ūrupā dar `aṣr-i Ṣafavī*. (Tehran: 1993).
Neçipoghlu, Gürlu. *The Age of Sinan: Architectural Culture in the Ottoman Empire*.

(London: 2005).
------. "Süleyman the Magnificent and the Representation of Power in the Context of Ottoman-Hapsburg-Papal Rivalry." In *Süleymân the Second and His Time*. Edited by H. Inalcik and C. Kafadar. (Istanbul: 1993), pp. 163–95.
------. "The Süleymaniye Complex in Istanbul: An Interpretation." *Muqarnas*. Vol. 3. (1985), pp. 92–117.
Netton, Ian Richard. "Suhrawardi's Heir? The Ishraqi Philosophy of Mir Damad." In *The Heritage of Sufism Vol. III: Late Classical Persianate Sufism (1501–1750) The Safavid & Mughal Period*. Edited by L. Lewisohn and D. Morgan. (London: 1999), pp. 225–46.
Newman, Andrew. "Fayd al-Kashani and the Rejection of the Clergy/State Alliance: Friday Prayer as Politics in the Safavid Period." In *The Most Learned of the Shi`a: The Institution of the* Marja` Taqlid. Edited by L. S. Walbridge. (New York: 2001), pp. 34–52.
------. "The Myth of the Clerical Migration to Safavid Iran: Arab Shiite Opposition to `Alī al-Karakī and Safawid Shiism." *Die Welt des Islams*. Vol. 33. No. 1. (1993), pp. 66–112.
------. "The Role of the Sādāt in Safavid Iran: Confrontation or Accommodation?" In *Oriente Moderno*. Vol. 18. (1999), pp. 577–96.
------. *Safavid Iran: Rebirth of a Persian Empire*. (London: 2006).
------. "Towards a Reconsideration of the 'Isfahan School of Philosophy': Shaykh Bahā'ī and the Role of the Safawi." *Studia Iranica*. Vol. 15. No. 2. (1986), pp. 165–99.
Nicholson, R. E. *Literary History of the Arabs*. (Cambridge: 1930).
Niewöhner-Eberhard, Elke. "Machtpolitische Aspekte des osmanische-safawidischen Kampfes um Bagdad im 16. /17. Jahrhundert." *Turcica*. Vol. 6. (1975), pp. 103–27.
O'Kane, Bernard. "From Tents to Pavilions: Royal Mobility and Persian Palace Design." In *Proceedings of the Symposium on Pre-Modern Islamic Palaces*. In *Ars Orientalis*. Vol. 23. (1993), pp. 249–68.
O'Leary, Stephen D. *Arguing the Apocalypse: A Theory of Millennial Rhetoric*. (Oxford: 1994).
Pārsādūst, Manūchehr. *Shāh Ismā`īl-i duvvum: Shujā` tabāh shudah*. (Tehran: 2002).
------. *Shāh Muḥammad: pādshāhi kih shāh na-būd*. (Tehran: 2002).
Paul, Jürgen. *Herrscher, Gemeinwesen, Vermittler: Ost Iran und Transoxanian in vormongolischer Zeit*. (Stuttgart: 1996).
Peirce, Leslie. *The Imperial Harem: Women and Sovereignty in the Ottoman Empire*. (New York: 1993).
Petrushevsky, I. P. *Islam in Iran*. Translated by H. Evans. (London: 1985).
Poonawala, I. K. "Apocalyptic II. In Muslim Iran." *Encyclypaedia Iranica*. Vol. 1. pp. 158–59.
Quinn, Sholeh. *Historical Writing During the Reign of Shah `Abbas: Ideology, Imitation, and Legitimacy in Safavid Chronicles*. (Salt Lake City: 2000).
Rabie, Hassanein. "Political Relations Between the Safavids of Persia and the Mamluks of Egypt and Syria in the Early Sixteenth Century." *Journal of the American Research Center in Egypt*. Vol. 15. (1978), pp. 75–81.
Rabino di Borgomale, H. L. *Coins, Medals, and Seals of the Shahs of Iran, 1500–1941*. (Hertford, U. K.: 1945).
Ray, Sukumar. *Humāyūn in Persia*. (Calcutta: 1948).
Renard, John. *Islam and the Heroic Image: Themes in Literature and the Visual Arts*. (Columbia, S. C.: 1993).
Reychman, Jan and Ananiasz Kajaczkowski. *Handbook of Ottoman-Turkish Diplomatics*. Translated by A. Ehrenkreutz. (The Hague: 1968).

Richard, Francis. *Catalogue des manuscrits Persans*. Vol. 1 (Ancien fonds). (Paris: 1989).

------. "Naṣr al-Solṭāni, Naṣir al-Din Mozahheb et la bibliothèque d'Ebrāhim Solṭān à Shirāz." *Studia Iranica*. Vol. 30. (2001), pp. 87–104.

------. "Quelques traités d'énigmes (*mo`ammâ*) en persan des XVe et XVIe siècles." In *Pand-o Sokhan: Melanges offerts à Charles-Henri de Fouchécour*. Edited by C. Balağ, C. Kappler, and Z. Vesel. (Tehran: 1995), pp. 233–42.

Richard, Yann. *L'Islam chi'ite: croyances et idéologies*. (Paris: 1991).

Richards, John F. *The New Cambridge History of India (Vol. 5.1): The Mughal Empire*. (Cambridge: 1993).

Ritter, Hellmut. *The Ocean of the Soul: Man, the World, and God in the Stories of Farid al-Din `Attar*. Translated by J. O'Kane. (Leiden: 2003).

Rizvi, Kishvar. "'Its Mortar Mixed with the Sweetness of Life:' Architecture and Ceremonial at the Shrine of Ṣafī al-Dīn Isḥāq Ardabīlī During the Reign of Shāh Ṭahmāsb." *Muslim World*. Vol. 90. Nos. 3/4. (2000), pp. 323–52.

Rizvi, Saiyid Athar Abbas. *A Socio-Intellectual History of the Isnā 'Asharī Shī'īs in India*. 2 Vols. (New Delhi: 1986).

Robinson, Francis. "Ottomans-Safavids-Mughals: Shared Knowledge and Connective Systems." *Journal of Islamic Studies*. Vol. 8. No. 2. (1997), pp. 151–84.

Roemer, Hans Robert. "Le Dernier Firman de Rustam Bahadur Aq Qoyunlu?" In *Bulletin de l'Institut Français d'Archeologie Orientale*. Vol. 59. (1960), pp. 273–87.

------. "Inshā'." *EI*[2]. Vol. 3. p. 1241–44.

------. *Die Niedergang Irans nach dem Tode Isma`ils der Grausamen (1577–1581)*. (Würzburg-Aumühle: 1939).

------. *Persien auf dem Weg in die Neuzeit: iranische Geschichte von, 1350–1750*. (Beirut: 1989).

------. "Das Türkmenische Intermezzo: Persische Geschichte zwischen Mongolen und Safawiden." *Archaeologische Mitteilungen aus Iran*. Vol. 9. (1976), pp. 263–97.

------. "Vorschläge für die Sammlung von Urkunden zur islamischen Geschichte Persiens." *Zeitschrift der Deutschen Morgenländischen Gesellschaft*. Vol. 104. (1954), pp. 362–70.

Rogers, J. M. "The State and the Arts in Ottoman Turkey, part 2: The Furniture and Decoration of Suleymaniye." *International Journal of Middle East Studies*. Vol. 14. (1982), pp. 283–313.

Röhrborn, K. M. *Provinzen und Zentralgewalt Persiens im 16. und 17. Jahrhundert*. (Berlin: 1966).

------. "Regierung und Verwaltung Irans unter den Safawiden." *Handbuch der Orientalistik*. Vol. 6. (1979), pp. 17–50.

Roxburgh, David. *Prefacing the Image: The Writing of Art History in Sixteenth-Century Iran*. (Leiden: 2001).

Rypka, Jan. "History of Persian Literature up to the Beginning of 20th Century." In *History of Iranian Literature*. Edited by. K. Jahn. (Dordrecht: 1968), pp. 62–352.

Sachedina, Abdulaziz Abdulhussein. *Islamic Messianism: The Idea of the Mahdi in Twelver Shi`ism*. (Albany: 1981).

------. *The Just Ruler* (al-sulṭān al-`ādil) in *Shī`ite Islam: The Comprehensive Authority of the Jurist in Imamite Jurisprudence*. (Oxford: 1988).

Sadan, Joseph. "Nouveaux documents sur scribes et copistes." *Revue des Études Islamiques*. Vol. 45. No. 1. (1977), pp. 41–87.

Savory, Roger. "The Consolidation of Safavid Power in Persia." *Der Islam*. Vol. 41. (1965), pp. 71–94.

------. "The Development of the Early Safavid State under Isma`il and Tahmasp, as Studies of the 16th Century Persian Sources." Unpublished D.Phil. Dissertation.

(University of London: 1958).
------. "Div Solṭān." *Encyclopaedia Iranica*. Vol. 7. p. 431.
------. "Djamāl al-Ḥusaynī." *EI*[2]. Vol. 3. p. 420.
------. "Esmā`īl I Ṣafawī. Biography." *Encyclopaedia Iranica*. Vol. 8. pp 628–35.
------. *Iran Under the Safavids*. (Cambridge: 1980).
------. "The Office of *Khalīfat al-khulafā* Under the Ṣafawids." *Journal of the American Oriental Society*. Vol. 85. (1965), pp. 497–502.
------. "The Principal Offices of the Ṣafawid State During the Reign of Ismā`īl I (907–30/1501–24)." *Bulletin of the School of Oriental and African Studies*. Vol. 23. (1960), pp. 91–105.
------. "The Principal Offices of the Ṣafawid State During the Reign of Ṭahmāsp (930–84/1524–76)." *Bulletin of the School of Oriental and African Studies*. Vol. 24. (1961), pp. 65–85.
------. "The Safavid State and Polity." *Iranian Studies*. Vol. 7. (1974), pp. 179–212.
------. "A Secretarial Career Under Shah Tahmasp I (1524–1576)." *Islamic Studies*. Vol. 2. No. 3. (1963), pp. 343–52.
------. "The Shī`ī Enclaves in the Deccan (15th–17th Centuries): an Historical Anomaly." In *Corolla Torontonensis: Studies in Honour of Ronald Morton Smith*. Edited by E. Robbins and S. Sandahl. (Toronto: 1994), pp. 173–90.
------. "The Significance of the Political Murder of Mirza Salman." *Islamic Studies*. Vol. 3. (1964), pp. 181–91.
------. "Some Notes on the Provincial Administration of the Early Ṣafawid Empire." *Bulletin of the School of Oriental and African Studies*. Vol. 27. (1964), pp. 114–28.
------. "The Struggle for Supremacy in Persia After the Death of Tīmūr." *Der Islam*. Vol. 40. No. 1. (1964), pp. 35–65.
------. "Ṭahmāsp." *EI*[2]. Vol. 10. pp. 108–10.
Sawar, Ghulam. *History of Shāh Ismā`īl Ṣafawī*. (Aligarh: 1939).
Schafiyha, Ahmad. "Das Grab des Seyhu'l-Islam Magdu'd-Din Abu'l-Futuh Ahmad Gazzali in Qazwin." *Oriens*. Vol. 34. (1994), pp. 348–53.
Schimmel, Anne-Marie. *And Muhammad is His Messenger: The Veneration of the Prophet in Islamic Piety*. (Chapel Hill: 1985).
------. *As Through A Veil: Mystical Poetry in Islam*. (Oxford: 2001).
------. *Islam in the Indian Subcontinent*. (Leiden: 1980).
------. *Mystical Dimensions of Islam*. (Chapel Hill: 1975).
------. *A Two-Colored Brocade: The Imagery of Persian Poetry*. (Chappel Hill: 1992).
Shani, Raya. "Illustrations to the Parable of the Ship of Faith in Firdausi's Prologue to the Shahnama." In *Shahnama Studies I (Pembroke Papers, 5)*. Edited by Charles Melville. (Cambridge: 2006), pp. 1–40.
------. "Noah's Ark and the Ship of Faith in Persian Painting: From the Fourteenth to the Sixteenth Century." *Jerusalem Studies in Arabic and Islam*. Vol. 27. (2002), pp. 127–203.
Ṣifātgol, Manṣūr. "Safavid Administration of Avqāf: Structure, Changes, and Functions, 1077–1135/1666–1722." In *Society and Culture in the Early Modern Middle East: Studies on Iran in the Safavid Period*. Edited by A. J. Newman. (Leiden: 2003), 397–408.
Simidchieva, Marta. "Imitation and Innovation in Timurid Poetics: Kāshifī's *Badāyi` al-afkār*, and its Predecessors, *al-Mu`jam* and *Ḥadā'iq al-siḥr*." *Iranian Studies*. Vol. 36. No. 4. (2003), pp. 509–30.
Simon, Udo Gerlad. *Mittelalterische arabische Sprachbetrachtung zwischen Grammatik und Rhetoric: `ilm al-ma`ani as-Sakkaki*. (Heidelberg: 1993).
Simpson, Marianne S. "Ebrāhim Mirzā." *Encyclopedia Iranica*. Vol. 8. pp. 74–75.

------. *Persian Poetry, Painting, and Patronage: Illustrations in a Sixteenth-Century Masterpiece.* (Washington: 1998).

Smyth, William. "Rhetoric and `Ilm al-Balagha: Christianity and Islam." *Muslim World.* Vol. 82. Nos. 3–4. (1992), pp. 242–55.

Soucek, Priscilla. "Calligraphy in the Safavid Period, 1501–1576." In *Hunt for Paradise: Court Arts of Safavid Iran, 1501–1576.* Edited by J. Thompson and S. Canby. (Milan: 2003). pp. 48–71.

------. "Nizami on Painters and Paintings." In *Islamic Art in the Metropolitan Museum of Art.* Edited by R. Ettinghausen. (New York: 1972), pp. 9–21.

------. "Solomon's Throne/Solomon's Bath: Model or Metaphor?" In *Ars Orientalis.* Vol. 23. (1993), pp. 109–33.

------. "Sultan Muhammad Tabrizi: Painter at the Safavid Court." In *Persian Masters: Five Centuries of Painting.* Edited by S. Canby. (Bombay: 1990), pp. 55–70.

------. "The Temple of Solomon in Islamic Legend and Art." In *The Temple of Solomon: Archaeological Fact and Medieval Tradition in Christian, Islamic and Jewish Art.* Edited by J. Gutmann. (Ann Arbor: 1976), pp. 73–123.

Soudavar, Abolala. "The Early Safavids and their Cultural Interactions with Surrounding States." In *Iran and the Surrounding World: Interactions in Culture and Cultural Politics.* Edited by N. Keddie and R. Matthee. (Seattle: 2002), pp. 89–120.

Stanfield-Johnson, Rosemary. "Sunni Survival in Safavid Iran: Anti-Sunni Activities during the Reign of Shah Tahmasp." *Iranian Studies.* Vol. 27. (1994), pp. 123–33.

------. "The Tabarra'iyan and the Early Safavids." *Iranian Studies.* Vol. 37. No. 1. (2004), pp. 47–71.

Stetkevych, Suzanne P. *The Poetics of Islamic Legitimacy: Myth, Gender, and Ceremony in the Classical Arabic Ode.* (Bloomington: 2002).

Stewart, Devin. "A Biographical Notice on Bahā' al-Dīn al-`Āmilī (d. 1030/1621)." *Journal of the American Oriental Society.* Vol. 113. No. 3. (1991), pp. 563–71.

------. "The First Shaykh al-Islām of the Safavid Capital Qazvin." *Journal of the American Oriental Society.* Vol. 116. No. 3. (1996), pp. 387–405.

------. "The Lost Biography of Baha' al-Din al-`Amili and the Reign of Shah Isma`il II in Safavid Historiography." *Iranian Studies.* Vol. 31. (1998), pp. 177–206.

------. "Notes on the Migration of `Āmilī Scholars to Safavid Iran." *Journal of Near Eastern Studies.* Vol. 55. No. 2. (1996), pp. 81–104.

------. "*Taqiyyah* as Performance: The Travels of Bahā' al-Dīn al-`Āmilī in the Ottoman Empire (991–93/1583–85)." In *Law and Society in Islam.* (Princeton: 1996), pp. 1–70.

Subtelny, Maria. "`Alī Shīr Navā'ī: Bakhshī and Beg." *Harvard Ukranian Studies.* Vol 3/4. (1979–80), pp. 797–807.

------. "Centralizing Reform and its Opponents in the Late Timurid Period." *Iranian Studies.* Vol. 21. (1988), pp. 123–51.

------. "Ektīār al-Dīn." *Encyclopædia Iranica.* Vol. 7. pp. 290–91.

------. "A Medieval Persian Agricultural Manual in Context: The *Irshād al-zirā`a* in Late Timurid and Early Safavid Khorasan." *Studia Iranica.* Vol. 22. No. 2. (1993), pp. 167–217.

------. "Mīr `Alī Shīr." *EI*². Vol. 7. pp. 90–93.

------. *Le monde est un jardin: aspects de l'histoire culturelle de l'Iran médiéval.* (Paris: 2002).

------. "The Poetic Circle at the Court of the Timurid Sultan Husain Baiqara, and Its Political Significance." Unpublished Ph.D. Dissertation. (Harvard University: 1979).

------. "Socioeconomic Bases of Cultural Patronage Under the Late Timurids." *International Journal of Middle East Studies.* Vol. 20. No. 4. (1988), pp. 479–505.

------. "A Taste for the Intricate: The Persian Poetry of the Late Timurid Period." *Zeitschrift der Deutschen Morgenländischen Gesellschaft*. Vol. 136. No. 1. (1986), pp. 56–79.

------. *Timurids in Transition: Turko-Persian Politics and Acculturation in Medieval Iran*. (Leiden: 2007).

------. "The Timurid Legacy: A Reaffirmation and a Reassessment." *Cahiers d'Asie Centrale*. Nos. 3–4. (1997), pp. 9–19.

Subtelny, Maria and Anas Khalidov. "The Curriculum of Islamic Higher Learning in Timurid Iran in the Light of the Sunni Revival Under Shāh Rukh." *Journal of the American Oriental Society*. Vol. 115. No. 2. (1995), pp. 210–36.

Szuppe, Maria. "Circulation des léttres et cercles littéraires entre Asie centrale, Iran et Inde du Nord (XVe-XVIIIe siècle)." *Annales (Histoire, Sciences Sociales)*. Vol. 59. Nos. 5-6. (2004), pp. 997–1018.

------. *Entre Timourides, Uzbeks et Safavides: Questions d'histoire politique et sociale de Hérat dans la première moitié du XVIe siècle*. (Paris: 1992).

------. "L'évolution de l'image de Timour et des Timourides dans l'historiographie safavide du XVIe au XVIIIe siècles." In *L'Héritage timouride Iran—Asie centrale—Inde XVe-XVIIIe siècles*. Edited by M. Szuppe. (Aix-en-Provence: 1997), pp. 313—31.

------. "Kinship Ties Between the Safavids and the Qizilbash Amirs in Late-Sixteenth Century Iran: A Case Study of the Political Career of Members of the Sharaf al-Din Oghlu Tekelu Family." In *Safavid Persia: The History and Politics of an Islamic Society*. Edited by C. Melville. (London: 1996), pp. 79–104.

------. "La participation des femmes da la famille royale à l'exercice du pouvoir en Iran Safavide au XVIe siècle (second partie): L'entourage des princesses et leurs activités politiques." *Studia Iranica*. Vol. 24. No. 1. (1995), pp. 61–121.

------. "Palais et jardins: le complexe royal des premiers Safavides à Qazvin, milieu XVIe-début XVIIe siècles." In *Sites et monuments disparu d'après les témoignages de voyageurs*. Edited by R. Gyselen. Appearing in *Res Orientales*. Vol. 8. (1996), pp. 143–77.

------. "Les résidences princières de Herat: problèmes de continuité fonctionnelle entre les époques timouride et safavide (1ère moitié du XVIe siècle)." In *Études Safavides*. Edited by J. Calmard. (Paris: 1993), pp. 267–86.

------. "Status, Knowledge and Politics: Women in Sixteenth-Century Safavid Iran." In *Women in Iran from the Rise of Islam to 1800*. Edited by G. Nashat and L. Beck. (Chicago: 2003), pp. 140–69.

Tājbakhsh, Aḥmad. *Tārīkh-i Ṣafaviyyah*. (Tehran: 1994).

Tavakoli-Targhi, Mohamad. *Refashioning Iran: Orientalism, Occidentalism, and Histioriography*. (New York: 2001).

Thackston, Wheeler. "The Diwan of Khata'i: Pictures for the Poetry of Shah Isma`il I." *Asian Art*. (Fall, 1988), pp. 37–63.

Al-Tikriti, Nabil. "The Hajj as Justifiable Self-Exile: Shehzade Korkud's *Wasīlat al-aḥbāb* (915–916/1509–1510)." *Al-Masaq*. Vol. 17. No. 1. (2005), pp. 125–46.

Tor, Deborah. "Toward A Revised Understanding of the `Ayyār Phenomenon." In *Iran: questions et conaissances* (Actes du IVe congrès Européen des études Iraniennes organisé par la Societas Iranologica Europaea, Paris, 6-10 Septembre 1999). Vol. 2 (Périodes médiévale et moderne). (Paris: 2002), pp. 231–54.

Vilāyatī, `Alī Akbar. *Tārīkh-i ravābiṭ-i khārijī-yi Īrān dar `ahd-i Shāh Ismā`īl Ṣafavī*. (Tehran: 1996).

Virani, Nargis. "'I am the Nightingale of the Merciful' Macaronic or Upside-Down: The Mulamma`āt of Jalāl al-Dīn Rūmī." Unpublished Ph.D. Dissertation. (Harvard University: 1999).

Walker, Paul. "The Resolution of the Shi`ah." In *Shi`ite Heritage*. Edited by L. Clarke

(Binghampton: 2001), pp. 75–90.

Walsh, J. R. "The Revolt of Alqāṣ Mīrzā." *Wiener Zeitschrift für die Kunde des Morgenlandes*. Vol. 68. (1976), pp. 61–78.

Watt, John. "Eastward and Westward Transmission of Classical Rhetoric." In *Centres of Learning: Learning and Location in Pre-Modern Europe and the Near East*. Edited by J. Drijvers and A. MacDonald. (Leiden: 1995), pp. 63–75.

------. "Syriac Rhetorical Theory and the Syriac Tradition of Aristotle's Rhetoric." In *Peripatetic Rhetoric After Aristotle*. Edited by W. Fortenbaugh and D. Mirhady. Rutgers University Studies in Classical Humanities. Vol. 6. (New Brunswick: 1994), pp. 243–60.

Watt, W. Montgomery. "The Queen of Sheba in Islamic Tradition." In *Solomon and Sheba*. Edited by J. B. Pritchard. (London: 1974), pp. 85–103.

Welch, Anthony. *Artists for the Shah: Late Sixteenth-Century Painting at the Imperial Court of Iran*. (New Haven: 1976).

------. "The Worldly Vision of Mir Sayyid Ali." In *Persian Masters: Five Centuries of Painting*. Edited by S. Canby. (Bombay: 1990), pp. 85–98.

Welch, Stuart Cray. *A King's Book of Kings. The* Shah-Nameh *of Shah Tahmasp*. (London: 1972).

------. "Le masğid-i ğami` de Qazwin." *Revue des Études Islamiques*. Vol. 41. (1973), pp. 199–229.

Wirth, Eugen. "Qazvin—Safavidische Stadtplanung und Qadjarischer Bazar." *Archäeologische Mitteilungen aus Iran und Turan*. Vol. 29. (1997), pp. 464–504.

Woodhead, Christine. "From Scribe to Litterateur: The Career of a Sixteenth-Century Ottoman Katib." *Bulletin of the British Society for Middle Eastern Studies*. Vol. 9. No. 1, (1982), pp. 55–74.

------. "Ottoman *Insha* and the Art of Letter-Writing: Influences Upon the Career of the Nishanchi and Prose Stylist Okccuzade (d. 1630)." *Osmanli arasstirmalari (Journal of Ottoman Studies)*. Vol. 7–8. (1988), pp. 143–59.

Woods, John. *The Aqquyunlu: Clan, Confederation, Empire*. New and revised edition. (Salt Lake City: 1999).

Yarshater, Ihsan. *Shi`r-i fārsī dar `ahd-i Shāh Rukh*. (Tehran: 1956).

Zakari, Mohsen. *Sasānīd Soldiers in Early Muslim Society: The Origins of the* `Ayyārān *and* Futuwwa. (Wiesbaden: 1995).

INDEX

Abarqūh, 25, 112
`Abbās (Shāh): accession of, 165; administration of, 177–8, 179; and the Bāgh-i Fīn, 123; and centralization, 176, 178–9, 180–1, 184–5, 189, 196–7, 202; documents and letters, 177, 181–97; and Gīlān, 179–80, 185–6, 242n115; and Ismā`īl II, 149; and the Perfect Man, 177; and Persian administrators, 177; and the Qizilbāsh, 163, 177; reforms of, 176, 177; and the Uzbeks, 178, 179–80, 187
`Abbās Mīrzā, 149, 162, 163, 165
`Abd al-Mu'min Khān, 183, 186–91, 259n279
`Abdāl `Alī Beg (Dada Beg), 22, 26, 35
`Abdī Beg Shīrāzī. *See also* Alexander the Great; Ardabīl: *`Ain-i Iskandarī,* 138, 201, 247n226, 247n235; and the battle of Gulistān, 23; and the conquest of Yazd, 26; and the image of Solomon, 122–3; *Jannat al-asmār,* 137, 138, 141, 201; *Jannat-i `Adan,* 106, 133, 137, 138, 246n226; letter to Murād III, 139–44; *Maẓhar al-asrār,* 138, 201, 247n226, 247n235; and religion in Ṭahmāsp 's court, 120; *Sarīḥ al-Milk,* 138; and the *tabarrā'iyān,* 24; *Takmilat al-akhbār,* 137, 138, 200
Abisaab, Rula, 145–6, 149, 175Ṭ
Abū al-Fatḥ Ṭahmāsp Mīrzā. *See* Ṭahmāsp
Abū Bakr: in the "Belt Letter," 84–5; and Fāṭima's ownership of Fadak, 228n74; and the Muḥājirūn, 230n119; `Umar, `Uthmān and, 75, 78–9; Uzbek acceptance of, 75
Abū Muslim nāmah: and the attack on Qāsim ibn Kathīr, 215n129; and *`ayyār,* 64; ban on the, 31, 72; recitation of, 23, 31
Abū Ṭālib Mīrzā, 163, 165
Achaemenian period, 3, 173, 202
Afūshtah-ī Natanzī, 123, 146, 150–1, 164, 196
`Alā' al-Daula Zū al-Qadar, 26, 32, 35-6
`Alī ibn `Abd al-`Alī al-Karakī (Shaikh), 137, 146, 149, 150
`Alī ibn al-Ḥusain al-Karakī: early career of, 71–2; *Jāmi` al-maqāṣid,* 72; *Maṭa`in al-mujrimiyyah fī radd al-ṣūfiyyah* ("Criminal Reproachments Regarding the Refutation of Sufism"), 101–2; *Masā'il-i mutaffariqah,* 109; and the Māzandarānī sayyids, 109–10; *Nafaḥāt al-lāhūt fī la`n al-jibt wa al-ṭāghūt,* 71, 72, 78; and Persian administrators, 70–2, 102–3; popularity of, 69–70; power of, 70–2; *Qāta'at al-lajāj fī ḥill al-kharāj,* 71; religious power of, 69, 72; *Risālah al-Ja`fariyya fī al-ṣalāt,* 70, 71, 109; Shāh Ṭahmāsp's endorsement of, 69; and Twelver Shi`ism, 67, 70, 71–88, 95, 101
Alexander the Great: in letters, 15, 53, 54, 58, 113–14, 121, 127, 131, 136, 191, 193; and the light of Alexander, 56; in the poetry of `Abdī Beg Shīrāzī, 247n238; in the poetry of Ismā`īl I, 214n110; in the work of Niẓāmī, 132, 190
al-Ghaurī (Sulṭān), 36–7
Alqāṣ Mīrzā (brother of Ṭahmāsp), 79–80, 104, 229n87
Amoretti, B.S., 150
Amīr Ḥusain Nīshāpūrī Mu`ammā'ī (Maulānā), 98, 99
Amīr Khusrau, 114–15
Amīr Qavām al-Dīn Mar`ashī (*laqab:* Mīr-i Buzurg), 107, 108
Amīr Zakariyā. *See* Muḥammad Kukajī (or Kujajī) Tabrīzī
Anatolia: and `Alā' al-Daula Zū al-Qadar, 26; bureaucratic culture in, 199; inflation in, 125; and "Jalālīs", 243n154; in the 1400s, 20–1; Sufi environment of, 201
Anūshīrvān: Ismā`īl I and, 32; in letters, 79, 168, 169, 171; in Safavid official documents, 3
Āqa Kamāl al-Dīn Ḥusain Musībī, 29, 49
Āq Qoyūnlūs: administration and the Safavids, 28–31, 44, 46, 50, 199, 201; and comparisons to mythical heroes and historical kings, 4; and the *dīvān-i a`lā,* 50; and the imprisonment of Ismā`īl I, 21; Ismā`īl I's conquering of, 23–4, 26; Ūzūn Ḥasan, 20, 233n173
Ardabīl: and `Abdī Beg Shīrāzī, 137–8; and the imprisonment of Ismā`īl I, 21; Safavid movement in, 23, 31, 100; Safavid shrine in, 106, 138, 239n53
Arjomand, Said, 69, 110, 224n14
Åṣaf ibn Barkhiya, 148, 164
`Aṭa Allāh Iṣfahānī, 51, 111, 177
Aubin, Jean, 20, 22, 46, 47, 48
āyah al-ṭathīr (Purification Verse), 85
Āzar Kaivān, 173
Āzarbāijān: Ottoman frontier in, 104; and

Persian administrators, 46; Āq Qoyūnlū in, 24; religion in, 20, 31, 38, 216n160; and the spread of Shi`ism, 83–4; Sufi environment in, 201, 219n220; taxes in, 117

Babayan, Kathryn: on religious and cultural hybridity in premodern Iran, 4, 197, 202; on the letter from Ṭahmāsp to Salīm II, 130, 134–5; on Mullā Muḥammad Zamān Zamānī, 261n347; *Mystics, Monarchs, and Messiahs: Cultural Landscapes of Early Modern Iran,* 4; on Ṭahmāsp's spiritual repentances, 110, 120; on politics in Safavid Iran, 59; on Safavid religious culture, 14, 31, 72–3; on shifting legitimacies in Safavid Iran, 5, 17; on *Tazkirah-yi Ṭahmāsp,* 69
Bagçi, Serpil, 122
Baghdad, 26, 28, 71, 200, 215n129
Bahā'ī al-Dīn `Āmilī (Shaikh), 110, 175, 191–3, 196, 261n333
Barkun, Michael, 29
Bashir, Shahzad, 39, 44, 100
Battle of Badr, 37
Battle of Chāldirān, 20, 28, 32, 46, 55
Battle of Jām, 61–6, 187, 201
Battle of Konya, 120, 125
Battle of Szigetvár, 129, 131
Bilqīs (Queen). *See* Sheba
Browne, E.G., 145, 206n41
Būdāq Munshī: on Ismā`īl I's administrative policies, 47; on Ismā`īl I's popularity, 24; on Jamāl al-Dīn `Alī Tabrīzī and Sayyid Ḥasan Farāḥānī, 110; *Javāhir al-akhbār,* 18; on Muḥammad Beg, 89; on Ṭahmāsp's coronation, 59; on royal garden and residential complex in Qazvīn, 105; on Shāh Ismā`īl II's coronation, 147–8

Caesar, 58
Calmard, Jean, 20, 31, 228n84
Circassia, 4, 21, 161, 162
Cohn, Norman, 29
Corbin, Henri, 173, 237n248

Darius: Ismā`īl I's manifestation of, 32; in Safavid documents, 3, 54, 56, 58, 113, 118
Daylam, 21, 179, 185
Dīv Sulṭān Rūmlū, 59, 60, 61
dīvān-i a`lā: and the changing climate at the Safavid court, 60–1; description of, 50; and differences from the *dīvān-i inshā,* 49–51; and diplomatic correspondence, 16; members of the, 28, 46, 61, 110–11, 138, 147, 152–4, 156, 162–5, 174, 177, 179–81, 239n59; and Persian administrators, 46–7, 49–51; Qizilbāsh in the, 89; and Qaḍī-yi Jahān Qazvīnī, 68, 89, 101, 102, 222n290
dīvān-i inshā: description of, 5, 50–2, 219n211; and differences from the *dīvān-i a`lā,* 49–51; members of the, 136, 163; and Shi`ite scholars, 79
divine kingship: as legitimization, 5, 64, 130–1, 167; and Ṭahmāsp, 82, 102, 117, 121, 124; and Persian administrators, 70; and Solomon, 123; and the Timurids, 197
Diyār Bakr, 23, 26, 28, 149
Doge of Venice, 90

Farīd al-Dīn `Aṭṭār, 36, 38, 124
Farrukh Yasār, 23
Fārs, 21, 25, 122
fatḥ nāmah, 27, 32–8, 185
Floor, Willem, 152
Fourteen Innocent Ones, the, 35, 109

Ghiyās̱ al-Dīn ibn Humām al-Dīn Khvāndamīr. *See* Khvāndamīr
Ghiyās̱ al-Dīn Manṣūr Dashtakī, 89, 103, 108, 173
Gholsorkhi, Shohreh, 146, 148
Gīlān: and a Gīlānī-Ottoman alliance, 179; and Ismā`īl I's imprisonment, 21; and Qahqaha Prison, 145; Safavid conquest of, 180, 185–8, 242n115; scholars in, 111; taxes in, 111

Ḥaidar (Sulṭān) (father of Ismā`īl I): as compared to family of the Imāms, 32, 33, 36, 214n108, 214n110; death of, 21; imprisonment of family of, 21; and millenarianism, 20–1, 31
Ḥamza Mīrzā, 161, 162, 163
Hanaway, William, 203n1
Ḥassān ibn Thābit, 171
Ḥātim Beg Urdūbādī: bureaucratic reforms of, 180–4, 190, 195, 196, 255n170; career of, 166, 179; and Mīr Dāmād, 193; and Shaikh Bahā'ī, 192, 193
Herāt: conquest of, 27, 76; and Emperor Humāyūn, 91, 93, 125, 235n198; Jāmī's shrine in, 89, 233n164; and Qulī Jān Beg, 27; and Safavid princes, 59, 160, 186, 222n281; and Khudābandah, 160–1; under Timurid rule, 26, 94, 95; and the Uzbeks, 59, 178, 180, 188
Herrmann, Gottfried, 29
Heywood, Colin, 3
Hillenbrand, Robert, 63
Hinz, Walter, 145, 153

Humāyūn (Emperor). *See also* Herāt: 91–4, 234n186, 235n198
Ḥusain `Abd al-Ṣamād al-Ḥārithī al-`Āmilī (Shaikh), 160, 175–6
Ḥusain Bāiqarā (Sulṭān): death of, 36; and Ikhtiyār al-Dīn, 212n69; letter from Ismā`īl I to, 33–5, 119; Timurid empire under, 26
Ḥusain Beg Shāmlū (Lala Beg), 22–3, 26, 35, 151, 212n73
Ḥusain Kār Kiyā, 25
Ḥusain Khān (Sulṭān), 162
Ḥusain Khān Shāmlū, 59–61, 68, 137
Ḥusain Qulī Rūmlū, 147, 149
Ḥusain Vā`iẓ Kāshifī: *Akhlāq-i Muḥsinī,* 13, 102; *Badāyi` al-afkār fī ṣanāyi` al-ash`ār,* 9, 99; *Futuvvat-i nāmah-yi sulṭānī,* 127, 244n169, 245n171; *Makhzan al-inshā,* 1, 90, 92, 135, 157, 183–4; *Risālah-yi al-`alīyya,* 231n128

Ibrāhīm Astarābādī (Maulānā), 112–13
Ibrāhīm Mīrzā: death of, 148–9; and decentralization of the Safavid court, 110–11; early life of, 222n281; and Ṭahmāsp, 148–9, 241n93; and Qāḍī Aḥmad, 166, 200; and Shi`ite conversion, 115–17
Ilyās Beg Aighūr-ūghlī, 22, 23
`Imad al-Dīn `Alī Qārī Astarābādī, (Mīr Kālān), 108–9
image of "the Pen" *(al-qalam),* 174
image of the cloak, 139–40
`Ināyat Allāh Iṣfahānī (Shāh), 148, 150, 152
Inshā-yi `alam ārā ("The World-Adorning Inshā"), 95–100, 199
`Īsā Khān, 115–16
Iṣfahān: as a centre of doctrinal and philosophical inquiry, 191; and the *Hārūn-i Vilāyat,* 48; and Ismā`īl I, 25, 28; and Ismā`īl II, 150; and the "Khalīfa" sayyids, 108; and religion, 39; relocation of the royal palace to, 180; and Safavid administration, 46–51, 56, 61
Iskander Beg Munshī: career of, 165–6; and epistolary texts, 200; and Ismā`īl II, 148, 151; and Ṭahmāsp, 125; and the Persian administration, 110–11; and the sayyids, 107, 109; and Ḥātim Beg Urdūbādī, 179–80; *Tārīkh-i `ālam ārā-yi `Abbāsī,* 5
Ismā`īl I (Shāh): administration of, 19–20, 28–30, 31, 46–58; campaigns of, 23–28; documents and letters, 19–20, 29–30, 31–46, 52–8, 119, 233n172; early life of, 21–2; and his time in Lāhījān, 21–2; and his tutor Shams al-Dīn Lāhījī, 21–2; and his *ẓuhūr,* 20-30, 45; as Mahdī, 5, 22, 24, 30–46; and millenarianism, 18–23, 30–46, 201, 214n107; and Persian administrators, 19, 28, 29, 31, 46–58, 201; poetry of, 19, 31–2, 214n107, 214n110, 214n121; popularity of, 24; propaganda for, 24, 31–8; and Shīrvān campaign (1500), 23–4; success of, 45; and Twelver Shi`ism, 4, 19, 22, 23, 24, 31, 47–8, 216n160, 218n194
Ismā`īl II (Shāh): campaign to realign the centrality and importance of Persian absolute monarchy, 146, 151; coronation of, 147–8; and the "court of justice" *(dīvān-i `adl),* 151–2; death of, 161; documents and letters, 154–8; incarceration of, 145, 147, 152, 239n53; and Persian administrators, 150, 151, 152, 153–4, 159, 196; and the royal family massacre, 145, 148–9, 158, 159; Sunnism and, 145–6, 149, 152, 153; ten-day interregnum, 147

Ismā`īl ibn Ḥaidar ibn Junaid Ṣafavī. *See* Ismā`īl I
Jalāl al-Dīn al-Davvānī, 13, 88–9, 122, 148, 161
Jalāl al-Dīn Muḥammad Tabrīzī Kukajī (Khvājah), 51, 60–1, 68
Jām, 59, 61–6, 187, 201
Jāmī: and kingship, 128; in letters, 76; popularity of, 100; *Shawāhid al-nubuwwat,* 84; shrine of, 28, 76, 89, 233n164
Joseph, 121, 140, 155
Joshua, 132
Junaid (Shaikh) (grandfather of Ismā`īl I), 20–1, 23, 31

Kabah Khalīfah Zū al-Qadar, 65–6, 200
Karbalā, 3, 23–4, 35, 85, 229n103
Kār Kiyā dynasty, 21, 119–20, 156–7, 179, 185–6
Kāshān: and the Bāgh-i Fīn, 123; and Ismā`īl I, 25, 28, 71; religion and, 39
Khādim Beg Ṭālish (Khulafā Beg), 22, 23
Khair al-Nisā Begum (Mahd-i `Ulyā) (wife of Shāh Khudābandah): death of, 162; and `Ādil Girāy Khān, 162; and `Khan Aḥmad Khān, 185; marriage of, 107; move to Qazvīn, 161; and Mīrzā Salmān Jābirī, 164; power of, 158, 159, 162, 252n99
Khalīl Allāh ibn Shaikh Ibrāhīm (Sulṭān), 21, 23, 29, 122, 213n81
Kamāl al-Dīn Maḥmūd Sāgharchī (Khvājah), 27, 48
Khān Aḥmad Khān of Gīlān: escape to

Istanbul of, 179; imprisonment of, 119; and Khair al-Nisā Begum, 185; letter from `Abbās to, 185–6; letter from Ismā`īl II to, 156–8; letter from Ṭahmāsp to (1567), 118–20
Khaṭā'ī, 31, 214n107
Khiḍr, 132
Khudābandah (Shāh) (Sulṭān-Muḥammad Mīrzā): abdication of, 163–4; accession of, 161; early life, 158–9, 160–1; letter to Murād III from, 122, 166–72; letters and documents of, 172–6; marriage of, 107; perceptions of, 159; and Persian administrators, 159, 162–3, 172; and religious personalities, 159
Khurāsān: and `Abbās, 186–90; and The Battle of Jām, 61–6; court activity in, 94–5; and Ismā`īl I's invasion of, 19, 26–8, 35, 45; and Mīrzā Shāh Vālī Iṣfahānī, 164; and Ṭahmāsp Mīrzā, 58–9; Persian administrators from, 46–52, 56, 90; style in letters, 55; and Sulṭan-Muḥammad Mīrzā, 160; and Sāvajī family, 222n293; and taxes, 117; and Timurid chancellery, 199; and the Uzbeks, 73, 76, 105, 174, 178–80
Khūrshah ibn Qubād, 18, 23, 27, 49, 59, 222n290
Khvāndamīr: *Ḥabīb al-siyar,* 5; *Makārim al-akhlāq,* 55, 200, 251n74; and Najm-i S̱ānī, 47; *Nāmah-yi nāmī,* 9, 52–5, 200, 220n229; and the 'Timurid Renaissance', 48; and Ḥusain Kiyā and Muḥammad Karrah, 25
Kurdistān, 26, 178, 188

Lāhījān, 21–2, 251n64
letters. *See also* `Abbās; Abū Bakr; `Abdī Beg Shīrāzī; Alexander the Great; Anūshīrvān; Babayan, Kathryn; Ḥusain Bāiqarā; Ismā`īl I; Ismā`īl II; Jāmī; Khān Aḥmad Khān; Khudābandah; Mecca; metaphors; Murād III; Salīm II; Sheba; Solomon; Sulaimān; Ṭahmāsp: to `Abd Allah Khān Uzbek, 193; allegory in, 74, 79, 80, 83, 84, 94, 98, 126, 174; antithesis in, 33, 57, 135; "Belt" Letter, the, 81–8, 91, 101, 201, 231n131; bird imagery in, 92, 123–7, 129, 190; historical events in, 90, 182, 190; *iqtibās* in, 33, 37, 77, 84, 99, 138, 140, 143, 205n37, 236n228, 243n143; "mosque" letter, 113–15; mythical and historical personalities in, 54–5, 58, 61, 79, 113–14, 142–3, 190; natural elements and agriculture in, 127, 170; religion in letters to western world, 91; rhyming in, 6, 41, 43, 56, 83, 92, 113, 121, 126, 129, 139, 144, 155, 195; Ṭahmāsp's court is described in letters, 91; *talmīḥ* in, 77, 99, 143
Losensky, Paul, 137

macaronic verse, 141–2, 144, 166, 227n64
Madrasah-yi Manṣūriyya, 88, 173
Mahdī: Ismā`īl I as the, 24, 30, 32, 45–6; Ṭahmāsp as the, 69, 96; Ṭahmāsp's dream of, 117–18; signs of the, 22, 23, 30
Mahd-i `Ulyā. *See* Khair al-Nisā Begum
Maidan-i Sa`ādatābād, 113, 115
Malcolm, Sir John, 145
Mar`ashī sayyids, 101, 107–10
Marlow, Louise, 124
Marv: defeat of the Uzbeks at (1510), 27, 32, 37–8, 187; defeat of the Uzbeks at (1529), 62–6
Mashhad as cultural centre, 111
Masjid-i Suleimaniye, 113
Ma`ṣūm Beg Ṣafavī, 110, 125, 145, 239n53
Māzandarān, 21, 105–12, 162
Mecca: and the Battle of Badr, 37; Ismā`īl I as the rightful lord of, 37; as metaphor in letters, 54; the Muḥājirūn in, 230n119; in the Qur'ān, 43, 74
Medina, 37, 74, 86–7, 230n119
Meisami, Julie Scott, 14, 15, 169, 262n357
Melikian-Chirvani, Assadullah Souren, 122, 242n124
Mélikoff, Irène, 22
Membré, Michel (Mikā'īl), 90
Messick, Brinkley, 198
metaphors: bodily metaphors in letters, 156–7; of kingly sovereignty and divine light, 53; metaphors and other literary devices in *inshā,* 97–8; pecuniary metaphors, 57; of predestined dominance of Islam, 58
metempsychosis *(tanāsukh),* 22, 32, 128, 261n347
Minorsky, Vladimir, 32, 69, 209n3, 242n124
mirrors-for-princes genre, 54, 55, 124, 154, 174
Modaressī-Ṭabāṭabā'ī, 108
Mohammed Reza Shah, 2
Moses: and Ismā`īl I, 21, 214n121; and the Khiḍr, 132; in Safavid documents and letters, 2, 77, 85, 139; and the Sixth Imām Ja`far al-Ṣādiq, 124; and Ṭahmāsp, 243n143
Mīr `Alī Shīr, 48, 84, 99, 100, 231n129
Mīr Fatḥ Allāh Shīrāzī, 172–3
Mīr Muḥammad Bāqir Dāmād (*laqab:* Mīr Dāmād), 110, 191, 193, 195

Mīr Sayyid `Alī Khaṭīb, 109, 138, 150, 247n233
Mīr Sayyid Ḥusain al-Karakī, 146, 149, 150, 152, 175–6
Mīr Sharaf al-Dīn Muḥammad. *See* Qāḍī-yi Jahān Qazvīnī
Mīrzā Hidāyat Allāh, 46, 165
Mīrzā Luṭf Allāh Shīrāzī, 153, 161, 165, 177, 178
Mīrzā Makhdūm Sharīfī, 145–6, 148, 150, 151, 152
Mīrzā Muḥammad Munshī, 152, 158, 163, 165, 177–8
Mīrzā Salmān Jābīrī, 153–5, 161–5, 174, 254n138
Mīrzā Sharaf Jahān (son of Qāḍī-yi Jahān), 88, 148
Mīrzā Shukr Allāh Iṣfahānī: and the chief accountancy, 178; as chief vizier, 148; and the "court of justice" *(dīvān-i `adl),* 152; demotion of, 154, 155; reappointment as *mustaufī al-mamālik,* 156, 249n25
Mīrzā Sulṭān Ḥaidar, 145, 147
Mughal Bābur, 28, 54
Mughals, 4, 10, 54, 182, 194, 235n198
Muḥammad al-Ḥusainī ibn Nāṣir al-Ḥaqq Nūrbakhshī (*takhalluṣ:* Sayyid), 95–100, 199
Muḥammad Amīn (Maulānā), 165, 166, 178
Muḥammad Kukajī (or Kujajī) Tabrīzī (Khvājah) (Amīr Zakariyā), 28–9, 46, 50
Muḥyī al-Dīn Aḥmad Shīrāzī (Shaikh). *See* Shaikhzādah Lāhījī
Mujtahid al-Zamān. *See* `Alī ibn al-Ḥusain al-Karakī
Mullā Ṣadrā, 110, 173, 191
Munsha'āt al-Ṭūsī, 50, 73
Murād III (Sulṭān): Caucasus invasions, 162; letter from Khudābandah to, 122, 166–72, 175, 200; letter from Ṭahmāsp to (1575), 138–44; letters from `Abbās to, 183, 185, 186, 188
mut`at al-ḥajj, 75–6
mut`at al-nisā, 75–6
Muẓaffar al-Dīn `Alī Injū (Shāh), 161

Nahj al-Balāgha, 82, 85, 97
Najm-i S̱ānī, 46, 47, 50, 53, 164
Naṣīr al-Dīn al-Ṭūsī, 161
Newman, Andrew, 146, 158, 175, 192, 218n194, 224n14
Ni`matullāhīs, 107, 176
Niẓāmī `Arūḍī Samarqandī, 9
Niẓāmī Ganjavī: and Alexander the Great, 132, 190; *Iqbāl nāmah,* 194; *Khamsah,* 194; *Khusrau va Shirīn,* 168; *Makhzan al-asrār,* 194; and Mullā Muḥammad Zamān Zamānī, 261n347; *Rāḥat al-ṣudūr,* 169; *Sharaf nāmah,* 190
Noah, 36, 74, 121, 124, 191
Nūrbakhshiyyah Order, 38–9, 44, 46, 95, 100–1

Parī Khān Khānum (daughter of Ṭahmāsp), 138–9, 158, 161, 249n19, 252n104
Pārsādūst, Manūchihr, 146, 163, 173
Peace of Istanbul, 178
Perfect Man, the, 5, 39, 177
Persepolis, 122
poetry: Alexander the Great in, 214n110, 247n238; anti-Sunni, 78; of Ismā`īl I, 19, 31–2, 214n107, 214n110, 214n121; of Khudābandah, 172; poetic riddles and acrostics in inshā, 99; as propaganda, 31–8
Prince Bāyazīd, 111, 115, 125–7, 243n148, 243n155
Prince Muṣṭafā, 125
pseudo al-Ghazālī, 154, 169–70, 174

Qāḍī `Abd Allāh of Khūy, 112, 164–5
Qāḍī Aḥmad al-Qummī: career of, 166; and the conversion of `Īsā Khān, 115; and the death of Khvājah `Abd al-Ḥayy Munshī, 30; description of Kabah Khalīfah, 65; description of Qāḍī Ulugh Beg Urdūbādī, 112; and the disbanding of Bāyazīd's militia, 125; father of, 111, 128, 136; *Gulistān-i hunar,* 181; *Khulāṣat al-tavārīkh,* 17, 40, 61, 128, 166, 196, 200–1; and Qaḍī-yi Jahān's family, 88–9, 222n290; *Shāh nāmah,* 135, 136
Qāḍī Muḥammad Kāshanī, 25, 29, 46, 47
Qāḍī-yi Jahān Qazvīnī: and al-Karakī, 70, 95; career of, 60–1, 68, 70, 88–95, 100–3, 222n290; imprisonment of, 60–1; influence over Ṭahmāsp, 105, 233n164, 234n186; and Ma`ṣūm Beg Ṣafavī, 239n153; release of, 68
Qahqaha Prison, 145, 147, 152, 157, 239n53
Qarā Pīrī Beg Qājār, 22
Qarā Qoyūnlūs, 20, 28, 50, 199, 201
Quinn, Sholeh, 5, 17, 55, 157, 196, 233n157
Qumm, 29, 34, 62, 70, 113

reincarnation, 22
Roemer, Hans Robert, 68, 145, 159, 173, 252n99

Röhrborn, Klaus-Michael, 158, 255n170
Roxburgh, David, 134
Rūmī, 169
Rustam, 2, 14, 29, 65–6, 93, 190–1

Sa`ādatābād, 105, 113–14, 130–3, 137, 147
Sachedina, Abdulaziz Abdulhussein, 102, 227n67
Sa`dī, 128, 167–71
Salīm I, 28, 53, 56–7
Salīm II (son of Sulaimān): accession of, 126; and the Battle of Konya, 120, 125; and Bāyazīd, 120, 125; death of, 138, 143, 144; letter from Ṭahmāsp to, 126, 128–37, 200
Sām Mīrzā (son of Ismā`īl I): biographical dictionary of, 31, 160; and Husain Khān Shāmlū, 59, 60; and Malik Maḥmūd, 51; and *mu`ammā,* 99; and Sharaf al-Dīn Ḥusainī Qummī, 137; tutors of, 52, 59
Sanā'ī, 140, 169, 170, 171
Sasanian period, 3, 173, 202
Savory, Roger, 145, 203n15, 252n100
Schimkoreit, Renate, 29
Shāh nāmah: in letters, 63–5, 133–4, 189, 190, 246n205; popularity of, 2, 4, 31; and the "Ship of Shi`ism", 74
Shāh nāmah-yi Shāh Ṭahmāsp: in letters, 63, 133–4; presented to Salīm II, 121, 129, 130, 133, 137; production of, 133–4, 137; and Ṭahmāsp's victory over the Uzbeks, 63–4
Shāh Rukh Khān Zū al-Qadar, 152–3

Shāhzādah Sulṭānum (sister of Ṭahmāsp), 108–9
Shaikhzādah Lahījī, 39–45, 95
Shams al-Dīn Lāhījī, 21–2, 29
Shams al-Dīn Muḥammad Lāhījī, 39, 44
Sharaf al-Dīn Maḥmūd Daylamī Qazvīnī, 28–9, 46, 50, 51
Sharīf al-Dīn `Alī Shīrāzī (Sayyid), 46
Sheba (Queen) (Bilqīs): conversion of, 128, 242n131; in letters, 64, 126–9; popularity of, 122–3; and Solomon's bird canopy, 245n171; and Solomon's Hoopoe bird, 126, 128, 244n162, 244n163
Shīrvān, 23–4, 105, 117, 162, 163, 178
Shīrāzī School, 95, 103, 161, 173, 175
Shujā` al-Dīn (son of Ismā`īl II), 149
Solomon. *See also* `Abdī Beg Shīrāzī; divine kingship; Queen Sheba: as exemplar in letters, 58, 64, 96, 113, 120–37, 140; and the Masjid-i Suleimaniye, 113
Soucek, Priscilla, 122, 242n132
Stewart, Devin, 146, 175, 196
Subtelny, Maria, 48
Sulaimān (Sulṭān): accession of, 53; and Bāyazīd, 120, 126, 243n148, 244n155; death of, 128, 131, 132; letter from Ismā`īl I to, 57–8; letter from Ṭahmāsp to, 79–81; letter from Ṭahmāsp to (1559 petition), 126; letter from Ṭahmāsp to ("Belt" Letter), 81–8; letter from Ṭahmāsp to ("mosque" letter), 113–15; and the Masjid-i Suleimaniye, 113–14; and the Treaty of Amāsya, 126, 136
Sulṭān-Muḥammad Mīrzā. *See* Shāh Khudābandah
Szuppe, Maria, 17, 196, 234n195

Ṭabaristān, 10, 21
Ṭahmāsp (Shāh): administration of, 51, 52, 60–1, 68, 71–3, 88–90, 112; campaigns of, 59; and divine kingship, 117; documents and letters, 61–6, 73–88, 90–5, 95–100, 113–20, 121–44, 228n84; early life of, 58–60; move to Qazvīn by, 104–11; and Persian administrators, 19, 46, 61, 64, 66–7, 68, 69, 70, 88–90, 100, 102; and the Qizilbāsh, 101; and *Tazkirah-yi Ṭahmāsp,* 5, 69, 243n143; and "the Takkalū disaster", 59–60; and Twelver Shi`ism, 5, 18, 69, 71–88, 95, 101–2, 104, 106, 110, 117, 234n186, 243n143
Ṭahmāsp Mīrzā (son of Khudābandah), 164
taqlīd, 74–5, 79
Ṭārum, 21, 112, 180
Tavakoli-Targhi, Mohamad, 2, 173
Treaty of Amāsya, 100, 104, 126, 135–6, 169–70

`ulamā, 69, 86, 150, 193, 197
`Umar, 75–9, 85, 191, 226n57
`Uthmān, 75, 77–9, 83, 85, 229n105

Venice, 90
Von Grunebaum, G.E., 3

Welch, Anthony, 110, 184
Woods, John, 50

Yazd, 25–6, 28–9, 39, 176–9

Zain al-Dīn Ziyāratgāhī, 27
Zainab Sulṭān, 162
Zoroastrianism, 1, 173
Zū al-Qadar, *See* `Alā' al-Daula Zū al-Qadar